Travels in Arabia Deserta, Vol. I (in two volumes)

CHARLES MONTAGU DOUGHTY

INTRODUCTION T.E. LAWRENCE

COSIMOCLASSICS

NEW YORK

Travels in Arabia Deserta, Vol. I (in two volumes)
First published in 1888
Current edition published by Cosimo Classics in 2010.

Cover copyright © 2010 by Cosimo, Inc.

Cover design by www.popshopstudio.com

Cover image, "An Arab Caravan outside a Fortified Town, Egypt"
by Jean -Léon Gérôme.

ISBN: 978-1-61640-516-8

Cosimo aims to publish books that inspire, inform, and engage readers worldwide. We use innovative print-on-demand technology that enables books to be printed based on specific customer needs. This approach eliminates an artificial scarcity of publications and allows us to distribute books in the most efficient and environmentally sustainable manner. Cosimo also works with printers and paper manufacturers who practice and encourage sustainable forest management, using paper that has been certified by the FSC, SFI, and PEFC whenever possible.

Ordering Information:
Cosimo publications are available at online bookstores. They may also be purchased for educational, business, or promotional use:
Bulk orders: Special discounts are available on bulk orders for reading groups, organizations, businesses, and others.
Custom-label orders: We offer selected books with your customized cover or logo of choice.

For more information, contact us at:

Cosimo, Inc.
P.O. Box 416, Old Chelsea Station
New York, NY 10011

info@cosimobooks.com

or visit us at:
www.cosimobooks.com

I passed for a seeker of treasure with some who had seen me sitting under the great acacia, which they believe to be possessed by the jan, at el-Hèjr; now they said to me, "Didst thou take up anything, Khalîl, tell us boldly?" and a neighbour whispered in my ear, "Tell thy counsel to me only, good Khalîl, and I will keep it close."

—from Chapter X, The Nomads in the Desert; Visit to Teyma

PREFACE TO THE FIRST EDITION.

*W*E set but a name upon the ship, that our hands have built (with incessant labour) in a decennium, in what day she is launched forth to the great waters; and few words are needful in this place. The book is not milk for babes: it might be likened to a mirror, wherein is set forth faithfully some parcel of the soil of Arabia smelling of sámn and camels. And such, I trust, for the persons, that if the words [written all-day from their mouths] were rehearsed to them in Arabic, there might every one, whose life is remembered therein, hear, as it were, his proper voice; and many a rude bystander, smiting his thigh, should bear witness and cry 'Ay Wellah, the sooth indeed!'

Little was known to me, writing apart from books and in foreign countries, of those few old Arabic authors that have treated, more Asiatico, of tribes and towns and itineraries in the vast Peninsula. I was too weary to inquire of aught beside my path, and learned men encouraged me to leave them to scholars. The like must be said of the writings of the two or three Europeans [Wallin, Palgrave, Guarmani] that before my time visited Hâyil and Teyma; and which, when I sojourned in Arabia, (and since,) were known to me only in A. Zehme's excellent treatise.

The first part of my work—the Inscriptions which I brought from Arabia—was published by the Académie, in Paris. From thence, the first of these volumes is

D. T.   *b*

*adorned by M. Renan's translation of the (Aramaic)
epitaphs of Medáin Sâlih or el-Héjr. At the end will
be found the Marquis de Vogüé's valuable note, of the
hewn architecture of those monuments. To the second
volume I have appended a ·notice of the geological
constitution of Arabia. A third part of my work is
the map, which is attached to these volumes.*

PREFACE TO THE SECOND EDITION.

O F surpassing interest to those many minds, which seek after philosophic knowledge and instruction, is the Story of the Earth, Her manifold living creatures, the human generations and Her ancient rocks.

Briefly, and with such views as these, not worldly aims, a disciple of the divine Muse of Spencer and Venerable Chaucer; having spent the best part of ten years of early manhood, sojourning in succession in most of the Continental countries, and lastly in Syria, and having wandered through the length and breadth of Palestine, I reached Egypt and Sinai; where with Beduin guides, I wandered on, through the most of that vast mountainous labyrinthine solitude of rainless valleys; with their sand-wind burnished rocks and stones and in some of them, often strangely scribbled Nabatean cliff-inscriptions (the names, the saws and salutations of ancient wayfarers). From thence gone up to Edom, I visited Petra; and at Maan settlement, which is a few miles beyond, heard of other Petra-like sculptured cliff-monuments, bearing many inscriptions, at Medain Salih. (That was a water-station of the Damascus yearly pilgrims' caravan, in their long desert way to Medina and Mecca;) lying some few days' journey southward from Maan, but difficult to be reached, at other times, for danger of the wild Beduins.

Medain Salih, i.e. cities of their reputed prophet Salih, so named by the pilgrims, being the subject of many Koran fables; but more properly, from antiquity, el-Héjr, (as it yet is in the mouths of the country nomads,) was at that time not known to Europeans.

What might be those inscriptions? I was unable to learn from my Arab companions, save that they were not Arabic. Interested as I was, in all that pertains to Biblical research, I resolved to accept the hazard of visiting them.

This was only accomplished later, after more than another year's fruitless endeavours; when finding none other means, I had taken the adventure of journeying thither, in the great Damascus caravan.

Arrived at the place, after three weeks' tedious riding, amongst that often clamorous, mixed and in their religion devout pilgrim-multitude; I found Medain Salih to be an old ruinous sand-plain, with sand-rock cliffs; where our encampment was pitched by a great cistern, defended from the interference of Beduins, by a rude-built Turkish fort or **kella**: whence it is the weary pilgrims draw to drink, for themselves and their numerous camels.

Hardly visible in the next cliffs, was some one of the sculptured monuments, which I was come thus far to seek. Upon the Western horizon appeared, (to me of hardly less interest,) the heads evidently by their forms, of some latent or extinct volcanoes.*

---

* In my later journeying in the high deserts, I found and visited the crater-hills of several more latent or spent volcanoes; and traversed wide harras or lava-areas, which, lying dispersedly as far down as the country above Mecca, came within my knowledge and observation: whose few wild creatures, in the long lapse of ages, have acquired (as I have seen the fox and gazelles) the swart hue of those cragged landscapes.

During those two months which remained till the returning of the pilgrimage, I visited the monuments and carefully impressed their formal superscriptions; which proved to be sepulchral and Nabatean, from a little earlier and a little later than the beginning of our Era: and found and transcribed some other few upon ancient building-stones, at the neighbour desert settlement, el-Ally, *which are Himyaric.**

The pilgrims come again, I did not return with them to Syria; but rode with a friendly sheykh of the district Beduins, to live with them awhile in the high desert. I might thus, I hoped, visit the next Arabian uplands and view those vast waterless marches of the nomad Arabs; tent-dwellers, inhabiting, from the beginning, as it were beyond the World.

Unto this new endeavour, I was but slenderly provided; yet did not greatly err, when I trusted my existence, (which could long endure, as in Sinai, with little more than Heaven's sun and air,) amongst an unlettered and reputed lawless tribesfolk, (with whom, however, I had already some more favourable acquaintance;) which amidst a life of never-ending hardship and want, continue to observe a Great Semitic Law, unwritten; namely the ancient Faith of their illimitable empty wastes. I might find moreover, in so doing, to add something to the common fund of Western knowledge. The name

---

* *Finding, when I returned home, no means of publishing the inscriptions, which I had painfully gathered in Arabia; I offered them to the Corpus Inscr. Semiticarum, then, as I learned, in course of publication in France: where, gladly accepted by the Académie des inscriptions et belles-lettres, they were photographically reproduced; and edited, (before their inclusion,) in a special 4° volume, with translations, by M. E. Renan.*

of Engleysy* might stand me at first in some stead, where known, perchance remotely, by faint hearsay, in some desert settlement. On the other hand, there must needs remain, as friendly Arab voices warned me, that predatory instinct of Beduins beyond their tents; besides the bitterness and blight of a fanatical religion, in every place.

In the adventure thus begun, there passed over me, amongst the thinly scattered, generally hostile and suspicious inhabitants of that Land of wilderness, nearly two long and partly weary years; but not without happy turns, in the not seldom finding, as I went forth, of human fellowship amongst Arabians and even of some very true and helpful friendships; which, from this long distance of years, I vividly recall and shall, whilst life lasts, continue to esteem with grateful mind. The haps that befel me are narrated in these volumes: wherein I have set down, that which I saw with my eyes, and heard with my ears and thought in my heart; neither more or less.†

These volumes, published originally by the Cambridge University Press, have been some time out of print.‡ A

---

* Kélamat Engleysy, *the word of an Englishman.*

† *It has, I am told, been asked: how could I take abundant notes in fanatical Arabia? I found no great difficulty in so doing. I was amongst them an Hakím: nor did I spare to make use of my inkhorn and reed pen in the illiterate leisure of the nomad tent; and when in the settlements, I wrote as I could. I did nothing covertly: thus I was able, "a son of the way," to pass forth with an honourable reputation and the good will of many, and finding always some helpful friends; to reach at length an happy ending of my travaillous voyage in Arabia.*

‡ *An abriged Edition, however, was published by Messrs. Duckworth.*

re-print has been called for; and is reproduced thus, at the suggestion chiefly of my distinguished friend, Colonel T. E. Lawrence, leader with Feysal, Meccan Prince, of the nomad tribesmen; whom they, as might none other at that time, marching from Jidda, the port of Mecca, were able, (composing, as they went, the tribes' long-standing blood feuds and old enmities), to unite with them in victorious arms, against the corrupt Turkish sovereignty in those parts: and who greatly thus serving his Country's cause and her Allies, from the Eastward, amidst the Great War; has in that imperishable enterprise, traversed the same wide region of Desert Arabia.

[I cannot here take leave, without recording my thankful memory of those good men (all are now passed from us), Henry Bradshaw, Librarian at that time of the Cambridge University Library, and W. Wright, University Professor of Arabic: who together with Robertson Smith, also Professor there of Semitic learning; powerfully persuaded the University Press Syndics, to undertake the costly printing and publishing of the MS. of this work.]

Charles M. Doughty.

SEPTEMBER, 1920.

CORRECTION.

Vol. I. p. 131; dele *The Rocks of J. Ethlib.*

CONTENTS TO VOL. I.

CHAPTER I.

THE PERAEA ; AMMON AND MOAB.

CHAPTER II.

THE MOUNTAIN OF EDOM ; ARABIA PETRAEA.

CHAPTER III.

CHAPTER IV.

CHAPTER V.

MEDÁIN SÂLIḤ AND EL-ʿALLY.

CHAPTER VI.

EL-ʿALLY, EL-KHREYBY, MEDÁIN.

Appendix to Chaps. IV. V. VI.

CHAPTER VII.

RETURN OF THE HAJ.

CHAPTER VIII.

THE NOMAD LIFE IN THE DESERT.

The Fejîr Beduins.

CHAPTER IX.

LIFE IN THE WANDERING VILLAGE.

CONTENTS.

CHAPTER X.

THE NOMADS IN THE DESERT ; VISIT TO TEYMA.

CHAPTER XI.

CHAPTER XII.

PEACE IN THE DESERT.

CHAPTER XIII.

MEDÁIN REVISITED. PASSAGE OF THE HARRA.

CHAPTER XIV.

WANDERING UPON THE HARRA WITH THE MOAHÎB.

Appendix to Chap. XIV.

CHAPTER XV.

NOMAD LIFE UPON THE HARRA.

CHAPTER XVI.

THE AARAB FORSAKE THE HARRA, AND DESCEND TO THEIR SUMMER STATION IN WADY THIRBA.

D. T. *c*

CHAPTER XVII.

THE MOAHIB SUMMER CAMP IN WADY THIRBA.

VISIT TO EL-ʿALLY.

CHAPTER XVIII.

THE FUKARA SUMMERING AT EL-HÉJR.

CHAPTER XIX.

TEYMA.

CHAPTER XX.

THE DATE HARVEST.

CHAPTER XXI.

THE JEBEL.

INTRODUCTION.

It is not comfortable to have to write about " Arabia Deserta."
I have studied it for ten years, and have grown to consider it a
book not like other books, but something particular, a bible of
its kind.   To turn round now and reckon its merits and demerits
seems absurd.   I do not think that any traveller in Arabia
before or since Mr. Doughty has qualified himself to praise the
book—much less to blame it.   The more you learn of Arabia
the more you find in " Arabia Deserta."   The more you travel
there the greater your respect for the insight, judgment and
artistry of the author.   We call the book " Doughty " pure and
simple, for it is a classic, and the personality of Mr. Doughty
hardly comes into question.   Indeed, it is rather shocking to
learn that he is a real and living person.   The book has no date
and can never grow old.   It is the first and indispensable work
upon the Arabs of the desert ; and if it has not always been
referred to, or enough read, that has been because it was exces-
sively rare.   Every student of Arabia wants a copy.

However, there is no need at this time of day to commend
Doughty to students.   They all know of him.   It is to the outside
public, willing to read a great prose work, the record of the
wanderings of an English poet for two years among the Beduins,
that this edition must make its appeal, and perhaps with them
that the verdict of present-day travellers in Arabia will have
weight.   I have talked the book over with many travellers, and
we are agreed that here you have all the desert, its hills and
plains, the lava fields, the villages, the tents, the men and animals.
They are told of to the life, with words and phrases fitted to them
so perfectly that one cannot dissociate them in memory.   It is
the true Arabia, the land with its smells and dirt, as well as its
nobility and freedom.   There is no sentiment, nothing merely
picturesque, that most common failing of oriental travel-books.
Doughty's completeness is devastating.   There is nothing we
would take away, little we could add.   He took all Arabia for
his province, and has left to his successors only the poor part of
specialists.   We may write books on parts of the desert or some
of the history of it ; but there can never be another picture of the
whole, in our time, because here it is all said, and by a great master.

There have been many well-endowed Englishmen travelling in Arabia, and most of them have written books. None have brought away a prize as rich as Doughty brought, and the merit of this is his own unaided merit. He had many things against him. Forty years ago the desert was less hospitable to strangers than it is to-day. Turkey was still strong there, and the Wahabi movement had kept fanaticism vivid in the tribes. Doughty was a pioneer, both as European and Christian, in nearly all the districts he entered. Also he was poor. He came down a lone man from Damascus with the pilgrim caravan, and was left behind at Medain Salih with scant recommendation. He struck out into the desert dressed like the very poor, travelling like the very poor, trying to maintain himself by the practice of rational medicine, in a society more willing to invest in charms.

Then he was a sick man. His health was weak when he started, and the climate of the plateau of Arabia is a trying one, with its extremes of heat and cold, and the poverty of its nourishment. He had been brought up in England, a fruitful country of rich and plentiful food. He came as a guest to the Arab tents, to share their lean hospitality, and to support himself on the little that sufficed them. They treated him to what they had themselves. Their skinny bodies subsisted well enough on a spring season of camel-milk, and rare meals of dates or meat for the barren months of the year, but such a diet was starvation for an Englishman. It would be short commons to a sedentary man; but Doughty was for ever wandering about, often riding from sunrise to sunset, if not for half the night, in forced marches across rocky and toilsome country, under a burning sun, or in keen exhausting winds. Travel in Arabia in the best circumstances, with a train of servants, good riding-beasts, tents and your own kitchen, is a trying experience. Doughty faced it native-fashion, in spite of his physical disadvantages, and brought home more booty than we all. The sheer endurance of his effort is wonderful.

Somewhere he half apologises for his defects, calling his book the seeing of a hungry man, the telling of a most weary man; nevertheless he seems to have recorded everything. We have all sometimes been weary in the desert, and some of us have been hungry there, but none of us triumphed over our bodies as Doughty did. He makes his hardships a positive profit to him, by distilling from them into his pages that sense of strain and desolation which will remind every Arabian traveller vividly of his own less fortunate moments. Yet even at such times, coming so often in these two dangerous years, Doughty's keenness of observation was not reduced. He goes on showing us the circumstances and the characters and the places of his tale, without any loss of interest : and that this could be so is a high testimony, not only to his strength of mind, but also to the imaginative appeal of Arabia and the Arabs to him and to us.

For his own strength of character his book stands unconscious witness. He has revealed himself to us in his pages indirectly (the book is never morbid, never introspective), almost unwillingly, for the way of telling is detached, making no parade of good or evil. He refused to be the hero of his story. Yet he was very really the hero of his journey, and the Arabs knew how great he was. I spent nine months in Western Arabia, much of it in the districts through which he had passed, and I found that he had become history in the desert. It was more than forty years ago, and that space of time would even in our country cause much to be forgotten. In the desert it is relatively longer, for the hardships of common life leave little chance for the body to recruit itself, and so men are short-lived and their memories of strangers, and events outside the family tree, soon fail. Doughty's visit was to their fathers or grandfathers, and yet they have all learned of him. They tell tales of him, making something of a legend of the tall and impressive figure, very wise and gentle, who came to them like a herald of the outside world. His aloofness from the common vexations of their humanity coloured their imagination. He was very patient, generous and pitiful, to be accepted into their confidence without doubt.

They say that he seemed proud only of being Christian, and yet never crossed their faith. He was book-learned, but simple in the arts of living, ignorant of camels, trustful of every man, very silent. He was the first Englishman they had met. He predisposed them to give a chance to other men of his race, because they had found him honourable and good. So he broke a road for his religion. He was followed by Mr. Wilfred Blunt and Miss Gertrude Bell, other strong personalities. They confirmed the desert in its view of Englishmen, and gave us a privileged position which is a grave responsibility upon all who follow them. Thanks to them an Englishman finds a welcome in Arabia, and can travel, not indeed comfortably for it is a terrible land, but safely over the tracks which Doughty opened with such pains. No country has been more fortunate in its ambassadors. We are accepted as worthy persons unless we prove ourselves the contrary by our own misdoings. This is no light monument to the memory of the man who stamped so clear an impression of his virtue on a nomad people in the casual journeyings of two years.

* * * * *

We export two chief kinds of Englishmen, who in foreign parts divide themselves into two opposed classes. Some feel deeply the influence of the native people, and try to adjust themselves to its atmosphere and spirit. To fit themselves modestly into the picture they suppress all in them that would be discordant with local habits and colours. They imitate the native as far as possible, and so avoid friction in their daily life. However, they cannot avoid the consequences of imitation, a hollow, worthless thing. They are like the people but not of the people, and their half-perceptible differences give them a sham influence often greater than their merit. They urge the people among whom they live into strange, unnatural courses by imitating them so well that they are imitated back again. The other class of Englishmen is the larger class. In the same circumstance of exile they reinforce their character by memories of the life they have left. In reaction against their foreign surroundings they take refuge in the England that was theirs. They assert their aloofness, their immunity, the more vividly for their loneliness and weakness. They impress the peoples among whom they live by reaction, by giving them an ensample of the complete Englishman, the foreigner intact.

Doughty is a great member of the second, the cleaner class. He says that he was never oriental, though the sun made him an Arab ; and much of his value lies in the distinction. His seeing is altogether English: yet at the same time his externals, his manners, his dress, and his speech were Arabic, and nomad Arab, of the desert. The desert inhibits considered judgments ; its bareness and openness make its habitants frank. Men in it speak out their minds suddenly and unreservedly. Words in the desert are clear-cut. Doughty felt this contagion of truthfulness sharply (few travel-journals show a greater sensibility to climate and geography than this), and among the tribes he delivered himself like them. Even in the villages he maintained an untimely and uncompromising bluntness, in a firm protest against the glozing politic speech of the town-Arabs. His own origin was from the settled country of England, and this preference for the nomad might seem strange ; but in practice the Englishman, and especially the Englishman of family, finds the tribes more to his taste than the villages, and Doughty everywhere is the outspoken Beduin. His " stiffness to maintain a just opinion against the half-reason of the world " was often unwise—but always respectable, and the Arabs respected him for it even where they resented it most.

Very climatic, too, are his sudden changes of tone and judgment. The desert is a place of passing sensation, of cash-payment of opinion. Men do not hold their minds in suspense for days, to arrive at a just and balanced average of thought. They say good at once when it is good, and bad at once when it is bad. Doughty has mirrored this also for us in himself. One paragraph will have a harsh judgment ; the next is warm kindness. His record ebbs and flows with his experience, and by reading not a part of the book but all of it you obtain a many-sided sympathetic vision, in the round, of his companions of these stormy and eventful years.

      *   *   *   *   *

The realism of the book is complete. Doughty tries to tell the full and exact truth of all that he saw. If there is a bias it will be against the Arabs, for he liked them so much ; he was so impressed by the strange attraction, isolation and independence of this people that he took pleasure in bringing out their virtues by a careful expression of their faults. " If one live any time with the Arab he will have all his life after a feeling of the desert." He had experienced it himself, the test of nomadism, that most deeply biting of all social disciplines, and for our sakes he strained all the more to paint it in its true colours, as a life too hard, too empty, too denying for all but the strongest and most determined men. Nothing is more powerful and real than this record of all his daily accidents and obstacles, and the feelings that came to him on the way. His picture of the Semites, sitting to the eyes in a cloaca, but with their brows touching Heaven, sums up in full measure their strength and weakness, and the strange contradictions of their thought which quicken our curiosity at our first meeting with them.

To try and solve their riddle many of us have gone far into their society, and seen the clear hardness of their belief, a limitation almost mathematical, which repels us by its unsympathetic form. Semites have no half-tones in their register of vision. They are a people of primary colours, especially of black and white, who see the world always in line. They are a certain people, despising doubt, our modern crown of thorns. They do not understand our metaphysical difficulties, our self-questionings. They know only truth and untruth, belief and unbelief, without our hesitating retinue of finer shades.

Semites are black and white not only in vision, but in their inner furnishing ; black and white not merely in clarity, but in apposition. Their thoughts live easiest among extremes. They inhabit superlatives by choice. Sometimes the great inconsistents seem to possess them jointly. They exclude compromise, and pursue the logic of their ideas to its absurd ends, without seeing incongruity in their opposed conclusions. They oscillate with cool head and tranquil judgment from asymptote to asymptote, so imperturbably that they would seem hardly conscious of their giddy flight.

They are a limited narrow-minded people whose inert intellects lie incuriously fallow. Their imaginations are keen but not creative. There is so little Arab art to-day in Asia that they can nearly be said to have no art, though their rulers have been liberal patrons and have encouraged their neighbours' talents in architecture, ceramic and handicraft. They show no longing for great industry, no organisations of mind or body anywhere. They invent no systems of philosophy or mythologies. They are the least morbid of peoples, who take the gift of life unquestioning, as an axiom. To them it is a thing inevitable, entailed on man, a usufruct, beyond our control. Suicide is a thing nearly impossible and death no grief.

They are a people of spasms, of upheavals, of ideas, the race of the individual genius. Their movements are the more shocking by contrast with the quietude of every day, their great men greater by contrast with the humanity of their mass. Their convictions are by instinct, their activities intuitional. Their largest manufacture is of creeds. They are monopolists of revealed religions, finding always an antagonism of body and spirit, and laying their stress on the spirit. Their profound reaction against matter leads them to preach barrenness, renunciation, poverty : and this atmosphere stifles the minds of the desert pitilessly. They are always looking out towards those things in which mankind has had no lot or part.

The Beduin has been born and brought up in the desert, and has embraced this barrenness too harsh for volunteers with all his soul, for the reason, felt but inarticulate, that there he finds himself indubitably free. He loses all natural ties, all comforting superfluities or complications, to achieve that personal liberty which haunts starvation and death. He sees no virtue in poverty herself ; he enjoys the little vices and luxuries—coffee, fresh water, women—which he can still afford. In his life he has air and winds, sun and light, open spaces and great emptiness. There is no human effort, no fecundity in Nature ; just heaven above and unspotted earth beneath , and the only refuge and rhythm of their being is in God. This single God is to the Arab not anthropomorphic, not tangible or moral or ethical, not concerned particularly with the world or with him. He alone is great, and yet there is a homeliness, an every-day-ness of this Arab God who rules their eating, their fighting and their lusting; and is their commonest thought, and companion, in a way impossible to those whose God is tediously veiled from them by the decorum of formal worship. They feel no incongruity in bringing God into their weaknesses and appetites. He is the commonest of their words.

This creed of the desert is an inheritance. The Arab does not value it extremely. He has never been either evangelist or proselyte. He arrives at this intense condensation of himself in God by shutting his eyes to the world, and to all the complex possibilities latent in him which only wealth and temptation could bring out. He attains a sure trust and a · powerful trust, but of how narrow a field! His sterile experience perverts his human kindness to the image of the waste in which he hides. Accordingly he hurts himself, not merely to be free, but to please himself. There follows a self-delight in pain, a cruelty which is more to him than goods. The desert Arab finds no joy like the joy of voluntarily holding back. He finds luxury in abnegation, renunciation, self-restraint. He lives his own life in a hard selfishness. His desert is made a spiritual ice-house, in which is preserved intact but unimproved for all ages an idea of the unity of God.

*   *   *   *   *

Doughty went among these people dispassionately, looked at their life, and wrote it down word for word. By being always Arab in manner and European in mind he maintained a perfect judgment, while bearing towards them a full sympathy which persuaded them to show him their inmost ideas. When his trial of two years was over he carried away in his note-book (so far as the art of writing can express the art of living) the soul of the desert, the complete existence of a remarkable and self-contained community, shut away from the currents of the world in the unchanging desert, working out their days in an environment utterly foreign to us. The economic reason for their existence is the demand for camels, which can be best bred on the thorns and plants of these healthy uplands. The desert is incapable of other development, but admirably suited to this. Their camel-breeding makes the Beduins nomads. The camels live only on the pasture of the desert, and as it is scanty a great herd will soon exhaust any one district. Then they with their masters must move to another, and so they circulate month by month in a course determined by the vegetation sprung up wherever the intermittent winter rains have this season fallen heaviest.

The social organisation of the desert is in tribes, partly because of original family-feeling, partly because the instinct of self-preservation compels large masses of men to hold together for mutual support. By belonging to a recognised tribe each man feels that he has a strong body of nominal kinsmen, to support him if he is injured ; and equally to bear the burden and to discharge his wrong-doing, when he is the guilty party. This collective responsibility makes men careful not to offend ; and makes punishment very easy. The offender is shut out from the system, and becomes an exile till he has made his peace again with the public opinion of his tribesmen.

Each tribe has its district in the desert. The extent and nature of these tribal districts are determined by the economic laws of camel-breeding. Each holds a fair chance of pasture all the year round in every normal year, and each holds enough drinking water to suffice all its households every year; but the poverty of the country forces an internal subdivision of itself upon the tribe. The water-sources are usually single wells (often very scanty wells), and the pasturages small scattered patches in sheltered valleys or oases among the rocks. They could not accommodate at one time or place all the tribe, which therefore breaks into clans, and lives always as clans, wandering each apart on its own cycle within the orbit of the tribal whole.

The society is illiterate, so each clan keeps small enough to enable all its adults to meet frequently, and discuss all common business verbally. Such general intercourse, and their open life beside one another in tents makes the desert a place altogether without privacy. Man lives candidly with man. It is a society in perpetual movement, an equality of voice and opportunity for every male. The daily hearth or sheikh's coffee-gathering is their education, a university for every man grown enough to walk and speak.

It is also their news-office, their tribunal, their political expression, and their government. They bring and expose there in public every day all their ideas, their experiences, their opinions, and they sharpen one another, so that the desert society is always alive, instructed to a high moral level, and tolerant of new ideas. Common rumour makes them as unchanging as the desert in which they live ; but more often they show themselves singularly receptive, very open to useful innovations. Their few vested interests make it simple for them to change their ways ; but even so it is astonishing to find how whole-heartedly they adopt an invention fitted to their life. Coffee, gunpowder, Manchester cotton are all new things, and yet appear so native that without them one can hardly imagine their desert life.

Consequently, one would expect a book such as " Arabia Deserta," written forty years ago, to be inaccurate to-day in such little respects, and had Doughty's work been solely scientific, dependent on the expression rather than the spirit of things, its day might have passed. Happily the beauty of the telling, its truth to life, the rich gallery of characters and landscapes in it, will remain for all time, and will keep it peerless, as the indispensable foundation of all true understanding of the desert. And in these forty years the material changes have not been enough to make them really worth detailed record.

The inscriptions at Medain Salih have been studied since his day by the Dominican fathers from Jerusalem, and some little points added to his store. The great stone at Teima which lay in the *haddaj*, was looked for by later travellers, and at last purchased and carried off to Europe. Doughty's collections of these primitive Arab scripts have been surpassed; but he holds the enduring credit of their discovery. His map, and some of his geographical information have been added to, and brought into relation with later information. People with cameras have wandered up and down the Aueyrid *harrat* in which he spent weeks, and of which he wrote so vivid a description. We know their outside face exactly, from photographs; but to read Doughty is to know what they make one feel. Crossley and Rolls-Royce cars have made a road of some of that Wadi Humth, whose importance he first made clear to Europe. Aeroplanes have quartered the hills in which he found such painful going. Unfortunately those in cars and aeroplanes are not able to write intimate books about the country over which they pass.

Another change in Arabia has come from the Hejaz Railway, which in 1909 was opened from Damascus to Medina, and at once put an end to the great army which used to perform the pilgrimage by road. The Emir el Haj and his people now go by train, and the annual pageant of the camel-caravan is dead. The pilgrim road, of whose hundreds of worn tracks Doughty gave us such a picture, is now gone dull for lack of all those feet to polish it, and the kellas and cisterns from which he drank on the march to Medain Salih are falling into ruin, except so far as they serve the need of some guard-house on the railway.

The Rashid dynasty in Hail has pursued as bloody a course since his day as before it. Saud, the last Emir, was murdered in 1920, and the sole survivor of the family is an infant, whose precarious minority is being made the play of the ambition of one and another of the great chiefs of the Shammar tribe. On the other hand, the Wahabi dynasty of Riath, which seemed in its decline has suddenly revived in this generation, thanks to the courage and energy of Abd el-Aziz, the present Emir. He has subdued all Nejd with his arms, has revived the Wahaby sect in new stringency, and bids fair to subject all the inner deserts of the peninsula to his belief. The Emir's younger son was lately in the Deputation he sent to this country, under the conduct of Mr. H. St. J. Philby, C.I.E., sometime British Resident at er-Riâth, during the Great War. Whilst in England they visited Mr. Doughty.

The Sherifate of Mecca, in whose humanity Doughty reposed at Taif at the end of his adventures, made a bid for the intellectual leadership of the Arabs in 1916 by rebelling against Turkey on the principle of nationality. The Western Arabs, among whom Doughty's ways had so long fallen, took a chivalrous part in the war as the allies of Great Britain and with our help. The Sherif's four sons put themselves at the head of the townsmen and tribes-men of the Hejaz, and gave the British officers assisting them the freedom of the desert. All the old names were in our ranks. There were Harb, Juheyma, and Billi, whom Doughty mentioned. His old hosts, the Abu Shamah Moahîb, joined us, and did gal-lantly. Ferhan, Motlog's son, brought with him the Allayda, and with the other Fejr they took Teyma and Kheybar from their Turkish garrisons, and handed them over to King Hussein.

Later the Shammar joined us, and volunteers came from Kasim, from Aneyza, Boreyda and Russ to help the common war upon the Turks. We took Medain Salih and El Ally, and further north Tebuk and Maan, the Beni Sakhr country, and all the pilgrim road up to Damascus, making in arms the return journey of that by which Doughty had begun his wanderings. "Arabia Deserta," which had been a joy to read, as a great record of adventure and travel (perhaps the greatest in our language), and the great picture-book of nomad life, became a military text-book, and helped to guide us to victory in the East. The Arabs who had allowed Doughty to wander in their forbidden provinces were making a good investment for their sons and grandsons.

In this great experience of war the focus of motive in the desert changed, and a political revolution came to the Arabs. In Doughty's day, as his book shows, there were Moslems and Christians, as main divisions of the people. Yesterday the dis-tinction faded ; there were only those on the side of the Allies, and those with the Central Powers. The Western Arabs, in these forty years, had learned enough of the ideas of Europe to accept nationality as a basis for action. They accepted it so thoroughly that they went into battle against their Caliph, the Sultan of Turkey, to win their right to national freedom. Religion, which had been the motive and character of the desert, yielded to politics, and Mecca, which had been a City of worship, became the temporal capital of a new state. The hostility which had been directed against Christians became directed against the foreigner who presumed to interfere in the domestic affairs of Arabic-speaking provinces.

*   *   *   *   *

However, this note grows too long. Those just men who begin at the beginning of books are being delayed by me from reading Doughty, and so I am making worse my presumption in putting my name near what I believe to be one of the great prose works of our literature. It is a book which begins powerfully, written in a style which has apparently neither father nor son, so closely wrought, so tense, so just in its words and phrases, that it demands a hard reader. It seems not to have been written easily ; but in a few of its pages you learn more of the Arabs than in all that others have written, and the further you go the closer the style seems to cling to the subject, and the more natural it becomes to your taste.

The history of the march of the caravan down the pilgrim road, the picture of Zeyd's tent, the description of Ibn Rashid's court at Hail, the negroid village in Kheybar, the urbane life at Aneyza, the long march across the desert of Western Nejd to Mecca, each seems better than the one before till there comes the very climax of the book near Taif, and after this excitement a gentle closing chapter of the road down to Jidda, to the hospitality of Mohammed Nasif's house, and the British Consulate.

To have accomplished such a journey would have been achievement enough for the ordinary man. Mr. Doughty was not content till he had made the book justify the journey as much as the journey justified the book, and in the double power, to go and to write, he will not soon find his rival.

T. E. LAWRENCE.

CHAPTER I.

THE PERAEA ; AMMON AND MOAB.

The Haj, or Mecca pilgrimage, in Damascus. The pilgrim camp in the wilderness at Muzeyríb. The setting forth. Hermon. The first station. The pilgrimage way, or Derb el-Haj. *Geraza. The Ageyl. Bashan. Umm Jemâl. Bosra. Jabbok, or the Zerka. Shebíb ibn Tubbai. Ancient strong towers in the desert. Punishment of a caravan thief. Aspect of the Peraean plains. The Beduins. Beny Sókhr. Beny Seleyta. Wélad Aly. Gilead. The Belka. Whether this fresh country were good for colonists.? Rabbath Ammon. Heshbon. Umm Rosás. The pilgrim-encampment raised by night. The brook Arnon. Lejûn. The high plains of Moab. Ruined sites. Dat Ras. Rabbath Moab. Kir Moab. "Heaps in the furrows of the field." The old giants. Agaba tribe. The land wasted by Israel. The ancient people were stone-builders. Kerak visited. Beny Hameydy tribe. Memorial heaped stones in the wilderness. Wady el-Hásy. The deep limestone valleys descending to the Dead Sea. Sheykh Hajellan.*

A NEW voice hailed me of an old friend when, first returned from the Peninsula, I paced again in that long street of Damascus which is called Straight ; and suddenly taking me wondering by the hand " Tell me (said he), since thou art here again in the peace and assurance of Ullah, and whilst we walk, as in the former years, toward the new blossoming orchards, full of the sweet spring as the garden of God, what moved thee, or how couldst thou take such journeys into the fanatic Arabia ? "

*   *   *

It was at the latest hour, when in the same day, and after troubled days of endeavours, I had supposed it impossible. At first I had asked of the *Wàly,* Governor of Syria, his license to accompany the *Haj* caravan to the distance of *Medáin Sálih.* The Wàly then privately questioned the British Consulate, an office which is of much regard in these countries. The Consul answered, that his was no charge in any such matter ; he had as much regard of me, would I take such dangerous ways, as of his old hat. This was a man that, in time past, had proffered to

---

The headpiece of this chapter represents a vine and pomegranate ornament, carved in relief upon a block of white marble, still lying in the ruinous wilderness of Moab.

show me a good turn in my travels, who now told me it was his
duty to take no cognisance of my Arabian journey, lest he might
hear any word of blame, if I miscarried. Thus by the Turkish
officers it was understood that my life, forsaken by mine own
Consulate, would not be required of them in this adventure.
There is a merry saying of Sir Henry Wotton, for which he
nearly lost his credit with his sovereign, " An ambassador is a
man who is sent to lie abroad for his country ; " to this might be
added, " A Consul is a man who is sent to play the Turk abroad,
to his own countrymen."

That untimely Turkishness was the source to me of nearly
all the mischiefs of these travels in Arabia. And what wonder,
none fearing a reckoning, that I should many times come nigh
to be foully murdered ! whereas the informal benevolent word,
in the beginning, of a Frankish Consulate might have procured
me regard of the great Haj officers, and their letters of commendation, in departing from them, to the Emirs of Arabia. Thus
rejected by the British Consulate, I dreaded to be turned back
altogether if I should visit now certain great personages of
Damascus, as the noble Algerian prince *Abd el-Kâder :* for
whose only word's sake, which I am well assured he would have
given, I had been welcome in all the Haj-road towers occupied
by Moorish garrisons, and my life had not been well-nigh lost
amongst them later at Medáin Sâlih.

I went only to the Kurdish Pasha of the Haj, Mohammed
Saîd, who two years before had known me a traveller in the
Lands beyond Jordan, and took me for a well-affected man that
did nothing covertly. It was a time of cholera and the Christians had fled from the city, when I visited him formerly in
Damascus to prefer the same request, that I might go down with
the Pilgrimage to Medáin Sâlih. He had recommended me
then to bring a firmân of the Sultan, saying, ' The *hajjàj*
(pilgrims) were a mixed multitude, and if aught befel me, the
harm might be laid at his door, since I was the subject of a
foreign government : ' but now, he said, ' Well ! would I needs go
thither ? it might be with the *Jurdy :* ' that is the flying provi-
sion-train which since ancient times is sent down from Syria to
relieve the returning pilgrimage at Medáin Sâlih ; but commonly
lying there only three days, the time would not have sufficed me.

I thought the stars were so disposed that I should not go to
Arabia ; but, said my Moslem friends, ' the Pasha himself could
not forbid any taking this journey with the caravan ; and though
I were a *Nasrâny,* what hindered ! when I went not down
to the *Harameyn* (two sacred cities), but to Medáin Sâlih ;
how ! I an honest person might not go, when there went down

every year with the Haj all the desperate cutters of the town ;
nay the most dangerous ribalds of Damascus were already at
Muzeyrîb, to kill and to spoil upon the skirts of the caravan
journeying in the wilderness.' Also they said ' it was but a few
years since Christian masons (there are no Moslems of the
craft in Damascus) had been sent with the Haj to repair
the water-tower or kella and cistern at the same Medáin
Sâlih.'

There is every year a new stirring of this goodly Oriental
city in the days before the Haj ; so many strangers are passing
in the bazaars, of outlandish speech and clothing from far
provinces. The more part are of Asia Minor, many of them
bearing over-great white turbans that might weigh more than
their heads : the most are poor folk of a solemn countenance,
which wander in the streets seeking the bakers' stalls, and I saw
that many of the Damascenes could answer them in their
own language. The town is moved in the departure of the
great Pilgrimage of the Religion and again at the home-coming,
which is made a public spectacle ; almost every Moslem household has some one of their kindred in the caravan. In the
markets there is much taking up in haste of wares for the
road. The tent-makers are most busy in their street, over-
looking and renewing the old canvas of hundreds of tents,
of tilts and the curtains for litters ; the curriers in their bazaar
are selling apace the water-skins and leathern buckets and
saddle-bottles, *matara* or *zemzemîeh;* the carpenters' craft are
labouring in all haste for the Haj, the most of them mending
litter-frames. In the *Peraean* outlying quarter, *el-Medân*, is
cheapening and delivery of grain, a provision by the way for
the Haj cattle. Already there come by the streets, passing
daily forth, the *akkâms* with the swagging litters mounted high
upon the tall pilgrim-camels. They are the Haj caravan drivers,
and upon the silent great shuffle-footed beasts, they hold insolently their path through the narrow bazaars ; commonly
ferocious young men, whose mouths are full of horrible cursings :
and whoso is not of this stomach, him they think unmeet for
the road. The *Mukowwems* or Haj camel-masters have called
in their cattle (all are strong males) from the wilderness to
the camel-yards in Damascus, where their serving-men are busy
stuffing pillows under the pack-saddle frames, and lapping,
first over all the camels' chines, thick blanket-felts of Aleppo,
that they should not be galled ; the gear is not lifted till
their return after four months, if they may return alive, from
so great a voyage. The mukowwems are sturdy, weathered
men of the road, that can hold the mastery over their often

1—2

mutinous crews ; it is written in their hard faces that they
are overcomers of the evil by the evil, and able to deal in
the long desert way with the perfidy of the elvish Beduins.
It is the custom in these caravan countries that all who are
to set forth, meet together in some common place without
the city. The assembling of the pilgrim multitude is always
by the lake of Muzeyrîb in the high steppes beyond Jordan,
two journeys from Damascus. Here the hajjies who have
taken the field are encamped, and lie a week or ten days
in the desert before their long voyage. The Haj Pasha, his
affairs despatched with the government in Damascus, arrives
the third day before their departure, to discharge all first
payments to the Beduw and to agree with the water-carriers,
(which are Beduins,) for the military service.

  The open ways of Damascus upon that side, lately encumbered with the daily passage of hundreds of litters, and all
that, to our eyes, strange and motley train, of the oriental
pilgrimage, were again void and silent ; the Haj had departed
from among us. A little money is caught at as great gain
in these lands long vexed by a criminal government : the hope
of silver immediately brought me five or six poorer persons,
saying all with great By-Gods they would set their seals to
a paper to carry me safely to Medáin Sâlih, whether I would
ride upon pack-horses, upon mules, asses, dromedaries, barely
upon camel-back, or in a litter. I agreed with a Persian,
mukowwem to those of his nation which come every year
about from the East by Bagdad, Aleppo, Damascus, to " see
the cities " ; and there they join themselves with the great
Ottoman Haj caravan. This poor rich man was well content,
for a few pounds in his hand which helped him to reckon with
his corn-chandler, to convey me to Medáin Sâlih. It was a last
moment, the Pasha was departed two days since, and this man
must make after with great journeys. I was presently clothed
as a Syrian of simple fortune, and ready with store of caravan
biscuit to ride along with him ; mingled with the Persians
in the Haj journey I should be the less noted whether by
Persians or Arabs. This mukowwem's servants and his gear
were already eight days at Muzeyrîb camp.

  It was afternoon when a few Arab friends bade me God-
speed, and mounted with my camel bags upon a mule I came
riding through Damascus with the Persian, Mohammed Aga,
and a small company. As we turned from the long city street,
that which in Paul's days was called " The Straight," to go up
through the Medân to the *Boábat-Ullah*, some of the bystanders
at the corner, setting upon me their eyes, said to each other,

" Who is this ? Eigh ! " Another answered him half jestingly,
" It is some one belonging to the *Ajamy* " (Persian). From
the Boábat (great gate of) Ullah, so named of the passing
forth of the holy pilgrimage thereat, the high desert lies before us those hundreds of leagues to the Harameyn ; at first
a waste plain of gravel and loam upon limestone, for ten
or twelve days, and always rising, to *Maan* in " the mountain of Edom " near to Petra. Twenty-six marches from
Muzeyrîb is el-Medina, the prophet's city (*Medinat en-Néby*,
in old time *Yathrib*) : at forty marches is Mecca. There were
none now in all the road, by which the last hajjies had passed
five days before us. The sun setting, we came to the little outlying village *Kesmîh :* by the road was showed me a white
cupola, the sleeping station of the commander of the pilgrimage,
Emir el-Haj, in the evening of his solemn setting forth from
Damascus. We came by a beaten way over the wilderness,
paved of old at the crossing of winter stream-beds for the safe
passage of the Haj camels, which have no foothold in sliding
ground ; by some other are seen ruinous bridges—as all is now
ruinous in the Ottoman Empire. There is a block drift strewed
over this wilderness ; the like is found, much to our amazement,
under all climates of the world.

We had sorry night quarters at Kesmîh, to lie out, with
fálling weather, in a filthy field, nor very long to repose. At
three hours past midnight we were again riding. There were
come along with us some few other, late and last poor foot wanderers, of the Persian's acquaintance and nation ; blithely they
addressed themselves to this sacred voyage, and as the sun began
to spring and smile with warmth upon the earth, like awaken-
ing birds, they began to warble the sweet bird-like Persian airs.
Marching with most alacrity was a yellow-haired young der-
wîsh, the best minstrel of them all ; with the rest of his
breath he laughed and cracked and would hail me cheerfully in
the best Arabic that he could. They comforted thémselves by
the way with tobacco, and there was none, said they, better in
the whole world than this sweet leaf of their own country.
There arose the high train of Hermon aloft before us, hoar-
headed with the first snows and as it were a white cloud hanging in the element, but the autumn in the plain was yet light
and warm. At twenty miles we passed before *Salâmen*, an old
ruined place with towers and inhabited ruins, such as those seen
in the *Hauran :* five miles further another ruined site. Some
of my companions were imaginative of the stranger, because
I enquired the names. We alighted first at afternoon by a cistern of foul water *Keteyby*, where a guard was set of two ruffian

troopers, and when coming there very thirsty I refused to drink,
" Oho ! who is here ? " cries one of them with an ill countenance,
" it is I guess some Nasrâny ; auh, is this one, I say, who should
go with the Haj ? "   Nine miles from thence we passed before a
village, *Meskîn :* faring by the way, we overtook a costard-
monger driving his ass with swagging chests of the half-rotted
autumn grapes, to sell his cheap wares to the poor pilgrims for
dear money at Muzeyrîb : whilst I bought of his cool bunches,
this fellow, full of gibes of the road, had descried me and " Art
thou going, cried he, to Mecca ?   Ha ! he is not one to go with
the Haj ! and you that come along with him, what is this for an
hajjy ? "   At foot pace we came to the camp at Muzeyrîb after
eight o'clock, by dark night ; the forced march was sixteen hours.
We had yet to do, shouting for the Aga's people, by their
names, to find our tents, but not much, for after the hundreds
of years of the pilgrimage all the Haj service is well ordered.
The mukowwems know their own places, and these voices were
presently answered by some of his servants who led us to their
lodging.   The morrow was one of preparation, the day after we
should depart.   The Aga counselled me not to go abroad from
our lodging.   The gun would be fired two days earlier this year
for the pilgrims' departure, because the season was lateward.
We had ten marches through the northern highlands, and the
first rains might fall upon us ere we descended to Arabia :
in this soil mixed with loam the loaded camels slide, in rainy
weather, and cannot safely pass.   There was a great stillness in
all their camp ; these were the last hours of repose.   As it was
night there came the waits, of young camp-followers with links ;
who saluting every pavilion were last at the Persians' lodgings,
(their place, as they are strangers and schismatics, doubtless for
the avoiding of strifes, is appointed in the rear of all the great
caravan) with the refrain *bes-salaamy bes-salaamy, Ullah yetow-
wel ummr-hu, hy el-âdy, hy el-âdy, Mohammed Aga!* " go in
peace, good speed, heigho the largess !   We keep this custom,
the Lord gave long life to him ; " and the Persian, who durst not
break the usage, found his penny with a sorry countenance.

The new dawn appearing we removed not yet.   The day
risen the tents were dismantled, the camels led in ready to
their companies, and halted beside their loads.   We waited to
hear the cannon shot which should open that year's pilgrimage.
It was near ten o'clock when we heard the signal gun fired,
and then, without any disorder, litters were suddenly heaved
and braced upon the bearing beasts, their charges laid upon
the kneeling camels, and the thousands of riders, all born in
the caravan countries, mounted in silence.   As all is up the

drivers are left standing upon their feet, or sit to rest out the latest moments on their heels : they with other camp and tent servants must ride those three hundred leagues upon their bare soles, although they faint ; and are to measure the ground again upward with their weary feet from the holy places. At the second gun, fired a few moments after, the Pasha's litter advances and after him goes the head of the caravan column : other fifteen or twenty minutes we, who have places in the rear, must halt, that is until the long train is unfolded before us ; then we strike our camels and the great pilgrimage is moving. There go commonly three or four camels abreast and seldom five : the length of the slow-footed multitude of men and cattle is near two miles, and the width some hundred yards in the open plains. The hajjàj were this year by their account (which may be above the truth) 6000 persons ; of these more than half are serving men on foot ; and 10,000 of all kinds of cattle, the most camels, then mules, hackneys, asses and a few dromedaries of Arabians returning in security of the great convoy to their own districts. We march in an empty waste, a plain of gravel, where nothing appeared and never a road before us. Hermon, now to the backward, with his mighty shoulders of snows closes the northern horizon ; to the nomads of the East a noble landmark of Syria, they name it *Towîl éth-Thalj* ' the height of snow ' (of which they have small experience in the rainless sunstricken land of Arabia). It was a Sunday, when this pilgrimage began, and holiday weather, the summer azure light was not all faded from the Syrian heaven ; the 13th of November 1876 ; and after twelve miles way, (a little, which seemed long in the beginning,) we came to the second desert station, where the tents which we had left behind us at Muzeyrîb, stood already pitched in white ranks before us in the open wilderness. Thus every day the light tent-servants' train outwent our heavy march, in which, as every company has obtained their place from the first remove, this they observe continually until their journey's end. Arriving we ride apart, every company to their proper lodgings : this encampment is named *Ramta.*

It is their caravan prudence, that in the beginning of a long way, the first shall be a short journey ; the beasts feel their burdens, the passengers have fallen in that to their riding in the field. Of a few sticks (gathered hastily by the way), of the desert bushes, cooking fires are soon kindled before all the tents ; and since here are no stones at hand to set under the pots as Beduins use, the pilgrim hearth is a scraped out hole, so that their vessels may stand, with the brands put under, upon the

two brinks, and with very little fuel they make ready their poor
messes. The small military tents of the Haj escort of troopers
and armed dromedary riders, *Ageyl*, (the most *Nejd* men), are
pitched round about the great caravan encampment, at sixty
and sixty paces : in each tent fellowship the watches are kept
till the day dawning. A paper lantern after sunset is hung
before every one to burn all night, where a sentinel stands with
his musket, and they suffer none to pass their lines unchal-
lenged. Great is all townsmen's dread of the Beduw, as if they
were the demons of this wild waste earth, every ready to assail
the Haj passengers ; and there is no Beduwy durst chop logic
in the dark with these often ferocious shooters, that might
answer him with lead and who are heard from time to time,
firing backward into the desert all night ; and at every instant
crying down the line *kerakô kerakô* (sentinel !) the next and the
next men thereto answering with *haderûn* (ready). I saw not
that any officer went the rounds. So busy is the first watch,
whilst the camp is waking. These crickets begin to lose their
voices about midnight, when for aught I could see the most of
their lights were out ; and it is likely the unpaid men spare
their allowance : those poor soldiers sell their candles privily
in the Haj market.

In the first evening hour there is some merrymake of
drum-beating and soft fluting, and Arcadian sweetness of the
Persians singing in the tents about us ; in others they chant
together some piece of their devotion. In all the pilgrims'
lodgings are paper lanterns with candles burning ; but the camp
is weary and all is soon at rest. The hajjies lie down in their
clothes the few night hours till the morrow gun-fire ; then to
rise suddenly for the march, and not knowing how early they
may hear it, but this is as the rest, after the Pasha's good
pleasure and the weather.

At half past five o'clock was the warning shot for the second
journey. The night sky was dark and showery when we removed, and cressets of iron cages set upon poles were borne to
light the way, upon serving men's shoulders, in all the companies. The dawn discovered the same barren upland before
us, of shallow gravel and clay ground upon limestone.

The *Derb el-Haj* is no made road, but here a multitude of
cattle-paths beaten hollow by the camels' tread, in the marching
thus once in the year, of so many generations of the motley
pilgrimage over this waste. Such many equal paths lying
together one of the ancient Arabian poets has compared to the
bars of the rayed Arabic mantle. Commonly a shot is heard
near mid-day, the signal to halt ; we have then a short resting-

while, but the beasts are not unloaded and remain standing.
Men alight and the more devout bow down their faces to say
the canonical prayer towards Mecca. Our halt is twenty minutes ;
some days it is less or even omitted, as the Pasha has deemed
expedient, and in easy marches may be lengthened to forty
minutes. " The Pasha (say the caravaners) is our *Sooltân*."
Having marched twenty miles at our left hand appeared *Mafrak*,
the second Haj road tower, after the great kella at Muzeyrîb,
but it is ruinous and as are some other towers abandoned. The
kellas are fortified water stations weakly garrisoned ; they may
have been built two or three centuries, and are of good masonry.
The well is in the midst of a kella ; the water, raised by a
simple machine of drum and buckets, whose shaft is turned by
a mule's labour, flows forth to fill a cistern or *birket* without the
walls. Gear and mules must be fetched down with the Haj
from Damascus upon all the desert road, to Medáin Sâlih.
The cisterns are jealously guarded ; as in them is the life of the
great caravan. No Aarab (nomads) are suffered to draw of that
water ; the garrisons would shoot out upon them from the
tower, in which, closed with an iron-plated door, they are
sheltered themselves all the year from the insolence of the
nomads. The kellas stand alone, as it were ships, in the im-
mensity of the desert ; they are not built at distances of camps,
but according to the opportunity of water ; it is more often
two or even three marches between them. The most difficult
passage of the pilgrim road before Medina, is that four or five
marches in high ground next above Medáin Sâlih ; where are
neither wells nor springs, but two ruined kellas with their great
birkets to be filled only by torrent water, so that some years,
in a nearly rainless country, they lie dry. A *nejjâb* or post,
who is a Beduin dromedary-rider, is therefore sent up every
year from Medáin Sâlih, bringing word to Damascus, in *ramathan* before the pilgrimage, whether there be water run in the
birket at *Dàr el-Hamra*, and reporting likewise of the state of
the next waters. This year he was a messenger of good tidings,
(showers and freshets in the mountains had filled the birket)
and returned with the Pasha's commandment in his mouth,
(since in the garrisons there are few or none lettered) to set a
guard over the water. But in years when the birket is empty,
some 1500 *girbies* are taken up in Damascus by the Haj administration, to furnish a public supplement of five days water
for all the caravan : these water-skins are loaded betwixt the
distant waterings, at the government cost, by Beduin carriers.

The caravaners pass the ruined and abandoned kellàs with
curses between their teeth, which they cast, I know not how justly,

at the Haj officers and say " all the birkets leak and there is no
water for the hajjàj ; every year there is money paid out of the
treasury that should be for the maintenance of the buildings ;
these embezzling pashas swallow the public silver ;   we may
hardly draw now of any cistern before *Maan,* but after the
long marches must send far to seek it, and that we may find is
not good to drink."   Turkish peculation is notorious in all the
Haj service, which somewhat to abate certain Greek Christians,
Syrians, are always bursars in Damascus of the great Mohammedan pilgrimage :—this is the law of the road, that all look
through their fingers.   The decay of the road is also, because
much less of the public treasure is now spent for the Haj
service.   The impoverished Ottoman government has withdrawn the not long established camp at Maan, and greatly
diminished the kella allowances ; but the yearly cost of the Haj
road is said to be yet £50,000, levied from the province of Syria,
where the Christians cry out, it is tyranny that they too
must pay from their slender purses, for this seeking hallows of
the Moslemîn.   A yearly loss to the empire is the *surra* or
" bundles of money " to buy a peaceful passage of the abhorred
Beduins : the half part of Western Arabia is fed thereby, and
yet it were of more cost, for the military escort, to pass " by
the sword."   The destitute Beduins will abate nothing of their
yearly pension ; that which was paid to their fathers, they
believe should be always due to them out of the treasures
of the ' Sooltan,' and if any less be proffered them they
would say " The unfaithful pashas have devoured it ! " the
pilgrimage should not pass, and none might persuade them,
although the *Dowla* (Sultan's Empire) were perishing.   It
were news to them that the Sultan of Islam is but a Turk
and of strange blood : they take him to be as the personage of
a prophet, king of the world by the divine will, unto whom
all owe obedience.   Malcontent, as has been often seen, they
would assault the Haj march or set upon some corner of the
camp by night, hoping to drive off a booty of camels : in
warfare they beset the strait places, where the firing down of
a hundred beggarly matchlocks upon the thick multitude must
cost many lives ; so an Egyptian army of Ibrahîm Pasha was
defeated in the south country by *Harb* Beduins.

Few hours westward of our march is Geraza, now *Jerash,*
where I had seen formerly stupendous Roman ruins ; and for
Mohammedans there is a grave of their prophet *Hûd,* who lies
buried in more places of Arabia. By five in the afternoon,
having journeyed thirty miles, we had sight again of our white
encampment pitched before us. The Haj alighting, there come

riding in from the horizon, with beating of tambours, the *Sayàl* troopers, our rear guard, and after them the squadron of *Ageyl*, which follow the Haj caravan at two miles distance, and wheeling they go to alight all round our ranges in the military tents. Also troopers march at the head of the caravan, with the Pasha and two field pieces borne upon mules' backs; other few, and sorry looking men they are, ride without keeping any order by the long flanks of the advancing column. The Ageyl are Arabians from the midst of the Peninsula, mostly *Kasîm* men of the caravan towns and villages *Boreyda, Aneyzy, el-Ayûn, el-Bukkarîa, el-Khubbera, er-Russ.* These, with all strangers cameleers of their nation, trafficking in Mesopotamia and in Syria, are called there the Ageyl and by the Beduins *el-Ageylát.* There are 150 dromedary riders, Ageyl, armed with matchlocks, appointed to the Haj service; bred up in land of nomads they boast themselves most able of all men to deal with the landloping Beduins. There is an elected sheykh of the Syrian Ageyl at Damascus, through whom they treat with the government; he was in my time *Sleyman abu Daûd*, a worthy man of Aneyzy family and had succeeded one lately deposed, of Boreyda: both were camel brokers in the Syrian city. The dromedary troop ride commonly singing some ribaldry in contempt of the Beduins, whom as oasis dwellers they hate naturally. Arabs of the blood, they are lean lithe bodies of swarthy and sorry aspect, unlike the broad white faces and sleek persons of Damascus citizens. The Damascenes hold them for little better than Beduw, they also accounting all the Nejd country people of the purer Arabian speech, and rightly, Beduins; so the great Emir *Ibn Rashîd* and the Waháby prince they say are "Beduins." These Arabian oasis men are mistrusted, for their foreign looks, by the inhabitants of cities: so on the road they say "Woe to the hajjy that fainting or lingering falls into the hands of the Ageyl! Ouff! they will cut his purse and his wezand!" Friends dissuaded me when at first I thought to have ridden with them, saying they would murder me when we were out of sight of Muzeyrîb. I have since known many of them, all worthy men; they are the Arabians that I have later visited in Nejd. The Arabs are always of a factious humour, and every condition will thus hardly accuse other.

In the spring of the year before, I had months long wandered through this country beyond Jordan and the Dead Sea. From hence to the eastward are the plains of Bashan, and a great antique city of basalt, her walls and roofs yet remaining, but since centuries not inhabited, *Umm Jemâl* (in Jeremiah Beth

Gamul) chief of many such basalt cities, now standing wide
from the inhabited land. In them all I saw churches with the
cross and Greek inscriptions, and read upon a lintel in the
tower of one of them, in this town without inhabitant, (the
letter-pits yet stained with vermillion,) [EN T]ȢTⲰ ✛ NIKΛS
BOHΘI—words of Constantine's vision. The narrow streets
and courts of Umm Jemâl are choked with great weeds, more
than the wild growth of the desert. Here are chambers and
towers, vaults and cellars ; the house doors, clean wrought flags
of basalt, yet roll heavily in their sockets of basalt, and ring if
you strike them as bells of an high tone. The ceiled chambers
are stonehenges ; the stone rafters not of length to ride upon
the walls, you see them thus composed (fig. *infra*). The basalt

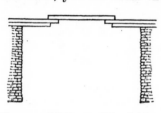

metal is eternal and the building
of great stones fairly laid, is " for
short time an endless monument,"
confirmed by its own weight.
Those plains now wilderness are
basalt, whereupon lies too shallow
earth for growth of timber ; the
people of Bashan had this lava by
them, which would yield to be riven in balks and flags ; and
it would cost them less than camel-borne trees which they
must have bought in Gilead.

Wide are the antique burying grounds of these dead cities,
the headstones standing of indestructible basalt ; the " old
desolate places " are not heaps and ruins, but carcases which
might return to be inhabited under a better government : perhaps thus outlying they were forsaken in the Mohammedan
decay of Syria, for the fear of the Beduins. There are some
of them in part reoccupied, as the Metropolis *Bosra*, full of great
old Romish and Christian buildings.

On the morrow we set forward at the same hour ; after ten
miles we rode by a column or tall milestone : all such are tokens
of an ancient road. At the wayside stands a dead village of stone
building, such as those in the Hauran. This journey was short ;
little after noon we came in sight of our city of tents, whitened
in the sun : from the wady brow I could overlook this Haj encampment, pitched in lower ground, as a military field measured
by the camp marshal. Their good order has grown up through
long generations, the tent rows and great pavilions standing
always in the same places : their number seemed to me about
two hundred. In each of them with the serving men might be
fifteen or twenty persons, many besides are the smaller tents.
We were here at the watering *Zerka*, the Biblical Jabbok, a

border of the children of Ammon in Moses' days. The caravan plashed through the rocky brook, running down towards the Jordan ; westward, that slender water of the desert is increased by springs : I have waded in June at a ford some hours lower, when the tepid water reached to our girdles.

A gunshot from the road stands a great old tower, *Kellat ez-Zerka.* This stronghold in the wilderness is, by the tradition, from the times before Mohammed ; the building is massy and not ruined. This is none of the Haj road forts, and is now seldom a night lodging of passengers or nomads and shelter for the Beduin folds. Here says the tradition was the residence of an ancient hero, *Shebîb ibn Tubbai ;* and from hence, one behind other, is a chain of such antique fortresses and watch-towers in the wilderness to *Shôbek,* nearly an hundred miles southward in Edom : at my former passing, in these deserts, I had seen some of them. Ibn Tubbai was Sultan of the land from below Maan, as they tell, unto mount Hermon. Two days from hence, south and west of the *Derb el-Haj,* I had passed an antique fortress in the desert side, which is also very considerable. " A Kasr (castle) of the old *Yahud* " (Jews) answered the *Beny Sôkhr* nomad who conveyed me on his *thelûl* (dromedary) ; he called it *Guwah* or *Kasr es-Shebîb,* and of a santon whose *makám* (sacred place of sepulture) is seen thereby, *Sheykh Besîr.* Sick I was then of long dieting with the Beduins ; if I alighted I could not easily have remounted, and as I entered the door, the fellow might forsake me, which he did the next day indeed. One told me who had been long in the road service at Maan, that better than all these is a tower he had seen two days south-east-ward from the *Kellat Belka,* whither for some danger, his Beduin company had led him far about, as he went to Maan. Said he " It is a *serai,* a very palace, and fresh (under this climate) as the building of yesterday ; " he was there by night and could not tell me if there were any engraved inscriptions. Was it a residence of some Ghrassanite prince ? Other lesser towers, which I passed not much below Kasr Besîr, were called by my companion *Mughraz* and *Risshán ;* more I have seen, appearing as watch-towers upon an high ridge towards *Kerak.* It is mentioned in the Hebrew scriptures of King Uzziah, who had much cattle, that he built towers and hewed cisterns in the desert ; such cisterns I have found in the wilderness of Hebron shelving to the Dead Sea. The tower was always the hope of this insecure Semitic world, so that Jehovah is lauded as " a Tower of Salvation, a strong tower from the enemy, a strong tower in His name." As for this antique name Ibn Tubbai, there is yet as I hear a small ancient nomad tribe, at the east part of the lake of Tiberias, *El-Klîb* or *Kleb*, whose sheykh's family name is *Ibn et-Tubbai.*

I was startled, where I reposed in my little travelling tent, by wailing cries and a rumour from the Persians' pavilion : in such a mukowwem's great canvas lodging might well assemble an hundred persons. In the midst is a square settle, which is carried in pieces, whereupon three personages may be seated cross-legged ; and housed within is all his gear and two camel litters. There entering, I was witness of a sorrowful execution. I took by the elbow one of this throng of grave faces, to know what was going forward. He whispered, " An *haràmy* " (thief). The accused was put to the torture—but if the wretch were innocent, for his health broken what god or human afterthought might make him amends !—Terrible in this silence sounded the handstrokes and his mortal groans. I asked again " Why is he beaten so ? " *Answer.* " Until he will confess where it is hidden, the cursed one ! "—" And if they beat on thus he will be dead ! " *Answer.* " Except he confess, they will leave no life in him." As I went through them, I heard that already four stout fellows had wearied their arms over him, and the fifth was now in the beginning of his strength. With an earnest countenance, he heaved in his two hands a tough plant and fetched down every stroke upon him with all his might. This malefactor was laid prone, men held down his legs, some kneeled upon his two shoulders and kneaded him, without pity. The writhing worm and no man, after the first cries drawn from him, now in a long anguish groaned hideously ; I thought, within a while he must be beaten in pieces and is already a broken man for his life after. It was perilous for me to tempt so many strangers' eyes, but as humanity required, I called to them, " Sirs I am an hakîm ; this man may not bear more, hold or he may die under your handling ! "—words which, besides their looking upon the speaker, were not regarded. Soon after I saw the grovelling wretch lifted from the earth, he had confessed his fault ; some then bearing up under his arms and all men cursing him, he walked as he could and was led forth. (Of that lying down to be beaten before the judge's face we read in Moses.) This was an Arab caravan servant of Bagdad and greyheaded : bursting a lock he had stolen the purse with £40 of his Persian master, a foolish young man, and hid it beside their tent in the earth.

This power of execution is with the chiefs of the pilgrim companies, and they repress the most dangerous spirits in the caravan : many among the haj servants are lurkers from justice and from the military conscription. " *Khalîl Effendi* " (said the

Persian when he found me alone) " what is this meddling with
the man's punishment ? wouldest thou to Medáin Sâlih, or no ?
This may be told to-morrow in the ears of the Pasha ; then
they will know you, and you will be turned back. Come no
more forth in the public view." But as an European I trod
every day upon the *mesquin* oriental prudence ; in camp he
would have me remain in my little tent separately. It is
perilous in the Haj to lodge alone at night, and I hired one of
the drivers, to cook my supper and set up the tent when we
alighted and at night to sleep by me.

The morrow was lowering and autumn showers delayed
us : it was two hours before mid-day when we heard the signal
shot to remove. The sun again shone forth cheerfully to dry
our wet coverlets and clothing ; we passed by an open limestone
country, here with many crooked trees, much like oaks, but
their leaf is ash-like ; the cooks and servants and every poor
man running, began to rend down and hew and make booty of
dry branches, and the Haj passing year by year it is a wonder
there should anything remain of them. I rode openly in the
caravan with my bags upon camel-back, and mused how I should
measure the way—by camels' paces ? but I found some camels
will step 50 and some 60 times in a minute, also the brute's
step is not at all hours alike. The Haj caravan hour I esteem
to be hardly above $2\frac{1}{2}$ miles. Afterward when even my watch
failed, I have computed distances in Arabia by camel journeys ;
nor in this manner so rude that the situation of any place in
so vast a country, may not be found by diligent cross reckoning,
with the largest error, I suppose, of thirty miles.

Beduins in these highlands are the Beny Sókhr, a strong
tribe and lately formidable, having many horsemen ; so that
none durst pass these downs, unless by night time or riding
in strong companies. Their intolerable Beduin insolence was
checked by a military expedition under the same Mohammed
Saîd now pasha-guardian of the pilgrimage, a valiant and
victorious captain, exercised in this manner of civil warfare
from his youth. The Aarab easily discouraged, whose most
strength is ever in their tongues, and none leading them,
were broken, and the Pasha mulcted them of horses and cattle.
The B. Sókhr being thus submitted to the Dowla, promised
for themselves to plough the land as the *fellahîn*. Those tribesmen are now the principal Beduin Haj carriers, from the north
down even to Mecca ; they are dispraised by their nomad
neighbours. Aarab of the borders, there is in them a double
corruption, of the settled land and the wilderness : other
Beduins speak of them a word in hatred, which is not to be

believed to the letter. "*Wellah* (by God) the Sokhûr will cut
the throat of a guest in the tent." To violate the guest, " the
guest of Ullah," in the religion of the desert, is the great
offence. Clients of the Beny Sókhr and partakers of their
country, are the Beny *Seleyta:* this weak nomad tribe are
a poor sort of people whom I have heard named treacherous ;
they pitch separately, (and, as the Beduins, after their kinships,)
in the same camp. I heard there are no marriages between them.

When the *Sókhry*, he of Shebîb's tower, abandoned me at
their sheykh's tent I found them kind : my complaint heard, the
sheykh vaulted with the long lance upon his mare, which stood
bound by the tent-side, and calling other two horsemen to
follow him, they parted at a gallop ; but not finding the traitor,
the Beduin cavaliers returned after an hour, when they had
well breathed their mares, saying ' that such had been the will of
Ullah ! ' Killing a sheep, he made the guest-supper at sunset
and entertained me with a noble hospitality and gentleness. The
morning being come as they were about to remove, he sent
me forward mounted on his own *thelûl*, with a black servant
to the sheykh of B. Sókhr ; but there I fared not so well.
When we arrived at his great booth, newly pitched and solitary
near the sculptured ruins *Umm Shetta* or *Meshetta* (also the
name of a *fendy* of the northern *Wélad Aly*), we found none
but women ; I saw two serpents slain in their tents' new ground,
they brought me milk and I sat down to await my adventure.
The sheykh *Effendy el-Fáiz* came first at afternoon ; he asked
them if I had eaten aught there. Then notwithstanding the
milk, he coveted a ransom, and began to threaten me ; at last
he said, if I would give him a present I might depart in peace.
I answered, " Let him give me another, his mare : " he bade
one lead his mare round and he would give her, but I condemned the jade, saying " I would not receive his old hackney
at a gift." The company that came with him, as elvish Arabs
laughed out, and seeing himself mocked this bell-wether found
no better counsel than to let me go. His dealing so with
a guest would certainly have been condemned as a cur's deed
by all Beduw. But strangely it is told that he himself is but
an incomer of the Arabs about Gaza (which are *Howeytát*) :
whereas in the right Arabian tribes the sheykh can be none
other than chief among the elders of the noble blood of their
patriarch. I saw in other B. Sókhr tents the goodly beduish
hospitality.

The Wélad Aly, of *Annezy*, are eastward, and their *dîra*
(nomad circuit) marches upon the Hauran. It is a half tribe
grown strong in the north, the rest of them remain in their

ancient seats between Medina and Medáin Sâlih. Even the Sokhûr were of old Southern Arabs, and their ancient dîra was by the same Medáin Sâlih, where it is fabled of them they are the offspring of those sandstone rocks (*sokhr*). These Peraean Beduw are more easy in their religion than the Wahabish tribesmen of Arabia ; they make little account of pattering the daily formal prayers, nor do they rightly know them. The women are not veiled, they mark their faces with some blue lines and spots, which I have not seen in Arabia Proper, and bind their doubled locks, combed upon their foreheads, with a fillet. The Aarab have no religious elders dwelling in their miserable encampments, nor have any of them learned letters : who then should teach the Beduw their religion.? Yet this was sometime endeavoured in Arabia under the old Waháby. The Wélad Aly are rich in cattle, they and their great sheykh *Mohammed ed-Dúgy,* are principal purveyors of the great haj camels.

Westward towards Jordan lies Gilead, a land of noble aspect in these bald countries. How fresh to the sight and sweet to every sense are those woodland limestone hills, full of the balm-smelling pines and the tree-laurel sounding with the sobbing sweetness and the amorous wings of doves ! in all paths are blissful fountains ; the valley heads flow down healing to the eyes with veins of purest water. In that laurel-wold country are village ruins, and some yet inhabited. There the settler hews and burns forest as it were in some far woods of the New World : the few people are uncivil and brutish, not subject to any government.—We came this day's march, riding twelve miles, by the ruined *Kella Blat,* where is seen some broken conduit ; soon after we entered our encampment.

These high limestone downs and open plains of Ammon and Moab, Reuben, Gad and Manasseh, are the *Belka* of the nomads, as much as to say Pied land ; highlands of a fresh climate, where all kinds of corn may be grown to plentiful harvests without dressing or irrigation. The shallower grounds, we may read in the Hebrew Scriptures, were at all times pastoral, " a good land for cattle." This is Shem (or Sham) the goodly North Country, where are waters fleeting above the ground : yet the camels are much vexed there with flies and, as the Beduins complain, mankind with fleas, in the many summer months. It may be known by the ruins, that the land was anciently inhabited in towns, hamlets and villages, rudely built, in the expedite Semitic wise. In none of them have I seen any inscriptions.

" The desert " (says the Hebrew prophet) " shall become a plough-land," so might all this good soil, whose " sun is gone

D. T.   2

down whilst it was yet day," return to be full of busy human
lives ; there lacks but the defence of a strong government. One
of the Damascene traders in the caravan said to me, " Seeing
that the Turks (which devour all and repair nothing) leave such
a fresh country in ruins, might not some of your ingenious
people of *Frankistan* lay an iron-way hither ? " Some in Europe
have imagined that Frankish colonies might thrive here, and
there is in sooth breadth of good soil to be occupied. But
perchance the event should not be happy, the laborious first
generation languishing, and those born of them in the land becoming little unlike Arabs. Who is there can wade through Jose-
phus's story of these countries without dismay of heart ! Were
not the sending of such colonists to Syria, as the giving of poor
men beds to lie on, in which other had died of the pestilence ?

Not distant from hence are proud Greekish ruins of Phila-
delphia, now *Ammàn,* anciently *Rabbath* (the metropolis of)
Ammon; the place, in a small open valley ground, I found
to be less that the site of some very inconsiderable English
town. A Roman bridge, of one great span, rides the river,
which flows from a mighty spring head, little above, of lukewarm water. " Why gloriest thou (says Jeremy) in thy
valleys, thy flowing valley ? " The kingdom of Ammon was
as one of our counties ; hardly threescore small townships
and villages. A few miles southward I found in some corn-
fields, which are tilled from the near-lying *es-Salt,* a sumptuous
mausoleum (el-Kasr) of white crystalline limestone blocks ;
within are ranged sarcophagi of the same marble and little
less than that great bed of Og which lay at the next town.
Such monuments of old civil glory are now an astonishment to
our eyes in a land of desolation and of these squalid Arabs.

We removed not before day, passing in the same open
country of loam upon limestone ; a wilderness which ploughed
might yield corn abundantly. Not far from hence is *Hesban,*
where I have seen but some platform and groundwall, as it
might be of a kella upon a rising ground, which is taken for
ruins of Heshbon of the Bible, Sihon's city. There beside
is a torrent-bed and pits, no more those fish pools as the eyes
of love, cisterns of the doves of Heshbon, but cattle ponds
of noisome standing water. Lower is *Umm Rosàs,* a rude
stone-built walled town in ruins : a mile before the place
stands a quaint tower of fair masonry, which may be seen to
lean from the plumb-line, and is adorned with many crosses,
by old Christian builders. The city walls and bastions, almost
fathom thick, are laid of the wild limestone blocks without
mortar, the midst filled in with rubbish. I saw the ruined

town fallen down in heaps, an horrid confusion, where-among
are straddling ogival arches, of their inner house walling yet on
foot, and in the manner of their house-building now at Kerak.—
Bright was the sky and the air, as we journeyed in the autumn
sun ; at the mid-afternoon we passed *Khan ez-Zeyt* where are
arches of an aqueduct. Not much further, after twenty-six
miles, we came to our encampment, in a bottom, beside the
lately repaired *Kellat el-Belka,* being here nearly due east of
Jerusalem, beyond the Dead Sea ; the land altitude is 2870 ft.

We were to depart betimes by the morrow, some enquiring of
the hour ; "At the cannon's word," answered a laughing Damascene of the Haj service. That shot is eloquent in the desert night,
the great caravan rising at the instant, with sudden untimely
hubbub of the pilgrim thousands ; there is a short struggle
of making ready, a calling and running with lanterns, confused
roaring and ruckling of camels, and the tents are taken up
over our heads. In this haste aught left behind will be lost,
all is but a short moment and the pilgrim army is remounted.
The gun fired at four hours after midnight startled many
wayworn bodies ; and often there are some so weary, of those
come on foot from very great distances, that they may not
waken, and the caravan removing they are left behind in the
darkness. Hot tea, ready in glasses, is served with much
sugar, in the Persian lodgings, also the slave will put fire in
their nargîlies (water-pipes) which they may " drink," holding
them in their hands, as they ride forward. Hajjies on horse-
back may linger yet a moment, and overtake the slow-footed
train of camels. There are public coffee sellers which, a little
advanced on the road, cry from their fires to the passengers,
Yellah ! Yellah ! Yellah ! yesully aly Mohammed, Ullah karîm,
which is " Come on, the Lord bless Mohammed, the Lord is
bountiful." So in all things the Semites will proffer God's
name whether for good or for evil. They pour their boiling
pennyworths to any that, on foot, can stand a moment to
drink and comfort the heart, in the cold night towards morning.
Some other sell Damascus flat-bread and dried raisins by the
way side : they are poor Syrians who have found this hard
shift to win a little every year, following the pilgrimage with
small wares upon an ass or a camel, for a certain distance,
to the last Syrian station Maan, or even through the main
deserts, where afterward they sell dates, to Medina and Mecca.
The camels seem to breathe forth smoke in the chill morning of
these highlands, clouds of dust are driven upon our backs
in the northern wind, and benighted, it seems many hours
till the day-spring with the sunbeams that shall warm us.

2—2

But the day was rainy, the pilgrims' bedding, commonly a
cotton quilt, in such a march is wetted through ; yet the
present evils cannot last and each moment we are nearer to the
sun of to-morrow. We journeyed almost forty miles to our
encampment, in a sandy place by the *Kella Katràn*, where
we drank at the cistern a sweet rain water. We pass in this
march by the dry *Wady Mojeb*, which is lower the brook
Arnon. Westward from hence is a four-square limestone-built
walled town in ruins, *Lejûn*, and such as Umm Rosàs, the
wall and corner towers of dry block building, at the midst of
every wall a gate. Among these ruins I saw many round
arches, turned without mortar : the ruins, as in the former
town, are within and without the walls. A little apart to
the southward I saw a square platform of masonry, with degrees all round, as it were a *suggestum* or *concionis locus*.   Is
Lejûn perchance Legio ? see we here a Roman military station,
stativa ? Months before, when I came riding hither in an even-
tide from Kerak, Beduin booths were pitched in the waste
without the walls ; the sun was setting and the camels wandered in of themselves over the desert, the housewives at the
tents milked their small cattle. By the ruins of a city of stone
they received me, in the eternity of the poor nomad tents, with
a kind hospitality.

We removed again at five in the morning. These are the
plains of Moab : not far, at our right hand, is Jebel Kerak,
high wilderness plains, in which are more ruined sites of hamlets
and townships than the Arabs can well number. In the former
year, besides the ruins of Rabbath Moab, I had visited in two
days riding near two score of them. Why should these countries
remain almost unknown ! might not a summer suffice to search
them through ? Nigh the pilgrim road are the ruined towns
Nikkel and *Ensheynish* : a little nearer Kerak I visited *Mehai*,
a double rising ground encumbered with wild ruins : there I
heard might be seen an effigy, some columns and inscriptions ;
but of all this I found nothing, and languishing with famine I
could not climb on through these fallen desolations of stones.
Mehai was a wide uplandish place without any curiosity of
building, but all is dry-laid masonry of the undressed limestone
and the great tabular flint blocks of these plains. I came in
half an hour from thence to *Medeybìa*, a smaller ruined town,
the building and the walls of wild massy blocks of lava ; for the
basalt here has broken up and flowed through the limestones of
the Belka. Of such vulcanic breaches there are many in these
limestone downs and in Edom, and more than all in the Jordan
and Dead Sea valley and that wide hollow land to the gulf of

Akaba. As I was riding towards Kerak, I espied a multitude
of pasturing camels ; my companion told me then, they were
of a tribe come hither from Ibn Rashîd's country : not unlikely
the *Fukara*, in migration, with whom I afterward dwelt about
Medáin Sâlih. South of Kerak, above the *W. el-Hâsy*, are certain
principal ruins, named by the Arabs, *Dat Ras.* There I found two
antique buildings, they are of just masonry and the stone is white
crystalline limestone or marble, as in the (Greekish) mausoleum
near Rabbath Ammon ; (the Belka chalk is changed by the
vulcanic heat, at the eruptions of basalt). The first, four-square,
might seem some small temple or imperial building : at the
sides of the door in the massy frontispiece are niches as it were
of statues, a few broken columns lie there : within the thickness
of the wall is a stair, of great marble blocks, to an upper terrace,
laid upon massy round arches : it was now the den of some wild
beast. " The pelican and the porcupine shall lodge in the upper
lintels thereof." There is a deep dry pool beyond and then
another, lined with rubble-work in mortar, and upon the next
rising ground are lower walls, also of marble masonry as of some
palace or beautiful Grecian building. The quarry, they tell me,
is a little beyond the wady. I could not search further for my
weariness nor loiter, for wide is now the desolation about so noble
ruins. We found a Beduin booth not far off, where the poor man
was much displeased that we could not stay to eat porridge with
him ; and commonly such nightly hospitality received us in the
wilderness.

I saw at Rabbath Moab cyclopean ground walls, laid without
mortar, and street lines of basalt pavement, a colonnade and
some small temple yet standing of Greekish building. If you
will believe them, under the next great heap of stones lies Great
Alexander, whom they call *Thû el Kurneyn* " of the two horns,"
and *meritò* as who in his life would needs be accounted an
offspring of the god Ammon, with his ram's head. Iskander is
now a saint among them and amongst the Greek Christians ; for
they will devoutly kiss his horned image appearing upon some
old denars. I have seen, built in the outer wall of one of their
churches in Palestine, an antique ornament of horned human
heads, it may be of the old Canaanitish Sun-worshippers. We
read in Genesis a like word, perhaps of the horned moon, Ash-
teroth *Karnaim*. Upon the hollow paved way from hence down
towards the Dead Sea, I hear is seen much Cyclopean building.
From this royal city of Moab, in which I found but booths
of summering Kerakers, whose flocks now lie down in the midst
of her, is not far to Kir of Moab, now Kerak, a rock marvellously
strong by nature; so that when all Moab was smitten and destroyed

by the confederate kings of Israel and Judah and Edom, yet it could not be taken and is inhabited at this day. It was here perhaps that the King of Moab in the siege and straitness took his eldest son, that should have reigned after him, and offered him his fearful burnt offering for the land upon the wall.

All the *khurbets* or ruined sites of this country are in the infirm heads of the Arabs, too supine and rude to cast a sum of them, "three hundred and sixty"; a round number of theirs, where they have one for every day in the year : but the now silent daughter of Moab was at all times a little poor uplandish maiden ; we read the Moabitish king "was a sheep master." The plots of khurbets are mostly small as hamlets ; their rude dry building is fallen down in few heaps of the common stones. I was so idle as to write the names of some of them, *Khurbet Enjahsah, Mehnuwara, el-Hahlih, Mehaineh, Meddáin, Negáes, Libbun, Jeljul, Nelnokh, Mehrud, Howihih, Gamereyn* (of the two moons) *Jarfa* (where a Mohammedan shrine and mosque ; anciently it was a church). An ancient paved way passes through the country under Rabba, which we crossed ofttimes in riding ; after their belief, (they have no tradition, of the land, before Mohammed) it is the ancient haj road. Wells and water-pits are many in all this high plain now wilderness : the eye falls everywhere upon stone heaps that the ancient husbandmen once gathered from off their plough-lands—"heaps in the furrows of the fields " says Hosea—which remain after them for ever. Here are very fertile corn lands, ploughed to a handdepth by the Kerakers : a few pounds will purchase a great field, and grain is in their town almost as the sand, that it cannot be sent abroad, for the excessive cost of camel carriage, which is as much as half the load to Jerusalem. Isaiah speaks of a great Moabitish multitude, and surely the ancient people were many in these fresh highlands. The Semites were wont to say of the old nations before them, that they were giants. The Nejd Beduins thus fable of the *B. Helál* of *Aad* and *Thamúd.* So before Moab were the Emim, sons of Anak, defeated by Chedorlaomer, whom Abram, with his three hundred young men, routed and the KING OF NATIONS and other kings two or three, which were in this outriding, with him. If Abraham alone had three hundred men, Abraham was a nomad tribe, and greater than many sub-tribes which are now-a-days in nomad Arabia. We read also of the children of Ammon that they succeeded to the giants, Zamzummim.

When this land came to be weakened, it would be soon partly forsaken, as lying open upon the Beduin marches : the few people would draw together in the stronger villages, the

outlying hamlets would be left without inhabitant. An insecure
country behind them, the fallen places would not be rebuilt. In
any such discouragement Semites are wont to emigrate, and
where they come they will settle themselves, with little looking
backward to return. After their tradition, under Shebîb ibn
Tubbai the land was not yet desolate ; the Aarab *el-Agaba*
destroyed all, they say, in times of Islam,—nomads from el-
Yemen which from strong beginnings are to-day a miserable
remnant of herdsmen under the sheykh of the town, inhabiting
about Kerak, and others of them by the Red Sea. Afterward
they say the B. Helál harried this country, in their passing
by to Egypt. Hither came David with the warfarers of Israel
in the ancient days, and having got the better of the Moabites
(whose king before had dealt very kindly with him, and saved
his father and mother from king Saul) " he cast them, we read,
to the ground and measured them in three parts with a line,
two parts he killed, the third left he alive." Moses, David,
Mohammed are all one in this ; as leaders of Semitic factions
they are ethnicides. With the sword of the destroying angel
they hew God's way before them in the wood of God's world.
In the legend of the kings of Israel when Jehoram and Jehoshaphat go up together with the king of Edom against the
king of Moab they hear that charge of Elisha, but contrary
to the word of Moses, " Smite ye every city of theirs, and fell
every good tree, and stop all wells of water, and mar every good
piece of land with stones " and they did so indeed.—" They
beat down the cities, and on every good ground every man
cast his stone, they stopped all the wells of water and felled
all the good trees." The plains of Moab are now last of all
trodden down by the Beduw, according to the cry of Jeremiah,
" Many pastors have destroyed my vineyard ; they have trodden
my pleasant portion under foot and made a desolate wilderness."
And now the gravelly waste face of the soil is cattle-trodden
and parched as it were to brick, under this burning sunshine.
Moab is called God's washpot, perhaps for the veins of water
in these limestones. But that which I have thought remarkable in these ruined village countries, is that their ancient
people were stone builders, whereas the Mohammedans inhabiting after them are at this day clay builders. The prophets of
old threatened to pour down their stones, and that they should
become as heaps in the fields and as plantings of a vineyard.

Kerak is now a small rude town and her people, of the
nomad speech, are perhaps of Moabitish blood and partly immi-
grants. It is so populous in the eyes of the dispersed nomads
that they call it *el-Medina*, The City. The site is a sharp plat-

form hill of limestone, environed by the winding of a deep
coomb. Ibrahîm Pasha, as he went up to Syria, took this place
with a bloody assault of his Egyptian and Albanian soldiery:
he shut up their sheykh in prison and left behind him a garrison;
but his men were after a few months overpowered by the
ferocious peasants, who jealous of their immemorial liberties,
and fearing lest they should be taxed as subjects to any foreign
power, are at all times rebels to the far-off Syrian government.
Their rock I saw might be taken without bloodshed, by cutting
off the only water, which springs in the deep without; or
Kerak could be occupied at unawares in the spring-time of the
year, when nearly all the villagers lie encamped abroad in tents
as the nomads, for the summering of their cattle. I found them
lodged in worsted booths in two main camps, as the Aarab, in
the desert before the town; and there is a third lesser camp
of Greek Christians which, of late times, are suffered to dwell
here in Beduin country, at the gate of Arabia; but they
are less worthy and hospitable than the Moslems, their formal
religion is most in pattering and dumb superstition. They
have a church building of St. George: a lickdish peasant priest
and another Syrian his deacon are their clergy. It is strange
here to see the Christian religion administered in the tents
of Kedar! I could not find that these gospellers had any conscience of the sanctity of Christ's lore: to the stronger Moslems
I would sooner resort, who are of frank mind and, more than
the other, fortified with the Arabian virtues. Nevertheless
Mohammedans esteem of the Christians and their priests' faith,
in the matter of a deposit; this is ever their fantasy of the
Nasâra. We have seen the pilgrimage treasurers are Christians,
and we always find aliens taken to these trusts, in the Mohammedan governments. Mohammed has made every follower of
his, with his many spending and vanishing wives, a walker upon
quicksands; but Christ's religion contains a man in all, which
binds him in single marriage. The Moslem town-sheykh deals
tolerantly with them, they are part of his " many," but the
Christians complain of vexations; they are all rude men
together. They have sometime attempted and had yet a mind
to go from the place, and buying the rights of the soil, that is
their peace, of the Beduins, for little money, to occupy Ammàn:
but they remain at Kerak where they were born and are townsmen, and there is less to fear. Besides there is a variance between
Mohammed the sheykh of the place and his next cousin Khalîl,
with their nearly equal factions, and each part speaks the
Christian neighbour fair, for the help that is rammed in their
matchlocks, and those Nasâra are hardy mountaineers. But

the rude Moslems look askance upon the Christians' unknown rites, as if they were some impure mysteries. These Moslems show a sepulchre of Noah, who is notwithstanding buried, at great length, in other places. The Christians' sheep are marked down the chine with a threefold cross ╾┿╾┿╾ . Near the town I entered two long ancient galleries, in the limestone rock : one of them, in the valley near Khanzîra, is hewn towards a spring head.

Mohammed Mejelly the sheykh is homeborn, but his father or else his grandsire was an incoming rich peasant-body from *J. el-Khalîl,* the mountains of Hebron ; for which cause any who are less his friends disdain him as a *sheykh fellàh,* " a peasant lord " they say " to rule them ! " He is strong handed, ambitious, a bird of prey ; and they, barbarous subjects who will not be guided by reason, are ruled by strength,—and that is ofttime plain violence. Upon such a sheykh lies all the daily burden of the public hospitality. This peasant duke, whom they call a " Sooltan," taxes the next village *Khanzîra* and holds the poorer sort of nomads in the country about at his obedience. The Beduins even of the *Ghror,* that deep under- lying Dead Sea plain, are his tributaries, a poor spirited folk consumed with fevers, and almost black of the much heat and moisture. So his name, as you alight at any tents of Moab, is first in every man's mouth ; for all this he is a prisoner in his own circuit, nor durst be seen, if he would, without safe con- duct, at Jerusalem or Damascus. Just he is and constant, a politic ruler, as are always the Arab sheykhs, among his own people. The Kerakers are half Beduish, and Mohammed had not learned letters. For the dispatch of his affairs he has commonly some stranger by him as his secretary. It was a Christian when I visited him, one newly escaped hither for an homicide, at Bethlehem, (Kerak, beyond the governed country, is a sure refuge ; such outlaws live of the public hospitality). I heard Mejelly speak a good word, some complaint being brought before him, ' that he would be no party in any dispute between Moslem and Nasrâny ; ' nevertheless the smooth Christian homicide, who behaved himself here as a person of civil integrity, whispered in my ear " Have thou a care of them, for these fear not Ullah." Mohammed, cock of this hill, of a haughty Arabian beauty, is, they say, a trembler in the field ; better him were to comb his beard delicately in a pedlar's glass with his wives at home, than show his fine skin to flying lead and their speary warfare.

Neighbours to the town upon the north are the *B. Hameydy :* a mere stone marks their bounds, *hajar missen,* which stands within

sight of Kerak. It is a tribe, as the rest, which had entered of old
by the sword.   The patriarch of the ancient Belka Arabs is named
Ab el-Ghrennem. With the Syrian Haj government they pass
for vile and treacherous, but are possessors of the most excellent
strains of Arab horses, and in this fresh and plain country there
is always plenty of wild pasture. Good friends were those in
the field with those of the town, until of late there fell among
them a savage division. It happened for the silver of the
Franks, who had treated with the sheykh of Kerak, for that
written stone which lay at *Dîbàn*, (Dibon) in the hills of Moab
and land of the B. Hameydy. I saw the place, there were
fallen down ruins as of some very small village and perhaps
a temple. Mohammed Mejelly, they told me, sent for this
(Moabite) stone ; which laid then upon two mules' backs was
borne to Jerusalem : and Mohammed, with a few bright Frankish
pounds, thought himself vastly well rewarded, since he had
only delivered a block, and that was not his own.   The
Hameydy hearing of his gains, their sheykhs rode to Kerak
to require of Mejelly a just partition of the price ; but when
any Arab has closed the hand upon a penny, for all his smiling
and grave goodly words it comes not forth again. Then the
B. Hameydy fell by night upon the tents of the Kerakers from
the north ; it was the Christians' camp, in which part lies their
inheritance : they killed five and took a score of matchlocks,
also there fell of the nomads three men. The Christians said
further, the Franks had sent other forty pounds, ' for their five
lives,' from Jerusalem. The Hameydy were now retired from
that side of the wilderness, and the townsmen durst no more
pass their embittered neighbours, except it were by night-time.
Mohammed Saîd Pasha, who was governor that year of the
Peraea, would show me by this example when I visited him, the
peril of my going down to Medáin Sâlih ; for said he, if I removed
some stone from thence, hurly-burlies might ensue and blood be
shed in that wild country ! threescore men he told me (magnify-
ing the numbers) had perished for the block carried from Dîbàn.

We marched this day, the seventh from Muzeyrîb, twelve
hours ; and before evening, descending in some coombs of these
limestone downs, I saw many heaps of stones, which whether to
mark a way, or graves, or places of cursing, or " heaps of witness "
are common in all the Semitic desert countries. We came
down upon a causey with a little bridge, made for the camels'
passage over the slippery loam, to our encampment in Wady
el-Hâsy, which divides the uplands of Moab and Edom : a sandy
seyl-strand or torrent, shelving out of the wilderness. In this
bottom stands the Haj kellâ ; lower it is a narrow valley and

deep, with a brook (perhaps the brook Zared of Moses) running out to the Dead Sea. Such deeps are all the limestone wadies descending from the eastern uplands, as Zerka, Mojeb, W. Kerak, beautiful with wild garden grounds and underwoods of the blossoming oleander, the pasture of the Christians' bees, (but thereof only a savourless honey,) to the Jordan and the alluvial lake valley. But where is the much stuff of these deep worn water furrows? how many solid miles of whitish loamy matter borne down by these brooks in the past milleniums, lie not spread out now upon the Jordan and Salt Valley bottoms! Under the kella is a new cistern to be filled by the freshet, for the well of stinking water within the tower is ruinous. After the long summer we found nothing in the birket to drink, but the shift of waterers was sent out, serving men which had gone all day upon their feet, to seek a cattle pool some miles lower in the valley and formerly known to me. It is a wild garden of rose-laurel and rushes, but from whence they brought again only water putrifying with the staling of the nomads' camels, which ever thus as they drink, envenom that little precious gift of water which is in the desert. This, which we could not drink, must now serve to our cooking. Other names of this valley are *W. Adîra* and *W. Fellah.* I found below the pools, at my former coming, in the first days of June, a wild pasture ground of thick grass nearly a yard high, where some Beduins but then arrived with their cattle; *Aarab el-Hajya,* a feeble tribe of Shobek. I was nobly entertained by their hearty old sheykh *Hajellán,* who killed a sheep to his guests' supper. Here were many wild boars, ravagers of the corn plots, then in the ear, of the kella soldiery : the brook below breaks from the oozy bed of the wady. In all these valley streams are a multitude of small fishes, not unlike fry of chub, of a leaden colour. The Kerak Christians are zealous to show to strangers a little cross-shaped bone in them, near the head, which they think to be divine testimony of the *Messîahi* religion. I found in the kella a garrison of five men, with their Kerak wives and families.

Old Sculptured Ornament in the Peraea.

CHAPTER II.

HERE the 19—20 November our tents were stiffened by the night's frost. Mount Seir or J. Sherra before us (*sherra* is interpreted high), is high and cold, and the Arabs' summer clothing is as nakedness in the winter season. The land is open, not a rock or tree or any good bush to bear off the icy wind ; it is reported, as a thing of a late memory, that wayfaring companies and their cattle have starved, coming this way over in the winter months. In the night they perished together, and the men were found lying by the cold ash-pits of their burned-out watch-fires. Not far from this wady, in front, begins that flint beach, which lies strewn over great part of the mountain of Esau ; a stony nakedness blackened by the weather : it is a head of gravel, whose earth was wasted by the winds and secular rains. This land-face of pebbles shines vapouring in the clear sun, and they are polished as the stones and even the mountains in Sinai by the *ajàj* or dust-bearing blasts. The wide-spread and often three-fathom deep bed of gravel, is the highest platform of land in all that province ; the worn flint-stones are of the washed chalk rock lying beneath, in which are massy (tabular) silicious veins : we see such gravel to be laid out in shallow

streaming water, but since this is the highest ground, from
whence that wash of water ? The land-height is 4000 feet above
the sea ! The Arabs name all this region *Ard Suwwan*, the
Flint-Ground ; the same which is in the old Geographers *Arabia
Petraea*. But, a marvel ! this gravel is not ancient, as the
antiquity of man ; I have found in it such wrought flint instruments as we have from some river and lake gravels and loams
of Europe. Journeying from this wady, we passed six or seven
ancient mile-stones by the wayside, without inscriptions. At
twelve miles' end we crossed the head of a deep and dry torrent
(or *seyl*) named by the Haj *Durf ed-Drawish* " butter-skins of the
poor Derwishes," whose course is not west to the Dead Sea-ward,
but eastward in the desert : so they say " all this land ' seyls ' (or
shelves, so that the shower-waters flow) towards the *Tchôl Bagdad*." In the hollow banks, when last I came by, I had found
a night's lodging. Further in our march we see the soil under
our feet strangely bestrewed with lava, whose edge is marked
upon the gravel-land as it were a drift which is come from the
westward, where we see certain black vulcanic bergs. Here,
and where we journeyed still for fifty more miles, Esau's land is
a great barrenness of gravel stones. We are in the marches of
the *Howeytát*, not a small Beduin nation, whose borders are the
two seas. They are liker nomad fellahîn than Beduins ; many
among them use husbandry, all are tent-dwellers.—I should not
wonder were they found to be Nabateans. *Ibn Jeysey* is sheykh
of the Howeytát *Daràwessha*, of the mountain of Edom ; in
his circuit is Petra. Early in the afternoon we passed by a
broken turret ; so small a sign of human hands is comfortable
to the eyes in this desolate country. From hence three hours
eastward upon the desert side, are the ruins of some considerable place, *Borma* or *Burma*.

Before sunset we came to encamp a little short of the
Kellat Anezy, where is but a cistern for rain water, kept by
two lubbers, sons of old Damascene tower-guards and of Shobek
mothers ; but commonly they live at home in their village.
My pilgrimage companions would hardly believe me that I had
drunk after rain the year before of this birket, they had never
found water there. Some miles from thence, westward, are
ruins of a place which the Arabs name *Jardania*, I went aside
to see it at my former passing : and that there is shadow and
shelter, it is often a lurking place of land-loping Beduw, so that
of the armed company with whom I rode, there was one only
who would follow me for a reward. I found a four-square town
wall nearly thirty feet high and dry building in courses, of the
wild lava blocks. There are corner towers and two mid-bastions

upon a side, the whole area is not great : I saw within but high
heaps of the fallen down lava house-building, a round arch in
the midst and a small birket. What mean those lofty walls ; is
not the site too small for a city ? neither is the soil very fit
hereabout for husbandry ; less town than fortress, it might be
a *praesidium*, in these parts, upon the trade road.   Thereby
stands a black vulcanic mountain which is a landmark seen
from Maan.   Here passing, in my former journeys, we saw
Aarab horsemen which approached us ; we being too many for
them, they came but to beg insolently a handful of tobacco.
In their camp such would be kind hosts ; but had we fallen
into their hands in the desert we should have found them
fiends, they would have stripped us, and perchance in a savage
wantonness have cut some of our throats.   These were three
long-haired Beduins that bid us *salaam* (peace) ; and a fourth
shock-haired cyclops of the desert, whom the fleetness of their
mares had outstripped, trotted in after them, uncouthly seated
upon the rawbone narrow withers of his dromedary, without saddle, without bridle, and only as an herdsman driving
her with his voice and the camel-stick.   His fellows rode
with naked legs and unshod upon their beautiful mares' bare
backs, the halter in one hand, and the long balanced lance,
wavering upon the shoulder, in the other.   We should think
them sprawling riders ; for a boast or warlike exercise, in the
presence of our armed company, they let us view how fairly
they could ride a career and turn : striking back heels and
seated low, with pressed thighs, they parted at a hand-galop,
made a tourney or two easily upon the plain ; and now wheeling
wide, they betook themselves down in the desert, every man
bearing and handling his spear as at point to strike a foeman ; so fetching a compass and we marching, they a little out
of breath came gallantly again.   Under the most ragged of
these riders was a very perfect young and startling chestnut
mare,—so shapely there are only few among them.   Never
combed by her rude master, but all shining beautiful and
gentle of herself, she seemed a darling life upon that savage
soil not worthy of her gracious pasterns : the strutting tail
flowed down even to the ground, and the name (*orfa*) was shed
by the loving nurture of her mother Nature.

The settled folk in Arabian country, are always envious
haters of the nomads that encompass them, in their oases
islands with the danger of the desert.   These with whom I
journeyed, were the captain of the haj road at Maan and
his score of soldiery, the most being armed peasantry of the
place, which came driving a government herd of goats, (the un-

willing contribution of the few unsubmitted Idumean villages)
to sell them at *Nablûs* (Sichem). Shots were fired by some of
them in the rear in contempt of the Beduw, whose mares,
at every gunfire, shrank and sprang under them, so that the
men, with their loose seats were near falling over the horses'
heads. " Nay Sirs ! " they cried back, " nay Sirs, why fray ye
our mares ? " The Beduw thus looking over their shoulders,
the peasantry shot the more, hoping to see them miscarry ; he
of the beautiful filly sat already upon his horse's neck, the
others were almost dislodged. So the officer called to them,
" Hold lads ! " and " have done lads ! " and they " Our guns went
off, wellah, as it were of themselves." And little cared they, as
half desperate men, that had not seen a cross of their pay in
sixteen months, to obey the words of their scurvy commander.
They marched with a pyrrhic dancing and beating the tambour :
it is a leaping counter and tripping high in measure, whilst
they chant in wild manner with wavings of the body and
fighting aloft in the air with the drawn sword. Those Beduins
roughly demanded concerning me " And who is he ? " It was
answered " A Nasrâny,"—by which name, of evil omen, the
nomads could only understand a calamity in their land : and
they arrogantly again in their throats " Like to this one see
ye bring no more hither ! " As I heard their word, I shouted
" Arrest, lay hands on them ! " They thought it time to be
gone, and without leave-taking they turned from us and were
quickly ridden under the horizon.

The pilgrimage set forward betimes on the morrow ; the
signal gunfire heard in front, a moment before the sun rising,
the caravan halted and we alighted a few minutes for the
morning prayer. Westward appeared the highlands of Shobek,
upon our left hand were low ranging hills in the desert. Seir
(interpreted rough woodland), this high and fresh country, was
of old times settled, upon all its western borders, (beyond the
wilderness of stones) ; the khurbets there of antique small
towns, villages and hamlets are not fewer than those of
J. Kerak. Beside Maan, the road station, the land is now
desolate, saving four or five good villages, which yet remain
from antiquity in the high and watered western coast, over-
looking the Ghror and Valley of Salt. Of these is Bosra
(*Buseira*), Amos threatens her palaces ; there, say the Arabs, are
tall standing (Roman) ruins. We held on over the black flint
gravel face of this limestone plain, always at an even height,
near 4000 feet, till two hours after noon, when we had sight
of Maan, and came where in a torrent bed are laid bare certain

great tubers (also common in the country next about) of the
lime rock underlying : these are " the carcases of ancient
kafirs." Here by the fable, stood an antique idolatrous city,
until a voice falling from heaven upon them, they became
these stark stones. I saw many pilgrims alighted to take
up pebbles and cast at the cursed stone kafirs ; whilst the Haj
service, grown old upon the road, having once cast their stones
as novices, pass by with a weary indifference.

Maan is a *merkez* (centre or rest station) of the haj road, another is Medáin Sâlih, before Medina. We arrive, saluted by
the firing of our artillery, mounted upon a rising ground, beside
the long moving lines of the caravan, which pass westward
of the village to their encampment, where little flags are flying
upon all the pavilions : over our Aga's great tent is the lean and
crippling lion of Persia. At Maan I was well known, since in
my former passage when I came hither from Egypt and Sinai,
I had stayed there twenty days. I dreaded the great Haj
officers would here remember me, in their leisure, and send
through the encampment to seek out the " Frenjy ", and I should
be turned back at the borders of Arabia :—and it was so, they
sought for me. Maan, the only village now upon this desolate side
of J. Sherra, began to be colonized, they say, in the last three
centuries ; when here, upon an old ruined site, was founded
a principal Haj station about the kella, made by the Sultan
Selím, a benefactor and builder upon the pilgrimage road.
Such a garrison station was old Maan, under the Romans and in
Mohammed's age, upon the highway of the Sabean traffic and
first in the brow of Syria to those ascending from Arabia.
A gunshot from Maan, upon the north, are ruins which they
call now *Hammam ;* there is a vast dry cistern, unlike the
work of this country, of brick walls, sixty paces upon a side,
which was fed by a little conduit pipe, now wasted, from
a spring at *Shemmîa.* Of the old town, only a few great
upright stones and waste walls are yet standing, some are laid
with mortar and even plastered within, but the most is dry-
building ; the good masonry has been broken up for stones to
build the kella : also I saw at Maan two chapiters of ancient
marble pillars, and upon them some sculptured barbaric ornament of basket or network. Hammam, if it be not Arabic,
resembles a biblical name Homam, which we read in the line
of Esau ; we read Shammah also in the lineage of Esau. Shemmîa is a sister village, half a mile west from Maan ; there are
five or six score inhabitants, and at Maan two hundred. Shemmîa is pleasanter and fruitful, her green corn-fields are watered
by a slender spring, her villagers are of a peaceful behaviour ;

her wells are many, the boughs of her fruit-trees hang over
the clay orchard walls into the inhuman desert. Shemmîa and
Maan are such doubtless as the " fenced cities " of old. They are
clay walled, but walls and towers are full of breaches, as in all
the Arab places. The Haj government established here in late
years a station of horse troopers and Ageyl riders, which should
keep the pilgrimage highway, and tame the insolence of the
Beduw. Maan was for a while full of tents, and quarters were
built at Shemmîa ; but this Turkish policy also was short lived.
At Maan the mukowwems and merchants leave a part of
their heavy wares and furnitures, because of the intolerable
cost of carriage upon the backs of camels. There is a sealed
storehouse and over it an officer, *Mudîr el-màl,* where their
goods are deposited. There is also in the Haj train certain
government carriage ; and first the camels charged with the
Sultan's yearly gift for the service (mostly fine oil for the lamps)
of the temples at Medina and Mecca ; then the year's rations of
all the kellats along the road. Corn might be had here at half
the Damascus price, from Kerak and Shobek ; but because
of the perpetual insecurity of the outlying country they keep
the old custom, to fetch all up from the Hauran to Damascus,
and carry it down again in the pilgrimage ; so that one sack
costs them as much as three sacks would be naturally worth,
at Maan. The shops at Maan are of small salesmen to the
Beduins ; they are mostly traders come over from Hebron.

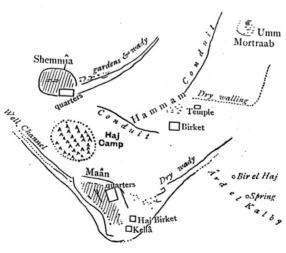

Map of Maan.

A lower quarter of the clay village, in the wady, stands lately
ruined ; it happened by the political malady of the Arabs.
There is a saying, if any stranger enquire of the first met
of Maan, were it even a child, " Who is here the sheykh ? " he
would answer him " I am he." They are very factious light
heads, their minds are divided betwixt supine recklessness and
a squalid avarice. When I formerly lodged here I heard with
discomfort of mind their hourly squabbling, as it were rats in
a tub, with loud wrangling over every trifle as of fiends in the
end of the world. It is a proverb here, that a man will slay
the son of his mother for an old shoe-leather. The breach was
this : some children disputed for an apple, the strife increased,
men rose from the clay benches, men came forth from the
thresholds, and drawing to their partialities, every hot head
cried down, despised and threatened his contraries. Men
armed themselves, and the elders' reverence was weak to
appease this strong sedition. Barbarous shoutings are answered
with bloody words ; they ran apart from both sides to their
quarters, and as every man entered his cottage there he shut
himself in and fortified the door ; then he mounted upon his clay
roof to shoot against the next hostile houses. None of them
durst come forth more in all that year, for their adversaries
would let shots fly at him from their house terraces. Upon
both sides they saw the harvest ripen and stand out so long,
without reapers, that all their bread was lost ; at length also
their pleasant autumn fruits, hanging ruddy in the orchards,
rotted before their eyes. There fell eight beleaguered champions, in eight months, beside some it was said who perished
with hunger. In this time many, not partisans, had abandoned
Maan ; the most went to settle themselves in the Hauran :
all the small traders removed to Shemmîa.—These Eve's sons
were lost for the apple at Maan ! even the peasant soldiery had
taken part with their seditious fellow-villagers, but the end was
near. The Pasha, at the returning of the Haj, enclosed their
place with the caravan guard, drew out the hunger-starved
rioters and binding their ringleaders and the sheykhs, carried
them, about twenty persons, to prison in Damascus. Strangers
count the people of Maan of Jewish blood, saying " The fairness
of their young women fades from the first child-bearing, and
the name *Harûn* is common among them ; "—but this is because
they are neighbours to Mount Hor, where is a shrine of Aaron.

East of the village is the desert ground *Ard el-Kelby* (also
the name of a very ancient tribe once in these quarters,) and
full of the limestone tubers, whereof they fondly imagine
hamlets and villages. The lesser knot-stones are like Holland

cheeses, " which the angels cast out of their hands from Heaven upon an impious generation " : a spring is seen there of ancient work hewn back in the limestone rock. A mile to the north is a ruined village *Mortrâb* upon a rising ground, the dry-built house-walls of stone yet standing ; the chambers are very small, as in all the ruined places. The air is most pure at Maan, the summer nights fresh, and in the ending of April were yet chill at this great altitude. In winter the snow lies commonly somewhile upon the ground. The *samn* or clari- fied Beduin butter of this droughty highland is esteemed above other, in Syria. Oftentimes in the forenoons, I saw a mirage over the flint plains ; within my experience, none could mistake the Arabian desert mirage for water. The spring is scant at Maan and failing ; it comes to them from an ancient dripping well-gallery, as it were a mine for water, (like those at Siena in Italy), and such are not seldom seen in these old dry countries opened to great length underground upon some vein of water, having many mouths to the air. Water in wells at Shemmîa and Maan lies at less than three fathoms ; the freshets go out in the desert. Walking in the torrent bed at Maan my eyes lighted upon,—and I took up, moved and astonished, one after another, seven flints chipped to an edge, (the before mentioned) : we must suppose them of rational, that is an human labour. But what was that old human kindred which inhabited the land so long before the Semitic race ? Does not the word of Isaiah, there imitating perhaps the people's *argot*, come to our hearts concerning them ?—" What was the rock whence ye were hewn, and the hole of the pit whence ye were digged ! " (see fig. pp. 36 and 37).

At that time I went over the moorland to Shobek in the village land of Edom. After fifteen miles is a principal ruined site *Utherah ;* the ancient town is built at a strong spring, welling forth in a great waterbrook. There are ground walls of squared stones and round arches of regular masonry, and small dry-built chambers of the old private houses. I saw a passage leading under the earth with a side chamber, of the best masonry ; also rude chapiters of pillars and fragments of white marble, of which all the best was, they say, carried to Damascus, long ago, for those beautiful pavements of the courts of their houses : there is an aqueduct ending in solid towers, which they call water-mills. In this good forsaken soil are outlying corn plots of Maan ; the harvest they must halve with the Beduins, who are lords of the desert. Here lay now a camp of them. The iniquitous sheykhs had put in their mares to graze the villagers' standing corn. Though in so good

Flint instruments found (1875) in the high land (flint) gravel of Mt. Seir ; freshet bed at Maan, 4200 ft. : reduced one-third.

a country, some among them I saw were so poor, that they had no booth to shield them from the weather ; only a little hair-cloth sail was set up before them upon a stake, to bear off the night blast. These Howeytát sat upon the three sides of a square before us in the sheykh's tent, which is usage of the fellahîn, half nomads, in the villages of Edom : their women are not veiled. Green is this upland, in the ending of May, under the Syrian sky, with wild grassy herbage. An hour beyond, are dry-built ruins of a fenced village, *Mottehma.* An hour later another, *Hetigy ;* an hour before Shobek at a brook-side, the ruins *Nejjel ;* the land is open limestone downs and coombs. A little more, and we came to the brink of the mountain of Esau, and looked down into the hazy deep of the sunken Dead Sea land and *Wady el-Araba :* the ground might be five thousand feet beneath us. The bluish dark saddlehead

of a sandstone mountain appeared a little wide to the southward below our feet, this is mount Hor (*Jebel Saidna Harûn*)
which stands behind Petra.   We came here to a summer camp
of the Shobekers, who like those of Kerak, are half the year
lodged abroad in the wilderness, in booths, as the nomads ;
rude good fellows and hospitable, not subject to any strange
government, very jealous of their liberties.   Shobek, *Mons
Regalis* of the crusaders, was over the next bent : but the
sheykh said I should never come in thither, except for much
money.   Then he promised I should see their deep old draw-
well and a Kûfic inscription.   It is from an obscure tradition of
the crusaders, that these unlettered peasants fanatically abhor
the name of Frengies.   The tall villager was not a lord born,
but by the bull force of his body and the armed support of
his partisans, had of late made himself sheykh.   " What wot
any man," exclaimed Strongbrawns, " that I was not one come
to spy their place, and the Frengies would enter afterward
to take the country ? "   This honest host fed us largely in his
great tent of a sheep boiled (such here is their marvellous
abundance) in butter-milk.   For Israel ascending from Sinai
this was a land that flowed with milk indeed.

The Idumean villagers are noted to be without formal
knowledge of religion.   It seems besides the shrine and chapel-
of-rags of Aaron upon Mount Hor they have no *mesjids* (mosques),
or any other canonical observance than to circumcise their male
children.   At Maan I have heard a tale of them that may seem
a fable.   " Years ago there came up a zealous elder from the
wilderness of Hebron to Bosra, where he saw some men warming
themselves in a field at a great fire they had made of olive
timber, and went and sat down by them.   After tidings, the
venerable man beginning to preach to them of the common
faith, he reproved their ignorance, lamenting to God that,
knowing not how to pray, and not fasting in ramadan, or yielding
tribute to lawful government, they were in danger to fall down,
at the last, into hell fire.   The peasants, who listened maliciously,
answered, ' We shall put thee in first, thou old man.   Fellows,
we have heard the words of him enough : more wood ! '   And
they thrust him in, and flinging on timber, let him lie and
burn, not fearing that this strange blood should ever be required
of them."

There are no more wine-fats at Bosra, but her fields are
even now fruitful vineyards.   The Hebrew prophets at all times
rail with bitter enmity of evil neighbourhood against the Peraean
countries : we may gather out of their words that these were
corn and vine lands.   Isaiah seems to signify that Edom was

full of small cattle ; they to-day abound upon this mountain
side. The greatest sheep flocks which I have seen of the Arabs
were in the rocky coomb-land (the country of Isaiah's rams of
Nebaioth) between Shobek and Petra, whither I now went.
The rock is full of beds and shelves of tabular flint : in the best-
sheltered places are corn plots of the neighbouring villagers, *ard
baal*, nourished only by the rain. Some outlying fallows are tilled
by a kind of nomad peasantry, dwelling hereabouts in tents at
all times, and not accounting themselves Beduins. One of them
being my muleteer in this journey, I passed a night in their
encampment ; but the tribe's name is not now in my remembrance. They inhabit the soil in peace, for they pay the " brothership " to all Beduins, even to those by Medáin Sâlih, two hundred
miles to the southward ; thus none preying upon them they
increase continually. I think I have seen flocks of five hundred
head couched at night before some tents of their households.
This limestone moorland, of so great altitude, resembles Europe,
and there are hollow park-like grounds with evergreen oak
timber. After nine miles upon a rising ground are rude dry-
built ruins *Khidàd*, and some limestone caverns ; the place is
like Kurmel, where Nabal dwelt, eastward below Hebron.
We may think these high borders were anciently hardly less
peopled than the best parts of settled Syria at this day. The
air was so light, the bright shining spring sun was little hot
here at noonday ; we passed by some other ruined sites, they
are always seen beside springs.

We began to descend over a cragged lime-rock, beset with
juniper, towards *Wady Mûsa*, Moses' valley, that is Petra, now
appearing as a deep cleft very far below us. We saw an
encampment of worsted booths, but not of Beduw. These were
summering peasants of W. Mûsa : their village is *Eljy* above
Petra. My guide whispered in my ear, " these were perilous
fellows that cared nothing for captain at Maan and haj-road
government ; it might be *Sheytàn* if they happened to detain
me." The sheykhs came out to meet us, but when we entered
the chief tent they said we should not pass to-day, and one
asked with the Arabs' maliciousness, if I had no mind to remain
a moon with them. They made coffee, but chided with my
driver protesting " that though the world besides might be open
passage, yet so is not W. Mûsa, no, wellah ! nor they men to be
commanded whether by Sultan or pasha ! " They were churls,
and whilst they pleased I should be here their captive guest.
Heavy is their long day of idleness, they slumber every hour and
smoke tobacco ; some of them I have seen toss pebbles in their
hard fists, to drive the time away. At length, the sun setting,

a mighty trencher is fetched in of porridge (*jerrîsh*), and all present are partakers of the bountiful poor mess. The night advanced, we lie down in our places on the earth, to sleep ; but then the sinners of goats trooping in from the night air, walked over our faces every hour till the morning light.

The worthy Burckhardt who in our fathers' time adventuring this way down to Egypt, happily lighted upon the forgotten site of Petra, found these peasants already of a fresh behaviour. He appeared to them as a Syrian stranger and a Moslem, yet hardly they suffered him to pass by the monuments and ascend to sacrifice his lamb upon Mount Hor. Europeans visiting Petra commonly lament the robber violence of these Eljy villagers ; but the same were now very good to me, since I came to them in a red cap from the part of the Dowla, and had eaten bread with them in the tents. When the sun is at half noon height, they break their fasts ; after that I departed, and they sent four men along with us, that no evil might betide me in that wild abysmal place which is desolate Petra. The limestone downs and coombs, where we descended, are like the country about Bath. *W. Faraôun* we see first, and far off under the sun Kasr Faraôun (Pharaoh's palace) : that is the only building in the valley of Petra, and much like a temple, which is of regular masonry. In this country every marvel is ascribed to Pharaoh who made himself, they told me, to be worshipped as a god and here resisted Moses and Aaron.

We have left the limestones with certain rude caverns above ; the underlying mountain rocks are ruddy sandstones and pictured often with green coloured and purple veins : lower in the same are the high cliffs of the hewn monuments. Descendingly deeply, we came by the principal of them, Greekish palatial frontispieces of two storeys now much decayed by the weather. There is nothing answerable within to the majestical faces, pompous portals leading but into inconsiderable solid halls without ornament ; now they are nightstalls of the nomads' flocks and blackened with the herdsmen's fires. The valley cliffs, upon both sides, are sculptured in frontispieces full of columns and cornices with their inner chambers ; the most are of a formal pattern, which I saw later at Medáin Sâlih, and there are other like to those few hewn monuments, which we see in the valley of Jehoshaphat at Jerusalem. A good part of the monuments are manifestly sepulchral, none I can think were houses ; and were all numbered together they would not be found very many. The city was surely in the midst and, to judge by that little we see remaining of stone ruins, of clay building. It is thus at Medáin Sâlih : in both towns they

might see their monuments standing round about them. We
made some chambers in the rock our night's lodging under a
little hewn cistern, *Ayn Músa,* and which only, of all here seen,
I can conjecture to have been a dwelling.

The men returned on the morrow, and as we passed on alone
through the solitary valley, some Beduins that had spied us from
the cliffs far off descended to make trouble. Four young men
stayed my mule, forbidding further passage ; they having but
one gun, I was for going by them. My driver said they would
then bring down many upon us, but these would be content to
depart for a little money, which I gave them ; and yet we could
not be quit of the fellows, they accompanied us now as friends.
The midday was not here hot, the land-height is perhaps as much
as two thousand feet. Near the head of the valley, we found a
Beduin and his wife with their flock, and sat down by the poor
man, who went and milked his goats for us bountifully. There a
side valley ascends to Mount Hor. I asked him, when we had
drunk, if he would not be my companion, and we would go now
upon the mountain. " He durst not," he answered, " had he fifty
men to accompany us with the guns, no nor for any reward " :
the villagers had forbidden me already, giving me to understand
that I should fall by their shot in so doing, although I had
many lives. From thence passing by the hewn theatre we
entered the *Sîk ;* this is a passage by a deep cleft in the valley
head, wherein are many wild fig trees. Near the mouth is that
most perfect of the monuments *Khasna* (treasure-house of)
Faraóun, whose sculptured columns and cornices are pure lines
of a crystalline beauty without blemish, whereupon the golden
sun looks from above, and Nature has painted that sand-rock
ruddy with iron-rust. Through the Sîk an old pavement may be
seen in the torrent-bed, and in the sides certain obscure and
singular tablets—we shall consider them later at Medáin Sâlih.
At the upper end (now in the limestone) are few other pyramidal
hewn monuments and side caverns. Above is the village Eljy
with a great spring *Ayn Harûn,* which leaving apart we mounted
by a cragged mountain way, and came after long miles to the
summer encampment of the other sheykh of Wady Mûsa ; upon
a high hill-side where the wind blew chill, and the nights
were yet cold. There by a spring are ruins of an antique
village *Mêrbrak.* Arriving as guests, we were entertained in the
sheykh's tent and regaled with new butter and cheese and *lében*
(butter-milk). Some, to make the strangers cheer, chanted
to the hoarse chord of the Arab viol ; so they make to themselves music like David, drawing out the voice in the nose,
to a demesurate length, which must move our yawning or

laughter. I found the most here diseased in the eyes, as are nearly all the Arabs, even from their childhood.

I returned on the morrow to view the rest of the monuments of Petra, and upon a tomb in the west cliffs of three columns whose hewn fore-wall is broken away beneath, I saw a large

perfect and beautiful ancient inscription of several lines ; it might be Nabatean. An hour from the Sîk is said to be another inscription, (above a hewn " casement " in the rock,) at a place called *Sabra.* Strange and horrible as a pit, in an inhuman deadness of nature, is this site of the Nabateans' metropolis ; the eye recoils from that mountainous close of iron cliffs, in which the ghastly waste monuments of a sumptuous barbaric art are from the first glance an eyesore. The villager, my companion, led me up over the coast to the vast frontispice *ed-Deir :* from those heights above, is a marvellous prospect of the immense low-lying Araba valley and of the sandstone mountain of Biblical memory, Mount Hor, rising nigh at our hand ; behind us is the high rugged coast of Seir. But the sun setting, we durst not loiter, the peasant strode down before me : when I came to him he was passionately pattering prayers and casting his hands to Heaven for our deliverance from that peril, which they imagine to be ever in so solitary a place. We hasted through the wild of rocks and blossoming oleanders : many startling rock partridges with loud chuck ! chuck ! flew up before us and betrayed our lonely footfall. The mule we found where we had left her, in Pharaoh's treasure-house. Then passing the Sîk, the fellow would have brought me to sleep in el-Eljy, at his own house. But when we came nigh and the villagers, who had knowledge of our expedition since the morning, heard a clatter of the mule's hoofs on the rocks above, a horrid clamour rose of wild throats below crying from all houses, ' out upon us,' forbidding that any Nasrâny should enter their place. Also this fellow of theirs that accompanied me, they named *Abu Nasrâny* (a father or abettor of Christians) ; and when they had found this bitter railing cry, it was shouted among them outrageously. The wretch, with me, plucked his hair, and with palms of supplication prayed in an agony to be delivered : he drove quickly upon the cold mountain side to come by them ; and so returning upward we rode late through the darkness to the tents again. Thus far I have spoken of the Petra monuments, that with these we might afterward compare Medáin Sâlih. Some credible persons have spoken to me of other like monuments, but they are few, which are seen in the Dead Sea country between J. Sherra and J. Khalîl ; that place is named *Medáin Lût*, the Cities of Lot. A lettered trader of my acquaintance who had sometimes passed there, said that those were frontispices without inscriptions.

Maan is only five hours from Petra ; returning, in the way thither I saw the dry-built ruins *Graaf*, which are the most considerable after Utherah in the high land of Esau ; where also they reckon, as in Moab, " three hundred and sixty," that is to say very many, khurbets. This country people, who have no antique tradition, will tell you again ' the antique citizens and builders before them were men of great stature.' Wisdom and understanding are ascribed in the scriptures to the inhabitants of Edom, of which wisdom it might be that their habitations were so simple, void of unnecessary things, seeing they possessed their lives, as the generations before them, but for a moment. Ammon, Moab, Edom were neighbour lands to the nomads, people of their kindred ; it were not likely they should use much more ambitious curiosity than the nomads in building their houses. Some of the inhabitants of Moab and Edom by the testimony of a psalm were tent-dwellers. Edom is in Isaiah the Land of Uz.

Edom and Jeshurun are rivals, and great was the cruelty of the Hebrew arms in these countries. When David was king, his sister's son Joab went and killed of Edomites in the Ghror twelve thousand men, and Joab's brother Abishai killed of them his eighteen thousand, if the Semitic numbers were aught ; Edom, be it remembered, and Moab and Ammon, were states to be compared with our smaller counties. Joab's sword went through Edom six months, until he had made an end of killing every male of Esau, and belike he made then sure of Doeg the king's adversary, and the righteous laughed to the ears, at his calamity ; but all was contrary to Moses' word " Thou shalt not abhor the Edomite for he is thy brother." David set garrisons in all Edom : after him in the generations of his house, Amaziah slew of

Edomites his ten thousand, in the same Ghror ; the Idumean mountain perhaps, with so high coasts was too hard for them. Other ten thousand, taken captives, he brought to the top of the rock (we have seen by Shobek, what fearful precipices are over the Ghror), and there he made them the king's tumblers, casting them headlong down together by the sharp rocks, that they were all broken in pieces. In the Hebrew scripture we hear a voice of the daughter of Edom detesting the bloody city, and crying " Down with it, down with it, to the ground." They exult in the ruin of Judah and Israel, and naturally desire also those now desolate neighbour lands, an heritage for themselves. And this is |" the controversy of Zion," whereof the Hebrew prophets are in pain, as of a woman in travail. ' Against Esau's land the Lord hath indignation for ever : his sword bathed in heaven shall smite down upon the people of his curse, even upon Idumea, and the land shall be soaked with blood. The day of the Lord's vengeance, his recompense for the controversy of Zion : he shall stretch upon Edom the line of confusion and the plummet of emptiness ; thorns, thistles, and nettles shall spring, and ghastly beasts, dragons, owls and a satyr, and the night raven shall dwell there. I am against thee, I will make mount Seir most desolate : *because thou hast a perpetual hatred* and hast shed the blood of Israel, in the time of calamity. I will fill thy mountains with the slain and make thee a perpetual desolation, *because thou saidest their two countries shall be mine.* Because thou didst rejoice over the inheritance of Israel that it was desolate : because Edom did pursue his brother with the sword and cast off all pity and kept his wrath for ever.' Malachi speaks of the land as already wasted. " I loved Jacob and hated Esau. Whereas Edom saith we will return to build the desolate places, the Lord saith they shall build, but I will throw down." We read in two of the prophets a proverbial refrain of the utter cutting off of Esau that there is nothing left. " If thieves come to thee by night would they not have stolen [but] till they had enough ? if the grape-gatherers come to thee would they not leave some gleaning of grapes ? " And his mouth was bitter which said " When the whole world rejoiceth, yet will I make thee desolate."

The pilgrims rested all the next day over in their encampment. And now I will briefly speak of the way from hence in Idumea to Ayla, (by Ezion Gaber) : in the same, after the Haj tradition, was the ancient passage southward of the great pilgrimage, which entered thus (at the head of the Akaba Gulf,) the Egyptian path to the sacred cities. That gulf is the *fjord*, or

drowned valley of the great Araba land-trough. As we would go
from Akaba upward to Edom, our path lies for few miles through
the open W. el-Araba ; then by a side valley enters the coast of

Head of the Gulf of Akaba and palm village of Ayla.

granite mountains, seamed with vulcanic dykes hundreds of
feet in height as in Sinai. And this is the *W. Lithm*, encumbered by mighty banks of ancient flood-soil. In the mouth is a
ruinous ancient dam, *es-Sid,* of wild blocks laid to a face in
mortar. After twelve miles we see above us the highest of these
granite bergs *Jebel Bakr*, of granite, and there we pass by a
stone scored over with a Nabatean inscription : the Arabs spoke
to me of some effigy that was here, of a human head or figure.
Thirty miles from Akaba being come upon a pleasant highland we
found some plough-lands in the desert, green with corn nourished
only of the rain ; the husbandry, I heard with wonder, of *Allowîn*
Howeytát Beduins. These desert men lean to the civil life, and
are such yeomen perhaps as Esau was. Other of their tribesmen I have seen, which are settled in tents, earing the desert sand
near Gaza ; their plough is a sharpened stake, shod with iron,
and one plough-camel draught. The Arab yeoman will lay
this plough-tree on his shoulder, and ride with a snivelling song
upon his work beast, to and from the ploughing. Later there
was warfare between their kindreds for those desert fallows ; and
the worsted part, (in the former time of my being at Maan,) fled
over to their kinsmen in J. Sherra, who, with the old humanity
of the desert, distributed to them of their own cattle. The
Howeytát speech savours of peasantry, even in the mouths of
those that live furthest in Arabia. All this noble open country
lies waste, of the best corn lands. At the next daybreak we came
by a broken cistern *Gueyrîa* and conduit, under *Jebel Shàfy,*
whose peak is of the motley and streaked sandstones of Petra.

And here upon the granite borders is the beginning of a great
sandstone country *el-Hisma* or *Hessma,* which stretches so far
into Arabia. In this place some of the barley-plot Beduins of

yesterday, had pitched their camp : *Ibn Jad* their sheykh, to
whom we now came, is lord of that country side. The generous
old lion (but as they be all, an ungenerous enemy,) came forth in
a red mantle to meet us, and with kind greeting he led me by
the hand into the shadow of a nomad booth. His people with
him were some thirty tents set out in an oval, which is their
manner in these parts. Ibn Jad told me the division of waters,
to the Red and the Dead Seas, lay " an hour " from that place
northward. We felt the spring mid-day here very hot. Unknown to me the old sheykh had killed a sheep for his guests ;
and all the men of the encampment assembled to the afternoon
guest-meal with us, when between two persons was fetched in a
lordly dish, the Beduin hospitality. His vast trencher was heaped
with the boiled mutton and with great store of girdle-bread hot
from the housewife's fire. All these tribesmen abound in bread-
stuffs of their own husbandry ; they know not hunger. Looking
upon that shoal of kerchiefed Howeytát heads, and they are rude-
limned peasant-like bodies, I thought I had not ever seen such
a strange thick-faced cob-nosed cobblers' brotherhood. Ibn Jad
rent morsels of the boiled flesh and lapping each portion in a
girdle-cake, he said a man's name and delivered it to him ; they
were too many to sit about the dish. The Hisma is here a forest
of square-built platform mountains which rise to two thousand
feet above the plain, the heads may be nearly six thousand feet
above sea level. It was evening when we rode from Ibn Jad :
after two dark hours we found another of their nomad encampments pitched under a berg of sandstone, whereupon (lightened
by the many camp-fires,) appeared strangely flitting tent-great
images of men and cattle. These were tents of *Saidîn* Howeytát, Aarab of the Ghror, come up hither for the better
spring pasture in their kinsman Ibn Jad's high country. There
seemed much nakedness and little welfare amongst them.
Remounting our camels we rode on that night ; the new day
lightening I saw a coast before us, which is here the edge of
J. Sherra. The sandstone earth under our feet is rusty and
might be compared by rude men with the redness of blood, *ed-
dumm,* which is this land's name *Edom.*

Here we ascend from the red sandstone country, in the
cragged Sherra side, which is clayey limestone with veins of
tabular flint. An hour or two above are wide ruins, *el-Bettera,*
in an open valley cumbered with low waste walls of dry building ; the principal with some columns are upon a rising ground.
Beyond in the desert, are seen the heaps of stones, gathered from
those once fruitful acres, by the diligence of the ancient husbandmen. For here were vine-lands and corn-lands, but " the

land now keepeth her sabbaths."—The Syrian lark rose up with
flickering wings from this desolate soil, singing before the sun ;
but little on height and faltering soon, not in loud sweetness of
warbles, nor in strength of flight as the sister bird in Europe. A
light breath was in the wilderness ; and we were few miles distant
from Maan. Now I saw a sorry landscape, the beginning upon
this side of the Flint Ground, strewed (from an eternity,) in the
sun and wind and which north and south may be fifty miles over :
eastward from Maan it lasts a day and a half, and may be, nearly
2500 square miles. We alighted in the first hollow ground to
lurk till nightfall ; my companions, an Egyptian and a Beduin,
durst not pass so open a landscape, whilst the sun shone, for the
often danger of scouring Beduin horsemen. We removed in the
twilight ; chill blew the fluttering night wind over these high
wastes : about midnight we arrived at Maan. The place lay
all silent in the night, we rode in at the ruinous open gateway
and passed the inner gate, likewise open, to the *sûk :* there
we found benches of clay and spread our carpets upon them
to lodge in the street. All Arabs are busy-headed and fearful of thieves in a strange place ; they use to tie their bags
before they sleep and lay any small things under their heads.
Glad of our rest we lay down soon, as men which had not closed
the eyes to slumber in three days and two nights tedious riding.
A pitiful voice called to us bye and bye out of a dark entry ; my
companions, too feverish with fatigue to sleep soon, started and
answered again " *Ent weled wala bint,* Thou beest a lad or a
maid ? "—There was none that answered, so they said " It is an
afrît (bogle) ,by Ullah." It was not long before I heard this
ghost by my bed's head ; sitting up I saw some squalid
stealing figure that uttered I perceived not what ; which when I
threatened, passed through a next doorway and seemed to shoot
the lock, the door I could not tell again when the day dawned.
I thought it might be some lunatic lad or squalid quean stalking
by night ; and that is not unseen in the Arabic places.

The pilgrim caravan lying at Maan, I lived in apprehension,
knowing that the Pasha sought for me : the Persian aga had
been called before the council, but he played the merchant and
they could learn nothing from him. I was blithe to hear the
second morning's signal shot ; it was eight of the clock when we
removed again. The Persians march, as said, in the rear ; and
we moving last up from our dismantled camping ground (the
ninth from Muzeyrîb) as I was about secretly reading the aneroid, I was not aware how we came riding to a bevy of persons,
that stood to observe us ; these being my old acquaintance the

Kurdy captain of the place with his red beard, and beside him Mahmûd the secretary. Perchance they were come out by order, to look for me. I perceived, I felt rather, that they noted me, but held on unmoved, not regarding them, and came by them also unhindered. They could not easily know me again, one of the multitude thus riding poorly and openly, clad in their guise and with none other than their own wares about me.

It was in my former coming hither I heard certainly of Medáin (cities of) Sâlih, of which also the villagers had spoken to me many marvellous things at Wady Mûsa, supposing that I arrived then from the southward by the haj road. Those "Cities" they said to be five, hewn likewise in the rocks! Of Mahmûd the secretary, a litterate person who had been there oftentimes, I learned more particulaly of the inscriptions and images of birds in the frontispieces; and with those words Mahmûd was the father of my painful travels in Arabia. ·Understanding that it was but ten marches distant, I sought then means to go down thither; but the captain of the station thwarted me, alleging the peril —he might be blamed, if there anything mishappened to a foreigner—of the long way in lawless land of the Beduins. He forbade also that any in the obedience of the Dowla, should further or convey me thither. I heard much also among the Maan soldiery but lately returned from an expedition against *Jauf,* of a certain great prince whom they named Ibn Rashîd, sultan or lord of the Beduin marches and of "sixty" date villages lying far inland, to the eastward. At Maan, under the climate of Jauf, are seen only few languishing palm stems, which stand but for an ornament of the earthen village. The plant may not thrive at this altitude; yet it is rather that both the earth and the water here are sweet.—The ten journeys hence to Damascus may be passed by dromedary post-riders, (nearly without drawing halter) in three and a half days.

As we marched a mirage lay low over the coal-black shining flint pebble-land before us, smelling warmly in the sun of southernwood. There is no sign, upon the iron soil, of any way trodden. The few seyls, as those at Maan, spend themselves shortly in the desert plain, which shelves, after my observation, eastward from the meridian of Maan.—Loud are the cries of poor firesellers by the wayside, to put a coal for money in the rich man's water-pipe; *Ullah mojûd, wa habîb-ak Mohammed en-Néby!* "God subsistent! and Thy beloved is the prophet Mohammed!" After eight hours we came to our encampment, standing ready in the plain, a place they called *Ghradîr Umm Ayásh,*—and every desert stead is named.

—Here a word of the camping grounds of Moses; all their names we may never find again in these countries,—and wherefore? Because they were a good part passengers' names, and without land-right they could not remain in the desert, in the room of the old herdsmen's names. There is yet another kind of names, not rightly of the country, not known to the Beduins, which are *caravaners' names*. The caravaners passing in haste, with fear of the nomads, know not the wide wilderness without their landmarks; nor even in the way, have they a right knowledge of the land names. What wonder if we find not again some which are certainly caravaners' names in the old itineraries!

Sculptured ornaments upon building stones in ruinous sites of Moab.

CHAPTER III.

THE HAJ JOURNEYING IN ARABIA.

Trooping gazelles. The brow of Arabia. Batn el-Ghrôl. *A fainting derwish. Pilgrim "martyrs".* The Ghrôl or Ogre of the desert. Iram. *Nomads B. Atîeh, or Maazy. "The maiden's bundle of money." The art of travel. Desert Arabia. The Haj pilot. Camels faint. Rocket signals by night. Aspect of the Desert* Medowwara. Hallat Ammar. *Thàt Haj. The "wild Cow".* Sherarát *nomads (B. Múklib). The Persian pilgrims. Persian dames in the Haj. The pilgrims might ride in wagons. Mule litter marked with a Greek cross. Comparison with the Haj of "the thousands of Israel."* The Mahmal. *The motley hajjàj.* The *foot service.* El-Eswad. The Muatterín. *The massacre of Christians at Damascus. A discourse of the novices. The Haj camels. The takht er-Rûm. Dying Persians carried in the camel-coaches. Pilgrimage of a lady deceased. Contradictions of the road. Camel-back muetthins. Persian hajjies, for defiling Mohammed's grave, burned at Medina. The Caravan thief. The imperial secretary. The Pasha. Pilgrim dogs from Syria. A cock on pilgrimage. Coursing desert hares. The* thôb. El-Kâ. *Night march to Tebûk. The ancient village. The Pulpit mountain. The villagers. The Pasha paymaster. The story of his life. The game of the road.* The Harra. El-Akhdar *station.* The Sweyfly. *Visit the* kella. The Kâdy's *garden.* W. es-Sâny. *The "bear".* Moaddam *station. Water is scant. Gum-arabic tree. Dar el-Hamra station. Cholera year in the Haj. A man returned from his grave to Damascus.* Abu Tâka. Mûbrak en-Nâga. *The miraculous camel. A cry among the Haj.*

THREE and a half hours after midnight we departed from this station :—from henceforth begin the great journeys of the Haj in Arabia. Little before day at a gunshot in front the caravan halted, and whilst we rested half an hour the great ones drink coffee. Two hours above the *Akaba* before us is a site, *Khân ez-Zebîb;* Mohammed Saîd Pasha in the last returning Haj, riding out upon his mare in advance of the caravan, (the Arabian spring already beginning), here lighted upon a great assembling of gazelles and killed with his pistol shots so many that venison was served that evening in all the great haj officers'

pavilions. We approached at noon the edge of the high limestone platform of J. Sherra, *Masharîf es-Shem* of the old
Mohammedan bookmen, " The brow of Syria or the North."
And below begins Arabia proper, *Béled el-Aarab :*—but these
are distinctions not known to the Beduish inhabitants.

The haj road descending lies in an hollow ground, as it were
the head of a coomb, of sharp shelves of plate-flint and limestone.
We are about to go down into the sandstones,—whereof are
the most sands of Arabia. A ruinous kella and cistern are here
upon our left hand. The caravan column being come to the
head of the strait passage, we are delayed in the rear thirty
minutes. The caravaners call such a place *Akaba,* " A going
up " ; this is named the Syrian or northern, *es-Shemîya.* I found
here the altitude 4135 feet. Upon a rock which first straitens
our descending way was seated, under a white parasol, the
Pasha himself and his great officers were with him : for here on
the 24th of November we met again the blissful sunshine and the
summer not yet ended in Arabia. The caravan lines are very
loose, and long drawn out in the steep, which is somewhat encumbered with rocks above. As the camels may hardly pass two
and two together the Pasha sees here at leisure the muster of the
hajjàj slowly passing ; the pilgrims have alighted from the cradle-
litters and their beasts' backs and all fare on foot. My unlucky new
camel, which had been purchased from the Beduins at Maan and
not broken to this marching, tied, burst her leading-string at the
Pasha's feet, which made a little confusion and I must run to bring
all in order again. But I was confident, although he had seen me
in Arabic clothing at Damascus, that he should not now know me.
The Akaba is long and, past the Pasha's seat, of little difficulty.
The Beduins name this going-down *Batn el-Ghrôl,* ' belly (hollow
ground) of the Ogre ' or else ' strangling place,' *fen yughrulún
ez-zillamy ;* a sink of desolation amongst these rusty ruins
of sandstone droughty mountains, full of eternal silence and
where we see not anything that bears life. The Akaba is
not very deep, in the end I found, where the pilgrims remounted, that we were come down hardly 250 feet. The length
of the caravan was here nearly an hour and there was no
mishap. Camels at a descent, with so unwieldy fore-limbs
are wooden riding ; the lumpish brutes, unless it be the more
fresh and willing, let themselves plumb down, with stiff joints,
to every lower step. These inhospitable horrid sandstones resemble the wasting sandstone mountains about *Sherm* in Sinai.

Below we are upon a sand bottom, at either hand is a wall of
sand-rock, the long open passage between them descends as a
valley before us. Upon the left hand, the crags above are

4—2

crusted with a blackish shale-stone, which is also fallen down to
the foot, where the black shingles lie in heaps shining in the sun
and burnished by the desert driving sand. This is the edge of
a small lava-field or *harra :* I had seen also erupted basalt
rock in the descent of the Akaba. After three miles the way
issues from the strait mountains and we march upon a large
plain *Debîbat es-Shem, Ard Jiddàr,* of sand ; heavy it is to
handle and oozing through the fingers. Few miles from the
road upon our right hand are cloud-like strange wasted ranges
of the desolate Hisma.

I saw one fallen in the sand, half sitting half lying upon
his hands. This was a religious mendicant, some miserable
derwish in his clouted beggar's cloak, who groaned in extremity,
holding forth his hands like eagles' claws to man's pity. Last in
the long train, we went also marching by him. His beggar's
scrip, full of broken morsels fallen from his neck, was poured
out before him. The wretch lamented to the slow moving lines
of the Mecca-bound pilgrimage : the many had passed on, and
doubtless as they saw his dying, hoped inwardly the like evil
ending might not be their own. Some charitable serving men,
Damascenes, in our company, stepped aside to him ; *ana mèyet,*
sobbed the derwish, I am a dying man. One then of our
crew, he was also my servant, a valiant outlaw, no holy-
tongue man but of human deeds, with a manly heartening
word, couched, by, an empty camel, and with a spring of his
stalwart arms, lifted and set him fairly upon the pack saddle.
The dying derwish gave a weak cry much like a child, and
hastily they raised the camel under him and gathered his
bag of scattered victuals and reached it to him, who sat
all feeble murmuring thankfulness, and trembling yet for fear.
There is no ambulance service with the barbarous pilgrim
army ; and all charity is cold, in the great and terrible wilderness,
of that wayworn suffering multitude.

After this there died some daily in the caravan : the deceased's
goods are sealed, his wayfellows in the night station wash and
shroud the body and lay in a shallow grave digged with their
hands, and will set him up some wild headstone by the desert road
side. They call any pilgrims so dying in the path of their religion,
shahûd, martyrs. But the lonely indigent man, and without succour, who falls in the empty wilderness, he is desolate indeed.
When the great convoy is passed from him, and he is forsaken of
all mankind, if any Beduw find him fainting, it is but likely they
will strip him, seeing he is not yet dead. The dead corses unburied
are devoured by hyenas which follow the ill odour of the caravan.
There is little mercy in those Ageyl which ride after ; none upon

the road, will do a gentle deed " but for silver."—If we have lived
well, we would fain die in peace ; we ask it, a reward, of God,
in the kind presence of our friends !—There are fainting ones
left behind in every year's pilgrimage ; men of an old fibre
and ill-complexion, their hope was in Ullah, but they living
by the long way only of unwilling men's alms, cannot achieve
this extreme journey to Mecca. The fallen man, advanced in
years, had never perhaps eaten his fill, in the Haj, and above two
hundred miles were passed under his soles since Muzeyrîb. How
great is that yearly suffering and sacrifice of human flesh, and
all lost labour, for a vain opinion, a little salt of science would
dissolve all their religion ! Yet, I understood, there is some pious
foundation remaining from the old Ottoman Sultans, to send every
year a certain number of poor derwishes with carriage and provision to the holy places. A camel and water-skin is allotted to
two or three derwishes, and a tent for every companionship of
them. They are few altogether ; or men, " wearers of rough
garments," ranters with long-grown locks, and " mad-fellows,"
would run from all the town-ends to the almoner at Damascus ;
to have themselves enrolled of the sons of the prophets, with the
poor beggars : it is so pleasant for this religious people to find a
shift for themselves in any other than their own purses. It
was told me the Haj of old were wont to descend not by the
Akaba but by another steep at the south-westward, where the
seyl waters flow down from J. Sherra. This is *Jiddàr ;* one
said, who knew, ' it is so easy that a coach road might be
made there.'

The *ghról* or *ghrûl* is a monster of the desert in which
children and women believe and men also. And since no
man, but Philemon, lived a day fewer for laughing, have here
the portraiture of this creature of the Creator, limned by a
nomad : ' a cyclops' eye set in the midst of her human-like
head, long beak of jaws, in the ends one or two great sharp
tushes, long neck ; her arms like chickens' fledgling wings, the
fingers of her hands not divided ; the body big as a camel's, but
in shape as the ostrich ; the sex is only feminine, she has a foot
as the ass' hoof, and a foot as an ostrich. She entices passengers,
calling to them over the waste by their names, so that they
think it is their own mother's or their sister's voice. He
had seen this beast, ' which is of Jin kind, lie dead upon the
land upon a time when he rode with a foray in the *Jeheyna*
marches ; but there was none of them durst touch her.' He
swore me, with a great oath, his tale was truth ' by the
life of Ullah and by his son's life.' He was a poor desert man,
one *Doolan,* at Medáin Sâlih, noted to be a fabler. The aga of the

kella believed not his talk, but answered for himself " It is true, nevertheless, that there is a monstrous creature which has been oft seen in these parts nearly like the ghrûl, they call it *Salewwa.* This salewwa is like a woman, only she has hoof-feet as the ass." Many persons had sworn to him, upon their religion, they had seen salewwas, and he knew fifteen tribesmen which had seen her at once. Again, " a great ghrazzu, eighty men of the *Sherarát,*

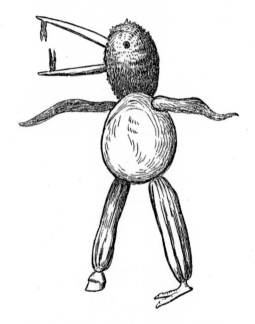

The Ghról ; drawn by Doolan the Fehjy at el-Héjr.

saw her as they alighted in an evening, but when their bullets might not do her scathe ; they took up firebrands to beat the woman-fiend, and they beat on her all that night."

Few miles westward of the road, I hear to be a site of considerable ruins, *Ayîna,* there are seen many ancient pillars. In that place are springs, and there grows much of the tamarisk kind *ghrottha.* Ayîna is a summer water station of the Beduins, and the rocks are written full of their *wasms.* According to Sprenger's researches, whose learned work *Die alte Geographie Arabiens,* was my enchiridion in these travels, IRAM might be nearly in this circuit, " the city of columns, the terrestrial paradise." Further in

Hisma, a little south of the midway between Maan and Akaba, is a ruined site *Kherbet er-Rumm*, at a great spring of water, with good wilderness soil about ; also in that place are fallen columns.

We came in the evening twilight to our encampment. Here are the nomad marches of the B. *Atîeh* tribesmen, which are called in the parts towards Egypt, after their patriarch, *el-Maazy* : Maaz is brother of *Anâz*, patriarch of the Annezy (the signification is goat, in both their names). A part of the Maazy nation is strangely dispersed beyond the Red Sea, they inhabit now those deserts over against Sinai named by the Arabs " Welsh Country," *Burr el-Ajam*, or of men speaking outlandish language, that is the great continent of Africa. There are in the ages many like separations and dispersions of the wandering tribes, and it is told of some far emigrated, that they had forgotten at length the soil from whence they sprung, but not the name of their patriarch, and by their wasm which remained they were known !

The B. Atîeh receive surra of the Haj administration for all kellas in the desert passage from hence down to Tebûk. The surra (every year the same sum is distributed) is paid to the sheykhs after their dignities, whose names are written in the roll of the treasurer at Damascus. It is almost incredible how the soul of these Semites is bound up with the prey of pennies, which they have gotten without labour ; therefore the pasha-general of the pilgrimage had needs be a resolute man of great Asiatic prudence, that is foxes' sleight with weighty courage (and such are plants of a strong fibre, which grow up out of the Oriental dunghill), to conduct his caravan through all adventures of the hot-hearted Beduins, in so long a way of the wilderness to the sacred cities. It is told how these tribesmen had, a score of years before, fallen upon the Haj at unawares so vehemently that they beat off the guard and seized many hundreds at once of the haj camels with their loads. The thing happened for a small displeasure, *surrat el-bint* " the maiden's bundle of money." The pasha-paymaster in that Haj giving out to the assembled sheykhs, at their station, the pensions of silver, presents of clothing and utensils, had denied them that which fell to her father's name, when he ascertained that the man had been dead a year or two, and his decease was hidden by fraud of Beduins. The good which was paid out for him in those years came to his orphan girl ; the fault now discovered, yet the kinsmen loudly claimed " the girl's due " ; her father had been nearly the last in the line of sheykhs, his surra was only six crowns. Of this the greedy and iniquitous Aarab caught occasion to set upon the caravan, and in that as if the pilgrim townsmen had been their capital enemies, killed some innocent persons.—Here is the sub-tribe *el-Ageylát* which are haj carriers between Maan and Tebûk.

And now come down to Arabia, we are passed from known landmarks. Two chiefly are the perils in Arabia, famine and the dreadful-faced harpy of their religion, a third is the rash weapon of every Ishmaelite robber. The traveller must be himself, in men's eyes, a man worthy to live under the bent of God's heaven, and were it without a religion : he is such who has a clean human heart and long-suffering under his bare shirt ; it is enough, and though the way be full of harms, he may travel to the ends of the world. Here is a dead land, whence, if he die not, he shall bring home nothing but a perpetual weariness in his bones. The Semites are like to a man sitting in a cloaca to the eyes, and whose brows touch heaven. Of the great antique humanity of the Semitic desert, there is a moment in every adventure, wherein a man may find to make his peace with them, so he know the Arabs. The sour Waháby fanaticism has in these days cruddled the hearts of the nomads, but every Beduin tent is sanctuary in the land of Ishmael (so there be not in it some cursed Jael). If the outlandish person come alone to strange nomad booths, let him approach boldly, and they will receive him. It is much if they heard of thee any good report ; and all the Arabs are at the beginning appeased with fair words. The oases villages are more dangerous ; Beduin colonies at first, they have corrupted the ancient tradition of the desert ; their souls are canker-weed beds of fanaticism.— As for me who write, I pray that nothing be looked for in this book but the seeing of an hungry man and the telling of a most weary man ; for the rest the sun made me an Arab, but never warped me to Orientalism. Highland Arabia is not all sand ; it is dry earth, nearly without sprinkling of the rains. All the soft is sandy ; besides there is rocky moorland and much harsh gravel, where the desolate soil is blown naked by the secular winds. The belts of deep sand country and borders about the mountain sandstones, which are called *Nefûds*, are perhaps of kin with those named, in England, "greensands." Commonly the Arabian desert is an extreme desolation where the herb is not apparent for the sufficiency of any creature. In a parcel of desert earth great as an house floor, you shall find not many blades and hardly some one of the desert bushes, of which the two-third parts are no cattle-meat but quite waste and naught.

There is after Maan no appearance of a trodden haj road in the wilderness, all is sea-room and our course is held by landmarks : but there is much natural way in hollow ground between Akaba and Mecca. Seldom I saw this ancient caravan path marked by any beacon of heaped stones, as it is by Maan and in the branching of the *Wady el-Akhdar.* There is one, *Dalîl el-haj,* who guides the pilgrimage, day and night, those nearly nine hundred miles from Muzeyrîb down to Mecca. This landcraft master was a Damascene, who had been yearly in this passage from his youth : a townsman is appointed to this office, they will trust the Haj conduct to no Beduins. I saw not anywhere the reported strewed skeletons of camels nor mounds of sand blown upon their fallen carcases. The Arabs are too poor so to lose cattle ; but these and the like, are tales rather of an European Orientalism than with much resemblance to the common experience. The Haj from Syria is the most considerable desert caravan of the Eastern world. There faint always some camels which have thinner soles, when these are worn to the quick, in the length of so great a journey. Any such bleeding-footed beast is sold for few crowns to the Beduins, and after some weeks' rest may be again a good camel ; but if there be no buyers at hand and he must needs be abandoned, they cut the throat in haste, to take his skin, and go forward. The hyena, the wolf, the fox, which follow the camp, finding this meat, the carcase is rent and the bones will be scattered. I have never seen any frame of bones lying in the desert or buried by the sand-driving wind, which blows lightly and only seldom in inner Arabia.

After Maan there is no rest for the Haj but day and night marches, and we departed at three and a half hours after midnight. At day-break we saw a rocket shot up in the van, for the halt to prayers and to rest ourselves a half-hour : all alighting, the most lie down upon the earth ; our backs are broken by the long camel riding. The camels, which cannot be unloaded, stand one behind another in every company, all tied for less labour of driving, which is the caravaners' manner, but not that of the Beduins. We are in a sand plain shelving before us but not sensibly ; westward continually, a few miles from the road, are the ruinous Hisma mountain skirts, showing by their forms to be sandstones. Upon the other hand are like-shaped low heights much more distant, in the Sherarát nomad country, also trending with the road. Under our feet is fine sand, in which for jollity, that we are come so far in the sacred way, the young Damascus serving men wallowed and flung one over other ; and sometimes the soil is a flaggy pavement of sandstones, rippled in the strand of those old planetary seas. An hour before the mid-day we ascended three miles through a low girdle of rocky sand-stones, which is a train from Hisma, and went down to pitch in the plain before

the kellat *Medowwara,* where we came to water. The place
lies very desolate ; the fort is built at a spring, defended now by
a vault from the Beduin's hostility. We felt the noon here very
sultry and the sun glancing again from the sand we were between
two heats.

At our right-hand is a part of the desert fabulously named
by the pilgrims *Hallat Ammár,* where of old they say stood a
city. Ammar was a mukowwem in the Haj, who going thither
to seek his provision of water in an extreme deadly heat,
found naught at all but steaming ground and smoke. Others
say better, " Hallet el-Ammar is at the cragged passage between
Medowwara and *Dzat (Thàt el-) Haj ;* where, the pilgrimage
journeying, the flaming summer heat dried up the oozing water-
skins, which seemed to vapour into smoke and the caravan
perished." Upon the rocks hereabout some told me they had
seen inscriptions. At six on the morrow, ascending from that
belt of low sandstone hills, we marched anew upon the plain
of shallow sliding sand. The sun rising I saw the first greenness of plants, since the brow of Akaba. We pass a gravel of
fine quartz pebbles ; these are from the wasted sand-rock. Fair
was the Arabian heaven above us, the sunny air was soon
sultry. We mounted an hour or two in another cross-train
of sand-rocks and iron-stone ; at four afternoon we came
to our tents, pitched by a barren thicket of palms grown wild ;
and in that sandy bottom is much growth of desert bushes, signs
that the ground water of the Hisma lies not far under. Here
wandered already the browsing trroops of those nomads' camels
which followed with the caravan. In this green place, pleasant
to Damascus eyes, stands the kella of good building with an
orchard of tall palms, Thàt-Haj, in the Beduins' talk *el-Haj.*
There are goodly vaulted cisterns of masonry, but only in a
lesser one of them was there stored water for the hajjàj, by
so much is this pilgrimage diminished from its ancient glory.
The water runs in from a spring at little distance ; the taste is
sulphurous. Surra is paid to the *Robillát,* a kindred of Beny
Atîeh. It was told me that the waters of J. Sherra seyl down
hither ;—believe it who will ! After the heat by day we found
the late night hours chilly. On the morrow very early the
waits came about again with the old refrain *bes-salaamy :* they
reckon at this station a third part accomplished of the long way
to Mecca.

At six we set forward, a great journey lay before us, the
desert soil is harder sand and hard ground, now with drift
of vulcanic pebbles. Westward, we see ever the same mountainous
Hisma coast, and eastward the same Sherarát sandstone hills. In

that country is found the " wild cow," a creature hitherto unknown in Europe ; it is an antelope. They company two and
three together, and run most swiftly in the waterless sand plains
where they never drink. The garrison at el-Haj bred up one
of them which had been taken by nomads, and this when
I was formerly at Maan, I might have purchased for ten pounds.
I heard later that the beautiful creature had been carried up
in the next Haj, caged in a mule litter, to Damascus, and sent
thence to Constantinople, a present from the imperial officer of
the pilgrimage to the Sultan *Abd el-Azîz.*—The Sherarát
are the *Beny Muklib* of the Beduin poets. The Sherarát are
not named, they have told me themselves, with any regard of
J. Sherra.

We rode through the hot day, bowing at each long stalking
pace upon the necks of our camels, making fifty prostrations
in every minute whether we would or no, towards. Mecca. The
Persian pilgrims about me, riding upon camels, were near seven
hundred ; peasants for the most part, as the richer and delicate
livers are ever less zealous to seek hallows than poor bodies
with small consolation in this world. Girded they are in
wadmel coats, falling below the knee, and thereunder wide
cotton slops ; upon their heads are high furred caps as the
Sclavonians. I heard that such an " honour of his head " may
cost a poor man three pound. The welfaring bear with them
a shaggy black mantle, woven of very fine and long goat's hair
or wool. These men, often red-bearded and red dye-beards, of
a gentle behaviour, much resemble, in another religion, the
Muscovite Easter pilgrims to Jerusalem. And these likewise
lay up devoutly of their slender thrift for many years before,
that they may once weary their lives in this great religious
voyage. Part are gazers also, that come far about to visit
the western cities, *el-mudden.* I was certainly assured that
there rode some amongst them whose homesteads lay in the
most backward mountains of Persia, and that ascending and
descending the sharp coasts they marched first three months
in their own difficult country ; so they have nearly twelve
months' journey from the setting out to the Holy City. A
client of the Persian age, who conducted for him upon that
side to Damascus and spoke willingly as being my patient, told
me he was himself every year eleven in the twelve months footing
upon the great road. When I asked how could he endure, he
answered as a Moslem " *Ullah !* " my sufficiency is of God. A
pined and jaded man he was before his middle days, and unlikely to live to full age. Better his mother had been barren,
than that her womb should have borne such a sorry travailous

life ! The Persian pilgrims are shod with the best wayfarer's sole, it is crimpled folds of cotton compacted finger-high, light and easy treading under the feet, and will outlast sole-leather. They are civil and ingenious (so is not the Semitic nomad race) ; but of a cankered ingenuity in the religion, sinners against the world and their own souls. If but thy shadow pass over their dish it is polluted meat, they eat not of it, neither willingly eat they with any catholic Moslem, an observer of the *Sunna* (the Mohammedan Talmud or canonical tradition). A metal ewer for water hangs at all their saddles, with which they upon every occasion go superstitiously apart to perform certain loathsome washings.

Upon a great haj camel rides but one person with his stuffed carpet bags, wherein, besides his provision, is commonly some merchandise for the holy fair at Mecca. I hear they use no camels in their own country, where there is much water in the mountain ways, but ride upon mules. A few in the great marches, which were clerks, took out their parchment written prayer-books, in which (as the orientals read) they chanted their devotion, becking the miles along, in the uneasy camel saddle, toward the holy places. I saw among them a woman, a negress, serving some ghastly Persian dames, clad as if they went to a funeral, which were borne in a litter before us, and a child was with them. Besides them I remember not to have seen women and little ones in the caravan. From Damascus there are many pious women pilgrims to Mecca, but now for the most part they take the sea to *Jidda;* the land voyage is too hard for them, and costly for their families ; and he is mocked in the raw Haj proverbs that will lead his querulous hareem on pilgrimage. Nevertheless the Haj Pasha will have sometimes with him a pious housewife or twain. Their aching is less which are borne lying along in covered litters, although the long stooping camel's gait is never not very uneasy. Also many pairs of cradle litters are borne upon mule-back, which is good riding, and even upon pack-horses.

We should think that if this people were in their minds, they might ride with all their things about them in covered wagons, as some sheykhs of Israel went so long ago wandering in the wilderness. All the way is plain, even the Akaba were not too difficult, where later the Jurdy descend with a brass field-cannon of five inches upon wheels ;—but it is not usage ! The Damascus litter is commonly a cradle-like frame with its tilt for one person, two such being laid in balance uplon a beast's back; others are pairs housed in together like a bedstead under one gay canvas awning. Swinging upon a stout mule's back, I saw one such every day little before us, whereupon a good Greek cross of red stuff was embroidered, whether a charm or an ornament. Sometimes Mohammedan women will sew a cross upon their lunatic or sick children's clothing and have them christened by the Greek priest for a charm and even be sprinkled themselves, (for fecundity !) and superstitiously drink holy water. Of the Persian folk a few which could be freer spenders came riding with their burning water-pipes, of the sweet Persian *tombac*, in the Damascene cradles. Greater ones were a mitred fellowship of two or three withered Persian lordlings for whom was pitched a wide pavilion in the stations : but for that little I met with them, I could imagine the solemn Persian gentlemen to be the most bad hearted dunghill souls of all nations. Our aga and his son came little behind them in the Persian birth of their minds, save that leading their lives in Damascus, they were pleasant smilers as the Arabs.

The breadth of our slow marching motley lines, in the plains, might be an hundred paces. What may we think of the caravan of Moses ? if we should reckon all Israel at 2,500,000 souls and four camels abreast, which, according to my observation, is more than might commonly pass in the strait valleys of Sinai encumbered with fallen quarters of rocks. The convoy of Israel should be four hundred times this Haj train or more than two hundred leagues long ; and from the pillar of cloud or fire to the last footman of Jacob would be more journeys than in the longest month of the year ! But what of their beasts in all that horrid labyrinth ? and suppose their camels to be 3,000,000 to 6000,000 and all their small cattle 7,000,000 ; they had besides oxen and asses ! Can we think that Sinai, which is the sorriest of all desert pastures, could bear them, or that there were enough for three days to feed such a multitude of cattle ?

I might sometimes see heaving and rolling above all heads of men and cattle in the midst of the journeying caravan, the naked frame and posts of the sacred *Mahmal* camel which resembles a bedstead and is after the fashion of the Beduish woman's camel-litter. It is clothed on high days with a glorious pall of green velvet, the prophet's colour, and the four posts are crowned with glancing knops of silver. I understand from grave elders of the religion, that this litter is the standard of the Haj, in the antique guise of Arabia, and yet remaining among the Beduw ; wherein, at any general battle of tribes, there is mounted some beautiful damsel of the sheykh's daughters, whose generous loud *Alleluias* for her people, in presence of their enemies, inflame her young kinsmen's hearts to leap in that martial dance to a multitude of deaths. In this standard litter of the

Haj is laid *eth-thôb*, the gift of the Sultan of Islam, that new silken cloth, which is for the covering of the *Kaaba* at Mecca, whereof " Abraham was the founder." I saw this frame in the stations, set down before the Pasha's pavilion : I saw also carried in our caravan a pair of long coffers in which were mast-great tapers for the shrine of Mohammed. And looking upon the holy Hajjàj it is a motley army, spotted guile is in their Asiatic hearts more than religion ; of the fellowship of saints in the earth are only few in their company. A wonder it was to me to see how the serving men, many of them of citizen callings, in which at home they sit still, can foot it forty days long to Mecca and Mona. Water is scant and commonly of the worst ; and these Syrians dwelling in a limestone country are used to be great drinkers of the purest water. Marching all day they hardly taste food but in the night stations, where they boil themselves a great mess of wheaten stuff ; they seldom buy flesh meat, with money out of their slender purses. But after the proverb, men know not all their sufferance but in the endeavour, also we may endure the better in company. There are very few who faint ; the Semitic nature, weak and quick metal, is also of a wonderful temper and long suffering in God. And every soul would hallow himself (even though he be by man's law a criminal) in seeking " God's house " : in returning again the sweet meditation upholds a man of seeing his home, his family, his friends.

The salary of a footman driver is about £8 English money to Mecca ; but since good part of the pilgrimage will go home by ship, the many dismissed servants must seek a new shift for themselves in returning upward. In our company of a score most of the lads were novices : the mukowwems are fain of such *ghrashîm*, or raw haj prentices which serve them without wages, receiving only the carriage of their food and water. But the foremen are every year in the Haj, and of this voyage is most of their living : besides there are many whom their old pain so enamours of the sacred way, that they will fare anew and cannot forsake it. And though the akkâms be reputed wild and rude, yet amongst our crew but one and another were brutish lads, and the rest poor young men of Damascus, commonly of an honest behaviour. Their *rayîs* or head received double money, or £16 English : this was a wayworn man, one *Abu Rashîd* a patten-maker, lean as any rake. Two-thirds part of the year he sat at home in their sûk, under the great cathedral mosque at Damascus : but the haj month come about (whereto their lent month last before, filling the body with crude humours, is but an evil preparation) he forsook all, and trudging four months re-

visited the blissful Harameyn and brought again of that
purgatory of fatigues a little money, to the sustenance of
his honest family. Second of our skilled hands was the
akkâm who served me ; one of those wild and well-bent hearts
of strong men that lean, by humanity of nature, to the
good, but which betrayed by some rheum that is in them of a
criminal rashness, are sooner drawn to evil ways in the
world. His companions called him *el-Eswad* for his generous
brown colour, yet which they hold for a deformity. He was of
the dangerous fellowships at Damascus called the *Muatterîn;*
men commonly of hardy complexion and overflowing strength,
who look to help their loose living by violence. Few years before having been drawn in the conscription he deserted, and since
travelled up and down out of sight of the law, and even sailed
hither and thither by sea ; now he lived secretly at Damascus,
an herb gatherer. Eswad had £12 of the mukowwem to Mecca :
there is no seeking for outlaws and evil doers in the Haj caravan.

All the Damascene servants in our Persian company knew
me to be a Nasrâny ; and contained their gossiping tongues,
less of good will than that we were divided by the Persian
multitude from the next companies of the Arabic language.
As ever our two misliving rufflers barked upon me, which was
hour by hour, Eswad snibbed them sharply with *fen dînak*,
' where is thy faith ? ' Nimbly upon the way he trode and upright as a wand ruling a camel-coach litter with undaunted
strength. In the great marches I alighted to walk some miles
that he might ride and rest awhile in my stead. The Arabs full
of their own vanities, are impatient of a stranger's contradiction,
and if sometime the fanatical persuasion, where every heart
is full of pain and unrest of the road, had made him nettlesome
with the Nasrâny, I said to him " What will *Abu Saad* think
upon it ! " This was a poor man of good estimation, a penitent
father of muatters and by adventure of my acquaintance at
Damascus : it chanced also he was Eswad's own master, so that he
named him father ; one in whom the old violence seemed to be
now mollified to religion, with devout fasting twice in the week.
But Abu Saad, with some of the old leaven, yet vaunted
' the muatters were sore a-dread of him ' : Eswad looked
upon me and was silent when I had named him. I knew
the man as a client of a Christian Damascus family. In that
massacre of Christians, now many years gone, one of the
household as he hasted by the street, was beset at a corner by
murderous Moslems who cried with one breath, " Out upon
a Nasrâny and kill him." And the trembling man might have
come then by his death, but he thought upon a wile ; he

touched one amongst those fiendly white turbans and, not knowing him, said to him *ana dakhîl-ak* " I am thy suppliant." The valiant muatter, thinking his honour engaged, plucked out the old horse-pistol in his belt, for all men were now in the streets with their arms, and bit it between his teeth. Then he heaved the Christian high upon his back, and bade men give him way or he would make one ; and he staggered forth as the Christian load showed him, until he set him down at the door of his own house. That family was saved, and now Abu Saad names them ' his brethren of Nasâra ' ; he visits them and they kindly entertain him some months in the year in their houses. He is a carrier of quarried stones, and they of their welfare bestow upon him at all times for his needs.

Many were the examples of Christians in that mortal extremity succoured by pitiful men of the Mohammedan poor people, for no hope of reward ; but only as they were taught of God and human kindness, especially in the open village quarter and trading with the Beduish country, el-Medân, among whose citizens is a savour of the venerable spirit of the Semitic desert. Some then piously took up poor Christian children in the ways, where they met with them, and kept them in covert in their own houses. The rich booty of the burning streets of Christian houses was soon too hot in the handling of rude Moslems ; all the best was sold, even jewels and gold, for a little ready money to the Jews, fain of the abominable lucre and foxes to keep these bloody stealths close. Also I have heard the Mohammedans complain " by Ullah all we did, we did it for the Yahûd (Jews), the Yahûd made the Moslemîn fools ! " Even certain considerable Christians which were saved, are said to have then enriched themselves of other poor Nasarenes' goods, carried for safety into their principal houses, when the owners having been slain there remained no record of the place of deposit ; for all gape in these Turkish countries to swallow other, even their own kind. Another of our lads was a bathier in the hammam by the Persian consulate, but man enough to step down three hundred leagues to Mecca ; and one was a miller's knave at *Bab Tooma* in the Christian quarter ; and one of *Hums* (Emesa) a great town towards Aleppo : he fleered and laughed all the way as he went. " It is a fool (said the companions) all the Humsians are alike sick of a devil." Of the other novices was one of an honourable mind and erect stature ; no pains of the road could ever move him from a gentle virtuous demeanour. One day in a resting-while the son of the Persian aga said amongst them " What think ye of the ₐNasâra ? theirs is a good religion men say, and they worship *Îsa* (Jesu) as we Mohammed and the Jews *Mûsa ;* who

may say that their religion is not well enough, or that we have
a better ? would ye change religions for a reward and cease
to be Moslemîn ? Would some man give me now a thousand
pound in my hand, I doubt whether I would not consent to
be of their religion." That novice spoke then a noble word ; " I
would not, said he, be divided from the Religion for any world's
good, for *ed-dinnia fàny,* the world fadeth away." "Khalîl
Effendi," said the young Persian Damascene ; " if you will come
over to our religion, go down now with us to Mecca and we will
show thee all the holy places, and this were better for thee
than to leave the caravan at Medáin Sâlih, where by God the
Beduw will cut thy throat as ever the Haj shall be gone by them."
I enquired what nomads were those at Medáin Sâlih : it was
answered " The *Fukara*, which according with their name (*fakîr*,
a poor man, a derwish) are liker gipsies than Beduins ; they
are so thievish we fear them more than other upon the road ;
by the life of God they are the worst of the Beduw. Be not so
foolhardy to trust thyself among them : but go to the kella and
there lodge, and the Pasha will bind the soldiery for thy safety
until the returning Haj."

The great haj camels, unlike the small Beduin cattle,
(which live only of that they may find in the dry desert,)
browse nothing on the road ; they are fed at the halts, as in
Syria, with boiled pulse, wrought into clots of which four or
five or six are crammed into the great weary beast's jaws,
and satisfy that frugal stomach. The masters buy also at some
desert stations a long knot-grass forage, *thurrm,* of certain
poor nomads (not Beduins), which their camels chaw in the
hours of repose. They are couched then in rows, their halters
running upon a ground-rope stretched between iron pins. Those
many novices marching with us were taken for side-men, under
the rayîs and Eswad, of the two *takhts er-Rúm* or camel-coaches,
in the equipage of the Persian aga, which are borne in such
sort that each is suspended by the four shafts, between the
withers of a fore and the shoulders of an after camel. By every
shaft there goes a lad, and in the midst a lad, upon both sides,
six for a takht. Where the wild road is unequal, with the
strength of their arms, they rule the sway of this high uneasy
carriage. The takhts are gallantly painted and adorned, there is
room in them that a man may lie at his length or sit up. The
Pasha and a few rich men ride to Mecca in such vehicles,
at great charges : and therefore I wondered to see these of the
Ajamy carried empty, but el-Eswad told me, he has therefore
a yearly exhibition from his government ; also I should soon
see some conveyed in them : for if any poor man sickened to death

D. T.   5

in the company, he would pay the one hundred piastres of daily hire to ride like a lord in the few hours that remained for him to live. Upon the bearing harness of the takht camels are shields of scarlet, full of mirrors, with crests of ostrich plumes, and beset with ranks of little bells, which at each slow camel's foot-fall jungle, sinking together, with a strange solemnity; it is the sound of the Haj religion wonderfully quaint and very little grateful in my hearing. The hind camel paces very unhandsomely, for that he may not put his muzzle through the glass panel, his head and huge long neck is drawn down under the floor-board of his unwieldy burden, which is under the height of his shoulders, with much distress of the weary beast in the long marches. Not a little stately are those camel litters, with the ladders and gay trappings, marching in the empty way of the desert;—they remain perchance of the old Byzantine pageantry. Journeying by day and by night the takhts are rarely disordered. All this sore travail of men and beasts, and great government expense, might well be spared, if palmers would take the sea to Mecca; but that were less meritorious: without this irrational wearing of the flesh in the worship of God the Giver of life they were not hajjies indeed. The aga and his son rode upon hackneys; but the carriage is costly, of their barley and much daily water. A Galla slave bore fire after them in an iron sling, for the nargîlies; whirling the smouldering coals they are presently kindled.

As we advanced I saw the takhts to be inhabited, and that they were the beginning of a man's funerals. Wrapped in his large hair cloak he was laid in them, soon to die, and the pompous litter was often his bier before evening. I saw none of those clay-white faces that came in there which left it again alive; they depart this life in the vehement labour of the way, without comfort of human kindness, amidst the litany of horrible imprecations, which are all moments in the mouths of the young Damascus drivers: and when a man was passed, any of them who looked in upon him said but to his fellows, *mât*, " he is dead ! " Arrived at the station they lifted out his corse, the dead man's heels knocking and training upon the ground, and bore it into the pavilion. In our riding, I often saw some wild headstone of a palmer's sandy grave. The strangest adventure in this Haj was the pilgrimage of a Persian lady deceased, who dying at Maan, would needs be laid in holy ground at Mecca thirty journeys in advance, and faithfully her serving man endeavoured to fulfil his dame's last request. He bought a camel (of our Persian camel-master), and the beast slaughtered, he sewed in the raw hide his dead mistress and lapped upon that

raw sheepskins ; then binding poles all round, he laid up this
bale of worm's meat in her cradle litter, and followed as hitherto
in the caravan. After some journeys, the tiding came to the ears
of the Pasha ; certain persons had seen the servant sitting under
a thorn tree, which he had made his night quarters, to keep the
wake by his ghastly baggage. The Pasha took counsel, and his
ordinance was that the uncouth funeral might follow with the
pilgrimage, but at a little distance ; also he forbad this man to
bring his dead lady, at the stations, within the encampment.—
As an impression in water will strike all round, so it is in every
mischief in the world ! for this chance I was also the worse, and
rode since Maan as one of the mourners ; it happened so that
the beast taken for the slaughter was the camel from under me.

Every day, since Muzeyrîb, the camel-master had murmured,
that my over-heavy load would break his camel's back; of this
or other cause the great brute suffered by the way and was
sick. Then at Maan they all told me, with mouths full of
great oaths, that my camel was dead. The camel-master bought
there, to mount me, a young black cow-camel, of the Aarab,
wild and untaught : this unlucky change of riding turned also
to my great torment. Unused to marching tied, and these long
journeys, under heavy burdens, she would fall upon her knees
and couch down amidst the moving lines, snap the leading
strings, and trouble all behind which came on riding over me.
It made me oftentimes a mark for the choleric exclamations of
too many weary persons, and there was danger thus, when all
is danger, in the dark night marching. I could have no redress,
and though this was against the faith of my Damascus con-
tract, they all cried upon me, that I had killed the man's camel.
The camel-master, hoping to extort somewhat, many times
refused to send me my camel at the removes ; when all the
rest were ready and the signal was heard to march, they have
left me alone in the desert, standing in the dark, by my bags.
When it happened thus, I laid hold of el-Eswad, and would not
let him go, for though they brought up the beast at last, I
had not strength to load on her single handed ; sometimes the
worst have sworn ' to leave my body under the sand where
I stood.' These shrews played an ill comedy ; the danger
urgent, I drew out before them my naked pistol : after other
days, they gave over thus to trouble me. They are wolves
to each other and what if some were hounds to me ? for the
distress of the way edges all men's spirits. And this is spoken
proverbially in Syria amongst Mohammedans as against the
Haj. " Ware of any neighbour of thine an hajjy ! Twice a hajjy,
keep thy door close ; an hajjy the third time, build up the door

of thy dwelling and open another upon the contrary part."
Commonly the fanaticism in religion is worn very near the
threads in old hajjies : they are come to some cold conceit
of their own religious matter ; for what sanctity perceive
they at Mecca ? where looking into the ark, they see but
bubbles burst, that seemed before pearls in Syria ! Yet there
are no hurly-burlies in the Haj, the fearful fantasies of townsfolk in Beduin country, draw them silently together where they
think there is no salvation out of the caravan.

The pilgrims the more earnestly remember their devotion as
they approach the sacred temples ; and in the forced marches
whilst we rode, at the hours, some pious men played the
Muetthins, crying to prayers from the rocking height of their
cattle. The solemn cry was taken up at the instant, with
vast accord by the thousands of manly throats, and the desert
side once a year bellows again, with this multitudinous human
voice. The Persians take up the cry in the rearward, yet putting in their confession before Mohammed, the name of Aly.
And that is a chief cause of their contention with the catholic
Mohammedans by whom they are named *Shîas*, and betwixt
shîas and sunnîs, when they meet, is commonly contention.
Their bickerings are not seldom in the Persian Gulf, among
the British steam-packet passengers, so that the English officers
must come between them. The litany of Mohammed's Arabian
religion must be said in his native tongue.—Oh what contempt
in religions of the human reason ! But it is a wonder to hear
these poor foreigners, how they mouthe it, to say their prayer
in the canonical strange speech, and only their clerkish men can
tell what ! There came in our crew, in fellowship with el-
Eswad, a young tradesman of Damascus ; these friends went by
the long way sporting, and (as southern folk) leaning on each
other's necks, and in that holy cry they shouted as good as ten
men in mockery for " our Lord Aly." Sometimes at Medina
there has befallen certain imprudent and embittered Persians
an extreme and incredible mischief ; this is when they would
spitefully defile Mohammed's sepulchre, in covertly letting fall
dung upon it ; yet not so privily but they were espied by
Argus-eyed sunnîs. Mahmûd at Maan, yearly wont to ride
with the Haj soldiery, had three years before my coming thither
seen such an hap at Medina. The denounced wretch was haled
forth to the raging execrations of the fanatic hajjàj. The sunnî
multitude condemned him to die in hell torments ; there was
fetched-to and heaped timber, and the fire kindled they thrust
him in ; and said Mahmûd, with a sigh of vengeance satisfied,
" we burned him the cursed one."

Among the light-mounted, I saw an old man, you might take him for some venerable sheykh of his village, sitting " as one of the governors," upon a white ass of Bagdad, and whenever I noted him he would pleasantly greet me, saying, " How fare you, Khalîl Effendi ? " and looking upon me the old eyes twinkled under his shaggy brows as stars in a frosty night. He rode somewhat bowed down with a stiff back upon his beast, and his face might well be less known to me, for it was he who had been so extremely beaten days before at W. Zerka. The conscience of the box-breaker was already whole after the suffered punishment, his ridge-bone not yet ; his fault known to all men, he was not ashamed.

The *Sir Amîn* is entitled *Emir el-Haj*, ' commander of the great pilgrimage,' an officer who, in old times, was often a Sultan's son ; but in our days it is some courtier warm from the delicate carpets of Stambûl, and little able to sustain the rudeness of camel-riding. I saw him carried softly in a varnished coach, between two stout even-pacing mules with trappings of scarlet ; a relay followed, and when it pleased him he mounted his beautiful horse with the Pasha, with whom lies all the charge of conducting the caravan. The gentleman was not wont to so early rising, and removing before dawn, and commonly his tardy litter overtook the caravan about day-break. As for the Pasha, although stepped in years, there was none so early or so late as he : *Muhàfiz* or guardian of the pilgrimage, he held also the office of paymaster, *kasra el-haj*, upon the road, to the Beduw. This resolute man of the sword, most robust, and hardened to sustain fatigues from his youth, sleeps but two hours, (thus his familiars say of him,) in the Haj journey. He rests, in the night marches, in his takht er-Rûm, borne by his own camels, and that is first in the train : there goes beside him the dalîl or pilot of the caravan. His passage in the day time was not so wearying as our slow march ; the Pasha then rides forth, freshly mounted upon his mare, with his officers and a few troopers, to two or three leagues in advance of the caravan ; there halting they alight, a fire is kindled and they sit down to drink coffee and the nargîly, until the pilgrimage is coming again by them ; and with another and another of these outridings the day is passed. A tent is pitched about noon for the Pasha, and a tent for the Sîr Amîn, where shadowed they may break their fasts ; and this sand country is often burning as coals in the winter's sun.

Strange to me was the daily sight of some half-score of Syrian street dogs, that followed with the pilgrimage : every year some Syrian hounds go down thus to Mecca, with the city of tents, and return from thence. The pious eastern-people charitably regard those poor pilgrim creatures, that are, in their beasts' wit, they think, among God's witnesses of the true religion. Eswad, if he saw any fainting hound, in the next halt he lured him, and poured out a little precious water, to the unclean animal, in the heel of his shoe. Strange hounds will be rent in pieces among them, if they enter another quarter in their own city ; at Mecca it is likely they remain abroad by the baggage encampment. The quaintest of our Persian fellowship was a white cock ; I thought, after the lion, this brave bird might be a standard of theirs, so gallantly rode chanticleer aloft, in a chain and pair of scarlet jesses. He stood pitching uneasily and balancing with his white wings upon the highest of the takht er-Rûm camel furnitures ; at night he roosted lordly in the coach, or chained, like a bear to a post, within the Persians' wide pavilion. *Chuck, chuck !* said this fluttering ghost that had no more a merry heart to hail us in the desert morning ; crestfallen was the pasha-bird, it was piteous that men carried none of his hareem along with him !— I could not read this riddle of a cock ; Eswad only answered me " the bird is mine." This fatigue of the journey cuts off a man's voice at the lips, and half his understanding ; more than this I could not learn, it might be a mystery of religion. Who will spend his spirits in the long march ? There is little uttered then besides curses, yet in the night station they will sit taling awhile under the stars about their supper fires.

The long hours passed, our march lay ever between the double array of mountains : the hajjies on camel-back slumbered as they sat bent and bowing in the hot sun. By the long way, is sometimes heard a sudden shouting, upon the flanks of the moving caravan ; there is a running out of the people and a shower of sticks and stones. A poor little startled hare is their quarry, more seldom the *thób ;* at every double she escaped many deaths until some violent bat bereft her dear life ; or I have seen poor puss hie her among the rabble of footmen, running back and doubling for shelter, among the legs of the camels and even fairly escape, by miracle. The thób is an edible sprawling lizard; the great-grown is nearly a yard long with his tail, and the Arabs say very sweet meat. A morsel of venison is so pleasant to poor folk in the caravans : the better provided carry some smoked and cured flesh which may be had good enough and cheap at Damascus. Mutton slaughtered by Beduins is set to sale at the principal stations. They only fare well which are of the Pasha's household, whose government mess is every day a yearling sheep ; these fattened at some kella stations we saw daily driven along with the caravan.

At the mid-afternooon there was some mirage before us : I saw it not again in nomad Arabia, which is nearly dewless, and without ground moisture ; there is mirage also of the wavering and smoking of thin heated air over the sun-stricken soil. Ten miles westward upon our right hand, is a ruined site *Gereyih,* of which the country Beduins recount strange fables, but I hear of trustworthy persons it is inconsiderable. We came soon after to the canvas ceilings of our tents, stretched without the skirts, in an open plain, *el-Ká.* That station was only for a short resting-while and to take food, for the night before us we were to join to this daylight's already long marching. I sent to the camp market for meat, but there was none held here, nor had any tradesman opened his bales of merchandise. The market in the journeying canvas city is also called *súk ;* it is a short street of caravan merchants' tents, and pitched in our descending march at the southward. There are set out wares for the Beduins, (which assemble from far upon both sides of the derb el-haj,) clothing and carpets and diverse small merchandise : also there are salesmen to the pilgrims of biscuit, prepared wheaten stuff and the like ; and if any private man would sell or buy anything by the cry of the running broker, it is done there. The clothing merchants go not all down to Mecca ; but certain of them descending every year in the Haj, to their several nomad districts, there remain until the returning upward. The most are of the Medân ; some of them were born of Beduin mothers. Their gross gain is not, they say, above twenty-five in the hundred ; but when the Aarab pay them in butter, there is a second advantage, at Damascus.

The desert closed over us with vast glory of fiery hanging clouds : the sun's great rundle went down, with few twinkling smiles, behind the mountains of Hisma. In these golden moments after we had rested out two hours and supped, a new gunfire warned the caravan to remove. We set forward in the glooming, which lasts but few minutes in Arabia, and it is dim night : other eleven hours we must journey forth to come to our rest-station at Tebûk. The moon lightened our march this third Sunday night ; which name to the heart born in land of Christians, in the most rumble, weariness and peril of the world is rest and silence. Near behind me there drove a Persian akkâm, who all night long chanted, to teach his rude fellow, now approaching the holy places, to say his canonical prayer, the Arabic sounding sweet upon his Persian tongue, *el-hamdu lillahî Rub el-alamîn ;* the words of the *fátha* or " opening " of the koran, " Unto God be all glory, the Lord of worlds " :—this lullaby they chanted ever among them till the morning light. Soon after midnight the shooting in the van of two rockets was the signal to halt ; we slept on the sand for an hour : at a new

warning shot we must rise again and set forward. When the
moon went down, at three in the morning, we marched by our
paper lanterns.   There was a signal again little before dawn
and we halted forty minutes : the sunrising in Arabia is naked
and not bathed in dewy light.   The caravan making forward
anew, in a purgatory of aching fatigue and betwixt sleeping and
waking, we came nodding at eight o'clock in the morning, in
sight of Tebûk. Of twenty-six hours, or more than a revolution of the planet, we had marched twenty-four, and left behind
us fifty miles at least : it is a great wonder how so many in the
caravan can hold out upon their feet.

The ancient village, built of raw clay, appears of an ochre
colour, pleasantly standing before a palm-grove, in a world of
weary desert, strewn with the sandstone quartz pebbles.   I
found the altitude 2900 feet ;   green corn-plots are before the
place in the irrigated sand. Far at our left hand, standing over
the wild bank of mountains, is the sharp Jebel head called by
the Syrian caravaners *Mumbir er-Rasûl*, the Apostle's pulpit,
for the form, which is of a tilted table, or such as the preacher's

munbir in the great mesjids. Mohammed passing
by Tebûk stood, they say,
upon that loft of the black
looking mountain, and
preached to the peoples
of Arabia : the Beduw
name this height *Sherôra*
it is a great land-mark,
and in marches of the
Sherarât (the head as I
might understand is lime-
stone, and the stack is
sandstone).—It were idle
to ask these land-names
of the caravaners : now the Hisma dies away behind us.   All
along by the haj road from hence were, as they tell, of old time
villages ; so that the wayfarer might at one break his fast, and
sup at another : no need was then to carry provision for the way.

We found here refreshment of sweet lemons, tomatoes,
pomegranates, and the first Arabian dates, but of a lean kind,
the best are fetched from *Teyma*. The villagers are named *el-
Humeydát* and they call themselves *Arab el-Kaabeny*, few and
poor people, their " forty households " only defended by the kella
from the tyranny of the Beduins ; and they are the kella
servants. The water here, flat and lukewarm, is little whole-

some ; this desert bottom is naturally a rising place of ground
waters. *Ayn* Tebûk is an ancient spring and conduit but
stopped by the ruin of great fallen stones. Surra for this
tower is received by the sheykh of B. Atîeh. Tebûk is an old
name ; nevertheless, the nomads say, the place was anciently
called *Yarmûk.* We should rest here the day over. As we
rode the last night, some troopers were come to enquire of me
what man I was ? I remained therefore in the tents, dreading
that my being in the caravan was now come to the Pasha's
ears, and he might leave me here. The Persians sit solacing in
the passing hours with sweet tea, which they make in such
brass machines as the Muscovites, and smoking the perfumed
nargîlies. Only the Pasha himself, who is paymaster of the
road, is all day most busy in the kella, with the Beduin sheykhs,
who are come into the place to receive their toll-money.

The paymaster's office fills yet higher the old man's heavy
purse : so he handles the disbursement that there shall remain
some rubbing of the serpent's scales in his hold. The Turkish
juggling by which one may be a public thief and yet an honest
stately citizen, is wonderful to consider ! The *mejîdy,* or ottoman crown piece was, say, twenty piastres government money,
and twenty-two or twenty-three in the merchants' reckoning at
Damascus. The sum of the Haj expenses is delivered to the
pasha paymaster, at the setting out, a crown for twenty piastres :
but he goes on paying the wild Beduw all the road along a
crown piece for twenty-two and a half piastres, swearing down
the faces of the nomad sheykhs, who are weak in art metric,
and taking witness of all men in their wits that the crown is
now so many piastres, by Ullah ! These Turkish souls seem
to themselves to be not alive in a corrupt world, but they
be still eating of the corrupt world somewhat : this pretty
device becomes a great man and makes him to be commended
in the fraternity of their criminal government. Here is no
leak in the chest, he diminishes not the Sultan's revenue, but
bites only the finger of the accursed Beduins. It is true he
deals in equal sort with the garrison's wages, and of their poor
bags he plucks out the lining ; but the soldiery can suffer smiling
this law of the road, since he also disburses to the tower wardens,
for more men than he will ever require of them, to be mustered
before him. And the stout old officer loves well the great fatigues
of his benefice, which can every year endow him so richly ; his
salary is besides 2000 Turkish pounds, with certain large allowances for the daily entertainment of many persons and cattle.

Mohammed Saîd was one the worthiest of his hand and most
subtle headed in all Syria. As all great personages in the

Arabic countries, I have found him easy to be spoken withal :
full of astute human humour, bearing with mildness his worshipful dignity. Of most robust pith he was ; yet all these strong
souls are born under no clearer star than to be money catchers.
In soil of such a government as theirs, there come up no patriots :
what examples see they ever in their youth of goodly deeds or
noble ends of men's lives ! And if any gentler spirit bred amongst
them, would suck some sweet comfort of his proper studies, in the
empty task of the Arabic letters, he should but grow downward.
The Kurdy Pasha to-day possessed funded property, all of his
own strong and sleighty getting at Damascus, (where he had built
himself a great palace,) of the yearly rent of more than 10,000
pounds, if you can believe them : his father was but a poor aga
before him. Like the most that are grown great ones amongst
them, he had been a man of brilliant violence and a blood-
shedder from his youth. Appointed upon a time governor of
Acre, when the Moghreby commander would not cede his place,
they took the event of battle upon it : such strife was there in
those lawless days, betwixt Kurds and the Moghrebies merce-
naries, and between either of them and the not less turbulent
Albanians ; their divisions were an old sore, in these parts of
the Turkish empire. Mohammed Saîd's part chased the other
to Tiberias, and held on killing and wounding, to Jacob's bridge
over Jordan ; his own brother fell there. A familiar friend of
the Pasha told me the government is tardy to go between these
bickerings of stubborn nations, whom they let thus spend themselves and spare for no human blood : the Turks rule also by
oppositions of religions ; it is thus they put a ring in the nose
of Syria.

The old Kurdy, yet more covetous in his office, was become
his own camel-master, in the caravan ; fifty of his beasts carried
the sacred stores, such as the yearly provision of oil for the
Harameyn ; and a load of the holy stuffs is only sixty *rotl*, the
ordinary being an hundred. Thus by the haj way he licked fat
from all beards, and was content to receive peace offerings even
of the poor kella keepers, their fresh eggs and chickens, presents
of sweet lemons and the like ! His children were an only
daughter, and he loved her dearer than himself. When I was
come again from the Arabian journey to Damascus, I went to
salute him at his marble-stairs palace ;—the unhappy father !
his dear child was lately dead. Alas weary man, a part of him
buried, for what more should he live ? and whose to be, ere
long, those gotten riches, when he should be borne out feet
foremost from his great house ! He had brethren ; I met with a
young brother of this old man, an under-officer of soldiery, little

before I took my journey, who hearing I would out with the Haj, answered with a fanatical indignation, "Ullah forbid it : shall any Nasrâny come in the *Hejâz!*"—The Kaimakàm at Maan is paid well with £20 a month, and he lives himself of his horse rations of barley. Besides, drawing the corn and wages of sixty men for the garrison, he holds but twenty, of whom only ten are Damascene men-at-arms, and the rest half-paid hirelings of the peasantry in the next villages. Here is forty men's living honestly spared, to be divided between himself and the crooked fingers of his higher officers ! This is the game of the derb el-haj, they all help each other to win, and are confederate together ; and the name of the Sultan's government is a band of robbers.

At a signal shot on the morrow the caravan removed ; two hours before day we were marching in a place of thorns and tamarisks, a token of ground-water ; we made good booty of firewood. The loose sand soil is strewed with black vulcanic pebbles, which are certainly from the *Harra.* The hills fade away eastward, the country is rising. Westward, are seen now, behind the low border train of sandstone bergs, rank behind rank, some black peaks of a mighty black platform mountain, and this is the Harra. Those heads are spent vulcanoes

of the lava-covered Harra-height, twenty miles backward ! After marching ten hours we pass a belt of hills, which lies athwart our road for an hour. Forty miles from Tebûk we encamped in open ground *Dàr el-Múghr* or *el-Kalandary ;* the Harra beyond is that of the *Sidenyîn* nomads, a division of B. Atîeh, whose women wear the forelock braided down in an horn, with a bead, upon their foreheads.

We were again hastily on foot at three in the dark morning. With what untimely discomfort and trepidation of weary hearts do we hear again the loud confused rumour of a great caravan rising! that harsh inquietude, upon a sudden, of the silent night camp and thousands of bellowing camels. We marched then through the belt of mountains in hollow ground, ascending till we came, at nine, to the highest of the way. We descend soon by the *Boghráz el-Akhdar*, a steep glen head, an hundred feet deep in thick bedded sandstone : dangerous straits were they beset by Beduins, there may hardly more than two camels pass abreast. I espied upon the face of a stone, at the wayside, some Nabatean inscription of two lines, the first I had seen in these countries : leaping from my camel, I would have hastily transcribed the strange runes, but in a moment was almost overridden by the tide of those coming behind, of whom some cursed the hajjy standing in the way and some went by me and wondered. The passage in an hour opens into a sandy valley-bottom one hundred and fifty feet lower, with green desert bushes : we arrived already an hour before noon, at the kellat el-Akhdar, to rest and watering. The Aarab name both the valley and tower *el-Khúthr*, and the neighbour Beduin sheykh, (*Meságed*, with his people of B. Atîeh), is surnamed *el-Khúthery*. *Saidna* (our Lord) *Khithr* is that strange running Beduwy of the Bible, Elijah theProphet ; a chapel-of-rags, under his invocation, is seen within the kella. Elijah, confounded also with St. George, is a mighty prophet with the Syrians, as well Mohammedans as Greek Christians : they all prognosticate from this year's day, in the autumn, the turning of the weather, which they are well assured never fails them. The fiery Tishbite taken up quick to heaven, has at sometime appeared to men in this forlorn valley ; the Moslemîn ignorant of our biblical lore say of him, " It is that prophet, who is in earth and also in heaven."

Over this kella doorway is an old Arabic inscription, engraved within a border, shaped as a Roman ensign board. The great cistern is triple ; and here only a third and least part was now in use ; the water is raised of a shallow well within the kella. The watering of a multitude of men and cattle is a strong labour, and these hardly-worn and weakly-fed serving men are of wonderful endurance. Beyond the haj-camp market I saw some wrtched booths, next under the kella, of certain nomads which inherit the office of foragers of the camel knot-grass to the Haj : no Beduins would lend themselves to this which they think an ignoble traffic. These despised desert families, the *Sweyfly*, are reckoned to the Sherarát. The head of this wady is in the district *er-Ràha* of the Harra, under the

high vulcanic hills *Sheybàn* and *Wítr*. From a cliff in the
valley head, there flows down a brook of warm water, which
where stagnant in lower places is grown about with canes ; in this
ponded desert water are little fishes. Here the Aarab draw for
their camels, but drink not themselves, the taste is brackish ;
the freshet runs little further, and is sunk up again. The valley
below now turns northward and goes out, so far as I could learn
from the nomads, in the circuit of Tebûk. Beduins that have
part ground rights of this tower, to receive surra and be haj
carriers are the *Moahîb*, afterward my friends, (Aarab of the
next lower Harra,) and the Fejîr or Fukara ; they are Annezy
tribes of the circuit of Medáin Sâlih.

Upon these valley coasts I saw cairns or beacons ; the akkâms
call them *mantar*. Many are the hasty graves of buried pilgrim
" witnesses " in this station ; upon the headstones of wild blocks
pious friends have scored the words which were their names. To
be accounted " witnessing," surely for civil souls, is the creeping
plague of Egypt. It is so many days and nights since poor men
change not their clothing, that those who inhabit by all the rivers
of Damascus are become as any derwishes. But if one cannot
for a set time withdraw his spirit from the like miseries, paying
the toll to nature for such difficult passages, let him not be
called a man : and who would be abashed if lions rose upon
him, he is not meet to be " a son of the way " in this horrid
country.

After nightfall I stole with el-Eswad through the camp, to
visit some inscriptions within the kella. We crept by the Pasha's
great pavilion, a greenish double tent, silken they say and
Engleysy, that is of the best Frankish work ; at every few paces
we stumbled over stretched cords and pins of the pilgrims' tents,
which, when struck, carry like spiders' threads an alarm within
and sleepers waken with a snatching sound and a rude bounce
in their ears. " Who he there ! " is cried out, and we had much
to do to answer softly " Forgive it, friends " and go on stumbling.
The kella was open, and in the doorway, lighting our lanterns,
he showed me the inscriptions, they were but few rude scorings
upon wall stones. There came to look on some of the loitering
garrison, which are Moors, and wondered to see one writing,
and when they spoke some piety of the Néby, that I answered
nothing, as I could not in conscience. We looked into Elias'
chamber-of-rags and hastily departed ; the caravan was again
about to remove, to march all this night, for there is no rest
upon pilgrimage.

At ten o'clock of the starry night we set forth, and rode
descending in a deep ground with cliffs, till two in the morning,

when the eastern bank faded into a plain before us. The night was open with cold wind ; footgoers made blazing fires of the dry bushes and stood by, a moment, to warm themselves. We passed an hour or two through a pleasant woody place of acacia trees named by the caravaners *Jeneynat el-Kâdy* " The justice's pleasure ground ; " and all greenness of bushes and trees is " a garden " in the desert. After twenty miles we were in a deep open valley ; a little before the sun rising the caravan halted forty minutes. And from thence we enter a long glen *W. Sâny*, whose cliffs are thick beds of a massy iron sandstone. That sand bottom is bestrewed with vulcanic drift, some bluish grey, heavy and hard, worn in the shape of whetstones, pumice, and black lavas. The drift ceasing, after some miles begins afresh ; I saw it fallen down over the shelves of the valley's western wall, and pertaining doubtless to the Harra, which although not in sight, trends with our long passage since Tebûk. The soil was even footing and many alighted here to walk awhile. Some Persians, my neighbours, ran to show me (whom they understood to be an hakîm) morsels which they had taken up of clear crystal, to know if they had not found diamonds ; for blunt men as they are further from home, think themselves come so much the nigher to the world's riches and wonders. Here Eswad promised to show me many inscriptions, I found only scorings of little worth, upon hard quarters of sandstone, that lay in the wady floor. Whilst I lingered to transcribe them, the caravan was almost half an hour gone from us, and there came by the Beduin carriers, men of lean swarthy looks, very unlike the full-of-the-moon white visages of Damascus. Ill clad they were, riding upon the rude pack furnitures of their small desert camels ; these Beduins were afterwards my hosts in the wilderness. The hajjies admire upon the east valley side above, a statue-like form *ed-dubb* " the bear," whether so made by rude art, or it were a strange mocking herself of mother Nature. It resembles, to my vision, a rhinoceros standing upon legs, and the four legs set upon a pedestal. One might guess it had been an idol ; I hear from some which had climbed, that the image is natural. The sandstones, in some places of iron durity, in others are seen wasted into many fantastic forms.

We came, always ascending in very high country, to our camp, at four in the afternoon, having marched nineteen hours. Here is *Birket Moaddam* and an abandoned kella, the fairest and greatest in all the road, with the greatest cistern ; a benefaction of the same Sultan Selím. The border is here between the Fejîr and' Khuthéra nomads ; the land height 3700 feet, and this

is a fresh station in the great summer heats. The birket
is ruinous, there is no water ; we make therefore great forced
marches, the only hope of water since el-Akhdar before Medáin
Sâlih, fifty leagues distant, being at the next station, *Dàr el-
Hamra*, where is commonly none. For there is also but a
cistern at a freshet bed to be flushed by the unceratin winter
rains ; and if there runs in any water, within a while it will be
vapoured to the dregs and teeming with worms. The Haj
journey, day and night, to arrive at their watering before the
cattle faint, which carry their goods and their lives. In such
continuous marching, 150 long miles, many of the wayworn
people die. I have seen hard caravan men, that I had thought
heartless, shudder in telling some of their old remembrances. It
is most terrible when in their lunar cycle of thirty years, the
pilgrimage is to be taken in the high summer ; the Arabian
heaven is burning brass above their heads, and the sand as
glowing coals under their weary feet. This year good tidings
were come to Damascus, showers were fallen, a seyl had filled
the cistern. *Khubbat et-Timathîl* is some rock nigh this station,
as the Beduins tell, scored over with inscriptions. The southern
Wélad Aly are from this stage Haj carriers ; their nomad
liberties are beside and below their kinsmen the Fukara, to
Sawra, the fourth station above Medina. Some four hundred
are their tents : they are unwarlike, treacherous, inconstant,
but of honourable hospitality. They having lately withheld
the tribute from Ibn Rashîd, the great prince of *Shammar*, and
betrayed *Kheybar* to the Turkish governors of Medina, Ibn
Rashîd came upon them this summer, in a foray, at Medáin
Sâlih, and took a booty of their camels and brought away the
tents and all their household stuff.

We removed about three hours after midnight ; a few miles
further we passed through belts of desert thorns, which tree is
the gum-arabic acacia. The caravan marched in an open sandy
plain, bordered along by hills at either hand : in the morning
I found the height 4000 feet. This land lies abandoned to the
weather, in an eternity, and nearly rainless ; in all the desolate
soil I have not perceived any freshet channel since our coming
down from the Akaba, the nomads may discern them, but not
our eyes : yet in some great land-breadths of desert Arabia there
are found none. In the next circuit of *el-Héjr*, that is Medáin
Sâlih, save a shower or two, there had not fallen rain these three
years. The wady ground before us is strewed with vulcanic
drift for many miles ; the Harra border, though hidden, lies not
very far from the road. Further the sand is strewn with
minute quartz grains, compared by the pilgrims to rice. East

by the way, stacks are seen of fantastic black sandstone pinnacles, that resemble the towers of a ruinous city.

Before the sunset we came to our white tents pitched beside the ruinous kella, without door and commonly abandoned, Dàr el-Hamra " the red house." Ruddy is that earth and the rocks whereof this water-castle is built. High and terrible it showed in the twilight in this desolation of the world. We are here at nearly 4200 feet. After marching above one hundred miles in forty-three hours we were come to the water,—water-dregs teeming with worms. The hot summer nights are here fresh after the sunset, they are cold in spring and autumn, and that is a danger for the health of the journeying pilgrimage, especially in their returning jaded from tropical Mecca. Eswad told me a dolorous tale of a cholera year, now the third or fourth past, in the ascending Ḥaj : he thought there died in the marches and in the night stations, an hundred (that is very many) every day. 'The deceased and dying were trussed with cords upon the lurching camels' backs until we reached, said he, this place ; and all was fear, no man not musing he might be one of the next to die, and never come home to his house ; the day had been showery, the rain fell all that night incessantly. The signal gun was fired very early before dawn and the Haj removed in haste, abandoning on the wet ground of the dark desert, he thought, one hundred and fifty bodies of dead and dying. At length those which survived of the pilgrimage, being come upon the wholesome Peraean highlands, were detained to purge their quarantine at ez-Zerka eight days.' He thought it was hardly the half of them which lived to enter again, by the Boábat Ullah, to the pleasant streets of Damascus. Many are their strange Haj tales of the cholera years, and this among them. ' There was a poor man who dying by the way, his friends, digging piously with their hands, laid him in a shallow grave ; and hastily they heaped the sand over their dead and departed with the marching caravan. Bye and bye in this dry warmth, the deceased revived ; he rose from his shallow burial, and come to himself he saw an empty world and the Haj gone from him. The sick staggered forth upon their footprints in the wilderness, and relieved from kella to kella, and from nomads to nomads, he came footing over those hundreds of waste miles to Damascus and arrived at his own house ; where he was but scurvily received by his nighest kin, who all out of charity disputed that it was not himself, since some of them but lately laid him in the grave, stark dead, in Arabia. They had mourned for him as dead ; now he was returned out of all season, and they had already divided his substance.'

We slept as we could, weary and cold, and removed an hour before the new daybreak; the country is an high ascending ground of cragged sandstones, bestrewn with rice-like quartz corns. The caravaners name the passage *Shuk el-Ajûz;* an ancient dame, as they say, once fallen in the rugged way, had given money to plane it. At the highest I found 4500 feet: now from hence is seen trending down mainly from the north, the solemn black front of the immense platform Harra mountain. We descended upon an easy shelving plain of sand, called by the nomads *Menzil el-Haj.* Twenty miles from Dàr el-Hamra is a part of the way, among sandstone crags and deep sand called *ez-Zelakát*, where we made halt almost an hour, and the day was sultry. I heard that here were seen inscriptions. The mountain at the left hand is called by the caravaners *Abu Tâka* and they say this rhyme *Jebel Abu Tâa fî ha arbaa asherîn zelâkat;* also upon some of these rocks is read a scoffing Syrian epigraph, deriding the folly of any pilgrim who will bring his querulous hareem upon this voyage, *Ibn el-karra, ellathi behâjiz el-marra.* The weary akkâms on foot about me, in the last miles' marching enquired every hour "Khalîl Effendi, seest thou yet the tents from the back of thy camel?" till I answered in their language *ana sheyif,* "I see them." We came down to our white camp in a sandy bottom environed with hills, and named in the caravan the Rice Beds, *Mufârish er-Ruz,* because the soil is all bestrewed with those white quartz grains. I was nearly now at the end of my journey with the Haj; the next station is that fabulous Medáin Sâlih, which I was come from far countries to seek in Arabia. The march is short, we should arrive on the morrow early; and there they come to water.

We removed again an hour after middle night: mild was the night air about us of the warm Arabia. At length in the dim morning twilight, as we journeyed, we were come to a sandy brow and a straight descending-place betwixt cliffs of sandstones. There was some shouting in the forward and Eswad bid me look up, "this was a famous place, *Mûbrak en-Nâk(g)a.*" The English of this name is 'where the cow-camel (nâga) fell upon her knees and couched down' (to die); this is the miraculous nâka born of a mountain at the intercession of the Arabian prophet Sâlih, of whom are named the *Medáin* or "Cities" now before us. By the little light I saw heaped stones upon the fallen-down blocks, a sign that it is a cursed place. The divine nâka was pierced to death in this passage, by the bowshot of some sons of Belial, therefore the hajjàj fire off here their pistols, and make hurly-burly, lest their cattle should be frighted by phantom-groans among the rocks of Néby Sâlih's camel. For the country Beduins,

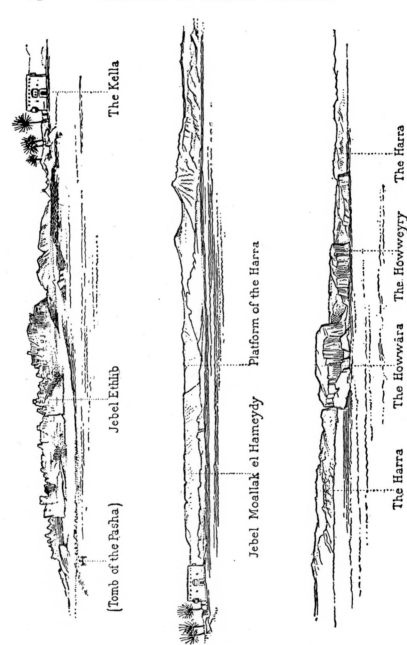

PANORAMA OF MEDÁIN SÁLIH (EL-HÉJR), v. CHAP. III. p. 83.

unwitting of these devout fables, the name of the strait is
el-Mezham " place of thronging." It is short, at first steep, and
issues upon the plain of el-Héjr which is Medáin Sâlih ; where
the sun coming up showed the singular landscape of this valley-
plain, encompassed with mighty sand-rock precipices (which
here resemble ranges of city walls, fantastic towers and castle
buildings,) and upon them lie high shouldering sand drifts.
The bottom is sand, with much growth of desert bushes ; and
I perceived some thin sprinkled vulcanic drift. Westward is
seen the immense mountain blackness, terrible and lowering,
of the Harra.

I asked " And where are the *Cities of Sâlih ?* " It was answered
" In none of these precipices about, but in yonder jebel," (Ethlib,)
whose sharp crags and spires shot up now above the greenness
of a few desert acacia trees, great here as forest timber. " And,
Khalîl, thou shalt see wonders to-day of houses hewn in the rock,"
some added, " and the hewn houses standing, wellah, heels uppermost, by miracle ! " Other plainer men said " This we saw not,
but Khalîl now thy way is ended, look, we have brought thee to
Medáin, where we say put not thyself in the danger of the
Beduw, but go thou in to lodge at the kella which thou seest
yonder with the palms ; it is a pleasant one."

The pilgrimage began on Sunday, this fair morning was
the fourth Sunday in the way, therefore the world for me was
peace, yet I mused what should become of my life, few miles
further at Medáin Sâlih. Whilst we were speaking I heard
this disastrous voice before me : " Now only another Nasrâny
is in the caravan, curse Ullah his father, he will be dealt
with presently." I demanded immediately of Eswad " what was
it ? " he did not answer again. I could but guess, that some
Christian akkâm had been discovered amongst them, and to
such the hajjàj were but a confederacy of murderers :—their
religion is murderous, and were therefore to be trodden out
as fire by the humanity of all the world ! I looked continually,
and would have attempted somewhat, I was also an European
and the caravan is full of reasonable men ; but I perceived
naught, nor might hear anything further of him. I remembered
the chance of a Syrian Christian *mukâry*, or muleteer carrier,
whose friends were known to me at Damascus ; and who had
many times been a driver in the Haj to the Harameyn. The
lad's partner on the Syrian roads, was a jolly Moslem that went
every year akkâm in the pilgrimage ; and would have his fellow
along with him, although it were to Mecca. The Christian was
willing, and the other taught him praying and prostrations
enough for young men of their simple condition. Thus the

6—2

circumcised and the uncircumcised went down year by year, and
returned to make a secret mock together : yet were any such in-
loper uncased in the Haj, he being but a poor subject of theirs,
and none to plead for him, he had sinned against his own soul ;
except he would abjure his faith, he must die like a dog, he
is " an unclean Nasrâny," for the despite done unto Ullah and
His Apostle.

CHAPTER IV.

MEDÁIN [THE "CITIES" OF] SÁLIH.

In a warm and hazy air, we came marching over the loamy sand plain, in two hours, to Medáin Sâlih, a second merkez on the road, and at the midst of their long journey; where the caravan arriving was saluted with many rounds from the field-pieces and we alighted at our encampment of white tents, pitched a little before the kella.

The Ajamy would have me write him immediately a full release and acquittance. I thought it were better to lodge, if I might, at the kella; the *kellájy*, surveyor of this and next towers, had once made me a promise in Damascus, that if I should ever arrive here he would receive me. The Beduins I heard to be come in from three days distance and that to-morrow they would return to their wandering menzils. I asked the Persian to transport my baggage, but because his covenant was out

he denied me, although my debtor for medicines which he
had upon the road freely, as much as he would. These gracious
Orientals are always graceless short-comers at the last, and therefore may they never thrive! Meanwhile the way-worn people
had bought themselves meat in the camp market of the Beduin
fleshers, and fresh joints of mutton were hanging soon before
all the Haj tents. The weary Damascenes, inhabitants of a
river city, fell to diligently washing their sullied garments.
Those who played the cooks in the fellowships, had gathered
sticks and made their little fire pits ; and all was full of business.

Here pilgrims stand much upon their guard, for this is, they
think, the most thievish station upon the road to Medina, which
" thieves " are the poor Beduins. A tale is told every year
after their cooks' wit, how ' the last time, by Ullah, one did
but look round to take more sticks and when he turned again
the cauldron was lost. This cook stepped upon his feet and
through the press he ran, and laid hand upon a bare-foot Beduwy
the first he met ; and he was he, the cursed one, who stole back
with the burning pot covered under his beggarly garment.'
Friendly persons bade me also have a care, I might lose a thing
in a moment and that should be without remedy. There came
in some of the poor nomads among us ; the citizen hajjies
cried upon them " Avaunt ! " some with staves thrust them,
some flung them headlong forth by the shoulders as wild
creatures ; certain Persians, for fear of their stealing, had armed
themselves with stones.—Yet afterward I knew all these poor
people as friendly neighbours, and without any offence. There
were come in some of their women, offering to sell us bunches
of mewed ostrich feathers, which they had taken up in the
desert. The ribald akkâms proffered them again half-handfuls
of broken biscuit ; yet are these fretted short plumes worth
above their weight in silver, at Damascus. Eswad, who was
a merry fellow, offended at this bargaining with a dishonest
gesture ; " Fie on thee, ah lad for shame ! " exclaimed the poor
young woman :—the nomads much despise the brutish behaviour
of the towns-people. I went through the encampment and came
under the kella, where sweetmeat-sellers, with stone counterpoises,
were selling pennyworths of dates upon their spread mantles ;
which wares are commonly carried in the desert journeys upon
asses. I spoke to one to lend me his beast for money that
I might fetch in my baggage. " My son, (answered the old
man, who took me for one of the Moorish garrison,) I have
therewith to do, I cannot lend him." I returned to the Ajamy ;
he would now lend me a mule, and when I had written him
his quittance, the cloudy villain changed to fair weather ; I saw

him now a fountain of smiles and pleasant words, as if he fed only with the bees among honey flowers, and bidding el-Eswad drive the load he brought me forward with the dunghill oriental grace and false courtesy. As I was going " Khalîl Aga (said the best of the akkâms) forgive us ! " they would have me not remember their sometimes rude and wild behaviour in the way. We found that kellâjy standing before the gate of his kella, (thereover I saw a well engraved Arabic inscription); busy he was receiving the garrison victual and caravan stores. He welcomed me shortly and bade me enter, until he should be out of hand. Loiterers of the garrison would hardly let me pass, saying that no strangers might come in there.

But what marvellous indifference of the weary hajjies ! I saw none of them set forth to view the monuments, though as much renowned in their religion as Sodom and Gomorrah, and whereof such strange fables are told in the koran. Pity Mohammed had not seen Petra ! he might have drawn another long-bow shot in Wady Mûsa : yet hardly from their camp is any of these wonders of the faith plainly visible. The palmers, who are besides greatly adread of the Aarab, durst not adventure forth, unless there go a score of them together. Departing always by night-time, the pilgrims see not the Cities of Sâlih, but the ascending Haj see them. Eswad came to the kella at nightfall, and bade me God-speed and to be very prudent ; for the tower garrisons are reputed men of violence, as the rest of the Haj service. So came the kellâjy, who surprised to find me still sitting obscurely within, by my baggage, assigned me a cell-chamber. One came then and called him forth to the Pasha ; I knew afterward that he was summoned upon my account. About mid-night the warning gunshot sounded in the camp, a second was the signal to remove ; I heard the last hubbub of the Haj rising, and in few more moments the solemn jingles of the takhts er-Rûm journeying again in the darkness, with the departing caravan. Few miles lower they pass a *boghrâz,* or strait in the mountains. Their first station is *Zmurrûd,* a forsaken kella ; in another remove they come to *Sawra* kella, then *Hedîeh* kella, *Sûjwa* kella, *Barraga, Oweynat el-Béden ;* there the Haj camp is pitched a little before Medina. In every step of the Mecca-bound pilgrims is now heart's rest and religious confidence that they shall see the holy places ; they have passed here the midst of the long way. In the morning twilight, I heard a new rumour without, of some wretched nomads, that with the greediness of unclean birds searched the forsaken ground of the encampment.

As it was light the Beduins came clamorously flocking into the tower, and for a day we were over-run by them. Said

Mohammed Aly the kellâjy " Wellah, we cannot be sure from hour to hour ; but their humour changing, they might attempt the kella ! " It was thus the same Fejîr Beduins had seized this kella few years before, when the Haj government established a new economy upon the pilgrimage road, and would have lessen- ed the nomads' former surra. The caravan gone by, the Aarab that were in the kella, with their sheykh *Motlog,* suddenly ran upon the weak guard, to whom they did no hurt but sent them in peace to *el-Ally.* Then they broke into the sealed chambers and pillaged all that might come to their hand, the Haj and Jurdy soldiers' srores with all that lately brought down for the victualling of this and the other kellas that stand under Medáin Sâlih. The tribes that year would hardly suffer the caravan to pass peaceably, and other kellas were in like manner surprised and mastered by them ; that next below Medáin, and Sújwa kella were robbed at the same time by the W. Aly. The Beduw said, they only sought their own ; the custom of surra or payment for right of way, could not now be broken. A squadron of Syrian cavalry sent down with the next year's Haj, to protect those towers, was quartered at el-Ally, but when the caravan was gone by, the Beduins (mostly W. Aly) went to surround the oasis, and held them besieged till the second year. I have said to the Beduins, " If the tower-keepers shut their plated door, what were all your threatenings against them ? " Arabians have not wit to burst iron-plate with the brunt of a beam, or by heaping fire-wood to burn the back timber of the door, nor any public courage to adventure their miserable lives under defended walls. They have answered me, " The kella could not be continually shut against us, the Beduins have many sly shifts ; and if not by other means yet by a *thubîha,* (gift of a sheep or other beast for slaughter,) we should not fail sometime to creep in."

In this kella an old Moor of Fez, *Haj Nejm,* was warden (*mohàfuz*) ; the other tower-keepers were *Haj Hasan,* a Moor of Morocco, who was before of this tower service, and coming in our pilgrimage from Damascus, had been stayed here again, at the entreaty of his countryman Nejm. Then *Abd el-Káder,* (Servitor-of-the-mighty-God) a young man named after the noble Algerian prince, and son of his deceased steward : he growing into fellowship with the muatterîn at Damascus, his " uncle " (whose venerable authority is absolute over all the Moorish emigration) had relegated the lubber into the main deserts for a year, in charge of Mohammed Aly. A fourth was *Mohammed,* a half Beduin lad, son of a former Damascene kella keeper, by a nomad housewife ; and besides, there was only a slave and another poor man that had been sent to keep the water together at the B. Moaddam.

Our few Moors went armed in the tower amonsgt the treacherous Beduins ; Haj Nejm sat, with his blunderbuss crossed upon his knees, amongst his nomad guests, in the coffee chamber. He was feeble and old, and Hasan the only manful sufficient hand amongst them. This stalwart man was singing all the day at his task and smiling to himself with un-abated good humour. Self-minded he was and witty of head to find a shift with any wile, which made all easy to him, yet without his small horizon he was of a barbarous understanding ; so that Mohammed Aly would cry out upon his strongheaded-ness, " Wellah thou art a *Berber*, Hasan ! " (The Berbers, often blue-eyed and yellow-haired, a remnant of the former peoples of Barbary.) Twelve years he had been in the East, and might seem to be a man of middle age, but in his own eyes his years were fifty and more, " And wot you why (he would say and laugh again), my heart is ever green." The Moors are born under wandering stars. Many wearing the white *burnûs*, come in every pilgrimage to Mecca ; thence they disperse themselves to Syria, to Mesopotamia, and to all the East Arabic world seeking fortune and service. They labour at their old trades in a new land, and those that have none, (they have all a humour of arms,) will commonly hire themselves as soldiers. They are hired before other men, for their circumspect acrid nature, to be caretakers of orchards at Damascus, and many private trusts are committed to the bold Moghrebies. These Western men are distinguished by their harsh ventriloqual speech, and foreign voices.

Nejm, now a great while upon this side of the sea, was grown infirm more than aged ; he could not hope to see his Fez again, that happier soil of which, with a sort of smiling simplicity, he gossiped continually. He had wandered through the Barbary states, he knew even the Algerian *sáhara ;* at Tunis he had taken service, then sometime in Egypt far upon the Nile ; afterward he was a soldier in Syria, and later of the haj-road service, in the camp at Maan : a fervent Moslem, yet one that had seen and suffered in the world, he could be tolerant, and I was kindly received by him. ' The *Engleys* (said he) at *Jebel Tar* (Gibraltar) were his people's neigh-bours over the strait.' He had liever Engleys than Stambûlies, Turks that were corrupted and no good Moslems. Only the last year the Sîr Amîn had left a keg of wine with them in the kella, till their coming up again : " a cursed man (he said) to drink of that which is forbidden to the Moslemîn ! " He was

father of two children, but, daughters, he seemed not to regard
them ; female children are a burden of small joy in a poor
Moslem family ; for whom the father shall at last receive but a
slender bride-money, when they are divided from his household.

Nature prepared for the lad Mohammed an unhappy age ;
vain and timid, the stripling was ambitious to be somewhat,
without virtuous endeavour. A loiterer at his labour and a slug
in the morning, I heard when Mohammed Aly reprehended him
in this manner : " It is good to rise up, my son (as the day is
dawning), to the hour of morning prayer. It is then the night
angels depart, and the angles of the day arrive, but those that
linger and sleep on still, Satan enters into them. Knowest thou
I had once in my house a serving lad, a Nasrâny, and although
he washed his head with soap and had combed out his hair, yet
then his visage always appeared swollen and discoloured, wellah
as a swine ; and if you mark them of a morning, you may see the
Nasarâ to be all of them as swine."

" Ignorant " (*jâhil*) more than ill-given was the young Abd
el-Kâder, and hugely overgrown, so that Hasan said one day,
observing him, " Abd el-Kâder's costard is as big as the head of
our white mule and nothing in it." They thus pulled his coxcomb in the kella, till it had done the poor lad's heart good
to have blubbered ; bye and bye he was dismissed to keep the
water with another at B. Moaddam.

Mohammed Aly, (by his surname) *el-Mahjûb*, surveyor of the
kellas between Tebûk and el-Medina, was an amiable bloody
ruffian, a little broken-headed, his part good partly violent
nature had been distempered (as many of their unquiet climbing spirits) in the Turkish school of government ; he was without
letters. His family had inhabited a mountain country (he said,
" of uncorrupted ancient manners ") in Algeria : in the conquest,
rather than become subjects of the Nasâra, they embarked at
their own election in French government vessels, to be landed
in Syria. There was a tradition amongst their ancestors, that
" very anciently they occupied all that country about Maan, where
also Moses fed the flocks of Jethro the prophet ; the B. Israel
had dispossessed them." Entering the military service, he
had fought and suffered with the Syrian troops, in a terrible
jehâd against the Muscovites, in the Caucasus, where he was
twice wounded. The shot, it seemed to me, by his own showing,
had entered from the backward, and still the old wounds vexed
him in ill weather. Afterward, at the head of a small horse
troop, he served in Palestine and the lands beyond Jordan,
attaching himself to the fortunes of Mohammed Saîd, from

whom he had obtained his present office. The man, half ferocious trooper, could speak fair and reasonably in his better mind ; then as there are backwaters in every tide, he seemed humane: the best and the worst Moslemîn can discourse very religiously. He held the valour of the Moghrebies to be incomparable, it were perilous then to contrary him ; a tiger he was in his dunghill ill-humour, and had made himself formerly known on this road by his cruelties. Somewhile being lieutenant at Maan, he had hanged (as he vaunted) three men. Then, when it had been committed to him to build a vault over the spring head at the kella Medowwara, and make that water sure from all hostility of the Aarab, he took certain of them prisoners, sheykhs accused of plundering the Haj, and binding them, he fed them every day in the tower with two biscuits, and every day he caused to be ground a measure of meal in an hand-mill (which is of intolerable weight) upon their breasts ; until yielding to these extremities, which they bore sometime with manly fortitude, they had sent for that ransom which he would devour of them. A diseased senile body he was, full of ulcers, and past the middle age, so that he looked not to live long, his visage much like a fiend, dim with the leprosy of the soul and half fond ; he shouted when he spoke with a startling voice, as it might have been of the ghrôl : of his dark heart ruled by so weak a head, we had hourly alarms in the lonely kella. Well could he speak (with a certain erudite utterance) to his purpose, in many or in few words. These Orientals study little else, as they sit all day idle at the coffee in their male societies : they learn in this school of infinite human observation to speak to the heart of one another. His tales seasoned with saws, which are the wisdom of the unlearned, we heard for more than two months, they were never ending. He told them so lively to the eye that they could not be bettered, and part were of his own motley experience. Of a licentious military tongue, and now in the shipwreck of a good understanding, with the bestial insane instincts and the like compunctions of a spent humanity, it seemed the jade might have been (if great had been his chance) another Tiberius senex. With all this, he was very devout as only they can be, and in his religion scrupulous ; it lay much upon his conscience to name the Nasrâny *Khalîl*, and he made shift to call me, for one Khalîl, five times Ibrahîm. He returned always with a wonderful solemnity to his prayers, wherein he found a sweet foretaste of Paradise ; this was all the solace here in the deserts of his corrupt mind. A caterpillar himself, he could censure the criminal Ottoman administration, and pinch at all their misdemeanours. At Damascus, he had his

name inscribed in the register of French Algerian subjects ; he
left this hole to creep into, if aught went hard with him, upon
the side of the Dowla ; and in trouble any that can claim their
protection in Turkish countries, are very nimble to run to the
foreign consuls.

The nomads have an ill opinion of Turkish Haj government,
seeing the tyrannical and brutish behaviour of these pretended
rulers, their paymasters. All townsmen contemn them again as
the most abject of banded robbers. If any nomad be taken in a
fault, the military command "Away with this Beduwy" is shouted
with the voice of the destroying angel "and bind him to the gun-
wheel." Mohammed Aly was mad, in his Moorish pride, and of
desperate resentment ; only the last year he durst contend here
in the deserts, with his Haj Pasha. In a ground chamber of the
kella are sealed government stores and deposits of the mukowwems' furnitures : with the rest was sent in by the paymaster-
Pasha a bag of reals, of the public money. When they came again,
the Pasha sent his servant to receive the silver. The man, as
he held it in his hand, imagining this purse to have leaked, for the
Arabs are always full of these canine suspicions, began to accuse
Mohammed Aly ; but the Moor, pulling out his scimitar, cut
down the rash unarmed slave, flung him forth by the heels, and
with frantic maledictions, shut up the iron door after him. The
Pasha sent again, bidding Mohammed Aly come to him and
answer for this outrage ; but the Syrian Moor, his heart yet
boiling, swore desperately he would not go until his humour
were satisfied.—"Away and say these words to the Pasha from
Mohammed Aly, If Mohammed Saîd have cannon, so have I
artillery upon the terrace of this kella,—by God Almighty
we will hold out to the last ; and let him remember that we are
Moghrâreba! " This was a furious playing out friends and
playing in mischief, but he trusted that his old service would
assure him with the robust Pasha ; at the worst he would
excuse himself, attesting his wounds suffered in the sacred cause
of their religion ; and after all he could complain " Wellah, his
head went not all times well, and that he was a Moghreby,"
that is one of choleric nature and a generous rashness : at
the very worst he could defy them, proving that he was a
stranger born and a French subject. His artillery (and such
is wont to be the worth of an Arabic boast) were two very
small rust-eaten pieces, which for their rudeness, might have
been hammered by some nomad smith : years ago they had been
brought from the *Borj,* an antique tower half a mile distant,
towards the monuments, and were said to have served in old
nomad warfare between Annezy and *Harb* tribesmen.

Before the departure of the Aarab, came their sheykh Motlog enquiring for me ; *Wen-hu, wen-hu,* ' where is he, this *dowlány* or government man ? ' He bounced my door up, and I saw a swarthy Beduin that stood to gaze lowering and strangely on one whom he took to be *gomány*, an enemy. Mohammed Aly had said to them that I was a Sîr Amîn, some secretary sent down upon a government errand. This was a short illusion, for as the Moslems pray openly and Khalîl was not seen to pray, it was soon said that I could not be of the religion. Mohammed Aly was a hater of every other than his own belief and very jealous of the growing despotism in the world of the perilous Nasâra ;—thus they muse with a ferocious gloom over the decay of the militant Islam. Yet he could regard me pleasantly, as a philosopher, in whom was an indulgent natural opinion in all matter of religion.—These were the inhabitants of the kella, a tower seventy feet upon a side, square built. Lurid within are these water-stations, and all that I entered are of one fashion of building. In the midst is the well-court, and about it the stable, the forage and store chambers. Stairs lead upon the gallery which runs round above, whereupon in the north and south sides are the rows of small stone dwelling chambers. Staircases lead from this gallery to the terrace roof, where the garrison may suddenly run up in any need to the defence of the kella.

This tower is built about an ancient well, the *Bîr en-Nâga* where the miraculous she-camel had been watered ; it is the only water that a religious man may drink, in the opinion of their doctors, in " the subverted country : " but by leaking of the cesspool, I fear this well is an occasion of grave vesical diseases. The *bîr*, as the other ancient wells that remain in the plain, is lined with dry-built masonry, twenty-six feet deep to the ground water, which comes up warm and reeking in a winter morning, at a temperature of 66 Fahr. ;—I never found well water not lukewarm in Arabia ! The *Ullema* teach that men's prayers may hardly rise to Heaven from the soil of Medáin Sâlih, and the most perfect of them carry their water over from the last stages, that even of the naga's well they refuse to drink. The kella birket without to the southward, measures eighteen by twenty-two paces ; the depth is three fathoms. Two mules from Damascus wrought singly, turning the rude mill-machine of the well, four and four hours daily ; but that was so badly devised, that nearly a third part of the drawn water as it came up in the buckets, which are hoops of chipwood like corn measures, was spilled back again ; and good part of that which flows out is lost, for all the birket floor leaked or the whole might be filled in ten or twelve days. For the renewing of the well gear of this and the next kellas stores are brought down here in every Haj from Damascus.

It is remarkable that all the haj-road kellas are said to have been built by Nasâra, nearly to Medina ; Christian masons a few years before repaired this tower of Medáin Sâlih ; I was not then the first Christian man seen within these distant kella walls : they were remembered to have been quiet and hospitable persons. The kella foundations are of stones without mortar laid upon the weak loamy bottom ; the walls above are rude courses of stones raised in clay ; the work is only pointed with mortar. Stone for burning lime must be fetched upon the backs of hired Beduin camels from *Jebel Îss*, which is a sandstone mountain overlaid with limestone in a wady of the same name, two journeys distant under the *Harreyry* or little Harra, below el-Ally. This is not that greater *W. el Îss* of antiquity, wherein are seen many springs with *dôm* palms and the ruins of villages, which descends from the *Jeheyna* country, beginning a long journey above *Yánba*, and goes out in the *W. el-Humth* or *W. Jizzl*.

In Damascus I had heard of the pleasant site of this kella with its garden of palms. Here were three grown female trees, with one male stem which made them fruitful. In the orchard plot closed with a clay wall, Haj Nejm passed his holiday hours in this immense Beduin wilderness, and raised his salads, his leeks and other pot-herbs to give a savour to his Arab messes. The tower stands solitary half a mile before the mountain Ethlib, almost in the midst of the valley-plain of Medáin. This is Hijr of the koran, el-Héjr of the Beduins. The place is Ἔγρα of Ptolemy's geography ; in his time an emporium of the caravan road between el-Yémen and Syria which is since become the derb el-haj. From the kella roof two may be descried of the greatest monuments, and the plain is seen as enclosed by cliffs. Only past Ethlib the plain appears open upon the left hand, with shelves of sand riding upon the short horizon to the south-eastward : it is there the haj road passes. Between us and the solitude of the desert, are the gate Arabs, certain nomad families whose tents were always pitched before the iron door of the kella. They are poor Fej(k)îr households, (which wanting camels cannot follow the wandering camps of their tribesmen,) and a half dozen ragged tents of *Fehját*, a small very poor kindred of *Heteym*, and despised almost as outcasts ; they are clients of the Fukara and from ancient times, at the service of the kella, and foragers like the Sweyfly at el-Akhdar, selling their camel loads of harsh knot-grass, to the pilgrimage caravan, for a

certain government price, which is set at a real. Of the
Fehját, Sweyfly, and the poor Humeydát of Tebûk, is chanted
a ribald rime in the Haj "We have companied with the daughters
of them for a crown." 'Another poor sort of haj foragers in
these parts are the *Bedówna,* they are also Heteym; their
home district is *Jebel Dokhàn* below el-Ally : they are fifty
families, sellers here, and at Sawra, of the same tall grass kind,
which grows in low sandy places under the desert mountains ;
the thurrm is not browsed by the small Beduin camels. The
Arabs blame this country as *Béled ej-jûa,* ' a land of hunger '
households seldom here cook anything, a handful of clotted
dates is the most of their commons : also they name it *Béled
el-haramîeh,* ' a land of robbers.' This plain is a path of many
ghrazzûs (ridings on warfare) of hostile tribesmen, so that few
days ever pass without alarms.

The *Medáin Sálih* are, in the koran fable, houses hewn in
the rocks of the idolatrous tribe Thamûd of the ancient
Arabians, which were destroyed already, according to their fantastic chronicles, in the days of Jethro, God's messenger to the
Midianites. Jethro, in the koran, preaches to his incredulous
tribesmen of the judgments that had overtaken other peoples
sometime despisers of holy prophets. *Hejra* in Ptolemy and
Pliny, is an oasis staple town of *the gold and frankincense
caravan road* from Arabia the Happy. In the next generations it must needs decay, as this trade road to the North was
disused more and more and at last nearly abandoned for the sea
carriage. In Mohammed's time, only five hundred years later,
the desolate city had so long passed away that the name was
become a marvellous fable. Mohammed going by, in the Mecca
caravans, was doubtless moved seeing from the road the archaic
hewn architecture of those " desolate places " : (no one can consider without emotion the severe and proud lineaments of these
solemn ranges of caverns !) also he beheld in them a divine
testimony of the popular tradition. The high sententious fantasy of the ignorant Arabs, the same that will not trust the
heart of man, is full of infantile credulity in all religious matter ;
and already the young religionist was rolling the sentiment
of a divine mission in his unquiet spirit. In his prophetic
life the destruction of Thamûd, joined with the like pretended cases of *Aad,* of Midiân and of the cities of Lot, that
had " rejected the apostles of Ullah," is become a capital argument in the koran ; words of present persuasion of fear not
easily to be answered, since their falsity could only be ascertained by the event. *El-Hijr* is entitled a chapter in the
koran, and one hundred and fourteen being all the koran

chapters, this legend is remembered in more than twenty of
them.

The dreary Semitic fable of Medáin is in this sort : Aad
defeated Thamûd (ancient peoples in el-Yémen or Arabia
Felix). Thamûd emigrating northward alighted upon the plain
el-Héjr, under mount Ethlib.　In later generations God's
warning is come to these sinners, which of a vain confidence had hewed them dwellings in the rocks, by the mouth
of Sâlih, a prince of their own nation.　The idolatrous Thamudites required of him a sign : ' Let the mountain, they said,
bring forth a she-camel ten months gone with young, and they
would believe him.'　Then the mountain wailed, as in pangs to be
delivered, and there issued from the rocky womb that she-camel
or nâga which they had desired of God's prophet.　Two months
after when she put down her calf, (for they go twelve months,) her
milk sufficed to nourish all the people of the plain.　But the
prodigious camel pasturing in the wilderness affrighted their
own cattle, moreover at her every third days' watering, she drunk
up all the well-waters of the malicious Thamudites.　They
growing weary of her, certain of them, wicked men, conspired to
bring her to mischance, and she was slain by their arrows, (as before said,) in the passage called Mûbrak en-Nâga.　It repented the
people of Thamûd when the divine camel was dead ; the prophet
bade them bring in her erring calf, and haply the fault might be
forgiven them.　But the calf lowed fearfully.　" The lowings, said
Sâlih, are three days ; remain in your dwellings, and after that
the calamity will come upon you."　At that time there went
forth wicked men to lie in wait for Néby Sâlih, but were baffled
of angels.　The days ended there fell a fearful wind, *sarsar*, the
earth shook, a voice was heard from heaven, and on the morrow
the idolatrous people were found lying upon their faces (as
the nomads use to slumber) all dead corpses, and the land was
empty of them as it had never been inhabited.　A like evil
ending is told of Aad, and of the Midianites.　The Syrian
Moslems show a mountainous crag (*el-Howwâra*) in this plain,
which opened her bosom and received the orphan calf again.

A week now we had been shut in the kella, and were still
weary of our journeys from Syria.　Mohammed Aly would not
let me go forth alone : but he had spoken with *Zeyd*, a principal
Beduin sheykh, who after other days would return and accompany
me to the monuments.　Haj Nejm said of Medáin, "It is a marvel,
that you may view their sûks, and even the nail-holes whereupon
were hanged their stuffs over the shop doors, and in many of
their shops the shelves, spences and little cellars where they laid

up their wares ; and, wellah, you may see all full of the
bones of *Kôm Thamûd ;* they were *kuffàr*, they would not
believe in God until they fell down dead men, when the blast
was come upon them." The worthy old Moor spoke between a
confused simplicity and half an honest thought that there failed
something in his argument : " and (said he to the aga) knowest
thou a new thing was found of late ; certain of the women
searching for gunsalt (saltpetre) in the ' houses,' have lighted
upon some drug-like matter, which cast on the coals yields an
odour of *bakhûr* (frankincense). Wellah, they have sold it for
such at el-Ally." He went and fetched us small crumbling pieces,
they were brown and whitish ; " and see you here, said he, three
kinds, *bakhûr, aud* and *mubârak.*" He cast them in the hearth
and there rose a feeble earthy smoke, with mouldy ill-smelling
sweetness of incense. Frankincense is no more of Arabia
Felix, and yet the perfume is sovereign in the estimation of all
Arabians. The most is brought now in the pilgrimage from the
Malay Islands to Mecca ; and from thence is dispersed throughout the Arabian Peninsula, almost to every household. The odour
comforts the religious soul and embalms the brain : that we think
the incense-odour religious, is by great likelihood the gentile
tradition remaining to us of this old gold and frankincense road.
The Arabians cast a morsel in a chafing dish, which is sent
round from hand to hand in their coffee drinkings, especially in
the oases villages in any festival days : each person, as it comes
to him in the turn, hides this under his mantle a moment, to
make his clothing well smelling ; then he snuffs the sweet reek
once or twice, and hands down the perfume dish to his neighbour.

The Beduins had departed. We sat one of these evenings
gathered in the small coffee chamber (which is upon the gallery
above), about the winter fire of dry acacia timber, when between
the clatter of the coffee pestle we thought we heard one hailing
under the loop-hole ! all listened ;—an hollow voice called wearily
to us. Mohammed Aly shouted down to him in Turkish, which
he had learned in his soldier's life : he was answered in the
same language. " Ah," said the aga withdrawing his head, " it is
some poor hajjy ; up Hasan, and thou run down Mohammed,
open the door : " and they hastened with a religious willingness to
let the hapless pilgrim in. They led up to us a poor man of a
good presence, somewhat entered in years ; he was almost naked
and trembled in the night's cold. It was a Turkish derwish
who had walked hither upon his feet from his place in Asia
Minor, it might be a distance of six hundred miles ; but though
robust, his human sufferance was too little for the long way.
He had sickened a little after Maan, and the Haj breaking up

from Medowwara, left this weary wight still slumbering in the
wilderness ; and he had since trudged through the deserts those
two hundred miles, on the traces of the caravan, relieved only at
the kellas ! The lone and broken wayfarer could no more overtake the hajjàj, which removed continually before him by forced
marches. Mohammed Aly brought him an Aleppo felt cloth, in
which the poor derwish who had been stripped by Aarab only
three hours before Medáin, might wrap himself from the cold.

Kindly they all now received him and, while his supper was
being made ready, they bade him be comforted, saying, The next
year, and it pleased Ullah, he might fulfil the sacred pilgrimage ; now he might remain with them, and they would find him,
in these two and half months, until the Haj coming again. But
he would not ! He had left his home to be very unfortunate
in strange countries ; he should not see the two blissful cities,
he was never to return. The palmer sat at our coffee fire
with a devout thankfulness and an honest humility. Restored to the fraternity of mankind, he showed himself to be
a poor man of very innocent and gentle manners. When we
were glad again, one of the gate-nomads, taking up the music of
the desert, opened his lips to make us mirth, sternly braying
his Beduin song to the grave chord of the rabeyby. This was
Wady of the Fejîr Beduins, a comely figure in the firelight company, of a black visage. He had lived a year at Damascus of
late, and was become a town-made cozening villain, under the
natural semblance of worth. Of sheykhly blood and noble easy
countenance, he seemed to be a child of fortune, but the wretch
had not camels ; his tent stood therefore continually pitched
before the kella : more than the flies, he haunted the tower
coffee chamber, where, rolling his great white eyeballs, he fawned
hour by hour with all his white teeth upon Mohammed Aly,
assenting with *Ullah Akhbar !* " God most high," to all the
sapient saws of this great one of the kella.

Lapped in his cloth, the poor derwish sat a day over, in this
sweetness of reposing from his past fatigues. The third morrow
come, the last of the customary hospitality, they were already
weary of him ; Mohammed Aly, putting a bundle of meal in
his hand and a little water-skin upon his shoulders, brought
him forth, and showing the direction bade him follow as he
could the footprints of the caravan, and God-speed. Infinite
are the miseries of the Haj ; religion is a promise of good
things to come, to poor folk, and many among them are half
destitute persons. This pain, the words of that fatal Arabian,
professing himself to be the messenger of Ullah, have imposed
upon ten thousands every year of afflicted mankind !

In the time of my former being at Maan there came a young Arab derwish, of those inhabiting the mixed Arabic-Persian border countries, beyond Bagdad. This " son of the way," clad only in a loose cotton tunic, arrived then alone afoot from Mecca, (more than six hundred miles distant,) almost six months after the returning Haj. He had been relieved at the kellas, and sometimes where he passed he met with Aarab and lodged awhile in their encampments. I asked him, How could he find his path and not be stripped by the Beduins ? *Answer:* "O man, I have no more than this shirt upon my shoulders and the wooden bowl in my hand." Strong and ruddy he was, it seemed he had not yet begun to be weary : from Damascus he was yet two hundred and fifty miles ; after that he must drudge other two months with some caravan to Mesopotamia, and foot it yet far beyond to his own home. Though the journey be never so great to Medina and Mecca, they will cheerfully undertake it upon their feet and with the greatest levity ! This young man, left behind sick at Mecca, lay long in an hospital, which is there of pious foundation, for the receipt of strangers.—Any who die destitute in the holy town, are buried of the alms which are found in the temple chest : upon any naked wretches is bestowed a shirt-cloth of the same public benefit.

Of the derelicts of the Haj was another already harboured in the kella, a poor soul of Emesa (in Upper Syria), that had been before of the trooping police service. On foot, without a piece of silver, he had put himself in the way to make his pilgrimage, and hired himself for diet to a camel master, to serve the camels. Hard is the service, he must waken at night after the long day marches. When he had gone five hundred miles his ankles swelled : he halted yet a march or two, then he let himself sink down by the wayside few miles from Medáin and the Haj passed by him. The Pasha himself found the wretch as he came riding in the rear : " What fellow art thou ? " said he. " It may please your worship my limbs can bear me no more ; mercy Sir, I have been in the soldiery, or I shall be dead here."—" Up ! (cried the military chief) rouse thee, march ! " and the Turk laid hardly upon him with his hide whip. " Alas ! I cannot go a step, and though your good worship should beat me till I die." The Pasha then bade a rider of the Ageyl take this man upon his thelûl and carry him to the kella : there he might remain till the Haj returned and the warden should give him his rations. Nasar was the man's name, a torpid fellow and unwelcome, since they were bound to entertain him, to the kella crew ; after the three days of hospitality they banished him from the coffee chamber and gave him quarters like a beast in the hay-house below. I

cured the poor man, who was very grateful to me ; for the little
vigour of his blood, nourished only of rice and water, he was
not well before the Haj returning.

Beduins soon came in who had seen our derwish slowly travelling upon the lower haj road : clear was the weather, the winter's
sun made hot mid-days, but the season was too chill for such a
weary man to lie abroad by night. Weeks after other Beduins
arrived from Medina, and we enquired if they had seen aught
of our derwish ? They hearing how the man was clad, answered
" Ay, billah, we saw him lying dead, and the felt was under
him ; it was by the way-side, by Sawra, (not far down,) almost
in sight of the kella." Sorry were his benefactors, that he
whom they lately dismissed alive lay now a dead carcase in
the wilderness ; themselves might so mishap another day in the
great deserts. All voices cried at once, " He perished for thirst ! "
They supposed he had poured out his water-skin, which must
hang wearily on his feeble neck in the hot noons. The sight
was not new to the nomads, of wretched passengers fallen
down dying upon the pilgrim way and abandoned ; they oftentimes (Beduins have said it in my hearing) see the hyenas stand
by glaring and gaping to devour them, as ever the breath
should be gone out of the warm body. They pass by :—in Beduins
is no pious thought of unpaid charity to bury strangers.—
Mohammed Aly told me there is no Haj in which some fail
not and are left behind to die. They suffer most between the
Harameyn, " where, O Khalîl ! the mountains stand walled up
to heaven upon either hand ! " In the stagnant air there is no
covert from the torment of the naked sun : as the breathless
simûm blows upon them they fall grovelling and are suffocated.
There is water by the way, even where the heat is greatest, but
the cursed Beduins will not suffer the wayfaring man to drink,
except they may have new and new gifts from the Turkish
pashas : there is no remedy, nor past this valley of death, is
yet an end of mortal evils. The camping ground at Mecca
lies too far from the place, the swarm of poor strangers
must seek them hired dwelling chambers in the holy city :
thus many are commonly stived together in a very narrow room.
The most arriving feeble from great journeys, with ill humours
increased in their bodies, new and horrible disorders must needs
breed among them :—from the Mecca pilgrimage has gone forth
many a general pestilence, to the furthest of mankind !

Enormous indeed has been the event of Mohammed's religious faction. The old Semitic currencies in religion were
uttered new under that bastard stamp of the (expedite, factious,
and liberal) Arabian spirit, and digested to an easy sober rule of

human life, (a pleasant carnal congruity looking not above men's possibility). Are not Mohammed's saws to-day the mother belief of a tenth part of mankind ? What had the world been ? if the tongue had not wagged, of this fatal Ishmaelite ! Even a thin-witted religion that can array an human multitude, is a main power in the history of the unjust world. Perilous every bond which can unite many of the human millions, for living and dying ! Islam and the commonwealth of Jews are as great secret conspiracies, friends only of themselves and to all without of crude iniquitous heart, unfaithful, implacable.—But the pre-Islamic idolatrous religion of the kaaba was cause that the soon ripe Mawmetry rotted not soon again.

The heart of their dispersed religion is always Mecca, from whence the Moslems of so many lands every year return fanaticised. From how far countries do they assemble to the sacred festival ; the pleasant contagion of the Arab's religion has spread nearly as far as the pestilence :—a battle gained and it had overflowed into Europe. The nations of Islam, of a barbarous fox-like understanding, and persuaded in their religion, that " knowledge is only of the koran," cannot now come upon any way that is good.

Other days passed, Mohammed Aly saying every evening, on the morrow he would accompany me to the monuments.' These were Turkish promises, I had to deal with one who in his heart already devoured the Nasrâny : in Syria he had admired that curious cupidity of certain Frankish passengers in the purchasing of " antiquities." " What wilt thou give me, said he, to see the monuments ? and remember, I only am thy protection in this wilderness. There be some in the kella, that would kill thee except I forbade them : by Almighty God, I tell thee the truth." I said ' That he set the price of his services, and I would deliver him a bill upon Damascus : '—but distant promises will hardly be accepted by any Arab, their world is so faithless and they themselves make little reckoning of the most solemn engagements.

Now came *Zeyd*, a sheykh of the Fejîr Beduins, riding upon a dromedary from the desert, with his gunbearer seated behind him, and the sheykh's young son riding upon his led mare. Zeyd had been to town in Damascus and learned all the craft of the Ottoman manners, to creep by bribes into official men's favours. Two years before when his mare foaled, and it was not a filly, (they hardly esteem the male worth camel-milk,) this nomad fox bestowed his sterile colt upon the Moorish wolf Mohammed Aly ; the kellâjy had ridden down on this now

strong young stallion from Syria. Zeyd had seen nothing
again but glozing proffers : now was this occasion of the Nasrâny,
and they both looked that I should pay the shot between them.
" Give Zeyd ten pound, and Zeyd will mount thee, Khalîl, upon
his mare, and convey thee round to all the monuments." The
furthest were not two miles from the tower, and the most are
within a mile's distance. Zeyd pretended there was I know not
what to see besides ' at *Bîr el-Ghrannem*, where we must have
taken a *rafîk* of *Billî* Aarab.'   Only certain it is that they
reckon all that the overthrown country of el-Héjr which lies
between Mûbrak en-Nâga and Bîr el-Ghrannem, which is thirty
miles nearly ; and by the old trade-road, along, there are ruins of
villages down even to el-Medina. But the nomads say with one
voice, there are not anywhere in these parts *byût* or *bébàn*,
that is, chambers in the rock, like to those of el-Héjr or Medáin
Sâlih.

Zeyd had been busy riding round to his tribesmen's tents
and had bound them all with the formula, *Jîrak* " I am thy
neighbour." If I refused Zeyd, I might hire none of them. The
lot had fallen, that we should be companions for a long time to
come. Zeyd was a swarthy nearly black sheykh of the desert,
of mid stature and middle age, with a hunger-bitten stern
visage, So dark a colour is not well seen by the Arabs, who in
these uplands are less darkish-brown than ruddy. They think
it resembles the ignoble blood of slave races ; and therefore
even crisp and ringed hair is a deformity in their eyes. We
may remember in the Canticles, the paramour excuses the
swarthiness of her beautiful looks, " I am black but comely, ye
daughters of Jerusalem, as the booths of the Beduw, as the tent-
cloths of Solomon ; " she magnifies the ruddy whiteness of her
beloved.   Dark, the privation of light, is the hue of death,
(*mawt el-aswad*) and, by similitude, of calamity and evil ; the
wicked man's heart is accounted black (*kalb el-aswad*). According to this fantasy of theirs, the Judge of all the earth in the
last judgment hour will hold an Arabian expedite manner of
audit, not staying to parley with every soul in the sea of
generations, for the leprosy of evil desert rising in their visages,
shall appear manifestly in wicked persons as an horrible blackness.   In the gospel speech, the sheep shall be sundered
from the goats,—wherein in some comparison of colour—and the
just shall shine forth as the sunlight. The Arabs say of an unspotted human life, *kalb-hu abiâth*, white is his heart : we in like
wise say *candid*. Zeyd uttered his voice in the deepest tones
that I have heard of human throat ; such a male light Beduin
figure some master painter might have portrayed for an

Ishmaelite of the desert. Hollow his cheeks, his eyes looked austerely, from the lawless land of famine, where his most nourishment was to drink coffee from the morning, and tobacco ; and where the chiefest Beduin virtue is *es-subbor*, a courageous for-bearing and abiding of hunger. " Aha wellah, (said Zeyd,) *el-Aarab fàsidîn* the nomads are dissolute and so are the Dowla " : the blight was in his own heart ; this Beduish philosopher looked far out upon all human things with a tolerant incredulity. A sheykh among his tribesmen of principal birth, he had yet no honourable estimation ; his hospitality was miserable, and that is a reproach to the nomad dwellers in the empty desert. His was a high and liberal understanding becoming a *mejlis* man who had sat in that perfect school of the parliament of the tribe, from his youth, nothing in Zeyd was barbarous and uncivil ; his carriage was that haughty grace of the wild creatures. In him I have not seen any spark of fanatical ill-humour. He could speak with me smilingly of his intolerant countrymen ; for himself he could well imagine that sufficient is Ullah to the governance of the world, without fond man's meddling. This manly man was not of the adventurous brave, or rather he would put nothing rashly in peril. *Mesquîn* was his policy at home, which resembled a sordid avarice ; he was wary as a Beduin more than very far-sighted. Zeyd's friendship was true in the main, and he was not to be feared as an enemy. Zeyd could be generous where it cost him naught, and of his sheykhly indolent prudence, he was not hasty to meddle in any unprofitable matter.

Zeyd (that was his desert guile) had brought five mouths to the kella : this hospitality was burdensome to his hosts, and Mohammed Aly, who thought the jest turned against him, came on the morrow to my chamber with a grave counten-ance. He asked me ' Did I know that all his corn must be carried down upon camels' backs from Damascus ? ' I said, not knowing their crafty drifts, that I had not called them ;—and he aloud, " Agree together or else do not detain him, Khalîl ; this is a sheykh of Aarab, knowest thou not that every Beduin's heart is with his household, and he has no rest in absence, because of the cattle which he has left in the open wilderness ? " I asked, were it not best, before other words, that I see the monuments ? ' It was reasonable,' he said, ' and Zeyd should bring me to the next bébàn.'—" And Khalîl ! it is an unheard-of thing, any Christian to be seen in these countries," (almost at the door of the holy places). I answered, laying my hand upon the rude stones of the kella building, " But these courses witness for me, raised by Christian men's hands."—" That is well spoken, and we

are all here become thy friends : Moslem or Nasrâny, Khalîl
is now as one of us ; wellah, we would not so suffer another.
But go now with Zeyd, and afterward we will make an accord
with him, and if not I may send you out myself to see the
monuments with some of the kella.''

We came in half a mile by those ancient wells, now a watering place of the country Beduins. They are deep as the well in
the kella, ten or twelve feet large at the mouth ; the brinks are
laid square upon a side, as if they had been platforms of the

The first monument entered.

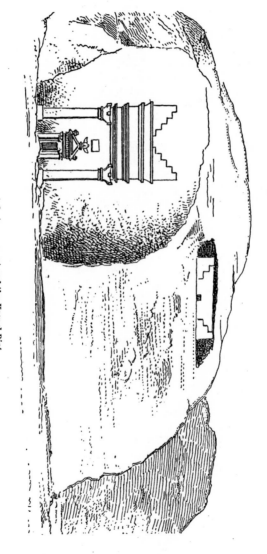

A first monument and the *Kasr el-Bint.*

old wheel-work of irrigation. The well-lining of rude stone
courses, without mortar, is deeply scored, (who may look upon
the like without emotion ?) by the soft cords of many nomad
generations. Now I had sight (*v.* p. 105) at little distance, of a first
monument, and another hewn above, like the head of some
vast frontispice, where yet is but a blind door, little entering
into the rock, without chamber. This ambitious sculpture,
seventy feet wide, is called *Kasr el-Bint*, " the maiden's bower,"
It is not, as they pretend, inaccessible ; for ascending some ancient
steps, entailed in the further end of the cliff, my unshod companions have climbed over all the rocky brow. I saw that tall
nightmare frontispice below, of a crystalline symmetry and
solemnity, and battled with the strange half-pinnacles of the
Petra monuments ; also this rock is the same yellow-grey soft
sandstone with gritty veins and small quartz pebbles. *Kasr*, in
the plural *kassûr*, has commonly the sense in Arabia of ' stable
habitation,' whether clay or stone, and opposite to *beyt shaar*,
the hair-cloth booth, or removable house, of the nomads. Thus,
even the cottages of clay, seen about outlying seed-grounds in
the wilderness, and not continually inhabited, are named kassûr.
At *Hâyil* and *er-Riâth* the prince's residence is named el-Kasr, as
it were " the castle." Kasr is also in some desert villages, a cluster
of houses, enclosed in one court wall ; thus they say of the
village *Semîra* " she is three kassûr." Any strong building for
defence and security, (such holds are very common in Arabia,)
is called gella, for kella. Borj (πύργ-), tower of defence, manifestly
a foreign word, I have not heard in Nejd Arabia.

Backward from the Borj rock, we arrived under a principal
monument (*v.* p. 104) ; in the face I saw a table and inscription,
and a bird ! which are proper to the Héjr frontispice ; the width of
sculptured architecture with cornices and columns is twenty-two
feet.—I mused what might be the sleeping riddle of those strange
crawling letters which I had come so far to seek ! The whole is
wrought in the rock ; a bay has been quarried in the soft cliff, and
in the midst is sculptured the temple-like monument. The aspect is Corinthian, the stepped pinnacles (& *v.* p. fig. 107)—
an Asiatic ornament, but here so strange to European eyes—I
have seen used in their clay house-building at Hâyil (*v.* the
fig.). Flat side-pilasters are

as the limbs of this body of
architecture ; the chapiters
of a singular severe design,
hollowed and square at once,
are as all those before seen at
Petra. In the midst of this counterfeited temple-face, is sculptured

PLATE I.

Frontispices in the Borj rocks.

[*To face p.* 107.

a stately porch, with the ornaments of architecture. Entering, I found but a rough-hewn cavernous chamber, not high, not responding to the dignity of the frontispice : (we are in a sepulchre). I saw in this dim room certain long mural niches or *loculi ;* all the floor lies full of driven sand. I thought then, with the help of a telescope, I might transcribe the epigraph, faintly appearing in the sun ; but the plague of flies at every moment filled my eyes : such clouds of them, said the Arabs, were because no rain had fallen here in the last years.

Sultry was that mid-day winter sun, glancing from the sand, and stagnant the air, under the sun-beaten monuments ; those loathsome insects were swarming in the odour of the ancient sepulchres. Zeyd would no further, he said the sun was too hot, he was already weary. We returned through the Borj

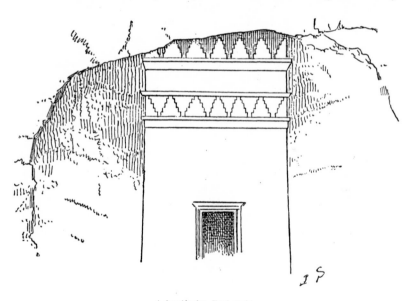

A frontispice, Borj rocks.

rocks ; and in that passage I saw a few more monuments (*v.* fig. and plate), which are also remarkable among the frontispices at el-Héjr : and lying nigh the caravan camp and the kella they are those first visited by any curious hajjies. Under the porch of one of them and over the doorway are sculptured as supporters, some four-footed beast ; the like are seen in none other. The side pedestal ornaments upon another are like griffons ;

these also are singular. The tablet is here, and in some other, adorned with a fretwork flower (perhaps pomegranate) of six petals. Over a third doorway the effigy of a bird is slenderly sculptured upon the tablet, in low relief, the head yet remaining. Every other sculptured bird of these monuments we see wrought in high natural relief, standing upon a pedestal, sculptured upon the frontispice wall, which springs from the ridge of the pediment : but among them all, not a head remains ; whether it be they were wasted by idle stone-casts of the generations of herdsmen, or the long course of the weather. Having now entered many, I perceived that all the monument chambers were sepulchral (see the plate). The mural loculi in the low hewn walls of these rudely four-square rooms, are made as shallow shelves, in length, as they might have been measured to the human body, from the child to the grown person ; yet their shallowness is such, that they could not serve, I suppose, to the receipt of the dead. In the rock floors are seen grave-pits, sunken side by side, full of men's bones, and bones are strewn upon the sanded floors. A loathsome mummy odour, in certain monuments, is heavy in the nostrils ; we thought our cloaks smelled villanously when we had stayed within but a few minutes. In another of these monuments, *Beyt es-Sheykh*, I saw the sand floor full of rotten clouts, shivering in every wind, and taking them up, I found them to be those dry bones' grave-clothes !

" Khalîl," said Mohammed Aly, " I counsel thee to give Zeyd three hundred piastres." I consented, but the sheykh had no mind to be satisfied with less than a thousand. If I had yielded then to their fantastic cupidity, the rumour would have raised the country and made my future travels most dangerous. But Zeyd departing, I put a little earnest gold into his hand, that he might not return home scorned ; and he promised to come for me at the time of the returning Haj, to carry me to dwell with him among the Beduw : Zeyd hoped that my vaccinating skill might be profitable to himself. The aga had another thought, he coveted my gun, which was an English cavalry carbine : a high value is set in these unquiet countries on all good weapons. " And so you give me this, Khalîl, I will send you every day with some of the kella till you have seen all you would of the monuments ; and I will send you to see more of these things, to el-Ally : and, further, would you to Ibn Rashîd, I will procure even to send you thither. "

I went out next with some of the kella to the Kasr el-Bint *bébàn* (*v*. p. 109). The bébàn ' row of doors,' are ranges of frontispices upon both sides round of this long crag ; the bird is seen

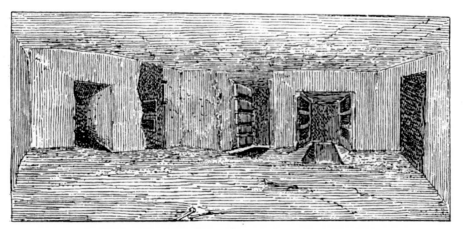

Sepulchral chamber within the portal with beasts: the cavern above man's height.

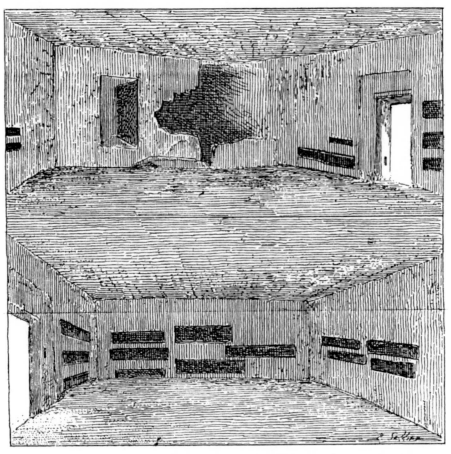

PLATE II. Another sepulchral cavern ; panorama.

[*To face p.* 108.

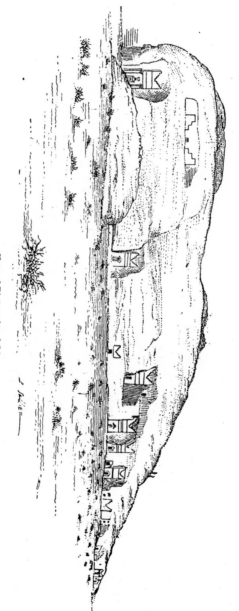

Kasr el-Bint rocks; *bébin.*

upon not a few of them and the epitaph. These are some of
the most stately architectural caverns at el-Héjr, the floors are
full of men's bones; but not all of them. Showing me a tall
monument, " This (said my companions) is the beyt of the father
of the bint, and look, Khalîl! here is another, the beyt of the
sheykh's bondman, where they all perished together." In this
last I saw the most strewed bones : they bade me admire
in them the giant stature of Kôm Thamûd. I saw them
to be ordinary; but they see in matter of religion less as men
with waking eyes than dreaming. Bare rock floors are found
in some chambers ; the loculi are not found in all. Near the
old hewn stair, in the end of the crag, is a double irregular
chamber, and this only might seem not sepulchral; yet upon
the party wall is a rude sepulchral inscription (Appendix no. 17).

We crossed then to visit the middle rocks (I distinguish them
in such manner for clearness), where are many more frontispices
and their caverns, but less stately (here are no sculptured
eagles, the stone also is softer, the cliff is lower), hewn in all
the face of the crag about. I

found here an epitaph tablet
above a door, banked up with
blown sand, so that a man might
reach to it with his hands.
Amongst them is seen an inconsiderable monument abandoned
in the beginning, where only the
head of the niche and the upper
parts are wrought out (see the
fig.). From thence we came to
that lofty frontispice within view
from the kella, *Beyt es-Sâny,* ' the
smith's house.' They showed me
' the smith's blood,' which is but
a stain of iron-rust, high upon
the battlements. ' This sâny, say
the nomads, dishonoured the *bint* or maiden daughter of the
sheykh of *The Cities.* Seeing her grow great with child, the
sheykh, her father, was moved to take cruel vengeance ; then the
valiant smith sallied with his spear to meet them, and in the
floor of the sheykh's bondman (that we have seen full of human
bones), they all fell down slain.' The porch is simple, and that
is marred, as it were with nail-holes, those which Haj Nejm
had mentioned ; the like we may see about the doorways of some
few other monuments (*v.* fig. p. 112). [Mr. James Fergusson
tells me that such holes might be made for pins by which

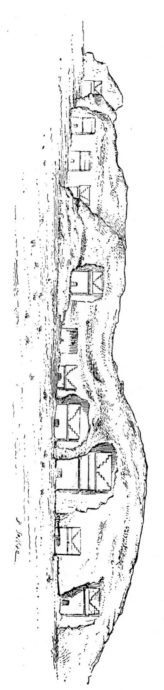

Western rocks; *bélkin.*

wooden cornices have been fastened in a few frontispices, where
the stone was faulty.]

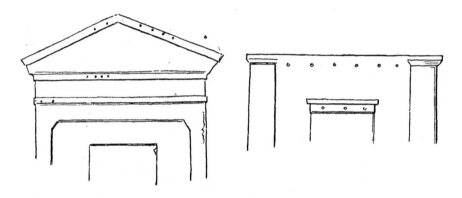

We visited then the western rocks, *K'ssûr* or *Kassûr B'theyny*
(*v.* p. 111) ;—this is a name as well of all the Héjr monuments,
" save only the Beyt es-Sâny." There are many more frontispices in the irregular cliff face and bays of this crag, of the
same factitious hewn architecture, not a few with eagles, some
are without epitaphs ; in some are seen epitaph tablets yet
unwritten. Certain frontispices are seen here nearly wasted
away and effaced by the weather.

The crags full of these monuments are " the Cities of
Sâlih." We were now five hours abroad : my companions,
armed with their long matchlocks, hardly suffered me to linger
in any place a breathing-while, saying " It is more than thou
canst think a perilous neighbourhood ; from any of these
rocks and chambers there might start upon us hostile Beduins."
The life of the Arabians is full of suspicion ; they turned their
heads with continual apprehension, gazing everywhere about
them : also Haj Nejm having once shed blood of the Wélad Aly,
was ever in dread to be overtaken without his kella. In this
plain-bottom where we passed, between cliffs and monuments,
are seen beds of strewed potsherds and broken glass. (See
the Map.) We took up also certain small copper pieces
called by the Beduins *himmarît* (perhaps *Himyariát*) of rusted
ancient money. Silver pieces and gold are only seldom found
by the Aarab in the ground where the camels have wallowed.
A villager of el-Ally thirty years before found in a stone
pot, nearly a bushel of old silver coinage. Also two W. Aly
tribesmen, one of whom I knew, had found another such treasure

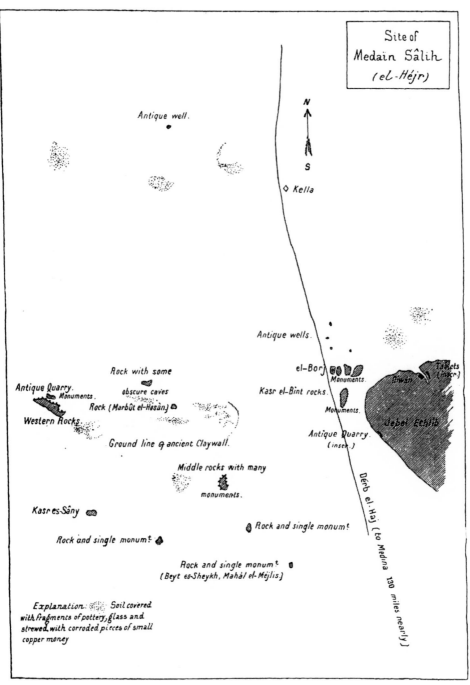

Site of
Medain Sâlih
(el-Héjr)

Antique well.

N
↑
S

◇ Kella

Antique wells.

el-Borj
Monuments.

Kasr el-Bint rocks.

Rock with some
obscure caves

Antique Quarry.
Monuments.

Rock (Marbût el-Hosàn.)

Western Rocks.

Monuments.

Ground line of ancient Claywall.

Antique Quarry.
(inscr.)

Tablets
(inscr.)

Dîwân

Jebel Ethlib

Middle rocks with many
monuments.

Dérb el-Haj (to Medina 130 miles nearly.)

Kasr es-Sâny

Rock and single monumt.

Rock and single monumt.

Rock and single monumt.
(Beyt es-Sheykh, Mahàl el-Méjlis.)

Explanation: ▒ Soil covered
with fragments of pottery, glass and
strewed with corroded pieces of small
copper money

PLATE III.

in late years. Of the himmarît, some not fully corroded show a
stamped Athenian owl, grossly imitated from the Greek moneys ;
they are Himyaric. Potsherds and broken glass, nearly in-

Himyarite trade money (in copper) found at el-Héjr (Medáin Sâlih): they are imitated from
the silver-pieces of Athens ;—see the head of Pallas, the owl and olive spray and AΘE.

destructible matter, are found upon all the ancient sites in
Arabia : none here now-a-days use these brittle wares, but only
wood and copper-tinned vessels. Arabia was then more civil
with great trading roads of the ancient world ! Arabia of our
days has the aspect of a decayed country. All nations trafficked
for gold and the sacred incense, to Arabia the Happy : · to-day
the round world has no need of the daughter of Arabia ; she is
forsaken and desolate.

Little remains of the old civil generations of el-Héjr, the
caravan city ; her clay-built streets are again the blown dust in the
wilderness. Their story is written for us only in the crabbed
scrawlings upon many a wild crag of this sinister neighbourhood,
and in the engraved titles of their funeral monuments, now
solitary rocks, which the fearful passenger admires, in these
desolate mountains. The plots of potsherds may mark old inhabited sites, perhaps a cluster of villages : it is an ordinary
manner of Semitic settlements in the Oasis countries that they
are founded upon veins of ground-water. A sûk perhaps and
these suburbs was Hejra emporium, with palm groves walled
about.

By the way, returning to the kella, is a low crag full of
obscure caverns, and without ornament. In this passage I had

D. T.   8.

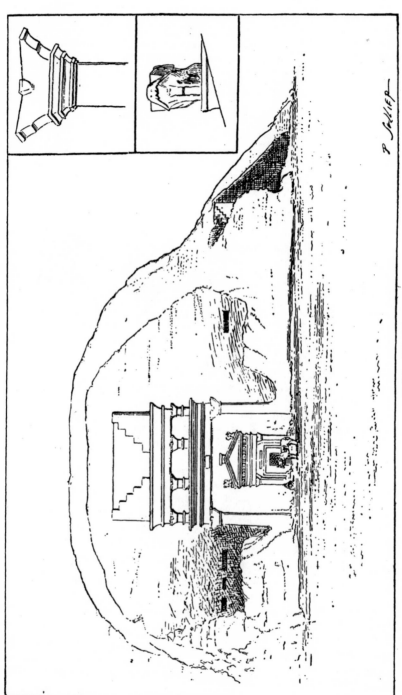

BEYT AKHREYMAT.

viewed nearly all the birds which are proper to the frontispices of Medáin Sâlih. The Arabs say, it is some kind of sea-fowl. The Syrian pilgrims liken them to the falcon; they are of massy work as in gross grained sand-rock, in which nothing can be finely sculptured. The pediments bear commonly some globular and channeled side ornaments, which are solid, and they are sculptured in the rock.

In other days, I visited the monuments at leisure, and arrived at the last outstanding. The most sumptuous is that, they call *Beyt Akhreymát*. Between the mural cornices there is sculptured an upper rank of four bastard pilasters. There is no bird but only the pedestal; instead of the channeled urns, there are here pediment side-ornaments of beasts, perhaps hounds or griffons. The bay of the monument (wherein are seen certain shallow loculi, like those found in the walls of the sepulchral chambers) is not hewn down fully to the ground; so that the heels of the great side pilasters are left growing to the foot of the rock, for the better lasting and defence of this weak sculptured sandstone. The spurious imitating art is seen thus in strange alliance with the chaotic eternity of nature. About the doorway are certain mouldings, barbarously added to the architecture. This goodly work appeared to me not perfectly dressed to the architectural symmetry; there are few frontispices, which are laboured with the tool to a perfect smoothfacedness. The antique craft-masters (not unlikely hired from Petra,) were of a people of clay builders; their work in these temple-tombs was imitation: (we saw the like in the South Arabian trade-money, p. 113). They were Semites, expeditious more than curious, and naturally imperfect workmen.— The interpretation of the inscriptions has confirmed these conjectures.

We were come last to the *Mahál el-Mejlis* or senate house, here the face of a single crag is hewn to a vast monument more than forty feet wide, of a solemn agreeable simplicity. The great side pilasters are in pairs, which is not seen in any other; notwithstanding this magnificence, the massy frontispice had remained unperfected. Who was the author of this beginning who lies nearly alone in his huge sepulchral vanity? for all the chamber within is but a little rude cell with one or two grave-places. And doubtless this was his name engrossed in the vast title

8—2

plate, a single line of such magnitude as there is none other, with deeply engraved cursive characters [now read by the learned interpreters, *For Hail son of Douna* (and) *his descendants:* Appendix no. 22.] The titles could not be read in Moham-

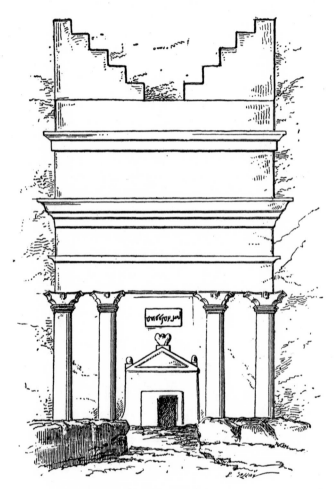

Mahál el-Mejlis.

med's time, or the prophet without prophecy had not uttered his folly of these caverns, or could not have escaped derision. The unfinished portal with eagle and side ornaments, is left as it was struck out in the block. The great pilasters are not chiselled fully down to the ground ; the wild reef yet remains before the monument, channeled into blocks nearly ready to be removed,— in which is seen the manner to quarry of those ancient stone-cutters. Showing me the blocks my rude companions said, " These were benches of the town councillors."

The covercles of the sepulchres and the doors of the " desolate mansions," have surely been wooden in this country, (where also is no stone for flags) and it is likely they were of acacia or tamarisk timber ; which doubtless have been long since consumed at the cheerful watch-fires of the nomads : moreover there should hinder them no religion of the dead in idolatry. Notwithstanding the imitating (Roman) magnificence of these merchants to the Sabeans, there is not a marble plate in all their monuments, nor any strewn marble fragment is seen upon the Héjr plain. It sufficed them to " write with an iron pen for ever " upon the soft sand-rock of these Arabian mountains. A mortise is seen in the jambs of all doorways, as it might be to receive the bolt of a wooden lock (see pl. between pp. 108—9). The frontispices are often over-scored with the idle wasms of the ancient tribesmen. I mused to see how often they resemble the infantile Himyaric letters.

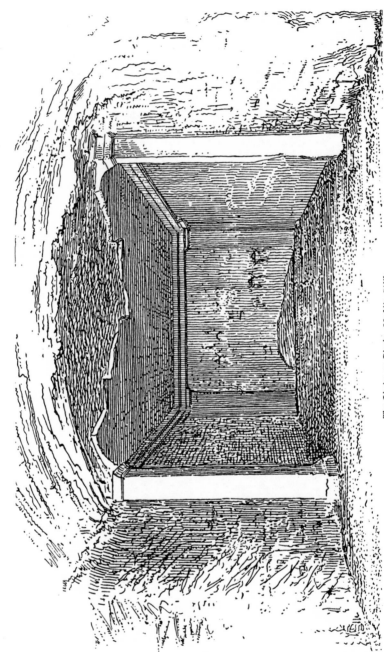

The Liwân or Diwân, Medâin Sâlih.

CHAPTER V.

MEDÁIN SÂLIH AND EL-ALLY.

The Diwán. *The Haj post. Beduins visit the kella. Cost of victualling and manning a kella. Syrian Kurds and Moorish tower guards. The desert tribes about el-Héjr. Nomad wasms. The day in the kella. Three manners of utterance in the Arabic speech. Their fable talk. The "Jews of Kheybar." Beny Kelb. Hunting the wild goat in the mountains. Antique perpendicular inscriptions. Bread baked under the ashes. Night in the mountain : we hear the* ghrôl. *The porcupine : the colocynth gourd. The ostrich. Pitted rocks. Vulcanic neighbourhood. Rude rock-inscriptions. Antique quarries. Hejra clay-built. The Cross mark. Ancient villages between el-Héjr and Medina. Colonists at el-Héjr. Christmas at Medáin. Sânies of Teyma. The way down to el-Ally. The* Khreyby *ruins. El-Ally. The Sheykh* Dâhir. *Sacramental gestures. The town founded by Barbary Derwishes. Voice of the muetthin. Dâhir questions the stranger. The people and their town. Arabic wooden lock. Beduins mislike the town life. The English Queen is the chief Ruler in Islam. El-Ally a civil Hejâz town. Ibn Saûd came against el-Ally. The Kâdy. Sickly climate. They go armed in their streets. Hejâz riots, battles joined with quarter-staves. History of the place. Rain falling. Dates. The women. Fables of Christians and Jews.*

HAVING viewed all the architectural chambers in those few crags of the plain, my companions led me to see the *Diwán*, which only of all the Héjr monuments is in the mount Ethlib, in a passage beyond a white sand-drift in face of the kella. Only this *Liwàn* or Diwán ' hall or council chamber,' of all the hewn monuments at el-Héjr, (besides some few and obscure caverns,) is plainly not sepulchral. The Diwán alone is lofty and large, well hewn within, with cornice and pilasters, and dressed to the square and plummet, yet a little obliquely. The Diwán alone is an open chamber : the front is of excellent simplicity, a pair of pilasters to the width of the hewn chamber, open as the nomad tent. The architrave is fallen with the forepart of the flat ceiling. The hall, which is in ten paces large and deep eleven, and high as half the depth ; looks northward. In the passage, which is fifty paces long, the sun never shines, a wind breathes there continually, even in summer : this was a cool site to be chosen in a sultry country. Deep sand lies drifted in the Diwán floor : the Aarab digging under the walls for " gun-salt,"

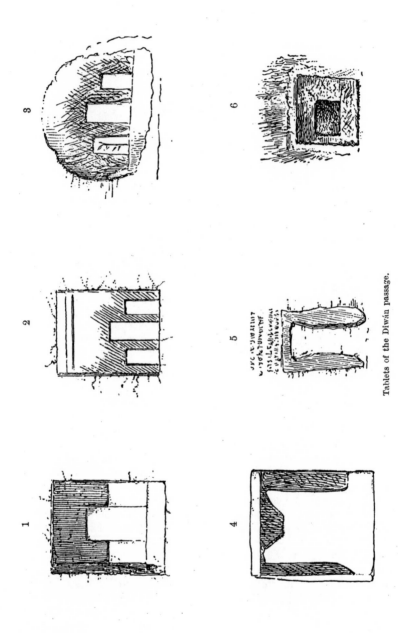

Tablets of the Diwán passage.

(the cavern is a noon shelter of the nomad flocks,) find no bones, neither is there any appearance of burials. The site resembles the beginning of the Sîk at Wady Mûsa, in which is the Khazna Jarôun ; in both I have seen, but here much more (pp. 120 and 122), the same strange forms of little plinths and tablets. The plinths are single, or two or three unevenly standing together, or there is a single plinth branching above into two heads (No. 4) ; a few have the scupltured emblems about them of the great funeral monuments : we cannot doubt that their significance is religious. There is a Nabatean legend lightly entailed in the rock above one of them (No. 5). [It is now interpreted *This is the mesgeda* (beth-el or kneeling stone) *made to Aera, great god.* This shows them to have been idol-stones.]—(Inscr. No. 1.)

We see scored upon the walls, within, a few names of old Mohammedan passengers, some line or two of Nabatean inscriptions, and the beginning of a word or name of happy augury ΕΥΤΥ-; these Greek letters only I have found at Medáin Sâlih. Also there are chalked up certain uncouth outlines in shepherd's ruddle, *ghrerra*, (such as they use to mark flocks in Syria,) which are ascribed to the B. Helál. Upon the two cliffs of the passage are many Nabatean inscriptions. Higher this strait rises among the shelves of the mountain, which is full of like clefts,—it is the nature of this sandstone. From thence is a little hewn conduit led down in the rocky side (so in the Sîk), as it were for rain-water, ending in a small cistern-chamber above the Diwán ; it might be a provision for the public hall or temple. Hereabout are four or five obscure hewn caverns in the soft rock. Two of the Fehját accompanied me armed, with Mohammed and Abd el-Kâder from the kella ; whilst we were busy, the kella lads were missing, they, having seen strange riders in the plain, had run to put themselves in safety. Only the Fehjies remained with me ; when I said to them, Will you also run away ? the elder poor man answered with great heart, " I am an *Antary* and this is an Antary (of the children of Antar), we will not forsake thee ! " (The hero Antar was of these countries, he lived little before Mohammed.) No Beduins were likely to molest the poor and despised Fehjies.

Fourteen days after the Haj passing, came *el-nejjàb*, the haj dromedary post, from Medina ; he carried but a small budget with him of all the hajjies' letters, for Damascus. Postmaster of the wilderness was a W. Aly sheykh, afterward of my acquaintance : he hired this Sherarát tribesman to be his post rider to Syria. The man counted eleven or twelve night

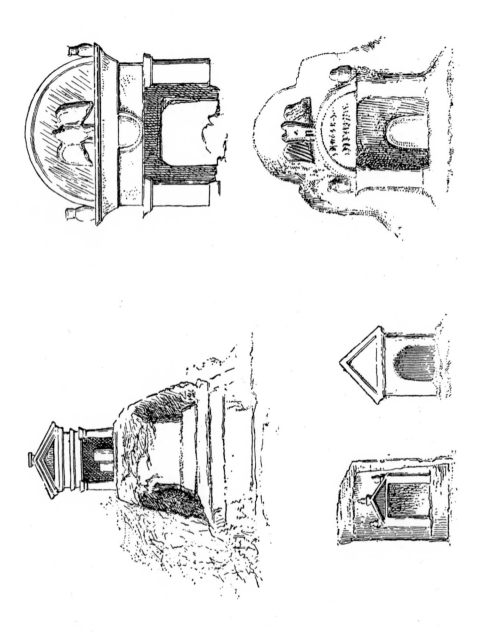

stations in his journey thither, which are but waterings and
desolate sites in the desert: *el-Jinny, Jeraida, Ghrurrub,
Ageyly, W. el-Howga, Moghreyra, Howsa, Bayir.* A signal
gun is fired at Damascus when the haj post is come in. The
day following the light mail bag is sealed again for the Harameyn. For a piece of money the poor man also carried my
letters with him to Syria.

Many were the days to pass within the kella : almost every
third day came Beduins, and those of the garrison entertained
them with arms in their hands ; in other days there were
alarms of ghrazzûs seen or of strange footsteps found in the
plain, and the iron door was shut. Not many Beduw are
admitted at once into the tower, and then the iron door is barred
upon their companions without. Besides Fejîr there came to us
Moahîb, nomads of the neighbouring Harra, and even Beduins
of Bíllî ; all sought coffee, a night's lodging and their supper
in the kella. The Bíllî country is the rugged breadth of the
Teháma, beyond the Harra. They pronounced *gîm* as the
Egyptians. Three men of Bíllî arriving late in an evening
drank ardently a first draught from the coffee-room buckets
of night-chilled water, and "Ullah be praised! sighed they, as
they were satisfied, wellah we be come over the Harra and
have not drunken these two days ! " They arrived now driving a
few sheep in discharge of a *khúwa,* or debt for " brotherhood," to
the Fukara, for safe conduct of late, which was but to come in to
traffic in the Haj market. Said Mohammed Aly, " Mark well the
hostile and necessitous life of the Beduw ! is it to such wild
wretches thou wilt another day trust thy life ? See in what
manner they hope to live,—by devouring one another ! It is
not hard for them to march without drinking, and they eat,
by the way, only, if they may find aught. The Beduins are
sheyatîn (of demon-kind ;) what will thy life be amongst them,
which, wellah, we ourselves of the city could not endure ! "

How might this largess of the kella hospitality be continually maintained ? " It is all at our own and not at the government cost," quoth the aga. The Aarab suppose there is certain
money given out of the Haj chest to the purpose ; but it seems
to be only of wages spared between the aga and the tower-
warden, who are of a counsel together to hire but half the
paid strength of the garrison. To the victualling of a haj-
road kella there was formerly counted 18 camel loads (three
tons nearly) of Syrian wheat, with 30 cwt. of caravan biscuit
(*ozmát*), and 30 of *bórghrol,* which is bruised, parboiled
wheaten grain, and sun-dried (the household diet of Syria)
with 40 lbs. of samn. But the old allowances had been now

reduced, by the reformed administration, to the year's rations
(in wheat only) of ten men (*nefer*), and to each a salary
of 1000 piastres, or £8˙sterling ; but the warden received for
two nefers : thus the cost of a kella to the Syrain government may be £220 English money by the year. There is no
tower warden on the road who has not learned Turkish arts ;
and with less pay they have found means to thrive with
thankful mind. The warden, who is paymaster for ten, hires
but five hands, nor these all at the full money. The Pasha
will never call for the muster of his ten merry men ; they
each help other to win and swallow the public good between them : all is well enough if only the kella be not lost,
and that the caravan find water there.—How may a kella,
nearly unfurnished of defence, be maintained in the land of
Ishmael ? How but by making the Beduw their allies, in the
sacrament of the bread and salt : and if thus one man's wages
be spent in twelve months, for coffee and corn and samn,
the warden shall yet fare well enough ;—the two mules' rations
of barley were also embezzled. But I have heard the old man
Nejm complain, that all the fat was licked from his beard by
Mohammed Aly.

Betwixt Wady Zerka in the north and Hedîeh midway from
Medáin upon the derb to Medina, are eleven or twelve inhabited kellas, manned (in the register) by one hundred and
twenty nefers, said Mohammed Aly ; this were ten for a kella,
but afterward he allowed that only seventy kept them. Thus
they are six-men garrisons, but some are less ; that which is
paid out for the other fifty in the roll, (it may be some £1300,)
is swallowed by the confederate officiality. In former times
five hundred nefers were keepers of these twelve towers, or
forty to a kella ; afterward the garrisons were twenty-five men
to a kella, all Damascenes of the Medân. But the Syrians
bred in happier country were of too soft a spirit, they shut
their iron doors, as soon as the Haj was gone by, ten months, till
they saw the new returning pilgrimage : with easy wages and
well provided, they were content to suffer fron year to year this
ship-bound life in the desert. The towers below Maan were
manned by Kurds, sturdy northern men of an outlandish speech
and heavy-handed humour : but a strange nation could have
no long footing in Arabia. After the Émir Abd el-Kâder's
seating himself at Damascus and the gathering to him there of
the Moorish emigration, Moghrâreba began to be enrolled for
the haj road. And thenceforth being twenty or twenty-five
men in a tower, the iron doors stood all daylights open. The
valorous Moorish Arabs are well accepted by the Arabians, who

repute them an " old Hejâz folk, and nephews of the Beny Helál." The adventurous Moors in garrison even made raids on unfriendly Beduw, and returned to their kellas with booty of snall cattle and camels.

These are the principal tribes of Beduin neighbours : Bílli (singular *Belúwy*) over the Harra ; next to them at the north Howeytát (sing. Howeyty) : south of them Jeheyna, an ancient tribe (in the gentile vulg. plur. *Jehîn*), nomads and villagers, their country is from Yánba to the derb el-haj. Some fendies (divisions) of them are *el-Kleybát* (upon the road between Sawra and Sujwa), *Aroa, G'dah, Merowîn, Zubbián, Grûn* and about Yánba, *Beny Ibrahîm, Sieyda, Seràserra.* Above Medina on the derb el-haj were the *Saadîn* (sing. *Saadànny*) of Harb ; westward is *Bishr* and some fendies of Heteym towards Kheybar. The successions of nomad tribes which have possessed el-Héjr since the Beny Helál, or fabled ancient heroic Aarab of Nejd, were they say the Sherarát, (also reckoned to the B. Helál)—

Wasms of some Beduin tribes

these then occupied the Harra, where the *dubbûs*, or club-stick, their cattle mark, remains scored upon the vulcanic rocks —after them are named the *Beny Saîd*, then the *Duffîr, sheykh Ibn Sweyd* (now in the borders of Mesopotamia), whom the Beny Sôkhr expelled ; the Fukara and Moahîb (now a very small tribe) drove out the B. Sôhkr from the *Jau.* The Moahîb reckon their generations in this country, thirteen : a sheykh of theirs told me upon his fingers his twelve home-born ancestors ; this is nearly four centuries. Where any nomad tribe has dwelt, they leave the wild rocks full of their idle wasms ; these are the Beduins' only records and they remain for centuries of years.

In such sort we passed a day in the kella ; as the morrow lightened every one in his narrow chamber chanted the first prayers with a well-sounding solemnity. A mule was yoked to the creaking *dulàb* or well-machine and a nefer drives with loud carter's shouting from the gallery above. The embers of the yester-evening fire are blown to a flame in the coffee-chamber hearth, where the warden with his great *galliûn* (tobacco-pipe), and the aga with his redoubtable visage and his snuff-box, take their old seats. Coffee is now roasted, brayed, and boiled for the morrow's bitter cup, as the custom is to-day of all Arabs ;—and yet this tower might be of older building than the first coffee-drinking in Asia ! About ten, each one withdrawing to himself, they breakfasted. The raising of the water is all the care of the kella : a mule wrought four hours and was unyoked ; the second wrought four afternoon hours. At mid-afternoon our household provision of water is taken and stored in well-buckets in the several dwelling cell-chambers. The gate Arabs' house-wives come in then to fill their water-skins, and after prayers those of the kella sit anew to make coffee. At sunset they supped, every man in his own chamber, after they had solemnly recited the evening prayer : when they rise from their simple grain or rice messes, they go to drink the evening coffee together. Every man took his own place again, upon the stone floor, about the coffee hearth ; and the long Arab evening is spent over their coffee pots and tobacco.

Mohammed Aly could not sit long silent, and when he had opened his mouth, we heard his tales for hours, all of good matter and eloquent, and (as unlettered men tell,) of the marrow of human experience ; then it was, since all is not wisdom in many words, that we could discover his mind. The other bold Moghrebies answered him with a sober mirth, admiring their argute and world-wise aga, sooner than loving him : the gate Arabs sat on silent and smiling. I have won-

dered how often the talk of these Moorish men in the East,
touched Europe! The Engleys were friends, said they, of the
Moslemîn. France rides but roughly in their necks in Barbary :
they thought it pearls to hear how that mighty state, which
had hardly mastered Moghreby Algeria in fourteen years, had
been vanquished in as many days by a nation of this new name,
Borusia : Mohammed Aly swore loud by Ullah that the ransom
of *Fransa* heaped together, might fill the four walls of this
kella ! The ingenious Franks are even here their merchants
(more than they were aware) ; Manchester clothes them in
part ; even the oriental coffee cups, the coffee pan and their
red caps were made for these markets in Europe. Haj Nejm,
sometimes turning to me with his old man's ingenuous smiles,
could say over a few words of the neighbour Frankish coast,
and current in Barbary, *sordi, muchacho, niño, agua ;* "such
(he added) are the words of them." He had seen our sea-
faring nations in the ports of this country ; Flamingies (Flemish
or Dutch) Americânies and the Taliân.—" The Taliânis were
slaves (this he thought, because of their Neapolitan and sea-
men's brown visages !) of the Engleys."

The aga unlettered but erudite in the mother tongue distinguished to us three kinds of the Arabic utterance : *el-aly*, the
lofty style as when a man should discourse with great personages ;
el-wast, the mean speech, namely for the daily business of
human lives ; and that all broken, limping and thread-bare, *ed-
dûn*, the lowly,—" and wellah as this speaking of Khalîl." Nevertheless that easy speech, which is born in the mouth of the
Beduins, is far above all the school-taught language of the town.
The rest of our conpany were silent Arabs, and when the aga's
talk was run out, he looked stourly about him, who should speak
next. Haj Hasan's wit was most in his strong hands, he had
little to say ; in the old man Nejm was an ingenuous modesty,
he could not speak without first spreading his lean palms to the
fire, and casting down the eyes when any looked upon him.
These men sat solemnly, with their great galliûns and " drank "
tobacco. " Ullah ! I am a friend, would cry Mohammed Aly, of
heart-easing mirth in every company." When he spoke all
feared his direful voice. " What ! has none of you any word ?
Then Khalîl shall tell us a tale. Say anything, Khalîl, only tell
us of your country, and whatso thou sayest it will be new and
very pleasant to us all. Arabs ! listen ; now Khalîl begins.
This is a tale you are to imagine of the land of Khalîl and
of the Engleys that are a great people, ay wellah, and only
little after the Dowlat of the Sûltàn." But I answered " There
is little voice in my chest, there is no tale ready upon my

tongue which is not current this year, you have said it yourselves : " and I thought this silence salutary, among so hot
heads of Moghrebies, until the Haj should be again at the door.
Then would he cry " What do you Arab to sit like the dumb ?
let us hear now some merry tale among you ; tell on only for
good fellowship." Mohammed Aly's soldiering life had been
much in the nomad borders of Syria ; well knew he their speech
and affected it here amongst them, and yet he told me that
when the Beduins were in the mid-sea-deep of their braying
rimes, he could not many times follow them. There are turns
and terms of the herdsmen poets of the desert which are
dark or unknown in any form to the townling Syrians. The
truant smiling Beduins have answered again, that they could
no tales, unless it were of their small cattle and camels, or
to tell of ghrazzûs. Their bare life is in the wastes : the wonderful
citizen world is almost out of their hearing. A coffee chamber
pastime was yet to tell upon their fingers the caravan journeys
and find at what station the hajjàj should arrive this day. From
hence to Medina the distance is perhaps one hundred and thirty
miles ; they count it three journeys for thelûl riders.

Mohammed Aly's tales were often fables, when he touched
common things out of his knowledge. He had been upon
an English ship-board, in the time of the fanatical troubles in
Syria, (the fleets of Europe lying then at Beyrût ;) and now he
told us, ' her guns were three hundred, and the length of every
gun nine yards, and so great that hardly three men's arms could
fathom them, one of her decks was a market, where he saw all
kinds of victuals sold ; her sea-soldiers were 25,000.' These
things he affirmed with oaths,—such are the Arabs' tales. I
had sat in amazement to hear of a strange country in Arabia,
southward of Mecca, a civil land of towns and villages only
in the last age converted to Islam, the province they named
Béled Jawwa. When of this I questioned Mohammed Aly, a
dim spirit but rolled in the busy world and free from the first
rust of superstition, he answered, " Ay ! Khalîl ! and I have seen
them in the pilgrimage at Mecca, they inhabit a country in
el-Yémen, the men have no beards on their faces." Later I
understood that this was spoken of the Javenese, whom they
supposed to be a people of the Arabian Peninsula. Again
the Harb are dreaded (their name is War) by the Syrian
pilgrims ; because the robber wretches and cutters of the caravans betwixt the Harameyn, are counted to this nomad nation.
" The Harb are terrible, it may be known by their customs, said
Mohammed Aly, more than any other. The male is not circumcised in childhood, but when he is of age to take a wife ;

then his friends send for surgery and the young man is pilled
from the pubis : the maiden also looking on, and if her lad
shrink or cast a sigh, wellah she will disdain him for an
husband." I have asked them, when I afterwards came to the
Harb, " Is it so among you ? " " Lord ! they answered, that so
strange things should be reported of us poor people ! but
Khalîl, these things are told of *el-Kahtán*,"—that is of a
further nation and always far off.

A common argument of the Syrian Haj fables are the *Yahûd*
(Jews of) *Kheybar ;* an ancient name indeed and fearful in the
ears of the more credulous pilgrims. Kheybar, now a poor village, (which later, with infinite pains, I have visited,) is a place
renowned in the Moslem chronicles, as having been first conquered in the beginning of the religious faction of Mohammed.
Kheybar is fabulously imagined to be yet a strong city, (which
was manifestly never more than a village and her suburbs), in
the further side of the desert ; and whose inhabitants are a
terrible kindred, Moslems indeed outwardly, but in secret cruel
Jews, that will suffer no stranger to enter among them. In
the midst of the town, as they tell, is a wonderful fortress, so
high, that even the summer sun cannot cast her beams to the
ground. And that cursed people's trade is fabled to be all in
land-loping and to be cutters of the Haj. Also in their running
they may pass any horse : so swift they are, because the whirl-
bone of the knee is excised in their childhood ; by nature they
have no calf under their shanks. There are told also many
enterprises of theirs, as this :—' Three Yahûd Kheybar being
taken in the manner, the Haj Pasha commanded to bury them in
the sand to the ears ; it was done, and the Haj passed from them.
There came a leopard in the night-time, which smelled to the
two former, and finding them dead, she left them, but the
third still breathing, she busily wrought with her paws, to
have digged him up ; the man then returning to himself and
seeing the grisly brute stand over, heaved himself for dread, and
the beast fled affrighted. This Yahûdy sprang out and ran
fast after the Haj, now a journey gone before him ; yet
reaching their camp the next night, he climbed by the stays
and from above entered the Pasha's pavilion. The great officer
lay sleeping with his head upon the treasury chest ; for all this,
the thief stole the government silver, as much as he might carry.
In the next night station the thief, returning to attempt the like,
was taken by the watch, and bound till the morning. Then being
led out to die, the Pasha commanded his soldiery to stand in
compass about him. The Yahûdy answered, " Sir, am I not he
whom ye buried ? and who robbed the chest but I this other night ?

D. T.   9

I fear thee not yet."—" And how cursed man, dost thou not fear me who have power to kill thee ? "—" There is no man can make me afraid ; "—and with a cast of his legs, the thief sprang quite over the circle of men's shoulders and ran from them faster than any trooper's pursuing.'

Wonders are told also in Arabia of the *Beny Kelb,* a tribe of human hounds. Kelb, " a dog," now an injury was formerly an honourable name in the Semitic tribes. They say " The Kelb housewives and daughters are like fair women, but the male kind, a span in stature and without speech, are white hounds. When they have sight of any guest approaching, the hospitable men-dogs spring forth to meet him, and holding the lap of his mantle between their teeth, they towse him gently to their nomad booths." Some will have it " they dwell not in land of Arabia, but inhabit a country beyond the flood ; they devour their old folk so soon as their beards be hoary." As this was told some day in our coffee talk at Medáin Sâlih, Doolan shouted, of a sudden, that in another of his distant expeditions he had met with the Beny Kelb—" Ay billah ! and they came riding upon thelûls." Then reminded that the B. Kelb dwelt over seas, and that the men were in likeness of hounds, he exclaimed, " Well, and this may be true, God wot ; wellah ! I thought I saw them, but, life of this coffee ! I might be mistaken." Doolan told me another day that the people of Kheybar were six hundred thousand men ;—and all was of the poor man's mag-nanimity that he would make them many in his fable talk. A very sober and worthy Fejîry who ever told me the truth within his knowledge, said " the country of the B. Kelb lies five or six days eastward from Mecca, but they are not right Moslems, their matchlock men are ten thousand." That were a tribe of fifty thousand souls !—there is not any so great nomad nation in all Arabia. The Annezy, which inhabit almost from Medina to the north of Syria, a land-breadth of more than fifteen thousand square miles, I cannot esteem to be fully half that number ; but their minds have little apprehension of the higher numbers : I have commonly found their thousands to signify hundreds, so that the tenth of their tale very nearly agreed with my own reckoning.

Haj Hasan, whose two hands wrought more than the rest of the garrison, would upon a day go a hunting to the jebel with some of the gate Arabs, and I should accompany them. In the way beyond the eastward cliffs of the plain, I heard there were inscriptions. As we crossed two and a half hours to the *Rikb el-Héjr,* before noonday, some of the Arabs of this land of famine complained already in the sun *ana ajizt,* their weak limbs were dull in the sand. Wady was amongst them, he went in rags, the custom in Ishmaelite Arabia of any who must adventure a little abroad, for dread of being stripped by any hostile ghrazzû. We passed the barrier cliff by a cleft banked with deep sand. The mountain backward is an horrid sandstone desolation, a death as it were and eternal stillness of nature. The mountain sandstone cloven down in cross lines, is here a maze of rhomboid masses, with deep and blind streets, as it were, of some lofty city lying between them. Of the square crags some that were softer stone are melted quite away from among them, leaving the open spaces. The heights of wasting rock are corroded into many strange forms of heads and pinnacles. [*v.* The rocks of J. Ethlib, p. 243.] The counterlines of sandstone sediment are seen at even height in all the precipices. We marched in the winter heat ; a thermometer laid, upon a white cloth, upon the sand at an height of 3700 feet, showed 86° F. : at the highest of the mountain labyrinth, sixteen miles from the kella, I found nearly 4000 feet. From thence we saw over a wide waste landscape northwards to a watering of the Fejîr nomads. We were distressed, stepping in the deep banked cliff sand, descending and ascending still amongst the perplexed cliff passages. As we went I found a first Himyarish legend of the desert, written upon the cliff, perpendicularly, with images of the ostrich, the horse and his rider, and of camels. [*Doc. Épigr.* pl. xx.] We came to a cave in a deep place of sand where there grew acacia trees. The sun now was setting and this should be our night's lodging.

We had brought dough tied in a cloth, to spare our water ; it had been kneaded at el-Héjr. Of this dough, one made large flat cakes (*abûd*) which, raked under the red-hot sand and embers of our earth, are after a few minutes to be turned. Our bread taken up half baked was crumbled with dates in the hollow of a skin pressed in the sand troughwise, with a little water, that we might feel the less need to drink and make not too soon an end of our little girby, being five persons. The nomads in this country after dates rub their palms in sand ; some ruder choughs wipe the cloyed fingers in their long elf locks. The bright night shone about us very cold, and half numbed we could not sleep ; before morning I found but 38° F. Once we heard a strange noise in the hollow of our cavern upward. Doolan, who came with us, afterward boasted " We had all heard, wellah, the bogle, *ghrûl*, (ay, and even the incredulous son-of-his-uncle Khalîl : " but I thought it only a rumble in the empty body of Wady's starveling greyhound, for which we had no water and almost not a crumb to cast, and that lay fainting above us. We rose from our

9—2

rocky beds after midnight with aching bones, to make up the
watch-fire. We broke our fast ere day of that which remained,
and each had a draught of water. Then taking up their
long guns they went to stalk the *bedûn*, or great wild-goats of
the mountain. I stayed by the water-skin in the way by which
we should return, whilst they climbed among the waste rocks.
Until noon, only Wady had fired at a running buck and
missed him, as the Beduins will nine times in ten. As we
went homewards, a troop startled before us of ten bedûn
and sprang upon the rocky shelves : our gunners went creeping
after for an hour, but the quarry was gone from them.

One day our hunters brought in a porcupine, *nís*, they find
his earth like a rabbit-burrow and with a stick knock him
on the head. An equal portion of this (the Arabs' religious
goodness) was divided to all in the kella. The porcupine is
not flayed, the gelatinous skin may be eaten with the flesh,
which has a fishy odour. They boiled the meat, and every one
after supper complained of heart-burning, I only felt nothing.
It is also the Arabs' fable, that the creature can shoot out
his pricks against an enemy. The goat, the ass, the porcupine, will eat greedily of the colocynth gourd, which to human
nature is of so mortal bitterness that little indeed and even
the leaf is a most vehement purgative ; they say it will leave
a man half dead, and he may only recover his strength, by
eating flesh meat. Surely this is the " death in the pot " of
Elisha's derwishes. Some Beduwy brought us in a great ostrich
egg, which dressed with samn and flour in a pan, savoured as
a well-tasting omlette. The ostrich descends into the plain
of Medáin Sâlih ; I have seen her footing in Ethlib. Doolan,
as many of his Heteym nation, was an ostrich hunter ; in the
season he mounted upon his thelûl and riding at adventure in
the wilderness, if God would he found an ostrich path, there he hid
himself, awaiting, all day, with lighted match, till the bird should
pass : but this patience is many times disappointed save when
the nest is found. Once he had brought home two ostrich chicks,
which grew up in the kella, but one day the young birds
fed of beans, and these swelling in their crops had choked them.
So poor was the man, he found not every day to eat, yet were
his hunter's tools of the best ; his matchlock was worth more
than other in that desert side, namely forty reals. Doolan had
most years his two skins ready against the Haj, in which is
wont to come down a certain Damascus feather merchant, who
buys all ostrich skins from the nomads by the pilgrim road, paying
for every one forty to forty-five reals. The ostrich feeds, pasturing from bush to bush, " like the camel." The hunters eat the

bird's breast, which is dry meat; the fat is precious, one of
their small coffee-cups full is valued at half a mejîdy; they
think it a sovereign remedy for heat and cold, and in many
diseases. Inhabitants of the air, here in this winter season,
were crows, swallows (black and grey), and blue rock pigeons.
All nights in the kella we were invaded by a multitude of
small yellow beetles, which fretted our butter-skins and preyed
upon all victuals: I have not elsewhere seen them in Arabia.

As the Arabs were accustomed to the Nasrâny I began to
wander alone, in all the ·site of Medáin Sâlih. Only the aga
bade me mount first with my glass upon the Borj rocks, and if
I saw no life stirring in all the plain, I might adventure. In
this exploring day by day, I saw more perfectly the several
frontispices and their chambers. The height of the Borj rocks is
pitted, as with shallow surface graves; the people of this rainless
country take. them for cisterns. They lie many there together,
some north and south, some east and west, but are not often a
span deep; only backward from the tower are seen plainly, two

grave-pits. Also certain bare shelves of rock are seen pitted
in the plain, with the like shallow grave-places ; as under the
Kasr el-Bint rocks, before the threshold of one of the fairest
frontispices (fig. p. 133). The Borj is a rude square-built low
tower laid of untrimmed stones without mortar, six paces by
five, of uncertain age : a yard is the thickness of the wall
diminishing upward ; outstanding flags have served within for
stairs.

In the plain, I saw everywhere drifted pebbles of lavas
and pumice, certainly from yonder black Harra, which I have
afterward found to be sandstone mountain overflowed with
a wonderful thickness of basaltic lava-streams ; and the black
hills seen thereupon, from hence, are craters of vulcanoes. Yet
there is no sign of any showers of vulcanic powder or cinders,
fallen of old time in the plain ;—such surely was not the cata-
strophe of el-Héjr. I found upon the wild rocks, and transcribed many old scored inscriptions. Upon the precipices I
often wondered to see, twenty-five feet high or more from the
ground, antique traced images of animals, which could be
reached now only by means of a long ladder : the tallest man
standing upon his camel could not attain them !—" Plainly
(say the Arabs) the men of former ages were of great stature ! "
The aga answered them " Yet there might be shrinking of the
soil, between weather and wind, in long course of time ; " but
neither can this be the cause, if we consider the doorsills of the
funeral monuments, for they appear at present at the ground
level. I found also millstones, of antique form, in black lava ; the

like I had seen before lying in the Petra valley. Half buried in
the sand, I saw also some stone vessels (*jurn* or *nejjar*) like font-
stones, and nearly a yard wide ; there is one now set up for a
drinking trough in the kella. In the plain under Ethlib, I found

an ancient quarry, upon whose wall is cut, as with a workman's chisel, this Himyaric legend, which is nearly singular among

the Nabatean inscriptions at Medáin Sâlih ; I found a second ancient quarry, backward from the western rocks.—Two very small quarries could not suffice for the stonework of a town ; and though they had some stone-waste from the hewing of the funeral monuments : but their town was clay-built and the clay house-walls were laid upon a ground-course or two of stones, rude and nearly unwrought. I have seen very few plots of antique houses remaining, in all the ancient site. I suppose not many are covered by the driven sand, but rather that all such provision of stones, lying ready to hand, has been taken up long since, for the building of the kella. Small were those ancient houses, we should not think them cottages ; no larger are the antique houses of rude stone building, which I have since seen yet standing, from Mohammed's time, about Kheybar.

Under the Borj rocks I have often stayed to consider the stain

of a cross in a border, made with ghrerra, or red ochre. What should this be ! a cattle brand ?—or the sign of Christ's death and trophy of his never ending kingdom ? which some ancient Nasrean passenger left to witness for the Author of his Salvation, upon the idolatrous rocks of el-Héjr ! The cross mark is also a common letter in the Himyaric inscriptions, which the ignorant Arabs take for a sure testimony, that all their country was of old time held by the Nasâra.—I have found no footstep of the Messianic religion in this country unless it were in a name in Greek letters, which I afterward saw scored upon the rocks of Mubrak en-Nâga, (ΚΥΡΙΔΚΟϹ).

El-Héjr was still a small village in the tenth century ; many villages were in the hollow ground from thence towards Medina, and full of people even in the times of our Crusades : to-day they are silent sites of ruins, there is no memory even of their names among the people of the country. By the Borj rocks are some broken palm-yard walls, with ruins of clay houses ; these are not so old as a century. Zeyd's grandfather, the great sheykh of his tribe, had brought husbandmen from Teyma to irrigate this fruitful loam and dwell here under his protection. Large were their harvests, and they had ready sale to the Beduins. The Teyma colonists were bye and bye thriving, although they paid a part of the fruit to their nomad landlords. The men having in few years gotten silver enough to buy themselves wells and palm grounds at home, returned to Teyma. I asked why they abandoned the place, where their labours prospered. Zeyd answered, " Because it is *khála*," the empty solitary waste where they were never in assurance of their own lives. Westwards a mile from the kella, I found great clay walls upon foundations of rude stone-laying without mortar ; those abandoned buildings were of old outlying granges, as we see them in some provinces of Nejd. The bare clay walling will stand under this barren climate for ages. The fatness of the Héjr loam is well known in the country ; many have sown here, and awhile, the Arabs told me, they fared well, but always in the reaping-time there has died some one of them. A hidden mischief they think to be in all this soil once subverted by divine judgments, that it may never be tilled again or inhabited. Malignity of the soil is otherwise ascribed by the people of Arabia, to the ground-demons, *jan*, *ahl el-ard* or earth-folk. Therefore husbandmen in these parts use to sprinkle new break-land with the blood of a peace offering : the like, when they build, they sprinkle upon the stones, lest by any evil accidents the workmen's lives should be endangered. Not twenty years before one of the Fehjies (of whom a few households are planters of small palm-grounds, without the walls of Teyma) enclosed some soil at el-Héjr within gunshot of the kella. He digged a well-pit and planted palms and sowed corn. The harvest was much and his pumpkins and water melons passed any that can be raised in the sand bottom at el-Ally ; but his fatal day overtook him in the midst of this fair beginning, and the young man dead, his honest enterprise was abandoned.

At Christmas time there fell a pious Mohammedan festival, *eth-thahîa*, when a sheep is slaughtered in every well-faring household, of which they send out portions to their poorer neighbours. The morning come, they all shot off their guns in the kella and sat down to breakfast together. The nomads devoutly keep this feast : there is many a poor man that for his father, lately deceased, will then slaughter a camel.

Certain *sânies* (Arabians of the smith's caste) arrived before noon from Teyma, who although it was a festival day sat down bye and bye to their metal trade ; their furnace-hearth is hollowed in the sand. One forges, another handles the pair of bellows-skins ; they were to tin all the copper vessels for the new year and mend the old matchlocks and swords of Haj Nejm, in the armoury of the kella : the infirm but valorous old Moor had taken the most of them in the pursuit of hostile ghrazzûs. The smiths, notwithstanding their soon smutched faces, were well-faring men at Teyma, where they dwelt in good houses and I afterward knew them. The witty-handed smiths and always winning, are mostly prudent heads ; and suffering themselves in the peevish public opinion, they are tolerant more than other men. They came about this country once a year, and sojourned three months tinkering at el-Ally ; they would thither this afternoon with some of the garrison who must go to the village to barter their government wheat for rice and fetch up the mules' forage. I thought also to visit the oasis in their company.

At *el-assr* (mid afternoon) we set forth ; Hasan and the lad Mohammed were those of the kella. These were perilous times ; the jehâd was now waged against a part of Christendom. At Damascus we had long time dreaded a final rising and general massacre of the Nasâra ; the returning post messenger might soon bring down heavy tidings. It was well I parted excellent friends from the aga, who followed me with these words : " Khalîl is as one, wellah, who has been bred up among us." I reminded Haj Nejm, as we joined hands, that we were neighbours in the West. " Ay, wellah, he answered, neighbours." Besides the sânies there went with us a bevy of Fehját women to the town, to sell what trifles they had found upon the ground of the Haj encampment ; but as Hasan would (for all the Arabs are thus evil tongued), sooner to make a dishonest commerce of themselves. One of these, *Kathâfa*, Doolan's daughter, strode foremost of the female company, bearing her father's matchlock upon her stalwart shoulder ; for all the way to el-Ally is full of crags, and the straits, a little before the town, are often beset by *habalîs*, thievish rovers from the Tehâma, mostly of the here dreaded Howeytát. Haj Nejm told us how he had been shot at in the boghrâz, a bullet thrilled his red cap, a second whissed by his cheek and spattered upon the rock nigh behind him. The last year Mohammed Aly was set upon there, as he went down with some of the garrison to el-Ally. Hostile Beduins rose suddenly upon them from the tamarisk thicket, braving with their spears, leaping and lulli-looing. If we were attacked said the strong Hasan, he would take to the mountain side ;—the Arabs think themselves half out of danger, when they have the advantage of ground, and can shoot down upon their adversaries.

Hasan and Mohammed riding at the mule's best pace, I bade them slack a little ; the aga had given order that we should mount by shifts, and little prosperous in health, I could not hold the way thus on foot with them. ' We durst not pass the straits, said Hasan, after the sun ; it was late already and if I could not go he must abandon me, like as by the living God he would forsake his own father which begat him ; if I mishapped he would say that robbers met with us and I was fallen in the strife. Am I, he cried, a man to obey the aga !' Laying hold of the mule furnitures I helped myself forward along with them, until past the middle way, when Hasan seeing I could go no further, bade the *askar* (soldier) lad dismount, whom he named to me in disdain " that Beduwy," and they helped me to the saddle. I enquired of the sânies " Where will ye lodge at el-Ally, in the sheykh's 'house ? " They answered " Where we are going there is no hospitality ; the people of el-Ally are hounds."—They keep not here, in lowland Hejâz, the frank and hospitable customs of Nejd or uplandish Arabia.

The latter way lies by the south-east corner of the Harra, and through a maze of sandstone crags *el-Akhma* which are undercliffs of the same mountain. Here was the former haj road, which passed by el-Ally ; and once not many years ago a haj pasha led his caravan, this way, to Bîr el-Ghrannem :—it was forsaken, as too dangerously encumbered with rocks and strait passages. The bottom is mostly deep sand ; in low places under the rocks there grow tamarisks, which taste saltish, and harsh bent grass. Four or five miles above el-Ally we came (always descending from el-Héjr) to little ancient wells of three fathoms, *el-Atheyb*, with corrupt water. Thirsting in the winter sun we halted, and Mohammed, as it is commonly seen in the East, climbed down to draw for us. Not far from thence begins that *Boghrâz el-Ally*, between the lofty sandstone cliffs *Moallak el-Hameydy*, of the Harra, and high ruddy precipices of that wild barrier of low mountains which closes the plain of Medáin Sâlih to the southward, *el-Hùtheba, J. Rumm, Moâtidal*. Under this left side in the boghrâz is seen a white bank of stone heaps mingled with loam ; plainly the antique ground of a town of stone houses, that are fallen down in the clay which united them.

This is that site they call *el-Khreyby* "The little Ruin," in the midst I saw the famous stone cistern, nejjar or jurn, shaped as those smaller which we have seen in the Héjr plain (fig. p. 134), which is called "the milking-pail of Néby Sâlih's nâga."

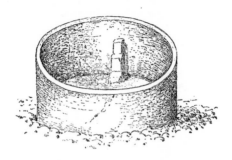

The sun setting, my companions hastened to pass. I saw as it were doorways hewn in those cliffs, they seemed to be of some funeral chambers. The company showed me upon the rocky height above, *el-Kella*, a square pinnacle, wherein they believe to be sealed some great treasure. Said Haj Hasan, "Khalîl! hast thou not an art to raise this wealth and so take it half for thyself and half for us? divide it thus, we are thy fellowship."

The outlying palms of the town were now before us; here is a range of pits, air holes, of a water-mine or aqueduct running underground to the oasis,—a work, as all such in these lands, of the antique Arabians. We crossed there the freshet bed which descends from Medáin Sâlih, almost never flushed with rain, the seyl goes out below to the great Hejâz wady, W. el-Humth; in these parts named as often W. el-Jizzl. We heard already the savage rumour of their festival, shots fired and an hideous drumming. The town yet hidden, my companions turned to ask me what heart I had to enter with them. I answered in their manner, that "I left all unto God." The Alowna are noted, by the Aarab, to be of a tyrannical humour within their own palms, and faint heart in the field. Indeed all town Arabs, among whom is less religion of guestship, are dangerous, when their heads are warm and their hearts elated, with arms in their hands. There wanted but some betraying voice from our company, some foolish woman's crying "Out upon this kafir!" and my life might be ended by a rash shot. Hasan said this maliciously in my ear, who displeased to-day with his aga, in any trouble had not perhaps stood by me: but he found it himself an awry world. Arrived before the town gate, at an open ground under the Harra side, where a throng of villagers was keeping holiday, one stepped forth to attach his white mule, for an ancient debt of Haj Nejm. Strenuous was then the guttural contention of the Moghreby's throat, and yet he durst not resist ; the hated Alowna were too many for him : the people thronged upon us. Hasan looked pale in the twilight ; and the two contentious went away together with an idle rabble, and the mule, to swear before the *kâdy* or village Justice.

With the lad Mohammed I passed through the glooming streets, to the house of the Sheykh of el-Ally, *Dâhir ;* and he there coming forth to receive me, I was surprised in that half light to see him a partly negro man, and to hear the African voice. Dâhir led me to his upper house, which for the dampness of the ground in these Hejâz oases, is their dwelling chamber. The lad Mohammed recited to him the aga's charge, and, taking off his kerchief-cord, he bound the sheykh's neck with it, saying that such was the bidding of Mohammed Aly, and that he bound him surety to answer for me. The Semitic life is full of significant gestures, and sacramental signs. The Christian religion has signs in this kind, of the noblest significance. The Christian is once washed from the old sinful nature, to walk in newness of life ; he eateth bread and salt with Jesus at the Lord's table ; such tokens being even declared necessary to salvation. Dâhir, who had the lips, the hair, the eyes of an Ethiopian with the form of the Arabs, boasted himself a sheykh of ancestry in the lineage of Harb. He was the sheykh here after his father, as the Beduin sheykhs succeed, by inheritance. I think there are few in the town who show not the mixture of African blood ; yet they will deny it and fetch their descent from old Moghreby colonists, and Jeheyna, and Harb, and Beny Sókhr : but the Moors might have been as well Moorish negroes, since the name of an Arabic tribe or nation is of both free and bond. The nomads think those squalid and discoloured visages to be come so of the working of their close valley climate. There are Harb settlers of the full blood, in those many hot oases betwixt the Harameyn, which are blackish as Africans ; but they have pure lineaments of Arabs.

The resettlement of the ground and foundation of el-Ally is ascribed to a palmers' fellowship of forty Barbary derwishes. Journeying upon the Syrian haj road, with their religious master, from Mecca and Medina, they were pleased with the solitary site, where they had found ruins. The holy man bade his disciples await him there, whilst he went up to pray in

Jerusalem. " How, they answered him, may we endure this desert place and there is nothing to drink ? " Then the saint struck his burdon in the sand, and there welled up a vein of water ; it is that lukewarm brook which waters their village : also his Jacob's staff put down roots and became a palm tree.

Dâhir regaled me with a little boiled rice ; slender supper fare to set before strangers in the hospitable eyes of the nomads : he made also coffee of a bean which had lost all savour, and with a shallow gracious countenance, bade me tell him truly if this were not good to drink. We see in the Arab's life that those which need most are of most hospitality. Famine is ever in the desert, it is therefore in men's eyes a noble magnanimity to set meat before the wayfaring man. The sheykh of el-Ally sat demurely in a mantle of scarlet ; such as it is the custom of the Dowla to bestow upon principal sheykhs in token of government favour. An astute sober man he was, very peaceable in his talk ; Dâhir waited among my words that he might imagine what countryman I was. In this there surprised me the impassioned solitary voice of a muetthin, intoned in the winter's night, from the roof of the village mosque (*mesjid*) next to us (here are no minarets) crying to the latter prayers ; and Dâhir, with an elation of heart, which is proper to their comfortable Mohammedan faith, said immediately with devout sighing the same words after him,—words which seem to savour for ever of the first enthusiasis of the néby of the Arabs, " *The only God, He is above all ; I do bear witness that there is no god but God alone, and I bear witness that Mohammed is the Messenger of God.*" Dâhir turned to watch me, that if a Moslem my heart also should have danced after the piper : when I looked but coldly upon it, this seemed to certify him ; for there is no Mohammedan, of whatever good or evil living and condition he be, whose heart is not knit to the fresh faith of the " Apostle's " religion and who will not pray fervently. Sheykh Dáhir said now very soberly, " If thou art not a Moslem, tell me what art thou, Khalîl ; I am as thy father, and is not this a town of the Moslemîn ? " He would say where is no Beduin wildness, but a peaceable civil life in God's fear, under the true religion.

Dâhir went out to his devotion in the mesjid ; and returning within a while the elder found his young housewife, and mother of his two younger sons, sitting in his place by the hearth, curious to discourse with a stranger, and hardly he rebuked her as if she had forgot her modesty. " Woman, and thou givest me every day a cause, I shall put thee away ! " he bid her remove, and sit further off in the gloom of the chamber ; thus their poor housewives are banished from the warmth and light of the cheerful coffee fire, the husband sitting alone with his friends, in their own houses, if the company be not some of their nigh kindred. In Nejd there is made, as in the nomad tent, a woman's apartment. Here I think not many men have more wives than one, those that I knew were all simple couples. When he questioned me again I answered " I hope it may seem nothing very hard to you, that I am of the Engleys, which are allies of the Sûltan, as you have heard, and they are Nasâra ; and I am a Nasrâny, does this displease you ?   So many Christians are in the Sûltan's country that Stambûl is half full of them." And he ; " Well, Khalîl, repose thyself here without carefulness of heart this night, we shall see what may be good to do on the morrow."

The morning come, as I walked upon the house terrace, I heard it cried by children from the next roofs " Aha ! he that neither prays nor fasts,—Aha, it is he."   I knew then that malicious tongues of some of the company from el-Héjr had betrayed me. As I heard this cry I would gladly have been out of the town, for it had been said over the coffee fire in the kella, that these free villagers are very zealous of their religion and would be ready to kill me.   The sheykh was abroad ; Hasan then coming in, who had slept at the kâdy's, I went out with him, and on through the narrow ways to the kâdy's *kahwa* (coffee-house) ; there the coffee-drinkers with sober cheer gave place to a stranger and the pourer-out handed me the cup of hospitality.   They sat with those pithless looks of the Alowna, as it were men in continual languor of fevers under that lurid climate ; and this is the Hejâz humour, much other than the erect bird-like mind and magnanimous behaviour of Nomad, that is Nejd Arabia. The young men abroad were perfumed, and sat idle in the streets in the feast day, which these townsmen keep till the third morrow ; their nails and the palms of their hands, they had now barbarously stained yellow with henna. This is their sight is an amiable quaintness of young gentlemen ; and some among them had dressed their fleecy locks in the fringe of many little cords, not as the bold nomads' few plaited locks, but in Ethiopian manner.

The narrow town ways are very clean but much darkened with over-building, less I can suppose because there is not much ground-room, than, in their stagnant air, for a freshness of upper chambers. At every door is made a clay bench in Arab-wise, where householders and passengers may sit friendly discoursing and " drink " tobacco. There is no filth cast in their streets, dogs may not enter the place, which is well-built and decent more than almost any Syrian village.   Here is an open bazaar, small wares of the daily provision are sold after sunrise at the street corners ;

butchers sell mutton and goat-flesh at half-afternoon without
the walls : everyone is a merchant, of the fruits of his own ground,
at home in his own house. Hasan when we were again in the
street, meeting with some of his late adversaries, began to chide
anew with them ; the great heart swelled in his Moghreby
breast that any Alowwy durst lay hand upon the white mule " to
detain the service of the Sooltàn." Among the next benchers
I sat down ; the people were peaceable and spoke friendly with
me, none reproached me. Dâhir's son came to call me to
breakfast, I saw as we went an Himyaric inscription very fairly
sculptured, in embossed letters, in the casement of one of the
over-built chambers ; whilst I stood to transcribe it, no one
molested me. Dâhir brought me afterward to his kahwa,
every sheykh has such a public chamber, where coffee is served
at certain hours. They are here ground chambers, and commonly under the stairs of the host's dwelling-floor above.

All the house building is here of rude stones, brought from el-
Khreyby, and laid in loam for mortar. El-Ally is a stone-built
Moslem village in the manner of antiquity, and though the
Mohammedan Arabs are nearly always clay-builders ;—nor is it
because their sandy loam will not bind into bricks. Their rafters
are of *ethl* (sing. *ethla*), the tall-growing kind of tamarisk, and
palm beams ; the doors of palm boards rudely fashioned with
the axe. In the midst of their street doors this sign (of which
no one would give me any interpretation,) is
often stained in red ochre or coaled with
charcoal ; it might, I thought, be the wasm
of nomad forefathers of the town. A koran
verset is often written above. The fasten-
ing, as in all Arabic places, is a wooden lock : the bolt is
detained by little pegs falling from above into apposite holes,
the key is a wooden stele, some have them of metal, with
teeth to match the holes of the lock : the key put in under,
you strike up the pegs and the slot may be withdrawn. To
the ringing of the coffee-pestle a company entered, of those
sitting idle upon the street benches. No one altered his behaviour as they saw the Christian come among them, they
talked and drank round ; but after the cup they said, " Here,
Khalîl, you are safe in a town of Islam. At el-Ally is good
company and all that one may need is at hand ; were it not
more pleasant to live here, than lodged with those askars in
the kella at el-Héjr ? " Thus they spoke, because there are
none, who have not an ill opinion of their town. The impatient nomads complain, as in all settled places, of *el-wákh'm*,
the filth, the garbage (though cast without the town walls), the

stagnant air, and the rotten-smelling (sulphurous) brook-water, of which if they drink but a hearty draught, they think themselves in danger of the oasis fever.

I would have returned with Hasan to Medáin, where I hoped to find some manner of scaling the high frontispices ; the aga had promised me the old well-shaft which lay in the kella, and might serve for a ladder. I should otherwise have thought it great peace and refreshment, to stay still shadowing out some days in pleasant discourse in the sweet lemon-groves at el-Ally.—But Hasan had loaded and was departed. When the coffee friends bore out my baggage to the gate, we saw him already far distant : the lad Mohammed, having a contention with him came loitering after. The villagers laid my bags upon his mule, but he flung them down, and when I insisted the cowardly lad thrust his matchlock to my breast. Dâhir bade me, let this worthless fellow go, and he would send me himself to the kella ; the Alowna, despised by the men of the garrison, have small goodwill towards the " nefers " again. We went homeward, and the sheykh said " There is now brotherhood between us, and thou art as my son, Khalîl."

Sitting on the benches they asked me questions in friendly sort and after their fiction of the world, as " What is the tax which ye, the Nasâra, must pay for your heads [as not Moslems] to the Sooltàn ? " I said, " Our Lady the Queen, Empress of India, is the greatest Sultan of el-Islam." And they : " But is not el-Hind a land of the Moslemîn ?—alas ! el-Islam *râhh*, passeth away ! What then is the poll-tax that the Moslemîn pay to the Nasâra rulers, eigh ! Khalîl ? " When I answered that all the subjects of the Sultana enjoy equal civil rights, of what nation soever they be or religion, this they found good, since it was to the profit of the Moslemîn : " But, Wellah ! (tell us sooth by God) what brings thee hither ? "—" I came but to visit el-Héjr." I wondered to see this people of koran readers, bred up in a solitary valley of desolate mountains amidst immense deserts, of that quiet behaviour and civil understanding. The most of the men are lettered but not all ; children learn only from the fathers : there are two or three schools held in the mosques, in the month of Ramadan. In that rude country the people of el-Ally (often called the Medîna or City) pass for great scripture-read scholars. The town pronunciation is flat like the rest of their nature, thus for *el-mà*, water, they utter an almost sheep-like *mé*." Some said to me, " Our tongue here is rude, we speak Bedúish." It is nearly I think that Hejâz Arabic which I heard afterward in the mouths of the Harb Beduins of Medina. El-Ally, in their opinion, is " the beginning of the Hejâz."

They are devout in religion, mild, musing, politic rather than fanatics, and such was Mohammed himself ; whereas Nejd men, of the nomad blood, are more testy and sudden in their fanaticism. These townsmen (whether partly descended from them or no) are of the religious rite of the Moghrebies, *el-malakîeh.* I saw many, the sheykh among them, scrupulous, as in abstaining from tobacco, rather than worthy men.

El-Ally was never made subject ; yet these villagers tax, themselves, their dates and corn every year and send this freewill offering " to the Néby," that is to the temple of Medina : they are content to be called friends of the Dowla. Once in the strong Waháby days nigh fifty years ago, Ibn Saûd came with his band and a piece of cannon to have occupied el-Ally. For a time they lay before the place and never could speed, their gun could not be shot off : so said the Waháby people, " This is the will of Ullah ; look now ! let us be going, it is in vain that we sit before el-Ally ; "—and they turned from them. The Beduins say, " the Alowna are confident within their plantations, but abroad they are less than women." The oasis, in *Wady Kurra,* is the third of a mile over (*v.* next page). W. Kurra (Kora) is all that hollow ground which lies from hence to Medina, and commonly called *W. Deydibbàn ;* although this be no true wady. It is the dry waterways of two descending wadies, which meet at the midst ; namely the W.. Jizzl from these northern parts, and the W. el-Humth which descends by el-Medina from above *Henakîeh,* passing betwixt the mount *Ehad* or *J. Hamzy* and their prophet's city.

The Alowna live quietly under their own sheykhs. Dâhir was sheykh by inheritance ; not much less in authority and in more esteem was the kâdy Mûsa ; his is also an inherited office, to be arbiter of the Arabs' differences. Mûsa, who could read, was a koran lawyer ; the village justices (which is admirable) handle no bribes nor for affection pervert justice, but they receive some small fee for their labour. Mûsa's was a candid just soul, not common amongst Arabs ; to him resorted even the nomad tribesmen about, for the determining of their differences out of " the word of Ullah " ; though they have sheykhs and arbiters of their own, after the tradition of the desert. The kâdy in such townships appoints the ransom for every lesser crime and the price of blood. They live here kindly together, surrounded by the hostile nomads ; human crimes may hardly spring in so lowly soil. Under this sickly climate, even their young men are sober ; most rarely is there any ruffling of rash heads among them. When homicide or other grave crime is committed, the guilty with his next kindred must flee from the

D. T. 10

place. After seven years are out, they may return and agree
for the blood at a price.

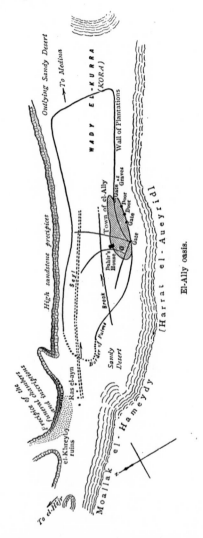

I walked unheeded in the streets of el-Ally and transcribed
the inscriptions [here all Himyaric] which I found ofttimes upon
building stones, or to which any friendly persons would lead me.
There were other, they said, in their inner walls of certain houses.

Yet some illiberal spirits blamed them, from their benches, where
we passed. I wandered now alone through the sûks or wards,
whereof twenty-four are counted in all the town, and whereso I
heard t o cheerful knelling of a coffee-pestle, (sign of a sheykh's
kahwa) I entered. Every public coffee-room is of a fraternity or
sheykh's partiality, where also any stranger, who is commonly the
marketing Beduwy, is welcome : there neighbours sit to discourse
soberly and " drink smoke " ; but small is their coffee, for all are
of the sparing hand at el-Ally. It is noted of the Alowna
that they go always armed in their own streets ;—that might
be from a time when these townsmen were yet few in land of
the Aarab. They pass by armed to prayers in the mesjids ; the
elders bear their swords or have some short spear in their
hands, poorer folk go with long oaken quarter staves, *nabût,* or
shûn. This is the people's weapon in Hejâz, and therewith certain factious sûks in Mecca keep the old custom (notwithstanding
the sanctity of the soil and the Turk's strong garrison), to break
each other's brows and bones, sometime in the round year,—
their riots must be dispersed by the soldiery. The fighting-bat is
an old Semitic weapon : hand-staves are mentioned in the book
of Samuel and by Ezekiel. The bedels and rake-hell band of
the chief priest came armed to the garden, to take Jesus, with
swords and staves. As they enter the mosque they leave their
bats standing in the entry where they put off their sandals :
these seen at a house doorway are to any stranger the sign of
an Ally kahwa. Upon their earthen floors is spread some
squalid palm matting, which is plaited by the women in all
palm settlements. Commonly I saw the *darraga,* target or
buckler, hanging at the foot of the house stairs, where I entered ;
this is also Hejâz usage, there are none seen in upland Arabia.
Those coffee drinkers have the sorry looks of date-eaters and
go not freshly clad. The nomad kerchief, cast loosely upon
their heads, is not girded with the circlet-band (*agâl*),—which is
the dignity of the Arab clothing. The calico tunics are rusty
and stiffened upon their backs with powder and sweat ; for soap
(from Syria) is too dear for them. The swarming of stinging
flies in the hot winter noon in the date village, was little less
than under the sepulchral rocks at el-Héjr.

Jid, or patriarch of el-Ally, (in the Semitic manner to
lead up every people from a sire,—thus Arabians have
asked me, " Who is he the Jid of the Engleys ? ") they name
Allowîy, whose people expelled the B. Sókhr. The place was
called then *Baith Naam,* some say *Shaab en-Naam.* Later
they find the town written in their old parchments *Búndur
Aulánshy* (*Alúshy*) or *Bundar Alût.* It is said there are

10—2

even now Beduin families of B. Sókhr, who draw their due of dates every year from el-Ally. The migration of the Beduin tribes is commonly upon some drought or warfare ; there are great changes thus in few centuries in the nomad occupation of the Peninsula.

Two days after my coming the morrow broke with thunder and showers ; the rain lasted till another morning : in nearly three years they had not seen the like. My lodging was always the sheykh's upper chamber, and almost every well-faring elder at el-Ally has two or three houses :—a dwelling-house for himself and his housewife, the house perhaps of his children by a former wife, or of his married son, and his store-house. Dâhir's upper-room walls were hanged with little flails of fine palm-straw ware, gauded with ties of scarlet and small sea shells, (surely African rather than the curiosity of Arabs !) and with mats of the same, *sufra*, which all Arabic villagers spread at meat under the tray of victuals. African in my eyes is the gibing humour of this Hejâz population. There is an industry here, amongst a few families, of weaving harsh white summer mantles of the Beduins' wool, *berdàn*.

The Arabians inhabit a land of dearth and hunger, and there is no worse food than the date, which they must eat in their few irrigated valleys. This fruit is overheating and inwardly fretting under a sultry climate ; too much of cloying sweet, not ministering enough of brawn and bone ; and therefore all the date-eaters are of a certain wearish visage, especially the poorer Nejd villagers, whereas well-faring men from the same oases are of a pleasant, so to say, honest aspect : a glance might discern among them all the countenance of the milk-drinking Beduins. Where the date is eaten alone, as they themselves say, human nature decays, and they drink a lukewarm ground-water, which is seldom wholesome in these parts of the world. I have nowhere in Arabia seen such an improbity, so to speak, of the facial lineaments (here infected with negro blood) as in this township of el-Ally, and though theirs be the best dates in the country. What squalor of bones ! the upper face is sunken and flattened, the jaw nearly brute-like and without beard. Yet a few families are seen of better blood, whitish and ruddy, as the kâdy Mûsa and his adherents descended (they pretend) from B. Sókhr. The faces of these townsmen are so singular, that I could find one Alowwy, even without his white mantle, in the thickest market press in Damascus.

The women go closely veiled, and live in the jealous (Hejâz or Moorish) tyranny of the husbands ; their long and wide wimples

are loaded with large glittering shards of mother-of pearl shells
from el-Wejh. The wives of my acquaintance, that I have
seen in their houses partly unveiled, were abject-looking and
undergrown, without grace of womanhood. The Semitic woman's
nose-ring, such as Abraham's steward brought to fair Rebekah,
(it moved the choler of the prophet Isaiah to see them in the
fair faces of his townswomen,) wide here as the brim of a coffee-
cup, is hanged in the right nostril and loaded with minute
silver money ; their foreheads are set out with like clusters in
the hair. They make, as the daughters of Jerusalem, a tinkle-
tinkle as they go, and perfume their clothing ; which may be
perceived as a sickly odour in the street where any woman has
lately passed. Timid they are of speech, for dread of men's
quick reprehending : the little girls wear a round plate of
mother-of-pearl suspended at the breast, their heads are loaded
with strings and bunches of small silver.

As I walked by the streets, if any children cried after me
" Aha ! the Nasrâny ! " the elder men turned to rebuke them.
Where I sat down in any kahwa, a confortable text was
commonly spoken among them, *kul wàhed aly dîn-hu*, " every
one in his own religion." The sheykhly persons, fearing to utter
ignorances before the people, forbore to question the stranger ;
but they lent a busy ear whilst the popular sort asked me
of many things, and often very fondly as " Wellah ! is there
not in the Christian seas, a land where they breed up black
men to eat them ? " One who had been in Damascus related
that the Christians in their great mid-winter festival (Christmas)
offered in sacrifice a Mohammedan ; but others who had visited
the north disputed with him, saying that it was not so. Some
of them said " the Nasâra be not so malignant towards the
Moslemîn, as the Yahûd ; the Jews are heathens and theirs
is a secret religion." Another answered, " Nay, but they worship
the *thôr*, steer, (that is Aaron's calf)." I said, " The Jews have
a law of God delivered by the hand of Moses, which you call
the *Towrat*, they worship God alone." It was answered, " If this
be so they do rightly, but the Yahûd are of cursed kind, and
they privily murder the Moslemîn."

CHAPTER VI.

EL-ALLY, EL-KHREYBY, MEDAIN.

A Jew arrived at el-Ally. A Turkish Pasha banished thither. The warm brook of the oasis. The orchards. The population. Abundance of rice from el-Wejh. Dâhir's talk. Abu Rashîd. An Arabic Shibboleth. Practice of medicine. Fanaticism in the town. Arabs have wandered through the African Continent very long ago. A Christian (fugitive) who became here a Moslem. The Khreyby is one of the villages of Hejra. Himyarite tombs and inscriptions. The Mubbiát. Korh. Antara, hero-poet. , Dâhir's urbanity. Return to Medáin. Violence of M. Aly. His excuses. Ladder-beam to scale the monuments. The epitaphs impressed. Rain in Arabia. The sculptured birds. Sculptured human masks. The Semitic East a land of sepulchres. The simple Mohammedan burial. " The sides of the pit " in Isaiah and Ezekiel. The Nabatean manner to bury. A sealed treasure upon the rock Howwâra : to remove it were the end of the world. A Moorish magical raiser of hid treasures. Miracles of the East. A Syrian Messiah in Damascus. Visit to the house of fools Blasphemous voice of the camel. Sepulchre of the prophet Jonas. The judgment of Europeans weakened by sojourn in the East. Hydrography. The nejjâb arrives. The Moslem and the European household life. All world's troubles are kindled by the hareem. They trust the Nasâra more than themselves. Beduin robbers of the Haj. A night alarm. Habalîs or foot robbers. Alarms continually about us. Contentious hareem corrected with the rod.

I HEARD here, from many credible persons, that a certain Yahûdy was once come to them some years before, they thought from the coast ; others said from Jerusalem. They had found a pleasure in the stranger's discourse ; for he was of the Arabic tongue, one well studied therein and eloquent : also they heard from him many admirable things of the Jewish Scriptures, " which were not far from their own thoughts, and agreeable with many places of ' God's word.' " Some of the principal persons had called him to eat with them. The Yahûdy went upon a day to visit Medáin Sâlih, and returned saying, those old monuments were of the Nasâra, (neither Jew nor Mohammedan has any natural curiosity in architecture). They could

not certainly tell me what became of him ; some thought
he had gone from them to Kheybar. Later at Teyma, the
sheykh spoke to me of a stranger who had passed there not
many years ago, and stayed a day or two in his house, " one who
would not travel upon the *sabt* " (Sabbath). When afterwards
I was at Kheybar, the villagers told me of a Yahûdy, who
came thither from el-Ally as they supposed ; for Arabs, so
remiss in the present, are commonly fatally incurious of all
time past. ' He remained in their valleys to seek for treasure ;
he had been found in fault with some woman of the place ;
he fell sick and perished,' I could not learn in what manner ;—
it might be they would not frankly tell me. When the coffee-
drinkers required me to speak some noble word out of my
religion, I said to them, " Honour thy father and thy mother,"
and with this they were very well pleased. Though a sober
and religious people, I saw card-playing used amongst them ;
this carding is spread to the Hejâz villages from the town coffee-
houses and dissolute soldiers' quarters of Medina. In Medina
there is much tippling in *arrak*, brutish hemp smoking and
excess of ribald living.

Dâhir was the more careful of me as he heard that the
Haj functionaries had charged the kella keepers for my safety.
He remembered, in his father's time, a certain pasha, fallen
into disgrace at Stambûl :—when the Sultan had demanded ' into
what extreme part of his dominions he might banish his courtier
out of the world for ever ; ' it was answered him, " There is
beyond Syria a little oasis of palms lying out by the haj road,
in land of the Beduw." The poor gentleman, relegated to
el-Ally, lodged two years in the house of the sheykh, Dâhir's
father. The Sultan after that time, remembering his ancient
kindness, sent for the sad exile and restored him, and commanded that money should be given to the village sheykh,
with his imperial firmàn, naming him " a well-doer to the
Dowla."

Their date-groves and corn-plots are in the breadth of the
W. el-Kurra, irrigated by the lukewarm brook, and by some other
lesser springs which rise in the midst of the oasis, all of flat and
ill-tasting tepid water, exhaling a mephitic odour, as the sulphurous stream at Palmyra. In all are the same small turreted
shells, and in this brook side I found much growth of a kind of
fresh-water sponges. The warmth of the strong-running channel
which is two and a half feet deep, I found to be constantly 92° F. ;
that was in the village three or four hundred paces from the
mouth of the conduit, and thrice as much perhaps from the
source. The watercourse reeks in the chill of the morning : in

it the townsmen wash themselves as they go to the mesjids, and there are made some enclosed bathing-places, above, for women. The height of the oasis I found equal to the land-height of Damascus! this I could not have guessed without the instrument, but the Arabs divined it; and Haj Nejm was constant in the opinion that the plain of Medáin must lie a little above the soil of Damascus. The outlying palms above the level of the springs, are watered out of well-pits dug to twenty-seven feet in the sand and twenty wide. This ground-water, which is cooler and brackish, is drawn by the walking to and fro of their small humped kine.

The orchards of palms and sweet lemons are very well hus-banded. The higher grounds of the shelving valley side are digged out deeply, to the irrigating spring level; so that the public paths seemed to be raised as wide walls which divide those plantations, and the beautiful spreading heads of palms, not here tall-growing, appear as rising from the floor of the ground. Many crooked palms spring together from one stem; they are old suckers let grow to trees when the mother stock is fallen. Here in the Hejâz they sell their refreshing sweet lemons to the Haj: but bargaining of fruits (not being food, as dates) would be unbecoming any honourable man in the near Nejd. The orange is unknown, so far as I have seen, in Arabia. There are not many vines, but every family has some plant or two, never pruned, climb-ing upon trees or in trellises, for their refreshment in the hot midsummer. Of stone fruit they have no more than the plum, though some of their young men go up every year to Damascus, to hire themselves as husbandmen. They cultivate upon the ground, as in the other Arabian villages, great pumpkins, *dibba*, of which gobbets, as it were fat flesh, are mingled with their weak porridge, and they think this a supper to set before guests. It is delicious to see all this beautiful burden of green upon a soil which is naturally naked loam-bottom, and driving desert sand. Besides the small humped kine for their field labour they have a few weak asses for carriage; almost every household has a milch goat or two and poultry. There were no more than two horses in the town; of what service should the warlike animals be to so unwarlike masters? The Alowna will pay no " brothership " to the Beduw for their town, which they never quit, unless to ride sometime in their lives, with the Haj, to the holy places, or ascend with the returning caravan to Syria.

All the cultivated oasis is nigh two miles, the town is narrow, upon the wady side, under the Harra. From those cliffs, I have seen all the houses together to be about four hundred. The population I had otherwise estimated at

1300 persons, yet the townspeople guess themselves to be 5000 or 6000 souls ! The Beduins say they are 1500 guns, that is, as I have commonly found in their reckonings, nearly the true tale of all souls, 1500 persons. They raise much more of their palms and corn grounds than suffices them ; that which is over they sell for silver to the Beduw, and many hoards of coffered reals are said to be lying in the town. They take up with their dates also much India rice, which is brought hither in the sack from el-Wejh (el-Wésh), the Red Sea coast village, and rice-*bundur* of all this north-west country ; this they sell again to the nomads. Middle men in the traffic are certain Bíllî Beduins : the Beduwy rice-carrier will take up his lading from the Wejh merchants, two sacks for a camel, at ten reals. For the same at el-Ally, six journeys after, through their own mostly peaceable dîra, he can have sixteen to twenty reals, or may load home dates in bales of palm matting, from this cheap market. Yet the poor Beduins are not much allured by such gains of their honest industry, neither think they again of the road whilst they have anything left to eat at home with their families. We see at el-Ally the simplest kind of trading and interchange of commodities. The price of rice inland from the coast, is so raised by the intolerable cost of camel-carriage, that it is hardly found so far as Teyma. The Beduins beyond use wheaten messes, or they draw *temmn*, that is river-rice from Mesopotamia. Of Ally dates the helw kind, soft and tasting almost like honey, is stored in old girby skins, *shenna, mujellad;* beginning to dry they crystallize. Many shennas are carried up every year in the Syrian Haj, and the honey-date of el-Ally is served for a sweetmeat to visiting guests in Mohammedan homes, at Damascus. The *bérni* date, long and wan, is their cheaper household food, and of this there are many kinds. The town is walled under the Harra, which dams from them the healthful western or sea winds, and open from the side of the orchards. There are two main gates, besides doors, from the desert, the woodwork in my time was ruinous ; they were never shut.

Long were the evenings at Dâhir's coffee fire, where there came no visiting guests. Dâhir was very discreet and covert to enquire what place I held in my own country ; that seeing me regarded by the Dowla, he knew not what manner of man might be under my Arab cloak. When he pressed me I answered, " I have none other than the trade of *fúlsifa* (φιλοσοφία), it is pleasant to secede from the town to the silent desert."—" And does this bring thee alone to el-Héjr, when thou wast well at home,—to this perilous land of the Aarab, to suffer

much disease ? "—" Why should we fear to live or to die, so
be upon a rightful way ? when the heart is warm all thin
appear light."—" Words, my son ; and thine is a bootless ta;
for thou art out of the way, not being in the saving religior
Dâhir could not gainsay me when I alleged " Solomon father
David," (this is as they ignorantly speak,) a name veneral
amongst them, or when I praised el-fúlsify, also an honoural
word with them, or magnified learning above the excellenc
in the world.   " What need, said he, of all this learning ? t
one thing is needful, a man should know Ullah to be t
only God and his messenger Mohammed ; and all the rest
of little advantage.   Were it not better for thee, forsaki
these vanities, to confess the faith of Islam ? from hencefoi
leading thy life in this mild and peaceable way of the religio
which will be well for thy soul's safety at the last." And Dâl
smiling religious solace to himself, sighed with a sidelong lo
and upcasting of the eyes ; he snuffled in his holy talk li
an honest Roundhead.

There were lodging at el-Ally two Damascus tradesmen
the Medân, that come down with clothing-stuffs for the Bedu:
in every pilgrimage. I went at their request to pass an eveni
with them.   The men were sons of old kella keepers at Med;
Sâlih. One of them, Abu Rashîd, had trafficked to Egypt, a
could tell marvels of great cities lighted with gas, of waterwoi
and railroads, all made he affirmed by the Engleys whom
praised as the most ingenious and upright of the Frank natio:
This year he would send his son, he told us, to the English scho
in Syria :—the new technic instruction, (by which only they thi
they fall short of the Europeans,) is all the present appet
of such up-waked Mohammedan Arabs.   Taking a soler
volume in hand, bound in red leather, in which he studied
ligion and philosophy, he read forth where mention was made
the Platonical sect.   The barbarous Arabic authors, withc
knowledge of the tongues or times, discourse with disdain
ineptitude of the noblest human spirits which lived alm«
a thousand years before their beginning, and were not ;
quainted with their néby Mohammed.   Abu Rashîd not:
my imperfect and unready speech, " These Franks labour, s;
he, in the Arabic utterance, for they have not a supple tongu
the Arabs' tongue is running and returning like a wheel, a
in the Arabs all parts alike of the mouth and gullet are orga
of speech ; but your words are born crippling and fall half de
out of your mouths.—What think you of this country tall
have you not laughed at the words of the Beduw ? what is t.
gòtar (went)—A-ha-ha !—and for the time of day their *gowu*

(the Lord strengthen thee) and *keyf'mûrak* (how do thy affairs prosper ?) who ever heard the like !' " He told this also of the Egyptian speech : a battalion of Ibrahîm Pasha's troops had been closed in and disarmed by the redoubtable Druses, in the *Léja* (which is a lava field of the Hauran). The Druses coming on to cut them in pieces, a certain Damascene soldier among them cried out " Aha ! neighbours, *dakalakom*, grant protection, at least to the Shwâm (Syrians), which are *owlàd el-watn*, children of the same soil with you ! " It was answered, ' They would spare them if they could discern them.' ' Let me alone for that, said the Damascene ;—and if they caused the soldiers to pass one by one he could discern them.' It was granted, and he challenged them thus, " *Ragel* (Egyptian for *Rajil*), O man, say *Gamel!* " every Syrian answered *Jemel ;* and in this manner he saved his countrymen and the Damascenes.

I thought to begin here the vaccination and my practice of medicine. But no parents brought me their children, only few sick persons visited me, and those were nearly desperate cases, to enquire for medicines ; even such went back again when they understood they must spend for the remedies, though it were but two or three groats. If I said, Are not medicines the gift of Ullah ? they answered, " We are trusting in Ullah."—" But, when another day the disease is amongst you and your children dying before your faces ? "—" There can happen nothing but by the appointment of Ullah." This is the supine nature of Arabs, that negligence of themselves, and expectation of heaven to do all for them, which they take for a pious acquiescence in the true faith : this fond humour passed into their religion we have named the fatalism of Mohammedans. At el-Héjr the gate Arabs desired of me *hijabs* or amulets ; such papers, written with the names of Ullah, they would steep in water, and think themselves happy when they had drunk it down.

When tumblers come to a town the people are full of novelty, but having seen their fill they are as soon weary of them ; so these few peaceable days ended, I saw the people's countenances less friendly; the fanatical hearts of some swelled to see one walking among them that rejected the saving religion of the apostle of Ullah. If children cried after the heathen man, their elders were now less ready to correct them. A few ill-blooded persons could not spare to crake where I passed from their street benches : " Say Mohammed rasûl Ullah ! " but others blamed them. In an evening I had wandered to the oasis side : there a flock of the village children soon assembling

with swords and bats followed my heels, hooting, " O Nasrâny !
O Nasrâny ! " and braving about the kàfir and cutting crosses
in the sand before me, they spitefully defiled them, shouting
such a villanous carol, " We have eaten rice with *halîb*
(milk) and have made water upon the *salîb* (cross)." The
knavish boys followed ever with hue and cry, as it were in
driving some uncouth beast before them, until I came again to
the town's end, where they began to stone me. There was a
boy among the troop of dastardly children who ever stoutly
resisted the rest, and cursed with all his might the fathers that
begat them. With great tears in his eyes he walked backwards
opposing himself to them, as if he would shelter me with his
childish body ; so I said, " See, children, this is a *weled el-halàl*
(son of rightfulness), think rather to be such, every one of you,
than to despise the stranger, the stranger is a guest of Ullah."
This behaviour in the children was some sign of the elders'
meaning, from whom doubtless they had heard their villanous
riming ;—the same that was chanted by the Mohammedan
children at Damascus, for few days before the atrocious fratricide of the Nasâra. And the Semitic religions would have
none draw breath of life in the earth beside themselves, and
keep touch with no man without :—extreme inhumanities that
Mohammed had noticed in his difficult times in the iniquitous
Jews.

A poor young man of the Alowna for his dollar or two may
ride to Damascus, 550 miles, upon some dromedary croup, with
the Ageyl riders : they often apprentice themselves in the Syrian
city to learn stone-building of the Nasâra. I found one here, a
tall fellow, who years past was gone a soldiering, in the jehâd,
to the Crimea. He told me it was far ways and over seas ;
and this is all that such men can report of any distant parts
they have visited, for the world's chart is always unknown
to them. There are Arabs who wander wide as the continents
and returning (as the unschooled and barbarous) cannot declare
to us their minds : Arabs have travelled very long ago over all
the face of Africa, without leaving record. I saw a young
Syrian living here covertly ; a conscript, he had deserted in
el-Yemen. The lad's town was Nazareth, and he was somewhat
troubled to see me.

Another day I wandered to the further border of the oasis,
where herd-lads were keeping the few goats of the village.—
Upon a sudden there started from the tamarisks a fiendly
looking Beduin whom the lads not knowing they cried out " He
is one of the Howeytât," and lifting their staves and taking
clods in their hands, they bade him stand off. The wretch

fastening two robbers' eyes upon me asked "What man is he! and is he of you?" I said to him, "Accursed be the villain thy father! away with thee!"—"Hî-hî-hî! I go," and he vanished, with a strange shouting, as if he called to lurking fellows of his in the thicket. "The enemies are upon us," said the lads, and hastily they drove their goats within the walls. Sheykh Dâhir reproved me gravely at evening, saying that I seemed to be, a man of some instruction, and yet was one unwise, foolhardy and daily disobedient to his better counsel. "Open thy eyes, Khalîl, and be advised ere there befall thee a great mischief; but I have forewarned thee." Dâhir added with an under-smile worthy of his inhuman faith, ' he were not then to be blamed,' (—there would be one kâfir less in God's world.) Another while as I sat without the town gate, under the Harra, with an Ally man, a shower of stones tumbled upon us : we went back and saw a sneaking wretch climbing in the cliff above. My companion, with the short indignation of the Arabs, levelling his match-lock, cried to him to cast again—. I would ere this have re-turned to el-Héjr; but Dâhir bade me have patience for a few days that Howeytát footsteps had been seen in the boghrâz. I asked how they could know the tribe thus?—"By the length of their foot, which is more than of any neighbouring Beduins:" yet those tribesmen are said to be "small-footed as women." The most nomads of these parts, going at all times without sandals, have heavy flat feet.

The sheykh was good enough to send me to see the Khreyby rocks and ruins, with one of the town who undertook the service willingly. This was *Sâlih el-Moslemany*, a principal tradesman to the marketing nomads in the town, and client of Dâhir. He was well affected to me because his father's kindred were Christians. *Sâlih's* father was come hither (a fugitive perhaps) from Egypt : to dwell at el-Ally he must needs become a con-fessor of Islam, and had then received the neophyte surname el-Moslemany. His son, who passed for a good Mohammedan, and had made more journeys than one to the prophet's city, tendered for his sake the name of the Nasâra. Sâlih challenged by some that he favoured the Nasrâny thought himself obliged to iterate immediately the confession of faith, saying solemnly in their hearing, "*La îlah ill' Ullah*" and with most emphasis, "*wa Mohammed rasúl Ullah.*" Sâlih excused himself, this morning, ' it was late, those who had gone to that part to gather sticks would be returning presently;' but Dâhir said we might go, and sent his nephew with us.

They came then girded in their old rent clothing, and carry-ing long matchlocks. We passed the outlying palms and the seyl

to the Ras el-Aŷn, or " fountain-head " of their brook, a dark pit
twenty-five feet deep to the under-rushing water. Then begin
the ruins, el-Khreyby ; so we came to the " Nâga's milking pail,"

The Harra.   Outlying palms   Cliffs of
Moallak el-Hameydy.   towards el-Héjr.   el-Khreyby.

mah'leb nâkat néby Sâlih, or *helwîat en-Néby,* " the prophet's
milk-bowl " (fig. p. 139). This is a rock which has been wrought
into a cistern. I found it twelve feet wide, and measured from
without it is seven and a half feet at the highest : within, a stair
is left in the stone of three tall steps ; the wall is massy, I think
thirteen inches at the lip. The colossal jurn within and without
is scored over with other cattle marks than those of the tribes
of nomads which now inhabit this country. Gross pot-sherds
are strewed in this heaped ground of ruins, where we passed
with difficulty over rugged banks of loose-building stones.
The antique houses were of sandstone blocks, mostly untrimmed,
laid in clay ; some clay-walling is yet seen obscurely under the
heaps, where stones have been lately carried : el-Ally was thus
built, but there remain more stones than might build again
their village. The ancient houses were smaller, and here has
been a town, it may be, of nearly four thousand inhabitants.
Lettered persons at el-Ally say that this is also *Keriat Héjr*,
and they recited for me the solemn words of God's great
curse over the villages of the plain that " they should never rise
again."

We came to the partly quarried cliff, in which were engraved
Himyaric embossed inscriptions of many lines. As I began to
transcribe the first we were startled by a voice, for every new
sight or sound is dreadful in the anarchy of the desert. Sâlih
exclaimed, " Wellah, *hess ez-zillamy*, I heard a man's voice ;" they
struck sparks and blew hastily the matches of their long guns.
Sâlih, though a sickly body, handled his tools with mettle and
stood up to fight like a man. We heard now, as they supposed, some " Howeyty come on singing " ; his robber companions might be behind him, and they hid themselves, as
was easy in that cragged place. The causer of our cares, who
went by, was none other than the unlucky negro servant of

Himyarite loculi and image-tablets: cliff between el-Khreyby and el-Ally.

Dâhir, a fugitive from Kheybar, the wretch had failed us to-day, and he was ever to me, as all the Kheyâbara, only an occasion of sorrow. We found the cliff full of scored inscriptions, and all were Himyaric ; whereas at Medáin Sâlih they are always Nabatean. My companions very impatiently reminded me in every passing moment, that the sun descended, and of our peril in that place. I transcribed all the antique Himyaric legends, saving those from which we had been untimely startled, and visited all the chambers. These are not many ; their mouths, as has been said, appear like dark windows in the cliff : a few other resembled rude caverns ; in some of which I found a small chamber and simple surface sepulchres. Every sepulchral cell in the precipice is but a four-square loculus, hewn back from the entry to the length of a human body, and in some obliquely ; it may be, that these old star-gazers were not without some formal observance of the heaven, in their burials, which look westward. At length we came to cells, the last towards ths south (*v.* p. 159), which are the most strange of all ; and being no more than a mile from the town, yet only single persons of the timorous Alowna had seen them in their lives. Upon the cliff at the upper corners of a middle one of them, which is hewn back obliquely, are certain square tablets with sculptured images, not unlike mummy-chests of Egypt. The nomads call them *benát,* " maidens," for have not these enigmatic sculptures (in their rude sight) bare shanks, body muffled and head wimpled, in the guise of towns-women ?

Betwixt the benát a small square tablet is entailed upon the smooth cliff-face, as it were for the epitaph, but void ; a title is chiselled upon the rock next beneath, but the Himyaric letters were a little beyond my sight. Further in the next bay of the cliff are two more sepulchral loculi, and over them an image-tablet of a pair of benát ; those benát's heads are sculptured a little otherwise : and besides these, so far as I could learn, " there are no more." Scored upon those rocks we found also an antique human figure ;—the Arabs to-day do not limn so roundly. The ancient Arabian wears a close tunic to the knee, upon his head is a coif. One brought to me at el-Ally, an  ancient image of a man's head, cut in sand-stone ; upon the crown was made a low pointed bonnet. When the finder demanded more than a little money, I thought prudent to re-ject it. I found also, in the Khreyby ruins, an antique tablet only fourteen inches wide, made with little hollowed basins ; it might be taken for a money changer's table or a table of offerings : three or four more of them I have seen built in house-walls in the town.

At el-Khreyby, then, the manner of building, of burial, of writing, are other than at el-Héjr only ten miles distant !

We found in the sand where an hyena had lately passed : Ṣâlih asked if I knew the slot. I have often seen the traces in these parts and in Sinai, but not in highland Arabia : one such land-loping wild beast may in a night time leave foot-prints through a whole district ; they must be few which sub-sist in a nearly lifeless country. The Alowna say very well of the Himyaric legends, " they are like the Hábashy " (Abys-sinian form of writing). A fanatical person once stayed me in the street saying, he had at home two volumes written in these letters ! I could not persuade him to let me see them, because he would do the kafir no pleasure.

The villagers and nomads spoke to me of a ruined site in these parts, *el-Mubbiát.* This is a plural word, and may signify the sites of several ruined hamlets in one oasis. They say buried treasures lie there, and it was of old a principal town. That ground, six miles from el-Ally, is a plain with acacia trees, separated from W. Kurra by a narrow train of the mountain : it is a loam and clay bottom crusted with salt. " Incense " is found there, and human bones as at Medáin, and potsherds and much broken glass in rings, " as it were of women's bracelets." There are ruined clay buildings, and a few of clay and stone ; but as Sâlih told me, faithfully, there are neither chambers hewn in the rock nor engraved inscriptions. Dâhir said he would send me thither, but I thought it beside the present purpose. Some Wélad Aly Beduins have found pieces of gold money at Mubbiát, I heard that the titles were in Kufic, " *There is no God but the Lord.*" We see there is no long tradition in Arabia; I found no memory in this country of the busy trading town *Ḳorḥ,* mentioned by some of the old Mohammedan travellers. I have enquired among all the nomads, but they had not heard it ; the lettered men of el-Ally had no notice of such a name. I hoped to have seen the wilderness southward as far as Zmurrûd with Mohammed Aly, who awaited orders to visit that ruinous kella. In the next mountain valleys towards Medina are not a few ruined sites of good villages ; in that sandstone country may be many scored inscriptions.

By Hedîeh, a haj-road kella at the W. el Humth, are re-ceived the waters seyling from Kheybar. Far to the south-east is a side valley descending to the W. Kurra or bed of the Humth, in which are notable ruins, *Ḳorḥ,* of a place greater, as

D. T.   **11**

the Beduins report, than el-Ally.   The ground is rugged between hills and somewhat wider than the valley at el-Ally.
There are seen many plots of old buildings, and among them a
ruined kella.   The B. Wahab have no tradition of Ḳorḥ, notwithstanding that the district is theirs from antiquity.   If
this were Ḳ(Gk)orḥ they would pronounce *Gorḥ*, or else *Jorḥ ;*
that which they say is plainly Ḳorḥ.   In these parts is the
country of the poet-hero Antara : none matched him of the
antique nomads, whether in warlike manhood, or in the songs
of the desert ; he is maker of one of the seven golden poems.
Near the next kella, Sújwa, is a mountain named *Istabal Antar,*
" Antar's stable."   At the mountain head, their fabulous eyes
see a " manger " great as a cistern, and the stony rings, " where
the hero's mares stood bound"; Antara they take to have
been a man of five or six fathoms in stature.   The Moor Haj
Nejm had seen there, he told me, " a railroad " ;—these simple
men believe in good faith that telegraph and railways be come
down to us from the beginning of the world.   The rock may be
sandstone, with certain veins of ironstone.

    I would hastily return to Medáin, to impress the epitaphs, and
make a good end of this enterprise.   The sheykh had more than
once agreed with marketing Beduins in the town, to convey me ;
but at the hour of departure they failed us.   Dâhir, sorry to see
his town authority no more set by in their eyes, reproached
them with this urbanity, " Thy name is Beduwy."   The townsfolk deal roughly with the common sort of ragged nomads
that come to el-Ally ; but they esteem their chiefs, the sheykhs
of the desert, who are their paymasters, and men of gentler
behaviour than any townsmen.   Dâhir was religious rather
than good-hearted ; his crabbed black visage drawn by moments into some new form, and the weakness of his authority,
were a discomfort to me ; I had no hope in him at all.   I asked
Dâhir had he travelled in the countries, had he seen Damascus ?
" What needeth me, he answered, to see es-Shàm, here are we
not well enough ? "—And it is true that Dâhir could not be
more urbane, nor is there more civil town life than theirs even
at Damascus.   I said now I would return on foot to el-Héjr.
" I will send you myself, said Dâhir, the Beduins are *akarît !* "—
that is a villanous (Medina) word to be found in honest
men's mouths !   Sâlih, hearing I would depart, asked me privately had I found by divination *tamyîs*, if the chance were
good for this day's journey ?   When I enquired of his art, " What !
said he, you know not this ? how, but by drawing certain lines
in the sand ! and it is much used here."   Dâhir bade me return,
in case I should be coldly received by those askars in the kella,

to pass with him the few weeks which remained with the Haj ;
yet with a waspish word he blessed us all in an irony, which
had been causes to him of this trouble ; " The Lord have mercy
upon Mohammed Aly's father, and upon the Dowla, and upon
the father of Khalîl's country ! " He had six guns ready, and
sent his son with them to accompany me as far as the wells : his
unlucky negro servant of Kheybar came on driving a weak ass
with my light baggage. At el-Khreyby I went aside to copy the
sculptured inscriptions, from which we had before been startled.
(*Documents Épigraphiques* Pl. xv.) The soil is good loam-
ground, and we found mere-stones set two and two together of
the ancient acres. My companions exclaimed, " Ha, these were
their old landmarks, and we have not minded them before ! "
They returning then, I continued my journey with the Kheybary.
Walking three hours through a wilderness of crags, we came
upon the plain brow of el-Héjr, where Ethlib appeared before us,
that landmark of mountain spires and pinnacles ; and soon we
discerned the cliffs, (called by the Alowna *J. Shakhúnab*, though
this, among the nomads, is the name of a mountain north of the
Mezham,) with their wonderful hewn architecture, the borj and
the haj-road kella.

Upon the morrow I asked of Mohammed Aly to further me
in all that he might ; the time was short to accomplish the
enterprise of Medáin Sâlih. I did not stick to speak frankly ; but
I thought he made me cats'-eyes. " You cannot have forgotten
that you made me certain promises ! "—" I will give you the gun
again." This was in my chamber ; he stood up, and his fury
rising, much to my astonishment, he went to his own, came
again with the carbine, turned the back and left me. I set
the gun again, with a friendly word, in the door of his chamber,—" Out ! " cried the savage wretch, in that leaping up and
laying hold upon my mantle : then as we were on the gallery
the Moorish villain suddenly struck me with the flat hand and
all his mad force in the face, there wanted little of my falling
to the yard below. He shouted also with savage voice, " Dost
thou not know me yet ? " He went forward to the kahwa, and
I followed him, seeing some Beduins were sitting there ;—the
nomads, who observe the religion of the desert, abhor the
homely outrage. I said to them, " *Ya rubbâ*, O fellowship, ye
are witnesses of this man's misdoing." The nomads looked
coldly on aghast ; it is damnable among them, a man to do his
guest violence, who is a guest of Ullah. Mohammed Aly,
trembling and frantic, leaping up then in his place, struck me
again in the doorway, with all his tiger's force ; as he heaped

11—2

blows I seized his two wrists and held them fast. "Now, I said, have done, or else I am a strong man." He struggled, the red cap fell off his Turk's head, and his stomach rising afresh at this new indignity, he broke from me. The sickly captain of ruffian troopers for a short strife had the brawns of a butcher, and I think three peaceable men might not hold him. As for the kella guard, who did not greatly love Mohammed Aly, they stood aloof with Haj Nejm as men in doubt, seeing that if my blood were spilt, this might be required of them by the Pasha. The nomads thought by mild words to appease him, there durst no man put in his arm, betwixt the aga and the Nasrâny. "—Aha! by Ullah! shouted the demon or ogre, now I will murder thee." Had any blade or pistol been then by his belt, it is likely he had done nothing less; but snatching my beard with canine rage, the ruffian plucked me hither and thither, which is a most vile outrage. By this the mad fit abating in his sick body, and somewhat confused as he marked men's sober looks about him, and to see the Nasrâny bleeding, who by the Pasha had been committed to him upon his head, he hastily re-entered the kahwa, where I left them. The better of the kella crew were become well affected towards me, even the generous coxcomb of Haj Hasan was moved to see me mishandled: but at a mischief they were all old homicides, and this aga was their paymaster, though he embezzled some part of their salary, besides he was of their Moorish nation and religion. If M. Aly came with fury upon me again, my life being endangered, I must needs take to the defence of my pistol, in which, unknown to them, were closed the lives of six murderous Arabs, who, as hounds, had all then fallen upon a stranger: and their life had been for my life. As we waken sometime of an horrid dream, I might yet break through this extreme mischief, to the desert; but my life had been too dearly purchased, when I must wander forth, a manslayer, without way, in the hostile wilderness. All the fatigues of this journey from Syria I saw now likely to be lost, for I could not suffer further this dastardly violence. The mule M. Aly came by and marking me sit peaceably reading at the door of my chamber, with a new gall he bade me quit those quarters, and remove with my baggage to the *liwàn*. This is an open arch-chamber to the north in Damascus wise; there is made the coffee-hearth in summer, but now it was deadly cold in the winter night at this altitude. He gave my chamber to another, and I must exchange to his cell on the chill side, which was near over the cesspool and open to its mephitic emanations when the wind lay to the kella. After this M. Aly sent the young Mohammed to require again, as *rahn*, a pledge, the gun

which had been left in my doorway. I carried the gun to M. Aly :
he sat now in his chamber, chopfallen and staring on the ground.

At half-afternoon I went over to the kahwa ; Haj Nejm and
M. Aly sat there. I must ascertain how the matter stood ;
whether I could live longer with them in the kella, or it were
better for me to withdraw to el-Ally. I spread my *biuruldi*, a
circular passport, before them, from a former governor of Syria.
—" Ah ! I have thirty such firmàns at home."—" Are you not
servitors of the Dowlat es-Sultàn ? "—" I regard nothing, nor
fear creature ; we are Moghràreba, to-day here, to-morrow
yonder ; what to us is the Dowla of *Stambûl* or of *Mambûl ?* "—
" And would you strike me at Damascus ? "—" By the mighty
God men are all days stricken and slain too at es-Shem. Ha !
Englishman, or ha ! Frenchman, ha ! Dowla, will you make me
remember these names in land of the Aarab ? "—" At least you
reverence es-Sèyid, (Abd el-Kâder)—and if another day I should
tell him this ! "—" In the Sèyid is *namûs* (the sting of anger) more
than in myself : who has namûs more than the Sèyid ? eigh, Haj
Nejm ? wellah, at es-Shem there is no more than the Sèyid and
Mohammed Aly (himself). I have (his mad boast) seven hundred
guns there ! "—" You struck me ; now tell me wherefore, I have
not to my knowledge offended you in anything."—" Wellah,
I had flung thee down from the gallery, but I feared Ullah : and
there is none who would ever enquire of thy death. Your own
consul expressly renounced before our Wàly (governor of Syria)
all charge concerning thee, and said, taking his *bernéta* in his
hand, you were to him nothing more than this old hat."—
" Such a consul might be called another day to justify himself."
—" Well, it is true, and this I have understood, Haj Nejm, that
he passed for a *khanzîr* (an animal not eaten by the Turks) among
our Pashas at es-Shem, and I make therefore no account of
him :—also by this time the nejjàb has delivered Khalîl's letters
in Damascus.—It is known there now that you are here, and
your life will be required of us." Haj Nejm said, " Ay, and this
is one of those, for whose blood is destroyed a city of Islam."
(Jidda bombarded and Syria under the rod were yet a bitter
memory in their lives.) " Mark you, I said, Haj Nejm, that
this man is not very well in his understanding." M. Aly began
now in half savage manner to make his excuses ; ' Servitor had
he been of the Dowla these thirty years, he had wounds in his
body ; and M. Aly was a good man, that knew all men.'—
" Enough, enough between you ! " cries Haj Nejm, who would
reconcile us ; and M. Aly, half doting-religious and humane
ruffian, named me already *habîb*, ' a beloved ' ! We drank round
and parted in the form of friends.—Later I came to know the

first cause of this trouble, which was that unlucky Kheybary elf of Dâhir's, whom I had, with an imprudent humanity, led in to repose an hour and drink coffee in the kella : once out of my hearing, although I had paid his wages at el-Ally, he clamoured for a new shirt-cloth from the aga. This incensed the Turkish brains of M. Aly, who thought he had received too little from me :—more than all had driven him to this excess (he pretended) that I had called the wild nomads to be my witnesses. When afterwards some Beduins asked him wherefore he had done this : ' That Khalîl, he answered, with a lie, had struck off his red bonnet ;—and wellah the Nasrâny's grasp had so wrung his delicate wrists that he could not hold them to heaven in his prayers for many a day afterward ; ' also the dastardly villain boasted to those unwilling hearers that ' he had plucked Khalîl's beard.'

This storm abated, with no worse hap, they of the kella were all minded to favour me ; and on the morrow early, leaving one to drive the well-machine, every man, with Haj Nejm, and Mohammed Aly upon his horse, accompanied the Nasrâny among the monuments, they having not broken their fasts, until the sun was setting ; and in the days after, there went out some of them each morning with me. Of Haj Nejm I now bought a tamarisk beam, that had been a make-shift well-shaft, fetched from el-Ally : the old man hacked notches in my timber for climbing, and the ladder-post was borne out between two men's shoulders to the bébàn, and flitted from one to other as the work proceeded. I went abroad with large sheets of bibulous paper, water, and a painter's brush and sponge ; and they rearing the timber at a frontispice, where I would, I climbed, and laboured standing insecurely at the beam head, or upon the pediment, to impress the inscription. The moist paper yielded a faithful stamp (in which may be seen every grain of sand) of the stony tablet and the letters. Haj Nejm would then accompany us to shore the beam himself, (that I should not take a fall,) having, he said, always a misgiving. In few days I impressed all the inscriptions that were not too high in the frontispices. [*v.* pl., p. 176.] We went forward, whilst the former sheets hanged a-drying in their title plates, to attempt other. In returning over the wilderness it was a new sight to us all, to see the stern sandstone monuments hewn in an antique rank under the mountain cliff, stand thus billeted in the sun with the butterfly panes of white paper ; —but I knew that to those light sheets they had rendered, at length, their strange old enigma ! The epitaphs are some quite undecayed, some are wasted in the long course of the weather. Our work fortunately ended, there remained more than a half score of the inscription tablets which were too high for me.

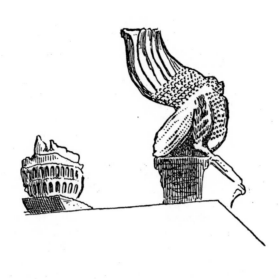

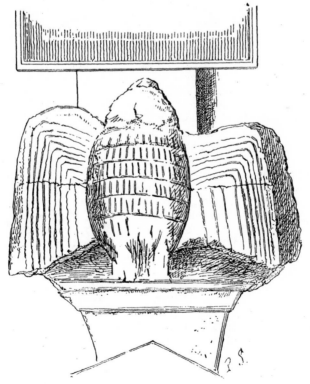

Our going abroad was broken in the next days by the happy fortune of rain in Arabia. A bluish haze covered the skirts of the Harra, the troubled sky thundered; as the falling drops overtook us, the Arabs, hastily folding their matchlocks under their large mantles, ran towards the kella. Chill gusts blew out under lowering clouds, the showers fell, and it rained still at nightfall. The Arâbs said then, " The Lord be praised, there will be plenty of samn this year." On the morrow it rained yet, and from the kella tower we saw the droughty desert standing full of plashes; the seyl of the Héjr plain did not flow for all this; I found there but few pools of the sweet rain-water. "—If only, they said now, the Lord shield us from locusts ! " which their old musing men foretold would return that year : they think the eggs of former years revive in the earth after heavy showers. Samn, the riches of the desert, was now after so long drought hardly a pint for a *real* or crown, at el-Ally.

But what of the sculptured bird in those frontispices of the sumptuous charnel houses ? (See p. 167.) It was an ancient opinion of the îdolatrous Arabs, that the departing spirit flitted from man's brain-pan as a wandering fowl, complaining thenceforward in deadly thirst her unavenged wrong; friends therefore to assuage the friend's soul-bird, poured upon the grave their pious libations of wine. The bird is called " a green fowl," it is named by others an owl or eagle. The eagle's life is a thousand years, in Semitic tradition. In Syria I have found Greek Christians who established it with that scripture, " he shall renew his youth as an eagle." Always the monumental bird is sculptured as rising to flight, her wings are in part or fully displayed.

In the table of the pediment of a very few monuments, especially in the Kasr el-Bint rocks, is sculptured an effigy (commonly wasted) of the human face. (See next page.) Standing high upon the ladder beam, it fortuned me to light upon one of them which only has remained uninjured ; the lower sculptured cornices impending, it could not be wholly discerned from the ground. I found this head such as a comic mask, flat-nosed, and with a thin border of beard about a sun-like visage. This sepulchral image is grinning with all his teeth, and shooting out the tongue. The hair of his head is drawn out above either ear like a long "horn" or hair-lock of the Beduins. Seeing this *larva*, one might murmur again the words of Isaiah, " Against whom makest thou a wide mouth, and drawest out the tongue ? " I called my companions, who mounted after me ; and looking on the old stony mocker, they scoffed again, and came down with loud laughter and wondering.

The Semitic East is a land of sepulchres ; Syria, a limestone country, is full of tombs, hewn, it may be said, under every hill side. Now they are stables for herdsmen, and open dens of wild creatures. " Kings and counsellors of the earth built them desolate places " ; but Isaiah mocked in his time those " habitations of the dead."—These are lands of the faith of the resurrection. Palmyra, Petra, Hejra, in the ways of the desert countries, were all less oases of husbandmen than great caravan stations. In all

is seen much sumptuousness of sepulchres ; clay buildings served for their short lives and squared stones and columns were for the life of the State. The care of sepulture, the ambitious mind of man's mortality, to lead eternity captive, was beyond measure in the religions of antiquity, which were without humility. The Medáin funeral chambers all together are not, I think, an hundred. An hundred monuments of well-faring families in several generations betoken no great city. Of such we might conjecture an old Arabian population of eight thousand souls ; a town such as *Aneyza* at this day, the metropolis of Nejd.

Under the new religion the deceased is wound in a shirt-cloth of calico, (it is the same whether he were a prince or the poorest person, whether villager or one of the restless Beduw,) his corse is laid in the shallow pit of droughty earth, and the friends will set him up a head-stone of the blocks of the desert. Ezekiel sees the burying in hell of the ancient mighty nations : hell, the grave-hole, is the deep of the earth, the dead-kingdom : the graves are disposed (as we see at Medáin Sâlih) in the sides of the pit about a funeral bed (which is here the floor in the midst). We read like words in Isaiah, " Babel shall be brought down to hell, to the sides of the pit." To bury in the sides of the pit was a superstitious usage of the ancient Arabians, it might be for the dread of the hyena. In what manner were the dead laid in the grave at el-Héjr ? We have found frankincense or spice-matter, the shreds of winding-cloths, and lappets, as of leathern shrouds, in certain monuments : in the most floors lies only deep sand-drift, the bones are not seen in all ; and the chamber floor in a few of them is but plain and bare rock. It is not unlikely that they buried the dead nearly as did the Jews about these times [*v. John* xix. 40, *Luke* xvi. 1], with odours, and the corse was swathed in one or several kinds of linen (I find three, finer and grosser webbed, brown-stained and smelling of the drugs of the embalmers) and sewed in some inner leather painted red, and an outer hide, which for the thickness may be goat or else camel-leather, whose welts are seamed with leathern thongs and smeared with asphalte. I saw no mummy flesh, nor hair. In peaceable country the monuments might be one by one explored at leisure. I never went thither alone, but I adventured my life.

In my dealings with Arabs I have commonly despised their pusillanimous prudence. When I told Mohammed Aly that those kassûr chambers were sepulchres, he smiled, though an arrow shot through his barbarous Scriptures, and he could forgive me, seeing me altogether a natural philosopher in religion. " *Yaw !* " said he, with a pleasant stare ; and he had seen himself the rocks plainly full of tombs in many parts of Syria : my word reported seemed afterward to persuade also the Syrian Jurdy and Haj officers, though their Mohammedan hearts despised a Christian man's unbelief.

Upon the landmark rock el-Howwâra in the plain of Medáin Sâlih lies a great treasure (in the opinion of the Moors in the kella) sealed in a turret-like stone chamber, in the keeping of an afrît (evil *genius loci*, a word spoken of the spirits of wicked men departed, which as flies to the dunghill haunt eternally about their places of burial). Fatal, they say, were the taking up of that treasure, " the kings of the world should strive together, the Aarab tribes should destroy one another. In that day a man will not spare his friend, nor his brother, the son of his father and his mother:" thus Haj Nejm. I have looked down upon the Howwâra cliff from the Harra, and can affirm that the head of it is plain, a black platform of lava ; the sandstone precipices all round are a hundred fathoms in height (see p. 82). Further Nejm told us how ' few years past there was come hither a certain Moghreby from Medina, somewhat after the pilgrimage ; he was on the way to Syria, and had stayed awhile in the kella. The wise man studying in his cabalistical book found that upon the Howwâra lay that wealth indeed ; but, he said, he durst not raise it. " I desire nothing for myself, also I find written that were those riches taken away, there should ensue great calamities." The same Moghreby, who by their saying, with all his dark lore, was a gentle soul, being afterward at Maan, was friendly entertained by the Kurdy aga of the place, he who had married the only daughter of Mohammed Saîd Pasha : and the wise guest, who would show as much courtesy to his host again, found somewhat for him, ere he departed, in those old ruins (el-Hammam), which are without the village. The guest and host stealing forth by night, the fortunate Kurdy filled his two saddle-bags with money, and all was red gold ; but the pleasant philosopher would take nothing for himself.—" All this, cried Mohammed Aly, I can confirm, for being at that time stationed at Maan, wellah, I saw that gold, and I was in the confidence of the aga."

Marvellous are the fables of the East ; and if the truth be in the mouth of many witnesses, it were hard not to believe them ; the world is yet full of miracles. In my time there were two Christs in Syria ; one of them, a second-sighted admirable person of the Persian religion, had been laid by the Ottoman government in " little-ease " at Gaza. The other was between ignorant block and mystical hypocrite, a religious dreamer at large. Born in the Christian religion, this man was by turns Jew and Mohammedan ; ' he had God's name, he told me in a terrific voice, sculptured between his two eye-brows.' This divine handwriting, be it understood, was in Arabic ; that is, he had rimples, as a triglyph, or somewhat resembling the trace الله—*Allah.* Herein, he would covertly convey, among us Christians, was his mystical name, divine ! and he was himself Messias of the second appearing. He was born in *Latákia*, and in this also, through barbarous ignorance of the Greek letters, he found a witness of the Scriptures unto himself. He prophesied to them with a lofty confidence, that the day was toward, when he should ride forth from the Damascus horse-market into his eternal glory ; and all things being fulfilled in himself, the children of Adam should return unto their Lord God, to be manifested in the whole world. He was a Moslem among the Moslemîn. I heard their ribalds deride this self-godded man upon a time as I walked with him in their cathedral mosque, and he went on saying (especially where we met with any simple hareem, near the gates) in an immense murmured voice, " How great is Mohammed ! yea, O ye people ! he is the Apostle of Ullah ! " They mocked him with " Hail, Néby ! " Of the Christians no man trusted him. Yet I have heard simple women, half in awe of a man of so high pretence, beg of him to foresay to them the event of these dangerous times,—" whether the Nasâra would be massacred ? " And he in mighty tones prophesied to them comfortable things ; he said they should have no hurt, these troubles should assuage shortly and Christ's kingdom be established. Also he could show, unto any faithful which resorted to him in certain hours, the testimony of miracles ; for with solemn gesture, the divine man and his wife prayed over a little water, then he breathed in mystic wise, and spread his hands, and behold it was made wine : and such had been seen by a simple Christian person of my familiar acquaintance. Upon a time finding him in the street I bade him wend with me, of his charity, to the house of fools, *el-Moristàn :* by his holy power with God, we might heal a mad body : he granted.—There entering, when we had passed bars and gates, he received from the porter a cup of water in his hand, and led me confidently to the poor men in durance. He had promised if we found any raging one, with the only name of Ullah, to appease him : but as all was still, he approached a poor man who sat in a cage, and enquired his name and country and condition. The sad prisoner answered to all things well and civilly ; and the blatant man of God, when he had cried *Ullah !* and breathed with an awesomeness upon the water, gave him through the bars his bowl, bidding him drink measurably thereof, and if the Lord would, he should come to his health : the un-happy man received it very thankfully. " Thou hast seen ! (said this doer of miracles,) now we may return." After a week he sent me his divine word that the dangerous madcap had mended, and ' was about to be sent home as a man in his right mind ;—and *did I not yet believe him ? '* This wonder-worker, after walking through all Christian sects and Judaism, had gone over to the Mohammedan profession, in that hoping, said his Christian neighbours, to come again by his own : and this was, after he had put out his little patrimony, at an iniquitous usury, to insolvent Moslems :—they having devoured the Nasrâny's good, derided him ; and a Christian has little or no hope in the Mohammedan judgment seats. The forlorn man had fallen between the stools of his natural and adopted religions, and his slender living was passed from his own into other shrews' hands ; and there was all his grief : the apostate found no charity in either. The Christian people's whisper even imputed to him an atrocious guilt. In better days a boy had served him, and he was known to beat the child more and more. Some while after, when the boy was not found, the neighbours said between their teeth, "he has murdered the lad and buried him ! " When I last saw him the religion-monger was become a sadder and a silent man ; the great sot had now a cross coaled upon his cottage door, in the Christian quarter. He said then with a hollow throat, ' he was but a sinner,' and denied to me, shaking out his raiment with an affected horror, that ever such as I alleged had been his former pretension. " Nay ah ! and ah nay ! " The sooth-sayer would persuade me that " all was but the foolish people's saying." I found him poring and half weeping over a written book, which he told me was " marvellous wise and healthful to the soul, and the copying it had cost him much silver." The argument was of God's creatures, the beasts, and showing how every beast (after that of the psalm, " Praise the Lord from the earth, all beasts, creeping things, and feathered fowl ") yieldeth life-worship unto God. He read me aloud his last lesson " Of the voices of the living creatures," and coming down to the camel, I said " Hold there ! every camel-voice is like a blasphemy : it is a very blasphemous beast." Said he : " Thou art mistaken, that brutish bellowing in his throat is the camel's making moan unto Ullah.—See further it is written here !—his prayer for patience under oppression, inasmuch as he is made a partner in man's affliction." Neighbours now told me the most sustenance of this sorrowful man, past the lining of his purse, to be of herbs, which cooling diet he had large leave to gather for him-self in the wild fields.

As I wandered in Palestine I came to a place where the Moslems show a sepulchre of the prophet Jonas. The respect-able blind sire who kept the chapel, when I would enter further than the ruinous chamber, forbade me ; and to the company he ralated how of late years two rash young men of the village had made bold to thrust into the Néby's tomb, " but ah ! Sirs, wellah, said he, they came forth blind ; " and the poor gaffer shook his head piteously again. Here credulous persons, having lighted upon a miracle, might have taken half the village to witness. Commonly the longer one lives in a fabulous time or country, the weaker will become his judgment. Certainly I have heard fables worthy of the Arabs from the lips of excellent Europeans too long remaining in the East. How often in my dwelling in that hostile world have I felt desolate, even in a right endeavour : the testimony of all men's (half-rational) understandings making against my lonely reason ; and must I not seem to them, in holding another opinion, to be a perverse and unreasonable person ? Many admirable things, unless you can misbelieve them all, fall out daily according to their faith, and their world is to thy soul as another planet of nature. Their religious wizards converse with the jan, the cabalistic discovery of hid things is every day confirmed by many faithful witnesses. Because they had some fond expectation even of me, a stranger, it was reported afterward, at Teyma, that I wrought miracles. Certain persons affirmed with oaths that " Khalîl had been seen by night uplifting stones, wellah of machinal weight, out of the great ruined well-pit, and with no more than the touch of his fingers ; " and yet at such hours I was sleeping, encamped with the Aarab, nearly half a mile distant.

If I asked any nomad of that great Harra in sight, of the *Ferrá* and the principal valleys, he began commonly, tracing with his camel-stick in the sand, or his finger in the powder of the kella floor, to show me the course of the wadies. All these parts seyl, they told me, into the W. Jizzl ; some said, " into the W. el-Humth ; " and then they said " the Jizzl and the Humth are one wady." The Humth valley descends from beyond Medina by Henakîeh. The Wady Jizzl, receiving the rain-streams from both sides of the Harra, goes out below el-Ally in the W. el-Humth, which passes westward through the Teháma, and issues to the Red Sea betwen Wejh and Yánba. The Humth is a great valley,—they compared it with W. er-Rummah. (See the map, Vol. I.) Later at Kheybar I heard that the W. el-Humth begins in Nejd above the Mecca country. These great valleys have each a length of nearly ten degrees and as all Arabian wadies they are continually waterless. That valley is called the Humth for the plenty there growing of the desert bush, *el-humth,* which is good camel-meat, and especially in the Teháma.

Now came the nejjàb : he had left all in quiet at Damascus. Overtaken by cold weather and fogs in the high *Ard es-Suwwan,* the Sherâry told us with oaths he could not see his hands in two days space, and he had nearly perished. A Wélad Aly lad was waiting here to ride on with his post-bags to Medina. —Letters were come from Damascus for Mohammed Aly, and the lad Mohammed was sent to hear them read at el-

Ally and bring word again. They thought I could read a post-script ; and whilst I studied it by the coffee-fire, said Nejm, " It might be a salaam from the hareem."—" Oh when (answered Mohammed Aly, turning upon him) do the hareem (whom they think to be only good for the house service) send their greeting ? or what man sends ever a greeting to the hareem ! "

In the household life there is a gulf betwixt us and the Arabs ; the open loving affection of our spouses-for-life, they esteem unmanly. Once Mohammed Aly touched this difference in my hearing :—" When I was stationed at Maan there arrived a Frenjy with his wife at W. Mûsa, and their accustomed long train of baggage camels and servitors; so that they appear to us persons of princely quality. Their truch-man in entering Moses' valley had paid out presents to the Howeytát sheykhs and to the village sheykh of el-Eljy. But whilst this Frank, leaving his wife to repose at the tents, was gone to view the next monuments, another ragged rout of the country Beduins ran down from the mountain, and came on with club-sticks and wild shouts to the Frenjy's camp ; where finding only the dame and none daring to oppose them, they laid on her their sun-blackened hands, crying fast *flûs, flûs*—money, money ! The husband hieing again to the clamour, the hooting Beduins, as ever they had sight of him, pulling out their cut-lasses, made as though they would carve his wife's neck ; and if he stood a moment, to make them signs, their swords were already at her throat. He called desperately then to his inter-preter to give them anything, all and whatsoever they would. So he comes up aghast, to see his lady so long forlorn in the midst of those demons, and they meant no more than to eat a little of his silver." He added, " ye may see how uxorious they are ! " Such for Mohammed Aly was Frankish travelling in Syrian countries,—and the contemptible marital affection, in (he said) " the not commendable Frankish life."

The time of the ascending Haj being nigh, the country was more than commonly insecure. Fehjy wives were gone upon a morning early with camels to fetch in their knot-grass stacked at some distance in clefts of the desert mountain. They were not come again at the fall of the evening, in which time they might have gone and returned twice ; we thought them certainly lost and the camels taken by a ghrazzu. The sun was gone down when we saw them coming. The women had lingered making holiday by the way ; but one of their husbands who had passed the last hours in extreme heaviness of his mind, cried out, " Wellah, all torments in men's lives be along of the cursed hareem!"—The weak must bear all burdens, and the poor hareem have all the blame, in the nomad life. This was a well-faring wretch, *Fardûs*, forged, like all his race, of an old world's likeness, and who made half our mirth with his sly gipsy humour. As he understood that Nasâra were truer men than the Moslemîn, he came to deposit in my cell-chamber, in presence of the aga, a sack of his beggarly gear, and in which was his money. I said I would not receive the trust, unless he gave me up the tale of his silver and would show in which part of the sack his wealth lay : he showed us then he had hidden it, eight reals gained of the Haj caravan, in the corner-knots of the sack's mouth, which the nomads use to tie upon a pebble stone. "Mark you, said Mohammed Aly, the deceitful arts of them ! *el-Aarab mukkarîn!* " Also a poor widow of the gate Arabs came upon a time as she went to the desert, to deposit with me her great cooking-pot, as much worth as her poor dowry ; and in the day of the Haj arriving Hasan came to pile half a score of loaded matchlocks in my cell, for the defence of that side of the kella, where also some camel loads of the Haj stores were left in my keeping ; so confident were they of truth in the Nasrâny. This honest opinion of theirs, after the first wild looks of Semitic intolerance, has oftentimes turned to my advantage, and my word was accepted without an oath in Arabia.

The birket-water mounted almost to a just level, which to maintain against the leaking floor, they must still drive half-days. One day when I had been abroad alone, coming early home I found many Beduins before the kella and the iron gate shut, and tardily admitted, said Hasan, " *Gôm*, Khalîl ! these are enemies, and what dost thou to be abroad in such dangerous times ? " They were of Wélad Aly, and brought a load of clothing stuffs of the Haj stores, which had been cast down from the camel that bore them by Beduins and robbed in our night march a little after el-Akhdar in the B. Atîeh country. The thieves could not then be known in the darkness ; but it was since understood that they were W. Aly tribesmen : the sheykhs must therefore procure their restitution, or else the worth of the goods would be charged against themselves in their next receipt of surra. The lost bales were brought in by a younger son of their great sheykh Motlog ; a lad wearing the government scarlet mantle, girded with a gunner's belt, and therein were a gay pair of old horse-pistols. They counted out their delivery in the kella, men's tunics, women's blue kirtles, a few mantles, eighty-two pieces ; but all the best were wanting. Such losses happen every year, and it is well if there be not some camels cut out in the night marches. In a former year, the

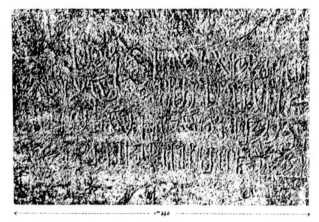

2

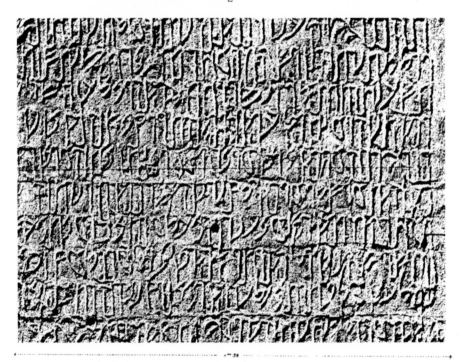

2 bis

Specimens (heliographs of the paper stamps) of the Nabatean Monumental Inscriptions at el-Héjr or Medáin Sálih :

No. 1.   Inscription above the idol-stone fig. 5, p. 130.
No. 2.   Width 29 inches nearly : epitaph of a monument in the Kasr el-Bint rocks.
No. 2 bis.   The name of the Architect which is scored immediately under no. 2.

[See these numbers in Appendix, p. 181.]

B. Atîeh fell upon the Haj convoy, one morning, under the same Pasha, and drove off about two hundred camels. Mohammed Saîd, who had passed his life victorious in this kind of running warfare, drew in his straggling soldiery whilst the Haj stood still : the field-pieces having been quickly mounted, he let a few shells fly over their heads, and sent his troopers to out-ride them. The Beduw then left their booty and held off ; all the camels were brought in again and the caravan set forward, —and great is the name of M. Saîd Pasha in the desert. The year of my leaving Arabia, Beduw set upon the descending pilgrimage betwixt the Harameyn, and killed (it is reported) a score of them, and took much booty ; the Aarab crying out that this seizing for themselves was forced upon them, foras-much as there had not been paid them their just surra. And little unlikely, there had been juggling in the covetous old Kurdy's disbursing of the government piastres, and that of some great ones' embezzling pence many poor and unarmed pilgrims came by their deaths. The great Stambûl officer of the year was sore affrighted, so that he durst return no more by the land-way, where he must see those sun-blackened faces again of the wild Beduw, but got him home upon shipboard.

A shouting without in the night made us start from slumbering on the cold stones ; the nomad dogs barked with all their throats, the gate Arabs from the booths cried to those in the kella ' a ghrazzu was upon them ! ' Our cut-throats ran now in the feeble moonlight, with their long matchlocks, upon the kella terrace. The cowardly young Mohammed, in this war-like rumour, when he had digged in the smouldering coffee-hearth a pan of coals, whereat to light their gun-matches, came braving after. The sickly M. Aly had cast on his military cloak, and standing in the door of his chamber, with a Turkish yell or rather the voice of some savage beast, gave the words of com-mand, "Run up, lads, and shoot at them, shoot!" himself came groping out on the gallery, and after them he stumbled with my carbine to the tower-head. Presently they heard it called from the tents that all was nothing,—a false alarm ; and Hasan ran down again, to sleep, with his gaggling Moorish laughter. Haj Nejm descended groaning, the valiant old man disliking this trouble in the night time ; their captain shouting terribly and all of them loudly attesting Ullah in their witless wild manner.

The W. Aly lad that had ridden post to Medina now re-turned to us, and his brother being here to meet him, this lovely pair would go a cattle-lifting. They having but a match-lock and an old blunt pike between them, went to scour the

country as foot-robbers, habalîs, and the elves desired me to
be in their company. When I denied them in mocking, they
were the more earnest to persuade me. ' Of what,' they asked,
' could I be afraid, seeing I had not feared to come hither ;
and having no riding beast, I might, going along with them, very
well light upon some thelûl.' They gaped for wonder when the
aga told them, soberly laughing, ' the Nasrâny was no robber,
nor one who would so much as receive any beast at a gift that
had been taken in a foray. You see, said he, that the Nasâra
are better than ye Beduins, for they can distinguish betwixt
the lawful and unlawful.'—" How it may be unlawful to rob
those that rob us we cannot tell, answered the young men ; such
at least is the custom of the Beduw." They took with them only
a bundle of dates, and a water-skin upon their shoulders, and
departed. I could imagine them to bear, in regard of me, a
heathenish mind ; to take the kafir's life, whilst I slept, had been
a good work in Beduin eyes ; it were to rid the country of a foreign
danger, and a poor spoil of clothing should be theirs, which is much
to those miserable inhabitants of the khála. Their stripping
the slain is like that (honourable) spoiling of armour in the
old world's enmities : they had been reckoned featy fellows so
they might have cut me off. One of these weleds came to my
chamber, saying with billahs he would give me notice of all
this country : then having a most elvish invention, he told me
over many ridiculous names of villages, and how in certain of
them, the people went clothed in silk, amongst them he placed
the Wady *Kheyt-beyt*, " valley of nullity." The like I have never
heard from Beduin body besides ; the nomads, so they be not
of the stuff of habalîs, are not wont to falsify this argument.
Having diligently written down the invention of his lips, I went
to read it in the coffee-chamber ; and the elder nomad present
solemnly reproved the young man's peevish levity, saying,
" Fearest not thou Ullah ! " These were W. Aly spirits, a very
slippery tribe, which continually set all the world by the ears.

It was time that my task should be done, and it was well
nigh ended. The Haj were already marching upward from the
Harameyn, and Jurdy descending from Syria, to meet them,
here, at the merkez of Medáin. And now the friendly nomads
drew hither from their dîras to be dealers in the Haj market.
Hostile Beduins hovered upon the borders to waylay them,
and our alarms were in these days continual. As fresh traces
of a foray of sixteen, habalîs, had been seen in the plain, not
a mile from the kella, a messenger was sent up in haste to
the kella shepherd Doolan, and his daughter, keeping those few

sheep and goats of the garrison in the mountains. He returned
the next evening, and the poor man came to my chamber,
bringing me a present of fresh sorrel, now newly springing
after the late showers ; a herb pleasant to these date-eaters
for its grateful sourness. Their mountain lodging was that
cold cavern where in our hunting we had rested out the night.
There they milked their goats upon sorrel, which milk-meat and
wild salads had been all their sustenance ; but I have learned by
experience that it may well suffice in the desert. Seeing the
skin of my face broken, he enquired quickly how I came by
the hurt. When I answered " That ogre ! " showing him with
my finger the door of Mohammed Aly's chamber ; said the son
of Antar between his teeth : " Akhs ! the Lord do so unto him,
the tyrant that is yonder man ; the Lord cut him off ! " Doolan
himself and the other gate Arabs dwelt here under the savage
tyranny of the Moghrebies, in daily awe of their own lives :
besides, they lived ever in little quietness themselves, as
wretches that had oft-days nothing left to put under their
teeth, and men can only live, they think, by devouring one
another. One day I heard a strife among the women ; soon
angry, they filled the air with loud clamouring, every one reviled her neighbour. Their husbands rated them, and cried
" Peace ! " the askars shouted (from the walls of the kella),
" Hush Hareem the Lord curse you ! " The young askar-lad
Mohammed sallied forth with a stick and flew bravely upon
them, and one after another he drubbed them soundly ; the
men of the tents looking on, and so it stilled their tongues none
caring to see his wife corrected.

When I came gipsying again to el-Héjr, after midsummer,
with the Fukara Arabs, *eth-Therryeh*, elder son of the sheykh,
always of friendly humour towards me, learning here of Mohammed Aly's outrage, enquired of me in his father's tent
' what thought I of the person.' I answered immediately, in
the booths of the freeborn, " He is a cursed one or else a madman ; " eth-Therryeh assented, and the prudent sheykh his father
consented with a nod. Zeyd said another while, " *Kubbak* (he
cast thee off) like a sucked lemon peel and deceived me ; very
God confound Mohammed Aly ! " M. Aly, whether repenting
of his former aggression, which I might visit upon him at
Damascus, or out of good will towards me, commended me now
with a zeal, to all nomads who touched at the kella, and later
to the servants of Ibn Rashîd that arrived from Hâyil and
Teyma, and warmly at length to the returning Pasha himself.
So Mohammed Aly, disposing all these to favour me, furthered
the beginning of my travels in Arabia.

APPENDIX.

THE NABATEAN INSCRIPTIONS UPON THE MONUMENTS DISCOVERED BY MR. DOUGHTY AT MEDÁIN SÂLIH: translated by M. ERNEST RENAN (*Membre de l'Institut*).

[From the vol. published by the *Académie des Inscriptions et Belles-Lettres*, "Documents Épigraphiques recueillis dans le nord de l'Arabie par M. Charles Doughty."]

*　　*　　*

....Quatre ou cinq groupes de faits, qui se rattachaient mal les uns aux autres, se trouvent ainsi réunis et expliqués. La paléographie sémitique en tirera les plus grandes lumières. Nos vingt-deux textes nabatéens, en effet, s'étagent, avec des dates précises, dans un espace d'environ quatre-vingts ans. On peut donc suivre la marche de l'écriture araméenne pendant près d'un siècle, et la voir, presque d'année en année, prendre un caractère de plus en plus cursif. L'écriture de nos monuments est comme le point central d'où l'on découvre le mieux l'affinité du vieil araméen, du caractère carré des Juifs, du palmyrénien, du sinaïtique, de l'estranghélo, du coufique, du neskhi.

L'histoire de l'écriture dans l'ancienne Arabie se trouve de la sorte éclairée en presque toutes ses parties. C'est là un progrès considérable, si l'on songe que, il y a soixante-quinze ans, l'illustre Silvestre de Sacy consacrait un de ses plus savants mémoires à prouver qu'on n'écrivait pas en Arabie avant Mahomet

ERNEST RENAN.

No 1. [*v. pl. facing p.* 176.]

De l'an 41 de J.-C.

Ceci est le *mesgeda* qu'a fait élever Serouh, fils de Touca, à Aera de Bosra, grand dieu. Dans le mois de nisan de l'an 1 du roi Malchus.

No. 2. [*v. pl. facing p.* 176.]
De l'an 2 de J -C.

C'est ici le caveau que firent faire Camcam, fils de Touallat, fils de Taharam, et Colcibat, sa fille, pour eux, pour leurs enfants et leurs descendants, au mois de tebeth de l'année neuvième de Hartat, roi des Nabatéens, aimant son peuple. Que Dusarès et Martaba et Allat...., et Menât et Keïs maudissent celui qui vendrait ce caveau, ou l'achèterait, ou le mettrait en gage, ou le donnerait, ou en tirerait les corps, ou celui qui y enterrerait d'autres que Camcam et sa fille et leurs descendants. Et celui qui ne se conformerait pas à ce qui est ici écrit, qu'il en soit justiciable devant Dusarès et Hobal et Menât, gardiens de ce lieu, et qu'il paye une amende de mille *selaïn*...., à l'exception de celui qui produirait un écrit de Camcam ou de Coleibat, sa fille, ainsi conçu : " Qu'un tel soit admis dans ce caveau."

Wahbélahi, fils de Abdobodat, a fait.

No. 3.
De l'an 40 de J.-C.

Ceci est le caveau qu'a fait faire Mati, le stratège, fils d'Euphronius, l'éparque, pour lui-même et pour ses enfants, et pour Vaal, sa femme, et pour ses fils, dans le mois de nisan de l'année quarante-huitième de Hartat, roi des Nabatéens, aimant son peuple. Que personne n'ose ni vendre, ni mettre en gage, ni louer ce caveau-ci.

Wahbélahi, fils de Abdobodat, a fait. A perpétuité.

No. 4.
Date illisible, vers 25 après J.-C.

Ce caveau a été fait construire par Seli, fils de Riswa, pour lui et pour ses fils et pour ses descendants en ligne légitime. Que ce caveau ne soit point vendu, qu'il ne soit point mis en gage, et quiconque fera autrement que ce qui est marqué ici, il sera redevable au dieu Dusarès, notre Seigneur, de mille *selaïn*... Dans le mois de nisan de l'année.....de Hartat, roi des Nabatéens, aimant son peuple Aftah le tailleur de pierre a fait.

No. 5.
Date illisible, au moins pour le premier chiffre, peut-être de l'an 16 après J -C.

Ce caveau a été fait construire par Tiemélahi, fils de Hamlat, pour lui-même, et il a donné ce caveau à Ammah, sa femme, fille de

Golhom. En vertu de l'acte de donation qui est dans sa main, elle peut en faire ce qu'elle voudra. En l'année 3 de Hartat, roi des Nabatéens, aimant son peuple.

No. 6.

Date en partie illisible ; de l'an 3, 13, 23 ou 33 de J.-C.

Ceci est le caveau que..........................et à leurs descendants et à quiconque viendra......................tout homme qui.....................................et quiconque le mettra en gage............................ Et quiconque fera autrement que ce qui est écrit, aura sur lui le double de la valeur de tout ce lieu-ci, et la malédiction de Dusarès et de Menât. Dans le mois de nisan de l'an....de Hartat, roi des Nabatéens, aimant son peuple. Et quiconque......dans ce caveau ou changera quelque chose à ce qui est écrit, il aura à payer à Dusarès mille *selaïn*....
Aftah [le tailleur de pierre a fait].

No. 7.

De l'an 3 avant J.-C.

C'est ici le caveau que fit Khaled, fils de Xanten, pour lui et pour Saïd, son fils, et pour les frères quels qu'ils soient de ce dernier, enfants mâles qui naîtraient à Khaled, et pour leurs fils et leurs descendants, par descendance légitime, à perpétuité. Et que soient enterrés dans ce caveau les enfants de Saïd..........Soleimat, fille de Khaled..................tout homme, hors Saïd et ses frères mâles, et leurs enfants et leurs descendants, qui vendra ce caveau et en écrira une donation ou..........à n'importe qui, excepté celui qui aurait un écrit en forme dans sa main,.....................
....
Celui qui ferait autrement que ceci devra au dieu Dusarès, notre Seigneur, une amende de cinquante *selaïn* d'argent...........notre Seigneur......Keïs. Dans le mois de nisan de la quatrième année de Hartat, roi des Nabatéens, aimant son peuple. Douma et Abdobodat, sculpteurs.

No. 8.

Date illisible ; vers l'époque même de notre ère.

Ceci est le caveau que firent Anam, fils de Gozeiat, et Arsacès, fils de Tateim le stratège...........et Calba, son frère. A Anamou appartiendra le tiers de ce caveau t sépulcre, et à Arsacès les deux autres tiers de ce caveau et sépulcre, et la moitié des niches du côté est et les *loculi* [qui y sont]. A Anemou appartiendra la moitié des niches du côté sud, et les *loculi* qui y sont. (Ces *loculi* appartiendront) à eux et à leurs enfants en ligne légitime. Dans le mois de tebeth de l'année..........de Hartat, roi des Nabatéens, aimant son peuple. Aftah, le tailleur de pierre, a fait.

No. 9.

A l'intérieur d'un cavèau ; de l'an 16 de J.-C.

Ce *loculus* a été fait par Tousouh, fils de.............., pour lui, de son vivant, et pour ses filles. Et quiconque le..........ou le tirera hors de la fosse,.................qu'il paye à notre Seigneur Hartat, roi des Nabatéens, ami de son peuple, mille *selaïn*....; et au dieu Dusarès, seigneur de tous les dieux. Celui qui.............. la fosse...............la malédiction de Dusarès et de tous les dieux....Dans le mois de............de l'année 23 de Hartat, roi des Nabatéens, ami de son peuple.

No. 10.

De l'an 77 après J.-C.

Ceci est le caveau de Hoinat, fille d'Abdobodat, pour elle, pour son fils et ses descendants, et pour ceux qui produiront en leur main, de la main de Hoinat, un écrit en cette forme : " Qu'un tel soit enterré en tel caveau."

Ce caveau a appartenu à Abdobodat,........................
....
à Hoinat ou Abdobokat, fils de Malikat,.......................... soit Abdobodat, soit Hoinat, soit tous ceux qui.................ce caveau..........l'écrit que voici : " Qu'il soit enterré dans ce caveau, à côté d'Abdobodat." Que personne n'ose vendre ce caveau, ni le mettre en gage, ni............dans ce caveau. Et quiconque fera autrement, qu'il doive à Dusarès et à Menât mille *selaïn* d'argent, et autant à notre Seigneur Dabel, roi des Nabatéens. Dans le mois d'iyyar de l'année deuxième de Dabel, roi des Nabatéens. Dans le mois d'iyyar de l'année deuxième de Dabel, roi des Nabatéens.

No. 11.

De l'an 61 de J.-C.

Ceci est le caveau qu'a fait construire Hoinat, fille de Wahb, pour elle-même, et pour ses enfants et ses descendants, à perpétuité. Et que personne n'ose le vendre, ou le mettre en gage ou écrire........ dans ce caveau-ci, et quiconque fera autrement que ceci, que sa part ....En l'année vingt et unième du roi Malchus, roi des Nabatéens.

No. 12.

Date illisible, antérieure à l'an 40 de notre ère.

Ce caveau a été fait par Maénat et Higr, fils de Amiérah, fils de Wahb, pour eux et leurs enfants et leurs descendants,..........

Maénat..........une part de ce caveau-ci..........dans le lieu de
Higr........une part......Maénat......il devra au dieu Dusarès
mille *selaïn* d'argent.............mille *selaïn*..................
la malédiction de Dusarès. Dans le mois de tisri de l'année........
de Hartat, roi des Nabatéens, aimant son peuple.

No. 13.
De l'an 6 de J.-C.

Cette fosse ....sa fille..............
tous ceux qui y seront enterrés...............................
dans toutes les fosses qui sont dans ce caveau autres que............
autre que cette fosse-ci.......................................
....
il devra à Dusarès cent *selaïn*......et à notre Seigneur le roi Hartat
tout autant. Dans le mois de thébet de l'année 13 de Hartat, roi
des Nabatéens, aimant son peuple.

No. 14.
De l'an 40 de J.-C.

C'est ici le caveau de Sabou, fils de Moqimou, et de Meikat, son
fils,......leurs enfants et leurs descendants légitimes, et de quiconque
apportera dans sa main, de la part de Sabou et de Meikat, un écrit
.... qu'il y soit enterré, ...enterré........
Sabou........ En l'année quarante-huitième de Hartat, roi des
Nabatéens, aimant son peuple.

No. 15.
An 49 de J.-C.

C'est ici le caveau de Banou, fils de Saïd, pour lui-même et ses
enfants et ses descendants et ses *asdaq*. Et que personne n'ait le
droit de vendre ou de louer ce caveau. A perpétuité. En l'année
neuvième du roi Malchus, roi des Nabatéens. Hono [fils de] Obeidat,
sculpteur.

No. 16.
Date illisible, entre 40 et 75 après J.-C.

Caveau destiné à Abda, à Aliël, à Géro, fils de Aut, et à Ahadilou,
leur mère, fille de Hamin, et à quiconque produira en sa main un
écrit ainsi conçu : " Qu'il soit enterré dans mon tombeau." A eux
et à leurs descendants. En l'année neuvième de Malchus.

No. 17.
Non datée

Ceci est le *loculus* qu'a fait Tahged pour Mesalmana, son frère, et
pour Mahmit, sa fille. Qu'on n'ouvre pas sur eux durant l'éternité.

No. 18.

De l'an 17 après J.-C.

Ceci est le caveau et tombeau que fit construire Maénat, fils d'Anban, pour lui-même et ses fils et ses filles et leurs enfants. En l'année vingt-quatrième de Hartat, roi des Nabatéens, aimant son peuple

No. 19.

De l'an 79 après J.-C.

Ceci est le caveau d'Amlat, fils de Meleikat, pour lui et pour ses enfants après lui. En l'année quatrième de Dabel, roi des Nabatéens.

No. 20.

Date illisible.

C'est ici le caveau de Higr, fils de ....et de ......ilat, pour eux-mêmes et pour leurs enfants et leurs descendants..............
En l'année.................................

No. 21.

Non datée.

Ce caveau est pour Sakinat, fils de Tamrat....et ses fils et ses filles et leurs enfants.

No. 22.

Pour Haïl, fils de Douna, (et) ses descendants.

Il est remarquable que dans cette liste on ne trouve aucun nom grec bien caractérisé. La civilisation nabatéenne avait cependant été pénétrée par la civilisation grecque, comme le prouvent certains noms propres, des mots tels que στρατηγός, ἔπαρχος et plus encore le style des monuments.

Le caractère des inscriptions de Medaïn-Salih témoigne d'un état social où l'on écrivait beaucoup et où les scribes se livraient à de grands caprices de calligraphie, ainsi que cela eut lieu plus tard pour l'écriture coufique.   E. R.

Medáin Sâlih.—*Note par M. Philippe Berger, Sous-Bibliothécaire de l'Institut.* [L'Arabie avant Mahomet d'après les Inscriptions : Conférence faite à la Sorbonne, *Mars* 1885.]—Voici toute une vallée pleine de sépultures de famille : car chacune de ces constructions n'est pas une sépulture particulière ; ce sont de véritables caveaux de famille, où les ayants droit sont spécifiés et qui sont entourés de toutes les formalités et de toutes les garanties que nous donnons à nos actes officiels.

Mais alors où étaient les maisons ?—Ce problème, qui nous embarrasse, a dû dérouter les Arabes du temps de Mahomet. On conçoit qu'en présence de ces monuments dont ils ne comprenaient plus la signification, ils se soient dit : ce sont les demeures des anciens habitants du pays, d'impies, de géants : les deux choses se touchent ; et que, pénétrant dans l'intérieur et voyant des cadavres, ils les aient pris pour les ossements des infidèles, frappés par le ciel dans leurs demeures. Ils ont dû être confirmés dans cette opinion par l'aspect de ces monuments. Les créneaux qui les surmontent et qui sont un des motifs habituels de l'architecture assyrienne, leur donnent un faux air de fortifications.

Un autre fait qui ressort clairement de ces légendes, c'est qu'à l'époque de Mahomet on ne comprenait plus ces inscriptions, dont on était séparé par cinq cents ans à peine, et *cela nous montre combien l'horizon des Arabes était borné du côté de ses origines.* Qui sait pourtant s'ils n'en ont pas eu encore un vague sentiment, au moins par tradition. Ces inscriptions, qui présentent un singulier mélange d'araméen et d'arabe, commencent par un mot qui n'est pas araméen, qui est arabe : *Dena Kafrâ* " Ceci est le tombeau." Or le même mot signifie en arabe *tombeau* et *impie.* Qui sait si, à une époque déjà éloignée de la dynastie nabatéenne, quand le souvenir de la langue araméenne commençait à se perdre, la confusion ne s'est pas faite entre les deux mots, et si, en répétant machinalement cette formule, les Arabes ne se sont pas dit : Voilà les mécréants écrasés par le ciel dans leurs demeures.

Il est un point sur lequel ils ne s'étaient pas trompés : c'est que ces anciens habitants du pays étaient bien des mécréants et des idolâtres. A l'une des entrées de la vallée de Medaïn-Saleh se trouve une gorge, taillée à pic, comme elles le sont toutes dans cette région. D'un des côtés on voit les restes d'une salle qui est creusée dans le roc ; seulement, au lieu d'être fermée par devant, elle est ouverte sur toute la largeur de la façade. Elle ne présente pas de niches : quelques figures, grossièrement dessinées au trait sur les murs ; rien de plus. C'est la seule construction qui n'ait pas de caractère funéraire. On l'appelle le Divan. Sur la paroi opposée de la gorge, au même niveau et dominant le précipice, on découvre toute une série de niches dans lesquelles se trouvent des pierres dressées, tantôt isolées, tantôt réunies par groupes de deux ou de trois. [*See above* pp. 120, 122.]

La vue de ces petits monuments, dessinés avec soin par M. Doughty, a été pour nous une véritable révélation. Nous avions déjà rencontré des monuments analogues à l'autre extrémité du monde sémitique. Il y a trois ans, on n'en connaissait qu'un exemple : un bas-relief, trouvé en Sicile, et qui représentait un homme en adoration devant une petite triade de pierre. Ce monument isolé était inexplicable ; mais il avait frappé l'attention de M. Renan, quand, quelque temps après (une découverte ne marche jamais seule), M. l'abbé Trihidez en rapporta plusieurs du même genre qui venaient d'Hadrumète, en Tunisie. Ces pierres, accouplées trois par trois, étaient des représentations divines, de véritables triades, il n'y avait pas de doute à avoir. S'il en restait encore, ils sont levés par les découvertes de M. Doughty. Voilà les dieux qu'allaient adorer les habitants de Medaïn-Saleh. Une inscription placée au-dessus d'une de ces niches le dit expressément :

" Ceci est le *mesgeda* qu'a fait élever Serouh, fils de Touca, à Aouda (ou Aera) de Bostra, grand dieu. Dans le mois de Nisan de l'an 1 du roi Malchus." [*No.* 5 : *see above* p. 121.]

Une autre niche porte une inscription analogue. Le *mesgeda*, c'est-à-dire la mosquée, n'est donc pas la salle située de l'autre côté du ravin, mais la niche avec la pierre qui est dedans. Voilà le Beth-El devant lequel les Nabatéens allaient se prosterner ; cette pierre n'est autre que le dieu Aouda.

* * *

On se demande où est, au milieu de tout cela, l'Arabe des Coréischites et de Mahomet ? Il nous apparaît comme un dialecte excessivement restreint, comme la langue d'une toute petite tribu, qui, par suite de circonstances, très locales, est arrivée à un degré de perfection extraordinaire. C'est à l'islamisme qu'elle a dû toute sa fortune.

L'islamisme de même a imposé sa langue avec sa religion à toute l'Arabie, et de là il s'est répandu de proche en proche, sur l'Afrique et sur l'Asie, créant, partout où il s'établit, une puissance qui pénètre tout, mais qui ferme la porte à tout ce qui n'est pas elle. Nulle part l'unité n'a été réalisée d'une façon aussi absolue. De là viennent les obstacles toujours renaissants que l'on trouve à pénétrer dans ces contrées fanatiques et désertes, obstacles si grands qu'on hésite à désirer que d'autres cherchent à les surmonter : le prix en est trop cher. Ils le seront pourtant, car il est une autre puissance que rien n'arrête, *c'est la force intérieure qui pousse l'homme à la recherche de la vérité.*

THE BAKHÛR, OR DRUGS OF THE EMBALMERS, MEDÁIN SÂLIH.— *Note by Prof. G. D. Liveing.*—A sample of gum resin which Mr. Doughty submitted to me for examination was subjected successively to the action of benzene, ether, alcohol and water, and the result found was that

2·35 per cent. of the substance was soluble in benzene,
5·45   ,,   ,,   ,,   in ether,
12·25   ,,   ,,   ,,   in alcohol,
27·36   ,,   ,,   ,,   in ·water.

There remained a considerable amount of residue after the ex-
traction by these menstrua. This consisted partly of sand with
some fibres of wood and other such substances. When burnt there
was altogether an amount of ash equal to 38·18 per cent. of the
whole sample.   G. D. L.

THE SHROUD CLOUTS, LEATHERN SHREDS, &c.—*Note by Prof. A.
Macalister.*—The pieces of cloth from the Nabatean tombs of Medáin
Sâlih are quite indistinguishable from the linen which was used in
Egypt for enwrapping mummies. The thicker leather is perhaps
camel-hide. The resinous matter [*bakhûr*] is of the same nature
as that so often found in Egyptian mummies.

THAMÛD : Hejra in Ptolemy is a town of Thamûd ; yet Medáin
Sâlih we understand by the epitaphs to have been of the Nabateans !
M. Sâlih is *Hijr* (Héjr) :—But what is Hijr ? El-Héjr, in the
tradition of the country Beduins and the Alowna, is all that valley
plain and valley ground (*v.* map in *Doc. Épigr.*, pl. xxx.) lying
between the Mezham and el-Ally (el-'Ola), and as far as Bîr el-
Ghrannem. Now el-Khreyby (*v.* p. 158) is likewise el-Héjr :—
the Khreyby we have seen in Himyaric or of the people from the
south, M. Sâlih is of the northern civil world. We might thus
conjecture that el-Khreyby is Hejra of Thamûd, and that Medáin
Sâlih, 10 miles to the N., is the Nabatean Hejra.

The name of Thamûd is found as late as the 5th century,
when certain Thamudite horsemen were numbered in the Roman
army. (*Die Alte Geogr. Arabiens* p. 28.) The earliest historical
notice which we have of the tribe of Thamûd has been read in the
Assyrian Monuments " in the list of tribes subdued by Sargon in one
of his expeditions into Arabia in about B.C. 715. The other tribes
mentioned in this passage are the Ibadid, Marsiman, Hayapa, the
country being named The Remote Bari (probably *bariyeh* [Arabic],
the Desert)."—*Letter from Sir Henry C. Rawlinson.*

THE MONEY OF ANCIENT ARABIA.—*Note by Mr. Barclay V. Head,
British Museum.*—The çoins of Arabia before Mohammedan times

may be divided into three great classes : (i) The money of Yemen or the so-called Himyaritic coins ; (ii) The money of the Nabathaean kings ; (iii) The coins of the various Arabian cities under the Roman empire.

(i) The coins of the Sabaeans and Homeritae (Himyarites) begin in the 4th or 3rd century B.C. and consist of imitations of the well-known Athenian tetradrachms and drachms. Most of these imitations come to us from Southern Arabia, and bear in addition to the Athenian types [the head of Pallas and the owl], Himyarite letters or inscriptions. In the 2nd cent. B.C. Alexander the Great's tetradrachms were also copied in South Arabia. In the second half of the first century B.C. the Athenian tetradrachms of the new style, with the owl seated on an amphora, served as models for the coins of the Sabaean kings. Of this class both gold and silver coins, the latter in large quantities, have been discovered at Sana. They bear on the obverse the head of a native king (afterwards superseded by a copy of the head of Augustus), and on the reverse the Athenian owl seated on an amphora, and inscriptions in a character which has not yet been read, accompanied by letters or monograms in the ordinary Himyaritic character. The copper coins [*of which specimens are here engraved*, p. 113] are contemporary with the silver above described. They are very rude (hardly recognisable) imitations of the Athenian silver money, and they were probably the copper currency of northern as well as Southern Arabia, indeed they come to us chiefly from the northern districts. During the first century A.D. the only money of Yemen was a small silver currency with inscriptions in the Himyarite character.

(ii) The money of the Nabathaean kings in Northern Arabia begins with Malchus I circ. B.C. 145 and ends with Malchus III circ. A.D. 67.

(iii) About the time of Hadrian, the Nabathaean currency was superseded by the local money of the Roman emperors struck at Bostra, Petra, Adraa, and other towns. These come to an end with the reign of Gallienus A.D. 268 or thereabouts.   B. V. H.

CHAPTER VII.

RETURN OF THE HAJ.

The last inscription. Whilst M. Aly with men of the garrison goes down to el-Ally, our flock is taken by robbers. Alleluia. "Hap" in Mohammedan mouths. The robbers' supper. Haj Nejm's valour. Nejm and the Arabian Prince Ibn Rashîd. The Emir's oratory. The Emir had shed blood of his next kinsfolk. Devout mis-livers. Riddling at the coffee fire. The robbers' tribe guessed. W. Aly wavering: alarms. New guests of the kella. Ibn Rashîd's gift-mare. The Jurdy arrive. Words of their chief. Ally fruit-sellers. Beduins would pilfer the camp Méhsan the Bountiful. The soldiery shooting at the Beduins. Mohammed "Father-of-teeth." A Jeheyna Beduwy arrested. Ibn Rashîd's messengers. Abd el-Azîz. Arabic cheer. M. Aly's saws to the Teyâmenâ. The Nejders, men of prayers. Cannon shot in the night-watches. The bitter night hours for the half-clad people abroad. Small-pox in the ascending Haj. Locusts gathered for meat. Tolerance of the multitude; the Nasrâny amongst them. Of his adven-turing further into Arabia. An Ageyly of East Nejd. The Pilgrim caravans are as corrupt torrents in the land of Arabia. The Haj arriving. The camp and market. The Persian mukowwem accused at Medina. The watering. A Beduin of Murra. M. Aly had been charged by the Pasha and the Sîr-Amîn for the Nasrâny. The Pasha and officers dissuaded Zeyd. Algerian derwishes. Nejd mares. Departure with the Haj from Medáin Sâlih. Beduin vaunting. Few slaves from the African Continent brought up in the Haj. Beduins stop their nostrils. A gentle derwish. Tidings of War. Saying of a Turkish officer. The Haj menzil. The military bone-setter. Giant derwish of the Medân. A meteor. Ageylies. The remove. Meeting with M. Saîd Pasha. Leave the Haj Caravan and enter the Beduin deserts. Zeyd's words to the stranger.

FOOTSTEPS of another ghrazzu of seven had been seen in the plain. In these days M. Aly would have me no more adventure out of sight from the kella: he forbad the gate Arabs to accompany me, ferociously threatening, Wellah, that the lives of them should be for mine: which he said in few days would be required of himself by Mohammed Saîd Pasha.

There remained a single frontispice crag, one of the last outlying monuments, which (since one might climb to the inscription without the ladder-beam) had been left hitherto. I had with difficulty M. Aly's licence to make a last excursion thither with a sure and sheykhly poor man of the Fejîr, *Mohammed ed-Deybis,* a near kinsman of Zeyd's. My com-

panion's eyes watched all round earnestly as we went, for said he
" I must answer for thee, and I am in dread of these ghrazzus ! "

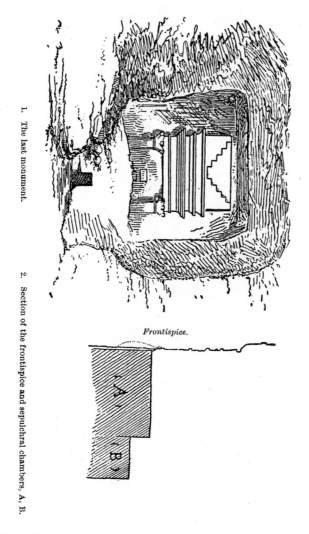

1. The last monument.

2. Section of the frontispice and sepulchral chambers, A, B.

Frontispice.

When the paper prints were long a-drying, for this sepulchre
looks to the north, I had leisure to visit the charnel within ;—
and the monument alone were a sufficient example of all that
may be seen at Medáin Sâlih !

Without is a single inscription tablet, which was engraved already when all the lower hewn architecture was yet to begin.

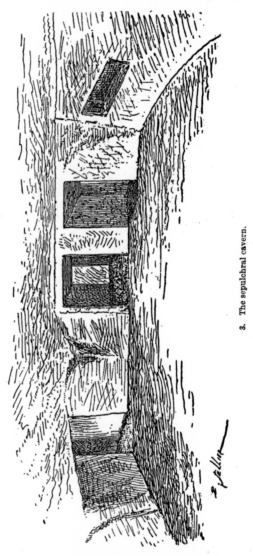

3. The sepulchral cavern.

The funeral chamber is fully perfected within as a long used burying place: here are loculi, sepulchral cells and sunken sepulchres, and an inner sepulchral chamber; but the fronti-

spice was only half ended in their time and has remained abandoned. Was this the eternal dwelling of some honest sheykhly
family, but not abounding in the world? [We may read now
the Epitaph (no. 4); and there appears in it a certain moderation
nearly without their formal and superstitious comminations.]

Mohammed Aly would visit el-Ally before the caravan,
to purchase helw dates for the Pasha and for the great Haj
officers. Because the last year he had been assailed in the
bóghrâz he would now ride strong and led every man of the
askars away with him; only Haj Nejm remained with me in the
kella. When they were gone I adventured to the monuments,
but in returning betimes there surprised me Aarab voices
among the rocks. Two Beduins came ambling upon a thelûl
from under Ethlib, and now they hailed me " *ya weled,* lad ho ! "
Not knowing them, whether friends or foemen, I made haste,
covered by the Maiden and Borj rocks, to be at home, and
when they overtook me it was in the open, within sight of the
kella. Our greetings were in this form : " Thou art who? "—
" And what be ye? and whence come ye? " Haj Nejm left alone,
the gate was sparred, and the old man made no speed to come
down and undo for us. Then as we sat to drink coffee the young
men, which were of W. Aly, reported how a little before they had
crossed many footprints of men and sheep together. " Out !
exclaimed Haj Nejm, the Lord avert !—then our flock is taken ! "
—The shepherd Doolan, his son, and a young Fehjy, had led
the flock that morning under Ethlib.

After their cups the Beduins rode further. There was no
lamentation ; if such kind of grief come upon them the
Moslem Arabs sit awhile astonished, and they speak in under-
tones without complaining : all is ruled, they muse, by the Will
above them ; the loss is theirs to-day, they also bring like evil
upon other. We watched on from the kella terrace, the afternoon passed, and yet we saw nothing. As the sun was going
down, the best eyes descried somewhat ; they said " It is the
sheep and the goats, with the herdsmen," which returned from
the contrary part, far under the Harra. The hareem of the gate
taking up their loud Alleluia *lullul-lullul-lullul-la !* children
shouted with them for joy, and there ran forth men and housewives to have the first tidings : but as the cattle and shepherds
approached, those that were to us for eyes said they could
see only about half their beasts returning, and fewer than the
people which went to meet them. Now they arrived, and
Doolan came shouting and protesting all the way up to our
coffee chamber, where with a sigh (which was all he gave to
grief), Haj Nejm already kindled the evening fire, and had

submitted himself, since there was no remedy, to the will of
Ullah. " *Shûf,* said he, *el-bakht,* that such a chance should betide
upon the only day of all the year when we could be taken unpro-
vided." Doolan began a passionate argument and loud defence
of himself. " The ghrazzu was nine on foot, all with guns !
wellah, he could know them by their speech to be Beny Atîeh ;
the last night they had lurked in Ethlib, and having watched
the departure of the aga with the askars, they rose from their
hiding-places to steal the flock of the kella." It was a place
of crags and sand-drifts : thus they came upon the shepherds
at unawares and unseen by them. For many days already
these robbers had been roaming in the plain, (it was their
strange footsteps we had seen) until for hunger they went down
to purchase dates at el-Ally ; where some ill-affected persons
taught them all the circumstances of our Héjr kella. Doolan
said to me, " And thou wast well-nigh fallen into their hands,
for as the robbers brought us forward with the *chessab* (booty)
we crossed the fresh footprints of Khalîl."

At first they would kill Doolan, saying, " he was a Fejîry ! "
and between these neighbours is perpetual blood fued.—" No, I
beseech you, for I am Doolan the Fehjy."—" If thou art Doolan,
open thy mouth, man, thou shouldest want the front teeth ; and
now put out thy tongue : " and the poor Fehjy told us betwixt
smiling and weeping, " They made me lob them out my
tongue ! "—" Ay ! he has the slit tongue ; fellows, this is he."—
The poor man had been maimed thus by a Ruwàlla lance-thrust
in the mouth, when riding in the North. Then the *agîd* or
leader of the crew, laying the sword-edge to his young son's
throat, bade Doolan say the sooth of God, whose these sheep
were and the goats every one. Such as he told them to be of
the kella they spared, saying, " We are friends of the Dowla."
To the poor Fehját at the gate they left a part of their own, and
took all the remnant, which were of Fukara tribesmen. Doolan's
loss was three head, the other Fehjies' six ; Haj Nejm had lost
three ; Wady two. " So four or five will fall to the agîd
(said Nejm) ; they will sup to-night of a sheep, and a goat or
sheep (the value of three or four reals) will be the lot of every
man." Afterward the bones were found of these hawks' suppers,
at the ashes of their evening fire, and by the signs it appeared
that they had swallowed five head between them, such hungry
wretches they were : this meal should refresh them homewards,
after a fortnight's deadly fatigue ; in which all days, wandering
as thieves in hostile country, they had jeoparded their own lives.
But such are pains they will undertake with cheerfulness in pursuit of an uncertain booty, and show themselves likely lads that

can attempt an hardy enterprise ; and with aught they bring
home, however small it be, they hold themselves rewarded. And
yet there is hardly a miserable Beduin in his ragged booth will
rise from lying along upon the ground and break his day's
slumber to make some small endeavour, for as good a reward certain. Such rovers when they come home often lie sick of their
past suffering and are in deadly weariness many long days after.

"Aha ! if Mohammed Aly," said Haj Nejm, (and he was not
content with M. Aly,) " had not taken every man along with
him ! *fuzzna* we had been up and after them." And the old man
sat gazing in the air and smoothing himself with wringing his
fingers ; the Moorish valour still bubbling in him and boiling
over with impatience.—" Wellah, by this time we had recovered
our cattle and taken some of their own from them, like as we
did that day—eigh, Wady ! eigh, Doolan !—to the ghrazzu of
Shammar ; but here (he told them on his fingers) be only Wady,
Doolan, the Fehjy lad, and Mohammed ed-Deybis, four guns
and I the fifth ; what can we do being so few ! " He spoke
of a small foray which in a former year had driven away the
kella flock, and finding some poor Fehját women gathering
sticks under Ethlib, stripped them bare out of their poor
smocks :—that indeed is reckoned a felony among Beduins ; but
many times in their haste they are not so nice observers of
the faith of the desert. Haj Nejm then, with another or
two, had pursued them all night until they came upon the
Beduin robbers, who, seeing " the Dowla *'* upon them, would not
stay to be shot at, but abandoning the slow-footed flock, made
haste to deliver themselves, and rode further. The fierce old
Moghreby, crying in the night like an afrît, took two thelûls
of theirs, which he afterwards sold to the Alowna ; the price of
them, he said, with much comfort, " he had eaten, and they were
now in his body." A gay embroidered dromedary headstall,
which had been theirs, the kind old man bestowed in later days
upon me, and where I rode in the desert it was the envy of
my nomad companions.

When Mohammed Ibn Rashîd was here, the past summer,
with his armed riders, and had taken the camp of the Wélad
Aly, he lay certain days at the wells under the Borj rocks, and
bid call the kellâjy, saying 'if he were a man afraid to come out
to him from the fort, he would send in one for him.' Haj Nejm
answered he feared naught ; and come to the Emir's tent,
about which the rest (Arabians in an expedition), lay abroad
barely upon the ground, the great prince of the Beduin countries asked gently of his welfare. " Well enough, said Haj
Nejm, well enough, ay el-Emir, were it not sometimes for

13—2

Beduw of yours (Shammar) : and if I had gotten them in my hold once I had chopped their necks, wellah, and it were (the word fell out of an old man's mouth) thine own self ! " The Shammar tyrant, whom the Aarab are wont to fear as the death, had never from a poor man such a rebuke. " Thou cut off my head ; thou ! " said the prince, rolling himself, and uncheerfully regarding the honest old Moor's countenance, who stood there stiffly for the Dowla before him. Mohammed, who had weathered waves of the world himself, and privily kept a good heart, even when his hands were stained with kinsmen's blood, and could show when he durst a pleasant mild humour, gave the Dowlâny a good new mantle and kerchief with a shirt-cloth (those he wore yet) and twenty mejîdies ; and to each of the men in the kella he bade give five, and a change of clothing.

The place of their camp about the wells was yet very apparent with the litter of a thousand camels. Haj Nejm in our days abroad showed me where the Prince's coffee-fire had been and where was his kitchen hearth, in a cleft of the wild sand-rock ; and the Emir's oratory,—a parcel of ground guarded from the common by a narrow horse-shoe of stones, the head bent towards Mecca. Such praying-places I saw often laid in the open deserts of Ibn Rashîd's country. Nejm told me how this man came to be prince, killing nigh a score of his kinsfolk. " Then, I asked, what has this man, or devil, to do with religion ? Wherefore should he pray ? who made his own brother childless, and killed his brethren ! does God hear murderers ? " Mohammed Aly answered me : " No, by God, and thou sayest rightly ; a man of blood can have no part in the religion." These sallies are never unwelcome to the Arabs, being as sparkles struck upon their own natural hearts, in the confused religious darkness of their Semitic conscience. When I heard it had been deliberated to give me poison in the dish at el-Ally,—they thought the Nasrâny could be come for no good so far hither, and he was " writing " their rocks—also that some of the kella and gate Arabs had asked license of the aga to make me away secretly, saying to Mohammed Aly, ' if only it should not hurt him at Damascus ; ' —and it had been done, but that they were in dread of an after-clap of the Dowla :—how ! I answered them who warned me, are these then so light to shed man's blood, who patter their daily prayers, as I hear them, most solemnly ? tell me whether such be good Moslemîn ! *Answer :* " Ha ! they pray, and their prayers are naught, God will not hear them, they are wicked men : but wot you, Khalîl, what they all say in this country, ' It is lawful to kill the Nasrâny, that were a deed well-pleasing unto Ullah ; he is God's adversary.' " Prayer to their understanding is to recite the canonical oration with unction at the hours, with washen hands and comely abasement of bowing and kneeling. At other times I have found some gospel (as of the true cleanness and fasting), which pulled down their malicious coxcombs, and they as Semites naturally of the religious mind, were pleased with these saws : so the best of them have then said, "Listen now ! that Khalîl *opens* (the religious understanding)."

But Doolan the herdsman for all his mighty oaths was not able to clear himself from the reproaches of the rest whose sheep he fed. Wady, a merely bad comely man, ceased not with dark looks to injure him every moment, and crying "Ha Fehjy !" Little blame belonged to the poor herdsman, who with a lad had been overpowered by nine desperate land-lopers. After the sheep were stolen the door was locked, and we passed three days committed to the kella. To drive the evenings in our now thin and silent company, the old man Nejm propounded riddles, over the coffee hearth. The Arabs were ready, they said theirs, and we guessed round ; when the word fell to me I set them the enigma of the sphinx, saying, this was the most famous riddle in the world. Haj Nejm told over in his palm, all the beasts of the wilderness, and wondered greatly what this strange thing should mean ; especially when I acknowledged that I had seen his footprints lately in the plain, not far off. When they could not unriddle that dark word-binding of the sphinx, they were delighted with the homely interpretation. Twice again I was taken in riddlers' company in Arabia, and have propounded my riddle, since I knew none other : a Beduin weled, son of Œdipus, sitting amongst the second wiseacres, unriddled me at the moment ; this kind of parabolical wisdom falls to the Semetic humour and is very pleasant to the Arabs.

The fourth day, came again M. Aly and the nefers in a rain from el-Ally. Shaking himself from the unwonted wet, he stamped mainly in his trooper's boots, and swore in Pilate's voice ' there should not a head of the sheep go lost, no ! nor of the goats neither. Every man should have his own again and that soon, by Ullah : and were those robbers any of B. Atîeh, Wellah ! as ever the Haj should be come to Tebûk he would bind the sheykhs of them to a cannon-mouth ! he had a mind also to wring from them some camel, in amends, for himself.' Only of their few words had been guessed the men's tribe and their fendy, that they were Khuthéra, of that dark looming northern Harra which is seen afar off from el-Héjr, and from whence are fetched the best basalt quern-stones (above the kellat el-Akhdar). All the idle nomads are diligent discerners of discourses ; those

men had said *kirra*, hire, which sounds more often *kirwa* upon
the Beduin tongue, *kerwa* at el-Ally.

Authors of the most alarms at Medáin Sâlih were the
W. Aly, in their perpetual defections and returning from one
to the other part ; they finding the Dowla a vain name to protect them in the desert, were now of a mind, forsaking again
the Dowla to be reconciled with Ibn Rashîd. I heard some
sherîf (or elder of the noble blood of Mohammed) from Medina
would be fetched up in the Haj to Medáin, to be a mean
between them. A great W. Aly market party coming in, in
these days, to meet the Haj, and alighting beside Kasr es-Sâny,
was alarmed by a rumour, in the ears of their evil consciences,
so leaving their market stuff on the ground, they hied in
panic fear upon the empty camels towards el-Ally. After
their amazement they found it had been nothing, yet durst no
more encamp there ; but loading their packs they entered the
rugged borders of the not distant Harra. The same day a
poor Fehjy had been stripped of his shirt and robbed of his
thelûl, in the plain. On the morrow some W. Aly were spoiled
near el-Héjr, by ten robbers. The young brothers habalîs,
lately gone out from us, not having returned, we thought them
lost. At a fortnight's end they came again, smiling with all
their white teeth, and leading in, to sell them in the Haj market,
three asses, which they had stolen by night-time whilst the
owners slept, from an encampment of Heteym far behind Kheybar, perhaps a hundred miles distant. They were deadly weary,
so long they had trudged, with peril of their lives, upon the
sharp lavas in an enemies' country, and having nothing to eat.

Certain traders, men born of Damascus fathers, arrived now
from Teyma and were guests in the kella : they would buy their
provision of clothing and coffee, for the year, in the Haj and
Jurdy markets. The same night came in the servants of Ibn
Rashîd, bringing the Emir's yearly present of a Nejd mare
for the Pasha. On the morrow, as we saw the Prince's gift-mare
standing in a horse-cloth of Arab mantle-stuff, weak, and un-
curried, she seemed to us hardly worth an ass, and our Moors
scoffed saying that this was wellah but a jade. The Jurdy was
about to arrive : the clerk of the Jurdy, called by the Aarab
the Jurdy pasha, riding out before them, knocked in the first
hours after midnight upon the iron door of the kella. This
was a Syrian Turk *Mohammed Tâhir Effendy*, and there came
with him the lieutenant of the military guard, a worthy
Turk ; he that had been stationed formerly with his troop to
repress the W. Aly at el-Ally. They saluted me with good

humour, glad to find me safe, and we all went to drink coffee together. Weary with the journey, quoth Mohammed Tâhir, as they sat down, *Ha wellah! ana shebaan min ummr-y,* " By the Lord I have now had my fill of life."—" What say'st thou ! " answered Mohammed Aly ; for who ever heard such a word in a fortunate man's mouth ?—" That I am full of my life, and that which is passed already, wellah, sufficeth me." Mohammed Effendy was a good man, careless of super- stitious ceremonial, of singular humour, one who spoke and wrought all, in the perplexed human life, from his heart ; as the Turks are not seldom, he was full of robust and, could they be well bestowed, of great natural qualities. In the grey of the morning rode in the Jurdy train ; in half an hour, a street of tent-shops and the white village of soldiers' tents was set up before the kella. The Jurdy pass the Beduin country in like military order, and paying a surra as the Haj before them. The Jurdy (*jerîd*, javelin) is sent down some time after the great pilgrimage, with relief of provisions from Syria, to meet them here at the midway returning from Mecca. That which was anciently a great convoy is now but a weary company of few private traders ; they journey guarded by forty horse troopers, and training on wheels a wide-mouthed short brass field-cannon, which was fired many times according to usage in their now arriving at the merkez, Medáin : the day was the 3rd of February. The same afternoon came fruit-sellers of the Alowna upon camels hired of the Wélad Aly, and alighted without tents under the kella ; with bushes they fenced in their encampment from the winter's night wind. The villagers brought dates and baskets of sweet lemons for the thirsty pilgrimage ; an hundred I have bought at el-Ally for half-a-crown.

Late in the day, as I sat in the tent of the Jurdy officer, upon a sudden, shots were fired in the camp : we rose and went out to see this chance. The soldiers of Syria, with savage levity, were shooting after a flying rout of Beduins, that had even now attempted to rob the Jurdy market, and were W. Aly tribesmen. I saw also the kella walls were manned, and that the feeble garrison fired off their matchlocks at those who fled and the iron gate was sparred. A trooper shouted hoarsely to slue the gun and let fly after them ;—as herdsmen and wolves, soldiers and Beduins may never agree together ; a shell was soon shot over their heads, which burst with a distant rumour in the sandy wilderness. Yet in the Jurdy pasha's tent there sat a great W. Aly personage, Mehsan the blind, next in dignity among them after his cousin, the head of the tribe ; he was rich among the sheukh of the desert, and the man's antique hospitality was chanted in the songs of the country side. Mehsan was a guest in camp to-day, waiting to go up with the Haj, to be treated for his cataract at Damascus. He hearing this stir sat on, rolling the pitiful dark eyeballs, and seemed to commiserate the sinister chance of his witless wild tribesmen. A robust man was he, now in elder's years, and very well bearded for an Arabian ; a sign among Beduins that in his honourable life he had never hungered. His diet was buttermilk of the flock, and he supped of a bowl of camel-milk from the cow at evening : and wide was the chest of this sheykh of the desert which harboured so large an heart.

Mehsan sat lordly clad in his new garments of honour, that he received every year of the Haj administration with his surra : the man was of not less understanding, with his good hearty humour ; he had been often a government guest in the towns. He knew at Damascus and el-Medina the settled life, and which until he pine again for the purer air is a refreshment to the for-wandered Beduin. Mehsan was afflicted in a part of his human nature which is to the Semitic affection a grave unhappiness : the man went childless, he was *ajjr (infecundus) ;* which the Arabs believe to follow upon some acute diseases. Mehsan's heirs were therefore his poorer tribesmen and strangers, all such being daily partakers of the bountiful man's mess. Mehsan had but one cheerless wife, for the dispense and service of his great household of hospitality. After Ibn Rashîd's late foray and the mischief of his tribe, he had divided (I heard said) five hundred reals to the more necessitous ; and though his own spacious Beduin booth and plentiful house-stuff had been carried away with the booty :—a great sum was this, that any nomad should have in his hand of ready money (his surra) : and how much public virtue was in this desert-born man, leading the vagabund life of the poor Beduin Arabs !

Every soldier emptied his sixteen-shotted carbine, but I could not hear that any of the Aarab was hurt ; yet it was said that one had been touched in the shoulder. Such shooting is cause that the nomads make light of the military fire-arms, as tools that shoot very fair and far off ; their beggarly matchlocks they are persuaded to be much the better pieces.

Now came in Bishr Beduins and strangers of other neighbour tribes, as Bílli and Jeheyna ; they would buy and sell in the Haj market : for this they paid, every one for himself, a real of brotherhood to some sheykh of the nomads of these marches. Landlords in their own right are, here, W. Aly, the Fejîr, and the Moahîb, all of Annezy stock. Among the Moahîb was a Morocco Moor formerly of the garrison at el-Akhdar, who forsaking that ill-paid service of the Dowla was become a rice-carrier from el-Wejh, and he lived now wived among the Aarab. His name was Mohammed, and they called him *Abu Sinûn*, or father of teeth, for his deformity of great canine tushes. An asthma made him seek the airy nomad life. Pleasantly smiling, he professed himself glad to meet, so far from the world, in this solitude, with an Engleysy; 'the Engleys were his people's neighbours! and if I visited him at any time in the Moahîb camp, he would show me yonder Harra and carry me to visit the sites of ruins in their nomad circuit.'

I saw a Beduwy arrested with cruel outcries in the kella. He was of Jeheyna : his fault was an ancient debt, and Haj Hasan stood threatening nothing less than to chop off his head. Some nomads entreated for the man, but his tormentors bound him and thrust back the hapless wretch into the dark forage-chamber, and locked the door upon him. The Jurdy pasha, who sat then by the well in the kella, shrinking his shoulders at the barbarous spectacle, looked up towards me to see how the European might bear it! Many guests were now lodged in the kella ; those from Hâyil and from Teyma, with daily con-course of Aarab and Alowna, so that there was no more room in the coffee-chamber.

The emir Ibn Rashîd's messengers were three freshly clad Nejders. Ahe principal was *Abd el-Azîz*, a prudent and honour-able person of the prince's confidence ; but although white as the Arabs I have understood he was not fully of the ingenuous blood, his parentage was from *el-Aruth* in the eastern Nejd. Many are the foreigners who have obtained some office, and stand now foremost in the tyrant's service at Hâyil. These white liber-tines in Arabia may be descended from Galla blood. A certain yellowness in their dim white skin, betrays them to be not pure Arabians. In Abd el-Azîz was a noble amenity, the Nejd manners and a substantial carriage, where a feminine sweetness of their humanity is mixed with a manly severity. He was also a maintainer here of his master's dignity : so when there entered some Ally villagers, in whose sorry dusky looks he could not be mistaken, Abd el-Azîz, with a lofty guesture, bade them with-draw. It should not become him, he said, to sit in one company with Alowna. This might be of an old Waháby grudge, in whose best days these abhorred Hejâz villagers had never bowed to the Nejd tyranny. Yet the same Abd el-Azîz could sit courting the W. Aly nomads, now the Prince's enemies. Friendly they sipped coffee of the same cups, and yet it was by this tribe's treacheries that had happened great damage of late, and slaughter of the Aarab in the emir's dominions. Ibn

Rashîd hoped to receive their submission ere long, since they could not always hold out against him. "Aha-ha," laughed Mohammed Aly, coming to my chamber; "O the strange fare that is amongst these Beduins! they would cut each other's throats, wellah, in the field, and here you may see them all drink kindly together." I went in to sit with them;—"Mehsan, said Abd el-Azîz, turning to the blind sheykh's ear, my counsel is to you that you hold the mountains, and remain in cragged places, where Ibn Rashîd may hardly attain you. Mehsan answered mildly, "Ay, ay, Abd el-Azîz, and this will we do."

The morning and evening hospitality, a vast metal charger heaped with twenty or thirty men's victuals, was led in between two bearers and set upon the gallery, and to this were bidden the guests of the kella. Haj Nejm's Arab cheer was buttered rice upon half-baked girdle-bread. Mohammed Aly could make himself pleasant to all his guests and strangers in the tower: of the Teyma men he subtilly enquired the situation of their town; 'was it plain or wady? and he would ride to visit them (when, a government man, he durst) some of these years.' To his forged Turkish words the frank Teyâmena knew to answer guardedly again; aware that the governors of Medina had meditated to take their oasis, in which they lived more to their minds under Mohammed Ibn Rashîd.

Abd el-Azîz visited me daily in my chamber; he discoursed with the stranger liberally, and so did those from Teyma; they had heard a good report of the Nasrâny in the kella, and understood me to be well affected towards the Moslemîn. He being a lettered man, examined also my books and, having never seen printed letters, he took them for manuscript, saying, "—very fairly written in language of the Nasara!" their own books, hagiography, quires of songs, and the koran, are mostly hand-written amongst them. Nejm and Mohammed Aly had boasted to them that the Nasrâny never lied, even were it to help himself; so he answered me with the truth and frankly, in all that I enquired of him. The beginning of the great Wady er-Rummah was, he said, in the Harrat Kheybar, and the going out at Zbeyer near to Bosra. He told me also I should see some inscriptions about Hâyil if ever I came thither. As he heard so much among them that I was Tom Truth, he returned to ask me again, Did I "drink" smoke,—for that is less than godly among Nejders. He with only two companions had ridden round upon thelûls by Teyma, leading the mare, in ten desert journeys; such is become the security of those Beduin districts, under the strong name of Ibn Rashîd. The men of Nejd and Teyma were very diligent in their often devotion; buckets had

been set for them, upon the kella terrace, for their washings
at the hours of prayer : then Abd el-Azîz, the prince's messenger, standing forth as *imâm* before them, led their formal
prostrations.

The Haj was late, and the Beduish multitude, which were
come to market without their booths, lay out sheltering under
the bushes in these bitter cold nights ; their cheerful watch-fires
appeared glimpsing up and down in the dark, nigh the camp, in
the wilderness. In the watch before midnight shells were shot
from the Jurdy cannon east and west over their treasonable
heads into the empty waste. Long now and chill at this altitude were the winter nights ; the gate Arabs these two months
could not sleep past midnight, but lay writhing, with only
their poor mantles lapped about them, in the cold sand and
groaning for the morning. But especially their women suffer
in the ragged tents : some of them, bare of all world's good,
have not more than a cotton smock upon their bodies ; for
where might they find silver to buy any mantle to cover them ?
Snow falls not in the plain, but some years it whitens the
Harra, above 3000 feet height. A dromedary rider, sent down
to meet the Haj, brought word that the pilgrims had been delayed, in their camps, by (tropical) rains, betwixt the Harameyn.
Now the caravan approaching, it was rumoured they brought
the small-pox among them. Beduins of my acquaintance, who
cared not to receive it before as a gift, now entreated me to sell
them vaccination ; and they reproached me when in this busy
stir and preparation to depart, I could not hear them.

The same evening we saw flights of locusts, an ill augury of
the opening spring season ; they would devour the *rabía*. The
people cried, " They come driving from el-Ally." The bird-like insects flittering upon their glassy feeble wings in the southern wind,
fell about the camp ; these locusts were toasted presently at all
watch-fires and eaten. The women on the morrow had gathered
great heaps, and were busy singeing them in shallow pits, with a
weak fire of herbs ; they give up a sickly odour of fried fish oil.
Thus cured and a little salt cast in, the locust meat is stived in
leathern sacks, and will keep a good long while : they mingle
this, brayed small, with their often only liquid diet of sour
buttermilk. Locust powder is not victual to set before guests ;
and I have seen poor nomads (more often women) a little out of
countenance to confess that (to beguile hunger) they were eating
this wretchedness. The best is the fat spring locust, and
" fretting every green thing," the Aarab account them medicinal.
The later broods, *dubba*, born of these, sexless, or imperfect
females, finding only a burned-up herbage, are dry and un-

wholesome. This early locust, toasted, is reckoned a sweet-meat in town and in desert.

In these days whilst we awaited the pilgrimage, so incurious were the weary Damascenes who came with the Jurdy, that only two parties, and they upon account of my being there, went a mile abroad to visit the monuments at Medáin Sâlih. The Jurdy pasha, with the Turkish lieutenant and his troop, Mohammed Aly guiding them, galloped another day to see what they were, for whose sake the Engleysy was come down, so far, from Syria. A lonely Christian in the midst of a stirring multitude of Moslemîn, assembled at el-Héjr, I lived among Syrians, and under that somewhat burdensome jealousy of the tolerant better sort of Arabians. Mohammed Aly also recommended me to everyone who might further my adventure in Arabia; from which, notwithstanding, all the friendly and well-disposed persons very heartily dissuaded me : it is not of their easy religious minds to attempt anything untried. ' Whither would I go, said they, to lose myself in lawless land, to be an outlaw, if only for my name of Nasrâny, and far from all succour ; where they themselves, that were of the religion and of the tongue, durst not adventure ? Khalîl, think better for thyself, and return with us, whilst the way is open, from this hunger-stricken wilderness and consumed by the sun ; thou wast not bred, and God calls thee not, to this suffering in a land which only demons, *afarît*, can inhabit ; the Beduw are demons, but thou art a Nasrâny,—there everyone that seeth thee will kill thee ! And if the Lord's singular grace save thy life to the end, yet what fruit shouldst thou have for all those great pains ? Other men jeopardy somewhat in hope of winning, but thou wilt adventure all, having no need." And some good hearts of them looked between kindness and wonder upon me, that born to the Frankish living, full of superfluity, I should carelessly think to endure the Aarab's suffering and barren life. And they said, " In a day or two we return to Syria, leave thou this purpose, and go up in our company : and is not Damascus a pleasant city to dwell in ? " The like said also the blind Mehsan, he too would honestly dissuade me, a man of the town-life, and a Nasrâny : " Hear," said he, " a friendly counsel ; return now, Khalîl, with the Haj to es-Sham : here is only a land of Beduw under no rule, and where thou art named Nasrâny ; do not jeopardy thy life : and yet I tell thee, wilt thou needs adventure, the Aarab are good folk, and thou wilt enlarge thy breast (feel thy heart to be free) amongst them." M. Aly answered, " Khalîl is a man too adventurous ; there may nothing persuade him." Said a sheykh, " If one go to the Aarab, he should carry his shroud under his arm with him ; " others said, " Khalîl, see thou trust not thyself to any of them all ; the Beduw are elfin." The Jurdy officers blamed me, saying, " And why cast your life away ? you know them not, but we know them ; the Beduins are fiends." And the lieutenant said, " Even we which are soldiers cannot pass, but by paying them surra. They are rebels, and (he added as a Turk) deserve to lose their heads. How durst they gainsay the authority of the Sûltàn ! " They asked me, " What think you of this desert ? " " I warrant you (answered M. Aly, the Algerian), if *Fransa* had it, there would be towns and villages." I told them I thought the country would not be worth the pains.

Secretary with the Jurdy was a swarthy Ageyly Arabian, a lettered man of the Waháby country, and very unlike all those Syrian faces about him. And yet the eyes of his dark visage regarded me with goodwill, without fanatical envy, as a simple Nasrâny traveller in land of the Arabs : he said he would tell me of a wonder in his country where I might come another day. " Write !....*Siddûs,* in *W. Halífa,* in the dîrat *Umseylmy* (Moseilima) *el-kithâb* (the false prophet), there is set up a *mîl* (needle, or pillar) with an unknown writing, no man can tell what ; but it was of those Nasâra or kafirs which in old time inhabited the land."

It was now ascertained that the Haj brought the small-pox among them. This terrible disease and cholera-fever are the destruction of nomad Arabia. In their weakly nourished bodies is only little resistance to any malignant sickness. The pilgrimage caravans, (many from the provinces of Arabia herself,) are as torrents of the cities' infection flowing every year through the waste Peninsula.

The eighth morrow of this long expectation, the Haj, which had journeyed all night, were seen arriving in the plain. The Jurdy troop mounted and galloped with their officers to salute the Pasha. The tent-pitchers came before : in few more minutes they had raised the pilgrims' town of tents, by the Jurdy camp. The jingles sounded again in our ears, measured to the solemn gait of the colossal bearing-camels, of the pageant-like (but now few returning) takhts er-Rûm. The motley multitude of the Haj came riding after. Their straggling trains passed by for half an hour, when the last of the company re-entered their lodgings. Twice every year stands this canvas city of a day, in the Thamudite plain, full of traffic ! Cobblers sat at the sûk corners to drive their trade ; they had by them raw soles of camels fallen by the way ; and with such they clouted shoes for those who fared so far on foot. The Jurdy street of tent-shops ·

was soon enlarged by the new merchants' tents. The price of
small commodities is, at this mid-way station, five to eight times
the market worth at Damascus. The Jurdy have brought down
Syrian olives, leeks and cheese and caravan biscuit. The Jurdy
baker was busy with his fire-pit of sticks in the earth and his
girdle-pans, *tannûr*, to make fine white flat-bread, for the pennies
of the poor pilgrims. The refreshing sweet and sour lemons
and helw dates, from el-Ally, I saw very soon sold out. The
merchants upon camels from Damascus opened their bales in the
tents and set out coffee-cups, iron ware, precious carpets (like
gardens of fresh colours and soft as the spring meadows,)—
fairings for great sheykhs! and clothing stuffs for the poor
Beduw. The returning Haj tradesmen bring up merchandise
from Mecca; now in their tent stalls I saw heaps of coffee from
el-Yémen (Arabia the Happy).

In little outlying tents I found spices set to sale from the
Malay islands, India or Mecca perfumes, and trifles in porcelain
from the China Seas; all brought by the Mohammedan pilgrims,
assembling to the Holy Fair, of mány strange distant nations.
The keeper of one of them cried to the Beduins, "Come up and
buy, *ya Aarab!*" women who went by, seeking for some drugs and
spicery, answered again very soberly, "What hast thou, young
man?" When they murmured at his price, "How is this? (exclaimed the seller) do ye take me for one that could defraud you,
a man coming up from beholding the temple of Ullah!"—Then,
seeing me, he stayed in his talk to salute me! the fellow made
me all the false smiling excuses in the world in the name of the
Persian Mohammed Aga, because he was not come this way
again (as his feigned promise had been to me, to convey me
to es-Shem), but gone about by sea to Bagdad. The Persian
feared in his conscience, I might another day accuse him at
Damascus. There I afterwards saw him again, when I had
returned in peace from Arabia; but so many world's waves
were gone over my head, that when he spoke to me in the
market-place I remembered him not, only of the cankered
visage there lingered some uneasy remembrance; he might be
sure that I intended no unkindness. "Ah! (he said then to my
companion, a Damascene) what have I suffered for your friend
because I conveyed him to Medáin Sâlih, at Maan and all along
the road! What happened to me then at el-Medina! Wellah!
I would not undertake the like again;—no, not for five times
the money. At Medina I was examined before their council,
day by day, and they regarded not my solemn oaths, but would
compel me to acknowledge where I had hidden the Nasrâny. I
was never in such trouble in my life."

Poor Beduins flitted up and down in the street of tent-shops, to sell their few pints of samn for silver, and hoping to have therefore a new mantle this year and a *shâmy* (Damascus ware) shirt-cloth. The pilgrims who have journeyed through the night are now reposing in the tents, and the pleasant water-pipe and the cup are made ready at a hundred coffee fires : but the large white faces of girded Damascenes, their heavy foreheads wound round with solemn turbans, their citizen clothing and superfluous slops, are now quaint to the eye disused a while in the wilderness. Great press of their waterers was about the birket, to fill the girbies and draw for the multitude of cattle. The kella cistern was already green and fermenting. Even the nomads (who are not wont to find good water), refused to drink ; it was become to us abominable by the nasty ablutions to prayerward of the odious Alowna, who made no conscience to go down and wash their bodies in the public water.

In this great company I met with a swarthy Beduwy of the Murra Aarab, a tribe far in the south, by Wady Dauâsir. The man was going up in the Haj caravan to Syria ! when I asked him of his country, he answered me with that common sorry saying of the Beduins, *Ma biha kheyr,* " little or no good to find in her." He would say, " an open soil without villages, land of dearth and hunger." *Béled biha kheyr,* " a good land," they use to say of a country whose inhabitants do eat and are satisfied.

I had been in friendly wise commended by the Jurdy officers, and praised by Mohammed Aly to the Pasha ; but I did not think it well so early in the busy day to visit him, who of my coming to Medáin Sâlih had formerly conceived a grave displeasure. From M. Aly, both in his better mind and in his angry moments, I had heard all that matter. In the December night of the Haj departure from Medáin, the Turkish Sîr Amîn and Mohammed Saîd Pasha had sent, before they removed, to call again M. Aly. " Wellah, they said to him, hast thou not hidden the Nasrâny, to send him secretly to Medina and Mecca ? " " God is my witness, no your lordships, but this man certainly has adventured hither only to see Medáin Sâlih : trust me he shall not pass a step further : in any case I shall know how to let him ; but I go to bring him before you : he shall answer for himself." " No," said the Pasha, " I will not see his face, and I have a dignity to keep." (It might be when I visited him in Damascus, I had not observed to call the old portly embezzler of public moneys " Your Magnificence ! ") Said the Sîr Amîn (of Stambûl), " Hearken, kellâjy ; if this Engleysy should follow us but one footstep further to Medina, thou art to bring me

the dog's head." [Englishmen, who help these barbarians at
Constantinople that cannot be taught, they would murder you
secretly, and let hounds live, at Medina and Mecca!] The
Pasha said to Mohammed Aly, " Let him remain with you in
the kella, and you are to send him round to all the monuments,
that no more Franks come hither hereafter.   Look to it,
that no evil befall this man : for wellah we will require his life
at thy hand." *Sir Amîn :* " By Almighty God, except we find
him alive at our coming again, we will hang thee, Mohammed
Aly, above the door of thine own kella." Sore adread are they
of late to be called in question for the life of European citizens.
—M. Aly looked stoutly upon it, and answered to their beards,
that ' he would obey his orders, but by High God, he was a
Moghreby, and not to be put in awe by living creature.' Now I
must ask a boon of the Pasha, namely, that he would commend
me to the wild Beduins of the road. When the caravan removed in the morning, I should go forth to wander with the
Aarab in the immense wilderness. The Jurdy officers had dissuaded Zeyd, so had even the Pasha himself ; but Zeyd hoped
to win silver, and they had no power at all with a free Beduin.

Some Algerian derwishes were evening guests at the kella.
Willingly they allowed to me—I might seem to them a Moslem
stranger,—that they had both liberty of religion, and justice,
under their Christian rulers. There were also Moorish askars
come in from the kellas to the southward ; for here they draw
their stipends, which upon the haj way are paid for the year beforehand, although all other men's wages of the Ottoman Dowla
be as much or more in arrear :—which of them would otherwise
remain cut off, in the midst of great deserts, waiting for his
pay ? that were much the same to them as if they should never
receive it. Merry were these men of the settled countries, used to
stout hackneys, to look upon the lean and scald gift-mare of the
Nejd prince. 'A beggarly scorn, to send this carrion, not worth
thirty crown pieces ; and the Pasha would not accept her ! ' Some
Beduins who were present boasted her worth to be thirty camels.
A Syrian said, " A month at Shem, and she will seem better than
now. A mare another year, lean' as a faggot, sent by this
Beduin emir, Ibn Rashîd or what you call him, grew in the
Pasha's stable, with plenty of corn and green provender, to be
big—ay as this coffee-chamber ! " The best brood-mares of pure
blood are valued in the Aarab tribes, where they are few, at
twenty-five camels, that is £130 at least, or at most £150
sterling ; and the worst at five camels, which is the price of the
best thelûls. The Beduin prince's yearly gift of a mare to

Mohammed Saîd was a sop in the mouth of the great Syrian pasha. The Pasha at his coming down again with the next year's pilgrimage sends his messenger from hence to Hâyil, bearer of counter-gifts for the Arabian emir. These are revolver pistols, rifle-guns, telescopes, and the like Western wares from Stambûl.

Upon the morrow at eight, when the signal gun was fired, the Haj caravan set forward, and I rode after them with Zeyd, upon a young camel he had bought me for thirty reals. In departing he asked Mohammed Aly to remember him at Damascus (for his gift-foal), and bring him down, in the next Haj, at least, a furred winter coat [the town guise : Syrian Aarab wear a warm jerkin of sheep skins ; Sinai Beduins a gazelle or other skin hanging from the neck, which they shift round their bodies as the wind blows]. Little the other answered again ; they were both deceivers, and we saw him no more. We journeyed through the Héjr plain, full of little sand-hillocks blown about *rimth* bushes. A Wélad Aly tribesman reviling me as we rode, (neighbours to Medina, they have I know not what ill savour of the town, with their nomad fanatical malignity,) said he, " Wouldst thou bring upon us the Muscôv ? O thou enemy ! (he levelled his matchlock ;) but know that thus will we do with them, we have many guns like this and every Beduwy in battle is worth, wellah, ten Muscovies." I said to him, " By my faith, one of them I can think were a match for many idle vaunters of you weleds ; I am no enemy, simpleton : there is no nation in all the world which envies you your sand deserts. I am of the part of the Sûltàn, and against those Muscôv, if they came hither." We alighted a moment, to let the caravan pass upward before Mubrak en-Nâga. It was a mirth to hear the solemn loud hooting and pistol firing of the devout hajjies. For the Beduw, ignorant of the koran mythology, here (as said) is but " The thronging place " : it might be such in former times when the pilgrimage was a multitude. As we rode I saw that the east cliff was full of antique scored inscriptions : but I could not now alight to transcribe them. Looking here from the height of my camel, I thought I saw the caravan much diminished ; hardly two-third parts returned of the Haj which had gone down to Mecca : there was not a Persian fur cap amongst them. The holy visitation accomplished, many go home by sea ; a few have died in the way. With the Haj returning from Mecca, are brought the African slaves, for all the north-west of the Mohammedan world, but gazing all day up and down, I could not count five among them.

D. T.   14

Seeing that some Beduins who marched with us had stopped their nostrils, I enquired the cause. The men told me 'they had never been inoculated, and they doubted sore to smell the Haj.' Nomads living always in an incorrupt atmosphere, are very imaginative of all odours. In entering towns, where they are sensible of diverse strange, pungent and ungrateful airs, it is common to see them breathe with a sort of loathing, through a lap of their kerchiefs. Sultry was that afternoon, and we were thirsty. A poor derwish, who went by on foot, hearing one say "water," laid hand, with a pleasant look, upon the bridle of my camel, and lifting his little girby he said heartily, "Drink of this, O pilgrim, and refresh thyself." Seeing but foul rotten water in the leathern bag and discoloured, I gave him his own again ; but he would not hear my excuses. It seemed by his looks he thought the rider on the camel had ill requited his religious gentleness, for all charity is cold in the struggle of the haj road. A moment he gazed in anger, his merit lost ; and passing on wearily might guess the man who would not drink water with other pilgrims to be no right Moslem.

The ascending Haj came to their camping-ground before sunset. We alighted and I went to commit my large roll of inscriptions, impressed at Medáin Sâlih, to Mohammed Tâhir ; he laid my commission in his camel-chests, and promised with good humour to deliver them at Damascus to the British Consulate :— and very honourably he did so, indeed. I enquired if there were any political tidings in Medina. He said thus : ' The Powers had exhibited certain requisitions to the Porte, threatening if they were not satisfied to make common cause against the Sûltàn.'— " And England ? "—" Ay, and Inghilterra ! Ha now ! who can tell how the world will go ? " There was standing by a young Turkish soldier of the Haj soldiery, and he said to me, " We know that the Frenjies talk these many years of dividing the Empire of the Sooltàn : but what says the Sooltàn ? ' Well, and it must be so, *hý yellah*, let them come, one or all together ; and unto whom it shall please the Lord, to them be the victory ! ' " He said this in a young man's melancholy, as if the divine decree were about to go forth and they must march soon to put all upon that final adventure.—The most fanatic and wild Mohammedan region lay before me, where the name of Nasrâny is only wont to be said as an injury ; how might I have passage amongst a frenetic and sanguinary population, and not be taken for a spy, one of their imagined hereditary enemies ? Because their political talk was full of solecisms, I judged the truth might be less, and thought not now to return from this enterprise. Was

this a year of the jehâd ? yet another time I might have no
list to travel in Arabia. The two officers turning at unawares looked to read in my looks how I received and did
digest this news of their dying religion, whether with no secret
exultation ? foreseeing the Christian triumph to be nearly ready
in the world : but when they marked evidently that I was not
glad of their sorrow, but pensive, this lifted me to the height of
their good opinion.

I awaited Zeyd ; when we alighted the guileful Beduin
would lead, he said, our camels to pasture ; and then we could
go together to find the Pasha. He eluded me till nightfall,
when weary and fasting since yesterday, I returned through the
sentinels to the fires of my Beduin company : there I found
Zeyd, who sat sipping coffee. He made me place, and with
smiles dissembled out the matter. Later, re-entering the Haj
menzil, I went alone to visit the Pasha ; but stumbling at the
cords of his pavilion, for the lights were out, I understood from
the watchman that the great man was already at rest. I saw
there the empty bearing-frame, standing without, of the Mahmal
camel ; and next to the great tent was made a small pole-and-
curtain court, " for an apartment of the hareem." I came then
to the military surgeon, whom they call *el-jábbar*, or the bone-
setter ; he had promised to read me a lesson in the art of
medicine. I found him a worthy person, and his few instructions
of one hour availed me long afterwards ; for I had lost my book
of pharmacy. I said the names over of my drugs, and wrote
down the simple usage of each of them, from his lips. At his
desire I had brought him, for a patient of his, a little laudanum
powder ; he was too weary himself to open his field-chests. I
enquired ' what to do if having given anyone many doses of
that medicine to keep by him, he in ignorance swallowed them
all together, *wa yuskut el-kalb ;* ' I would have said, " and
his heart ceased to beat," but all for weariness I pronounced
simple *k*, (not *k* with a guggle in the throat,) for *heart* mis-
saying, " and the *dog*, is silenced." My false word tumbled
to the mind of the pleasant hakîm : after the first smiles,
stroking down a russet beard, the algebrist composed his rising
mirth, which he held over (I am in dread) till the morrow,
when he should be sitting at the pasha's dish. In this there
enters a young derwish of the Medân, a giant of stature, and
who had very often seen me, a Frenjy, pacing in that open
quarter of Damascus. He came in to ask men's alms, some
biscuit for his supper ; and, having eyes seven feet above his
heels, he stood gazing to see one so like me sitting there in the
Haj, and in this array. " Biscuits (ozmát) are dear," quoth the

14—2

charitable surgeon, " but to-morrow and the day after they will
be at better price, then I will buy, and so come thou to
me." Carried upon camels, the price of all provisions in the
caravan sûk, is after every march enhanced or diminished as the
Haj is nearer the midst or the ends of their journey. Ozmát
were sold at Medáin for seven times their worth at Damascus.

Challenged civilly by the sentinels, I passed out of the camp
to the Arabs' firelight, and came again to our Beduin bush ;
where in the pure sand, with their camel-saddles piled against
the wind, we had our night's shelter. In this company sat a
devout Fejîry, who had been to the Harameyn and now returned
with the pilgrimage ; he was busily kneading a barley cake,
when upon a sudden, a clear great meteor sliding under the stars,
with luminous train, casting a broad blue gleam, drooped and
brake before our eyes. " Eigh ! (sighed the man full of the religious sight of Mecca) these things, my God, be past understanding, of Thy wonderful works ! " Then having raked the cake
under the ashes, and his fingers still cloyed, he rose quickly,
seeing a nâga staling, and ran to take water in the hollow of his
hands and rinsed them :—their cattle's excrement is pure in the
opinion of the nomads. Then I understood the perpetual penury
of waters in yonder desert land, where we should come on the
morrow. I found with our Beduins some Kasîm men ; who, leaving the Syrian Haj service, would go this way home, more than
three hundred miles, upon their feet, by Teyma and Jebel Shammar. They told me if ever I went to their country, I might
thrive there by my medicines. " But wherefore, said they,
proclaim thyself Nasrâny ? this thou mayest do at Damascus,
but not in Nejd, where the people having no notice of the world,
it will endanger thee." And as we drank round, they bade me
call myself a " Misslim," and in my heart be still of what opinion
I would, (this indulgence is permitted in the koran to any per-
secuted Moslemîn)—words not far from wisdom ; and I have
often felt the iniquitous fortune of travelling thus, an outlawed
man (and in their sight worthy of death), only for a name, in
Arabia. It had cost me little or naught, to confess Konfuchu
or Socrates to be apostles of Ullah ; but I could not find it in
my life to confess the barbaric prophet of Mecca and enter,
under the yoke, into their solemn fools' paradise.

At the last gunfire, before dawn, the Beduins charged their
camels and departed. I saw by the stars our course lay much
over to the eastward. Because the Aarab are full of all
guile which may profit them, I had then almost a doubt of
my company, until the light breaking I espied the B. Sókhr
haj-carriers, coming on disorderly with their wild Beduin canti-

cles ; the main body of the caravan, far in the rear, was not yet
in sight ; I saw also the old wheel-ruts of the Jurdy cannon,
and knew thereby certainly, that we were in the road. But
for more surety, I dismounted to walk ; and took an oath of
Zeyd, who yesterday had not kept touch, to ride with me before
the Pasha. By and by we had sight of the Pasha, riding far
in front, with his officers and a few soldiery ; it was near
Shuk el-Ajûz. I mounted then with Zeyd on his thelûl, (my
camel was sick,) and we rode to them at a round trot. Zeyd
greeted with the noble Beduin simplicity in his deep stern tones,
and as a landlord in his own country, " Peace be with thee."
Mohammed Saîd, hearing the Beduish voice behind him, said
only " Ho ! " again, without turning, but looking aside under the
sun, he saw and knew me ; and immediately with good humour
he said to my Beduin companion,—" I commit him to thee, and
(laying the right hand over his heart,) have thou a care of
him as of mine own eye." So he said to me, " Have you ended
all at Medáin Sâlih ? The epigraphs, are what ? believe you
there be any in your countries able to read them ? And what
of the houses ? have you not said there were no houses, but
sepulchres ?—But have you not found any treasure ?—Good
bye." I delayed yet, I spoke to the Pasha of the sick
camel which Zeyd had bought for me : so he said to Zeyd,
" Hearken ! thou shalt restore the camel to his owner, and
require the money again ;—and (he said to me) if this Beduwy
do not so I myself will require it of him at Damascus.—(To
Zeyd) Where be now your Aarab ? "—" About a day eastward of
this, and the face of them is toward Teyma." The Pasha asked
me anew, " And where are you going ? "—" To Teyma, to Hâyil,
I hope also to Kheybar." The Pasha drew a breath ; he misliked my visiting Kheybar, which is in the circuit of Medina :
he answered, " But it is very difficult." Here Mohammed Tâhir,
who came on riding with the Pasha, said friendly, " He has the
vaccination with him, and that will be for his security among
the Aarab ; I saw it myself." He added, " Are all your inscriptions together in the roll which you have committed to me ? "
I answered immediately, " All are there, and I trust in God to
show them one day to your worships at Damascus." The Pasha
answered gravely, *Insha 'lla,* ' if the Lord will,' doubtless his
thought was that I might very hardly return from this Arabian
adventure.—Afterwards Zeyd, reporting the Pasha's discourse in
the nomad tents, put in my mouth so many Beduin *billahs*
(' by-Gods '),. and never uttered, that I listened to him as one
who dreams.

Departing from them, we rode aside from the haj-road, and

went to fill our girby at a pool of sweet rain-water.   Then entering eastward in the wild sandstone upland *Borj Selmàn,* we
found before us an infinite swarm of locusts, flying together and
alighting under all the desert bushes, it is their breeding time ;
the natural office accomplished, it seems they by and by
perish.   As we went fasting, Zeyd found a few wild leeks and
small tubers, *thunma* or *sbeydy,* which baked are not unlike the
potato.   He plucked also the twigs of a pleasant-tasting salad
bush, *thalûk,* and wild sorrel, and offered me to eat ; and taking
from his saddle-bags a piece of a barley-cake, he broke and
divided it between us.   " This, he said, is of our surra ; canst
thou eat Beduins' bread, eigh Khalîl ? "   The upland through
which we passed, that they call the Borj Selmán (an ancient
name from the heroic time of the Beny Helál), is a waste land-
breadth of gravel and sand, full of sandstone crags.   This, said
Zeyd, showing me the wild earth with his swarthy hand, is the
land of the Beduw.   He watched to see if the townling were discouraged, in viewing only their empty desert before him.   And
he said, " Hear, O Khalîl ; so thou wilt live here with us, thy
silver may be sent down to thee year by year with the Haj, and
we will give thee a maiden to wife : if any children be born
to thee, when thou wouldest go from hence, they shall be as
mine own, billah, and remain with me."—Also of his stock he
would give me a camel.

CHAPTER VIII.

THE NOMAD LIFE IN THE DESERT.

The Fejîr Beduins.

WE journeyed taking turns to walk and ride, and as Zeyd would, changing our mantles, till the late afternoon; he doubted then if we might come to the Aarab in this daylight. They often removing, Zeyd could not tell their camping-ground within a dozen or score miles. One of the last night's Ageylies went along with us; armed with a hammer, he drove my sick camel forward. As we looked for our Aarab we were suddenly in sight of the slow wavering bulks of camels feeding dispersedly under the horizon; the sun nigh setting, they were driven in towards the Beduin camp, *menzil*, another hour distant. Come to the herdsmen, we alighted and sat down, and one of the lads receiving our bowl, ran under his nâgas to milk for us. This is

kheyr Ullah (the Lord's bounty "), not to be withheld from
any wayfaring man, even though the poor owners should go
supperless themselves. A little after, my companions enquired,
if I felt the worse; " because, said they, strangers commonly feel
a pain after their first drinking camel-milk." This somewhat harsh thin milk runs presently to hard curds in the
stomach.

In approaching the Beduin tents I held back, with the
Ageyly, observing the desert courtesy, whilst our host Zeyd preceded us. We found his to be a small summer or " flitting-tent "
which they call *héjra*, " built " (thus they speak) upon the desert
sand. Poor and low, it seemed, unbecoming a great sheykh,
and there was no gay carpet spread within : here was not the welfaring which I had known hitherto, of the northern Beduins. Zeyd
led me in with his stern smiling ; and, a little to my surprise, I
must step after him into the woman's apartment. These sometime emigrated Beduins, have no suspicion of Nasrânies, whom
they have seen in the north, and heard them reputed honest folk,
more than the Moslemîn. There he presented mé to his young
wife : " Khalîl (said he), here is thy new " aunt " (*ammatak*,—
hostess) ; and, *Hirfa*, this is Khalîl ; and see thou take good care
of him." Before the morning the absent tribesmen had returned from the haj market ; the nomads lodged yet one day in
the Borj Selmàn : the third morrow we removed. The height
of this country is nearly 4500 feet.

The removing of the camp of the Aarab, and driving
the cattle with them from one to another pasture ground, is
called *ráhla*. In their yesterday's mejlis they have determined
whither and how early ; or was it left in the sheykh's hand,
those in the neighbour booths watch when the day is light, to
see if the sheykh's hareem yet strike his tent ; and, seeing this,
it is the ráhla. The Beduish housewives hasten then to pluck
up the tent-pegs, and their booths fall ; the tent-cloth is rolled
up, the tent-poles are gathered together and bound in a faggot :
so they drag out the household stuff, (bestowed in worsted
sacks of their own weaving,) to load upon the burden-camels.
As neighbours see them and the next neighbours see those, all
booths are presently cast in the wide dispersed menzil. The
herdsmen now drive forward ; the hareem [plur. of *horma*,
woman] mount with their baggage ; the men, with only their
arms, sword or matchlock, hanging at the saddle-tree behind
them, and the long lances in their hands, ride forth upon their
thelûls, they follow with the sheykh :—and this is the march of
the nomad village. But if the sheykh's tent remain standing
and it is already an hour past sun-rising, when their cattle

should be dismissed to pasture, the people begin to say, " Let the beasts go feed then, there will be no ráhla tó-day."

This dawn, about the 16th February, was blustering and chill in that high country. *Shîl*, ' load now ! ' cried Zeyd ; and Hirfa, shivering and sighing, made up their household gear. Sheykhly husbands help not their feeble housewives to truss the baggage ; it were an indignity even in the women's eyes. The men sit on, warming themselves over any blazing sticks they have gathered, till the latest moment, and commonly Zeyd made coffee. The bearing-camels are led in and couched between the burdens ; only the herdsman helps Hirfa to charge them upon the rude pack-saddles, *hadàj*, a wooden frame of desert acacia timber, the labour of some nomad sâny or Solubby. The underset pad of old tent-cloth, *wittr*, is stuffed with some dry herbage, and all is girded under the camel's belly with a simple cord. Zeyd called to help lift the loads, for they were over-heavy, did it grudgingly, murmuring, ' Was a sheykh a porter to bear burdens ? ' I also helped them to stay up the weighty half-loads in the sides of the saddles until both were laid even and coupled. Zeyd was a lordling in no contemptible tribe. Such a sheykh should not in men's sight put the hand to any drudgery ; he leaves it to his hind. A great sheykh may take upon him part care of his own mare, in the menzil, whilst the hinds are all day herding in the field ; yet having led her to the well, if there be any, by, of the common tribesmen the sheykh will call him to draw her water. Nevertheless sheykhs' sons whilst they are children, and later as young men armed, are much abroad with the tribes' cattle and companions with the herdsmen. I have seen Zeyd go out with a grass-hook to cut his mare's forage and bring again a mantle-full on his back, and murmuring, with woe in his black visage, it was Selím his son's duty : and the boy, oftentimes disobedient, he upbraided, calling him his life's torment, *Sheytàn*, only never menacing him, for that were far from a Beduin father's mind.

We removed hardly ten miles, and pitched four hours to the eastward of Dàr el-Hamra. The hareem busily " build " their tents ; but the men, as they have alighted, are idle, that when not herding or riding in a foray sit all day at home only lazing and lording. " The *jouwár* (Bed. housewives), say they, are for the labour of the household and to be under discipline." Zeyd, with a foot-cast in the sand-bank where we had taken shelter from the gusty wind till the *beyts* were standing, had made an hearth ; then he kneeled with the Beduin cheerfulness to kindle our gipsy fire. Selím gathered sticks, and we sat down to warm ourselves and roast locusts.

Here we lodged two days, and removed anew five hours eastward through the same sandy moorland, with mild weather, and pitched in the camping-ground *el-Antarieh.* Sweet and light in these high deserts is the uncorrupt air, but the water is scant and infected with camel urine. Hirfa doled out to me, at Zeyd's commandment, hardly an ounce or two of the precious water every morning, that I might wash "as the townspeople." She thought it unthrift to pour out water thus when all day the thirsty tribesmen have not enough to drink. Many times between their waterings, there is not a pint of water left in the greatest sheykhs' tents ; and when the good-man bids his house-wife fill the bowl to make his guests' coffee, it is answered from their side, " We have no water." Too much of a great sheykh's provision is consumed by his mare ; the horse, of all cattle in the desert, is most impatient of thirst. Zeyd used oftentimes this fair excuse, (being miserable even in the poor dispense of coffee,) " There is no water." Motlog the great sheykh coming one of these mornings to visit me, enquired first, " Hast thou drunk coffee ? "—" Not to-day, they say *there is no water.*"—" What ! he asked, has not Zeyd made you coffee this morning ? " for even poorer sheykhs will not fail to serve the morrow's cup, each one to his own fellowship. Motlog knew his cousin Zeyd, and smiled, saying, " What is this, Zeyd has no water ! but, Khalîl, come over to us, and I will make thee coffee." He led me to his tent, which was not far off, where, sitting at the hearth, and being himself the sheykh of his tribe, he roasted, brayed and boiled, and prepared this cup of hospitality for the Christian stranger. In that place it chanced Zeyd to lose a camel, which had been frayed by wolves. He mounted his mare at the morrow's light, and rode forth with the long shivering horseman's lance upon his shoulder to follow her traces. The day after Zeyd returned to us, driving in his lost beast: he had found her near Birket Moaddam.

After three days the Aarab removed south-eastward twelve miles, and pitched at the camping-ground *Khussherkîsh.* It was now the 22nd February, and we found here the rabîa, or new spring of sweet blossoming herbage ; the most was of wild rape kind, pimpernel and sorrel, *humsîs.* The rabîa is the yearly refreshment, nay, the life, of the nomads' cattle. Delightful to the eye, in the desert land, was that poor faery garden of blossoms. When the Beduins saw me pensive, to admire the divine architecture of those living jewels, they thought it but childish fondness in the stranger. If I did but ask the names of the simples it was roughly answered, " The name of them all is *el-usshb,* ' the spring forage,' very good for our small cattle and camels." This high droughty country is plain for some days' journeys ; mostly sand soil and sandstone gravel, without furrows of seyls or wadies ; it is an upland, which in the light Arabian rains never runs down with water.

Zeyd knew that at el-Héjr I transcribed inscriptions. There are many scored in the cliffs of the desert, and he said, "To-morrow, we will walk down to *M'kuttaba,*" there he would show me a multitude. Makuttaba is a natural cistern in the sand rocks, and named (as the " Written Valley " in Sinai) because those cliffs are overwritten with a thousand legends scored in wild Himyaric letters : every one is but a line or twain, idle names perhaps of ancient waterers, with many antique images of camels. The soft rock is much corroded, there is seldom any legible inscription ; it is common thus to find them about desert waterings, which were at all times loitering places. The antique nomads,—for by likelihood so rude inscriptions were theirs, had then (which to-day have not the Mohammedan Bedu-ins) a knowledge of letters ? or were all these the handiwork of ancient passengers ? The antique outlined images are all round and lively, though somewhat long drawn. The Beduins now-a-days portray only such squalid effigies (left by idle herdsmen upon the desert rocks), as we see of children's scrawling. Zeyd called the inscriptions *Temathîl el-Helalát,* " Imagery of Beny Helál."

The camels now feeding of the sappy rabîa were *jezzîn* or 'not drinking.' In good spring years they are in these dîras almost two and a half months jezzîn, and not driven to the watering. Then the force of life is spent of the herb lately so fresh upon the ground, and withering under the sun it is dried up. If, after some shower, the great drinkless cattle find rain-water lodged in any hollow rocks, I have seen them slow to put down their heavy long necks ; so they snuff to it, and bathing out the borders of their flaggy lips, blow them out and shake the head again as it were with loathing. The nomads' camels are strong and frolic in these fat weeks of the spring pasture. Now it is they lay up flesh, and grease in their humps, for the languor of the desert summer and the long year. Driven home full-bellied at sunset, they come hugely bouncing in before their herdsmen : the householders, going forth from the booths, lure to them as they run lurching by, with loud *Wolloo-wolloo-wolloo,* and to stay them *Wòh-ho, wòh-ho, wòh-ho !* they chide any that strikes a tent-cord with *hutch !* The camels are couched every troop beside, about, and the more of them before the booth of their household ; there all night they lie ruckling and chawing their huge cuds till the light of the morrow. The Aarab say that their camels never sleep ; the weary brute may stretch down his long neck upon the ground, closing awhile his great liquid eyes ; but after a space he will right again the great languid carcase and fall to chawing. In this fresh season they rise to graze anew in the moonlight, and roam from the booths of the slumbering Aarab ; but fearful by nature, they stray not then very far off. Sometimes wakening after midnight and seeing our camels strayed, I went out to bring them in ; but the Beduins said, " Sleep on, Khalîl, there is no cause ; let them go feeding as they will." They would see them pasture now all they can ; but not seldom they are bereaved thus of their cattle by prowling night-robbers. Camels, the only substance of the nomads, are the occasion of all their contending. " *Neshîl*, we load, say they, upon them, and we drink halîb, the milk, of them." The cows go twelve months with young ; now was their time of calving, which falls at the beginning of the rabîa. The nomad year is divided in this sort : *er-rabîa*, springtime of three months ; *el-gâyth*, midsummer, three months ; *es-sferry*, fall of the year, three months ; *es-shitá* (pronounce *és-sh'tá*), winter. To be a ready man in this kind of lore, is clerkship with the Beduw, and to have a wayfarer's knowledge of the stars. When they found good pasture the Beduins encamped, and we lodged upon that ground mostly till the third or fourth morrow. The nomads dwelling, the day over, in any place, they say "el-Aarab *umjemmin*" (*j* for *k* guttural), or the camp is standing. The herdsmen bring word of the pasture about them, and as the sheykhs determine in the mejlis the people will remove again, it was commonly to twelve or thirteen miles distance ; and now their " face was toward " Teyma.

If the ráhla be short the Beduw march at leisure, the while their beasts feed under them. The sheykhs are riding together in advance, and the hareem come riding in their trains of baggage camels ; if aught be amiss the herdsmen are nigh at hand to help them : neighbours will dismount to help neighbours and even a stranger. The great and small cattle are driven along with their households. You shall see housewives dismount, and gossips walk on together barefoot (all go here unshod,) and spinning beside their slow-pacing camels. But say the Beduin husbands, " We would have the hareem ride always and not weary themselves, for their tasks are many at home." The Fukara women alighted an hour before noon, in the march, to milk their few ewes and goats. Every family

and kindred are seen wayfaring by themselves with their cattle.
The Aarab thus wandering are dispersed widely ; and in the
vast uneven ground (the most plain indeed but full of crags),
although many hundreds go on foot together, commonly we
see only those which go next about us. The Beduins coming
near a stead where they will encamp, Zeyd returned to us ; and
where he thought good there struck down the heel of his tall
horseman's lance *shelfa* or *romhh*, stepping it in some sandy
desert bush ; this is the standard of Zeyd's fellowship,—
they that encamp with him, and are called his people. Hirfa
makes her camel kneel ; she will ' build ' the booth there :
the rest of Zeyd's kindred and clients coming up, they alight,
each family going a little apart, to pitch their booths about him.
This is " Zeyd's menzil " and the people are Zeyd's Aarab. The
bearing-camels they make to kneel under their burdens with
the guttural voice, *ikh-kh-kh !* The stiff neck of any reluctant
brute is gently stricken down with the driving-stick or an hand
is imposed upon his heavy halse ; any yet resisting is plucked
by the beard ; then without more he will fall groaning to his
knees. Their loads discharged, and the pack-saddles lifted,
with a spurn of the master's foot the bearing-camels rise heavily
again and are dismissed to pasture. The housewives spread
the tent-cloths, taking out the corner and side-cords ; and
finding some wild stone for a hammer, they beat down their
tent pegs into the ground, and under-setting the tent-stakes or
" pillars " (*am'dàn*) they heave and stretch the tent-cloth : and
now their booths are standing. The wife enters, and when she
has bestowed her stuff, she brings forth the man's breakfast ;
that is a bowl of léban, poured from the sour milk-skin, or it
is a clot of dates with a bowl of the desert water : for guest-
days it is dates and buttermilk with a piece of sweet butter.
After that she sits within, rocking upon her knees the *semîla* or
sour milk-skin, to make this day's butter.

As Zeyd so is every principal person of these Beduins, the
chief of a little menzil by itself : the general encampment is
not disposed (as is the custom of the northern Aarab) in any
formal circuit. The nomads of these marches pitch up and
down in all the " alighting place " at their own pleasure. The
Fejîr or Fukara never wandered in *ferjàn* (*j* for *k* guttural)
or nomad hamlets, dispersedly after their kindreds, which is
everywhere the nomad manner, for the advantage of pasture ;
but they journey and encamp always together. And cause was
that, with but half-friends and those mostly outraged upon their
borders, or wholly enemies, there were too many reckonings
required of them ; and their country lies open. Zeyd's Aarab

were six booths : a divorced wife's tent, mother of his young and
only son, was next him ; then the tent of another cast-off housewife, mother of a ward of his, *Settàm*, and by whom he had
himself a daughter ; and besides these, (Zeyd had no near
kinsfolk,) a camel-herd with the old hind his father, of Zeyd's
father's time, and the shepherd, with their alliance. Forlorn persons will join themselves to some sheykh's menzil, and there was
with us an aged widow, in wretchedness, who played the mother
to her dead daughter's fatherless children, a son so deformed that
like a beast he crept upon the sand [*ya latîf*, " oh happy sight ! "
said this most poor and desolate grandam, with religious irony,
in her patient sighing]—and an elf-haired girl wonderfully foul-
looking. Boothless, they led their lives under the skies of God,
the boy was naked as he came into the desert world.   The
camel upon which they rode was an oblation of the common
charity ; but what were their daily food only that God knoweth
which feedeth all life's creatures. There is no Beduwy so impious
that will chide and bite at such, his own tribesfolk, or mock
those whom God has so sorely afflicted ; nor any may repulse
them wheresoever they will alight in the common wilderness
soil. Sometimes there stood a stranger's booth among us, of
nomad passengers or an household in exile from the neighbour tribesmen : such will come in to pitch by a shekyh of
their acquaintance.

Hirfa ever demanded of her husband toward which part
should " the house " be built. " Dress the face, Zeyd would
answer, to this part," showing her with his hand the south, for if
his booth's face be all day turned to the hot sun there will come
in fewer young loitering and parasitical fellows that would be
his coffee-drinkers. Since the sheukh, or heads, alone receive
their tribe's surra, it is not much that they should be to
the arms coffee-hosts. I have seen Zeyd avoid as he saw
them approach, or even rise ungraciously upon such men's
presenting themselves, (the half of every booth, namely the
men's side, is at all times open, and any enters there that will,
in the free desert,) and they murmuring he tells them, wellah,
his affairs do call him forth, adieu, he must away to the mejlis, go
they and seek the coffee elsewhere. But were there any sheykh
with them, a coffee lord, Zeyd could not honestly choose
but abide and serve them with coffee ; and if he be absent
himself, yet any sheykhly man coming to a sheykh's tent,
coffee must be made for him, except he gently protest, ' billah,
he would not drink.' Hirfa, a sheykh's daughter and his
nigh kinswoman, was a faithful make to Zeyd in all his sparing
policy.

Our menzil now standing, the men step over to Zèyd's coffee-fire, if the sheykh be not gone forth to the mejlis to drink his mid-day cup there. A few gathered sticks are flung down beside the hearth : with flint and steel one stoops and strikes fire in tinder, he blows and cherishes those seeds of the cheerful flame in some dry camel-dung, sets the burning sherd under dry straws, and powders over more dry camel-dung. As the fire kindles, the sheykh reaches for his *dellàl,* coffee-pots, which are carried in the *fatya,* coffee-gear basket ; this people of a nomad life bestow each thing of theirs in a proper *beyt,* it would otherwise be lost in their daily removing. One rises to go fill up the pots at the water-skins, or a bowl of water is handed over the curtain from the women's side ; the pot at the fire, Hirfa reaches over her little palm-full of green coffee-berries. We sit in a half ring about the hearth ; there come in perhaps some acquaintance or tribesmen straying between the next menzils. Zeyd prepared coffee at the hours ; afterward, when he saw in me little liking of his coffee-water, he went to drink the cup abroad. If he went not to the mejlis, he has hidden himself two or three hours like an owl, or they would say as a dog, in my little close tent, although intolerably heated through the thin canvas in the mid-day sun. It was a mirth to see Zeyd lie and swelter, and in a trouble of mind bid us report to all comers that ' Zeyd was from home ': and where his elvish tribesmen were merry as beggars to detect him. *Mukkarîn el-Beduw !* " the nomads (say the settled Arabs) are full of wily evasions."

The sheykhs and principal persons assemble at the great sheykh's or another chief tent, when they have alighted upon any new camping-ground ; there they drink coffee, the most holding yet the camel-stick, *mishaab, mehján* or *bakhorra,* as a sceptre, (a usage of the ancient world,) in their hands. The few first questions among them are commonly of the new dispositions of their several menzils : as, " *Rahŷel !* (the sheykh's brother), *fen ahl-ak?* where be thy people (pitched) ?—*Eth-Therrŷeh* (the sheykh's son), *fen ahl-ak ?—Mehsan* (a good simple man, and who had married Zeyd's only sister,)—*Khálaf* and the rest, where be your menzils ?—Zeyd is not here ! who has seen Zeyd ?—and *Mijwel,* where are his Aarab ? " for every new march displaces these nomads, and few booths in the shortness of the desert horizon are anywhere in sight. You see the Beduins silent whilst coffee is being made ready, for all their common talk has been uttered an hundred times already, and some sit beating the time away and for pastime limning with their driving-sticks in the idle sand. They walk about with these gay sticks, in the daytime : but where menzils are

far asunder, or after nightfall, they carry the sword in their
hands : the sword is suspended with a cord from the shoulder.
The best metal is the Ajamy, a little bent with a simple crossed
hilt (beautiful is the form), wound about with metal wire ; next
to the Persian they reckon the Indian blade, *el-Hindy.*

In nomad ears this word, Aarab, signifies " the people."
Beduin passengers when they meet with herdsmen in the
desert enquire, *Fen el-Aarab ?* " where is the folk ? "   Of the
multitude of nomad tribes east and west, they say in plural
wise, *el-Arbán*. This other word, Beduin, received into all our
languages, is in the Arabian speech Bedùwy, that is to say inhabitant of the waste, (*bâdia,*) in the plural *Bedaùwy* (*aù* dipth.),
but commonly *él-Bêduw*. As we sit, the little cup, of a few black
drops, is served twice round. When they have swallowed those
boiling sips of coffee-water, and any little news has been related
among them, the men rise one after other to go home over the
hot sand : all are barefoot, and very rarely any of those Aarab has
a pair of sandals. So everyone is come again to his own, they say
the mid-day prayers ; and when they have breakfasted, they will
mostly slumber out the sultry mid-day hours in their housewife's closed apartment. I have asked an honest wife, " How
may your lubbers slug out these long days till evening ? "   and
she answered, demurely smiling, " How, sir, but in solace with
the hareem ! "

The héjra, or small flitting-tent, laid out by the housewife,
with its cords stretched to the pins upon the ground, before the
am'dàn or props be set up under, is in this form :

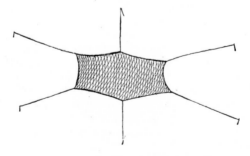

to every pair of cords, is a pair of stakes ; there are three stakes
to every pair of cords in the waist of the tent. Greater booths
are stayed by more pairs of waist-cords, and stand upon taller
staves. The Aarab tent, which they call the *beyt* [pl. *byût*]
es-shaar, " abode, booth, or house of hair," that is of black

worsted or hair-cloth, has, with its pent roof, somewhat the form of a cottage. The tent-stuff, strong and rude, is defended by a list sewed under at the heads of the am'dàn, and may last out, they say, a generation, only wearing thinner : but when their roof-cloth is threadbare it is a feeble shelter, thrilled by the darting beams of the Arabian sun, and casting only a grey shadow. The Arabian tent strains strongly upon all the staves, and in good holding-ground, may resist the boisterous blasts which happen at the crises of the year, especially in some deep mountainous valleys. Even in weak sand the tents are seldom overblown. Yet the cords, *tunb el-beyt*, which are worsted-twist of the women's spinning, oft-times burst : who therefore (as greater sheykhs) can spend silver, will have them of hempen purchased in the town. In all the road tribes, they every year receive rope, with certain clothing and utensils, on account of their haj surra. The tent-stuff is seamed of narrow lengths of the housewives' rude worsted weaving ; the yarn is their own spinning, of the mingled wool of the sheep and camels' and goats' hair together. Thus it is that the cloth is blackish : we read in the Hebrew Scripture, " Black as the tents of Kedar." Good webster-wives weave in white borders made of their sheep's wool, or else of their gross-spun cotton yarn (the cotton wool is purchased from Medina or the sea coast).

When the tent-cloth is stretched upon the stakes, to this roof they hang the tent-curtains, often one long skirt-cloth which becomes the walling of the nomad booth : the selvedges are broached together with wooden skewers. The booth front is commonly left open, to the half at least we have seen, for the *mukaad* or men's sitting-room : the other which is the women's and household side, is sometimes seen closed (when they would not be espied, whether sleeping or cooking,) with a fore-cloth ; the woman's part is always separated from the men's apartment by a hanging, commonly not much more than breast or neck high, at the waist-poles of the tent. The mukaad is never fenced in front with a tent-cloth, only in rain they incline the am'dàn and draw down the tent eaves lower. The nomad tents are thus very ill lodging, and the Beduins, clothed no better than the dead, suffer in cold and stormy weather. In winter they sometimes load the back-cloth ground-hem with great stones, and fence their open front at the men's side with dry bushes. The tent side-cloths can be shifted according to the wind and sun : thus the back of the Beduin booth may become in a moment the new front. A good house-wife will bethink herself to unpin and shift the curtain, that

her husband's guests may have shadow and the air, or shelter.
—In the picture are shown a sheykh's and a widow's tents of
Bíllî Beduw in the Teháma.

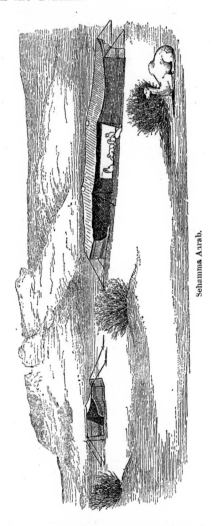

Sehamma Aarab.

Upon the side of the hareem, that is the household apartment, is stored all their husbandry. At the woman's curtain
stand the few tent-cloth sacks of their poor baggage, *él-gush* :
in these is bestowed their corn and rice if they have any

certain lumps of rock salt, for they will eat nothing insipid ;
also the housewife's thrift of wool and her spun yarn,—to be
a good wool-wife is honourable among Aarab women ; and some
fathoms perhaps of new calico. There may be with the rest
a root of *er'n* or tan wood, the scarlet chips are steeped
in water, and in two or three days, between ráhlas, they
cure therein their goat-skins for girbies and semîlies, besides
the leather for watering buckets, watering-troughs and other
nomad gear. The poorest wife will have some box, (commonly,
a fairing from the town,) in which are laid up her few household medicines, her comb and her mirror, *mèrguba*, her poor
inherited ornaments, the ear-rings and nose-ring of silver or even
golden (from the former generations) ; and with these any
small things of her husband's, (no pockets are made in their
clothing,) which she has in her keeping. But if her good-man
be of substance, a sheykh of surra, for his bundle of reals and
her few precious things she has a locked coffer painted with
vermilion from Medina, which in the ráhla is trussed (also · a
mark of sheykhly estate) upon her bearing camel.—Like to this,
I have mused, might be that ark of things sacred to the public
religion, which was in the nomad life of B. Israel.

Commonly the housewife's key of her box is seen as a glittering pendant, upon her veil backward ; and hangs, with her thimble
and pincers, (to pluck the thorns out of their bare soles,) by
a gay scarlet lace, from the circlet of the head-band. Their
clotted dates, if they have any, are stived in heavy pokes of
camel-hide, that in the ráhla are seen fluttering upon the
bearing-cattle with long thongs of leather. This apparel of
fringes and tassels is always to the Semitic humour ; of the like
we read in Moses, and see them in the antique Jewish sculptures. Of their old camel sack-leather, moisty with the juice of
the dates, they cut the best sandals. The full-bellied sweating
water-skins are laid, not to fret at the ground, upon fresh
sprays of broom or other green in the desert ; amongst all stands
the great brazen pot, *jidda*, tinned within by the nomad smith,
or by the artificer in their market village. They boil in it
their butter, (when they have any, to make samn,) and their
few household messes ; they seethe the guest-meal therein in
the day of hospitality.

The Aarab *byût shaar* are thus tents of hair-cloth made
housewise. The "houses of hair" accord with that sorry landscape ! Tent is the Semitic house : their clay house is built in
like manner ; a public hall for the men and guests, and an inner
woman's and household apartment. Like to this was Moses'

15—2

adorned house of the nomad God in the wilderness. Also the firmament, in the Hebrew prophet, is a tabernacle of the one household of .God's creation. These flitting-houses in the wilderness, dwelt in by robbers, are also sanctuaries of "God's guests," *theûf Ullah*, the passengers and who they be that haply alight before them. Perilous rovers in the field, the herdsmen of the desert are kings at home, fathers of hospitality to all that seek to them for the night's harbour. "Be we not all, say the poor nomads, *guests of Ullah ?* " Has God given unto them, God's guest shall partake with them thereof : if they will not for God render His own, it should not go well with them. The guest entered, and sitting down amongst them, they observe an honourable silence, asking no untimely questions, (such is school and nurture of the desert,) until he have eaten or drunk somewhat at the least, and by "the bread and salt" there is peace established between them, for a time (that is counted two nights and the day in the midst, whilst their food is in him). Such is the golden world and the "assurance of Ullah" in the midst of the wilderness : travelled Beduins are amazed to see the sordid inhospitality of the towns ;—but where it were impossible that the nomad custom should hold.

Zeyd told us one day his old chance at Damascus (the tribe was then in the North) ; and how he had disputed in this sense with a government man (Dowlâny) of late, some Haj officer, *Whether were nigher unto God the life of townsfolk or of the Aarab.—Officer :* "Some of you neither pray nor fast, the Beduw are incessantly riding in forays ; ye are manslayers for a little booty, and violent reavers of other men's goods. God wot, and though your mouths confess the Prophet, ye be little better than the *kuffâr* (heathen,—Jews and Christians). Ye discern not betwixt the *halàl* and the *harrâm ;* but we, knowing the good and the evil, are the better Moslemîn," *Zeyd :* "All this I can grant ; but hearken ! a stranger alighting at a Beduin booth, we welcome him, and are busy to serve him and we prepare the guest-supper ; and when he has eaten, in the same place he sleeps, in the assurance of Ullah, and with the morning light he rises up refreshed to hold on his journey. But ha ! when I came to es-Sham, riding upon my thelûl, it was an evening (at the supping hour), and passing weary and hungry by the sûk, I alighted before some door where I thought to take my night-lodging. As I knocked, one cries within, *Min ?* Who ? who ? I answered ' *Thaif !* (a guest) and O thou behind the door, open quickly ! ' But the voice said, ' O thou which standest knocking, seek further down the sûk, where is many a house, and there is nothing here ; go in peace, good man.'

This is the manner with them all, and they are not ashamed, billah! Then, not having tasted food that day (the wayfaring nomad eats not till his alighting), I lay me down in the dust of your street, slain with hunger and seeking to slumber. This is their dealing with strangers which enter your towns!—And wellah the Dowlâny allowed our life to be nigher unto God, because of the hospitality." So much they hold of this godly human virtue, as wherein a man may be just before the "Bountiful Ullah," and like to a poor player of the Divine Providence. With all this, there lacks not Arabic hospitality in the good city of Damascus; it is little less than I have afterwards seen in the upland Arabian towns. There are worthy sheykhs in the Medân, that village quarter of es-Shem, men of the antique simplicity, which keep nearly the open hospitality of the outlying villages.

This sheykh's name at the full is *Zeyd es-Sbeychan el-Fejîry ;* this signifies son of Sbeyk(ch)an, of the fendy or kindred el-Fejîr, which is in their tribe the kinship of sheykhs ; after the now common custom, the name of the sheykhly kin is attributed to the tribe. The Fejîr [*j* for *k* guttural, but in the pl. form el-Fúkàra] are last to the north of the *Ahl Gibly* or Southern Aarab. Their fendies are *Sâlih* or .el-Fejîr (all sheykhs), *el-Moghrassîb, Zuâra, Hamdán, Hejûr, Ainàt, 'Sgoora ;* and the plebeian fendy, since grown almost to half of the *ashîrat* (tribe), *el-Khamâla.* This tribe's old sheykhly name is the *Menâbaha,* from whom also *el-Hosseny,* now Arabs of the north near Aleppo, and of them is the lately famous princely family of East Nejd, Ibn Saûd, the Waháby.—Thus say the Fukara : it is otherwise said, in Nejd, that Ibn Saûd is of *Beny Hanîfa,* ancient Arabs, also of Annezy, in the wady of that name, since the time of Mohammed. Ishmaelites, yet fetch they partly their Annezy stock,—so do also their neighbours and capital foemen Maazy or Beny Atîeh—in the female line from *Kahtan,* the noble southern blood of Arabia (Moses' *Yoktan,* if you will trust the Ullema). *Wâil* (the common *jid* or patriarch) is the son of *Núshud el-Jemàl* and a *Kahtanite* woman ; his sons are *Anâz* and *Maaz,* fathers of the noble Ishmaelite nation Annezy, greatest of all Arabian *ashîrats* that now are, and Maazy. *Musslim,* a son of *Anâz,* is ancestor of the *Beny Wâhab,* which are the Menâb'ha, to-day el-Hosseny, el-Fejîr, and the Wélad Aly : also the Bishr, *Jellas* and Ruwàlla, all Annezy, are sometimes counted to B. Wáhab :—thus Zeyd. Fendies of W. Aly in the south are *et-Toála,* (most numerous), then *Thueyba, Taifát, Umshitta, 'Mraikhàn, Jebbâra, Erbeylát, Khâlid ;* the sheykhs are *Allàyda.*

The waste circuit of the Fukara begins about Dàr el-Hamra and reaches to Bîr el-Ghrannem : it is not less wide from the derb el-haj eastward to the mountain Birrd, at the border of Nejd. This is as much as certain of our English counties ; and they are nearly eight hundred souls. Their tents are two hundred ; I have been able to survey them at once, when we were summering later about the wells of el-Héjr. Small is these nomads' horizon ; few of them know much land beyond their own dîras or out of common ways, as the paths to Hâyil their political or Medina their religious metropolis. In distant forays they must hire a dalîl or land-pilot to ride with them ; he is commonly some former exile or guest in that country of which he will now betray the hospitality. Seldom (as in any general migrations) do they come to a knowledge of strange dîras. The whole world they can hardly imagine to be other than their Arabian sun-stricken wilderness, with little water and few palm-villages, with perhaps some populous border city, as Mecca. Nomad children have bid me tell them ' how many were the camels of ed-Dòwla ? ' The Ottoman Empire they could only think to be a tribe, whereof they see the Haj descending by them every year. The eldest son of the great W. Aly sheykh, who may live to be the head of that tribe after him, a wooden-headed young man, having enquired of me in which part of the world lay the dîrat of the Engleys, would know further the name of our market village ; and said earnestly, " Tell me, Kkalîl, the names of the tribes your foemen : " if he heard them he thought he might happen to know them. He could understand that we were kafirs, but not that we should be other than the tribes of Arabs.

And now to speak of Zeyd's household. He had another wife, but she was fled from him—this is common, in their male tyranny of many marriages—and now dwelt in her mother's tribe, the Bishr ; they were pasturing nigh before us in this wilderness. Zeyd rode over to his neighbours, and with pleasant promises, which well he knew to forge and feign, he wooed her home again. A sheykh told me she was beautiful, " she has egg-great eyes ; " but that, when I saw her, was all her pallid beauty. The returned wife would not pitch with us, where jealous Hirfa was, but " built " her booth with some kindred in another menzil. Zeyd and Hirfa were next cousins ; Hirfa was a sheykh's orphan, whom it seems he had taken partly for her few inherited camels. Hirfa was an undergrown thick Beduin lass, her age might be twenty ; the golden youth was faded almost to autumn in her childish face, but not unpleasing ; there was a merry wooden laughter always in her mouth, which ended commonly, from the unsatisfied heart, in sighing. ' The woman sighs (says the proverb) who has an ill husband.' Hirfa sighed for motherhood : she had been these two years with an husband and was yet *bint*, as the nomads say, ' in her girlhood ; ' and she wept inwardly with a Semitic woman's grief. Zeyd and Hirfa were as Isaac and Rebecca ; with the Beduin simplicity they sat daily sporting lovingly together before us, for we were all one family and friendly eyes, but oftentimes in the midst Hirfa pouted ; then Zeyd would coldly forsake her, and their souls were anew divided. Hirfa in her weary spirit desired some fresh young husband, instead of this palled Zeyd, that she mistrusted could not give her children. Again and again they bade the Christian stranger deliver judgment of their fruitless marriage, whether it had been lawful, as betwixt brothers' children. Hirfa, a testy little body, of her high birth in sheykhs' booths was a *sheykha* among the hareem, and so even by the men regarded ; all the principal sheukh were her nigh kinsmen. In the Arabian small tribes and villages there is a perpetual mingling of kindred blood : to-day after so many generations who may think this Semitic race has been impaired thereby ?— but truly we see not few brain-sick and cripples amongst them.

Self-minded, a bold-faced wench, mistress Hirfa cast as she should not a pair of eyes upon their herdsman, a likely young man, whom in her husband's absence she wooed openly and in Zeyd's despite ; but he was prudent, and faithful to his sheykh's service. Here, and though bordering the jealous Hejâz and the austere Waháby Nejd, the Fukara women go open-faced, and (where all are kindred) I could never perceive amongst them any jealousy of the husbands. In this tribe of date-eaters, there was not almost a well-grown man, besides the sheykh Motlog and his sons, nor any comely woman. Zeyd would tame his little wilful wife ; and upon a time he corrected her with the rod in the night.

The comedy of Hirfa and Zeyd was become matter of daily raillery in the mejlis of the coffee-drinking sheukh their cousins ; where, arriving alone, I might hear them say, " Eigh ! here comes Khalîl : *márhabba*, welcome, O Khalîl ; make place for Khalîl ; pass up, Khalîl, and sit thou here beside me."—" Well met, Khalîl ! but where is thine uncle Zeyd to-day ? "—" Zeyd is *zahlán*, or melancholy ; he lies in this mood wilfully slumbering out the day at home : "—in the lands of the sun men willingly sleep out their sorrow. " But tell us, knowst thou was Hirfa beat ? what news to-day ? Khalîl, do you love your uncle ? " One said who did not love him (*Khálaf Alláyda*, an exile, of the sheukh of W. Aly), " Zeyd is not a man, who beats his wife ; it

is a *marra*, woman, that will strike a *marra*; do your people
so, Khalîl?" I answered, "Nay, surely; unless it be some ungracious wretch." And he, "It is thus amongst us Beduw, *ayb*,
a shame, wellah." The wales of Zeyd's driving-stick were
ever in her stubborn little spirit; and at the next alighting
from a ráhla, when she had hastily built the booth and Zeyd
was walked to the mejlis, leaving all, Hirfa ran back embittered
into the wilderness. A devout Beduin of our menzil, he of the
meteors, held awhile her two little hands, beseeching her to
return to her patience; but, a sheykh's daughter, she would not
be held and peevishly she broke from him.

Of a disaffected Beduin wife, such is the public remedy; to
show herself to be alienated from her husband, and ready to
forsake his wedlock and household, thus putting upon him a
common scorn, because he will not dismiss her. There followed
after Hirfa, as soon as he heard the tidings, her next kinsman
of the mother's side, one that resembled Hirfa as if he had been
her brother: she was running like an ostrich alone in the wild
desert. An hour passed till he led her home to us, and left her
again sorrowful at her own and Zeyd's tent. "Ha, Khalîl," said
he, "what wilt thou give me now that I have fetched in thine
aunt again, who pours thee out léban and water? and (showing
me his cutlass), Wellah, I have brought her *bes-seyf* by constraint of the sword." Zeyd, displeased, now ranged some nights
to his Bishr wife's booth; and jealous Hirfa, not suffering this
new despite, another day, even in the presence of strangers,
Zeyd's guests, fled forth in the gall of her heart from the newly
pitched tent when the people alighted at a menzil; Zeyd sat
on, as a man aggrieved, only looking after her, but not hindering
(in their eyes it had been unseemly, that man's life is free).
The fugitive Beduin wife has good leave to run whithersoever
she would; she is free as the desert, there is none can detain
her. Hirfa hied then to her mother's kindred, and sat down, all
sighs, in her aunt's booth; and in what beyt soever a running
wife have taken refuge, not her own wedded husband may
honestly appear to reclaim his part in her.

The strangers departed, and Zeyd sat by his now desolate
booth in long heaviness of mind; but to show any lively resentment, only by occasion of a woman, had been ill nurture
and unmanly. He stretched himself upon the sand to sleep
out his grief, and slumbered with his head in the scalding
sun. The nomads make religion, to observe this mildness and
forbearance in the household life! "God's peace" is in that
parcel of the great and terrible wilderness, which is shadowed by
every poor herdsman's booth. By and by I shook him and

said, " It is not good so to sleep and swoon in the sun." We
went then together to seek coffee at the mejlis, where, some
malicious ones smiling at his sadness and new troubled looks,
Zeyd complained in his great, now untoned voice, ' that he had
no longer an household,—unless it were that Khalîl (their guest)
would fetch Hirfa home.' Every tiding is presently wide blown
in all the open tents of a nomad menzil, and there is no idle
tale that will not ride upon the tongues, light as leaves, of witless
Beduins, to drive the empty hours.

The common voice blamed Hirfa's second flight : " How, they
said, abandon Zeyd's tent in the presence of guests, and they
were strangers ! "—" Ha ! " there answered an aged mother of our
menzil to the old hind her husband, " dost dear, Sâlih ? The
hareem be good for little now-a-days,—ay, billah ! I say they are
all corrupted-like ; but it be only myself !" Those strangers were
certain Howeytát (*Terabîn*) Beduw and merchants, from the
Syrian seaboard desert, under Gaza, and who every spring-time
return hither, as camel-brokers, among the Aarab. They passing
by us in the end of the ráhla, Zeyd had called them from his
menzil to alight with him and rest themselves. They sat down
on the sand, whilst the tents were building, and he brought them
forth the midday commons of their wretched country, a bowl of
musty dates and another of the foul desert water. They, seeing
this hap of the host's renegade wife, as men that could their
courtesy, dispatched themselves and rising from the slender
breakfast, gave thanks ; yet a little with that unhandsome
citizens' humility which is not in the easy carriage of the
nomads : Beduins bless the host and yield their thanks unto
Ullah ; but these were border countrymen, and had almost the
daunted looks of townspeople, in the deep wilderness. They
purchase only of the best beasts : although they bid high prices
the Aarab are never very willing to sell them. The camel they
think is a profitable possession, a camel will bring forth the
camel, but money is barren good that passes quite away in the
using. Commonly they will sell of their beasts only when they
have some present need of reals, and then sooner of the males ;
but they are the better for carriage.

For robust he-camels of good stature was paid, by the
brokers, as much as fifty reals ; the half told in the hand, the rest
is counted out in calico, which the nomad may readily sell away
again, for shirt cloths, in the desert. This the traders brought
from Syria ; and, selling here at the price of Teyma, they gain
for their risks and charges not above the fourth part. The
purchased camels they will sell again in Egypt and Syria.
Such brokers travel, most years, through all parts of the upland

Arabia, to buy for the border countries, and thereby the price of camels had been doubled within few years ; it is now almost one throughout the northern country : and any need rising in the border lands, as for a war declared with Abyssinia, Arabia might be searched in few weeks by these emissaries, and an advance offered, there could be brought forth many thousands of camels. But this is very costly carriage in an expedition, since six camels' backs must be set under every ton burden.

The Howeytát asked me what I did there in that Beduin world ? I told them I had visited their country, and lodged in their circle villages of tents, and seen how they plough the wild sand with camels. " To-morrow's dawn (said they, friendly) we ride homeward. Were it not better for thee to return with us ? "

The Howeytát nation inhabit all the wilderness country above the Sinai Peninsula betwixt the two seas and deep inland : they come down in the Tehámá border, by the Red Sea, to Wejh. Their Mediterranean seabord town in the north is Gaza, a granary of cheap corn to the tribes of Sinai, and for the nigher Arabian nomads. About Gaza we have seen them (*Tiáha, Seydeîn*), husbandmen tent-dwellers ; in the Tehámá their nation are nomad herdsmen : but certain of their tribesmen dwelling there in valley grounds and low bottoms, are also husbandmen of palms and sowers of grain, in little hamlets of standing tents. We have seen them, in the Hisma, barley sowers ; in the *Nefúd* and old Amalekite soil betwixt Gaza and Egypt, their clans (*Terabín, Suâki*) are nomads. The Howeytát tent-villagers of Palestine are nearly as the other Syrians, there are many of them that follow merchandise, trafficking more especially with the Beduw ; of these tribesmen are some which have also store-houses of clay. There are mere Beduin tribes which use clay housing, even in Arabia ; as the Fukara and Wélad Aly sheykhs have clay summer-houses at Kheybar ; where they are landlords but not land-tillers. The station is to the forwandered Beduins, *keyif*, a cheerful refreshment ; they have little or no aversion to take up the settled life. Certainly all the villages and towns in the breadth of nomad Arabia, were at first colonies of Beduins, whose inhabitants yet remember their nomad tribes ; and we see up and down in the open nomad country the Beduwy will become half an husbandman where he may have good easy thrift. Thus the best valleys upon both sides the Harra, next el-Héjr, are sown all years by some of the Moahîb Aarab. Their harvest up, they strike the hamlets of tents, and with their cattle go forth to wander a while as the nomads.

The Howeytát are commonly clownish bodies, having the
large bony frame of wheat-eaters, and raw visages, much resembling the Syrian peasantry of outlying villages, (such are
even those which I have seen from the Teháma in Arabia,)
sooner than the lithe-limbed and subtle-brained and supple-
tongued Arabians of land-inward Nejd. All that I could
learn, often enquiring, of their ancestry, 'was only that they
are variously reported to descend from two brethren, as some
will, of Harb, who came of old time into that upper Red
Sea country from el-Yémen. But it is otherwise commonly
told of them that they are descended from Nasâra : which may
be interpreted, ' they remain in the same seats which they
already occupied in fore-Islamic (to the Arabs pre-historic)
times under another religion.' This is the old circuit of the
western Nabateans. Be the Howeytát—traders even now
and husbandmen—descended from Nabateans ? I enquired
of those dealers, how they hoped to pass safely with their
merchandise to Howeytát country, which begins about two
hundred and fifty miles from hence at J. Sherra ? They told
me, " We have taken a *rafîk* from every tribe upon the way
thither." The Arabian rafîk, often an enemy, is a paid brother-
of-the-road, that for a modest fee takes upon him to quit
the convoy from all hostile question and encounter of his own
tribesmen. Thus Arabian wayfarers may ride with little dread
through hostile marches, and be received even to their enemies'
hospitality.

When I understood in our menzil that this is the guest's
honourable office, I went the next afternoon to call Hirfa home
to Zeyd's household ; where else she had been abashed to return
of herself and they to seek her. I found Hirfa a little shame-
faced, sitting in the midst of her gossips ; old wife-folk that had
been friends of her dead mother ; they were come together to the
aunt's booth to comfort her, and there were the young men her
cousins. Sad-faced sat the childless young wife, she was playing
fondly with a neighbour's babe. ' Khalîl, she said, must fill her
great tobacco pipe, galliûn, or she would not hear my words.'
The old wives cried out, " Thou art, Khalîl, to fill all our galliûns
(they are great tobacco ' bibbers '), and else we will not let Hirfa
go." The young men said they would keep Hirfa, and marry
her themselves, and not give her again " to that wicked Zeyd."
The tobacco distributed, I took Hirfa by the little Beduish
hand (never labouring, they have all these little hands), and
bidding her rise, the little peevish housewife answered me,
' But she would not be held, Khalîl must let go her hand.' I

said then, " I will bring thee home, hostess, return with me ; and else I must alight to pitch my tent by thee, from the next ráhla." *Hirfa :* " That do, Khalîl, and welcome : I and thou will go,—ah ! where we shall eat a camel together (she would say a bountiful household), only fill thou again my galliûn." *The Aunt :* " And mine, Khalîl ; or Hirfa is ours, ay, and we will not let her go." Having filled the galliûns of them all, I asked if our mistress Hirfa were not now coming. A young cousin said " I am her father, and Hirfa is mine, Khalîl ; no ! we will not give her more to Zeyd." Said her aunt : " Well, go over, Khalîl ; Hirfa follows, and all we (the bevy of old women) accompany her " (to bring her home honourably). Soon after, arriving before my tent door, they called me out to pay them another dole of tobacco :—And Hirfa sat again in her own beyt.

The woman's lot is here unequal concubinage, and in this necessitous life a weary servitude. The possession in her of parents and tutors has been yielded at some price, (in contempt and constraint of her weaker sex,) to an husband, by whom she may be dismissed in what day he shall have no more pleasure in her. It may be, (though seldom among nomads their will is forced,) that those few flowering years of her youth, with her virginity have been yielded to some man of unlikely age. And his heart is not hers alone ; but, if not divided already, she must look to divide her marriage in a time to come with other. And certainly as she withers, which is not long to come, or having no fair adventure to bear male children, she will as thing unprofitable be cast off ; meanwhile all the house-labour is hers, and with his love will be lost. What oneness of hearts can be betwixt these lemans, whose lots are not faithfully joined ? Sweet natural love may bud for a moment, but not abide in so uneven ways. Love is a dovelike confidence, and thereto consents not the woman's heart that is wronged.

Few then are the nomad wives whose years can be long happy in marriage ! they are few indeed or nearly none that continue in their first husband's household. Such are commonly mothers of many children, or wedded in needy families, so that the house-fathers are not able to maintain another housewife. But substantial and sheykhly persons will have done betimes with these old wives, and pass to new bride-beds, or they were not Moslemîn ; and being rich men they spend cheerfully for new wives as they will spend for the seasonable change of clothing. The cast housewife may be taken up by another worthy man, in favour of some old liking, or pass to the new marriage and household service of some poorer person. The woman's joy and her comfort is to be mother of sons, that at least she may remain a matron in her boy's tent, when even his hard father shall have repudiated her. It was thus with *Ghrobny*, Zeyd's young son Selím's mother. Zeyd, pitying her tears, had found her another husband of poor Khamâla folk, by whom she had now a new babe : but the man dealt unkindly with her ; wherefore returning to her young son, she was pitched again as an uncheerful widow to live by Zeyd. A day dawned, and Ghrobny's booth was away ! the Arabs stood half laughing and wondering, for it was a poor-spirited creature, that had been a fair woman in her youth, till we understood of Selím she had loaded upon her camel in the night-time and was stolen away to the Khamâly in a distant menzil. The wretch, the day before, coming hither, had kissed her and vowed like a smooth lover to receive her again. But after two days the poor fond woman, and now little pleasing, returned to us with red eyes, to embrace her child, who had remained in the meanwhile confused with his father ; and from the next ráhla, the drivelling and desolate wife alighted as before to encamp by Zeyd.

These Aarab say, " the hareem are twice the men, in number." If that be so, natural reason should teach that a man may have more wives than one ; and I can think that the womankind exceed them. From spring months to spring months, nine months in the year, the most nomad women are languishing with hunger : they bear few children ; of two at a birth I have heard no mention among them. They are good mothers, and will suckle the babe very long at their meagre breasts, if they be not again with child. In Zeyd's encampment was a little damsel of four years, not yet weaned ; and the mother said, " We have no goats, there is naught in this waste, and what else might I do for my little bint ? " They wash their babes in camel urine, and think thus to help them from insects : it is acrid, especially when the cattle have browsed of certain alkaline bushes, as the rimth. And in this water they all comb out their long hair, both men and women, yet sometimes thereby bleaching their locks, so that I have seen young men's braided " horns " grizzled. There is a strange custom, (not only of nomad women, but in the Arabic countries even among Christians, which may seem to remain of the old idolatry among them,) of mothers, their gossips, and even young maidens, visiting married women to kiss with a kind of devotion the *hammam* of the male children.

In all Arabia both men and women, townsfolk and Beduins, where they may come by it, paint the whites of their eyes blue, with *kahl* or antimony ; thus Mohammed Ibn Rashîd has his bird-like eyes painted. Not only would they be more love-looking, in the sight of their women, who have painted them, and that braid their long manly side-locks ; but they hold that this sharpens too and will preserve their vision. With long hair shed in the midst, and hanging down at either side in braided horns, and false eyes painted blue, the Arabian man's long head under the coloured kerchief, is in our eyes more than half feminine ; and in much they resemble women.

Townswomen of well-faring families, in all the old government of the Waháby are taught the prayers ; and there are some that have learned to read. In the nomad tribes women are seldom seen to pray, except in *ramathán*, the month of bodily abstinence and devotion : they are few which know the prayers ; I suppose even the half of. the men have not learned them. The Beduwy, in Arabia, passes for as good as a clerk that can say his formal devotion : the nomads which have much praying amongst them, are the more ill-natured. Women pray not as the men, falling upon their faces ; but they recite the form of words with folded arms and kneeling. " *El-entha*, the female (mild to labour and bringing forth the pastoral riches) is, of all animals, the better, say the Arabians, save only in mankind." Yet this is not an opinion of all Arabs, for the *hurr*, or dromedary stallion, is preferred for his masculine strength by the Moors or Western Arabs. Upon the human entha the Semites cast all their blame. Hers is, they think, a maleficent nature, and the Aarab complain that " she has seven lives." The Arabs are contrary to womankind, upon whom they would have God's curse ; " some (say the Beduw) are poisoners of husbands, and there are many adulteresses." They, being full of impotent iniquity themselves, too lightly reproach the honest housewives, although not without some cause : but what might not those find to tell all day again of the malignant inconstancy of husbands ? The *horma* they would have under subjection : admitted (they say) to an equality, the ineptitude of her evil nature will break forth. They check her all day at home, and let her never be enfranchised from servitude. If the sapient king in Jerusalem found never a good woman ; many a better man has found one better than himself. The veil and the jealous lattice are rather of the obscene Mohammedan austerity in the towns : among the mild tent-dwellers in the open wilderness the housewives have a liberty, as where all are kindred ; yet their hareem are now seen in the most Arabian tribes half veiled. When some asked me, at Zeyd's coffee-fire, if our hareem went veiled, I answered, " No ! they are open-faced, there is no need of face-clouts among honest folk ; also I think among you Aarab, they which have their women's faces veiled, are the more dissolute tribes." The Beduins are always glad to hear other tribesmen blamed. It was answered, " Ay, billah, they are corrupted." I asked Zeyd, " Art thou of this opinion ? " " Khalîl—he said in his heart, ' Thou thinkest as the kuffâr '— the face of a wife should be seen of no man besides her own husband."

The woman's sex is despised by the old nomad and divine law in Moses ; for a female birth the days of her purification are doubled, also the estimation of her babe shall be at the half. Did she utter any vow, it is void if her husband say no. But the Semitic mother of a son is in honour. We read : " Let a man obey his mother and his father," the Semitic scribe writing his mother first. And commonly it is seen amongst rude Arabs, the. grown son has a tender regard toward his mother, that she is his dam, before the teeming love even of his fresh young wife. So the mother's love in the tribes is womanly, tender ; and naming her sons she will add some loving superstitious saw, as *el-agal Ullah*, " The Lord preserve them ! " The nomad hareem are delivered as other mothers, with pangs, after a labour of certain hours. It is a fond opinion that the daughters of the desert are as the wild creatures, that suffer not in child-bearing. But her household and nation is migratory ; there is no indolent hope before her of comfort and repose. The herb is consumed daily about them, the thirsty cattle are ever advancing to pasture and water, the people is incessantly removing : in the camping-ground of to-day, they cannot perhaps lie upon the morrow. Their bed is a mantle or tent-cloth spread upon the earth ; they live indeed in the necessitous simplicity almost of the wild creatures. The nomad woman has therefore, of custom, of necessity ! another courage. Are the Aarab in a journey when her time is come ? her family halt, and alight-ing, they build the booth over her. Are the tribesmen en-camped ? with certain elder women friends she steals forth to be delivered, apart in the wilderness. The nomads about jour-neying, when it were peril to be left behind, she is gently lifted and seated as any other sick and infirm person in a nest made of her carpet or her tent-cloth wound down upon the camel pack-saddle, to follow riding with them in the râhla : and that they pass their lives thus nomads feel little fatigue, but rather take rest in riding.

In the *Jahaliat* or " olden time of heathen ignorance," there was an horrible custom in the desert, nearly to the generation of Mohammed, to bury maid-children living (which signifies also that the female births among them were more numerous). The woman is not born to manage the sword, but her hand is

for the silly distaff, she neither strengthens the ashîra nor is
aught to the increase and building of her father's household,
but an unprofitable. mouth is added to the hungry eaters of a
slender substance : and years long he must wear a busy head
for the keeping of a maiden ; the end of all is an uncertain
bride-money (therewith he buys for her again some household
stuff, and it is her dower), when she will go forth as a stranger to
another house. The father hid himself, in the day of her birth,
from his common acquaintance.

When I have questioned the Beduw, had they heard
of this by tradition ? they have answered, marvelling, "They
could not imagine there had ever been such a cursed custom
in the country." Daughters when past the first amiable infancy are little set by in the Arabic households. The son is
beloved by his father, till he be grown, above the wife that
bare him, before his own soul, and next after the man's own
father : and the young child in an household is hardly less
beloved of his elder brethren. God has sent a son, and the
father cannot contrary him in anything, whilst he is a child.
This it is that in time to come may comfort his age, and in his
last end honourably bury him ; and year by year after, as the
nomads in their journeys be come again, offer the sacrifice
of the dead and pray over him : so shall his name be yet
had in remembrance among the living. Much sooner then,
would a man give a buffet to his wife, or twenty, than lay
hand-strokes upon the back of the perverse child their son,
and turn away the mind of him for ever. In bitterness of a
displeasure he will snib his disobedient son with vehement
words, but his anger shall pass no further to break the house-
peace ; after years this child shall be better than himself, and
therefore he is one whom he durst not now offend. There be
fathers, say the nomads, that rule with the rod. I cannot
believe them. A son dying, a father's spirit is long overcast, he is
overborne awhile with silent sorrow ; but the remembrance of a
deceased daughter, unless her life were of any singular worth
or goodly promise untimely broken, is not very long enduring.
Moslemîn, (this is to say, *The Submitted-to-the-divine-govern-
ance-of-the-world*,) the men make no lamentation for the dead ;
only they say, "He is gone, the Lord have mercy upon him ! "

I found also among these Beduins, that with difficulty they
imagine any future life ; they pray and they fast as main duties
in religion, looking (as the Semitic Patriarchs before them)
for the present life's blessing. There is a sacrifice for the dead,
which I have seen continued to the third generation. I have
seen a sheykh come with devout remembrance, to slaughter his

sacrifice and to pray at the heap where his father or his father's father lies buried : and I have seen such to kiss his hand, in passing any time by the place where the sire is sleeping, and breathe out, with almost womanly tenderness, words of blessing and prayer ;—and this is surely comfort in one's dying, that he will be long-time so kindly had in his children's mind. In the settled Semitic countries their hareem, and even Christian women, go out at certain days to the graves to weep. I have seen a widow woman lead her fatherless children thither, and they kneeled down together : I saw the mother teach them to weep, and she bewailed her dead with a forced suffocating voice and sobbing, *Ya habîby,* " Aha ! aha ! my beloved ! " The Aarab children are ruled by entreaties ; the nomad girls are often wayward at home, the boys will many times despise the mother's voice. I have known an ill-natured child lay a stick to the back of his good cherishing mother; and asked why she suffered this, she answered, sighing, " My child is a kafir," that is, of an heathenish froward nature : this boy was not of the full Beduin blood, his father being Abu Sinûn the Moor. Some asking if our children too were peevish, when they heard from me the old dreadful severity of Moses' law, they exclaimed, " But many is the ill-natured lad among us that, and he be strong enough, will beat his own father." The Arabs babble, and here also it were hard to believe them. Savages inure their sons ; but Beduin children grow up without instruction of the parents. They learn but of hearing the people's saws, in the worsted tents, where their only censor is the public opinion. There are devout Beduins full, in that religious life of the desert, of natural religion, who may somewhiles reprove them ; but the child is never checked for any lying, although the Arabians say " the lie is shameful." Their lie is an easy stratagem and one's most ready defence to mislead his enemy. Nature we see to be herself most full of all guile, and this lying mouth is indulged by the Arabian religion.

CHAPTER IX.

LIFE IN THE WANDERING VILLAGE.

THE camels now jezzîn, we wandered without care of great watering places ; the people drinking of any small waters of the *suffa*, or ground rock. There are in all this ·desert mountain soil pit-like places of rock choked with old blown sand. In these sand-pools a water, of the winter rains, is long time preserved, but commonly thick and ill-smelling in the wet

sand, and putrefying with rotten fibres of plants and urea of
the nomads' cattle, which have been watered here from the beginning. Of such the Aarab (they prefer the thick desert water
to pure water) now boiled their daily coffee, which is not then
ill-tasting. The worst is that blackish water drawn from pits
long forsaken, until they have been voided once; and sooner
than drink their water I suffered thirst, and very oft passed the
nights half sleepless. Strange are the often forms in this desert

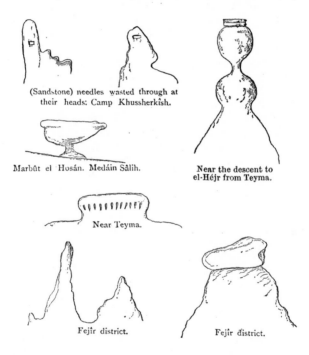

(Sandstone) needles wasted through at
their heads: Camp Khussherkìsh.

Marbût el Hosán. Medáin Sâlih.

Near the descent to
el-Héjr from Teyma.

Near Teyma.

Fejîr district.

Fejîr district.

of wasted sand-rock, spires, needles, pinnacles, and battled
mountains, which are good landmarks. I asked Zeyd, ' Did he
know them all?' *Answer:* "From my childhood, I know as
good as every great stone upon all our marches," that may be
over three or four thousand square miles. Mountain (*jebel* in
the settled countries) is commonly *thulla*—" rib," (and dim.
thulleya,) with the nomads;—we say *coast* almost in like
wise. Any tall peak, berg or monticule, serving for a landmark, they call *towîl;* a headland is *khusshm*, "naze, snout;"
(khusshm is said in Arabia for man's nose.) Some hilly
mountain-coasts are named *huthb; bottîn* in the mouths of the

16—2

Moahîb Beduins is said of any blunt hilly height. The desert waste is called *khála*, " the land that is empty ; " the soil, *béled.* —And such is desert Arabia.

—But to speak now of the nomad inhabitants and how they lead their lives. El-Beduw *ma yetaabun,* " toil not " (say they,) that is not bodily ; but their spirits are made weary with incessant apprehension of their enemies, and their flesh with continual thirst and hunger. The necessitous lives of the Aarab may hardly reach to a virtuous mediocrity ; they are constrained to be robbers. " The life in the desert is better than any, *if there were not the Beduw,*" is said proverbially by oases' Arabians ; the poor Beduins they think to be full of iniquity, *melaun el-weyladeyn,* " of cursed kind, upon both sides, of their father and mother." Pleasant is the sojourn in the wandering village, in this purest earth and air, with the human fellowship, which is all day met at leisure about the cheerful coffee fire, and amidst a thousand new prospects. Here, where we now alighted, is this day's rest, to-morrow our home will be yonder. The desert day returning from the east, warns the Beduin awake, who rises to his prayers ; or it may be, unwitting of the form, he will but murmur toward heaven the supplication of his fearful human nature, and say, " Ah Lord my God ! " and, " Oh that this day may be fortunate ; give Thou that we see not the evil ! " Of daily food they have not half enough, and if any head of the cattle be taken !—how may his household yet live ? Bye and bye the herdsman is ready, and his beasts are driven far from his sight.

No sweet chittering of birds greets the coming of the desert light, besides man there is no voice in this waste drought. The Beduins, that lay down in their cloaks upon the sandy mother-earth in the open tents, hardly before the middle night, are already up and bestirring themselves. In every coffee-sheykh's tent, there is new fire blown in the hearth, and he sets on his coffee-pots ; then snatching a coal in his fingers, he will lay it in his tobacco-pipe. The few coffee-beans received from his housewife are roasted and brayed ; as all is boiling, he sets out the little cups, *fenjeyl* (for *fenjeyn*) which we saw have been made, for the uningenious Arabs, in the West. When, with a pleasant gravity, he has unbuckled his *gutía* or cup-box, we see the nomad has not above three or four fenjeyns, wrapt in a rusty clout, with which he scours them busily, as if this should make his cups clean. The roasted beans are pounded amongst Arabs with a magnanimous rattle—and (as all their labour) rhythmical—in brass of the town, or an old wooden mortar, gaily studded with nails, the work of some nomad smith. The water bubbling in the small dellàl, he casts in his fine coffee powder, *el-bunn*, and withdraws the pot to simmer a moment. From a knot in his kerchief he takes then an head of cloves, a piece of cinnamon or other spice, *bahar*, and braying these, he casts · their dust in after. Soon he pours out some hot drops to essay his coffee ; if the taste be to his liking, making dexterously a nest of all the cups in his hand, with pleasant clattering, he is ready to pour out for the company, and begins upon his right hand ; and first, if such be present, to any considerable sheykh and principal persons. The *fenjeyn kahwa* is but four sips : to fill it up to a guest, as in the northern towns, were among Beduins an injury, and of such bitter meaning, " This drink thou and depart." Then is often seen a contention in courtesy amongst them, especially in any greater assemblies, who shall drink first. Some man that receives the fenjeyn in his turn, will not drink yet,—he proffers it to one sitting in order under him, as to the more honourable : but the other putting off with his hand will answer *ebbeden*, " nay, it shall never be, by Ullah ! but do thou drink ! " Thus licensed, the humble man is dispatched in three sips, and hands up his empty fenjeyn. But if he have much insisted, by this he opens his willingness to be reconciled with one not his friend. That neighbour, seeing the company of coffee-drinkers watching him, may with an honest grace receive the cup, and let it seem not willingly : but an hard man will sometimes rebut the other's gentle proffer.

Some may have taken lower seats than becoming their sheykhly blood, of which the nomads are jealous ; entering untimely, they sat down out of order, sooner than trouble all the company. A sheykh, coming late and any business going forward, will often sit far out in the assembly ; and show himself a popular person in this kind of honourable humility. The more inward in the booths is the higher place ; where also is, with the sheykhs, the seat of a stranger. To sit in the loose circuit without and before the tent, is for the common sort. A tribesman arriving presents himself at that part, or a little lower, where in the eyes of all men his pretension will be well allowed ; and in such observances of good nurture, is a nomad man's honour among his tribesmen. And this is nigh all that serves the nomad for a conscience, namely, that which men will hold of him. A poor person approaching from behind, stands obscurely, wrapped in his tattered mantle, with grave ceremonial, until those sitting indolently before him in the sand shall vouchsafe to take notice of him : then they rise unwillingly, and giving back enlarge the coffee-circle to receive

him. But if there arrive a sheykh, a coffee-host, a richard amongst
them of a few cattle, all the coxcomb companions within will
hail him with their pleasant adulation, *taad hennéyi*, " Step thou
up hither."

The astute Fukara sheukh surpass all men in their coffee-
drinking courtesy, and Zeyd himself was more than any large
of this gentleman-like imposture : he was full of swaggering
complacence and compliments to an humbler person.   With
what suavity could he encourage, and gently too compel a man,
and rising himself yield him parcel of another man's room !   In
such fashions Zeyd showed himself a bountiful great man,
who indeed was the greatest niggard.   The cups are drunk
twice about, each one sipping after other's lips without misliking ; to the great coffee sheykhs the cup may be filled more
times, but this is an adulation of the. coffee-server.   There are
some of the Fukara sheukh so delicate Sybarites, that of those
three bitter sips, to draw out all their joyance, twisting, turning
and tossing again the cup, they could make ten.   The coffee-
service ended, the grounds are poured out from the small
into the great store-pot that is reserved full of warm water : with
the bitter lye the nomads will make their next bever, and think
they spare coffee.

—This of the greater coffee gatherings : but to speak rather
of the small daily company in a private sheykh's menzil, drawn
together to the clatter of the good man's *surbût* or coffee-pestle.
Grave, with levity, is the indolent nomad man's countenance.
As many Beduin heads, so many galliûns or tobacco-pipes, with
commonly nothing to put in them.   Is any man seen to have
a little of the coveted leaf, knotted in his kerchief, he durst
not deny to divide it with them,—which if he withheld, yet
pretending mirth, the rest would have it from him, perforce.
If there be none found among them, they sit raking the old
filth out of their galliûns and, with sorry cheer, put the coal
upon that, which they have mixed with a little powdered dry
camel-dung or some sere herbage : thus they taste at least a
savour (such sweetness to them) of tobacco, whereof, when
they are any while deprived, I have seen them chop their pipe-
stems small for the little tobacco moisture which remained
in them ; and laying a coal upon this drenched wood they
" drink " in the fume with a last solace.

The best pipe-heads are those wrought in stone by the
hands of the Beduins, the better stone is found two days below
Héjr, and by Teyma.   Besides they use the *sebîl*, or earthen-
ware bent tube of the Syrian haj market.   Their galliûn stem is
made of the branch of some wild fig-tree, grown by desert

waters, or of plum-tree from the oasis ; they bore it with a red-hot iron over the evening watch-fires. Comfortatives of the brain and vital spirits, and stay of importunate hunger, we find the Arabian nomads abandoned to the usage of coffee and tobacco ; in both they all observe the same customs and cere- mony, which we might imagine therefore, without book, to be come down in their generations from some high antiquity. So much are they idly given to these tent pleasures, that many Beduins think they may hardly remember themselves of a morning, till they have sipped coffee, and " drunk " upon it a galliûn of tobacco. The coveted solace of the grape, in the veins of their old idol-worshipping fathers, is no more re- membered by the Beduin tradition ; even their former artillery, the bows and arrows, hardly two centuries laid down, I have found almost out of mind amongst them. We see the Arabian race lasting without change, only less than their eternal deserts ; but certain inventions (guns, tobacco, coffee) sprung up in the world, and falling, like their religion, to the national humour, have as hastily prevailed among them. Even the outlying great waste Peninsula is carried by the world's great changes ! History shows a marvellous levity of their hundred tribes ; part fearing for themselves, and partly in the hope of booty, converting (so they will ever to the stronger), in one generation, from their ancient idols to the new and soon grown faction of Mohammed in religion.

Coffee, we hear, had been brought first into el-Yémen from " Abyssinia " (that is Galla-land or further *Hábash*). Galla men sold into slavery in Arabia have related to me that, in their country are " trunks of wild coffee-trees great as oaks " ; and very likely those secular stems were living before the first drinking of kahwa in Asia, which from Mecca must soon spread (with every returning pilgrimage) to the whole Moham- medan world. In Galla-land the fallen coffee-beans are gather- ed under the wild trees and roasted in butter : coffee is only drunk by their elders ; younger men, they said, " would be ashamed " to use, at their years, the caudle drink. Tobacco, brought in the English cloth-merchants' ships to Constantinople in James I.'s days, is now (save the reformed soil of Nejd) sown up and down in the Arabian oases. The Beduins love well to ' drink ' the fume of a strong leaf till the world turn round, yet will they say, after the Waháby doctrine, " Tobacco is *bawl iblís*, the devil's water." Nevertheless the evil use is tolerated (so a man burn the " unbecoming " leaf within his own house) in all Nejd, without the (now small) Waháby state and in some utter fanatical tribe as the Kahtân. I have known

brothers of the galliûn, which had been little less than abandoned to their darling tobacco, wean themselves from the
irreligious and uncomely use, upon a sudden frank deter-
mination, and not tempt it again. These were for the most
part fanatics. I remember one comely villager, who forsook
it because the pipe-stem deformed the grace of his lips, would
bring too soon his age upon him, and endangered an amorous
breath. He had a fair wife or twain at home, and was besides a
lover at large, a heartless seeker of new marriages, even in the
desert. There are also Beduins which have a natural aversion
from the tobacco drug, others again indifferent ; and some
at the first having been " beaten from it " by their fathers,—poor
men who would not have their lads, which as herdsmen must
labour in the sun for their living, to grow up, as loitering flies, in
camp, about the coffee-tents,—they continue in this abstinence.
So there are many which find no taste in coffee, or of an
abstinent humour, that will indulge themselves in nothing, they
drink not, fearing it should abate their manly courage. The
most mejlis men abuse these drugs, which distemper their weak
bodies ; many thus are *umbratiles* in the booths, and give themselves almost to a perpetual slumber.

For the Beduins sitting in the coffee-tent of their menzil,
when the sun mounts, it is time to go over to the mejlis, " sitting,"
the congregation or parliament of the tribesmen. There also is
the public coffee-drinking, held at Motlog's or some other one of
the chief sheykhs' worsted " houses " ; where the great sheykh
and the coffee companions may that morrow be assembled : for
where their king bee is found, there will the tribesmen assemble
together. The mejlis-seekers wending through the wide encampment, enquire of any they meet, " The mejlis, where ?
eigh weled ! hast thou seen the sheukh sitting ? " In this parliament they commune together of the common affairs ; they
reason of their policy in regard to Ibn Rashîd, the Dowla, the
tribes about them. Here is reported what any may have
heard of the movement of foemen, or have signs been seen of a
ghrazzu : tidings from time to time are brought in of their own
or foreign waters ; householders tell of the pasture found yesterday by their dispersed herdsmen. Let him speak here who will,
the voice of the least is heard among them ; he is a tribesman.
The mejlis forecast the next journeys of the tribe, whereof a
kind of running advice remains in all their minds, which they
call *es-shor ;* this is often made known to their allies, and is very
necessary to any of themselves that are about to take a journey.

This is the council of the elders and the public tribunal :
hither the tribesmen bring their causes at all times, and it is

pleaded by the maintainers of both sides with busy clamour ; and everyone may say his word that will. The sheykh meanwhile takes counsel with the sheukh, elder men and more considerable persons ; and judgment is given commonly without partiality and always without bribes. This sentence is final. The loser is mulcted in heads of small cattle or camels, which he must pay anon, or go into exile, before the great sheykh send executors to distrain any beasts of his, to the estimation of the debt. The poor Beduins are very unwilling payers, and often think themselves unable at present : thus, in every tribe, some households may be seen of other tribes' exiles.

Their justice is such, that in the opinion of the next governed countries, the Arabs of the wilderness are the justest of mortals. Seldom the judge and elders err, in these small societies of kindred, where the life of every tribesman lies open from his infancy and his state is to all men well known. Even their suits are expedite, as all the other works of the Arabs. Seldom is a matter not heard and resolved in one sitting. Where the accusation is grave and some are found absent that should be witnesses, their cause is held over to another hearing. The nomad justice is mild where the Hebrew law, in this smelling of the settled countries, is crude. In the desert there is no human forfeit, there is nothing even in homicide, if the next to the blood withhold not their assent, which may not be composed, the guilty paying the amends (rated in heads of cattle). The Hebrew law excised the sores in the commonwealth, and the certainty of retaliation must weigh and prick in the mind of evil-doers. The Beduwy has no more to fear before him than a fine afar off ; he may escape all if his evil heart sufficeth him, only going from his own kin into perpetual exile.

Towards noon, in days when the camp is standing, as the mejlis is ended, the company begin to disperse. The bare-foot Beduwy returns lonely over the hot sand, and will slumber, in his booth, till vespers, el-assr. The nomads are day-sleepers : some of the Beduins will turn upon their sides to slumber, as if the night were come again, by ten o'clock. But if a man fall asleep, sitting in the coffee circle, it is unbecoming ; let him go apart and lie down in the sides of the tent. Is any overcome at unawares amongst them, the rest will shake him and say, " Up, man ! what dost thou here to slumber ? " Yet in the midst of their murmuring discourse, and being feeble with fasting, I not seldom fell asleep, upon a sudden, sitting to drink coffee ; which weakness of nature they saw in a stranger with wondering piety and humanity ! All the Arabs reverence a man's sleeping ; he is as it were in trance with God, and a truce of his waking solicitude : in their households they piously withdraw, nor will any lightly molest him, until he waken of himself. Only from el-assr till the sun set, they sleep no more, that such they think were unwholesome. Of their much slumbering, they are more wakeful in the dark night hours, which time in the open wilderness is troubled with alarms ; the hounds often bark at the wolf till the morning light, and the habalîs are afoot. Some will talk the mid-day hours away lying out in the next cliff's shadow, or under the thin shade of some gum-acacia tree, or in the sheykh's great tent. At vespers the Beduin bestirs himself ; he goes forth again, murmuring some words of pious preparation, to say his afternoon prayer : falling on his knees, he claps his palms upon the sand before him, and rubs them, then drawing them down from the forehead, he washes thus the two sides of his visage, for there is no water. Rising again from his devotion, he walks abroad to look for any new smoke rising, which is a sign of the coffee fire and cheerful fellowship. A sheykh who would far over the wide encampment, will leap upon his mare's bare back to ride thither. Most officious of the afternoon coffee-hosts was *Burjess,* a rich young sheykh among certain sheukh of W. Aly, malcontents living now with the Fukara ; his was the most spacious tent in our encampment. If the mejlis assembled again for any public business, or after a ráhla, the afternoon company was more numerous, many of the shepherds at that hour coming in.

As for the head of the tribe, Motlog, he was a personable strong man and well propórtioned, of the middle stature, of middle age, and with a comely Jewish visage ; and thereto the Arabian honour of a thick black beard, and he looked forth with a manly assurance under that spacious brow of his sheykhly moderation. A fair-spoken man, as they be all in fair weather, full of the inborn Beduin arts when his interest was touched. Simple in his manners, he alone went with no gay camel-stick in his hand and never carried a sword ; by which politic urbanity, he covered a superfluous insolence of the nobleman, which be-came him well. When the mejlis assembled numerous at his booth, he, the great sheykh and host, would sit out with a proud humility among the common people, holding still his looks at the ground ; but they were full of unquiet side-glances, as his mind was erect and watching. His authority slumbered, till, there being some just occasion, he ruled with a word the unruly Beduw. A rude son of the desert sat down by me in the mejlis at my first coming, the shepherd of Zeyd's menzil. I asked him in his ear, "Which of them is Motlog?" *Answer:* "Yonder is Motlog!" and he added boisterously, to the stranger, "The man there is our

Pasha; for right as the haj pasha, this Motlog governs the Aarab. When he says 'The ráhla!' we all mount and set forth; and where he alights there we pitch our booths.—Oho, thou Motlog! speak I not well to this Nasrâny?—and, Khalîl, if he would, he might cut off the heads, wellah-billah, of us all." Motlog lifted his eyes upon us for a moment with half a smile, and then reverted to himself. The sheykh of a nomad tribe is no tyrant; a great sheykh striking a tribesman he should bruise his own honour: man-striking is a very bestiality, in their sight, at home.

The sheukh (*pl.* of sheykh, an elder) are nobles of the blood, of a common ancestor, the reputed Jid or father of the tribe; the great sheykh's dignity he has of inheritance. Motlog *el-Hameydy* succeeded his father Hameydy, who fell in a foray, and was sheykh of the Fejîr, as all his fathers before him, ascending to the patriarch; and this dignity, which in their sight is a disposition of Providence, there is no man certainly who will gainsay. No commoner, nor any of strange blood, even though he surpassed all men in wealth and sufficiency, can come to be the head of a nomad ashîra, or even to be named of the sheykhly kindred, which, as has been said, are a noble lineage in the tribe. Sheukh match sooner with sheykhs' daughters; and between all the Fejîr was now a certain, so to say, feminine resemblance of voice and manners: the sheukh were here about the fifth part of the ashîra. The sheykh of the tribe is as well, agîd, of his own right, conductor of the general ghrazzus; his is the fourth part of the booty. If he ride not himself, he will send a son or another of the sheukh, his deputy, it might be Zeyd, who leads for him. I asked Zeyd, " But if the inheriting sheykh doted, or he were a man notoriously insufficient?" Zeyd had not heard of such a chance. " He would be set aside," he answered, " and the next after him would become our sheykh."

The sun setting, the loitering coffee-companions turn again homeward to pray and to their suppers. At first, when the Aarab saw me wander in the cool of the evening, I heard them say " Khalîl goes forth to pray after his religion;" but bye and bye, since I would not by any feints deceive my hosts, they began to account me a prayerless one of the heathen, living in the world without conscience of Ullah. An hour or two passed, the sheukh companions will *sayer*, " sally" or stray away, again to coffeeward and the evening mejlis, where they will linger on till midnight. For dread they have of treading in the darkness upon serpents, a sheykh may be seen then to draw on some quaint pair of old boots, such as he may have long since purchased at Medina. Arabian Beduins are not wearers of the high red clanking boots, which are a proud token of sheykhly estate in Syria.

The Fukara are of the fanatical tribes; but they are nearly all thus in Arabia. Motlog, the sheykhs and tribesmen, had been displeased with Zeyd that (for his cupidity, so well known to them,) he had brought in a kafir, and none such as those home-bred Nasrânies, which they had seen themselves in Syria, but of a formidable foreign nation and government, (the sheykh heard this from the Jurdy and Haj officers,) to wander amongst them. And yet, even the great sheykh's authority could hardly go between any hospitality of the poorest tribesman among them. But now as they knew me better, they welcomed the Nasrâny with friendly words at all their coffee fires, and I sat every day with Zeyd in the mejlis. Only Zeyd would have me often remember it was only himself, who sheltered me from the murderous wildness of the Beduins. He would not have me venture, even with himself when he went abroad, after the day's light, but sit at home by our tent-fire with Hirfa and the men of our menzil: 'what if some wretch, he said, stabbed me in the darkness, and the doer of it might never be known.' Those of our encampment, with whom I had eaten bread and salt, confirmed Zeyd's words, with may billahs, bidding me not trust to any creature, beside themselves. The Arabs are full of great words; and I did not disquiet myself for their fanatical wild talk. " Wellah ! " said Zeyd, " it was never seen before that any Nasrâny should sit in the Beduins' mejlis, or be seen riding aloft upon a camel and to follow the râhla."

My practice in medicine was yet to begin ; now, in most unhappy hour, my vaccination failed me ! The lymph was purchased of a fawning Christian vaccinator of Damascus : I had more sent to me by the Jurdy ; but, exposed in open quills, the virtue was lost even before they could be delivered to me at Medáin Sâlih. I had used the lately learned art with good success in Syrian villages. For the benefit of vaccination, the Beduw would have almost pardoned my misbelief ; and I might have lived thereby competently in a country where it is peril of death to be accounted the bearer of a little silver. No more than a sick camel now remained to me, and little gold in my purse, and I began to think of quitting this tedious soil, where henceforth without a pretext, I must needs appear as a spy intruded among them ; and—since it were impossible for me to conform to their barbaric religion—where my neck would be for every lawless and fanatic wretch's knife ; and in what part soever I should pass, with great extremities, every soul would curse me.

I was not the first Christian vaccinator in land of the

southern Aarab. They had all to tell me of one *Abu Fâris,* who came to them with this craft many years before me : a man of an uplandish Syrian village, part inhabited by Nasâra. He was well remembered among the Aarab : for his sake I can think them, where I came, to have been often less fanatically minded towards me.—And who comes after me may, I confide in God ! find the (before reproachful) Christian name respectable over large provinces of the fanatical Peninsula. Abu Fâris led a year of his life with the nomads ;—only touching at the towns, for doubt of their less tolerant humanity. Teyma he visited and Hâyil ; he was even in Kasîm, and had vaccinated at Aneyza. There was after him a second Abu Fâris : he came to the tribes ten years later, also a Nasrâny ; his own name was *Sleymàn,* but, professing the art of Abu Fâris, he was called by the nomads Abu Fâris.

Vaccination they understand to be come from the north : therefore if lymph be brought from the southward and the Harameyn (which is seldom) it is little esteemed : neither are there Moslem vaccinators in the north, but Nasâra only. The Beduw upon the Syrian borders are served from Damascus, where there are three or four professors. I found them to be drapers in the bazaar ; they had learned to win also by this leechcraft. As the spring is come, they go on circuit to the country villages : more rarely, at their earnestly entreating him, some one of them will adventure two or three days journey eastward to the Syrian nomads. Abu Fâris, not timid as the demiss Damascene Christians, but of the hardy mountaineers, was the first to descend with the nomads into Arabia. Well accepted had he been in the "houses of hair"; a man that could frankly repress the petulance of the ill-meaning sort, and even (they tell me) in reasonable cause laying his heavy hand upon some of them: and they, for their parts, were content to see this sturdy manhood in the Christian man. The same. Abu Fâris, later in Hâyil, being led by the steward of the Prince's hall through the castle-yard to dinner, some light spirits of the household bade the Nasrâny halt a moment and read them a writing, if he could, which was painted in ochre above the inner tower gateway. " Ay, said he, I can read, my masters."—" Then tell us what is this scripture," (feigning themselves they knew no letters.) " I see written '*there is none other God but Ullah.*'" —" And then—?"—" Well, and then there is that, which ye say, '*Mohammed messenger of Ullah.*'" And likewise, many years afterward, at the same place, they called me to read ; and as I read it in a breath, " Khalîl, cried the malicious witlings, has not refused to read all, but—ha-ha-ha !—ye remember the word here of Abu Fâris, ' *That which ye say*, Mohammed rasûl Ullah ! ' "

The later Abu Fâris was less a man of his meat among the Beduw : when word was brought to the mejlis of the massacre of the Nasâra in Syria, they saw him, between grief and fear, sobbing and sighing before them. When the kind Beduw said, " *Meskîn !* poor man, why will he lament thus ? Abu Fâris, take thy heart again, dost thou not believe, also in thy religion, that althing is from Ullah ? " he answered them, " Alas I am thinking of my parentage, ah Lord God ! and lie they now dead ? woe is me, all cruelly murdered ! " and half womanized he added, " *Ya rubba*, Aha ! this friendly company, will ye now slay me also ? *La, la, dakhîlakom*, nay, nay, do it not ! I cast myself upon you, I do entreat you ; " then abjectly, so that the citizens of the wilderness laughed out, " *Udkhul hareemakom*, I do enter even to your women, that they protect me ! " " Wellah, answered the Aarab, the man is *mejnûn*, beside himself. Now look up man ! Abu Fâris ! How, thou Sleymàn ! " And said many magnanimous desert voices, " Hast thou not eaten with us the bread and salt ? *bess !* it is enough, *khàlas !* all doubts are ended between us ; as for this doing in es-Shem, we judge not whether it were good or evil ; but *henna* (we are) *el-Beduw*, we make no account of the Shwâm (Damascenes). Let no fear be in thee here amongst us, thy friends ; *henna el-Beduw, wa eth-thaif azîz*, and the guest is as one dearly beloved."

It was Khálaf Allàyda who had fetched and fathered this Sleymàn the vaccinator, *mujeddir*. They came riding down together upon his thelûl with the Haj from Syria, and the Beduin's share was to be a third in this profitable adventure. I heard the tale from Khálaf's mouth ; he had since a mind to have fetched another mujeddir ; but the poor man's heart failed him when he saw the Beduwy's gaunt thelûl at his door and ·only the wilderness before him.—The Aarab had been faithful to Abu Fâris, nor envied they the man's good fortune ; every one of them paying gladly the ransom for his life from the horrible sickness, the fourth part of the mejîdy, or a shilling. His year ended, they sent him home in peace, with not a little substance, which he had gathered amongst them : his cattle were driven up before him, by the Beduin herdsmen, to Syria.

The Arabs, until now using inoculation, being once vaccinated, are in no fear of the disease for the rest of their lives. If I said " It is not so sure," they answered, " But it has been approved among hundreds, and whosoever was vaccinated with the *taam* (lymph) of Abu Fâris, when the *jídery* (small-pox) was in again, wellah *ma sâb-hu*, it never attained him." The

Aarab are cured in their maladies by the hareem, who have all some little store of drugs, spices and perfumes, fetched from Medina, and their grandam's skill of simples, which are not many to find in their desert dîras. The nomads had little expectation of better remedies in the hands of Khalîl, which were dearer " government medicines " and strange among them. They bade me show my drugs to the hareem who, they supposed, should certainly know them. The practice of the poor affectionate women, is not all (in some malignant husbands' surmising) to their health ; men too often ascribe their slow and obscure maladies to ' witchcraft of the hareem.' " See, Khalîl, some patient has said, how dead is my body and wasted : I am in doubt of a jealous wife, and that she has given me some cold drink." Poisoning is familiar to the criminal imagination of all the Arabs. They call medicaments *dawwa*, as in the settled countries ; and the Beduins give the name to those few herbs and condiments which they put to their food to give a pleasant savour and colour.

Hirfa, as a principal sheykh's daughter, was reputed to be seen in leechcraft. Hirfa one day calling her gossips together, they sat down before me to see my medicine-box opened. The silly bewildered hareem took my foreign drugs in their hands, one by one ; and, smelling to them, they wavered their heads with a wifely gravity. And all these they allowed to be to them unknown, but sure they were they had smelled out *haltîta*, or gum asafœtida, a drug which the Arabs have in sovereign estimation. But what was their wonder to see me make an effervescing drink ! Hirfa oftentimes entreated me to show her gossips this marvellous feat of " boiling water without fire." It is strange how, for remedies, the Arabs make no more a nice account of halàl and harrâm ; they will take of the unclean and even abominable, saying : " dawwa ! it is medicine." These Beduins give the sick to eat of the *rákham* or small white carrion eagle. Upon a day I found a poor woman of our menzil seething asses' dung in the pot ; she would give the water to drink with milk, to her sick brother : the Arabs think the ass unclean, but especially the excrement.

Now were I to speak of my medical practice plainly, I think it a desperation to cure the Arabs, and that a perfect physician would hardly be praised amongst them. He is lost whose science is slow, and the honest man of few promises ; they will despise his doubts and his tentatives. He who would thrive must resemble them, some glozing Asiatic that can file his tongue to the baseness of those Semitic minds. Their wild impatience

looks to see marvels : the right physician, only handling a
pulse, they think, should be able to divine a man's state and
all his past infirmities ; and some specific must he have for every
disease, because ' there is a salve in Nature for every sore ' ; yet so
knavish are they that for all his skill they would pay him only
upon a day which is ever to come. The Arabians are ill
nourished, and they think themselves always ailing. The nomads live nearly as the wild creatures, without certain diet, and
they drink infected waters. Few have not some visceral infirmities—*el-kibd ;* and, the wind breathing upon their nearly
naked bodies, they are crazed with all kinds of rheums, *er-rîhh ;*
a name they give to all obscure, aching diseases. Every sickness they name *wajjâ,* " pain, disease ;" the patient *wajjân.*

Inured from his youth to bodily extremities, the Beduwy
can suffer a painful malady of years, and will sooner pine still,
than put away his penny for uncertain cures to the *Mudowwy,*
or man of medicine. For these Semites, feeling themselves such
shrews, have no confidence in man, but in God only : they
would all see the leech's skill proved upon some other than
themselves. Thus hardly do any come to the man of medicine till
he be about to depart from them ; when commonly only the most
intractable or hopeless cases will be brought before him. Notwithstanding, they all love to bibble-babble their infirmities, in
the wholesome ears of the hakîm. As I have walked in Arabian
villages, some have caught me by the mantle to enquire, "Eigh !
thou the apothecary ! canst thou not restore their sight to the
blind ? " So everywhere they besought me to help some whose
eyes were perished. It is lawful, they think, to come to the physician, and merit to supinely endure a disease, which (by the will
of Ullah) is come upon them. If I said I had little or no hope
to relieve them, they responded cheerfully : " *El-Hakîm* (the
Physician is) *Ullah,* He is all-cure ; "—yet some, full of melancholy,
" *Ma ly ghreyr Ullah,* what then remaineth unto me but the
Lord ? " They will give to Ullah the praise of all human service,
and not pay the apothecary : and they say, " I will pay for no
medicines, I will pay for the cure ; trust me, Mudowwy, I will
requite thee at that time as thine own heart can desire."

It is said in the towns, " *the Beduwy's mind is in his eyes.*"
Negligent and impatient, they judge, as they are passionately
persuaded, in the seeing of the moment, and revert to their
slumbering indolence. They cannot be persuaded that a little
powder of quinine should be truly sold for a silverling, when their
housewives buy their hands full of beggarly drugs at Medina,
for a piece of small money. Others imagined the Mudowwy
himself had made all the medicines, of some common earths and

simples. Where they proved some marvellous effect of a remedy, as morphia (a grave anguish relieved with one drop of the medicine-water), neither could this move them : for all is as nothing, in comparison of God's miracles. Nor enquired they for it again of the man of medicine ; since they must pay the second time, if only with the gift of a little rice, or with the promise of a bowl of sour butter-milk. Others, having received my medicines, the elves withheld the price ; for all that the Beduin can catch of another man's good is his booty. There were some so ungracious ones that they have stolen away the cups in which, with much pains, I had charitably mixed them medicines ; poor losses, but that cannot be repaired in the desert. So said the men at our homely evening fire, " The people come to Khalîl's tent for medicines ; and Khalîl, not distinguishing them, will give to all of them in trust : the people *yegôtarun,* go their ways, and he sees them no more, wellah ! Khalîl, there is no wit in thee at all for buying and selling."

And were I to wander there again, I would carry with me only a few, that are called quack-salving medicines, of an easy application and like to specific remedies. Who has not made the experience, can hardly think how tedious it is to prepare medicines in the wilderness ; in that sun-stricken languishing and indigence of all things and often confusion of the nomad tent, to weigh out grains in the balance, the sand blowing, and there is no pure water : but when the potions are ready and the lotions, your nomad patients will hardly be able to find any phial, *garrôra,* to receive them. After my return a friend said to me, " Your Beduins have a good custom,—I would God we had it here ! Let physicians be paid only upon the patients' amendment ! A bold man to take upon you an art unlearned ! "—" I relieved many, the most part freely ; I hurt none ; I have deluded no man."

All the Aarab would have hijabs sooner than medicaments, which they find so unprofitable in the hands of their hareem. The Moghrâreba, Moors or " Occidental Arabs," are esteemed in Arabia, the best scriveners of these magical scriptures ; and the people suppose them to be of a wonderful subtlety, in the finding of hid treasures. There are hijabs for the relief of several diseases, and against possession of the jan or earth-demons ; also hijabs which should preserve life in dangers, as hijabs written against lead. *Metaab Ibn Rashîd,* prince of Shammar after his brother *Tellâl,* had worn one of this kind of amulets ; and his murderous nephews, who thought they might not prevail with common shot, killed him therefore with a silver bullet. The lieutenant of Turkish soldiery at Kheybar told in my hearing, long after, of one who, taken in a revolt at Medina, had been sentenced by the military court to be shot. Brought forth to execution, the bullets which struck the condemned fell down as from a wall, and he remained unwounded : so one fired a pistol in his bosom, but the lead fell from him. The unhappy man cried out in his suffering, " Sirs ! I have no defence against iron ! " so they bound him to a cannon's mouth, and at the blast, he perished. The Turk swore to us mighty oaths he was there, he had seen the thing with his eyes ; and others said they had known the like, " ay, billah ! "—Such are everyday miracles, heard and confirmed and believed in among them.

The same men catch after charms, that will not pay for medicine : every wiseacre of them would purchase a hijab with reals, even were they the last in his slender purse. The hijabs of famous magical men are dear worth ; those grave foreheads make it strange, and will profess themselves wonderfully unwilling. They are composed (as all things among them take colour of religion) out of " God's word," texts chosen in the koran, written cabalistically. And more than half confident is the well-nosed man, who has such a talisman suspended from his flesh, even in the greatest hazards. Also hijabs (some of the quaintest you shall find were written by Jews) have been used in mediæval Europe ; so are they yet among Oriental Christians. In the Arabic border lands there is hardly a child, or almost an animal, which is not defended from the evil eye, by a charm.—What ! do we not see the like even at this day in Europe ? in all the priests' countries yet in bondage.—Such were often their words : " We will pay for no medicines, the Arabs are poor folk ; but here is my three reals—wellah, I would bring five and lay them down, so thou write me an hijab such as I desire : " and before other they would have philters of dishonest love. They could well imagine, that the outlandish Nasrâny man might write them a quick spell, more than another : and they thought it a marvel, poor as they saw me, that I constantly denied them sharply, when with the draught of a reed I might have enriched myself. Yet if I said, " Should a man meddle in things pertaining to the Providence of Ullah ? " then the best among them, as Moslems, assented devoutly.

Beduins sometimes gave me their hands, supposing I should be skilled in palmistry, and prayed me to read their life-lot, ' whether it were fallen well to them.' Some vain young men would have me divine of their faces, saying, ' Saw I any likeness in them to lucky persons ? ' Mankind, after the Arabs' opinion, may be vexed in their bodies and mind by possession of the jan, of which they say " half are malignant and a half good demons, ay and Moslemîn." They inhabit seven stages, which (as the seven heavens above) is the building of the under-world. Strange maladies and lunatic affections are ascribed to their influence ; scorned and bewildered persons are said to be " be-jinned," mejnûn, demoniacs. Every disease asketh a remedy, and there are also exorcists for the mejnûns in Arabia :—be there not some, in these days, in our bell-and-candle Europe !—By " reading " powerful spells, out of the " scripture of God " over those sick persons, they would have us believe they can " put in fear and drive out " the possessing demons. Many have come and entreated me to use that ability, to the relief of some of their next kindred ; and these persons received, with hateful looks, my simple denial, protesting hardly, " it was but of an evil meaning towards them that I would not vouchsafe this kindness to the Moslemîn."

The nomad's mind is ever in the ghrazzu ; the knave would win, and by whose loss he recks not, neither with what improbity : men in that squalid ignorance and extreme living, become wild men. The Aarab are not all thus ; but, after their strait possibility, there are virtuous and higher human spirits, amongst them ; especially of the well-faring and sheykhs, men enfranchised from the pining daily carefulness of their livelihood, bred liberally and polished in the mejlis, and entertainers of the public guests. Human life, where the poor hardly find passage by foul and cragged ways, full of cruel gins, is spread out more evenly before them. These are the noblemen of the desert, men of ripe moderation, peacemakers of a certain erudite and subtle judgment.

Pleasant, as the fiery heat of the desert daylight is done, is our homely evening fire. The sun gone down upon a highland steppe of Arabia, whose common altitude is above three thousand feet, the thin dry air is presently refreshed, the sand is soon cold ; wherein yet at three fingers' depth is left a sunny warmth of the past day's heat until the new sunrise. After a half hour it is the blue night, and clear hoary starlight in which there shines the girdle of the milky way, with a marvellous clarity. As the sun is setting, the nomad housewife brings in a truss of sticks and dry bushes, which she has pulled or hoed with a mattock (a tool they have seldom) in the wilderness ; she casts down this provision by our hearthside, for the sweet-smelling evening fire. But to Hirfa, his sheykhly young wife, Zeyd had given a little Beduin maid to help her. The housewife has upon her woman's side an hearth apart, which is the cooking-fire. Commonly Hirfa baked then,

17—2

under the ashes, a bread-cake for the stranger : Zeyd her husband, who is miserable, or for other cause, eats not yet, but only near midnight, as he is come again from the mejlis and would go in to sleep.

At this first evening hour, the Beduw are all *fî ahl-ha,* in their households, to sup of such wretchedness as they may have ; there is no more wandering through the wide encampment, and the coming in then of any persons, not strangers, were an unseemly " ignorance." The foster-camels lie couched, before the booth of hair : and these Beduins let them lie still an hour, before the milking. The great feeble brutes have wandered all day upon the droughty face of the wilderness ; they may hardly crop their fills, in those many hours, of so slender pastures. The mare stands tethered before the booth at the woman's side, where there is not much passage. Such dry wire-grass forage as they find in that waste, is cast down beside her. When the Arabs have eaten their morsel and drunken léban of the flock, the few men of our menzil begin to assemble about the sheykh's hearth, where is some expectation of coffee. The younger or meanest of the company, who is sitting or leaning on his elbow or lies next the faggot, will indolently reach back his hand from time to time for more dry rimth, to cast on the fire, and other sweet resinous twigs, till the flaming light leaps up again in the vast uncheerful darkness. The nomads will not burn the good pasture bushes, *gussha,* even in their enemies' country. It is the bread of the cattle. I have sometimes unwittingly offended them, until I knew the plants, plucking up and giving to the flames some which grew in the soil nigh my hand ; then children and women and the men of little understanding blamed me, and said wondering, " It was an heathenish deed."

Glad at the fall of the empty daylight, the householders sit again to make talk, or silent and listless, with the drooping gravity of brute animals. Old men, always weary, and the herdmen, which were all day abroad in the sun, are lying now upon an elbow (this is the right Aarab posture, and which Zeyd would have me learn and use), about the common fire. But the reposing of the common sort at home is to lie heels out backward, about the hearth, as the spokes of a wheel, and flat upon their bellies (which they even think appeases the gnawing of hunger) ; and a little raising themselves, they discourse staying upon their breasts and two elbows ; thus the men of this lean nation will later sleep, spreading only their tattered cloaks under them, upon the wild soil (béled), a posture even reproved by themselves. Béled, we saw in the mouth of the

nomads, is the inhabited soil of the open desert and also of the
oasis ; they say of the dead, " He is under the béled." Dîra, the
Beduin circuit, is heard also in some oases for their town settlement.—I asked Zeyd, " Then say ye the béled is our mother ? "—
" Ay well, and surely, Khalîl ; for out of the ground took God
man and all return thither." They asking me of our custom,
I said " You are ground-sitters, but we sit high upon stools
like the Tûrk."—The legs of chair-sitters to hang all day they
thought an insufferable fatigue. " Khalîl says well," answered
Zeyd, who, a sheykh of Aarab, had been in high presence of
pashas and government men at Damascus ; and he told how
he found them sitting in arm-chairs and (they are all cross
leg Orientals) with a leg crossed over the other, a shank or
a foot : ' a simple crossed foot is of the under functionaries :
but to lap a man's shin, (Zeyd showed us the manner,) he
said to be of their principal personages.' The Arabs asked
me often, if we sat gathered in this kindly sort about our
evening fires ? and if neighbours went about to neighbour
byût, seeking company of friends and coffee-drinking?

Sitting thus, if there anyone rises, the mare snorts softly,
looking that it is he who should now bring her delicious bever
of warm camel-milk, and gazing after him, she whinnies with
pleasance. There is a foster camel to every nomad mare, since
they taste no corn, and the harsh desert stalks could not else
sustain her : the horse, not ruminating and losing much moisture
by the skin, is a creature very impatient of hunger and thirst.
His mare is therefore not a little chargeable to a sheykh in
the desert, who must burden oftentimes another camel with her
provision of water. Twice she will drink, and at the hottest of
the summer season, even thrice in a daylight ; and a camel-load
of girbies may hardly water her over two days. Who has wife
or horse, after the ancient proverb, may rue, he shall never be
in rest, for such brittle possessions are likely to be always ailing.
Yet under that serene climate, where the element is the tent of
the world, the Beduw have little other care of their mares ; it is
unknown in the desert so much as to rub them. They milk
first for the mare and then (often in the same vessel) for
the nomad household. She stands straining upon her tether,
looking toward the pleasant sound of milking : the bowl frothing from the udder is carried to her in the herdsman's hand
and she sups through her teeth the sweet warm milk, at a long
draught. The milking time of camels is but once in the day, at
evening, unless a little be drawn for some sick person or stranger
in the morning, or for any wayfaring man in the daytime. The
small cattle, *ghrannen* or *dubbush*, are milked at sunset ; only in

rich spring districts, the housewives may draw their teats again in the morning. The dubbush are milked by their housewives, the milch camels by the men and lads only. Spring is the milky season, when men and beasts, (if the winter rain failed not) fare at the best in the wilderness. With small cattle, it lasts only few weeks from the yeaning till the withering of the year be again upon them, when the herb is dried up ; but the camel kine are nearly eleven months in milk.

So needful is the supplement of milk to the desert horses, that when, in the dry summer or at some other low times, the camels are driven wide from the standing menzil to be *azab*, absent certain days, that is in quest of pasture, the mare also is led along with them in her master's troop, to drink the foster milk. But if the sheykh have need of his mare then at home, he will nourish her, as he may, without the wet-nurse, mixing at evening a bowl of *mereesy* or dry milk rubbed in water. Mereesy is the butter-milk of the flock, dried by boiling to the hard shard, and resembles chalk. It is a drink much to thank God for, in lean times, and in the heat of the year, in the wilderness ; in the long dead months when there is no milk, it is every day dearer and hard to be come by. Excellent to take upon journeys, mereesy is gipsy drink and no dainty in the border countries ; but in the Arabian oases it is much esteemed to use with their unwholesome date diet, which alone were too heating. Mereesy (' that which rubbed between the palms of the hands, can be mingled with water,') or dry milk, is called by many other names in the provinces of Arabia, as *thiràn* and *bùggila, baggl,* in West Nejd ; in the South and towards Mecca, *mùthir.* Butter is the poor nomads' market ware : with this they can buy somewhat in the towns for their household necessities. Having only mereesy in the saddle-bags and water before us every third day on the road, I have not doubted to set out upon long voyages in the khála. Mereesy will remain unaltered till the next season ; it is good in the second year, only growing harder. The best were to grind it to flour, as they do in Kasîm ; and this stirred, with a little sugar, in a bowl of the desert water is a grateful refreshment after the toil and heat of the desert journey.

A pleasure it is to listen to the cheerful musing Beduin talk, a lesson in the travellers' school of mere humanity,—and there is no land so perilous which by humanity he may not pass, for man is of one mind everywhere, ay, and in their kind, even the brute animals of the same foster earth—a timely vacancy of the busy-idle cares which cloud upon us that would live peaceably in the moral desolation of the world. And pleasant

those sounds of the spretting milk under the udders in the Arabs'
vessels ! food for man and health at a draught in a languishing
country. The bowl brought in foaming, the children gather to
it, and the guest is often bidden to sup with them, with his
fingers, the sweet froth, *orghra* or *roghrwa*, *irtugh :* or this milk
poured into the sour milk-skin and shaken there a moment,
the housewife serves it forth again to their suppers, with that
now gathered sourness which they think the more refreshing.

The nomad's eyes are fixed upon the crude congruity of
Nature ; even the indolence in them is austere. They speak of
the things within their horizon. Those loose " Arabian tales "
of the great border-cities, were but profane ninnery to their
stern natural judgments. Yet so much they have of the Semitic
Oriental vein, without the doting citizen fantasy, that many
dream all their lives of hidden treasures ; wealth that may fall
to them upon a day out of the lap of heaven. Instead of the
cities' taling, the Aarab have their braying rhapsodies, which
may be heard in every wild nomad hamlet, as those of the
Beny Helál. The Arabs are very credulous of all that is told
beyond their knowledge, as of foreign countries. All their
speech'is homely ; they tell of bygone forays and of adventures
in their desert lives. You may often hear them in their tale
quote the rhythms between wisdom and mirth of the *kasasîd*
(riming desert poets without letters) ; the best are often widely
current among the tribes. In every tribe are makers : better
than any in this country were the kassâds of Bishr. The *kassâd*
recites, and it is a pleasant adulation of the friendly audience to
take up his last words in every couplet. In this poetical elo-
quence I might not very well, or hardly at all, distinguish what
they had to say ; it is as strange language. The word *shâer*, he
that ' *feeleth*,' a poet, is unused by them ; the Beduins knew not
the word, Zeyd answered " it is *nadêm*." The Beduin singer
draws forth stern and horrid sounds from the rabeyby or viol of
one bass string, and delivers his mind, braying forcedly in the
nose. It is doubtless a very archaic minstrelsy, in these lands,
but a hideous desolation to our ears. It is the hinds, all day
in the wilderness with the cattle, who sing most lustily in
their evening home-coming to the humanity of the byût. I
often asked for a *kasîda* of Abeyd Ibn Rashîd, and have found
no singer in this country who was not ready with some of
them. The young herdsmen of Zeyd's menzil would chant for
the stranger the most evening-times the robust *hadû*, or herding-
song. [This word *rabeyby* is perhaps the Spaniard's *rabel*, and
that was in Ancient England *revel*, *rebibel*.] The Beduw make
the instrument of any box-frame they may have from the towns :

a stick is thrust through, and in this they pierce an eye above for the peg ; a kid-skin is stretched upon the hollow box ; the hoarse string is plucked from the mare's tale ; and setting under a bent twig, for the bridge, their music is ready.

The nomad's fantasy is high, and that is ever clothed in religion. They see but the indigence of the open soil about, full of dangers, and hardly sustaining them, and the firmament above them, habitation of the Divine salvation. These Ishmaelites have a natural musing conscience of the good and evil, more than other men ; but none observe them less in all their dealings with mankind. The civil understanding of the desert citizens is found in their discourse (tempered between mild and severe manly grace) and liberal behaviour. A few turns and ornaments of their speech, come suddenly to my remembrance : gently in contradiction, *la ! Ullah yesellímk*, "Nay, the Lord give thee peace;" in correction, *la ! Ullah hadîk*, "The Lord lead thee;" and in both, *Ullah yerham weyladeyk*, "The Lord show mercy to thy deceased parentage ;" or *yuhâdy weyladeyk il' ej-jínna*, "Lead in thy parents to the paradise." Wonder, as all their Semitic life, has the voice of religion, *Ullah !* "The Lord !" *Ana ushhud*, "I do bear witness !" *Yukdur Ullah !* "The Lord is able." *Rahmat Ullah !* "The Lord His mercy !" and very often the popular sort will say, (a Beduinism that is received with laughter in the towns,) *ana efla yowwella !*—which I leave to Arabists. When weary they sigh *ya Rubby !* "Ah my Lord !" Lovers of quietness at home, their words are peace, and still courteous in argument ; *wa low*, "And if it were so ;" *sellímt*, "I grant it you." Confession of faulty error through ignorance, *udkhul al' Ullah*, "If I said amiss, the Lord is my refuge." A word of good augury to the wayfaring and stranger ; *Ullah yuwasselak b'il-kheyer*, "God give thee to arrive well." *Insh' Ullah ma teshûf es-shurr*, "It may please the Lord that you see not the evil !" *Ullah yethkirak b'il-kheyer ?* "The Lord remember thee for good !" Beduish giving of thanks are : *âfy aleyk, el-âfy*, "I wish thee heartily health !" or, *jizak Ullah kheyer*, "God give thee good chance !" The nomads, at leisure and lively minds, have little other than this study to be eloquent. Their utterance is short and with emphasis. There is a perspicuous propriety in their speech, with quick significance. The Arabian town-dwellers contemn this boisterous utterance of the sons of the wilderness ; they themselves are fanatic sectators of the old koran reading. Asiatics, the Aarab are smiling speakers. All Beduin talk is one manner of Arabic, but every tribe has a use, *loghra*, and neighbours are ever chiders of their neighbours' tongue. "The speech of them,

they will say, is somewhat ' awry,' *awaj*." In the mouth of the
Fukara sheykhs, was a lisping of the terminal consonants. The
Moahîb talk was open and manly. In that dry serenity of the
air, and largely exercised utterance of the many difficult articu-
lations of their language, the human voice, *hess*, is here mostly
clear and well-sounding; unless it be in some husk choking
throat of heart-sore misery.

There is as well that which is displeasing in their homely
talk. The mind is distempered by idleness and malice : they
will hardly be at pains to remember suddenly, in speech,
their next tribesman's name ; and with this is their barbarous meddling curiosity, stickling mistrust one of another
and beggarly haggling for any trifle, with glosing caresses,
(would they obtain a thing, and which are always in guile,) impudent promises and petulant importunity. And their hypocrite
iniquitous words, begetting the like, often end in hideous
clamour, which troubling " the peace of Ullah " in the nomad
booth, are rebuked by the silent impatience of the rest, of whom
the better will then proffer themselves as peace-makers. The
herdsmen's tongue is full of infantile raillery and, in sight and
hearing of the other sex, of jesting ribaldry : they think it
innocent mirth, since it is God that has founded thus our nature.
Semites, it is impossible that they should ever blaspheme,
in manner of those of our blood, against the Heavenly Providence. Semitic religion is the natural growth of the soil in
their Semitic souls ; in which is any remiss, farewell life's luck,
farewell his worldly estimation : their criminal hearts are capa-
ble of all mischief, only not of this enormous desperation to lede
the sovereign majesty of Ullah. Out of that religious persuasion of theirs that a man's life should be smitten to death,
who is rebel unto God and despiser of the faith, comes the
sharp danger of our travelling among them ; where of every ten,
there is commonly some one, making religion of his peevish
bestiality, who would slay us, (which all men may do religiously
and help divine justice). But otherwise they all day take God's
name in vain (as it was perhaps in ancient Israel), confirming
every light and laughing word with cheerful billahs. The
herdsmen's grossness is never out of the Semitic nature, the
soul of them is greedy first of their proper subsistence and then
of their proper increase. Though Israel is scattered among the
most polite nations, who has not noted this humour in them ?
Little Joseph is a tale-bearer to their father of his brethren's
lewd conversation in the field ; such are always the Semitic
nomads. Palestine, the countries beyond Jordan and Edom,
given to the children and nephews of Abraham, spued out the

nations which dwelled before in them, and had defiled the land : the Beny Israel are admonished, lest the soil cast out them also. In Moses is remembered the nomad offence of lying with cattle ; the people are commanded to put away guiltiness from the land by stoning them : in Arabia that is but a villanous mock, and which the elder sort acknowledge with groans and cursing. The pastoral race being such, Israel must naturally slide back from Moses' religion to the easy and carnal idolatry of the old Canaanites.

To speak of the Arabs at the worst, in one word, the mouth of the Arabs is full of cursing and lies and prayers ; their heart is a deceitful labyrinth. We have seen their urbanity ; gall and venom is in their least ill-humour ; disdainful, cruel, outrageous is their malediction. " Curse Ullah, thy father (that is better than thou), the father of the likes of thee ! burn thy father ! this is a man fuel for hell-burning ! bless thee not God ! make thee no partaker of His good ! thy house fall upon thee ! " I have heard one, in other things a very worthy man, in such form chide his unruly young son : " Ullah rip up that belly in thee ! Curse the father (thy body) of that head and belly ! Punish that hateful face ! " And I have heard one burden another thus ; " Curse thee all the angels, curse thee all the Moslemîn, let all the heathen curse thee ! " The raging of the tongue is natural to the half-feminine Semitic race. The prophet prayeth against some which disquieted him : " Pour out their blood by the sword, let their children consume with famine, their women be childless and their wives widows : they shall cry out from the houses as the ghrazzu is suddenly upon them. Forgive not, Lord, their trespass, give to them trouble of spirit, destroy them from under the heaven, and let Thy very curse abide upon them." Another holy man curses to death petulant children. The Aarab confirm all their words by oaths, which are very brittle, and though they say *Wa hyât Ullah,* " As the Lord liveth," or a man swear by himself, *aly lahyaty,* or *Wa hyât dúkny,* " Upon (the honour of) my beard." He will perform such oaths if they cost him nothing, this is if he be not crossed in the mean while, or have become unwilling. If a man swear by his religion, it is often lightly and with mental reservation. For the better assurance of a promise they ask and give the hand ; it is a visible pledge. So in Ezekiel, the sheukh of the captivity promise and plight their hands. A Beduin will swear to some true matter Wellâhi, or doubly, which is less to trust, Wellâhi-Billâhi. It is a word he will observe if he may, for nothing can bind them against their own profit ; and they may lawfully break through all at an extremity. Another form is Wullah-Bullah, often said in mocking uncertainty and hypocrisy. That is a faithful form of swearing which they call *halif yemîn :* one takes a grass stalk in his fist, and his words are : " *Wa hyât hátha el-aûd,* By the life of this stem, *wa'r-rubb el-mabûd,* and the adorable Lord." When I have required new wayfaring companions to swear me this at the setting out, and add *inny mâ adeshurak,* " I will not (for any hap) forsake thee," they have answered, " Our lot is one whilst we are in the way, whether to live or die together ; and what more can I say, I will conduct thee thither, but I die, and by very God I will not forsake thee." I laid hold on their hands and compelled them, but they swore (to a kafir) unwillingly ; and some have afterward betrayed me : when then I reproached them to the heart, they answered me, " Oaths taken to a kafir be not binding ! " Magnanimous fortitude in a man, to the despising of death, where his honour is engaged, were in their seeing the hardihood of a madman : where mortal brittleness is fatally overmatched we have a merciful God, and human flesh, they think, may draw back from the unequal contention.

To clear himself of an unjust suspicion one will say to the other, " There is nothing between us but Ullah." Like words we hear from gentle Jonathan's mouth, in his covenant with the climbing friend David. Certain oaths there are, which being received by the custom of the tribes as binding, are not violated by any honourable person. And, to tell the little which I have ascertained in this kind,—a Beduin, put in trust of another man's cattle, often some villager, will give up his yearly tale of the increase without fraud, under a solemn obtestation which he durst not elude, the owner having also traced a ring about him with his sword. If aught be missing in the nomad menzil, the owner of that which is lost or strayed may require of whom he will an oath of denial, as Ahab took an oath of his neighbours, who are called " every nation and kingdom," that his subject and enemy, Elias, was not found amongst them. I have seen some under an inputation go with the accuser to the hearth to give his answer ; this they call to swear upon their swords. It is over certain lines, which they trace with their weapon in the ashes ; a cross mark in a circle ⊕ ; therewith taking a handful from the ash-pit. It is an oath such, that the complainant must thereafter yield himself satisfied. Zeyd accused of devouring his neighbours' substance, which was not seldom, would cheerfully, with a faultless countenance, spread and smooth out upon the soil the lap of his mantle, and clapping down his flat palm upon it, he cried, " Ha ! " and proffered himself all ready to swear

that this was not so, there was nothing of the other's ownership,
Wellah! in his hold. Oaths of the desert there are some held
binding between enemies. I knew a B. Atîeh man guesting with
the Moahîb, who in time when they lay friendly encamped together with the Fejîr, was admitted to converse freely amongst
these his natural foemen, when he had sworn his oath at the
hearth, before Motlog, that he would not practise against them.
This matter of oaths is that in the nomad commonwealth which
I have least searched out ; even the solemn forms, conjuring
quarter and a magnanimous protection. Although Beduins
often questioned me, what our words were in these cases, yet
ever, as God would have it, to the last, I neglected to enquire
the like of themselves again. At every moment, when they
gave me their minds, I had rather ascertain all that I might
of the topography of their country ; having less care of the rest,
as never thinking to entreat for my life of any man.

Besides, there are certain gestures used among them, which
are tokens of great significance. I smooth my beard toward
one to admonish him, in his wrongful dealing with me, and have
put him in mind of his honour. If I touch his beard, I put him
in remembrance of our common humanity and of the witness of
God which is above us. Beard is taken in Arabia for human
honour, and to pluck it is the highest indignity ; of an honest
man they say, *lahyat-hu taîba,* " His is a good beard ; " of a vile
covetous heart *mâ lihu lahya,* " He has no beard." The suppliant who may bind, as I have heard, a certain knot in the
other's kerchief, has saved himself : and were the other the avenger
for blood, yet he must forbear for God ! Kiss an angry man's
forehead, and his rancour will fall ; but the adversary must be
taken by surprise, or he will put forth stern hostile hands to oppose thee. Surely a very ancient example of the Semitic sacramental gestures is that recorded of Abraham, who bids his
steward put the hand under his thigh, to make his oath sure.
A simple form of requiring an honourable tolerance and protection is to say ; *Ana nuzîlak,* " I have alighted at thy tent," or
say where thou fearest treachery, *ana nusîk,* and again, *Ana bi
wejhak ya sheykh,* " Sir, I am under thy countenance ; " more
solemnly, and touching him, *Terâny billah ya sheykh ; wa bak
ana dakhîlak,* which may signify, " By the Lord thou seest me,
and I do enter, Sir, under thy protection." In my long dangerous
wanderings in the Arabian peninsula I have thrice said this one
word *dakhîlak :* twice when, forsaken in the deserts, I came to
strange tents of Heteym (they are less honourable than Beduins,
and had repulsed me) ; once to the captain of the guard at
Hâyil, when I was maltreated by the emir's slaves in the market-

place. He immediately drove them from me ; and in the former
adventure it made that I was received with tolerance.

As above said, the nomads will confirm every word with an
oath, as commonly *wa hyât*, ' By the life of ;' but this is not in
the Waháby country, where every oath which is by the life of
any creature they hold to be " idolatry." They swear *wa hyât*,
even of things inanimate ; ' By the life of this fire, or of this
coffee,' *hyâtak*, " By thy life," *wa hyât rukbaty*, " By the life of
my neck," are common affirmations in their talk. *Wa hyât ibny*
men rarely say, and not lightly, " By my son's life." *Wa hyât
weyladich*, " Life of thy child," is a womanish oath of Bíllî
mothers one to another at every third word ; and a gossip
says tenderly, *wa hyât weylady*, " By my child's life :" I have
heard a Beduin woman testify to her child thus, " By the
life of thy father, who begat thee upon me ! " In the biblical
authors, Joseph makes protestation to his brethren " By
the life of Pharaoh," and later that is common in them " as
the Lord liveth;" Jehovah promises under the same form,
" As I live, saith the Lord." In every tribe there is a manner, even in this part of their speech. The Moahîb, who, like
their Bíllî neighbours, are amiable speakers, use to swear,
not lightly, by the divine daylight and the hour of prayer, as
wa hyât el-missîeh hâtha, " By this (little) sun-setting hour."
The Beduw will put off importunity with much ill humour,
saying, *furrka* or *furr'k ayn abûy*. Unruly children are checked
with *subbak !* they will answer *yussbak ent*. Full of ribaldry, the
Aarab will often say in a villanous scorn *kuss marrathu*, " his
wife's nakedness for him," or *ummhu*, " his mother's nakedness."
My Medina host at Kheybar, who otherwise was a good worthy
man, would snib his only son tyrannically and foully with this
reproach of his deceased mother, whom he had loved. The biblical Saul, justly incensed, also reviles his son by the nakedness
of his mother, a perverse and rebellious woman, and Jonathan
her son rose from his father's dish and departed in fierce anger.

The Aarab's leave-taking is wonderfully ungracious to the
European sense, and austere. The Arab, until now so gentle a
companion, will turn his back with stony strange countenance
to leave thee for ever. Also the Arabs speak the last words as
they have turned the back ; and they pass upon their way not
regarding again. This is their national usage, and not of a
barbarous inhumanity ; nay, it were for thee to speak when any
departs company, saying : " Go in peace." You have not eaten
together, there was nothing then between you why this must
take his leave ; all men being in their estimation but simple
grains, under the Throne of God, of the common seed of

humanity. But the guests will say as he goes forth, and having
turned his face, with a frank simplicity, *nesellem aleyk*, " We bid
thee peace." The Arabs are little grateful for the gift which is
not food, receive they with never so large a hand ; " So little !
they will say, put to, put to ; " but the gentler spirits will cry out
soon, *bess ! wâjed ! keffy !* " enough, there is found, it sufficeth
me heartily."

CHAPTER X.

THE NOMADS IN THE DESERT; VISIT TO TEYMA.

A formidable year for the Fukara. The tribe in the North. Enigma of the Nasrâny. The Sâiehh or World's Wanderer. Damascus the ' World's Paradise.' The Nasrâny, whether a treasure seeker, or a spy. ' The Lord give victory to the Sooltân.' The horses of the Nasâra are pack-horses. The Fejîr reckoned a tribe of horsemen. They dread, hearing of our armed multitudes. The War in the Crimea. ' The flesh of the Nasâra better than theirs.' How should the Nasâra live not having the date in their land? The Nasâra inhabit land beyond seven floods. ' The stranger to the wolf.' The Nasrâny in the land of the Beduw. They wondered that we carry no arms in our own country. The Lappish nomads and the Arctic dîra. The land of the Nasâra very populous. Shooting stars fall upon the heads of the kuffâr. Art-Indian. The camel wounded beyond cure. The " desert fiends." Nomad deposits in the deserts. The Solubbies. Precept of their patriarch. Their land-craft and hunting in which they surpass the Aarab. They want not. Journey for provisions to Teyma. The Beny Kelb. The green oasis in sight. The orchard towers. Teyma, a colony of Shammar, very prosperous. Their wells are of the ancients. Teyma of the Jews, (the Biblical Tema). The townspeople. The Nejd coffee fire. The coffee hall. The viol forbidden in the estates of Ibn Rashîd. Rahŷel, marriage of a Beduwy sheykh and a townswoman. The moon eclipsed. Ibn Rashîd's Resident. Stately carriage of the Shammar Princes. The slave trade. A building of antique Teyma. Inscription. The Hadàj. The Suâny. Sleymàn and the hareem of his household. An untimely grave. Teyma husbandry. Teyma fruits given to any stranger, but not sold. Teyma dates. Dates are currency. Sons of Damascenes at Teyma. Kasr Zellûm. Inscription with eyes. The oasis a loam bottom. Way to Jauf. The evening company. They blame the religion of the Nasâra. Religion of the Messiah. A wedder of fifteen wives. The Mosaic commandments. The ancient scriptures they say to be falsified by us. " The People of the Scriptures." Biblical Teyma. The tribesmen depart from Teyma by night. The Fukara in fear of Ibn Rashîd forsake their dîra.

THIS was a formidable year for the Fukara: they were in dread of Ibn Rashîd; they feared also that Kheybar would be barred to them,—" Kheybar the patrimony of Annezy," from whence those tribes in the South eat (the date fruit), eight in the twelve months. Besides it was a year of locusts. The tribesmen

disputed in the mejlis, " should they go up anew to the Hauran,"
the land of bread ; and that which they call, (nearly as nomad
Israel coming from the lower deserts,) " The good Land of the
North, where is milk enough ; " this is Shàm or High Syria.
They would remain as before in the *Niggera* (Batanea,) which is
in the marches of their kinsmen the northern half-tribe of W. Aly :
they count it fifteen removes, journeying with all their cattle
and families, beyond Teyma. They had few years before forsaken
their land upon this occasion : the Fejîr in a debate with their
sister tribe, the southern W. Aly, had set upon them at Dàr
el-Hamra, and taken their camels. Many were slain, and the
mishandled kinsmen, appealing to Ibn Rashîd, the Prince gave
judgment that satisfaction be made. The Aarab will hardly
restore a gotten booty, especially where there is evil meaning
between them ; and to live without fear of the Emir, they
withdrew to a far-off Syrian country, where slenderly clad
and not inured to that harsh and longer winter, and what for a
contagious fever which happened in the second year, there
perished many among them ; the most, as it is the weak which
go to the wall, were poor Fehját, wretches whom the iniquity
of fortune ceases not to pursue until the end of all natural
evils.—The Fehját buried, in the north, the half of their
grown males, which were twenty persons. There is always
living with the northern W. Aly, a body of the Fukara, *el-
Kleyb, sheykh Fendy*, which for a blood feud with Bishr, might
not inherit their own country.

The presence of the Nasrâny in land of the Aarab was an
enigma to them ; they put me to the question with a thousand
sudden demands, which were often checked by the urbanity of
the rest. ' At what distance (they enquired), in which pàrt lay my
country ? ' I said, " A thelùl rider might alight among my neighbours, a little before the year's end."—They had not thought
the world was so large ! So they said, " Khalîl's country lies at
very great distance, and can it be he has passed all that great
way, only to visit the Aarab ! now what can this mean ? Tell us
by Ullah, Khalîl, art thou not come to spy out the country ?
For there will no man take upon himself immense fatigues
for naught. Khalîl, say it once, what thy purpose is ? Art
thou not some banished man ? comest thou of thine own will,
or have other sent thee hither ?—Khalîl loves well the Moslemîn, and yet these books of his be what ? Also, is he not
' writing ' the country as he has ' written up ' el-Héjr and el-
Ally ? " I said, " I was living at Damascus and am a *Sâiehh ;* is
not the sâiehh a walker about the world ?—and who will say him
nay ! also I wander wilfully."—" Now well ! Khalîl is a *Sûwahh ;*

wander where you list, Khalîl, and keep to the settled countries, there is nothing to hinder ; but come not into the wilderness of the Beduw ; for there you will be stripped and they will cut thy throat : wellah, in all the desert no man fears to kill a stranger ; what then when they know that thou art a Nasrâny !—A sûwahh ! eigh ! but the Aarab are so ignorant that this will not help thee ; a day may come, Khalîl, the end of all this rashness, when someone will murder thee miserably ! "—*Sâiehh* in the Mohammedan countries is God's wanderer, who, not looking back to his worldly interest, betakes himself to the contemplative life's pilgrimage. They would not hold me for a derwish. "Nay, said they, derawîsh are of small or no regard ; but Khalîl was a care to the Dowla." Also they had word I was some rich man in Damascus. How then, they wondered, could I forsake Damascus, *jinnat ed-dinnea,* "the world's garden or paradise," to dwell in the waste land of the Aarab !—It is always a melancholy fantasy of the upland Arabians, who have seen or heard anything of the plentiful border provinces, to complain of their own extreme country. The Southern Arabs lead their lives in long disease of hunger and nakedness : to see good days in the northern land, which is watered with seasonable rains and is wet with the dew of heaven, they think should be a wonderful sweetness. The "garden" of all is Damascus, the Arabs' belly-cheer "paradise" ; for there is great cheap of all that can ease a poor man, which is food and raiment. And such, as Semites, is all they intend, in their word of Damascus, "the garden or paradise."

I passed for a seeker of treasure with some who had seen me sitting under the great acacia, which they believe to be possessed by the jan, at el-Héjr ; now they said to me, "Didst thou take up anything, Khalîl, tell us boldly ? " and a neighbour whispered in my ear, " Tell thy counsel to me only, good Khalîl, and I will keep it close."—" There is no lore, I answered, to find treasures ; your finders are I know not what ignorant sots, and so are all that believe in their imposture."—" God wot it may be so ; Khalîl is an honest-speaking man ;—but in roaming up and down, you lighted upon naught ? Hearken ! we grant you are disinterested—have patience ! and say only, if you find a thing will you not give some of it to your uncle Zeyd ? "—" The whole, I promise you."—" Wellah, in Khalîl's talk is sincerity, but what does he, always asking of the Aarab an hundred vain questions ?—Though thou shouldst know, O Khalîl, the name of all our camping grounds and of every jebel, what were all this worth when thou art at home, in a far country ? If thou be'st no spy, how can the Aarab think thee a man of good understanding ? " In other

times and places whilst I was yet a stranger little known among
them, the Beduin people did not always speak so mildly, many
murmured and several tribesmen have cruelly threatened that
' could it be known, I came about spying the land, they would
cast me, billah, on a fire, with my books, and burn all together.'
In such case, they might break the cobweb customs of hospitality : the treacherous enemy is led forth, and drawn to the
hindward of the tent there they cut his throat. Many times
good Beduin friends predicted to me this sharp ending of
my incurable imprudence, when leaving their friendly tribes I
should pass through strange dîras : but as I lingered long in
the country, I afterward came almost no-whither, where some
fair report was not already wafted before me. " Friends, I have
said, I am come to you in no disguises ; I have hidden nothing
from you ; I have always acknowledged myself a Nasrâny, which
was a name infamous among you." And they : " Well, but the
war with those of your kindred and the Sooltân !—Is he not
killing up the Nasâra like sheep flocks ? so God give him the
victory !—say this, Khalîl, *Ullah yunsur es-Sooltân.*"

As we hearken to strange tales, so they would ask me of the
far Nasarene country ; were we *ahl tîn,* ' a people dwelling in clay
(houses),' or else *ahl byût shaar,* ' wandering Aarab dwelling in
houses of hair ' ? When I answered, " We have no other nomad
folk, than a few gipsies ; "—" it is plain (they said) that Khalîl's
Arabs are *hâthir,*" or settled on the land : and they enquired
which were our cattle. It was marvels to them, that in all our
béled was not one camel.—" Lord ! upon what beasts do they
carry ? "—" Ours is a land of horses, which are many there as your
camels ; with a kind of labouring horses we plough the fallows :
besides, we have the swiftest running horses of stature as your
thelûls." There lives not an Arab who does not believe, next
to his creed, that the stock of horses is only of the Arabs, and
namely, the five strains, educated in Arabia. ' And to which
of these (they would know) reckoned we our horses ? ' It perplexed and displeased them that our béled should be full of
horses :—' had Ullah given horses also to the Nasâra ! '—" Listen !
(said Zeyd, who loved well to show his sharp wit,—the child's
vanity not dead in the saturnine grown man,) and I can declare
Khalîl's words ; it is that we have seen also in es-Sham : Khalîl's
coursers be all *kudsh,* or pack-horses." When I answered, ' he
was mistaken ; ' they cried me down ; " Khalîl, in other things
we grant you may know more than we, but of horses thou canst
have no knowledge, for they are of the Aarab." The Fejîr are
reckoned a tribe of horsemen, yet all their mares were not a
score : Beduins of tribes in which were very few horses I have

found mistrustful of their own blunt judgment ; they supposed
also I might tell them many subtle skills from a far country.

They enquired of our ghrazzus, and what number of fighting
men could we send to the field. Hearing from my mouth that
many times all the Haj were but a small army of our great
nations, they gasped for fear, thinking that el-Islam was lost ;
and " wherefore, they asked quickly, being such multitudes, did
we not foray upon them (as they would have overridden us) :—
Ah God ! (they cried), help Thou the Moslemîn ! " " Comfort
yourselves, I answered, that we, being the stronger, make no
unjust wars : ours is a religion of peace ; the weak may live
in quietness for us."—" It is good that God has given you this
mind, to the welfare of el-Islam, yet one Moslem (they confided)
should be able to drive before him an hundred of the Nasâra."
I told them we had made the great war of *Krîm* (the Crimea)
for the Sûltàn and their sake ; in which were fallen the flower
of our young men, and that women yet weep for them in our
land." They enquired coldly, " Were your dead two or three
hundred, or not so many ? " When I said their number might
be 60,000, (and they believing I could not lie,) as men confounded they cried, " Ah Lord God ! is not that more than all
the men together in these parts ? " (there may not be so many
grown males in the nomad tribes of upland Arabia !) " And
have your people any great towns, Khalîl ! "—" Great indeed, so
that all the Beduw gathered out of your deserts might hardly
more than fill some one great city."—" God (they exclaimed) is
almighty ! but have we not heard of Khalîl's people, is it not of
them that is said *el-Engreys akhuâl es-Sûltàn* (the English are
uncles of the Sûltàn on the mother's side) ; the Sûltàns do well
to ally in their friendly Christian blood,"—which always they
esteem above their own. They say in Arabia, " the Nasâra never
ail anything in their lives, nor suffer in their flesh, but only in the
agony of dying ; their head aching, it is a sign to them that they
are nigh their end : the flesh of the Nasâra is better than ours."
Beduins have curiously observed me in their camps, waiting to
see the truth of their opinion fulfilled, if at any time I sat wearily
with the head in my hand ; some would then say, " Eigh ! what
ails thee ? does thy head ache ?—it is likely that he will die,
poor Khalîl ! "

And our béled, " a land without palms," this was as a
fable to them.—" There are no dates ! How then do your people
live, or what sweetness taste they ? Yet Khalîl may say sooth :
companions, have we not found the like in the North ? Which
of us saw any palms at Damascus ? Khalîl's folk may have
honey there, and sugar ;—the sweet and the fat comfort the

18—2

health of the ill dieted under these climates. We too have
seen the north country ; all that grows out of the soil is there,
and that oil of a tree which is better than samn." These hungry
Beduins being in the Hauran, where they had corn enough,
yet so longed in the autumn for the new date berries, that it
drew them home to their empty desert, only " to eat of their
own palms at Kheybar." The nomads think they cannot be in
health, except they taste this seasonable sweetmeat ; although
they reckon it not wholesome diet.

The Beduw very often asked me " Beyond how many floods
lies the land of the Nasâra ? " They heard say we dwelt behind seven floods ; other said, " It is three, and if you will not
believe this, ask Khalîl." "Ullah bring thee home, Khalîl!
and being come again to thy house, if the Lord will, in peace,
thou wilt have much to relate of the Aarab's land ? and wilt thou
not receive some large reward ? for else, we think, thou wouldst
never adventure to pass by this wilderness, wherein even we,
the Beduw, are all our lives in danger of robbers : thou art
alone, and if thou wast made away, there is none would avenge
thee. There is not, Khalîl, a man of us all which sit here, that
meeting thee abroad in the khála, had not slain thee. Thy camel
bags, they say, are full of money, but, billah, were it only for the
beast which is under thee ; and lucky were he that should
possess them. *The stranger is for the wolf!* you heard not this
proverb in your own country ? "—" By God (one cries), I had
killed Khalîl!"—"And I" (said another).—"Wellah, I had waylaid him (says another) ; I think I see Khalîl come riding, and
I with my matchlock am lurking behind some crag or bush ; he
had never seen it :—*deh!* Khalîl tumbles shot through the
body and his camel and the gear had been all mine : and
were it not lawful, what think ye ? to have killed him,
a God's adversary ? This had been the end of Khalîl." I
said, " God give thee a punishment, and I might happen to
prevent thee."—" Wellah (answered the rest), we had not spared
him neither ; but beware thou, the Beduw are all robbers.
Khalîl ! the stronger eat the weaker in this miserable soil,
where men only live by devouring one another. But we
are Zeyd's Aarab, and have this carefulness of thee for Zeyd's
sake, and for the bread and salt : so thou mayest trust us, and
beside us, we warn thee, by Ullah, that thou trust not in any
man. Thou wilt hardly receive instruction, more than one
possessed by the jan ; and we dread for thee every morrow lest
we should hear of thy death ; the people will say, ' Khalîl was
slain to-day,'—but we all wash our hands of it, by Ullah ! The
Aarab are against thee, a Nasrâny, and they say, ' He is spying

the country : ' and only we are thy friends which know thee
better. Khalîl may trust to the Dowla, but this is a land under
no rule, save only of the Lord above us. We but waste breath,
companions; and if God have blinded this man, let him alone;
he may die if he will, for who can persuade the foolhardy ? "
When I told them that far from looking for any reward, I
thought, were I come home, I might hardly purchase, at need,
the livelihood of a day with all this extreme adventure, they
answered, ' Were the Nasâra inhospitable? '

The Arab travels with his rafîk, they wondered therefore how
I came unaccompanied : " Khalîl, where is thy companion, that
each might help other ? " They wondered hearing that all ours
was peaceable land, and that we carried no arms, in our own
country. " Khalîl, be there no Beduins at all, in the land of
the Nasâra? " I told them of the Lapland nomads in the
cold height of the north, their round hoop-tents of skins, and
clothing of the same : some bid me name them, and held that
' they had heard such a name.' " What are their cattle in
so cold a béled ? the winter snow lying the more months
of the year, it were unfit for camels ! "—" You will not believe me : their beasts are a kind of gazelles, big as asses,
and upon their heads stand wide branching horns, with those
tines they dig in the snow to a wort, which is their daily
pasture. Their winter's night, betwixt the sunsetting and the
sunrising, is three months ; and midsummer is a long daylight, over their heads, of equal length. There I have seen the
eye of the sun a spear's height above the face of the earth at
midnight." Some thought it a fabulous tale that I told in scorn
of them. " We believe him rather," said other. Nothing in
this tale seemed so quaint to them, as that of those beasts'
branching horns, which I showed them in the sand with my
camel-stick ; for it is the nature of horns, as they see any, to be
simple. They asked, " Should not such be of buffalo kind ? "
But of that strange coming and going of the sun, the herdsmen's mirth rising, " How, laughed they, should those Aarab
say their prayers ? would it be enough to say them there but
once, in a three-months' winter night ! "

" And are your settled countries so populous ? tell us, wellah,
Khalîl, have you many villages? an hundred? "—" Hundreds,
friends, and thousands : look up ! I can think as many as these
stars shining above us : " a word which drew from them long
sighing eighs ! of apprehension and *glucks !* upon their Beduish
tongues, of admiration. Meteors are seen to glance at every few
moments in the luminous Arabian night. I asked, " What say
the Aarab of these flitting stars ? " *Answer :* " They go to tumble

upon the heads of the heathen, O Khalîl! fall there none
upon the Nasâra? Ullah shortly confound all the kuffâr!" Zeyd
said with a sober countenance, "Your towns-folk know better
than we, but ye be also uncunning in many things, which the
Aarab ken.—Khalîl now, I durst say, could not tell the names of
the stars yonder," and pointing here and there, Zeyd said over
a few names of greater stars and constellations, in what sort the
author of Job in his old nomad-wise, "The Bear, Orion and the
Pleiades." I asked, "How name you this glorious girdle of the
heavens?"—"*El-Mujjir*;" and they smiled at our homely name,
"The Milky Way." I told them, This we see in our glasses to
be a cloud of stars; all our lore is not to call a few stars by their
names. Our star-gazing men have numbered the stars, and set
upon every one a certain name, and by "art-Indian," they may
reckon from a hundred ages before our births, or after our
deaths, all the courses of the host of heaven.—But those wandering stars stedfastly shining, are like to this earth, we may see
seas and lands in them." Some of the younger sort asked then,
"Were there Aarab in them?—and the moon is what, Khalîl?"

There is a proverb which says, "Misfortunes never come
single;" my vaccination had failed, and now *Abán*, my camel,
failed me. Abán (to every beast of their cattle is a several
name, as these are of camels: *Areymîsh, Ghrallàb, er-Rahîfa, ed-
Dònnebil, Dánna, el-Màs, Aitha, Atsha*) was a strong young he-
camel and rising in value; but Zeyd had it in his double mind
to persuade me otherwise, hoping in the end to usurp it himself.
Upon a morrow the unhappy brute was led home, and then we saw
the under-jaw bleeding miserably, it was hanging broken. It happened that a great coffee company was assembled at Zeyd's, from
the sunrise, and now they all rose to see this chance. The groaning camel was made to kneel; some bound the limbs, and with
strength of their arms careened and laid this great bulk upon the
side; and whoso were expert of these camel masters searched the
hurt. Zeyd laid his searing irons in the embers ready for firing,
which is seldom spared in any practice of their desert surgery.
All hearkened to the opinion of a nomad smith, which kindred
of men are as well the desert farriers and, skilled in handling
tools, oftentimes their surgeons. This sâny cured the broken jaw
with splints, which he lapped about with rags daubed with rice
cinder and red earth. The camel, said he, being fed by hand,
might be whole in forty days. The like accident, I heard it said
among them, had happened once in their memories to a tribesman's camel, and the beast had been cured in this manner; but I
felt in my heart that it might never be. The wound was presently

full of flies, and the dressing, never unbound, bred worms in so great heat ; the dead bone blackened, and in few days fell away of itself. My watch also failed me, by which I made account of distances : from thenceforth I have used cross-reckonings of camel journeys.

It was March ; already the summer entered with breathless heat, and in face of these contradictions of fortune, I thought to depart out of the desert country. I would return to el-Ally, and there await some rice-caravan returning to Wejh, from whence by any of the small Arab hoys, upon which they use to ship camels, I might sail for Egypt. But Zeyd and Motlog bade me have patience, until after the spring season ; when the tribe in their journeys should again approach the Héjr country, from which we were already very far divided. ' The forsaken deserts behind us being now infested by habalîs, I should not find any willing, and they moreover would suffer none to accompany me.' The habalîs, ' desert fiends,' are dreaded by the nomad tribesmen, as the Beduw among settled country and oasis folk. Commonly the habalîs are some young miscreants that, having hardly any head of cattle at home, will desperately cast themselves upon every cruel hazard : yet others are strenuous solitary men, whose unquiet mettle moves them from slothing in the tent's shadow to prowl as the wolf in the wilderness. These outlaws, enduring intolerable hardships, are often of an heathenish cruelty, it is pretended they willingly leave none alive. Nearly always footmen, they are more hardly perceived, lurking under crag or bush.

The waste (sand-plain) landscape of these mountain solitudes is overgrown with rare pasture bushes. The desert bushes, heaped about the roots with sand, grow as out of little hillocks. The bushes dying, the heaps which were under them remain almost everlastingly, and they are infinite up and down in all the wilderness : in some is the quantity of two or three or more wagon loads. These nomads bury in them their superfluous carriage of dates every year, as their camels come up overloaded with the summer gathering from Kheybar : that they may find their own again they observe well the landmarks. Some sheykhs will leave their winter beyt thus committed to the sand of the desert : in the hot months, with scarcity of pasture, and when the cattle are least patient of thirst, if they would not have them lean they must lessen their burdens. These nomad deposits lying months in the dry ground are not spoiled ; and there is none of their tribesmen that will ever disturb them : the householder shall be sure to find his own again where he buried it. The nomad tribes have all this manner

of the summer deposit ; some leave their cumber in the villages
with their hosts, and such trust is (in nearly all men's hands)
inviolable.   The Moahîb have a secret cave known to none
living but themselves, in their desolate Harra ; there they lay
up, as in a sanctuary, what they will, and a poor tribesman may
leave his pound of samn.—Passing through a valley apart from
the common resort in the solitudes of Sinai, I saw a new
Beduin mantle, hanging on a thorn.   My nomad camel-driver
went to take it down, and turning it in his hand " Ay billah (said
he), a good new cloak enough ! " and hanged it on the bough
again : such goods of tribesmen are, as it were, committed
to God. So we came to some of those Sinai stone cottages,
which they call ' Nasarene houses ' (they would say, of the antique
people of the land, before the Moslemîn), in which they use to
leave their heavy quern-stones ; and there are certain locked
barns of the few traffickers bringing in corn from Gaza, among
the Beduw. We entered one of them, and as I was looking at
something of their gear, my companion, with altered looks, bade
me put it up again ; as if even the handling were sacrilege.
Sheykhs receiving surra of the haj road, have also their stores of
heavy stuff and utensils in the kellas, as those of the Fejîr
at Medáin ; and I heard they paid a fee to Haj Nejm, one
real for every camel load.   The sand upon all this high inland
is not laid in any ripples (as that at the Red Sea border, rippled,
in this latitude, from the north) ; here are no strong or prevail-
ing winds.

As we went by. to the mejlis, "Yonder (said Zeyd) I shall
show thee some of a people of antiquity."   This was a family
which then arrived of poor wanderers, *Solubba*. I admired the
full-faced shining flesh-beauty of their ragged children, and have
always remarked the like as well of the Heteym nomads.
These alien and outcast kindreds are of fairer looks than the
hunger-bitten Beduw.   The Heteym, rich in small cattle, have
food enough in the desert, and the Solubba of their hunting and
gipsy labour : for they are tinkers of kettles and menders of
arms, in the Beduin menzils.   They batter out upon the anvil
hatchets, *jedûm*, (with which shepherds lop down the sweet
acacia boughs, to feed their flocks,) and grass-hooks for cutting
forage, and steels for striking fire with the flint, and the like.
They are besides woodworkers, in the desert acacia timber,
of rude saddle-trees for the burden-camels, and of the thelûl
saddle-frames, of pulley reels, (*máhal*) for drawing at any deeper
wells of the desert, also of rude milk vessels, and other such
husbandry : besides, they are cattle surgeons, and in all their trade

(only ruder of skill) like the smiths' caste or *Sunna*. The Solubba obey the precept of their patriarch, who forbade them to be cattle-keepers, and bade them live of their hunting in the wilderness, and alight before the Beduin booths, that they might become their guests, and to labour as smiths in the tribes for their living. Having no milch beasts, whereso they ask it at a Beduin tent, the housewife will pour out léban from her semîla, but it is in their own bowl, to the poor Solubba : for Beduins, otherwise little nice, will not willingly drink after Solubbies, that might have eaten of some *futîs*, or the thing that is dead of itself. Also the Beduw say of them, "they eat of vile insects and worms:" the last is fable, they eat no such vermin. Rashly the evil tongue of the Beduw rates them as ' kuffâr,' because only few Solubbies can say the formal prayers, the Beduins are themselves not better esteemed in the towns. The Solubba show a good humble zeal for the country religion in which they were born, and have no notice of any other ; they are tolerant and, in their wretched manner, humane, as they themselves are despised and oppressed persons.

In summer, when the Beduw have no more milk, loading their light tents and household stuff, with what they have gained, upon asses, which are their only cattle, they forsake the Aarab encampment, and hold on their journey through the wide khála. The Solubby household go then to settle themselves remotely, upon some good well of water, in an un-frequented wilderness, where there is game. They only (of all men) are free of the Arabian deserts to travel whithersoever they would ; paying to all men a petty tribute, they are mo-lested by none of them. Home-born, yet have they no citizen-ship in the Peninsula. No Beduwy, they say, will rob a Solubby, although he met him alone, in the deep of the wilder-ness, and with the skin of an ostrich in his hand, that is worth a thelûl. But the wayfaring Beduwy would be well content to espy, pitched upon some lone watering, the booth of a Solubby, and hope to eat there of his hunter's pot; and the poor Solubby will make the man good cheer of his venison. They ride even hunting upon ass-back. It is also on these weak brutes, which must drink every second day, (but otherwise the ass is hardly less than the camel a beast of the desert,) that they journey with their families through great waterless regions, where the Beduwy upon his swift and puissant thelûl, three days patient of thirst, may not lightly pass. This dispersed kindred of desert men in Arabia, outgo the herdsmen Beduw in all land-craft, as much as these go before the tardy oases villagers. The Solubbá (in all else ignorant wretches,) have inherited a land-lore from sire

to son, of the least finding-places of water. They wander upon
the immense face of Arabia, from the height of Syria to el-
Yémen, beyond *et-Tâif*, and I know not how much further!
—and for things within their rat-like understanding, Arabians
tell me, it were of them that a man may best enquire.

They must be masters in hunting, that can nourish themselves in a dead land ; and where other men may hardly see a
footprint of venison, there oftentimes, the poor Solubbies are
seething sweet flesh of gazelles and bedûn, and, in certain sand
districts, of the antelope ; everywhere they know their quarries'
paths and flight. It is the Beduw who tell these wonders of
them ; they say, " the S'lubba are like herdsmen of the wild
game, for when they see a troop they can break them and
choose of them as it were a flock, and say, ' These will we have
to-day, as for those other heads there, we can take them after to-
morrow.' "—It is human to magnify, and find a pleasant wonder,
this kind of large speaking is a magnanimity of the Arabs ; but
out of doubt, the Solubba are admirable wayfarers and hardy
men, keen, as living of their two hands, and the best sighted of
them are very excellent hunters. The Solubba or *Slèyb*, besides
this proper name of their nation, have some other which are
epithets. West of Hâyil they are more often called *el-Khlúa* or
Kheluîy, " the desolate," because they dwell apart from the
Kabâil, having no cattle nor fellowship ;—a word which the
Beduw say of themselves, when in a journey, finding no menzil
of the Aarab, they must lie down to sleep " solitaries " in the
empty khála. They are called as well in the despiteful tongue
of this country, Kilâb el-Khála, ' hounds of the wilderness.'
El-Ghrúnemy is the name of another kindred of the Slèyb in
East Nejd ; and it is said, they marry not with the former. The
Arabians commonly suppose them all to be come of some old
kafir kind, or Nasâra.

—Neither are the Sherarát and Heteym nomads (which are
of one blood) reckoned to the Beduin tribes. The dispersed
kindreds of Sunna are other home-born aliens living amongst
the Aarab, and there is no marrying between any of them. *Má
li-hum asl,* say the Beduw, " They are not of lineage," which can
be understood to signify that ' not descended of Kahtân, neither
of the stock of Ishmael, they are not of the Arabs.' And if any
Arabians be asked, What then are they ? they answer : " Wellah,
we cannot tell, but they come of evil kin, be it Yahûd or Nasâra "
(this is, of the Ancients which were in the land before Mohammed, and of whom they have hardly any confused tradition). As
often as I met with any Solubba I have asked of their lineage :
but they commonly said again, wondering, " What is this to en-

quire of us *mesquins* dwelling in these deserts ? we have no
books nor memory of things past ; but read thou, and if anything of this be written, tell us." Some said the name of their
ancestor is *M'aibî;* the Beduw also tell of them, that which is
read in Arabic authors, how they were the *Aarab Jessàs,* once
Beduins : being destroyed in their controversy with the *Aarab
K'leyb* and bereaved of all their cattle, they for their livelihood took up this trade of the hammer, and became Solubba.
Later in the summer I found some Solubba families pitched
under the kella at el-Héjr, who were come over the Harra and
the Tehám̨a from Wejh, their own station. At that season
they make a circuit ; last year they had wandered very far
to the south, and I saw their women grinding a minute wheaten
grain, which they had brought from a wady near Mecca !
They (as coast and Hejâz dwellers) were of more civil understanding than the uplandish Solubba. To my questions the
best of them answered, " We are Araab K'fâ, of old time possessors of camels and flocks, as the Beduw : those were our villages,
now ruins, in the mountains southward of el-Ally, as *Skeirát*
in *Wady Sódr;* but at last our people became too weak to maintain themselves in an open country, and for their more quietness, they fell to this trade of the Solubba. Said one of them,
" We are all *Beny Murra,* and fellowship of *Sálim Ibn ez-Zîr,*
from the hill *Jemla,* a day on the east side of Medina ; we
are called *Motullij* and *Derrúby.*" Haj Nejm laughed as I came
again, at " this strange fantasy of Khalîl, always to be enquiring
somewhat, even of such poor folk. Khalîl ! these are the *Beny
Morr,* they are dogs, and what is there besides to say of them ? "

When Beduins asked me if I could not tell them by book-
craft what were the Solubba, it displeased ̨them when I answered, " A remnant, I suppose, of some ancient Aarab ; " they
would not grant that Solubbies might be of the right Arabian
kindred. All who are born in the Arabs' tongue are curious
etymologers ; a negro, hearing our discourse, exclaimed,. "Well,
this is likely that Khalîl says ; is not Solubba to say *Sulb el-
Arab,* the Arab's stock ? " The poor soul (who had spoken a
little in malice, out of his black skin, for which he was dispraised
amongst the white Arabs) was cried down by the other etymologers, which were all the rest of the company, and with great
reason, for they would not have it so. " The Solubba are rich
(say the Arabs), for they take our money, and little or nothing
comes forth again ; they need spend for no victuals. They have
corn and dates enough, besides samn and mereesy, for their
smith's labour." The Solubby has need of a little silver in his
metal craft, to buy him solder and iron ; the rest, increased to a

bundle of money, he will, they say, bury in the desert sooner than carry it along with him, and return perhaps after years to take it up again, having occasion it may be to buy him an ass. Yet there are said to be certain Solubba, keepers of a few cattle, towards Mesopotamia ; living under their own sheukh, and riders upon dromedaries. I have seen a sheykhly northern man, honourably clad, at Hâyil, who was a Solubby ; he invited me (I think at the great Emir's bidding) to ride with him in the next mountains, seeking for metals. I asked, "Upon what beast?" He said I should ride upon an ass, " we have no other." I would gladly have ridden out of Hâyil into the free air ; but I thought a man's life was not to trust with abjects, men not of the Beduin tradition in faithful fellowship. Even the Solubba hold to circuits, and lodge by their tribes and oases. There are Solubby families which have their home station, at some settlement, as Teyma ; but the most remain in the desert.—The Sunna are some settled in the villages, and some are wandering men with the tribes, leading their lives as nomads, and possessors of cattle. The Solubba outcast from the commonwealth of mankind, and in disgrace of the world, their looks are of destitute humility. Their ragged hareem, in what encampment they alight, will beg somewhat, with a lamentable voice, from beyt to beyt, of the poor tolerant Beduw : yet other (as those from Wejh) are too well clad, and well-faring honest persons, that their wives should go a-mumming. I have seen young men, which were Slèyb, in the Syrian wilderness, clad in coats of gazelle-skins. The small Solubby booth is mostly very well stored, and they have daily meat to put under their teeth, which have not the most poor Beduins.

Wandering and encamping, we had approached Teyma ; and now being hardly a journey distant, some of our people would go a-marketing thither, and Zeyd with them, to buy provisions : I should ride also in the company with Zeyd. We set out upon the morrow, a ragged fellowship, mostly Fehját, of thirty men and their camels. We passed soon from the sandy highlands to a most sterile waste of rising grounds and hollows, a rocky floor, and shingle of ironstone. This is that extreme barrenness of the desert which lies about Teyma, without blade or bush. We passed a deep ground, *M'hai*, and rode there by obscure signs of some ancient settlement, *Jerèyda*, where are seen a few old circles of flag-stones, pitched edgewise, of eight or nine yards over, seeming such as might have fenced winter tents of the antique Aarab, sheltered in this hollow. In the Moallakát, or elect poems of ancient Arabia, is some mention of round tents, but the

booths of all the Arab nomads are now foursquare only. The
company hailed me, " See here ! Khalîl, a village of the *Auellîn*,
those of old time."—"And what ancients were these?"—"Some
say the Sherarát, others the *Beny Kelàb* or *Chelb*, and theirs,
billah, was the Borj Selmàn and the ground *Umsheyrifa*." Zeyd
added: " This was of the *Ahl Theyma* (not Teyma), and sheykh
of them *Aly es-Sweysy the* Yahûdy." Come upon the highest
ground beyond, Zeyd showed me the mountain landmarks,
westward *Muntar B. Atîeh*, next *Twoyel Saîda, Helaima* before
us, in front *el-Ghrenèym*, which is behind the oasis. Some
murmured, "Why did Zeyd show him our landmarks?"—"I
would have Khalîl, said he, become a Beduwy."

Delightful now was the green sight of Teyma, the haven of
our desert; we approached the tall island of palms, enclosed
by long clay orchard-walls, fortified with high towers. Teyma
is a shallow, loamy, and very fertile old flood-bottom in these
high open plains, which lie out from the west of Nejd. Those
lighthouse-like turrets, very well built of sun-dried brick, are from
the insecure times before the government of Ibn Rashîd, when,
as the most Arabian places, Teyma was troubled by the sheykhs'
factions, and the town quarters divided by their hereditary
enmities. Every well-faring person, when 'he had fortified his
palms with a high clay-brick wall, built his tower upon it;
also in every sûk of the town was a clay turret of defence and
refuge for the people of that street. In a private danger one
withdrew with his family to their walled plantation: in that
enclosure, they might labour and eat the fruits, although his
old foes held him beleaguered for a year or two. Any enemy
approaching by day-light was seen from the watch-tower. Such
walling may be thought a weak defence; but for all the fox-like
subtlety of Semitic minds, they are of nearly no invention. A
powder blast, the running brunt of a palm beam, had broken up
this clay resistance; but a child might sooner find, and madmen
as soon unite to attempt anything untried. In the Gospel para-
bles, when one had planted a vineyard, he built a tower therein
to keep it. The watch-tower in the orchard is yet seen upon all
desert borders. We entered between grey orchard walls, overlaid
with blossoming boughs of plum trees; of how much amorous con-
tentment to our parched eyes! I read the oasis height 3400 ft.
We dismounted at the head of the first sûk before the *dàr*, house
or court of a young man our acquaintance, *Sleymàn*, who in the
Haj time had been one of the kella guests at Medáin. Here he
lived with his brother, who was Zeyd's date merchant; we were
received therefore in friendly wise, and entertained. The hareem
led in Hirfa, who had ridden along with us, to their apartment.

As the coffee pestle (which with the mortars, are here of limestone marble, sunna's work, from Jauf,) begins to ring out at the coming of guests ; neighbours enter gravely from the sûk, and to every one our sheykh Zeyd arose, large of his friendly greeting, and with the old courtesy took their hands and embraced them.

Teyma is a Nejd colony of Shammar, their fathers came to settle here, by their saying, not above two hundred years past : from which time remain the few lofty palms that are seen grown to fifteen fathoms, by the great well-pit, *Haddàj;* and only few there are, negroes, who durst climb to gather the fruits of them. All their palm kinds have been brought from Jebel Shammar, except the helw, which was fetched from el-Ally. Theirs is even now, in another dîra, the speech of Shammar. Here first we see the slender Nejd figures, elated, bold tongued, of ready specious hospitality, and to the stranger, arriving from the Hejâz, they nearly resemble the Beduins. They go bare-footed, and bravely clad of the Hâyil merchandise from *el-Irâk,* and inhabit clay-built spacious houses, mostly with an upper floor ; the windows are open casements for the light and air, their flooring the beaten earth, the rude door is of palm boards, as in all the oases. This open Shammar town was never wasted by plagues, the *burr* or high desert of uncorrupt air lies all round about them from the walls : only Beduins from the dry desert complain here of the night (the evaporation from irrigated soil), which gives them cold in the head, *zikma.* Here are no house-ruins, broken walls and abandoned acres, that are seen in the most Arabian places. Prosperous is this outlying settlement from Nejd, above any which I have seen in my Arabian travels. If anyone here discover an antique well, without the walls, it is his own ; and he encloses so much of the waste soil about as may suffice to the watering ; after a ploughing his new acre is fit for sowing and planting of palms, and fifteen years later every stem will be worth a camel. Teyma, till then a free township, surrendered without resistance to the government of Ibn Rashîd. They are skilful husbandmen to use that they have, without any ingenuity : their wells are only the wells of the ancients, which finding again, they have digged them out for themselves : barren of all invention, they sink none, and think themseves unable to bore a last fathom in the soft sand-rock which lies at the bottom of the seven-fathom wells. Moslemîn, they say, cannot make such wells, but only Nasâra should be good to like work and Yahûdies. Arabian well-sinkers in stone there are none nearer than Kasîm, and these supine Arabs will call in no foreign workmen. They trust in God for their living,

which, say the hearts of those penny-wise men, is better than
to put their silver in adventure.

There was none here who asked alms in the street ; indeed
it is not common to see any destitute persons in West Nejd. I
knew in Teyma but one such poor man, helpless with no great age.
In what house he entered at supper time, he might sit down with
the rest to eat and welcome, but they grudged that he should
carry any morsel away. There were in the town one or two
destitute Beduins, who entered to sup and " to coffee " in which
households they would, no man forbidding them. At night they
lay down in their cloaks, in what coffee hall they were ; or
went out to sleep, in the freshing air, upon some of the street
clay benches.

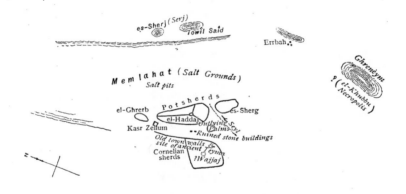

Old Teyma of the Jews, according to their tradition, had
been (twice) destroyed by a flood. From those times there remain some great rude stone buildings ; the work is dry-laid
with balks and transoms of the same iron-stone. Besides, there
is a great circuit (I suppose almost three miles) of stone walling, which enclosed the ancient city. This *sûr* lies somewhat
above the oasis. The prince of old Mosaic Teyma is named
in their tradition *Béder Ibn Jòher*. Nomad masters of new
Teyma were at first B. Sókhr, unto whom even now they
yield a yearly khûwa ; and else they should not be delivered from
their distant foraying. Fever is unknown at Teyma. Their
water, and such I have found all Arabian ground water, is flat,
lukewarm and unwholesome. Of this they think it is that
amongst them almost no man is seen of robust growth ; but
they are the lean shot-up figures of Nejd, with the great
startling eyes, long oval shallow faces, and hanging jaws : you

might think them Beduins. The women are goodly, more than
the men, loose-fleshed large village faces, but without ruddiness,
they have dissonant voices : as the neighbour tribeswomen of
the B. Wáhab, they go unveiled. I saw in the town no aged
persons. Of the two hundred houses here, are three sheykhs'
sûks or parishes and fifteen *hârats* or smaller wards ; in every one
there is some little mesjid or public oratory (often but a pent-
house) of poor clay walling without ornaments, the flooring is
of gravel. Such are as well places of repose, where the stranger
may go in to sleep under a still shadow, at the gate of heaven.
But the great mosque, whither all the males resort for the
Friday mid-day prayers, preaching, and koran reading, stands a
little without the sûks to the eastward. It is perhaps the site
of some ancient temple, for I found certain great rude pillars
lying about it. At el-Ally, (a Hejâz oasis, and never entered
by the Waháby,) I saw the mosques nearly such as are those
in the Syrian villages.

We were led round to drink in the coffee-halls of other householders, with whom Zeyd dealt, for some part of his victual of
grain and dates. As they have little fuel of that barren land
about them, and out of their plantations no more than for the
daily cooking,—the palm timber is besides " as vinegar to the
teeth and smoke to the eyes " in burning—they use here the
easy and cleanly Nejd manner of a charcoal coffee-fire, which is
blown in a clay hearth with a pair of smith's bellows : this coal is
brought by men who go out to make it, in the further desert.
The smiling oasis host spares not, sitting at his coals, to blow
and sweat like a Solubby for his visiting guests : and if thou his
acquaintance be the guest of another, " Why, he will ask thee
with a smooth rebuke, didst thou not alight at my dàr ? "
Coffee is thus made, with all diligence, twice or thrice over in
an hour : prepared of a dozen beans for as many persons, their
coffee drink is very small at Teyma. The coffee-hall, built
Nejd-wise, is the better part of every house building. The
lofty proportion of their clay house-walls is of a noble simplicity,
and ceiled with ethl or long tamarisk beams, which is grown in
all the oases for timber. The close mat of palm stalks laid upon
the rafters, is seen pleasantly stained and shining with the
Arabs' daily hospitable smoke, thereabove is a span deep of
rammed earth. The light of the room is from the entry, and in
many halls, as well, by open casements, and certain holes made
high upon the walls. The sitting-place (múkaad) of the earthen
floor and about the sunken hearth, is spread with palm mat
or nomad tent cloth. Upon the walls in some sheykhs' houses
is seen a range of tenter-pegs, where guesting sheykhs of

the Aarab may lay up their romhh or long horseman's lance.
In these dàrs you shall hear no minstrelsy, the grave viol sounds
in Waháby ears are of an irreligious levity, and the Teyámena
had received a solemn rescript from Ibn Rashîd, forbidding
them to sound the rabeyby! *Khálaf,* the emir, a liberal-minded
person, told it to some Beduins in my hearing, not without a
gesture of his private repugnance.

We met Motlog's brother in the streets ; he was come into
Teyma before us. I marked how preciously the nomad man
went, looking upon the ground, I thought him dazing in the
stagnant air of the oases, and half melancholy : *Rahÿel* might be
called in English the complete gentleman of his tribe ; a pensive
and a merry errand he had now upon hand. The sheykh was
come in to wed a town wife : for as some villager, trafficking to the
nomads, will have his Beduwîa always abiding him in the desert,
so it is the sick fantasy of many a Beduwy to be a wedded man
in the market settlement, that when he is there he may go home
to his wife, though he should not meet with her again in a round
year. At evening we heard loud hand-clapping, the women's
merrymaking for this bridal, in one of the next houses. This is a
general and ancient Semitic wise of striking sounds in measure,
to accompany the lively motions of their minds ; in the Hebrew
Scriptures it is said, ' The floods and the trees of the field clap
their hands.' The friends of the spouse fired off their matchlocks. This pairing was under a cloud, for there happened
at the moment a strange accident ; it was very unlucky I came
not provided with an almanac. Seeing the moon wane, the
housewives made great clangour of pans to help the labouring
planet, whose bright hue at length was quite lost. I began
to expound the canonical nature of eclipses, which could be
calculated for all times past and to come. The coffee drinkers
answered soberly, " It may well be true, but the Arabs are
ignorant and rude ! We cannot approach to so high and perfect kinds of learning."

Upon the morrow, whilst we sat at coffee, there enters one,
walking stately, upon his long tipstaff, and ruffling in glorious
garments : this was the Resident for Ibn Rashîd at Teyma.
The emir's gentleman, who seemed to have swallowed a stake,
passed forth, looking upon no man, till he sat down in his
solemnity ; and then hardly vouchsafed he to answer the
coffee-drinkers' cheerful morning greetings. This is the great
carriage of Hâyil, imitated from the Arabian prince Ibn
Rashîd, who carries his coxcomb like an eagle to overawe the
unruly Beduw. The man was Saîd, a personage of African

blood, one of the libertines of the emir's household. He sat
before us with that countenance and stiff neck, which by his
estimation should magnify his office : he was lieutenant of the
lord of the land's dignity in these parts. Spoke there any man
to him, with the homely Arabian grace *ya Saîd!* he affecting
not to look again, seemed to stare in the air, casting eyes over
your head and making merchants' ears, bye and bye to awaken,
with displeasure, after a mighty pause : when he questioned any
himself he turned the back, and coldly averting his head he
feigned not to attend your answer. Saîd was but the ruler's
shadow in office for this good outlying village : his was the pro-
curation and espial of his master's high affairs ; but the town
government is, by the politic princely house of Shammar, left in
the hands of the natural sheykhs. Saîd dwelt in a great Teyma
house, next by the Haddàj : miserably he lived alone to himself
and unwived ; at evening he sparred the door, and as he went
not forth to his master's subjects, so he let in no coffee-fellowship.
The Prince's slave gentleman has a large allowance, so much
by the month, taken upon the tribute of the town : unlettered
himself, a son was here his clerk. Now he thought good to
see that Nasrâny come to town, who was dwelling he heard,
since the Haj, amongst the Beduw of Ibn Rashîd. Saîd, with
a distant look, now enquired of the company " Where is he ? "
as if his two eyes had not met with mine already. After
he had asked such questions as " When came he hither ?—
He is with thee, Zeyd ? " he kept awful silence a set space ;
then he uttered a few words towards me and looked upon
the ground. " The Engleys, have they slaves in their country ? "
I answered, " We purge the world of this cursed traffic, our ships
overrun the slave vessels in all seas ; what blacks we find in
them we set free, sending them home, or we give them land and
palms in a country of ours. As for the slave shippers, we set
them upon the next land and let them learn to walk home ; we
sink their prize-craft, or burn them. We have also a treaty with
the Sûltàn : God made not a man to be sold like an head
of cattle. This is well, what thinkest thou ? " The gross
negro lineaments of Saîd, in which yet appeared some token
of gentle Arabic blood, relented into a peaceable smiling, and
then he answered pleasantly, " It is very well." Now Saîd had
opened his mouth, his tongue began to wag : he told us he
had gone once (very likely with Nejd horses) as far as Egypt,
and there he had seen these Frenjies. So rising with lofty
state, and taking again his court countenance, he bade Zeyd
bring me presently, and come himself to his dàr, to drink
coffee.

When we arrived thither, Saîd had doffed his mockery of
lordship, and sat but homely in old clothes in his own house.
He led me to the highest place; and there wanting leaning
pillows, he drew under my elbow his *shidâd*, or thelûl saddle,
as is the usage in the nomad booths. These Beduin manners are seen in the oases' coffee-halls, where (the Semites
inventing nothing of themselves) they have almost no other
moveables.—And seeing them in their clay halls in town and
village one might say, " every Arab is a wayfaring man, and
ready for the journey." Saîd brought paper and ink, and
a loose volume or two, which were all his books; he would
see me write, So I wrote his name and quality, *Saîd Zélamat
Ibn Rashîd;* and the great man, smiling, knew the letters
which should be the signs of his own name. So when we had
drunk coffee, he led me out beyond his yard to a great building,
in stone, of ancient Teyma, hoping I might interpret for him
an antique inscription; which he showed me in the jamb of the
doorway, made (and the beams likewise, such as we have seen in

the basaltic Hauran) of great balks of sandstone. These strange
characters, like nothing I had seen before, were in the midst
obliterated by a later cross-mark. Saîd's thought was that this
might be the token of an hid treasure; and he told us " one
such had been raised at Feyd,"—a village betwixt Shammar
and Kasîm.—Is not this a mad opinion? that the ancients,
burying treasure, should have set up a guidestone and written
upon it! Returning, I found in the street wall near his door,
an inscription stone with four lines sharply engraved of the
same strange antique Teyma writing.

Zeyd went out to buy his provision, and no one molesting me, I walked on through the place and stayed to consider their great well-pit, El-Haddàj ; a work of the ancients which is in the midst of the new Teyma. That pit is unequally four-sided, some fifty feet over, and to the water are seven fathoms. The Haddàj is as a great heart of Teyma, her many waters, led outward to all sides in little channels, making green the whole oasis ; other well-pits there are only in the outlying hamlets. The shrill draw-wheel frames, *suâny*, are sixty, set up all round, commonly by twos and threes mounted together ; they are seldom seen all in working, at once. The well-camels walking downwards from the four sides of the pit, draw by their weight each one a vast horn-shaped camel-leather bucket, *dullû:* the lower neck is an open mouth, which, rising in the well, is sustained by a string, but come to the brink, and passing over a roller the dullû belly is drawn highest, whilst the string is slackened, and the neck falling forward, pours forth a roaring cataract of water. Afterward, I saw the like in India. The shrieking suâny and noise of tumbling water is, as it were, the lamentable voice of a rainless land in all Nejd villages. Day and night this labour of the water may not be intermitted. The strength of oxen cannot profitably draw wells of above three or four fathoms and, if God had not made the camel, Nejd, they say, had been without inhabitant. Their Haddàj is so called, they told me, " for the plenty of waters," which bluish-reeking are seen in the pits' depth, welling strongly from the sand-rock : this vein they imagine to come from the Harra.

Returned to the coffee-hall I found only Sleymàn ; we sat down and there timidly entered the wives and sisters of his household. The open-faced Teyma hareem are frank and smiling with strangers, as I have not seen elsewhere in Arabia : yet sometimes they seem bold-tongued, of too free manners, without grace. The simple blue smock of calico dipped in indigo, the woman's garment in all the Arab countries, they wear here with a large-made and flowing grace of their own ; the sleeves are embroidered with needlework of red worsted, and lozenges sewed upon them of red cotton. The most have bracelets, *hadŷd*, of beautiful great beads of unwrought amber, brought, as they tell me, anciently from Hâyil. The fairer of them have pleasant looks, yet dull as it were and bovine for the blindness of the soul ; their skin, as among the nomads, is early withered ; spring-time and summer are short between the slender novice and the homely woman of middle age. Tamar's garment of patches and party-colours was perchance of such sort as now these Arabian women's worked gown. His old loving father made for little Joseph a motley coat : and it may seem more than likely, that the patriarch seamed it with his own hands. Amongst the nomads men are hardly less ready-handed to cut, and to stitch too, their tunics, than the hareem. *Sleymàn:* " See Khalîl, I have this little sister here, a pretty one, and she shall be thine, if thou wouldest be a wedded man, so thou wilt number me the bride-money in my hand ; but well I warn thee it is not small." The bevy of hareem, standing to gaze upon a stranger, now asked me, " Wherefore art thou come to Teyma ? "— " It were enough if only to see you my sisters." But when their tongues were loosed, and they spoke on with a kine-like stolidity, Sleymàn cried full of impatience, "Are your hareem, Khalîl, such dull cattle? Why dost thou trouble thyself to answer them ? Hence, women, ye stay too long, away with you ! " and they obeyed the beardless lad with a feminine submission ; for every Arab son and brother is a ruler over all woman-kind in the paternal household. This fresh and ruddy young man, more than any in the town, but not well minded, I found no more at my coming again : he lay some months already in an untimely grave ! " Where (I asked) is Sleymàn ? "—" *Ràhh* (they answered in his house), he is gone, the Lord have mercy upon him."—" Oh, how did he die ? "—" Ah, Khalîl, of a wajja " (a disease), and more than this I might not learn from them. His brother called me to eat of a sheep, the sacifice for the dead, in which we remembered Sleymàn. " Khalîl, said the elder brother's wife (the fairest among women of the Teyâmena) rememberest thou Sleymàn ? ah, he died a little after your being here, *mesquin !* Ullah have mercy upon him ! " When I responded, " Have mercy upon him, Ullah ! " they looked upon me a little wondering, to hear this friendly piety out of the mouth of a kafir : they abhorring us as miscreants, suppose that we should desire of God to damn them in their deaths also.

The oasis ways lie between orchard walls ; but where I entered, I saw their palm grounds very well husbanded. A pond fed by the irrigating channels from the Haddàj is maintained in the midst of every plantation, that ground moisture may be continually about the roots of the palm-stems (almost to be reckoned water plants). Their corn plots are ploughed, in the fall of the year, with the well-camels, and mucked from the camel-yards ; a top-dressing is carried upon the land from loam pits digged in the field's sides. There is not so good tillage in the Syrian villages. Naturally this land is fat, and bears every year corn, now one now another kind of grain ; but they sow only for one harvest in the year, since all their irrigation afterward is no more than enough

for the palm plantations. Wheat and barley harvest is here in
the first week of April; they grow also, as in all the Arabian
country, the tall flag-like millet *thùra,* and a minute Nejd grain,
which is called *dúksa.* Besides their *bread plants,* they grow
enough of the "indecent" leaf of tobacco. It is a wonder that
the Shammar prince has not forbidden them! In this we may
see that Nejd-like Teyma is not Nejd. Fruit-trees, not to usurp
the room of the food-palm, they plant beside their irrigating
channels; the plum, the pomegranate, the fig, the great citron,
the sweet and sour lemons : the vine is seen at most of their
wells, a great trellis plant, overspreading the long enclosed walk
of the draft camels with delicious shadows. The Teyâmena will
liberally bring of their pleasant fruit in this thirsty land to any
passing stranger, but they will sell them none ; yet grapes are
sold in the Nejd village-country of Kasîm. They might plant
here all the tree-kinds of the paradise of Damascus ; but to
what advantage ? —for their own using ? The poor should not
tempt Ullah with delicate eating : such as they have may well
suffice, the rest they desire not, and rather can despise them
with religious indolence. The many kinds of Teyma dates are
of very excellent quality and savour. The stems very tall and
robust, and great fruit bearers. But all their dates are *harr,* or
heating ; they should be eaten with mereesy or with the nomads'
sour butter-milk, which are cooling drinks. The Teyâmena
hold all dates, (although the most of their diet,) in a kind
of loathing. Twenty small Teyma pottles, *sah* (pl. *suah*), were
given this year for a real, almost as much as by the Beduins'
estimation may serve a man, with a little milk, for the days of a
moon. Of their small-grained Arabian wheat, yet sweet and
good, only six such standard measures were sold for the same.
These villagers raise corn enough to sell to the nomad neighbours. Of other cattle than camels, they have but a few head
of small humped kine from el-Ally ; they have plenty of poultry ;
dogs are not seen here, house-cats I have not seen in Nejd.

Here is little current money, most of their buying and selling
is reckoned in sahs, and great bargains in camel-loads, of the
date staple. Barter is much of all Arabian traffic. Silver
comes to them from the desert, in the hands of the nomads,
who have it by the sale of some of their camels to the brokers ;
but it is mainly, in the haj-road country, of the surra, paid to
their sheykhs in good Turkish mejîdies. This yearly receipt
of silver, is nearly all taken up again from the village dealers
for the government tax, which for Teyma is four thousand
reals by the year, gathered after the date harvest ; certain of
the sheykhs then ride with it to Hâyil, and bring this tribute

into the treasury of the emir. There are a few strangers here, tradesmen, from J. Shammar : they sell Bagdad clothing, and the light and cheaper gulf calico, *saleyta*, in hired chambers and houses. These Hâyil citizens went about in Teyma with a lofty gait of the Nejd metropolis. A half-stranger or two sold Syrian clothing wares, and they were Damascenes by the father's side. Such was one Mahmûd, come a child to Teyma with his Medânite father, in the year of the massacre of the Nasâra. In this young man was now the aspect of the Nejders. The second was son of an old kella keeper. No shops are seen in the sûks, the land-owners are sellers of their corn and dates at their own houses.

Sultry seemed this stagnant air to us, come in from the high desert, we could not sleep in their clay houses. My thirst was inextinguishable ; and finding here the first clean water, after weeks of drought, I went on drinking till some said, " Khalîl is come to Teyma only to drink water ; will he drink up the Haddàj ? " When Zeyd returned not yet, I went out to visit some great ancient ruin, *Kasr Zellûm*, named after a former possessor of the ground. A sturdy young half-blooded negro guided me, but whose ferocious looks by the way, brain-sick and often villanous behaviour, made me pensive : he was strong as a camel, and had brought a sword with him, I was infirm and came (for the heat) unarmed. We passed the outer walls, and when I found the place lay further in the desert, and by the eyes and unsettling looks of this ribald I might divine that his thought was in that solitary way to kill me, I made some delay ; I saw a poor man in a field, and said, I would go over to him, and drink a little water. It was a nomad, building up an orchard clay wall for the villager's hire, paid in pottles of dates. In this, there came to us from the town, a young man of a principal sheykhly family, *er-Romàn*, and another with him. They had been sent after me in haste by Zeyd, as he had news in what company I was gone :—and in a later dissension Zeyd said, " I saved thy life, Khalîl ! rememberest thou not that day at Teyma, when the black fellow went out to murder thee ? " I knew these young smilers, so not much trusting them, we walked on together. I must run this risk to-day, I might no more perhaps come to Teyma ; but all that I found for a weapon, a pen-knife, I held ready open under my mantle, that I might not perish like a slaughter-beast, if these should treacherously set upon me.

Kasr Zellûm I found to be a great four-square fort-like building ; it may be fifty or sixty paces upon a side. The walls are five feet thick, in height fifteen feet, laid of dry masonry.

A part within is divided into chambers, the rest is yard, in the midst they think a great wall lies buried. The site of the kasr is a little below those great town walls of ancient Teyma, which are seen as sand-banks, riding upon the plain ; the head of the masonry only appearing. In the midst of the kasr wall, I found another inscription stone, laid sideways, in that strange Teyma character ; and above the writing, are portrayed human eyes.—We read that the augurs of the antique Arabs scored two lines as eyes, the wise men naming them their " children of vision."   At the rendering of Teyma to Abeyd Ibn Rashîd, he left this injunction with the Teyâmena, " Ye are not to build upon the walls of that kasr ! "

All this oasis—shallow *jauf* or flood - bottom in the high desert, and without outlet—has been in other time of the world (it is likely) a winter meer : seven torrent channels (not all sensible to our eyes) flow therein. I write the names only for example of their diligent observation : *el-Hosenîeh, Khóweylid, Heddajor, Seyfîeh, el-Toleyhat, er-Rotham* and *Zellûm.* Striped bluish clays and yellow-brown loam may be seen in their marl pits. In the grounds below the last cultivated soil, are salt beds, the famous *memlahát Teyma.* Thither resort the poorer Beduins, to dig it freely : and this is much, they say, " sweeter " to their taste than the sea-salt from Wejh. Teyma rock-salt is the daily sauce of the thousand nomad kettles in all these parts of Arabia. Poor Fukara carry it to el-Ally, and receive there four reals for their camel-load. The most lower grounds in these deserts are saltish, of the washing down from the land above ; after the winter stand-ing-water may be found a salty crust,—such I have seen finger-thick, taken from near the mountain *Misma,* for the provision of Hâyil. At *Gerish,* a *jau* or low-ground watering and mountain, half a day's riding in the north from Teyma, is digged a kind of black rock-alum, *shubb ej-Jemâl* and used as medicine for their

sick camels. From Teyma, the nomads reckon six nights out to
Jauf; the way is seldom trodden; the Nefûd lying between is here
but a journey over. The stages are, *Ubbeyt,* a principal summer
station of the Sherarát (and there is some ruined site), the water
rises where they dig with their hands; then *Thulla Helwàn,*
(other than the Helwàn mountain, which is one day eastward
from Teyma); *Areyj,* in the Nefûd, *Towîl, 'Sfàn* or *el-Jeyn,* ed-
Dâha. Rarely any ride from hence to Maan, the nomad journeys
are—1. *Thulla Thafýa,* 2. *Dubbel,* 3. *el-Agel,* 4. *el-Agab* (of
Akaba): they hold *J. Tobey(k)ch,* at the distance of half a day or
more upon the right hand, a mountain, they say, standing east
and west, and greater than *Irnàn.* The snow lies long upon
J. Tobeych in winter; it is two nights out from Maan.

At evening we were gathered a great coffee company at our
host's fire, and some beginning their talk of the Christian religion, were offended that " the Nasâra worship idols, and this not
only, but that they blaspheme the apostle." Also they said, " It
is a people that know no kind of lawful wedlock, but as beasts,
they follow their natural affection; the lights quenched in
their religious assemblies, there is a cursed meddling among
them in strange and horrible manner, the son it may be lying
in savage blindness with his own mother, in manner, wellah, as
the hounds :—in such wise be gotten the cursed generation of
Nasrânies, that very God confound them! (the speaker dared to
add) and this Nasrâny I durst say cannot know his own father.
Besides, they have other heathenish customs among them, as when
a Christian woman dies to bury her living husband along with
her." Almost the like contumelies are forged by the malicious
Christian sects, of the Druses their neighbours in the mountain
villages of Syria. " Friends, I answered, these are fables of a
land far off, and old wives' malice of things unknown; but listen
and I will tell you the sooth in all." A Fejîry Beduin here
exclaimed, " Life of this fire! Khalîl lies not; wellah even though
he be a Nasrâny, he speaks the truth in all among the Aarab;
there could be no Musslim be more true spoken. Hear him!—and
say on, Khalîl."—" This is the law of marriage given by God in
the holy religion of the *Messîah,* 'the son of Miriam from the
Spirit of Ullah,'—it is thus spoken of him in your own Scriptures."—" *Sully Ullah aley-hu* (they all answered), whom the
Lord bless, the Lord's grace be with him," breathing the accustomed benediction as the name is uttered in their hearing of a
greater prophet.—" As God gave to Adam *Hawwa,* one woman,
so is the Christian man espoused to one wife. It is a bond of
religion until the dying of either of them; it is a faithful fellowship in sickness, in health, in the felicity and in the calamity of

the world, and whether she bear children or is barren : and that
may never be broken, saving because of adultery."—" But, said
they, the woman is sooner old than her husband ; if one may not
go from his wife past age to wed another, your law is not just."
One said, laughing, " Khalîl, we have a better religion, thy rule
were too strait for us ; I myself have wedded one with another
wives fifteen. What say you, companions ? in the hareem are·
many crooked conditions ? I took some, I put away some, ay
billah ! until I found some with whom I might live."

Certain of them now said, " But true is that proverb, ' There
are none so little Moslems as the Moslemîn ' and God for their
sins cannot bless them ; be not the very kafirs better than we ?
Yet tell us this, Khalîl,—is not in every place of your worship a malediction pronounced daily, upon God's messenger
Mohammed ? "—" Some of you (I said) are not good ; I am
weary of your malicious fables. Mohammed we do not blaspheme, whom ye call your prophet : but a prayer is offered
for you daily in all our Churches that God may have mercy
upon you. Tell me when did Mohammed live ? Six ages
after the Missîeh : it was time then to teach your gross idolatrous fathers ;—are you better than your fathers ? "—" God wot
we are better : our fathers were in *the Ignorance.*"—" But we
no ; you are newly come up, we are as your elder brethren :—as
for me I take every religion to be good, by which men are made
better. I can respect then your religion." Said he of the many
marriages, " Ha ! the Nasrânies are good folk, and if they say
a word they will keep it, and are faithful men in every trust,.
so are not we ; somewhat I learned too of their religion from
Abu Fâris—who remembers not Abu Fâris ? We heard from
him that, before all, they have certain godly precepts, as
these : kill not, steal not, covet not, do no adultery, lie
not, which you see how religiously they keep ! " They enquired then of the Towrat (the roll of Moses' books), and
the *Engîl* (Evangel), which they allow to be of old time
kelam Ullah, 'God's word;' but since falsified by the notorious
ill-faith of Yahûd and Nasâra, only in envy and contempt of
el-Islam ; and now annulled by the perfect koran sent down from
heaven, by the hand of Mohammed, " The *Seal of the prophets* and
the Beloved of Ullah." The Mohammedan world is generally
therefore merely ignorant of our Scriptures. This is cause why
their ghostly doctors blunder to death in the ancient histories
and their hagiology : the koran itself is full of a hundred mad
mistold tales and anachronisms. Yet because the former Books
of God's word were revealed to the Jews and Christians, we are
named by their writers " People of the Scriptures," and in the

common discourse " Teachers," as from whom is derived to them
the elder body of religious tradition and all human learning.
(This title, *Muâllem*, I have not heard spoken in the wholly
Mohammedan Arabia.) They lay to our charge that we " *make
God partners*," dividing the only Godhead and sinfully worship-
ping idols. The root of religion is affection, the whole stands
by opinion ; the Mohammedan theology is ineptitude so evident
that it were only true in the moon : to reason with them were
breath lost, will is their reason. Good Moslems have often
commiserated my religious blindness, saying, " Alas ! that a veil
was before my eyes, but God so willed it."

They listened at my saying, " Teyma is mentioned in the
Towrat." They asked under what name ?—" *Tema* "; also
Tema is one of the sons of Ishmael, called by the name of his
village. Teyma is intended in Isaiah, from whence the caravaners of Dedan, scattered before the bow and the sword of
the Beduw, are relieved with bread and water. My hearers
answered, " But the old name was *Tôma*."

Nejd Beduins are more fanatic, in the magnanimous ignorance of their wild heads, but with all this less dangerous than
the village inhabitants, soberly instructed and settled in their
koran reading. There was a scowling fellow at my elbow who
had murmured all the evening ; now as I rested he said, ' I
was like a fiend in the land, akhs ! a Yahûdy ! ' As I turned
from him, neighbours bade me not to mind this despiteful
tongue, saying " Khalîl, it is only a Beduwy." The poor man,
who was of Bishr, abashed to be named Beduwy among them in
the town, cast down his eyes and kept silence. One whispered
to Zeyd, " If anything happen to him have you not to answer to
the Dowla ? he might die among you of some disease." But
Zeyd answered with a magnanimity in his great tones, " *Hénna
mà na sadikîn billah*, Are we not confiding in God ! "—The
company rose little before midnight, and left us to lie down
in our mantles, on the coffee-house floor. Sleymàn said a last
petulant word, ' How could I, a civil man, wander with the wild
Beduw that were melaun el-weyladeyn, of cursed kind ? '

It was not long before we heard one feeling by the walls.
Zeyd cried, " Who is there ? " and sat up leaning on his elbow in
the feeble moonlight. " Rise, Zeyd, (said an old wife's voice,)
I come from Hirfa, the Aarab are about removing." Zeyd
answered, wearily stretching himself, " A punishment fall upon
them : "—we must needs then march all this night. As we stood
up we were ready ; there is no superstitious leave-taking among
them ; and we stepped through our host Sleymàn's dark gate

into the street, never to meet with him again, and came at the
end of the walled ways to the Beduins, who were already loading in the dark.   Zeyd, reproving their changeable humour,
asked a reason of this untimely wandering; "We would not,
they answered, be longer guests, to eat the bread of the
Teyâmena." They being all poor folk, had seen perhaps but cold
hospitality.

We held south, and rode soon by some ruins, "of ancient
Teyma, (they told me) and old wells there." They alighted near
dawn ; discharging the beasts, we made fires, and lay down to
slumber awhile.   Remounting from thence, after few miles, we
passed some appearance of ruins, *Burjesba*, having upon the south
a mountain, *J. Jerbûa.* At the mid-afternoon we met with our
tribesmen marching ; they had removed twice in our absence :
the Aarab halted to encamp few miles further. As said, this year
was big with troubles, the Fukara were now fugitives.   The
Beny Wáhab, as borderers, having least profit of Ibn Rashîd's
government, are not cheerful payers of his *zikâ*.   The Fejîr had
withheld the light tax, five years, until the Emir, returning last
summer with his booty of the W. Aly, visited them in the
wilderness, and exacted his arrears, only leaving them their own,
because they had submitted themselves. The Fukara were not
yet in open enmity with the Wélad Aly, as the Prince had
prescribed to them, only they were "not well" together ; but
our Fejîr were daily more in mistrust of the terrible Emir.
Every hour they thought they saw his riders upon them, and
the menzil taken.   They would go therefore from their own
wandering ground, and pass from his sight into the next Bishr
dîra.

CHAPTER XI.

IN this menzìl, because the people must march from the morrow, the booths were struck and their baggage had been made up before they slept. The Beduin families lay abroad under the stars, beside their household stuff and the unshapely full sweating water-skins. The night was cold, at an altitude of 3600 feet. I saw the nomads stretched upon the sand, wrapped in their mantles : a few have sleeping carpets, *ekîm*, under them, made of black worsted stuff like their tent-cloth, but of the finer yarn and better weaving, adorned with a border of chequerwork of white and coloured wool and fringes gaily dyed. The ekîms of Teyma have a name in this country.

It was chill under the stars at this season, marching before the sun in the open wilderness. The children of the poor have not a mantle, only a cotton smock covers their tender bodies; some babes are even seen naked. I found 48° F., and when the sun was fairly up 86°. It was a forced march ; the flocks and the herds, *et-tursh*, were driven forth beside us. At a need the Beduw spare not the cattle which are all their wealth, but think they do well to save themselves and their substance, even were it with the marring of some of them ; their camel kine great with young were now daily calving, The new-yeaned lambs and kids, the tottering camel-calf of less than five days old, little whelps, which they would rear, of the hounds of the encampment, are laid by the housewives, with their own children, upon the burden camels. Each mother is seen riding upon a camel in the midst of the roll of her tent-cloth or carpet, in the folds lie nested also the young animals ; she holds her little children before her. Small children, the aged, the sick, and even bed-rid folk, carried long hours, show no great signs of weariness in camel-riding. Their suffering persons ride seated in a nest of tent-cloth ; others, who have been herdsmen, kneel or lie along, not fearing to fall, and seem to repose thus upon the rolling camel's bare back. It is a custom of the desert to travel fasting : however long be the ráhla, the Aarab eat only when they have alighted at the menzil ; yet mothers will give their children to drink, or a morsel in their mouths, by the long way.

Journeying in this tedious heat, we saw first, in the afternoon horizon, the high solitary sandstone mountain J. Birrd. " Yonder thulla," cried my neighbours in their laughing argot, " is the *sheykh* of our dîra." Birrd has a height of nearly 5000 feet. At the right hand there stretches a line of acacia trees in the wilderness plain, the token of a dry seyl bed, *Gô*, which descends, they said, from a day westward of Kheybar, and ends here in the desert. In all this high country, between Teyma and Tebûk and Medáin Sâlih, there are no wadies. The little latter rain that may fall in the year is but sprinkled in the sand. Still journeying, this March sun which had seen our ráhla, rising, set behind us in a stupendous pavilion of Oriental glories, which is not seldom in these Arabian waste marches, where the atmosphere is never quite unclouded. We saw again the cold starlight before the fainting households alighted under Birrd till the morrow, when they would remove anew; the weary hareem making only a shelter from the night wind of the tent-cloths spread upon two stakes. It was in vain to seek milk of the over-driven cattle with dry udders. This day the nomad village was removed at once more than forty miles. In common times these wandering graziers take their menzils and dismiss the cattle to pasture, before high noon.—Hastily, as we saw the new day, we removed, and pitched few miles beyond in the Bishr dîra; from hence they reckoned three journeys to Hâyil, the like from Dàr el-Hamra, a day and a-half to Teyma.

A poor woman came weeping to my tent, entreating me to see and divine in my books what were become of her child. The little bare-foot boy was with the sheep, and had been missing after yesterday's long ráhla. The mother was hardly to be persuaded, in her grief, that my books were not cabalistical. I could not persuade the dreary indifference of the Arabs in her menzil to send back some of them, besides the child's father, to seek him : of their own motion they know not any such charity. If the camel of some poor widow woman be strayed, there is no man will ride upon the traces for human kindness, unless she can pay a real. The little herd-boy was found in the end of the encampment, where first he had lighted upon a kinsmen's tent.

We removed from thence a little within the high white borders of the Nefûd, marching through a sand

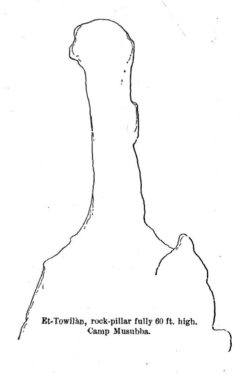

Et-Towilàn, rock-pillar fully 60 ft. high.
Camp Musubba.

country full of last year's plants of the " rose of Jericho." These
Beduw call them *ch(k)ef Marhab*. *Kef* is the hollow palm, with
the fingers clenching upon it. Marhab is in their tradition
sheykh of old Jewish Kheybar. We found also the young herb,
two velvet green leaves, which has the wholesome smack of
cresses, and is good for the nomad cattle. The Aarab alighted
afterward in the camping ground *Ghrormùl el-Mosubba;* known
from far by the landmark of a singular tower-like needle of sandstone, sixty feet high, the *Towîlan.* (See p. 303.) The third day
we removed from thence, with mist and chill wind blowing, to
J. Chebàd: from Chebàd we went to the rugged district *el-
Jebàl.* After another journey, we came to pitch before the
great sandstone mountain chine of Irnàn, in Nejd. Beyond
this we advanced south-eastward to the rugged coast of *Ybba
Moghrair;* the Beduins removing every second or third day,
journeyed seven or eight miles and alighted. I saw about
el-Jebàl other circles of rude flag-stones, set edgewise, as
those of Jerèyda. In another place certain
two cornered wall-enclosures, of few loose
courses ; they were made upon low rising
grounds, and I thought might have been a sort
of breastworks ; the nomads could give me no
account of them, as of things before their time
and tradition. East of Ybba Moghrair, we passed
the foot of a little antique rude turret in the
desert soil. I showed it to some riding next me in the ráhla.
"Works (they answered) remaining from the creation of the
world ; what profit is there to enquire of them ? " " But all
such to be nothing (said Zeyd) in comparison with that he
would show me on the morrow, which was a marvel : the
effigy of *Abu Zeyd,* a fabulous heroic personage, and dame
Alîa his wife, portrayed upon some cliff of yonder mountain
Ybba Moghrair."

Wandering in all the waste Arabia, we often see rude trivet
stones set by threes together : such are of old nomad pot-fires ;
and it is a comfortable human token, that some have found to
cheer themselves, before us, in land where man's life seems
nearly cast away, but at what time is uncertain ; for stones, as
they were pitched in that forsaken drought, may so continue
for ages. The harder and gravel wilderness is seen cross-lined
everywhere with old trodden camel paths ; these are also from
the old generations, and there is not any place of the immense
waste, which is not at some time visited in the Aarab's wanderings ; and yet whilst we pass no other life, it may be, is in
the compass of a hundred miles about us. There is almost

no parcel of soil where fuel may not be found, of old camel dung, *jella,* bleaching in the sun ; it may lie three years, and a little sand blown upon it, sometime longer. There is another human sign in the wilderness, which mothers look upon ; we see almost in every new ráhla, little ovals of stones, which mark the untimely died of the nomads : but grown persons dying in their own dîras, are borne (if it be not too difficult) to the next common burying place.

On the morrow betimes, Zeyd took his mare and his lance, and we set out to visit Abu Zeyd's image, the wonder of this desert. We crossed the sand plain, till the noon was hot over us ; and come to the mountain, we rounded it some while in vain : Zeyd could not find the place. White stains, like sea-marks, are seen upon certain of those desolate cliffs, they are roosting-places of birds of prey, falcons, buzzards and owls : their great nests of sticks are often seen in wild crags of these sandstone marches. In the waterless soil live many small animals which drink not, as rats and lizards and hares. We heard scritching owls some-times in the still night ; then the nomad wives and children answered them with mocking again *Ymgebâs! Ymgebâs!* The hareem said, " It is a wailful woman, seeking her lost child through the wilderness, which was turned into this forlorn bird." Fehjies eat the owl; for which they are laughed to scorn by the Beduw, that are devourers of some other vermin.

We went upon those mountain sides until we were weary. A sheykh's son, a coffee companion from his youth, and here in another dîra, Zeyd could not remember his landmarks. It was high noon; we wandered at random, and, for hunger and thirst, plucking wild dandelions sprung since some showers in those rocks, we began to break our fast. At length, looking down at a deep place, we espied camels, which went pasturing under the mountain: there we found Fehját herdsmen. The images, they said, were not far before us, they would put us in the way, but first they bade us sit down to refresh ourselves. The poor men then ran for us under the nâgas' udders, and drew their milk-skin full of that warm sustenance.—Heaven remember for good the poor charitable nomads ! When we had drunk they came along with us, driving the cattle : a little strait opened further, it was a long inlet in the mountain bosom, teeming green with incomparable freshness, to our sense, of rank herbage. At the head of this garden of weeds is an oozy slumbering pool ; and thereabove I perceived the rocks to be full of scored inscrip-tions, and Abu Zeyd's yard-high image, having in his hand the crooked camel stick, bakhorra, or, as the Aarab say, who cannot

D. T.   20

judge of portraiture, a sword : beside him, is a lesser, perhaps a female figure, which they call " Alîa his wife." It is
likely that these old lively shapes were battered, with a stone,
upon the sandstone ; they are not as the squalid scrawling
portraiture of the Beduw, but limned roundly to the natural
with the antique diligence. Here are mostly short Himyaric
legends, written (as is common in these deserts) from above
downwards ; the names doubtless, the saws, the salaams, of many
passengers and cameleers of antique generations. *Ybba*, is
said for *Abu*, father, in these parts of Arabia, and at Medina ;
Moghrair, is perhaps cave. I bade Zeyd let me have a milch
nâga and abandon me here with Abu Zeyd. Zeyd answered
(with a fable), he had already paid a camel to Bishr, for license
to show me their Abu Zeyd. The Fehját answered simply, " A
man might not dwell here alone, in the night time, the demons
would affray him."

As we came again, Zeyd lighted upon a natural sanded basin
among the rocks, under the mountain, and there sounding with
his hands to the elbow, he reached to a little stinking moisture.
Zeyd smiled vaingloriously, and cried, ' Ha ! we had discovered a
new water. Wellah, here is water a little under the mire, the hind
shall come hither to-morrow and fill our girbies.' Thereby grew
a nightshade weed, now in the berry ; the Beduin man had not
seen the like before, and bade me bear it home to the menzil,
to be conned by the hareem :—none of whom, for all their wise
looking, knew it. " A stranger plant (said they) in this dîra : "
it is housewifely amongst them to be esteemed cunning in
drugs and simples. Lower, we came to a small pool in the rock ;
the water showed ruddy-brown and ammoniacal, the going down
was stained with old filth of camels. " Ay (he said) of this
water would we draw for our coffee, were there none other."
Upon the stone I saw other Himyaric legends. And here sat
two young shepherd lasses ; they seeing men approach, had left
playing, their little flock wandered near them. Zeyd, a great
sheykh, hailed them with the hilarity of the desert, and the
ragged maidens answered him in mirth again : they fear none of
their tribesmen, and herding maidens may go alone with the
flocks far out of seeing of the menzil in the empty wilderness.
We looked up and down, but could not espy Zeyd's mare,
which, entering the mountain, he had left bound below, the
headstall tied back, by the halter, to an hind limb in the nomad
manner. Thus, making a leg at every pace, the Beduin mare
may graze at large ; but cannot wander far. At length, from
a high place, we had sight of her, returning upon her traces to
the distant camp. " She is thirsty (said Zeyd), let her alone and

she will find the way home : "—although the black booths were
yet under our horizon. So the nomad horses come again of themselves, and seek their own households, when they would drink
water. Daily, when the sun is well risen, the Beduin mare is
hop-shackled with iron links, which are opened with a key, and
loosed out to feed from her master's tent. The horses wander,
seeking each other, if the menzils be not wide scattered, and
go on pasturing and sporting together : their sheykhly masters
take no more heed of them than of the hounds of the encampment, until high noon, when the mares, returning homeward of
themselves, are led in to water. They will go then anew to
pasture, or stand shadowing out that hot hour in the master's
booth (if it be a great one). They are grazing not far off till
the sun is setting, when they draw to their menzils, or are
fetched home and tethered for the night.

There hopped before our feet, as we came, a minute brood of
second locusts, of a leaden colour, with budding wings like the
spring leaves, and born of those gay swarms which, a few weeks
before, had passed over and despoiled the desert. After forty
days these also would fly as a pestilence, yet more hungry than
the former, and fill the atmosphere. We saw a dark sky over
the black nomad tents, and I showed Zeyd a shower falling
before the westing sun.—" Would God, he answered, it might
reach us ! " Their cattle's life in this languishing soil is of a
very little rain. The Arabian sky, seldom clear, weeps as the
weeping of hypocrites.

We removed from hence, and pitched the black booths upon
that bleakness of white sand which is, here, the Nefûd, whose
edge shows all along upon the brown sandstone desert : a seyì
bed, *Terrai*, sharply divides them. The Aarab would next
remove to a good well, *el-Hŷza*, in the Nefûd country, where in
good years they find the spring of new pasture : but there being
little to see upon this border, we returned another day towards
the *Helwàn* mountain ; in which march I saw other (eight or
nine yards large) circles of sandstone flags. Dreary was this
Arabian ráhla ; from the March skies there soon fell a tempest of
cold rain, and, alighting quickly, the Beduin women had hardly
breath in the whirling shower to build their booths :—a héjra
may be put up in three minutes. In the tents, we sat out the
stormy hours upon the moist sand in our stiffened wet mantles ;
and the windy drops fell through the ragged tilt upon us. In
the Nefûd, towards el-Hŷza, are certain booming sand hills,
Rowsa, Deffafîat, Subbîa and *Irzûm*, such as the sand drift of
J. Nagûs, by the sea village of *Tor*, in Sinai : the upper sand
sliding down under the foot of the passenger, there arises, of

20—2

the infinite fretting grains, such a giddy loud swelling sound, as when your wetted finger is drawn about the lip of a glass of water, and like that swooning din after the chime of a great bell, or a cup of metal.—*Nagûs* is the name of the sounding-board in the belfry of the Greek monastry, whereupon as the sacristan plays with his hammer, the timber yields a pleasant musical note, which calls forth the formal *colieros* to their prayers : another such singing sand drift, *el-Howayrîa,* is in the cliffs (east of the Mezham,) of Medáin Sâlih.

The afternoon was clear ; the sun dried our wet clothing, and a great coffee party assembled, at Zeyd's tent. He had promised Khalîl would make *chai* (tea), "which is the coffee-drink, he told them, of the Nasâra.—And, good Khalîl, since the sheykhs would taste thy chai, look thou put in much sugar." I had to-day pure water of the rain in the desert, and that tea was excellent. Zeyd cried to them, "And how likes you the kahwat of the Nasâra ? " They answered, "The sugar is good, but as for this which Khalîl calls *chai*, the smack of it is little better than warm water." They would say " Thin drink, and not gross tasting" as is their foul-water coffee. Rahŷel drank his first cup out, and returned it mouth downward (a token with them that he would no more of it), saying, " Khalîl, is not this *el-khamr ?* the *fermented* or wine of the Nasâra : " and for conscience sake he would not drink ; but the company sipped their sugar, drink to the dregs, and bade the stranger pour out more. I called to Rahŷel's remembrance the Persians drinking chai in the Haj caravan. Beduins who tasted tea the second time, seeing how highly I esteemed it, and feeling themselves refreshed, afterward desired it extremely, imagining this drink with sugar to be the comfort of all human infirmities. But I could never have, for my asking, a cup of their fresh milk ; they put none in their coffee, and to put whole milk to this *kahwat en-Nasâra* seemed to them a very outlandish and waste using of God's benefit. When I made tea at home, I called in Hirfa to drink the first cup, saying to the Beduins that this was our country manner, where the weaker sex was honourably regarded. Hirfa answered, " Ah! that we might be there among you ! Khalîl, these Beduw here are good for nothing, billah, they are wild beasts ; to-day they beat and to-morrow they abandon the hareem : the woman is born to labour and suffering, and in the sorrow of her heart, it nothing avails that she can speak." The men sitting at the hearths laughed when Hirfa preached. She cried peevishly again, "Yes, laugh loud ye wild beasts !— Khalîl, the Beduws are heathens ! " and the not happy young wife smiled closely to the company, and sadly to herself again.

Evening clouds gathered ; the sheykhs going homewards had wet mantles. The mare returned of herself through the falling weather, and came and stood at our coffee fire, in half human wise, to dry her soaked skin and warm herself, as one among us. It may be said of the weak nomad horses, that they have no gall. I have seen a mare, stabling herself in the mid-day shadow of the master's booth, that approached the sitters about the coffee hearth and putting down her soft nose the next turned their heads to kiss her, till the sheykh rose to scold his mare away. They are feeble, of the slender and harsh desert forage ; and gentle to that hand of man, which is as the mother's teat to them in the wilderness. Wild and dizzy camels are daily seen, but seldom impetuous horses, and perverse never : the most are of the bay colour. The sheykh's hope is in his mare to bear him with advantage upon his enemy, or to save him hastily from the field ; it is upon her back he may best take a spoil and outride all who are mounted upon thelûls. Nor she (nor any life, of man or beast, besides the hounds) is ever mishandled amongst them. The mare is not cherished by the master's household, yet her natural dwelling is at the mild nomad tent. She is allied to the beneficent companionship of man ; his shape is pleasant to her in the inhospitable khála. The mildness of the Arab's home is that published by their prophet of the divine household ; mild-hearted is the koran Ullah, a sovereign Semitic housefather, how indulgent to his people ! The same is an adversary, cruel and hard, to an alien people.

The nomad horse we see here shod as in Syria with a plate open in the midst, which is the Turkish manner ; these sheukh purchase their yearly provision of horse-shoes in the Haj market. I have seen the nomads' horses shod even in the sand country of Arabia : yet upon the Syrian borders a few are left without shoes, and some are seen only hind-shod. The sâny who followed our tribe—he was accounted the best smith, in all work of iron, of that country side, not excepted Teyma—was their farrier. One day I went with Zeyd to see his work. We found the man-of-metal firing Rahyel's mare, which had a drawn hind leg, and as they are ready-handed with a few tools he did it with his ramrod of iron ; the end being made red-hot in the fire, he sealed and seared the infirm muscles. I saw the suffering creature without voice, standing upon three legs, for the fourth was heaved by a cord in stiff hands. The Beduw, using to fire their camels' bodies up and down, make not much more account of the mare's skin, how whole it be or branded. They look only that she be of the blood, a good breeder, and able to serve her master in warfare. Rahŷel quitted the sâny's hire ; Zeyd, who waited for the ends of the smith's labour, had brought his hands full of old horse-shoes, and bade him beat them into nails, against his mare should be shod. Zeyd went to pull dry sticks, kindled a bonfire, and when it had burned awhile he quenched all with sand ; and taking up the weak charcoal in his mantle, he went to lay it upon the forge fire (a hearth-pit in the sand). Then this great sheykh sat down himself to the pair of goat-skin bellows, and blew the sâny a blast. It was a mirth to see how Zeyd, to save his penny, could play the Solubby, and such he seemed sweating between two fires of the hot coals and the scalding sun at high noon, till the hunger-bitten chaps were begrimed of his black and, in fatigue, hard-favoured visage. Finally, rising with a sigh, " Khalîl, he said, art thou not weary sitting abroad in the sun ? yonder is Rahŷel's booth, let us enter in the shadow ; he is a good man, and will make us coffee." Thus even the Beduins are impatient of the Arabian sun's beating upon their pates, unless in the râhla, that is, when the air about them is moving.—" Peace be with thee, Rahŷel, I bring Khalîl ; sit thee down by me, Khalîl, and let us see thee write Rahŷel's name ; write ' Rahŷel el-Fejîry, the sheykh, he that wedded the bint at Teyma : ' " they kneeled about me with the pleased conceit of unlettered mortals, to see their fugitive words detained and laid up in writing.

There arrived at our camp some Beduin traders, come over the Nefûd from Jauf : they were of Bishr. And there are such in the tribes, prudent poor men, that would add to their liveli-hood by the peaceable and lawful gain of merchandise, rather than by riding upon ungodly and uncertain ghrazzus. The men brought down samn and tobacco, which they offered at two-thirds of the price which was now paid in these sterile regions. Yet the Aarab, iniquitous in all bargains, would hardly purchase of them at so honest and easy a rate ; they would higgle-haggle for a little lower, and finally bought not at all ; —sooner than those strangers should win, they would pay double the money later at el-Ally ! and they can wait wretchedly thus, as the dead, whilst a time passes over them. A little more of government, and men such as these traders would leave the insecure wandering life, (which all the Aarab, for the in-cessant weariness and their very emptiness of heart, have partly in aversion,) to become settlers. Beduins complain in their long hours of the wretchedness of their lives ; and they seem then wonderfully pensive, as men disinherited of the world. Human necessitous malice has added this to the affliction of

nature, that there should be no sure passage in Arabia : and
when there is dearth in any dîra, because no autumn rain has
fallen there, or their hope was devoured by the locust, the land-
traffic may hardly reach them.

The destitute Beduw, in their idle tents, are full of musing
melancholy ; if any blame them they answer in this pensive
humour : " Aha, truly the Aarab are *bahâim*, brute beasts ;
mesakîn, mesquins ; *kutaat ghranem*, *dubbush*, a drove of silly
sheep, a mixed herd of small cattle ; *juhâl*, ignorant wretches ;
mejanîn, lunatic folk ; *affinîn*, corrupt to rottenness ; *haramîyeh*,
law-breakers, thieves ; *kuffâr*, heathen men ; *mithil es-seyd*,
like as the fallow beasts, scatterlings in the wilderness, and not
having human understanding." And when they have said all,
they will add, for despite, of themselves, *wellah, el-Aarab kilâb*,
" and the nomads are hounds, God knoweth." But some will
make a beggarly vaunt of themselves, " the Aarab are jinnies
and sheyatîn," that is witty fiends to do a thing hardily and
endure the worst, without fear of God. Between this sorry
idleness in the menzils and their wandering fatigue they all
dote, men and women, upon *tittun*, tobacco. The dry leaf
(which they draw from el-Ally and Teyma) is green, whether,
as they say, because this country is dewless, or the Arabian
villagers have not learned to prepare it. They smoke the
green dried leaf, rubbed between the palms from the hard
stalks, with a coal burning upon it. I have seen this kind
as far as the borders of Syria, where the best is from Shobek
and J. Kerak, it is bitter tasting ; the sweetest in this country
is that raised by Beduin husbandmen of the Moahîb, in *Wady
Aurush*, upon the sea side of the *Aueyrid* Harra, over against
el-Héjr.

Our wandering village maintained a tobacco seller, an
Ally villager, who lived amongst them in nomad wise in the
desert, and was wedded with a tribeswoman of theirs. The
man had gathered a little stock, and was thriving in this base
and extortionate traffic. It irked the lean Beduin souls to
see the parasite grow fat of that which he licked vilely from their
beards. Seeing him merry they felt themselves sad, and for a
thing too which lay upon their consciences. The fault bewitched
them ; also they could not forbid a neighbour the face of the
free desert. Thus the bread of the poor, who before had not
half enough, was turned to ashes. He let them have here for
twelve pence only so much as was two penny-worth at el-
Ally ; the poor soul who brought him a kid in payment, to-day,
that would be valued before the year was out at two crowns,
comforted himself with his pipe seven days for this loss of a head

of cattle, having a half groat to " drink " of the villager's tobacco,
or rather the half of two pence, for, wetting the leaves, that
malicious Alowwy had devised to make the half part fill his
pint measure. After the men, I saw poor tobacco-sick hareem
come clamouring to his tent, and holding in their weak hands
bottoms of their spun wool and pints of samn which they have
spared perhaps to buy some poor clothing, but now they cannot
forbear to spend and ' drink ' smoke : or else having naught,
they borrow of him, with thanksgiving, at an excessive usury.
And if the extortioner will not trust one she pitifully entreats
him, that only this once, he would fill her cold galliûn, and
say not nay, for old kindness sake. Zeyd though so principal
a sheykh would buy no tobacco himself, but begged all day,
were it even of the poorest person in a coffee company : then
looking lovely he would cry, min y'ámir-ly, " Who (is he the
friend) will replenish (this sebîl) for my sake ? " For faintness of
mind in this deadly soil they are all parasites and live basely one
upon another : Beduins will abjectly beg tobacco even of their
poor tribeswomen. Zeyd came one day into the mejlis complaining of the price of tittun, and though it cost him little or
naught ; and sitting down he detested, with an embittered
roughness in his superhuman comely voice, all the father's kin of
Alowna. " Ullah ! (he cried) curse this Sleymàn the tittun-seller !
I think verily he will leave this people erelong not even their
camels ! " Tobacco is this world's bliss of many in the idle desert,
against whom the verses of a Beduin maker are currently recited
in all their tribes : " For three things a man should not ' drink '
smoke : is not he a sot that will burn his own fingers (in taking
up a coal from the hearth to lay it in his pipe-head), and he that
willingly wasteth his substance (spending for that which is not
bread), and withal he doth it ungodly.

The Fejîr wandered in the strange Bishr marches not without apprehension and some alarms,—then the sheykhs pricked
forth upon their mares, and the most morrows, they rode out
two hours to convoy the pastúring great cattle of the tribe,
el-'bil. The first locusts had devoured the rabiâ before us ;
there was now scarcity, and our Beduins must divide themselves into two camps. Motlog removed with his part, in
which were the most sheykhs, making half a journey from us
to the westward. Zeyd remained with his fellow Rahŷel, who
had the sheykh's charge in this other part. We marched and
encamped divided, for many days, in before determined and
equal manner.

I saw often the samhh plant growing, but not abundantly ;

now a leafless green wort, a hand high, with fleshy stems and branches full of brine, like samphire. At each finger end is an eye, where, the plant drying up in the early summer, a grain is ripened. In the Sherarát country, where the samhh grows more plentifully, their housewives and children gather in this wild harvest. The dry stalks are steeped in water, they beat out the seed with rods ; and of this small grain their hareem grind flour for the daily mess. I had eaten of this wild-bread at Maan ; it was black and bitter, but afterward I thought it sweet-meat, in the further desert of Arabia. The samhh porridge is good, and the taste " as camel milk : " but the best is of the flour, kneaded with dates and a little samn, to be eaten raw :—a very pleasant and wholesome diet for travellers, who in many open passages durst not kindle fire.

Now I was free of the Beduins' camp, and welcomed at all coffee hearths ; only a few minds were hostile still, of more fanatical tribesmen. Often, where I passed, a householder called me in from his booth, and when I sat down, with smiles of a gentle host, he brought forth dates and léban : this is ' the bread and salt,' which a good man will offer once, and confirm fellowship with the stranger. The Aarab, although they pardoned my person, yet thought me to blame for my religion. There happened another day a thing which, since they put all to the hand of Ullah, might seem to them some token of a Providence which cared for me. Weary, alighting from the ráhla in blustering weather, I cast my mantle upon the next bush, and sat down upon it. In the same place I raised my tent and remained sheltered till evening, when the cripple child of our menzil came to me upon all fours for his dole of a handful of dates, but at my little tent door he shrieked and recoiled hastily. He had seen shining folds of a venomous serpent, under the bush,—so they will lie close in windy weather. At his cry Zeyd's shepherd caught a stake from the next beyt, and running to, with a sturdy stroke he beat in pieces the poisonous vermin. The viper was horned, more than two feet long, the body swollen in front, with brassy speckled scales and a broad white belly, ending in a whip-like tail. A herdsman had been bitten, last year, by one of this kind in a ráhla ; they laid him upon a camel, but he died, with anguish and swelling, before the people were come to the menzil. A camel stung " will die in an hour," and the humour in so desiccated a soil must be very virulent, yet such accidents are seldom in the nomad life. I had certainly passed many times over the adder, the Beduwy bore it away upon a stick, to make some " salve very good for the camels." We had killed such an

adder at Medáin. Haj Nejm was with us; they called it
Umm-jeneyb, 'that moves upon her side.' The lad Mohammed divided the head with a cutlass stroke, as she lay sleeping deafly in the sand against the sun, in many S-shaped
boughts: the old Moor would have her horns. "Wot ye, in
the left horn lies the venom, and the antidote is in her
other, if it be drunken with milk:—or said I amiss! let
me think in which of them—: well lads let her be, for I
have not this thing certainly in mind." There is a horned
adder in the deserts of Barbary. This tale was told immediately in the nomad camp, 'the Nasrány escaped from the
poisonous serpent,' and some asked me in the mejlis, How
"saw" I the adventure? Zeyd answered them, "It was God's
mercy indeed." There was sitting by our fire a rude herding-
lad, a stranger of Ruwàlla, one of those poor young men of
the tribes, who will seek service abroad, that is with other
Beduins: for they think, in every other dîra may be better
life, and they would see the world. "Auh! said he, had she
bitten thee, Khalîl, thou shouldst never have seen thy mother
again." 'The guilty overtaken from Heaven upon a day,' such
is the superstition of mankind; and in such case the Beduins
would have said, "Of a truth he was God's adversary, the event
has declared it."

Surely these pastoral people are the least ingenious of all
mankind; is any man or beast bitten, they know nothing better
than to "read" over him (*el-kirreya*). Some spells they have
learned to babble by heart, of words fetched out of the koran;
the power of "God's Word," (which commandeth and it is made,)
they think, should be able to overcome the malignity of venom.
Some wiseacre "reader" may be found in nearly every wandering
village; they are men commonly of an infirm understanding
and no good conditions, superstitiously deceiving themselves
and not unwilling to deceive others. The patient's friends send
for one, weeping, to be their helper: and between his breaths
their "reader" will spit upon the wound, and sprinkle a little
salt. The poor Beduins are good to each other, and there is
sometimes found one who will suck his friend's or a kinsman's
poisoned wound. Yet all availeth less, they think, than the
"Word of God," were it rightly "read;" upon their part, the
desert "readers," without letters, acknowledge themselves to be
unlearned. There is also many a bold spirit among the Aarab,
of men and women, that being hurt, snatching a brand from the
hearth, will sear his wounded flesh, till the fire be quenched in the
suffering fibre: and they can endure pain (necessitous persons,
whose livelihood is as a long punishment,) with constant fortitude.

The ligature is unknown to them, but I once found a
Solubby who had used it: when his wife had been bitten in the
shin by an adder, he hastily bound the leg above the knee,
and sucked the venom. A night and a day his wife lay
dead-like and blackened ; then she revived little and little, and
came to herself : the woman recovered, but was for a long while
after discoloured. Charity, that would suck the bite of a serpent,
must consider is there no hurt in her own lips and mouth, for so
one might envenom himself. There came to me a man seeking
medicine, all whose lower lip to the chin was an open ulcer :
huskily he told me, (for the horrible virus corrupted his voice,)
that the mischief came to him after sucking a serpent-bite, a year
past. I said, I hoped to help him with medicines, and freely, as
his courage had deserved ; but the impatient wretch disdained a
physician that could not cure him anon. I saw him six months
later at Teyma, when he said, " See thou ! I am well again ; " all
the flesh was now as jasper, where the wound had been, which
was healed in appearance.

As we, or our nurses, so have they their blood-stones to stay
bleeding : and among these Beduins is another superstitious
remedy of snake-stones, in which they think (because the
stones are few in the world and precious,) there should be
some recondite virtue to resist the working of venom. The
Oriental opinion of the wholesome operation of precious stones,
in that they move the mind with admirable beauties, remains
perhaps at this day a part of the marvellous estimation of
inert gems amongst us. Those indestructible elect bodies, as
stars, shining to us out of the dim mass of matter, are comfortable to our fluxuous feeble souls and bodies : in this sense all
gems are cordial, and of an influence religious. These elemental
flowering lights almost persuade us of a serene eternity, and
are of things, (for the inestimable purity,) which separate us
from the superfluous study of the world. Even those ancient
divining stones, which were set one for a tribe, in the vesture
of the chief priest of Israel, we may suppose to have been partly
of like significance. Some snake-stones which I have seen were
cornelian, some were onyxes ; the rough pebbles had been rubbed
to a smooth face. Not all of one kind were in like estimation,
but that was according to their supposed virtue of healing ;
thus certain snake-stones, " which had wrought many great
cures," were renowned in the country. There came certain
of these snake-stone men to the Nasrâny, and showed me
their relics apart from common eyes. They had them curiously
wrapped in clouts, which they took commonly from a bag
hanging in their bosoms. Turning them to the light in my

hand, I enquired, "What is in these stones more than in all
the stones of the desert ? if you have more wit than small
children, let these toys be, and take to the ligature." But then
the masters, with less friendly looks, put up their things
hastily, repenting to have shown the pretended charms to any
uncunning and profane person. There are many free-minded
men amongst the Beduins, who do not much believe in anything, beside the circumstance of their religion, and such have
answered, "If any have made wonderful cures with their snake-
stones, we have not seen it ourselves ! " but as I said to the
possessors, "Are you then imposters ? " they answered me
soberly, "Nay truly ; we can bring many witnesses that
persons bitten by serpents have been saved by these stones,
that you speak against ; but thou wast not born in this
country, and art in such things mistaken." Some men, they
told me, were owners of stones, with which, "again and again,
the bites had been cured of most dangerous ' worms ;' and
from each person who recovered they had received for their fee,
a camel."

All the souls of a tribe or oasis are accounted *eyyal amm*
" brothers' children," and reputed brethren of a common ancestry. Also kindreds, be they even of other lineage, admitted
into a tribe, become eyyal amm with them ; as the Moahîb,
which are of the blood of Annezy, engrafted upon Bíllî, are
esteemed Bíllî, and they are "brothers' children " upon both
sides. It is an adulation in the tribes, when equals in age
name each other in their discourse, *weled ammy,* "mine
uncle's son." Amm is my father's brother ; also amm is the
householder, whose guest I am ; and amm is the step-father
of a wife's child by her former husband. Amm, in the
mouth of a servant or bond-servant, is the patron of his
living, (so the Spanish say, after the Moors in Europe, *amo*).
One who is elder, to another, and the tribesman to a guest
in his tribe, may say *ibn akhy,* son of my brother : *abúy,*
"my father," is a reverend title spoken by a lesser to the
more considerable and worshipful person, as his householder,
(so David, then a captain of outlaws, to the lawful head of
his people, king Saul). Full of humanity is that gentle persuasion of theirs from their hearts, for thy good, *ana abûk*
"my word is faithful, I am thy father," or *ana akhûk,* " I
am thy brother," *akhtak,* " thy sister," *ummak,* " thy mother :"
and akin to these is a sublime word in Moses, which follows
the divine commandments, " I am the Lord thy God."
Although tribesmen live together in harmony, the Beduins

are factious spirits; the infirm heads of the popular sort are
sudden to strive, and valiant with the tongue as women. Some
differences spring daily in the wandering village, and upon the
morrow they are deferred to the mejlis. The oasis dwellers, as
birds in a cage, are of more sober understanding. Oftentime it
is a frenetic dispute to ascertain whose may be some trifling
possession; wherein each thinks his soul to lie in the balance;
as " Whose kid is that ? " (worth twelve pence)—" Wellah, he is
mine."—" Nay, look, all of you bystanders, and bear witness;
Wellah, is not this my mark cut in his ear ? " The blood is
eager, of these hearts which lead their lives in famine and
apprehension, and soon moved : there is a beggarly sharp-set
magnanimity in their shallow breasts, the weaker of fortune
mightily disdains to be wronged. Also, from their childhood, there is many an old slumbering difference to be voided.
—But such are sooner in the ruder herding sort than in the
sheykhly kindred, whose displeasures are worn away in the daily
mejlis and familiar coffee fellowship. A burning word falls
perhaps from the incontinent lips of some peevish head, the wildfire kindles in their hearts, and weapons are drawn in the field.
Then any who are standing by will run in to separate their contention : " No more of this, for God ! (they cry) ; but let your
matter be duly declared before the sheykhs ; only each one of
you go now to his place, and we accompany you ; this dissension
can rest till the morning, when justice shall be done indifferently between you both." The nomad sheykhs govern with a
homely-wise moderation and providence ; they are peace-makers
in the menzil, and arbiters betwixt the tribesmen.

One evening a man was led to me bleeding in the arm, he
had but now received a sword-cut of a Fehjy : they strove for a
goat, which each maintained to be his own. The poor Fehjy,
thinking himself falsely overborne, had pulled out his cutlass
and struck at the oppressor,—neighbours running in laid hands
upon them both. Zeyd murmured at our fire, "—That any
Fehjy should be an aggressor ! (The Fehját, born under a
lowly star, are of a certain base alloy, an abject kind amongst
the Aarab.) It was never seen before, that any Fehjy had lifted
his weapon against a Fejîry." That small kindred of Heteym
are their hereditary clients and dwellers in their menzils. The
Fukara sheykhs on the morrow, and Zeyd a chief one with
them, must judge between the men indifferently : and for aught
I have learned they amerced the Fejîry, condemning him to
pay certain small cattle ; for which, some time after, I found
him and his next kinsmen dwelling as exiles in another tribe.
Satisfaction may be yielded (and the same number will be

accepted) in any year to come, of the natural increase of his
stock, and the exiles reestablish themselves : for the malicious
subtlety of ursury is foreign to the brotherly dealing of the
nomad tribesmen.

Passengers in the land say proverbially of these poor
Fehját, " The Fehjies are always blithe." And what care should
he have who lives as the fowls of the air, almost not hoping
to gain or fearing to lose anything in the world : and commonly they are full of light jesting humour, and merry as
beggars. Their father is that Marhab, say they, sheykh
next after the Mohammedan conquest of ancient Kheybar.
—Are they then the Yahûd Kheybar ? I have seen Doolan,
the prowest and the poorest of these Antarids, cast down a
night and a day after his lips had uttered to us this magnanimous confession ; as his grandsire Antara could proudly
acknowledge his illiberal blood of the mother's side, and be a sad
man afterward. Believing themselves such, they would sometime
have the Nasrâny to be an ancient kinsman of theirs ; and being
accused for the name of my religion, this procured me the good
will of such persons, which were themselves the thralls of an
insane fortune. Sometimes they said I should take a wife
of the fairest daughters amongst them ; and Fehjiát (Heteym)
were, I think, the only two well favoured forms of women in
this great encampment. As I rode in the midst of a rahlá, the
husband of one of them hailed me cheerfully—I had hardly
seen them before—" Ho there, Khalîl ! "—" *Weysh widdak ya zillamy*, O man, what is thy will ? "—" I say, hast thou any liking to
wed ?—is not this (his wife) a fair woman ? " And between
their beggarly mirth and looking for gain, he cries in merry
earnest, " Wellah, if this like you, I will let her go (saying the
word of divorce) ; only Khalîl, thou wilt *sûk* (drive up cattle,
that is, pay over to me) five camels,"—which he swore fast
he had given himself for her bride-money. Tall was this
fair young wife and freshly clad as a beloved ; her middle
small girt with a gay scarlet lace : barefoot she went upon
the waste sand with a beautiful erect confidence of the hinds,
in their native wilderness. "And what (I asked) is thy mind,
my sister ? " She answered, " So thou wouldst receive me,
Khalîl, I am willing."—Thus light are they in their marriages,
and nearly all unhappy ! I passed from them in silence at the
pace of my thelûl. Another day, seeing her come to a circumcision festival, I saluted her by name, but for some laughing
word maliciously reported she showed me, with a wounded look,
that I was fallen under her beautiful displeasure.

Wandering with the Fehjîr we have seen some malcontent

sheukh, Allayda, of the W. Aly. Certain households of the
Fukara were in like manner exiles with the W. Aly. Those
Allaydies' quarrel had been with Motlog Allayda, their great
sheykh and kinsman, for the partition of the Haj surra. Motlog
held that his part was less than enough, and that they received
more than their due. He then, of his sheykh's authority,
which is only controlled by the public opinion, would have
seized their camels. Good men they were not, which is Motlog
Allayda, by the common report : in a calamity of the W. Aly
by the enemies' ghrazzus, when I said in those sheykhs' tents,
I was sorry to hear of their tribesmen's mishap, they answered
coldly, "But not we, we would God Bishr had brought them
to greater mischance." There were besides in the Fukara
menzil two or three households of half-tribesmen, sons of
former Damascene kella-keepers ; after their fathers' day they
were become nomads and petty traders with their mothers'
kindred. Others of their brethren had passed to the civil
life in the paternal city ; we have seen how they traded yearly
hither, in the Haj, from Syria. Those which remained in the
desert were become as the nomads ; but whiter skinned men
of foreign looks, and of less franchise than the Beduw. Those
half-blooded Beduins returned every year, in the summer months,
(weary of their desert wandering,) to pitch their booths before
the old kella (where they were born) at el-Héjr. Yet one
of these was the boldest pricker in the tribe. He rode
a-foraying, as often as he might find any like minded
with himself, and he being agîd there must fall to him,
of any booty, the leader's share. Then he scoured again the
empty wilderness, consumed in the sunny drought. Such
ghrazzuing wretches descrying any byût of hostile Aarab,
dismount and lurk till nightfall, when they will creep in,
having left their thelûls kneebound out of hearing, and
they hope thus to take some camels ; but commonly these
riders returned home fainting from their perilous courses,
and brought nothing with them. The man was a valiant
jade. In all their chevying in the desert, his rafîk must be
his eyes ; I found his own half closed with crusts of an old
running ophthalmia.

Long were our sultry days since the tribe was divided, and
without mejlis ; yet the fewer neighbours were now more
friendly drawn together. Zeyd was always at home, to his beyt
resorted the sheukh companions, and he made them coffee.
All cousins together, the host far from all jealousy, and Beduins
fain to be merry, their often game was of the late passages
betwixt Hirfa and Zeyd ; they twitted the young wife's demure

ill humour. " Hirfa ho ! Hirfa, sittest thou silent behind the curtain, and have not the hareem a tongue ? Stand up there and let that little face of thine be seen above the cloth, and clear thyself, before the company. Hirfa ! what is this we hear of thee, art thou still contrary to Zeyd ? Didst thou not forsake Zeyd ? and leave Zeyd without an household ? and must Khalîl bring thee home again ? what hast thou to answer for thyself ? " *Khálaf Allayda :* " Say thy opinion, Khalîl, of my mare colt. She is well worth thirty-five camels, and her mother is worth twenty-five ; but Zeyd's mare is not worth five camels :—and hast thou seen my *jâra* (housewife) ? tell us now whether Hirfa be the fairer faced, or she that is mine." Hirfa, showing herself with a little pouting look, said she would not suffer these comparisons ; " Khalîl, do not answer." The Aarab playing thus in the tent-life, and their mouths full of the broadest raillery, often called for the stranger, to be judge of their laughing contentions : as, " Is not this a gomâny (enemy) ? Khalîl, he is a *hablûs ;* what shall be done to him ? shall I take off his head ?—and this old fellow here, they say, is naught with his wife ; for pity, canst thou not help him ? is there not a medicine ? "—And the old sire, " Do not listen to these young fools." So they said, " This Zeyd is good for nothing, why do you live with him ? and Hirfa, is she good to you ? she pours you out léban ; and she is beautiful, *mez'ûna ?* " Hirfa herself, were there no strangers, would come in at such times to sit down and jest her part with us : she was a sheykha, and Zeyd, a manly jaded man, was of this liberality more than is often seen among Beduins. Sometimes for pastime they would ask for words of my Nasrâny language, and as they had them presently by heart, they called loud for Hirfa, in plain English, " *Girl, bring milk !*—by thy life, Hirfa, this evening we have learned Enghreys." *Hirfa :* " And tittun, what is it in the tongue of Khalîl ? "—" Tobacco."—" Then give me some of this good word in my galliûn, fill for me, Khalîl ! "—Another day, a tribesman arriving sat down by Hirfa, in her side of the booth ; and seeing the stranger, " Tell me, he said, is not Hirfa mez'ûna ? oh, that she were mine ! " and the fellow discovered his mind with knavish gestures. Hirfa, seeing herself courted, (though he was not a sheykh,) sat still and smiled demurely ; and Zeyd, who could well play the shrew in other men's wedlock, sitting by himself, looked manly on and smiling.

Zeyd might balance in his mind to be some day quit of Hirfa, for what a cumber to man's heart is an irksome woman !—As we sat, few together, about another evening fire, said Zeyd, " Wellah, Khalîl, I and thou are brethren. In proof of this, I ask thee, hast thou any mind to be wedded amongst us? See, I have two wives, and, billah, I will give thee to choose between them; say which hast thou rather, and I will leave her and she shall become thy wife. Here is thy hostess Hirfa; the other is the *Bishrîa*, and I think thou hast seen her yonder."—Perhaps he would have given me Hirfa, to take her again (amended) at my departure and in the meanwhile not to miss her camels; for it seemed he had married the orphan's camels. To this gentle proffer I answered, 'Would they needs marry me, then be it not with other men's wives, which were contrary to our belief, but give me my pretty *Rakhyeh:*' this was Zeyd's sister's child, that came daily playing to our booth with her infant brothers. "Hearest thou, Hirfa? answered Zeyd; I gave thee now to Khalîl, but he has preferred a child before thee." And Hirfa a little discontented: "Well, be it so, and I make no account of Khalîl's opinions."—The great-eyed Bishr wife, meeting me some day after in the camp, proffered, betwixt earnest and game, without my asking, to take me for her husband, 'as ever her husband would divorce her: but I must buy some small cattle, a worsted booth, and camels; we should live then (she thought) in happy accord, as the Nasârines put not away their wives.' Sometimes in the coffee tents a father proffered his child, commending her beauty, and took witness of all that sat there; young men said they gave me their sisters: and this was because Zeyd had formerly given out that Khalîl, coming to live with him, would ride in the ghrazzus and be a wedded man.—For all their jealousy is between themselves; there had no man not been contented with the Nasrâny parentage, since better in their belief is the Christian blood; and the white skin betokens in their eyes an ingenuous lineage, more than their own. Human spirits of an high fantasy, they imagine themselves discoloured and full of ailing; this is their melancholy. I have known Beduin women that disdained, as they said, to wed with a Beduwy; and oasis women who disdained to wed among their villagers. They might think it an advancement, if it fell to them to be matched with some man from the settled countries. Beduin daughters are easily given in marriage to the kella keepers.

Only young hinds, abiding in the master's booth, and lads under age, can worthily remain unmarried. A lonely man, in the desert tribes, were a wretch indeed, without tent, since the household service is wholly of the hareem: and among so many forsaken women, and widows, there is no man so poor who may not find a make to 'build' with him, to load, to grind, to fetch water and wood: he shall but kill a sheep (or a goat, if he be of

so little substance,) for the marriage supper. Incredible it seems
to the hareem, that any man should choose to dwell alone, when
the benefit of marriage lies so unequally upon his part. Gentle
Beduin women timidly ask the stranger, of very womanhood, "And hast thou not hareem that weep for thee in thy
land ?"—When the man's help is gone from their indigent
house of marriage, they are left widows indeed. It is a common
smiling talk to say to the passenger guest, and the stranger in
their tents, *nejowwazak bint*, "We will give thee a maiden to
wife, and dwell thou among us." I have said, "What should she
do in my country ? can she forget her language and her people
leading their lives in this wilderness ?" And they have answered,
"Here is but famine and thirst and nakedness, and yours is a
good béled ; a wife would follow, and also serve thee by the way,
this were better for thee : the lonely man is sorrowful, and she
would learn your tongue, as thou hast learned *Araby*." But some
murmured, "It is rather a malice of the Nasâra, Khalîl will none,
lest the religion of Islam should grow thereby." Others guessed
'It were meritorious to give me a wife, to this end, that true
worshippers might arise among them, of him who knew not
Ullah.' Also this I have heard, "Wed thou, and leave us a
white bint, that she may in time be for some great sheykh's
wife." Large is the nomad housewives' liberty. The few good
women, sorted with worthy men, to whom they have born sons,
are seen of comely, and hardly less than matronly carriage.
In hareem of small worth, fallen from marriage to marriage,
from one concubinage to another, and always lower, is often
found the license of the nomad tongue, with the shameless words
and gestures of abandoned women. The depraved in both sexes
are called by the tribesmen *affûn*, putrid or rotten persons. The
maidens in the nomad booths are of a virginal circumspect
verecundity, wards of their fathers and brethren, and in tutelage
of an austere public opinion. When daughters of some lone
tents must go herding, as the *Midianite* daughters of Jethro,
we have seen, they may drive their flocks into the wilderness
and fear no evil ; there is not a young tribesman (vile though
many of them be,—but never impious,) who will do her oppression. It were in all their eyes harrâm, breach of the
desert faith and the religion of Islam ; the guilty would be
henceforth unworthy to sit amongst men, in the booths of the
Aarab.

Now longwhile our black booths had been built upon the
sandy stretches, lying before the swelling white Nefûd side : the
lofty coast of Irnàn in front, whose cragged breaches, where is

any footing for small herbs nourished of this barren atmosphere, are the harbour of wild goats, which never drink. The summer's night at end, the sun stands up as a crown of hostile flames from that huge covert of inhospitable sandstone bergs ; the desert day dawns not little and little, but it is noontide in an hour. The sun, entering as a tyrant upon the waste landscape, darts upon us a torment of fiery beams, not to be remitted till the far-off evening.—No matins here of birds ; not a rock partridge-cock, calling with blithesome chuckle over the extreme waterless desolation. Grave is that giddy heat upon the crown of the head ; the ears tingle with a flickering shrillness, a subtle crepitation it seems, in the glassiness of this sun-stricken nature : the hot sand-blink is in the eyes, and there is little refreshment to find in the tents' shelter ; the worsted booths leak to this fiery rain of sunny light. Mountains looming like dry bones through the thin air, stand far around about us : the savage flank of Ybba Moghrair, the high spire and ruinous stacks of el-Jebâl, Chébàd, the coast of Helwàn ! Herds of weak nomad camels waver dispersedly, seeking pasture in the midst of this hollow fainting country, where but lately the swarming locusts have fretted every green thing. This silent air burning about us, we endure breathless till the assr : when the dazing Arabs in the tents revive after their heavy hours. The lingering day draws down to the sun-setting ; the herdsmen, weary of the sun, come again with the cattle, to taste in their menzils the first sweetness of mirth and repose. —The day is done, and there rises the nightly freshness of this purest mountain air : and then to the cheerful song and the cup at the common fire. The moon rises ruddy from that solemn obscurity of jebel like a mighty beacon :—and the morrow will be as this day, days deadly drowned in the sun of the summer wilderness.

The rugged country eastward, where we came in another remove, was little known to our Beduins ; only an elder generation had wandered there : and yet they found even the lesser waters. We journeyed forth in high plains, (the altitude always nearly 4000 feet,) and in passages, stretching betwixt mountain cliffs of sandstone, cumbered with infinite ruins of fallen crags, in whose eternal shadows we built the booths of a day. One of these quarters of rock had not tumbled perhaps in a human generation ; but they mark years of the sun, as the sand, a little thing in the lifetime of the planet !

The short spring season is the only refreshment of the desert year. Beasts and men swim upon this prosperous tide ; the cattle have their fill of sweet pasture, butter-milk is in the

booths of the Aarab; but there was little or none in Zeyd's
tent. The kids and lambs stand all tied, each little neck in a
noose, upon a ground line which is stretched in the nomad
booth. At day-break the bleating younglings are put under the
dams, and each mother receives her own, (it is by the scent)—she
will put by every other. When the flock is led forth to pasture,
the little ones are still bound at home; for following the dams,
they would drink dry the dugs, and leave no food for the Arabs.
The worsted tent is full all day of small hungry bleatings, until
the ghrannem come home at evening, when they are loosed
again, and run to drink, butting under the mother's teats, with
their wiggle tails; and in these spring weeks, there is little rest
for their feeble cries, all night in the booths of the Aarab: the
housewives draw what remains of the sweet milk after them.
The B. Wáhab tribes of these open highlands, are camel-
Beduins; the small cattle are few among them: they have new
spring milk when their hinds have calved. The yeaning camel-
cow, lying upon her side, is delivered without voice, the fallen
calf is big as a grown man: the herdsman stretches out its
legs, with all his might; and draws the calf, as dead, before the
dam. She smells to her young, rises and stands upon her feet
to lick it over. With a great clap of the man's palm upon
that horny sole, zôra, (which, like a pillar, Nature has set
under the camel's breast, to bear up the huge neck,) the calf
revives: at three hours end, yet feeble and tottering, and after
many falls, it is able to stand reaching up the long neck and
feeling for the mother's teat. The next morrow this new
born camel will follow to the field with the dam. The cow
may be milked immediately, but that which is drawn from her,
for a day or two, is purgative. The first voice of the calf is a
sheep-like complaint, bâh-bâh, loud and well sounding. The
fleece is silken soft, the head round and high; and this with a
short body, borne arch-wise, and a leaping gait upon so long legs,
makes that, a little closing the eyes, you might take them for
fledglings of some colossal bird. Till twelve months be out they
follow the teat; but when a few weeks old they begin, already,
to crop for themselves the tops of the desert bushes: and their
necks being not yet of proportionate reach, it is only betwixt
the straddled fore legs, that they can feed at the ground. One
evening, as I stroked the soft woolly chines of the new-born
camels, "Khálîl! said the hind (coming with a hostile face), see
thou do no more so,—they will be hide-bound and not grow well;
thou knowest not this!" He thought the stranger was about some
maleficence; but Zeyd, whose spirit was far from all superstition
with an easy smile appeased him, and they were his own camels.

The camel calf at the birth is worth a real, and every month rises as much in value. In some " weak " households the veal is slaughtered, where they must drink themselves all their camel milk. The bereaved dam wanders, lowing softly, and smelling for her calf ; and as she mourns, you shall see her deer-like pupils, say the Arabs, ' standing full of tears.' Other ten days, and her brutish distress is gone over to forgetfulness ; she will feed again full at the pasture, and yield her foster milk to the Aarab. Then three good pints may be drawn from her at morning, and as much to their supper : the udder of these huge frugal animals is not greater than I have seen the dugs of Malta goats. A milch cow with the calf is milked only at evening. Her udder has four teats, which the southern nomads divide thus : two they tie up with a worsted twine and wooden pegs, for themselves, the other they leave to the suckling. The Aarab of the north make their camel udders sure, with a worsted bag-netting. Upon a journey, or when she is thirsting, the nâga's milk is lessened to the half. All their nâgas give not milk alike. Whilst the spring milk is in, the nomads nourish themselves of little else. In poorer households it is all their victual those two months. The Beduins drink no whole-milk, save that of their camels ; of their small cattle they drink but the butter-milk. The hareem make butter, busily rocking the (blown) sour milk-skin upon their knees. In the plenteous northern wilderness the semîly is greater ; and is hanged to be rocked in the fork of a robust bearing-stake of the nomad tent. As for this milk-diet, I find it, by proof in the Beduin life, to be the best of human food. But in every nomad menzil, there are some stomachs, which may never well bear it ; and strong men using this sliding drink-meat feel always an hungry disease in their bodies ; though they seem in never so good plight. The Beduins speak thus of the several kinds of milk : " Goat milk is sweet, it fattens more than strengthens the body ; ewe's milk very sweet, and fattest of all, it is unwholesome to drink whole :" so they say, "it kills people," that is, with the colic. In spite of their saws, I have many times drunk it warm from the dug, with great comfort of languishing fatigue. It is very rich in the best samn : ewe butter-milk " should be let sour some-while in the semîly, with other milk, till all be tempered together, and then it is fit to drink." Camel milk is they think the best of all sustenance, and that most, (as lightly purgative,) of the *bukkra*, or young nâga with her first calf, and the most sober of them add with a Beduish simplicity, " who drinks and has a jâra he would not abide an hour." The goat and nâga milk savour of the plants where the cattle are pastured ; in

some cankered grounds I have found it as wormword. One of
those Allayda sheykhs called to me in the ráhla, "Hast thou
not some Damascus *kaak* (biscuit cakes) to give me to eat?
wellah, it is six weeks since I have chewed anything with the
teeth ; all our food is now this flood of milk. Seest thou not
what is the Beduin's life ; they are like game scattered in all
the wilderness." Another craved of me a handful of dates;
"with this milk, only, he felt such a creeping hunger within
him." Of any dividing food with them the Beduins keep a
kindly remembrance ; and when they have aught will call thee
heartily again.

The milk-dieted Aarab are glad to take any mouthful of
small game. Besides the desert hare which is often startled
in the ráhlas, before other is the thób ; which they call here
pleasantly 'Master Hamed, sheykh of wild beasts,' and say he
is human, *zillamy*,—this is their elvish smiling and playing—
and in proof they hold up his little five-fingered hands. They
eat not his palms, nor the seven latter thorny rings of sheykh
Hamed's long tail, which, say they, is man's flesh.' His pasture
is most of the sweet-smelling Nejd bush, *el-arrafej*. Sprawling wide and flat is the body, ending in a training tail of
even length, where I have counted twenty-three rings. The
colour is blackish and green-speckled, above the pale yellowish
and dull belly : of his skin the nomads make small herdmen's
milk-bottles. The manikin saurian, with the robust hands,
digs his burrow under the hard gravel soil, wherein he lies
all the winter, dreaming. The thób-catcher, finding the hole,
and putting in his long reed armed with an iron hook, draws
Hamed forth. His throat cut, they fling the carcase, whole,
upon the coals ; and thus baked they think it a delicate roast.
His capital enemy among beasts, "which undermines and de-
vours him, is, they say, the *thurbàn*," I know not whether a living
or fabulous animal. The *jerboa*, or spring rat, is a small white
aery creature in the wide waterless deserts, of a pitiful beauty.
These lesser desert creatures lie underground in the daylight,
they never drink. The hedgehog, which they call *kúnfuth*,
and *abu shauk*, 'father prickles,' is eaten in these parts by Fejír
tribesmen, but by their neighbours disdained, although they be
one stock with them of Annezy. Selím brought in an urchin
which he had knocked on the head, he roasted Prickles in
the coals and rent and distributed the morsels, to every one his
part. That which fell to me I put away bye and bye to
the starveling greyhound ; but the dog smelling to the meat
rejected it. When another day I told this tale in the next
tribes, they laughed maliciously, that the Fukara should eat

that which the hounds would not of. The porcupine is eaten by all the nomads, and the *wabbar*. I have seen this thick-bodied beast as much as an heavy hare, and resembling the great Alpine rat; they go by pairs, or four, six, eight, ten, together. The wabbar is found under the border of the sand-stone mountains, where tender herbs nourish him, and the gum acacia-leaves, upon which tree he climbs nimbly, holding with his pad feet without claws; the fore-paws have four toes, the hind paws three: the flesh is fat and sweet: they are not seen to sit upon the hind quarters; the pelt is grey, and like the bear's coat.

Rarely do any nomad gunners kill the wolf, but if any fall to their shot he is eaten by the Beduins, (the wolf was eaten in mediæval Europe). The Aarab think the flesh medicinal, "very good they say for aches in the shins," which are so common with them that go bare-legs and bare-footed in all the seasons. Zeyd had eaten the wolf, but he allowed it to be of dog's kind, "Eigh, billah (he answered me), the wolf's mother, that is the hound's aunt." The fox, *hosseny*, is often taken by their greyhounds, and eaten by the Fejîr; the flesh is "sweet, and next to the hare." They will even eat the foul hyena when they may take her, and say, "she is good meat." Of great desert game, but seldom slain by the shot of these pastoral and tent-dwelling people, is the bédan of the mountains (the wild goat of Scripture, *pl.* bedûn; with the Kahtân *waûl*, as in Syria). The massy horns grow to a palm-breadth, I have seen them two and a half feet long; they grow stretching back upon the chine to the haunch. The beast at need, as all hunters re-

Horn of the (Bed.) *Wothîhi*, (vulg.) *Bakr el-Wdhashy* or "Wild Ox" [discovered by Mr. Doughty at Maan in Edom, May, 1875] which is probably the *Reem* of the Hebrew Scriptures, translated (from the Septuagint) "UNICORN." The length of the horn shown above [from the Sherarāt Country near Teyma, Oct. 1877] is 23 inches.

late, will cast himself down headlong upon them backwards : he is nigh of kin to the stone-buck of the European Alps.

The gazelle, *ghrazel*, pl. *ghrazlán*, is of the plains ; the Arabians say more often *thobby* (the N. T. Tabitha). They are white in the great sand-plains, and swart-grey upon the black Harra ; these are the roes of the scriptures. There is yet a noble wild creature of the Arabian deserts, which was hitherto unknown among us, the *wothýhi*, or "wild cow" above mentioned (p. 59). I saw later the male and female living at Hâyil ; it is an antelope, *Beatrix*, akin to the beautiful animals of Africa. It seems that this is not the "wild ox" of Moses : but is not this the (Hebr.) *reem*, the "*unicorn*" of the Septuagint translators ?—Her horns are such slender rods as from our childhood we have seen pictured "the horns of the unicorns." (See p. 327.) We read in Balaam's parable, "EL brought them out of Egypt ; He hath as it were the strength of a *reem :*" and in Moses' blessing of the tribes, "Joseph's horns are the *two* horns of reems." In Job especially, are shown the headstrong conditions of this *velox* wild creature. "Will the reem be willing to serve thee—canst thou bind the reem in thy furrow ? " The wounded wothýhi is perilous to be approached ; this antelope, with a cast of her sharp horns, may strike through a man's body ; hunters await therefore the last moments to run in and cut their quarry's throat. It was a monkish darkness in natural knowledge to ascribe a single horn to a double forehead ! —and we sin not less by addition, putting wings to the pagan images of gods and angels ; so they should have two pairs of fore-limbs ! The wothýhi falls only to the keenest hunters : the wothýhies accompany in the waterless desert by troops of three and five together.

Of vermin, there are many snakes and adders ; none of them eaten by these tribes of nomads. *Jelámy* is that small brown lizard of the wilderness which starts from every footstep. Scorpions lurk under the cool stones ; I have found them in my tent, upon my clothing, but never had any hurt. I have seen many grown persons and children bitten, but the sting is not perilous ; some wise man is called to "read" over them. The wounded part throbs with numbness and aching till the third day, there is not much swelling. Many are the cities, under this desert sand, of seed-gathering ants ; I have measured some watling-street of theirs, eighty-five paces : to speed once this length and come again, loaded as camels, is these small busy-bodies' summer day's journey.

Besides, of the great predatory wild animals, most common is the *thùbba*, hyena ; then the *nimmr*, a leopard, brindled black and brown and spotted ; little common is the *fáhd*, a wild cat no bigger than the fox ; he is red and brown brindled, and spotted. In these Beduins' memory a young fáhd was bred up amongst Bishr, which (they are wonderfully swift-footed) had been used by his nomad master to take gazelles. In all the Arabic countries there is a strange superstition of parents, (and this as well among the Christian sects of Syria,) that if any child seem to be sickly, of infirm understanding, or his brethren have died before, they will put upon him a wild beast's name, (especially, wolf, leopard, wolverine,)—that their human fragility may take on as it were a temper of the kind of those animals. Hawks and buzzards are often seen wheeling in the desert sky, and *el-ágab*, which is a small black eagle, and *er-rákham*, the small white carrion eagle,—flying in the air they resemble sea-mews : I have not seen vultures, nor any greater eagle in the deserts (save in Sinai). These are the most of living creatures, and there are few besides in the wilderness of Arabia.

CHAPTER XII.

UPON a morrow, when there was a great coffee-drinking at Zeyd's, one cries over his cup, *bahhir!* " Look there !—who come riding yonder ? " All shadowing with their hands, and fixing the eyes, it was answered, " Are, they not tradesmen of Teyma, that ride to sell calico ; or some that would take up well camels ; or the sheukh perhaps, that ride to Hâyil ? " The Beduw make no common proof that I can find of extraordinary vision. True it is, that as they sit the day long in the open tents, their sight is ever indolently wavering in the wide horizon before them, where any stirring or strangeness in the wonted aspect of the desert must suspend their wandering cogitation. But the Arabs also suffer more of eye diseases than any nation. It was not long before the weak-eyed Arabs discovered the comers, by their frank riding, to be Beduins ; but only a little before they alighted, the company knew them to be their own sheykh Motlog and his son, and a tribesman with them. Motlog had mounted very early from the other camp. Our company, of nigh fifty persons, rose to welcome their chief sheykhs ; Motlog re-entered cordially amongst them, with a stately modesty ; and every man came forward in his place, to salute them, as kinsmen returning from an absence, with *gowwak ya Motlog*, ' The Lord strengthen thee.' *Answer : Ullah gowwîk*, ' May He give thee strength :' so, falling upon each other's necks, they kiss gravely together, upon this and upon the other cheek. Room now is made for them in the highest place, where they sit down, smiling easily ; and the Fukara sheukh, noblemen born, of somewhat an effeminate countenance, excel, as said, in specious and amiable mejlis manners : yet their Asiatic hearts are full of corruption inwardly, and iniquity. Roasting anew and braying and boiling are taken in hand, to make them coffee ; and Zeyd, as an host, brings them forth a bowl of his musty dates to breakfast, (he would spend for none better at Teyma,) and another of butter-milk, and those in small measure ;—it was Hirfa and Zeyd's known illiberality, for which cause, there alighted almost no guest at Zeyd's beyt in the round year. This is the goodly custom in the wilderness, that somewhat be served immediately, (however early it be,) to the guest alighting from his journey. The sheykhs consented to join our camps from the next ráhla, and we should remove further into the Bishr country.

Bishr is a main partition of the Annezy nation, and certain of their great kindreds, as the *W. Sleymàn* in Nejd, might be compared with whole tribes. High sheykh of all the Nejd Bishr, is a warlike man of my later acquaintance, *Misshel* (called after his fendy) *el-Auájy ;* and entitled, Sheykh of the seven Kabâil (tribes, Kabîlies). Their kinships or fendies are, said Zeyd :

W. Sleymàn.	*Khumsha.*
Sweylmát.	*Sìllimat.*
Jiáfera.	*Hósenny.*
el-Aly.	*Sbá.*
Gathowra.	*Feddán.*
S'goor.	*Ammarát.*
Shemlán.	

Zeyd seemed to reckon the Ruwàlla Annezy with Bishr. They inhabit by the Nefûd, under Jauf, and westwards toward Syria ; they are Beduins of raw and simple manners. Their

kindreds are : *Aarab Ibn Muzzeyed, el-Hósenny, el-Musellíkh.*
Incorporate of old with the Ruwàlla, are the ancient Annezy
Aarab, *el-Jellàs ;* of whom a wady of Kheybar, their former posses-
sion, long forsaken by them, is yet named. Their kindreds are:

el-Nussír ; Noàsera.	*Deraan.*
Shalán.	*Unseir.*
Ribshàn.	*Belais.*
Sualma.	*B'dúr.*
Ferujja.	*Aarab Ibn Mahjil sheykh el-Essàjir.*
Koatcheba.	*Aarab Ibn Jíndal sheykh es-Suàlmo.*
Gaaja.	*Aarab Ibn Umjeyd sheykh Abdillah.*
Dogmàn.	*Kleyfát.*

As our Aarab were pitched together again, there arrived a
principal sheykh of Teyma, *Abd el-Azíz er-Román,* riding round
to the Aarab, to buy well camels. The price is two or three
camel-loads of dates or a load of corn, *aysh,* for a good nâga.
He alighted at Motlog's, and I went down to the coffee meeting,
to hear the country news. Motlog welcomed me graciously, and
called, " Bring a shidàd for Khalîl." The Teyma sheykh was
a well clad, comely, stirring man, in the favour of Ibn Rashîd,
collector of the prince's revenue in his oasis ; presumptuous,
penetrating-malicious, and, " as all the Teyâmena," in the
opinion of the nomads, *jáhil,* of a certain broken-headed ineptitude, and rusticity. In the nomad-like village, he had not
learned letters : Motlog, among Beduins, was the friend of his
youth. As we sat on, Abd el-Azîz, turning abruptly, demanded
of me, ' What did I there in the wilderness, and wherefore had I
banished myself from all world's good,' (that is, from the shadow
by day, bread and dates sure, and water enough, and the stable
dwelling). " I take the air."—" If this be all, thou mightest as
good take the air upon yonder top of Irnàn." His rafîk enquired in his ear, yet so that I heard it, " Is not this a
Yahûdy ? "—" Jew, there is no doubt (answered Abd el-Azíz),
or what they tell me Nasrâny, a difference in the names
only." The other then, with a ghastly look, as if he beheld a
limb of Sheytan, " Lord, for thy mercy ! and is this—akhs !—a
Yahûdy ? Ullah confound all the kuffâr." Abd el-Azîz, when I
came again to Teyma, had put on a new courtesy, since he heard
the stranger had publicly pronounced him, " Ignorant ass, and
sheykh of all the Yahûd of Teyma : " for the Arabs, who covet
to be praised, are tender as vain women of men's opinions.
They brought tidings of a disaster at home, the Haddàj was
fallen ! yet he looked merrily upon it, because his two or three
draw-wheels and the side which belonged to his own sûk, were
yet standing ; the loss was not of his faction.

The knavish Beduins heard unmoved of the mischance of
the Teyâmena; those merchants of dates and corn, that beguile, they think, their uncunning with false measures.   Of
some who came later from the oasis, we heard that the townspeople and fanatics laid all to the charge of the Nasrâny.
' The Haddàj fell only few days after my being there, I had overthrown it with mine eye;' but the graver sort said, 'it was not
fallen but by the permission of Ullah.'   I asked a plain worthy
man of the town, "How could I have cast down your well?"
And he: "Khalîl, I believe not it was thy doing; (he added
darkly,) I think rather it was of Ibn Rashîd!"   The prince
and his riders (perhaps three hundred men), returning from
the raid upon W. Aly, had encamped without Teyma walls a
day or twain.   He added, "The multitude of them was as the
sand, *ouff!*"—"Was it the tread of their waterers about the
Haddàj?"—"Not this, but *el-áyn*, the eye!"   The evil eye
is part of the Semitic superstition.   The darling of the body is
the eye, the window of the soul, and they imagine her malign influence to stream forth thereat.   Fanatical nomads, from that
day, looked upon me as a yet more perilous ' God's adversary.'

One of these evenings there rode into our encampment a
main ghrazzu, eighty men of Bishr, that had mounted to go set
upon their foemen W. Aly ; they passed this night as guests of
the Fukara, in their own dîra.   They were friendly entertained,
and heard after their suppers the latest advice of the W. Aly's
being pitched about the wells *Mogeyra;* about eighty miles
from hence, at the haj road, a journey below el-Héjr.   I enquired
of Zeyd, Would they not send this night to warn their cousins
of the sister tribe ?   *Answer:* "Ha, no ! but let them all be
taken, for us."   Months later, being with some W. Aly tribesmen I heard them censure this treacherous malice of the
Fukara ; and yet being full of the like themselves, which in
truth is the natural condition of Beduins.   Of the Annezy
nation, unto which all these tribes belong, and that is greatest
of all ashîrats in the Peninsula, it is spoken in proverb, " God
increased Annezy, and He has appointed divisions among them:"
there is no time when some of the kindreds are not *gôm*, or
robber enemies, of some other.   The Annezy have been compared with B. Israel ;   they are not without resemblance.
The seat of this people, in the first Mohammedan ages, was,
according to their tradition, the dîra lying a little north of
Medina, which is now of the W. Aly.   Then they conquered
Kheybar, whose feverish palm valleys became their patrimony
to this day.

It happened strangely that whilst Bishr was out against
them a main ghrazzu of the Wélad Aly had mounted to go
and set upon Bishr. These hostile squadrons by a new adventure met with each other in the wilderness. An hundred
thelûl riders cover the ground of a regiment. It is a brave
sight, as they come on with a song, bowing in the tall saddles,
upon the necks of their gaunt stalking beasts, with a martial
shining of arms. The foemen in sight, the sheukh descend
with the long lances upon their led horses ; and every sheykh's
back-rider, radîf, who is also his gun-bearer, now rides in the
thelûl saddle. Those thelûl riders, upon the slower sheep-
like beasts, are in comparison of their few light horsemen,
like a kind of heavy infantry of matchlock men. The nomad
cavalier, sitting loosely upon a pad without stirrups, can carry
no long and heavy firearm, which he could not reload. Only
few amongst these southern sheykhs are possessors of some old
flint horse-pistols, which abandoned in our grandsires' time, have
been sold away from Europe. Their hope is in the romhh or
shelfa, the Beduin lance : the beam, made of a light reed of the
rivers of Mesopotamia, is nearly two of their short horse-lengths ;
they charge them above their heads. Agîd or conductor of the
W. Aly part, was a beardless and raw young man, Fáhd, their
great sheykh's son ; and Askar of the other, son of Misshel, the
great sheykh above mentioned : these young hostile Annezy
leaders were sisters' sons. Fáhd, tilting impetuously, pierced
his cousin Askar ; but, overborne by strong men's hands, he
was himself taken alive. The W. Aly, glorious and confident in the tents, were seized with panic terror in the field,
in presence of the warlike Auájy, the most big of bone and
resolute of that country Beduins ; in each of whom they
looked for an avenger of the blood slain before Kheybar. They
cried out therefore that they were brethren ! and those W. Aly,
which were one hundred and twenty riders with arms in their
hands, submitted to the eighty lion-like men of Bishr ; every
one pitifully intreating his spoiler, " akhyey, ya akhyey, ah,
little brother mine ! take thou then my thelûl, have here my
arms, and even my mantle ; take all, only let me go alive."
No more than a few sheykhs of them, who were horsemen,
escaped that day upon their mares. Yet of the thelûl riders
there broke away three hardy men, mountaineers ; they were
Moahîb, that had ridden with them in hope to divide the spoils
of the common enemy.—Before the year was out, the Moahîb
by the same Bishr were miserably bereaved, in one day, of all
their cattle. The sheykhs upon all sides were, at some time, of
my acquaintance ; and I had this tale among them.

The Bishr received their *dakhils* to quarter ; they would not, only remembering the vengeance, make a butchery of their kinsmen ; and, as the southern Aarab use not to take human lives to ransom, they let their enemies go, in their shirts, to ride home to their wives, upon their bare feet. It is contrary to the Arabian conscience to extinguish a kabîla. There are tribes of neighbours, cruel gomânies since their granddames' days, as the Fejîr and B. Atîeh, that have never met in general battles, when, in a day, they might void so long controversies, by the destruction of one of them. Even the Beduins' old cruel rancours are often less than the golden piety of the wilderness. The danger past, they can think of the defeated foeman with kindness ; having compassion of an Arab lineage of common ancestry with themselves. When men fall down wounded in a foray the enemies which had the upper hand will often send again far back, and bear them to their menzil : and there they nourish their languishing foemen, until they be whole again ; when they give to each a water-skin and say to him *ruhh*, " depart," without taking promises, putting only their trust in Ullah to obtain the like at need for themselves. But Fáhd was led away with the Bishr, since he must answer for the life of Askar : if his cousin died he must die for his death, unless the next of kin should consent to receive the blood ransom ; he would be entertained in the meanwhile in his hostile kinsmen's tents. Askar recovered slowly, in the next months. I asked, " When those shearers of W. Aly came home shorn, with what dances and lullilooing will the hareem sally forth to meet them ! " It was answered, " Ay billah, they had merited the women's derision ! "—" But how, being one hundred and twenty strong, had they submitted to the fewer in number ? " *Answer :* " Are they not W. Aly ? and this is the manner of them." They are unwarlike, but the Fejîr, the sister tribe, were never contemned by their enemies, which are all those strong free tribes behind them, B. Atîeh, Howeytát, Bíllî, Jeheyna.

The clouds of the second locust brood which the Aarab call *am'dàn*, ' pillars ' [it is the word we read in Exodus—the *ammud* of cloud and fire], wreathing and flickering as motes in the sunbeam, flew over us for some days, thick as rain, from near the soil to great height in the atmosphere. They alight as birds, letting down their long shanks to the ground ; these invaded the booths, and for blind hunger, even bit our shins, as we sat at coffee. They are borne feebly flying at the wind's list, as in the Psalms, " I am tossed up and down as the locust." There fell of them every moment upon the earth, and were dashed

upon the stones.   After this we saw them drifted to the southward : and the Aarab, knowing they must now devour Kheybar,
where their dates would be lost, came forth, and stood to gaze after
them with a fatal indifference ; and with *aha !* they went in to sit
down again, leaving their lot in the hands of Ullah, who they
say is Bountiful.   And oftener than no, the Arabs will smile in
such mishaps, over their own broken hopes, with a kind of godly
melancholy.   The children bring in gathered locusts, broached
upon a twig, and the nomads toast them on the coals ; then
plucking the scorched members, they break away the head,
and the insect body which remains is good meat ; but not of
these latter swarms, born in time of the dried-up herbage.   A
young man at our fire breaking the toasted body of the first,
there fell out a worm, and he cast it from him with loathing ; and
cried, 'akhs! Wellah this cured him of all locust eating.'   Yet
women went out to gather them ; they were of some poor households.   The coffee-drinkers asked of me, " Eat you the locusts
in your béled, Khalíl ; tell us, be they wholesome ? "   (We read
in Leviticus that the children of Jacob might eat the kinds of
locust.)   Nearly every seventh year, in the Arabians' opinion, is
a season of locusts.—This year was remembered for the locust
swarms and for the great summer heat.   The male insect is
yellow, spotted brown, the female somewhat greater and of
a leaden colour.   The pair of glassy wings are spotted, the
inner pair are wide and folded under.   Her length to the end
of the closed wing is nearly three inches.   The Beduins say,
" This is not the eye which appears such, in the head, but that
clear spot under the short first legs."   I took a pen and made the
outline of a locust, and upon the next leaf was another of Abu
Zeyd: all the Arabs came to see these two pictures.   "Very
well, Khalíl," said the simple gazers, " and ha ! his image wellah,
without any difference ! "   And one smutched the lines of the
locust with his fingers, seldom washed, to know if this lay even
upon the smooth paper, and *yeteyr* quoth he " it will rise and
fly ! "   And ever as there came coffee-bibbers to Zeyd's menzil,
they asked for Khalíl, and " Let him show us Abu Zeyd and
his book of pictures;" these were a few prints in my book
of medicine.   Then they wondered to look through my telescope, in which, levelling at any camel a mile distant, they
saw her as it were pasturing before their faces.   Nevertheless,
as a thing which passed their minds, they did not learn to covet
it ; and yet to sharpen their vision the best sighted of them,
seeing as falcons, would needs essay all my eye-washes; for
there is no endowment of nature so profitable to them in this
life of the open wilderness.

Only the starveling hounds of the menzils, in these days, greedily swallowing up locusts, seemed to be in better plight, running gaily in the encampment, sleeping with their fills, and now sullenly careless of the Aarab. Their hounds, say the nomads, " bite the wolf:" they waken all night whilst the Aarab slumber. With the Fejîr, Beduins of a " camel dîra," the " wolf-eaters " are not many, and those of currish kind, nearly like the street dogs of Syria. The best I have seen with any Aarab, were the great shagged dogs of Bíllî, in the Teháma. The common nomad hound is yellowish, shaped as the fox ; the like is seen over most wild parts of the world. A few Beduins have their greyhounds, l'ght with hunger, and very swift to course the hare ; and by these the gazelle fawn is taken. The common barkers of every Beduin village (for they go not out with the flocks), in tribes where the house-mothers have little or no milk to give them, are carrion lean, and· in hunger-times they receive no sustenance of man's hands but a little water : it were hard to say of what uncleanness they then live. Only for a few days once in the long year they are well refreshed : these are in the date-gathering at Kheybar, when the fruit abounding in the Beduins' not improvident hands (above that they may carry,) they give to the camels and asses their fill of dates, and fling also to their wretched hounds largely.

The hounds for their jealous service have never a good word. It is the only life mishandled at home by the gentle Aarab, who with spurns and blows cast out these profane creatures from the beyt, and never touch them (unless it be the unweaned whelps) with their hands. If any dog be an house-thief, a robber of human food, he is chased with hue and cry, and will be most cruelly beaten ; the men swear great oaths ' he shall be dead, he has it well deserved.' This makes that the parasite creature, in these countries, is of more diffident behaviour, towards his masters : only to the nomad greyhound is granted, as of noble kind, to lie down in the booth. The hounds watch all day in the menzil, every one by his household, *ahlahu.* They follow in the ráhla with the baggage-train and their mistress ;. pacing, with a half reasonable gait, in the shadows of the lofty moving camels : impatient of heat and the sand burning under their paws, where they spy any shelter of crag or bush, there they will go in to pant awhile. At the alighting, the booth-cloth is hardly raised, when (if suffered—this is in the sheep-keeper tribes) they creep into the shadow and scrabble the hot sand, and dig with their paws under them, to make their lair upon the cool soil beneath. A dog strayed at the menzil, and running by strange tents, is hooted—*ahl-ak, ahl-ak !*

'to thy household, sirra!' The loud nomad dogs, worrying about the heels of all strange comers, are a sort of police of the nomad encampment. A few of them are perilous snatchers with their teeth ; a man may come by, skirmishing with his camel-stick behind him, and the people call off their dogs. But if there be only hareem at home, which do but look on with a feminine malice, a stranger must beat them off with stone-casts. Some woman may then cry, " Oh ! oh ! wherefore dost thou stone our dog? " And he, " The accursed would have eaten me."—" But, O thou ! cast not at him."—" Then call him in thou foolish woman and that quickly, or with this block now, I may happen to kill him."—" Eigh me ! do not so, this eats the wolf, he watches for the enemy, he is the guard of our beyt and the ghrannem ; I pray thee, no, not another stone."—" Mad woman, before he eat me I will break all the bones in his skin, and cursed be thy tongue ! with less breath thou canst call him off !" In such case, I have not spared for stones, and the silly wife thought herself wronged ; but the men answered, " It was well enough." The hareem, as to whom little is attributed, are naturally of infirmer reason, and liker children in the sentiment of honour ; so there are tents, where the passing guest may not greatly trust them, nor their children.

The sharp-set nomad hounds fall upon aught they may find abroad, as the baggage (when sometimes it is left without the booth) of any stranger guest : then they rend up all with their eager teeth and sharp claws ; therefore to carry in the guests' bags is accounted a charitable deed. Men who are pilferers of others' provision, are often called " hounds " by the Beduins. Hirfa called one of these mornings at my tent door, " Where art thou, Khalîl? I go abroad, and wilt thou the while mind my household ? "—"And whither will my hostess to-day ? "—" I go to buy us yarn : Khalîl, open the eyes and beware, that there come no dogs to my beyt." When she returned some hours after, Hirfa came to chide me, " Ha ! careless Khalîl, the dogs have been here ! why hast thou not kept my beyt ? and did I not bid thee ? "—" I have watched for thee, Hirfa, every moment, by thy life ! sitting before the booth in the sun, and not a hair of any dog has entered."—" Alas, Khalîl does not understand that ' the dogs ' are men ; tell me, Khalîl, who has been here whilst I was out ? "—" There came two men, and when I saw them sheltering in thy apartment, I guessed them to be of kindred and acquaintance ; could I suppose there would any tribesmen steal from a tribesman's beyt ? "—" But these have stolen, said she, a peck of dates, and all by thy fault." In the popular sort of nomads is little or no conscience to rob food (only) ; they holding it as common, kheyr Ullah.

The cheerful summer nights are cool from the sunset in these dry uplands. As they have supped, men wander forth to talk with neighbours, coffee drinkers seek the evening cup : in the mejlis coffee company, the Aarab gossip till midnight. Often in our menzil only the herdsmen remains at home, who wakens to his rough song the grave chord of the rabeyby.

Some moonlight evenings the children hied by us : boys and girls troop together from the mothers' beyts, and over the sand they leap to play at horses, till they find where they may climb upon some sand-hillock or rock. A chorus of the elder girls assemble hither, that with hand-clapping chant the same and ever the same refrain, of a single verse. Little wild boys stripping off their tunics, and flinging down kerchiefs, or that have left all in the mothers' beyts, run out naked ; there being only the *haggu* wound about their slender loins : this is the plaited leathern ribbon, which is worn, and never left, by all the right Arabians, both men and hareem. Every boy-horse has chosen a make, his *fáras* or mare; they course hand in hand together, and away, away, every pair skipping after other and are held themselves in chase in the moonlight wilderness. He kicks back to the horses which chevy after them so fast, and escapes again neighing. And this pastime of Aarab children, of pure race, is without strife of envious hearts, an angry voice is not heard, a blow is not struck among them. The nomads are never brutal. This may last for an hour or two : the younger men will sometimes draw to the merry-make where the young maidens be : they frolic like great camels amongst the small ghrannem ; but not unclad, nor save with the eyes approach they to that chanting bevy of young damsels; an ill-blooded nature appearing in any young man, he shall have the less estimation among them. After the child's age, these indolent Arabians have not any kind of manly pastime among them. Of Ahl Gibly, or southern nomads, I have not seen horsemen so much as exercise themselves upon their mares. Child's play it were in their eyes, to weary themselves, and be never the better. They have none other sport than to fire off their matchlocks in any household festivals. Herdsmen, they are naturally of the contemplative life : weakly fed, there can be little flushing of gross sanguine spirits in their veins, which might move them to manly games ; very rarely is any Beduin robust. Southward of Hâyil I did not see any young woman with the rose blood in her cheeks ; even they are of the summer's drought, and palled at their freshest age.

Now in the mild summer is the season of *muzayyins*,
the Nomad children's circumcision feasts : the mother's booth
is set out with beggarly fringes of scarlet shreds, tufts of
mewed ostrich feathers, and such gay gauds as they may
borrow or find.   Hither a chorus assembles of slender daughters of their neighbours, that should chant at this festival
in their best array.   A fresh kerchief binds about every
damsel's forehead with a feather ; she has ear-rings great as
bracelets, and wears to-day her nose-ring, *zmèyem*:   they are
jewels in silver ; and a few, as said, from old time are fine gold
metal, *thahab el-asfr*.   These are ornaments of the Beduin
women, hardly seen at other times (in the pierced nostril, they
wear for every day a head of cloves), and she has bracelets
of beads and metal finger-rings.   The thin black tresses loosed
to-day and not long, hang down upon their slight shoulders, and
shine in the sun, freshly combed out with camel urine.   The
lasses have borrowed new cloaks, which are the same for man
or woman.   Making a fairy ring apart, they begin, clapping
the palms of their little hands, to trip it round together,
chanting ever the same cadence of few words, which is a single
verse.   Hungered young faces, you might take them for some
gipsy daughters ; wayward not seldom in their mother's households, now they go playing before men's eyes, with downcast
looks and a virginal timidity.   But the Aarab raillery is never
long silent, and often the young men, in this daylight feast,
stand jesting about them.   Some even pluck roughly at the
feathers of the lasses, their own near cousins, in the dance,
which durst answer them nothing, but only with reproachful
eyes : or laughing loud the weleds have by and by divided
this gentle bevy among them for their wives ;   and if a
stranger be there, they will bid him choose which one he
would marry among them.   "Heigh-ho ! what thinkest thou
of these maidens of ours, and her, and her, be they not fair-
faced ? "   But the virgins smile not, and if any look up, their
wild eyes are seen estranged and pensive.   They are like
children under the rod, they should keep here a studied demeanour ; and for all this they are not Sirens.   In that male
tyranny of the Mohammedan religion regard is had to a distant
maidenly behaviour of the young daughters ; and here they
dance as the tender candidates for happy marriage, and the
blessed motherhood of sons.   May their morrow approach !
which shall be as this joyful day, whose hap they now sing,
wherein a man-child is joined to the religion of Islam ; it
is better than the day of his birth. The nomad son is circumcised being come to the strength of three full years ; and then

as the season may serve without any superstition of days, and as the mother shall be able to provide corn or rice enough for her guests' supper. They sometimes put off the surgery till the mor ow, in any rough windy weather, or because of the Aarab's ráhla.

. The friends of the father will come in to be his guests : some of them have adorned themselves with the gunner's belt and gay baldric, rattling with the many little steel chains and brass powder-cases ; and they bear upon their shoulders the long matchlocks. Therewith they would prove their hand to shoot, at the sheep's skull, which the child's *babbu* has sacrificed to ' the hospitality.' Every man kills his sacrifice, as in the ancient world, with his own hands, and the carcase is flayed and brittled with the Arabs' expedition. Nomads are all expert fleshers ; the quarters hang now upon some bush or boughs, which wandering in an open wilderness, they have sought perhaps upon a far mountain side. As the sun goes low the meat is cast into the caldron, jidda. The great inwards remain suspended upon their trophy bush. After the flesh, a mess is cooked in the broth of such grain as they have. The sun setting, the maidens of the ring-dance disperse : the men now draw apart to their prayers, and in this time the cattle of every household are driven in. The men risen from their prayers, the supper is served in the tent : often thirty men's meat is in that shield-wide wooden platter which is set before them. A little later some will come hither of the young herdsmen returning boisterous from the field ; they draw to the merry noise of the muzayyin that feel a lightness in their knees to the dance. A-row, every one his arm upon the next one's shoulder, these laughing weleds stand, full of good humour ; and with a shout they foot it forth, reeling and wavering, advancing, recoiling in their chorus together ; the while they hoarsely chant the ballad of a single verse. The housewives at the booth clap their palms, and one rising with a rod in her hand, as the dancing men advance, she dances out to meet them ; it is the mother by likelihood, and joyously she answers them in her song : whilst they come on bending and tottering a-row together, with their perpetual refrain. They advancing upon her, she dances backward, feinting defence with the rod ; her face is turned towards them, who maintain themselves, with that chanted verse of their manly throats, as it were pursuing and pressing upon her.—The nomads imagine even the necessity of circumcision : graziers, they will allege the examples of all cattle, that only in the son of Adam may be found this manner of impediment. When they questioned me I have said, " You can amend then the work of Ullah ! "—" Of

that we speak not, they answered, but only of the expediency."
Questioned, What be the duties of a Moslem? they responded
" That a man fast in the month, and recite his daily prayers ; "—
making no mention of the circumcision, which they call " purification."

The 15th of April, after a morning wind, blustering cold
from the north-eastward, I found early in the afternoon, with
still air and sunshine, the altitude being 4000 feet, 95 deg. F.
in the booth's shelter. The drooping herb withered, the summer
drought entering, the wilderness changed colour ; the spring
was ended. The Beduins removed and lodged in their desolate
camps : upon a morrow, when the camels had been driven forth
an hour, an alarm was given from the front, of gôm. A herdsman came riding in, who had escaped, upon a thelûl, and told
it in the mejlis, " él-'bil, the camel-herds are taken." The
sheukh rose from the hearth and left their cups with grave
startled looks : all went hardily out, and hastily, to find their
mares. Hovering haramîyeh had been seen yesterday, and
now every man hied to take arms. The people ran, like angry
wasps, from the booths : some were matchlock men, some had
spears, all were afoot, save the horsemen sheykhs, and hastened
forth to require their enemies, which could not be seen in
that short desert horizon : bye and bye only the housewives,
children and a few sick and old men were left in the encampment. Some asked me would I not ride to set upon the
thieves ; for Zeyd's talk had been that Khalîl would foray with
them. " Khalîl (cried the housewives), look for us in your wise
books ; canst thou not prophesy by them (shûf f'il ghraib) :
read thou and tell us what seest thou in them of these gomânies.—A punishment fall upon them ! they certainly espied
the people's watch-fires here this last night, and have been
lurking behind yonder mountain until the camels were driven
out."—The long morning passed over us, in the cold incer-
titude of this misadventure.

Motlog had ridden days before to Hâyil to treat with the
emir, and left Rahŷel to govern the tribe ; a man of perplexed
mind in this sudden kind of conjuncture. The armed tribesmen returning after midday, we went to sit in the mejlis and
talk over this mishap. I heard no word spoken yet of pursuing ;
and enquiring of my neighbour, " Ay, they would mount their
thelûls, said he, so soon as the 'bil were come home at evening ; "
for all the great cattle were not taken, but those which had been
driven forth from the north side of the menzil. Celerity is
double strokes in warfare, but these Beduins sat still the long

day and let the robbers run, to wonder what they were ; they
all said, "some Aarab of the North," for they had seen them
armed with pistols.   They reasoned whether those should be
Sherarát or Howeytát Ibn Jàsy (Beduins from about Maan) ; or
else of the Ruwàlla. " Hear me, and I shall make it known to
you, said Zeyd (who had this vanity among them), what they
were.   I say then, *es-Sokhûr*, and ye shall find it true."   The
few words which had fallen from the foemen's lips were now
curiously examined.   They had challenged the camel herds,
" What Aarab be ye—ha ! the Fejîr ? " but this could not suffice
to distinguish the *loghrat* of a tribe.   The gôm were thirteen
horsemen, and twenty riders upon thelûls.   In driving off the
booty a mare broke loose from them, and she was led into the
encampment, but of that nothing could be learned, the nomad
sheykhs not using to brand their horses with the tribe's cattle-
mark.   This mare, by the third day, perished of thirst ! that
none would pour out to her of their little water.   If a tribesman's goat stray among them, and her owner be not known,
none will water her.   In the time when I was with them, I saved
the lives of a strayed beast or two, persuading some of my
patients to give them drink.

They now reckoned in the mejlis the number of camels
taken, saying over the owners' names : Zeyd kept count,
scoring a new line for every ten in the sand ; so he told them
and found six score and seven camels—the value of £600' or
more.   All this tribes' camels were not so many as 2000,
nor I think fully 1500 ; and the whole fortune of the Fukara
Beduins in the field, two hundred households, their great
and small cattle with the booths and utensils, I suppose, not
to exceed £17,000.   Besides which is their landed patrimony
at Kheybar, that may be worth £7000 more.   A household of
these poor southern Beduins may thus, I think, possess the
capital value of £120 sterling ; and much like to them are their
nomad neighbours about.   In the same small tribe there are
nobles and commons, the sufficient livelihood, and the pittance,
and abject misery.   The great sheykh Motlog, possessing more
than other men, had not so many of his own as twenty-five camels.
There is difference also between tribe and tribe ; the great
tribes of the north, as the Annezy in Syria, and the northern
Shammar upon Mesopotamia, wandering in plenteous country,
are rich in cattle and horses : so also may be reckoned Kahtân
and *Ateyby* of the southern tribes, (their dîras we shall see are
watered by the yearly monsoon ;) but these middle tribes of
nomads, in a rainless land, are " weaker."   Those at the haj
road which receive a surra, are the most coffee-lazing, beggarly

and pithless minded of them all. The Fejîr sheukh divided between them, every year, I think about £600 of these payments! whereof almost an hundred pounds fell to Zeyd, who received his father's surra, and £160 to Motlog : besides some changes of clothing, grain, and certain allowances for their tents, and utensils ; yet poor they all were, and never the better. Motlog's halàl, or ' lawful own ' of cattle, his mare and his tent and household gear together, were worth, I think, not £300 : add to this for his funded property at Kheybar, and we may find he possessed hardly above £500.

The Aarab trifled time which could never be theirs again ; the housewives made some provision ready for those that should mount at evening. This mounting is at every man's free will, and yet the possessor of a thelûl cannot shun the common service and keep his honest name. Rahŷel led the pursuit. Some as they sat boasted, " This night or towards morning, when the haramîyeh think themselves come in security, and are first reposing, we shall be suddenly upon them, and recover our own, if the Lord will, and take their beasts from under them." As camels are driven off in a foray, the robbers chase them all that day at a run before them, hoping to outgo the pursuit ; and now as the sun was setting, these might be gotten almost fifty miles in advance. The last words were, as they rose, " Please God, every camel of those taken shall be couched again, to-morrow about this time, before the booth of his household : " and with this good augury the company dispersed, going to their suppers, and afterward the riders would take their thelûls, the sheykhs (for a long pursuit) not leading their mares with them. Zeyd sat still at home ; he had two thelûls, he said " they were ailing." Khálaf sat also close in his booth, a man who, though vaunting his mare's worth at so many camels and himself of the principal W. Aly sheykhs, had not a beast to mount. A weak reason is found too light in the balance of public estimation ; and Zeyd all the next day sitting melancholy, sipping much coffee, vehemently protested to be ever since sorry, by Ullah, that he was not ridden along with them.

His camels were saved that day, feeding on the other side of the desert ; but a calamity as this is general, and to be borne by the tribe. None which had lost their cattle to-day would be left destitute.; but the governing sheykh taxing all the tribesmen, the like would be rendered to them, out of the common contribution, in a day or two. He will send some round as assessors to the menzils, where every man's state being known, the computation is made of the cattle of every household. There was levied of Zeyd the next day, of less than twenty that he had, a camel, and the value of certain head of small cattle. The nomad tribes we have seen to be commonwealths of brethren, ruled by their sheykhs with an equitable moderation. They divide each others' losses, and even in such there is community between whole tribes. Mischief is never far from them, an evil day may chance which has not befallen them in many years, when a tribe is stripped at a stroke, of nearly all its cattle, as later in my knowledge, the Moahîb.—And what then ? The next Billî of free-will gave them, of their own, much cattle.

If cattle be robbed of any strangers dwelling in the tribe, the tribesmen are not bound, as neither upon those should fall any contribution for the losses of their hosts : yet there are magnanimous tribes, (I have heard it told of Shammar,) that will give somewhat, of free-will, to him who has long time lived in fellowship amongst them, in his afflicted case. If any villager has entrusted beasts to a nomad, to graze with his own cattle, and they are reaved by the tribe's enemies, the villager will demand his own, and scurvily attach the Beduwy, as his debtor, if he may take him again in his village : but the Beduwy, whose law does not bind him to such restitutions, will be ware, and no more adventure thither. These controversies are long-lived, and often the old grudges are inherited among them, to the third generation.—The law of Israel is for the villager in this case, and enjoins the grazier's restitution of the entrusted cattle. There is also amongst Beduins a loss without remedy, when a man's beasts are taken and the sheykhs in the mejlis find that the loss is his own, and not in the public abventure of the tribe. The unhappy tribesmen bitterly calls his sheykhs unjust, he is bare and they will not repair his undoing out of the public stock : I have known some such, sad men for life. I have known also well-faring Beduins suddenly come to poverty, when their camels had all died of a murrain. As in the whole world, so among this poor folk, it is much, in the evil day, to be well befriended. At the good and liberal man's need, every one of his fellowship will bring him a head of the flock in his hand ; so may he come to a little strength again.

Their ghrazzus and counter-ghrazzus are the destruction of the Aarab. Reaving and bereaved they may never thrive ; in the end of every tide it is but an ill exchange of cattle. So in the eyes of nomads, the camel troops of the Fukara were all " mingled " cattle and uneven, that is, not home-born-like, but showing to be robbed beasts out of several dîras. Motlog's son said to me, he who should be great sheykh after him, " Ay,

wellah! all our camels are harràm, (of prey taken in the forays,)
and not our lawful own." The Fejîr were impoverished of late
years, by their neighbours' incursions : Bishr, and after them
the W. Aly, had taken their flocks ; but they lost most by a
murrain, in these hot sandy marches, a kind of colic, in which
there had died nearly all the remnant of their small cattle.
A year before, Zeyd had a great mixed herd of goats and
sheep, so that Hirfa, the last spring time, made a camel
load and a half (as much as £18 worth) of samn.　Now I saw
but an ewe and two milch goats left to them, which yielded in
the day but a short bowl of milk, and, discouraged, he would
not buy more.　Zeyd had inherited òf his father, who was the
former great sheykh's brother, a large landed patrimony of
palm-stems at Kheybar : the half fruit being to the negro
husbandmen, his own rent was, he told me, nearly 200 reals.
Thus Zeyd, with his surra, had spending silver for every day, in
good years, of nearly two reals, the value of a goat, which is
much money in the khála : yet the man was miserable, and
loving to defer payments, he was always behind the hand with
old usury.　Sheykhs of the B. Wáhab lay up their money,
tháhab, (spared from the haj surra,) at el-Ally ; out of this, one
who is low will increase his " halàl " silently, and may sometime
go to the bottom of his bag to purchase him a new mare.

Rahŷel's pursuing party was three nights out.　The
men left in camp being now very few, they came continually
together to drink coffee.　The affectionate housewives sat abroad
all day watching : at mid-afternoon, the fourth after, we heard
the hareem's jubilee, *lullilu!*—but the merry note died away in
their throats when, the longer they looked, they saw those that
came riding in the horizon were leading nothing home with
them.　The men rose together, and going forth, they gazed
fixedly.　" What, said they, means this cry of the hareem ? for
look, they arrive empty-handed, and every man is riding apart
to alight at his own household ! " so returning to their fatal
indolence, they reentered as men that are losers, and sat down
again.　" Some of them, they said, will presently bring us
tidings."　Rahŷel soon after dismounted at his tent, pitched
near behind us.—The housewife comes forth as her husband
makes his thelûl kneel ; she receives him in silence, unsaddles
the beast, and carries in his gear.　The man does not often
salute her openly, nor, if he would to the mejlis, will he
speak to his wife yet ; so Rahŷel, without entering his tooth,
stepped over to us.—" Peace be with you ! " said he from a dry
throat ; and seating himself with the sigh of a weary man, in

some sadness, he told us, ' that in the second day, following the enemy upon the Nefûd, they came where a wind had blown out the prints,' and said he, " So Ullah willed it ! " They turned then their beasts' heads,—they had no list to cast further about, to come again upon the robbers' traces. " Ha well ! God would have it so ! " responded the indolent Aarab. A weak enemy they thus faintly let slip through their fingers, for a little wind, though these were driving with them nearly a tithe of all their camels. But Rahŷel, to knit up his sorry tale with a good ending, exclaimed, ' Wellah, they had found water at the wells el-Hŷza in the Nefûd ; and as they came again by Teyma, he heard word that some of the gôm had touched there, and they were of the Sherarát : "—Rahŷel, with his troop, had ridden nearly two hundred idle miles. " By and by we shall know (said the Beduins) which tribesmen robbed our camels ; then will we *ghrazzy* upon them, and God willing, take as many of them again." But the ghrazzus often return empty : a party of Fukara, " twenty *rikáb* " or warfaring thelûls, which rode lately upon the Beny Atîeh, had taken nothing.

Every man leans upon his own hand in the open desert, and there will none for naught take upon him a public service. The sheykh may persuade, he cannot compel any man ; and if the malcontent will go apart, he cannot detain them. The common body is weak, of members so loosely knit together, and there befalls them many an evil hap, which by a public policy might have been avoided.—" Why send you not out scouts, (thus I reasoned with Zeyd,) which might explore the khála in advance of your pasturing cattle ? or cannot you set some to watch in the tops of the rocks, for the appearing of an enemy ! Why commit yourselves thus to wild hazard, who are living openly in the midst of danger ? " When Zeyd gravely repeated my words in the mejlis, the sheykh's son answered readily, " Ay, and that were very well, if we might put it in practice ; but know, Khalîl, there are none of the Beduw will thus adventure themselves by twos or threes together, for fear of the habalîs, we cannot tell where they lie until thou hearest from behind a crag or bush *deh !* and the shot strikes thee."

Later in the week Motlog came again from Hâyil : he had not before been thither, nor his companions ; but they crossed an hundred miles over the open khála guided by sight only of the mountain landmarks, which they had enquired before-hand. We had shifted ground many times in his absence ; and it was strange for me to see them ride in, without having

erred, to our menzil. As the journeys of the tribesmen are
determined beforehand, they might reckon, within a day's
distance, where riding they should fall upon our traces, which
finding they will follow the fresh footing of our late ráhla ;
and climbing on all heights as they come, they look for the black
booths of the Aarab. Thus these land-navigators arrive by
and by at the unstable village port of their voyage. All the
tribesmen which were not abroad herding, assembled to parliament, where they heard Motlog was gone down, to his brother
Rahŷel's tent, to hear their shekyh give account of his embassy
to the emir, which imported so much to the policy of their
little desert nation.—Every man had armed his hand with the
tobacco-pipe, and, said each one arriving, "Strengthen thee,
O Motlog!" and to the great sheykh he handed up his galliûn.
Motlog sat freshly before them, in his new apparel, the accustomed gift of the emir, and he filled all their pipe-heads
benignly, with the aromatic tittun *el-Hameydy* of Mesopotamia ;
of which he had brought with him a few weeks' cheer, from
the village capital. The coffee was slowly served round, to
so great an assembly. Burdensome was that day's heat, and
now the mid-day's sun overhead, yet there was none who
thought of going to his slumber, or even to eat ; such was
all the people's expectation to hear the mind of the terrible
emir. They sat this day out, no man moving from his place,
and yet fasting, except only from coffee and tittun, till the
evening.—The prince licensed them to return, without fear, into
their own dîra.

The vassals of Ibn Rashîd receive, after the audience, a
change of clothing ; besides, the emir bestowed sixty silver
reals upon Motlog, and gave ten pieces to each of his way-
fellows. These are arts of the Arabian governors, to retain,
with a pretended bounty, the slippery wills of the wild Beduw ;
and well sown is the emir's penny, if he should reap, in the
next years, ten-fold. Motlog was sheykh of one of the tribu-
tary tribes, a little wide of his reach. The tax upon the
nomads is light, and otherwise it could never be gathered ; a
crown piece is payment for every five camels, or for thirty head
of small cattle. Of the Fukara was levied thus but four
hundred reals, which is somewhat as eight or nine shillings for
every household : yet the free-born, forlorn and predatory Beduw
grimly fret their hearts under these small burdens ; the emir's
custom is ever untimely, the exaction, they think, of a stronger,
and plain tyranny : yet yielding this tribute, they become of
the prince's federation, and are sheltered from all hostility of
the Aarab in front. Motlog was a prudent man, of reach and

sight ; but he could not see through sixty reals. This was a
pleasant policy of the emir, and by the like the wisest man's
heart is touched ; and the nomad sheykh brought back, in
his new smelling clothes, a favourable opinion, for the while, of
the flattering prince, and Hâyil government ; and thought in
his heart, to be the prince's liegeman, for the present, of whom
he had received so gentle entertainment. But the haughty
Mohammed Ibn Rashîd, who paid the scot, had another opinion
of him ; the emir afterward told me, with his own mouth, that
he misliked this Motlog.

Blithe were the Fukara to return to their home marches,
and better to them than all this high desolate country, which
(said they) is ' *ghror*, a land wherein is nothing good, for man
nor cattle.' Also, they think that dîra better, by which the
derb el-haj passes ; they say, " We have a kella," that is
a house of call, and store-chambers, the caravan market is
held there, and their sheukh receive súrra. On the morrow
we marched ; and the Beduins henceforth removed every day
by short journeys ; now their face was homeward. Behind us we
left J. Misma, then some mountain which I heard named *Roaf* :
the third day we came to drink upon the upland, at a wide
standing water, in a gravel bed, which in winter is a lake-plash,
of the ponded rain, *Therrai*.

We marched then in a sandstone country, where, for
crags, thick as loaves in a baker's oven, we could not see
the next riders about us. From the fifth march, we
alighted again under Birrd, to water, in the natural deep chaps
of the precipitous sandstone mountain : the herdsmen, digging
shallow pits with their hands in the fetid sand, took up in
buckets, with their waterer's song, a sandy foul water. We
removed now daily, loading before dawn, and alighting at high
noon. In another march we came, under the flaming sun, over
the high open plain, a barren floor of gravel, towards a great
watering place and summer station of the tribe, *el-Erudda*.
These uplands are mostly without growth of the desert acacia
trees : woe is therefore the housewife, for any tent-peg lost
in the ráhla. Yet now appeared a long line of acacias, and a
white swelling country, these are the landmarks of el-Erudda ;
and here, at the midst of their dîra, is a *mákbara*, or common
burying-place of the tribe, with few barren plants of wild
palms. It is hardly a journey from hence to el-Héjr : the
Beduins would be here umjemmîn, for many days.

Camels strayed the next night from Zeyd's menzil ; the
owners scoured the country, hoping to have sight of them, for
where all the soil was trodden down with innumerable foot-

prints of the tribe's cattle, they could not distinguish the traces. It was not that they feared their beasts, losing themselves, must in few days perish with thirst : the great dull and sheep-like cattle have a perfect conscience of all watering places of their home dîra; though, for all their long necks, in but very few of them might they attain to drink. Three years before, when the Fukara were in Syria, some camels of theirs, frayed and lost near the Hauran, had been recovered by tribesmen returning later in the year from Medina, who, crossing their own dîra, found these beasts feeding about a watering, in the border of the Hejâz. The men knew them, by the brand, to be some of their tribe's cattle, and brought up again those fugitive camels, which had fled to their native marches, over seven geographical degrees.

We had no more notice of the haramîyeh.—Then, by a Solubby family which arrived from over the Harra, there came uncertain tidings, that their cattle had been retaken by the Moahîb : a small Moahîb foray riding in the north had crossed the robbers; (hostile ghrazzus, meeting in the wilderness, hail each other, *ya gôm !* "ho ! ye enemies,") but not able to over-take the main body of them, they had cut off but fifteen camels. The custom of one real salvage, for a head, is paid between friendly tribes, and they are restored to the owners.

At length we understood that the robbers, as Zeyd fore-told, had been a party of Beny Sókhr, who from their tents in Syria, to the place where they met with us had ridden out not less than four hundred miles; and in their company there rode a few men of the Sherarát nomads who are part friends, part "not well" with the Fejîr. As for the Sokhûr, our Beduins reckoned them thitherto neither friends nor enemies ; yet certain Fukara households, of the northern migration, were wandering with that tribe to this day. A ragged rout of B. Sókhr, carriers to the Haj, must every year pass, with the caravan, through the Fukara country.—On behalf of the Fejîr a young sheykh, *Mijwel,* was sent after this to the North, to treat peace-ably with the B. Sókhr for the restitution of his tribe's camels. The elders of B. Sókhr responded in the mejlis, "They that had reaved the Fukara cattle were a company of ignorant young men ; but their ignorance to be less blameworthy because they found the Fejîr wandering out of their own dîra." The sheykhs promised that good part of the cattle should be brought again with the Haj ; the rest they would have conceded to the turbu-lent young men, "which must be appeased, with somewhat for their pains, and that for an end of strife." More might not Mijwel obtain : and this is as much justice as may commonly be had in the world.

Now, arrived at el-Erudda, my mind was to forsake the Beduin life and pass by el-Ally to the sea coast at el-Wejh. My friends bade me speak with Motlog in the matter of my camel. Why did not Zeyd obey the pasha's injunction ?—and then this mischief had not chanced. I had not the price of another camel,—hard must be my adventure henceforth in land of Arabia. The custom of the desert is that of Moses, ' If any man's beast hurt the beast of another man, the loss shall be divided.' Frolic in the succulent spring herbage, the great unwieldly brutes rise in the night with full cuds to play their whale-sports together ; some camel then, as the Beduins held, had fallen upon the neck of my gaping young camel : whether it happened then, or in the camels' bouncing forth to their morning pasture, it was among Zeyd's troop of camels. I must bring witnesses : but who would give testimony against a sheykh of his tribe, for the Nasrâny ? Amongst Mohammedans, and though they be the Beduins of the wilderness, there is equity only between themselves. I found Motlog in his tent, who with a woollen thread was stitching in his mare's saddle-pad. " A pity, said the sheykh, that any controversy should grow betwixt Khalîl and Zeyd, who were brethren, but the Pasha's words ought to have been observed." Zeyd was disappointed in me of his greedy hopes ; fortune had given us both checkmate since the hope of my vaccination had failed ; there remained only my saddle-bags, and his eyes daily devoured them. Great they were, and stuffed to a fault, in a land where passengers ride without baggage. Heavy Zeyd found their draught, and he felt in them elbow-deep day by day, which was contrary to the honourable dealing of an host ;—besides my apprehension that he might thus light upon my pistol and instruments, which lay hidden at the bottom in our menzils.

For these displeasures, in the last râhla I had forsaken Zeyd, and came on walking over the waste gravel, under the scalding sun many miles till the Aarab alighted. Zeyd found in his heart that he had done me wrong, I had not deceived him, and he respected my person : I also heedfully avoided to rake up the wild unknown depths of their Mohammedan resentment. I entered Motlog's tent, the sheykhly man sat playing with his children, he was a very affectionate father. Thither came Zeyd soon and sat down to drink coffee ; then raising his portentous voice said he, " If I had not intended to devour him, wellah, I had not received the Nasrâny ; I would not have suffered him to accompany the Aarab, no not in a râhla. The Nasrâny gave sixty reals (a fable) to Mohammed Aly, and I require the like to be paid me in this hour." " No,

(Motlog answered from behind the women's curtain, whither he was gone for somewhat,) this is not in thy hand, O Zeyd." Zeyd complaining that my being in his menzil was an expense to him, I proved that Zeyd had received of me certain reals, and besides a little milk I had taken of him nothing : but his meaning was that I brought too many coffee guests, who all came thither to see the stranger. Zeyd had bought two reals worth in the haj market. " Here (I said) is that money, and let Zeyd trust further to my friendly possibility. Zeyd complains of me with little cause ; I might complain with reason ; should one treat his guest's baggage as thing which is taken in the ghrazzu ? he seeks even in my purse for money, and in my belt, and ransacks my bags."—"Ha ! how does Zeyd ? " said some sheykh's voice. I answered, in my haste, " Billah, like an hablûs." Motlog shrank at the word, which had been better unsaid ; the Beduins doubted if they heard Khalîl aright : the worst was that Zeyd in all his life came so near to merit this reproachful word, which uttered thus in the mejlis, must cleave to him in the malicious memory of his enemies. He rose as he had sipped the cup and left us. In our evening mirth the hinds often called to each other, hablûs ! hablûs ! which hearing, and I must needs learn their speech of the Arabs, I had not supposed it amiss : but Zeyd vaunted himself sherîf. When he was gone out some said, so had Zeyd done to such and such other, Zeyd was a bad man ; (the Beduw easily blame each other). Said Motlog, ' in the question of the camel I must bring witnesses, but he would defend me from all wrongful demands of Zeyd.'

As we sat, one came in who but then returned from an absence ; as the custom is he would first declare his tidings in the mejlis, and afterward go home to his own household. He sat down on his knee, but was so poor a man, there was none in the sheykhly company that rose to kiss him : with a solemn look he stayed him a moment on his camel-stick, and then pointing gravely with it to every man, one after other, he saluted him with an hollow voice, by his name, saying, " The Lord strengthen thee ! " A poor old Beduin wife, when she heard that her son was come again, had followed him over the hot sand hither ; now she stood to await him, faintly leaning upon a stake of the beyt a little without, since it is not for any woman to enter where the men's mejlis is sitting. His tidings told, he stepped abroad to greet his mother, who ran, and cast her weak arms about his manly neck, trembling for age and tenderness, to see him alive again and sound ; and kissing him she could not speak, but uttered little cries. Some of the coffee-drinkers

laughed roughly, and mocked her drivelling, but Motlog said,
" Wherefore laugh ? is not this the love of a mother ? "

Selím came soon to call me from his father ; " Well, go with
Selím, said Motlog, and be reconciled to Zeyd ; and see that
neither require aught of the other." Zeyd invited me into his
wife's closed apartment, where we sat down, and Hirfa with us, to
eat again the bread and salt together. Zeyd soon returned from
these rubs, when he could not find his ' brother ' in fault, to the
Beduin good humour, and leaning on his elbow he would reach
over, pledge of our friendship, the peaceable sebîl, I should
' drink ' with him tobacco :—and such are the nomads. Our late
contention was no more mentioned, but it was long after branded
in Zeyd's mind, that Khalîl had called him hablûs. In the
autumn of this year, when the Fukara lay encamped at el-Héjr,
and I was again with them, as I passed by Zeyd's menzil, he
called me from the beyt, " *ya Khalîl taal!* come hither," I
greeted him, and also the housewife behind the curtain
" *gowwich Hirfa*, the Lord strengthen thee."—Zeyd answered,
" It is the voice of Khalîl, and the words of a Beduwy ; " and he
rose to bring me in to eat a bowl of rice with him, which was
then ready. After meat, " he was glad to see me, he said, once
more here in his beyt, it was like the old times ; " then a little
casting down his eyes he added, " but after our friendship I was
wounded, Khalîl, when you named me hablûs, and that before
the sheukh."—" Because you had threatened and displeased me ;
but, Zeyd, let not this trouble thee ; how could I know all the
words of you Beduins ? Seest thou these black worsted tents ?
Are they not all booths of hablûses ? " We walked down to the
mejlis, where Zeyd related, smiling, that my meaning had been
but to name him " thou Beduwy."

—When I reasoned with Zeyd, " Why didst thou not do as
the Pasha commanded ? " cried he, " Who commands me ! *henna*
(we are) *el-Beduw :* what is Pasha, or what is the Dowla here?
save only that they pay us our surra, and else we would take it
by force."—" What is your force ? were an hundred of you, with
club-sticks, lances, and old matchlocks, worth ten of the haj
soldiery ?"—"We would shoot down upon them in the boghrazát."
" And how far may your old rusty irons shoot ? " Zeyd answered,
between jest and solemnity, " *Arbaa saa,*" to four hours distance : Saat is with the Aarab ' a stound,' a second or third space
between the times of prayer. Often they asked me, " How many
hours be there in the day ? We know not well *saa.*" Their
partitions of the daylight are *el-féjr*, the dawning before the
sun ; *el-gaila*, the sun rising towards noon ; *eth-thôhr*, the sun
in the mid-day height ; *el-assr*, the sun descended to mid-after-

noon ; *ghraibat es-shems,* the sun going down to the setting :
—*mághrib* is a strange town speaking in their ears.

The nomads' summer station at el-Erudda was now as an
uncheerful village. In the time of wandering since the Haj, the
sheykhs had spent their slender stores of coffee ; and " where
no coffee is, there is not merry company," say the Aarab. Their
coffee hearths now cold, every man sat drooping and dull,
fi ahlahu, in his own household. Said Zeyd, " This was the life
of the old nomads in the days before coffee." The sheukh would
soon send down for more coffee of theirs which was stored at
Medáin ; and Zeyd must go thither to fetch up a sack of rice,
which he had also deposited in the kella : I would then ride
with him, intending to pass by el-Ally to the Red Sea coast.
The wilderness fainted before the sunny drought ; the harvest
was past, and I desired to be gone. The Aarab languished lying
in the tents ; we seemed to breathe flames. All day I gasped and
hardly remained alive, since I was breathless, and could not
eat. I had sometimes a thought in the long days to teach Selím
letters : but when his son had learned the alphabet Zeyd would
no more, lest the child should take of me some faulty utterance ;
my tongue he said was not yet "loosed." Having a vocabulary
in my hand, now and then I read out a page or two to the
company. Certainly I could not err much in the utterance of
many words that were before well known to me ; but no small
part of these town and bookish terms were quite unknown to all
my nomad hearers ! of some it seemed they had not the roots,
of many they use other forms. They wondered themselves, and
as Arabs will (who have so much feeling in their language and
leisure to be eloquent) considered word after word with a patient
attention. Thus when simple tribesmen come sometime in
their lives to enter any good town in the border-lands, the city
speech sounds wonderfully quaint in their hearing, ' they wot
hardly, they complain, what these townspeople should mean.'
The bookish speech is raised upon the old koran Arabic, which
was a lowland language, and never perhaps the tongue of the
upland Aarab. [If this were doubted, it seems to be confirmed by the learned Interpreters of the desert inscriptions,
v. p. 187 and *Doc. Épigr.*]

The evening before our departure, Mehsan had sacrificed a
sheep, the year's-mind of his father here lying buried, and
brought us of his cooked meat ; he was Zeyd's brother-in-law,
and we were a homely company. I made them sweet tea ; and
distributed presents of the things which I had. As we sat

I asked these Beduins if my *gaûd* (young camel) with the broken mouth could carry me a hundred and fifty miles to el-Wejh ? One sitting with us proffered, so I would give him ten reals, to exchange his own nâga for mine. Zeyd and Mehsan approving, I gave the money ; but the meditations of the Arabs are always of treachery. The poor man's wife and children also playing the weepers, I gave them besides all that I might spare of clothing, of which they have so much need in the desert ; but after other days I saw my things put to sale at Teyma. I bought thus upon their trust, a dizzy camel, old, and nearly past labour and, having lost her front teeth, that was of no more value, in the sight of the nomads, than my wounded camel. I was new in their skill ; the camels are known and valued after their teeth, and with regard to the hump. They are named by the teeth till the coming of the canines in this manner: the calf of one year, *howwar ;* of two, *libny ;* the third, *hej ;* the fourth, *jitha ;* the fifth, *thènny ;* the sixth, *ròbba ;* the seventh, *siddes ;* and the eighth, *shâgg en-naba, wafîat, mùfter.*

CHAPTER XIII.

MEDÁIN REVISITED. PASSAGE OF THE HARRA.

WHEN the day dawned, we departed: and soon there appeared before us the immane black platform of the Harra mountain; the large desert lying between seeming a hollowness below our feet, in which passes the haj road. Some miles further we saw two or three men skulking among the rocks far off, where we entered a cragged country; our company of five or six persons took them for habalîs. We found before us the new sprung herb and better pasture than we had seen of late; but this soil is seldom visited by the Beduw, ' unless, said Zeyd, when sometimes we are removing and encamping together with the W. Aly.' Here near a main passage from the north, they were, although in their own dîra, in too much danger of robbers. In this sinking upland, grew certain tall white toadstools; some of our fellowship gathered them, and these, being boiled with alum in the urine of camels that have fed of the bush el-humth, yield they told me the gay scarlet dye of the Beduin wool-wives.

At mid-afternoon we passed before a wall of rock, where I perceived a well-traced antique inscription, nearly in the Naba-

tean character of Medáin Sâlih ; this only, of all the desert
legends, is contained in a border. As I leapt down of a sudden,

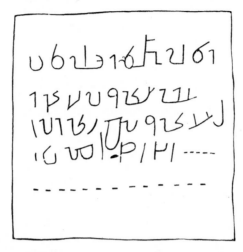

my dizzy camel fled from me, but was out-ridden and turned
by Zeyd upon his thelûl. This I could conjecture to be some
wayside inscription. A little more, and we come plainly into an
ancient way, which is marked through this coast of mountains,
down to the plain of el-Héjr, by heaps of stones. " They were
to show the road,' said my companions. This is the old way between Héjr and Teyma. The old haj road, say the Beduins,
passed by Teyma, and we know that a branch of the antique
trade-road ascended thus to Syria. [Sprenger *Alte Geogr. Arabiens.*] A droughty southern wind blew all that day against
us, which parches the throat, without refreshment : the Aarab
marching, covered their faces, to the eyes, with a lap of the
kerchief. This is the hot blast of thin air, which they call " the
pestilent," simûm. The sun was set as we came down by a
sandy steep, near the strange landmark (fig. p. 243) of a sandstone rock which resembles a pawn at chess, to the plain-
bottom of Medáin, here much beset with great-grown desert
bushes. Among these sand mounds and undergrowths, we met
in the darkness with another Beduin party, and challenged
them ; they knowing our voices, hailed us cheerfully again, they
were marketers of our tribesmen, returning from el-Ally.

It was the third hour of the night when we beat at the iron
plate door of the kella. Haj Hasan ran, at the noise, with the
lad Mohammed, upon the tower head, and looked from the

battlements, and fiercely they called down to know what men we were, that troubled their rest at these hours. Then, hearing our voices, the flung down stairs with immoderate laughter, and came to unspar the door for us ; we entered, welcomed as old friends, and ascended to the coffee chamber. Haj Nejm came shuffling down in his sandals, with a host's smile to see us. The fire was blown again in the hearth, and he sat to make his guests coffee ; as we drank, and were long talking, Haj Nejm fetched us in a great dish of girdle-bread, which his wife in this while had baked and buttered, for the guests' supper. "Poor fare (quoth the hospitable old man) to set before you, but ye come late, and what is there in the kella ! "—" Would you treat us then (said Zeyd) as strangers ? are we not here at home, Naj Nejm ? " It was friendly answered, nevertheless the jealous old tower-keeper winced, for a sting that came in the tail of it, he might remember when those Fejîr sheykhs had seized the kella.—" And Khalîl, thou art come again, *murabba*, fat of the spring pasture ? (cries the young half Beduin lad Mohammed). Aha, the spring ! the pleasant spring! Oh then is the milk-season in the khála, and it is good to be with the Aarab." Zeyd, making his words at first flow softly with some praises and caresses, which Beduins of sheykhly urbanity put before the stab, fell into a long complaint of the small profit he had received by Khalîl, who, for reward of his kindness, had called him *hablús!* The Moghrebies laughed out ; Zeyd the Beduwy and a shrew, could here win no favour, he spoke to ears that were of old hardened against him. Also the lad Mohammed, going out of door, had found my toothless nâga ; and with this new mirth, breaking Zeyd's tedious discourse, Hasan and the lad went with loud laughing to their rests. Then when Zeyd, turning to Nejm, impudently discovered to him all the dark labyrinth of his robber-like mind, the honest old Moor, saying but this word, " Khalîl, all the Beduw are sheyatîn ! " ceased to give him audience ; and spreading down his mantle evenly before him, he went upon his knees, beginning with the solemn Mohammedan devotion to say the latter prayer : —Zeyd babbled on, without any heeding. Haj Nejm rising, brought a piece of tent-cloth to spread upon the hard stone under me, and departed, bidding me rest well.

Early, as it was day, Zeyd's hind had loaded his goods from the store-chamber, and the Beduw, standing by their beasts without the kella door, were ready to depart ; so Nejm bade them in to breakfast, and I was left alone : Zeyd wondering remained still, he would not willingly forsake me thus,—nay, had the Moghrebies showed me dangerous looks, I doubt not, Zeyd had conveyed me again safe to the friendly liberty of his Beduin booth in the desert. But much other was the good old neighbour's mind ; a moment after, he returned to call me, where he had prepared my breakfast apart and, sign of his good will, with much samn. Soon the expeditious Beduins were risen to depart, and, saying to their host, " We bid thee peace," they mounted to return to el-Erudda. Nejm had received me well, a western man ; but commonly it were to put their tolerance to a dangerous proof, to return upon any Moslemîn : then the alien in religion may find with confusion of heart, that those which were before his friends, are fallen out of charity with him, to the insane inhumanity of religious fanaticism ! I would descend immediately to el-Ally ; but Nejm persuaded me to lodge awhile in the kella, and meanwhile he would enquire for me of convoys to el-Wejh, or till he might send me in some safe company, upon the Harra to the Moahîb, where I should find Abu Sinûn, who trafficked very often thither.

Now was the first week in May, the oasis fever was begun at el-Ally and, for the flies, a camel could not lie there above two days together ; and there being but the briny rimth and no wholesome bushes in the Héjr plain, I sent again my nâga to pasture with the Beduw. The sultry heat of the open highland, in the nomad booths, seemed here somewhat abated between stone walls, the afternoon heat being about 88° Fahrenheit. The Arabian day ended, the evenings brought refreshment, the thermometer sinking till near the day-break ; when I found commonly about 68° Fahrenheit. Flaws of hot wind from the southward came upon us, with heat-drops in the sultry afternoons, whirling high dust clouds against the kella. These are blasts of the valleys, at a season when there are but light-floating airs in the high desert. The mid-day sun was so nigh vertical, that it shined-in no more over my threshold, which looked to the south. I found the birket dry, and the floor of sand a garden, plotted in beds of irrigation, and overrun with a lusty generation of water-melons, which Nejm had sown after the Haj. The kerchiefs of those of the kella were now rolled up into turbans, and their coffee fire was kindled abroad in the shadow :—this was their new summer world.

I would now visit Mubrak en-Nâga, in which I had seen so many antique inscriptions. Haj Nejm dreaded for me, and Hasan gainsaying with his wonted heat, blamed " The heartless folly of Khalîl, that would trust himself alone with a Beduwy ! " I reminded him that Mohammed ed-Deybis who would accompany me was his own father-in-law. " Ay, Khlaîl, and a Beduwy !—if he intend no harm, yet thinkest thou at the sight

of an enemy he would not forsake thee ? " Finally Haj Nejm
was for indulging me, saying, " Khalîl must not be mewed in the
kella, and please God no harm may come of it." As we were
setting forth at afternoon he recommended us to lodge this
night well out of the way, and go with the first light of the
morrow to the place, and stay there not an hour, and hasten away.
Arabs of the settled countries have always too ill an opinion of
the faith of the poor nomads. My rafîk was startled, when they
said they would bind his son for me in the kella till our coming
again safe. The man was become my *akhu*, or brother-in-fee,
by the gift of a crown for a new shirt-cloth, a sober, constant,
and manly Beduwy ; and such he seemed perhaps more than he
was indeed. An hundred times I have entrusted my lonely life,
when I could not otherwise go forward, to a Beduin companion,
unknown to me, and for great distances. Might not his
treacherous sword-stroke, whilst I slept, have ended my days
in the world ? but this were fratricide in the faith of the
Arabian desert : none have offered me violence ; but when
the way was too hard for them, I have by some been abandoned.
The murderer of his rafîk would be infamous whilst he lived,
no faithful man in the Beduin menzils ought to suffer him to sit
in his beyt. Yet there are some found, atrocious spirits, in
every people, that cannot be bridled by any custom : also the
most Moslems, when they cannot otherwise excuse themselves,
will impiously maintain that " their law is not binding, save
within the religion of the Moslemîn."

Mohammed's livelihood was mostly of his akhuship : he was
akhu, with another tribesman, of Teyma ; if any Teymâny were
wronged by Fejîr tribesmen, they would be his defenders and
orators, to reclaim and recover for him in the mejlis. He received upon every well of the Teyâmana six sahs of dates, about
fourteen pence worth, by the year. Those Shammar villagers,
being no close dwellers at home as the Alowna, but riders in
the deserts, to hire well-camels, must needs have such alliance
in all the Beduin tribes about them. Besides he was akhu for
the poor Fehjies ; if any Fehjy were aggrieved in the tribe,
Mohammed was his advocate in the mejlis.

The way is three hours, and arriving near the passage at
the fall of the evening, we went aside to shelter in a deep
winding cleft of the Héjr mountain. We might kindle the
supper fire there unspied, and hobbling her fore-legs Mohammed dismissed our camel to pasture. He climbed then
before the sun set, to seek a troop of wild goats, whose fresh
traces we had crossed below ; but the bedûn, which he found

couched only a little above, were too nimble for the unready
Beduin hunter. As the next day was breaking, he followed

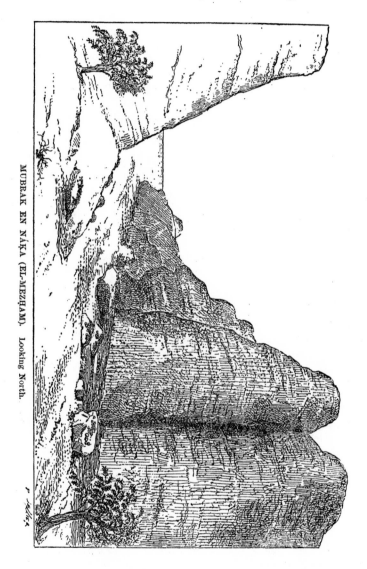

MUBRAK EN NÁKA (EL-MEZHAM). Looking North.

the game anew, but returned without venture. Small is the
cunning, and little the perseverance of these herdsmen carrying

matchlocks : when they see the head of game, they must kindle
their match, and by that they have blown it, the venison is
sped out of a man's sight: yet the Solubba, with the same unhandsome tools, take desert game enough.

We mounted our nâga, and came shortly to the Mezham.
This is a passage, certainly, of the old gold and frankincense
road from Arabia the Happy : there is none other such from the
Héjr plain, to the highlands above, for loaded camels. The free-
way lies under the eastward cliff, which we have seen to be full
of old inscriptions. Every one of the shallow legends, upon the
soft sand-rock, was battered, it is very likely, with an idle stone :
some of these antique scorings are yet white and clear, as any
made ᵤof late years, others are wasted with the wasting rock.
[*Doc. Épigr.* pl. xviii, xix.] The most are single rows of Himyaric letters ; a few are Nabatean : among the rest were two or
three lines upon which I dwelt in some confusion of mind,—
because I could read them (Hebrew ! or were they Christian
names ?) in Greek ! ΔΒΗΒΖΙ—ΔΒΗϹΔΚΙΟ̌—ΥΙΟ̌ ΒΕΝΙΔΜΗΝ—ΖΗΘΟϹ—
ΙΝΓΕΝ —Κ𝖵ΡΙΔΚΟϹ. With all the pains in the world, I could faithfully transcribe only a good part, which were legible, of that multitude of inscriptions. Here the old ascending passengers might
look back a last time to the Nabatean plain ; and those arriving
from the north had their first sight from hence of Hejra city : all
perhaps alighted in this place, and there might one and another
take up a stone (where he saw many had traced their legend
before him), to beat out his own remembrance.—At this day,
looking backward to el-Héjr, upon the green line of beautiful
acacias grown to forest trees by the dry seyl-bed, the eyes seem
to dwell still upon the antique trade settlement !—In our
returning, as I spoke of the Haj surra, Mohammed answered
stoutly, " Though their askars be the better armed, the Beduw
are of greater heart : " yet he allowed that the poor Beduins
were not able to stand before soldiery in the plain field. As
we approached the kella, his children ran from the booth, to
meet their father ; and with Beduin affection he took his
little son upon the saddle, to ride home with us.

The gate Arabs had of late robbed more than a dozen young
falcons from the eyries in Ethlib. I saw two or three at this
time in every tent, tied by a foot to their perches, set up in
the sand, and heard them all day querulously complaining.
Their diet was small desert vermin, lizards, rats and insects, as
their mewers might find ; or finding naught they maintain them
with a little dough : in the nomad life they pluck for them
those monstrous bluish blood-sucker ticks which cleave to the

breasts of their camels. Hawks (*sókr*) to take the hare are in
estimation among the Beduins ; it is some pastime for an idle
man, with pith in him ; and a good falconer may almost daily
mend the weak fare of his nomad household. The least is
worth a real, they will hardly sell the best at the price of a
thelûl. All these were gentle hawks ; in the same mountain
cliffs were buzzards, gledes, and other bastard kinds. The
Arabs, as I have seen everywhere, have excellent heads to
adventure themselves at a height : our barefoot climbers had
hardily trodden some precipices, which I was giddy to look
upon. But after my coming they borrowed a cord of me,
the less to endanger themselves. Every one was very jealous
of his own birds, gotten of the peril of his neck, and the
jars of the poor souls for their hawks too often troubled the

Cliffs of Ethlib.

kella. One day at our coffee hearth Wady raised his voice,
scolding with Doolan ; they shouted together for the head
of an hare, which each affirmed to be his sókr's meat. The
Arabs in their griefs, clamour like mad bodies, as if the persuasion should be in their much and loud crying. An uproar
of nomads within the guarded tower set our jealous Moorish
world by the ears. Nejm reeled in his seat ; then he started
upon his feet trembling ; and, casting to heaven his meagre
hands, the chafed old man swore there should no more Aarab
enter the kella. Wady cried fast, Doolan brayed with all
his throat, to excuse themselves, and hideous wàs this strife ;
until Hasan, with the brazen voice of a trumpet, bid them
" Have done and peace ha ! if they were not all beside themselves." The nomads now in disgrace gathered their ragged
cloaks about them, and silently stepped down the broken

stairway and out of doors, glad to be so come abroad without
blood ; and not to re-enter till a day of reconciliation, which,
with Haj Nejm, was not many hours distant.   And Hasan,
when he had put them forth and flung-to the iron door behind
them, returned to coffee with the wonted ventriloqual laughter,
and his great galliûn, and " he-he-he ! wellah, Haj Nejm, mine
uncle, now art not thou a little too hot-headed ? "   And the
other, " Should these bring their quarrels, Hasan, to our coffee-
fire ? "   Haj Nejm was full of this infirmity of sudden anger ;
once upon a time in such a fit, he had pulled out his horse-
pistols, and shot dead two W. Aly sheykhs, where they stood in
this kella, because when he cried *ho!* they had dared put forth
their hands to take a little corn out of the government sacks
which stood in the court below.   Hasan in that murderous
extremity to save the kella, had played with his knife under
the ribs of another, and flung him dead forth and sparred the
iron door.

Cliffs of Ethlib.

Another business of the idle gate Arabs was to go into the
wilderness for " gunsalt."   They gather tempered earth, when
they have tried it by the tongue, under any shadowing rocks
that since ages have been places of lying down at noon, of
the Beduin flocks.   This salt-mould they boil at home in
their kettles, and let the lye of the second seething stand
all night, having cast in it a few straws :—upon these yellow
nitre crystals will be found clustered in the morning.   With
such (impure) nitre they mingle a proportion of sulphur,
which is purchased in the haj market, or at Medina.   Charcoal they prepare themselves of certain lighter woods, and
kneading all together with water, they make a cake of gunpowder, and when dry, they cut it with the knife crosswise
into gross grains ; such powder is foul and weak, and they load
with heavy charges.   The Arabs buy nothing when they can
help themselves, and they are all in this sort gunpowder
makers.

I visited all the Héjr monuments anew, and saw nothing
that was not well known to me ; but searching the clefts in

Ethlib, I found other inscriptions : all are upon the side of the antique town ; there were none in the hinder part of the mountain : Doolan was my companion. We gathered, in the plain upon the potsherd sites, many small pieces of corroded copper money : he dug with his hands in a loamy heap, which perhaps remained of some fallen clay building, by the rock *Marbût el-hosàn*, and showed me charcoal of the ancient fires, which, by the grain, seemed to be burnt palm wood.

Returning one of those days I went to cut tent-pegs at the great solitary acacia tree which stands nigh the kella ; here the goats and sheep of the garrison lie down at noon after the watering. Clear gum-arabic drops are distilled upon the small boughs ; that which oozes from the old stock is pitchy black, bitter to the taste, and they say medicinal : with this are caulked the Arab coasting hoys which are built at Wejh. Hither I saw Doolan leading his flock, and waited to ask him for his bill, or else that he would cut down the sticks for me. He answered, " Wellah, O son of mine uncle, ask me anything else, but in this were mischief for us both. No ! I pray thee, break not, Khalîl, nor cut so much as a twig of all these branches, thou art not of this country, thou art not aware : look up ! seest thou the cotton shreds and the horns of goats which hang in these boughs, they are of the Beduw, but many fell in the late winds. And seest thou these nails ! certain of the Haj knock them into the stem whilst they pray ! " As I laid hand anew on a good bough and took my knife, Doolan embraced me. " No ! Khalîl, the man who cuts this tree, he said, must die."—" What is this folly ! are you afraid of trees ? "—"Ah me ! she is possessed by a jin ; be not so foolhardy. Wullah, I tell thee truth, a Beduwy broke but a bough and he died within a while and all his cattle perished. Khalîl, the last evening a little girl of the booth that is newly pitched here, gathered some of these fallen sticks, for her mother's fire, and as they kindled, by-thy-life ! the child's arm stiffened : they carried her immediately into the kella, where Haj Nejm hanged some charms about her, and by the mercy of God the child recovered."

Doolan was fallen out of favour in the kella, since those sheep and goats had been robbed out of his hand, and he imagined the world to be cruelly set against him. One day in this melancholy, as he lamented the many human wrongs not to be redressed, sitting with heavy sighs upon my threshold, I said to him, " Doolan, weep not, thou art an Antary ! " The destitute man, the despised Fehjy, hearing himself named in earnest son of Antara, could not contain his heroic heart ;

he would hide a great starting tear, which fell down upon
his breast, and with a sobbing laughter he went out to weep.
He would no more enter to drink the Moors' coffee, but
at evening he solaced his proud grief in his own tent with
many a mighty song to the groaning chord of the rabeyby :
thus he put all care away and hunger,—and surely there survived
in this poor Fehjy shepherd a magnanimous wild breath of the
ancient Arabians. Doolan every day that he lived was an
hungry man ; and it is hard to understand how nature may be
sustained, in these famished human bodies. He would often
show that he had nothing left to eat with the gesture of the
nomads, in crackling the thumb-nail, from the backward, upon
the upper front teeth; they would signify with the herdman
prophet, "He has given them cleanness of teeth." When he
understood that to the soldiery of the Sultan were appointed
daily rations, rice enough with flesh of boiled mutton, he thought
them well living in the world ; and "Oh! (he said) that a
man might have here to eat every day and be filled, as those
askars!" The inhabitants of the border lands are wont to say
of the hungered life of the nomads, "Their living is like dying,"
mithil el-mawt.

An evening as the Arabs stood looking for the new moon,
a little before the sunset, we heard a rushing sound in the
heaven afar off. It was *nejm* a star-stone, (said the Arabs,)
which had fallen they thought upon the mountains Rikb el-
Héjr. They told me some have in their time fallen visibly
in the country, and when they came to the place they
found the rocks shattered, but not the 'star' which they
supposed to have beaten deep into the earth. The new moon
was welcomed by the men with devout exclamations, and by
these poor nomad women with carols in the first hours of the
night. This is the planet of way for the wayfaring Semitic
race. The moon is indeed a watch-light of the night in the
nomad wilderness ; they are glad in her shining upon the great
upland, they may sleep then in some assurance from their
enemies. The hareem chanted their perpetual refrain of a
single verse, and danced for an hour or two. Moses appointed
his priests to 'blow up the horns in the new noons:'—they are
rams' horns, I have seen, which are sounded at these times, in
the Jews' solemnities in Syria.

All the locusts were not yet past ; once again they alighted
here from the evening wind, on all green bushes and in
the few palms of the kella. Haj Nejm ran up hooting on
his terrace, and stretching his weak arms, armed with long
palm branches, from the battlements to brush his date-trees,

he cried frenetically, "Burn Ullah their fathers!" and sent some of the gate Fehjies, who were partners with him in the fruit, to climb to the palm tops: this battle lasted till nightfall. In the oases, where they have fewer hands than can defend all their trees, the villagers suffer much damage. They lost this year a half of all their date fruits at Teyma. The immense plantations at Kheybar, were in the summer almost destroyed; the villagers can but kindle fires of green sticks under most of the stems.

On the morrow a number of Beduin horsemen rode to the door; alighting they tethered their mares, and leaning up their lances to the walls, knocked loud upon the iron plate, which had been closed when they were seen approaching. These were sheykhs of W. Aly, who upon their mares preceded the general ráhla. The tribesmen came down from wandering (for fear of Ibn Rashîd) upon the Harra with the Moahîb; and now two months before the time, for their better security, they would descend to Kheybar. Their riders had lately lost, to the Bishr ghrazzu, eighty dromedaries, well worth £1500 sterling, tamely surrendered, with their arms; whereby the tribe was left almost bare of defence, and to-morrow they would call in at el-Ally, to buy or take upon credit what matchlocks and swords they might find in the town; this noon they pitched in the midway about the wells of el-Héjr. Only a part were presently admitted. They had been but few years before dangerous gôm; and there was the blood betwixt them and Haj Nejm, of which the careful old host was ever in mind, who now stepped down in his best array and smiled with a grim kindness to meet them: the holster of two flint pistols, with which he had slain some of them, lay in a baldric upon his breast, and a flint blunderbuss was ready on his arm. Thus a man in trust or having anything to lose of his own, must converse with the men of rapine that are Beduins from home; he must watch their sliding faith, lest they who are in seeming and pleasant words your friends, an occasion being given before you have eaten together, should suddenly rise upon you as enemies. They look themselves to be dealt with thus, and he is respectable in their opinion, in whom is this giving heed against their treachery. There is much in their eyes in the ceremonial of receiving honourably a man's guests, and though it be done in half-hypocrisy: Nejm rolled a pair of Turkey carpets after him, that seemed sumptuous possessions in the eternal squalor of the desert; and these he spread for his guests upon the gallery.

So Wady came up to them, and all the gate nomads, in their holiday best. One after another, Wady fell upon the necks of his sheykhly kindred, smacked a Judas kiss in a man's two cheeks and he folds down his comely black head like a bulrush on their rusty shoulders. The others stand manly to greet the W. Aly sheukh, who rise to them with a distant gravity ;—because of Kheybar, and for Ibn Rashîd's sake, all is " not well " between these light and treacherous twin tribes. By this they are all solemnly seated again, and waiting to drink coffee. Hasan is our coffee master at the hearth ; he who in that sudden fray had killed one and swayed-to the iron door with his single main strength against many. Even now he was secretly armed; and showed me after their departure, with his inextinguishable gaggling laughter, both that blade and the pistol which he had ready in his wide slops, lest there should have fallen out among them any new desperate adventure. So must they that man the kellas, eat bread unquietly in the Ishmaelite country. Nejm had always a musing uneasy conscience of that blood hastily spilt: *ed-dumm thekîl*, would he say, " The burden of blood is very sore: " and were any cruder counsel moved at our coffee fire, Nejm would give his voice against it, commending milder ways and saying " It is good to look with indulgence upon men's faults, so they be without malice." I have heard him murmur to himself that ' he was hospitable and had a white heart.' When he was before of the tower at Sawra, in their dîra, he had fortified himself with a W. Aly marriage ; yet by her father's side, his wife was of the old kella keepers' daughters. She was of womanly worth, and hospitable, and only sometimes impatient of his close citizen discipline, which the absolute old Moor would lay upon a faithful jâra in the desert.

Motlog Allayda, the great sheykh, was a grey-headed man, and with homely gentle manners he seemed a fatherly personage ; when about to depart, he came to seek me out in my chamber. Bred in a civil society, it is likely he would have been, for all the world, a perfectly good man ; but the necessitous livelihood of the wilderness must cast him into many perplexities, out of which they will unwind themselves by any shift, which always they think better than fighting in the plain field ; and though some of their fox-like expedients be but base treachery. But there is no public dishonour in the desert ; all is reckoned human policy, that is done within the tribesmen's common interest, and contrary to the world, which is all without their tribe. Thus every Beduwy has two faces, this of gentle human kindness at home, the other of wild misanthropy and his teeth set against the world besides. All things are much as we esteem them; they think themselves, comparing themselves among themselves, honest men enough, whom we take to be most dangerous wretches and arrant thieves. The double treacheries of this unwarlike tribe had fallen back, twice, upon their own pates in the last twelvemonths' time, which made their false hearts cold.

The elders departed by and by to go to their menzil. The younger spirits lingered on, that for change of idleness would sit this day out in the kella, drowsing through the middle hours as though they were weary in the wilderness of their own minds: and hardly they roused themselves at the end of the day's quarters, when they found, by the shadow, it was time to say again the same formal prayers: then they rekindled their galliûns, and a blithe new knelling of the pestle and mortar relivened the company; yawners shook off sloth and sat up to sip the cup again. Thus they stayed, as the Beduins only can, still fasting, and making patience with cheerful slothing, till the evening. Cock on the hoop, of this younger company, was Fáhd the sheykh's son, a wooden-headed young man lately leader of that ghrazzu in which he rashly wounded the Bishr sheykh's son. Fáhd sent for me to come to him. He sent again. "Up (said the fellow his messenger), the sheykh calls thee to show him thy pictures." I bade him come to me, if he would aught of me, in my chamber. He entered, with a haughty brow, which, seeing I despised, he fell to entreating me would I show him my pictures (now famous in the country). It was he who, hearing my nation named, would understand which was our market village; now I said to him, "Young man, ours are a thousand villages, and many thousands;" Nejm a little before had boasted to them that the Nasrâny never said a word but the truth, and therefore the stolid younker could not wholly disbelieve me. The old Moor went by upon the gallery, and hearing our discourse, "Neither is this (he said to them) anything incredible which Khalîl tells; in the Moors' country be also great towns, and plenty of good villages, that is a wide land full of a multitude of people, and not such as you Aarab inhabit. What nakedness is this here of the sun and waste earth, with hardly some village weakly inhabited!—a land which only Beduw, and the afarît, may dwell in; but we are men of the West:—is it not so, Hasan? Ay! we have seen the world." The sun setting, these coffee guests departed—observing the good manners of the desert—and went then to their worsted menzils to breakfast.

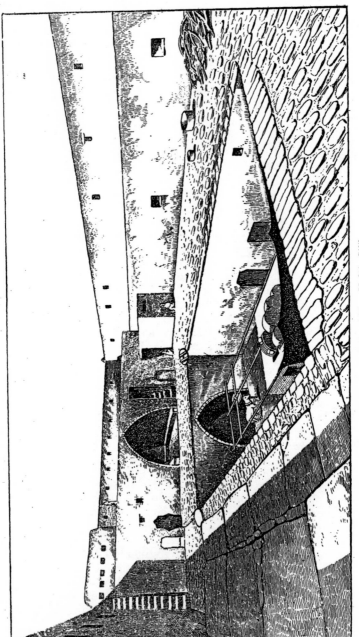

Picture of the kellà within: Medáin Sálih.

The old Moor Nejm had taken of late a greater aversion to the half Beduwy askar lad, his wife's brother; and all dreading his quick sanguinary humour, we led a careful life in the kella. Nejm had bred him from a child to the garrison service. We have seen this stronghold once already taken by surprise, and occupied by the Beduw: with so few hands under him, he must jealously guard against all the besetting dangers of the desert. He looked with a fierce care, by day and night to keep the gate. The craven lad Mohammed, with a braving negligence, made too light of his "uncle's" jealous bidding; and he, tyrannical and timorous, saw in this draw-latch his labour lost, and the kella committed to him by the Dowla, with his neck and livelihood in it, endangered; and every day, he hated more the boy's spurious metal. One of these nights we were hardly gone from the coffee-hearth to rest, when our peace was troubled with a savage altercation. The young Mohammed had stolen forth, leaving the kella iron door ajar at that hour, to the Fehjies' tents, only to quarrel with Doolan; and was scolding with the Fehjy women about some trifle of corn betwixt them, an imprudence likely to cost him all too dear—it might cost him his unprofitable life. For Haj Nejm, hearing this rumour, and a wrangling without, was risen, and as he knew certainly the brabbling voice he came forth in a frenzy upon the terrace, and as if his tower were now betrayed he yelled like a fiend to shut the door. The lad stole in again, and having softly laid up the spar, would then sneak up the stairs to his chamber; but the old man, spreading his arms in the moonlight, sware by his religion, and by his *Ghrarb*, or West country, that the boy was a Yahûdy (he could find no worse name for him). Haj Nejm sprang back to his quarters, and came again handling his glittering carbine. He yelled then, " Up, Hasan, I say, up ! " in a half suffocated and less than human voice :—Hasan he called to be witness at the Yahûdy's death; or he intended perhaps that, raging thus, Hasan should play peace-maker and come between them, to hinder him. Nejm would make all hearts this once afraid of him, with the horror of manslaughter in the night: from the opposite part, the puling miserable lad appealed to him weeping, " O uncle !—it is thyself that hast brought me up." But the old man rejected him, crying terribly again, " I am none of thine uncles; die ! Yahûdy, die ! " and as he levelled his gun at him, Mohammed ran by in the ghastly moonshine (the Arabs shoot not at flying), at the further side of the kella : so old Nejm, handling his shining blunderbuss, descended slipslop, with a stiff tread upon the stairs, from the terrace-roof, and terribly he made after him. Haj Hasan had stepped upon his feet at this ado and looked from his cell-chamber; now with the voice of a trumpet he outshouted them all. "*Bess*, enough, 'nuncle, and now ho! what is this fare, wouldest thou shed blood so hastily! and in with thee, Mohammed, thou foolish weled, to thy chamber; what, boy-fool! have not I an hundred times warned thee, as a father, and art thou always troubling the kella? And thou Haj Nejm go sleep; I say there will be time to look at the lad's fault to-morrow.—Have done Mohammed! do not answer thine uncle, but give the Lord thanks that thou seest the end of this night's work, and nothing worse is happened unto thee." By this the infirm old man's spirits were nigh spent; all again was still in the kella, and they returned to their rests till the morrow's light, only the puling askar lad yet blubbered as he passed the sill of his "beyt," 'He would tell the Pasha, and he would tell Mohammed Aly, as ever the Haj should be come again:' it was well that the testy old Moghreby did not overhear him.

The sun risen I went to the hearth to make tea with much sugar; in hope to call them friendly together: and the strife was laid till mid-day, when Doolan drove in their few sheep to drink at the troughs. Haj Hasan spoke to him some sober warning from above;—a word half uttered were enough for the wise, but twenty cannot admonish the imprudent—there broke then from the poor Fehjy's breast, he could not forbear, a bitter complaint and loud, as when the rude herdsmen are holloaing far over the desert. The foolish lad Mohammed came running to the cry, and sent out his brabbling voice against him: this brought down the kella, every man rose from his place. Looking up we saw that Haj Nejm had taken his blunderbuss; he came on shrieking, like one half beside himself, "Yahûdy! Yahûdy!" he trampled down by the stairs to them on the gallery, and set forward at a feeble run. The gate Arabs, that were in the kella to drink coffee, made after him, misdoubting the old Moor's frenetic humour and entreating him. Wady coming from behind caught Haj Nejm by the middle, and detained our "uncle" as it were a shuffle-footed old witch, casting his arms and struggling. Nejm gasped, and horribly he still threatened the lad.—Then he wrested himself free, ran from them, and anew levelled his gun, but so they were upon him again; he dragging them they contained his arms, and held strongly his impotent striving; thus they chased horribly up and down. Nejm, his strength failing, looked ghastly now about him, and panted in their strong arms. His wife stood above, weeping, and yet durst not proffer a woman's word for her unworthy young brother, that she dreaded might be slain, by her old husband, here before her face ; but now Hasan protested to him, "Wellah, have done Haj Nejm! what old fool, is not this to fare like a mad body ? ho! ho! an askar kill an askar!" (war against a man's own household). Also the nomads which held him entreated with the gentleness of the desert, "Let be, let be! Haj Nejm, nay it is thine own boy ; nay! and the Lord shall lengthen out thy days."—"An end of this, ho!" shouted Hasan, and as his senile strength gave out, they forced back ' our uncle ●into his chamber.

It was yet in my mind how I had nearly fallen here under the bestial Turkish fanaticism ; and I looked to heaven for a day to go again from this infernal cage to the freeborn Aarab, where no more hideous hurly-burlies should be in my ears of these hot-hearted Moghrebies : I promised my soul, once flown, never to re-enter these sordid kella walls to lodge in them. In this superstitious darkness of our lives, I could have imagined that some god had given me favour in the sight of the man, and allowance amongst them all. The same Haj Nejm, was to me always of an indulgent mildness, provident, for my good, to warn me with wise counsels where he thought me too little prudent, and which is but rare in their religion, disinterested : he seemed to regard me with a sort of neighbourly affection. But if upon a time there should fall any distaste between us, and he forgot his duty to the Dowla (his fanaticism in that day remembering only my religious disability), then certainly I had not long to live.

Fear and barbarous contention in lawless country (where a man must shout loud for the mastery, since there is little or no hope to move men's minds by reason) and sickness, had marred the virtuous good nature of Haj Nejm : surely in some less iniquitous circumstance of things, and under a holier discipline of religion, he had been of an excellent goodness, so much was there in him of uprightness with a modest simplicity ; and if in the smile of an Arab, which is in general sweet, we may divine anything of the primitive temper of his soul, Nejm might have been a saint also. If any censure this outrageous humour of the Moorish adventurers in the East, they will answer, in their milder mood, "You are to know that we are Western men, Moghrâreba." The Arabian men's blood has been tempered in the Occidental world. In stature of the mind and of the body, the Moors have outgrown the lazing, little in-

genious population of the old peninsula ; even if we should
compare them with the civil˙and industrious people of el-
Kasîm, they are superior, as Occidentals, to the less strenuous inhabitants of the East.   Men of hardy resolution, with
some civil ingenuity, honest industry and civil cohering together, they bring to pass even new enterprises.   A people of
the West, they have the harsh Occidental man's cautelous mind
and only little hospitable.   As all Arabs, they are born under
wandering stars : they are strenuous men more than the people
of the Peninsula.   The Arabian villager is less patient to labour
than they, and easily discouraged ; as for the empty-bodied
slugging Beduwy, he is very short-breathed, and, after an heady
effort, would return to his contemplative leisure, and lay him
down again out of mind of all world's cares.   It seems that some
like alteration is happened in the Barbary strains of Arabian
horses, which are grown to be of more fibre and courage in the
West.

The next days were peaceable ; Mohammed would go to his
nomad mother, and take the air awhile with the W. Aly.   The
boy had lately paid the bride-money and wedded a girl-wife
from Jeheyna ; but neither could she many days abide with her
unlucky groom, the coward had already beaten her : she fled one
of these morrows into the desert and ran down ten miles to
el-Ally.   Shut in a kella, among unkind strangers, the home-
sick Beduin bint came upon a time to enquire of me with
girlish simplicity ' if, when her young husband sent her away,
I would not receive her in marriage.'   I was now three weeks
lodged in a haj road tower this second time, we heard of no rice
caravaners arrived at el-Ally : my purpose was therefore to
ascend to the Moahîb, upon yonder cool platform, in sight, of the
Harra mountain ; but because all desert ways are perilous for
solitary passengers, I could find no man to ride with me thither.
We had tidings of a *kúfl* (convoy) of the Fejîr about to go down
for rice to Wejh, the second morrow they would set out from
el-Erudda ; a friend had sent me my nâga, by tribesmen who
went by, marketing, to el-Ally, and I might return in their
company.   I distributed small presents, and found a new
Damascus gown for Haj Nejm : the good old man would needs
put that gay headstall and bridle, which his own hand had
taken out of the hand of the Shammarite, upon my camel ; and
when the men came at evening, I departed with them.

The hot sun-light forsook the world, and we ascended, in the
calm night shadows, through the border of sandstone mountains, beyond the valley-plain of el-Héjr.   We came on in

the long night hours, when others sleep ; the air breathed more
chilly from the highlands, as the night increased. When the
sun was rising, we alighted and made a fire to warm ourselves.
After other two hours wayfaring, we came abreast of the
pasturing nomad cattle ; and seeing me, cries a rough shepherd,
" How now, fellows ! and wherefore have ye brought this Dowlâny ? " They answered him, " He is of you, and this is Khalîl."
The Fejîr yet lay about el-Erudda. The many small water-pits
are sunk there to man's height in the low sand ground, and
well lined with old dry building, of the wild stones. Water in
them, which is flat to the taste, never fails.

We rode by Zeyd's menzil, where was Mehsan only, who
came to take my hand. My companions of the way dispersed,
and I must make forward to Motlog, who was pitched at nearly
another hour's distance. A negro freewoman, a chideress, who
came with us, and was of Rahȳel's menzil, guided me thither ;
footing before, upon the soon burning sand, with the bridle in
her hand, impatient of my delays,—I could not drive for weariness—at every step she plucked the headstall of my jaded nâga.
Some of these women's smocks are made open sidewise, as it
were but a shirt-cloth, through whose midst the head is put ;
so only hanging from the neck, the stuff is gathered in
under their arms, and no fault is discerned, even though they
move hastily. But in the disorder of her tongue, and the
groaning nâga's resistance, it is likely she forgot her mind,
a flaw of wind in the still air blew out her summer frock from
the neck ; and besides the haggu, or girding lace of leathern
plait, they have nothing else upon their bodies. Lithe were
the negroid limbs, shining in the heat, and notwithstanding
the alloy of African blood, perfectly well shaped, she seemed a
statue of bronze. With a quick word, the negress caught in
her calico again, and turned with ruffled looks, to understand
if she were not mocked ; but as she marked how the kafir
came on riding with a discreet indifference, there was no more
tryanny of her tongue in the way : she ever owed me much
good will, that this was a mirth untold in the Beduin booths ;
and since she journeyed unquietly up and down to the market
villages, it chanced we rode some other times in the same
company.

When we approached Motlog's booth, the convoy was already departing, which we had heard would set out on the
morrow : I had hoped to repose here the day over, and thought
I could not have ridden further an hour,—and yet my journey
was but in the beginning. Only the last beasts of the kúfl
were now in sight. " Hasten forward, said the Arabs, if thou

wouldst come up with them."—Said Motlog, "Thou art late, but mayst overtake them." Men ran from the next tents, holding out their hands to the new comer to receive a little tobacco ; but, for all my need, I could hardly persuade any one to bring me a little of their léban, to drink. The Arabs are at such time unready, and even minded to lay load upon thy sore burden. I asked Motlog, who marked my drooping spirits, "How far will this journey last to-day ?"—"They will alight at mid-day, or before the half-afternoon ; ride forward ! "—but these are the pleasant forged promises of deceitful Beduins. Motlog vaulted upon his mare's bare back, he rode with headstall and bridle, the bit is unknown in these deserts. "See, (said the more friendly voices about me,) the sheykh is before thee, beat forward the nâga, or thou wilt be left behind them ; he is gone to recommend thee to them, and will bind the Bíllî sheykh's son (who conducted the kúfl) for thy safety." Motlog, as I came up, delivered me *teslím*, a trust from himself, to the young Bíllî rafîk. One hundred and fifty more miles' march were before me, almost without rest, in a deadly heat, and the languishing life was already almost at my lips. From time to time, I could hardly maintain myself in the saddle : departing from Medáin I had taken no water, and had not an ounce of food with me. The breathless sultry day was again upon us. At two hours distance, they stayed by a small watering place of shallow pits, lined with dry building, like those of el-Erudda. I hardly knew two or three faces of the tribesmen caravaners, whom I saw here mustered together ; the most being Khamâla, which, though a great fendy of Fejîr, are a sort of rude unfriendly commons, living withdrawn from the sheykhs, and not often coming to the mejlis.—This air was suffocating ! I alighted as they were ready to depart again, and would bathe my head in a little water which remained in a waterer's leather after the cattle drinking ; but the savage wretch forbade me, saying, ' Nay !—he feared Ullah ; ' and taking up his gear, he cast out the water, crying, with the dreary eyes of his ignorant fanaticism fastened upon me, ' Should he draw for a Nasrâny, one that was accursed of Ullah ? was the sun hot to-day, and I fainted ? he would God that I died also.'

We were not come far in the wilderness, when the peevish tongues of two light young Beduin women in the company, screeched to the men about me, " Look there, lads, is not that the kafir riding ? will ye not cut the wezand of him in the way ? " I bestowed, in my haste, a Beduin curse upon them, but it needed not ; the men marching nigh me answered gravely, " He is the son of our brother," because I had been a guest of some of their tribes-

men. Again the black immane platform and mountain-wall of
the Harra appeared standing to the burning heaven many hours
before us ;—and the kúfl not to halt until, living or dying, we
should arrive thither. The train descended to cross the hollow
plain under the cragged border, called by the haj caravaners
Shuk el-Ajûz, and by the nomads *el-Agorra*. We marched in a
dead dry air *el-hummu*, that is a scalding tempest of sun's rays,
which strikes up again, parching the eyeballs, from the glowing
sand. How slowly the raging summer sun fulfils his large arc
to descend at length till the blissful shadows of yonder Harra
cliffs shall cover us ! With the skin of the hands, neck and face,
and of the shins and feet, broken and peeled, I rode in a
sort of trance, and half burned. Sometime hearing a welter
behind me of their full-bellied girbies, I asked of the passenger
owners to pour out a little water, but they denied me. Another
who followed, of better heart, yielded grudgingly : I took up his
bowl of water to my lips, but for the throat's dryness in the
withering heat I could not swallow a draught. Seeing I had
but sipped,' as he received it again, the fellow cast out the water
upon the sand, for he said, " Who would drink after a Nasrâny ! "
Their large sweating girbies were swelling full of water, and
they would come to wells again on the morrow at this hour.
Friendly is their hospitality at home ; but in the way with
them you · may find among the same Arabs the behaviour of
enemies : yet ever there are some honourable men, who will at
all times be as good as themselves. It was late in the day
when we approached the Harra : there we entered a sandstone
breach in the mountain, and were sheltered from the burning
eye of the sun. The bottom is overspread with an outborne
drift of lighter pumice, mingled with an infinite cumber of
broken-up lava and some basaltic blocks. We ascended further
by a steep place of sand-drifts, in the undercliffs of the mountain (always sandstone) : the nomads alighted, the better to let
their beasts climb. To relieve my old feeble nâga, I rode upon
a hired camel. The owners bade me also dismount ; but seeing
me too weak to go upon my feet, they would not insist ; for the
Arabs, in your using anything that is theirs, can be gentle
and humane. " Why march thus (I enquired of one) in all
the day's heat and not in the night shadows, sparing your
own strength and the cmels ? "—" Ay, ay, it were better
thus ; but Khalîl, el-Beduw ! they are always affinîn, corrupt
to rottenness, and whatsoever they do, it will be found good
for naught."

When in the broad shadows I a little revived out of that
aching weariness in the way, which is a long dying without

death, I found of a very small thing a new affliction. A bint rode to us whose mother's was my hired camel; though her chitty-face was fairest of all their company, nothing in her was maidenly but the mask: the witch scritched like a jay, hooting me over hill and dale to the end of the journey, with "Ho! Kafir, aha! the Nasrâny! this is a Jew man." The nigh riding Beduins were malignant more than generous, none caring to admonish her. This day grew dim, at length it was sunset in the wilderness. The Arabs drew bridle in a sheltered place; the great camels kneeled down under them, and we all alighted for that night. I had mounted yesterevening at el-Héjr about this time, and riding through a summer night and the long day, had not tasted food or repose until now. The night is a most sweet respite from the sunlight and heat: the mountain air breathing upon us, I alighted, infirm indeed, but light as from sleep. The camel back is uneasy more than wearing: but what for the infelicity of nature, human malice and the devilish iniquity of religions, I hoped not to spend many other such days in the world,—that should be an hell suffering.

In the starlight, calling the peevish damsel, who with her brethren had alighted next beside us, I put a gift of tittun in her hand, for the witch her mother. I said to her, " Thou art a pretty little wolf; but come sweet-heart, that is forgiven; tomorrow wilt thou be my bride?"—'Well (said the poor Beduish lass) she was willing to "take me ; she would serve me in my voyage and follow me to my far country, and never give me again unrest of her brabbling, only I must promise not to put her away.' With this half earnest nomad jest my ears were lightened of a hussy's railing tongue for the morrow. Now it was night, the wayfaring Arabs sat about their watch-fires, and I lay beside my saddle-bags to rest. Later two young men passed by us, going back to their places, and I overheard them very well, as one said to his companion, "Here lies the kafir!" and the other answered him, "Look, there wants but one *whish* with the sword, and a man might come by all that good (my baggage)."—I knew the voice of the last speaker; he was the worthy Bíllî sheykh's unworthy son, who rode rafîk, for his father, with our caravan. As the new day lightened, the Arabs broke up in haste. I had overnight agreed for the hired camel; but now the owners denied me, alleging for themselves a shrew's proverb, (perhaps of the ancient Arabians, which may hardly now excuse them when they drink no wine,) " Promises made in the night be not binding by daylight."

I must load to go over the Harra, upon my jaded nâga. The main of the convoy had departed: those few that yet

lingered about me, threatened to abandon me ; but some alighted
to help the stranger when they saw that alone I could not lift
up my baggage. An hour further, of their own returning
weather-cock wills, they let me have the camel again ! We began
to be in steep cragged paths of the mountain : now we ascended
and descended all the half-hours till noon, engaged in the many
basalt coombs and crooked folds of the Harra mountain, yet
always passing upwards. All about us is an iron wilderness ;
a bare and black shining beach of heated vulcanic stones. Few
green stems of wormwood and southernwood, *shâeh*, springing on
the sharp lava shelves, give up a resinous sweetness under this
withering broad sunshine : the last is gathered and dried by the
hareem, for the hot cordial savour ; they mix a little with their
cold léban and mereesy. In all the deeper vulcanic bottoms
are tamarisks, and by the stony dry seyl-bed sides I saw woody
green groves of the desert acacia. Of other timber a few stone-
oaks grow upon the Harra ; I have seen their heavy club-sticks
cut of this wood. Some of the poorer Beduins and Fehját
sought in thickets of the acacia thorns whilst we passed, for the
clear drops, and whitey bunches of gum-arabic ; for such, they
said, would be given sixpence a pottle at el-Wejh.

The long-necked camels snatch as we ride at these thorny
boughs of sweet mimosa-like leaves. It is a wonder that the
hard finger-long sharp spines should not stab the great soft
pharynx !—thorns which will strike at once through their horny
soles, and wound so cruelly the nomads' bare feet that I have
known men long bedridden by such accidents. When I asked
some Beduins of this, " The world, they answered, is full of the
wonderful works of God ! and the Lord hath made every creature
to his proper livelihood. Yet if one will examine within the
mouth when any camel is slaughtered, he will find a skin-
substance, tender-like, but deep as your finger, and of such
toughness that a thorn might not readily pierce it." The Beduin
goat-herds, where there are acacia trees, carry out a bill with
them, and lop down the under boughs to their stock, more
especially for the young kids. Tólh trees with such cut wash-
boughs, hanging maimed and sere, are seen in all the desert ;
and the desert dust is often trodden down about the thorny
mimosa bushes by beautiful wild feet of the gazelles. This
tree, which they say grows quickly, seldom comes to great
timber. A spreading tólh-tree head is no hospitable covert,
but a greenish lattice of spray-wood and thorns with rare
minute leaves, which casts a thin sprinkled dimness, like a
shadow, and her old thorns upon the glaring waste ground.
The acacias give up to the air a hardly sensible wholesome

sweetness; the little yellowish flower-tufts are seen in all the midsummer months, and after the knops, the crooked cods before the summer time.   In *Wady Thirba* I have found the flowering tree full of murmuring bees of the desert (*athubba*) and casting a weak perfume, as the sweetness of flowering vine-yards.   To chaw the leaves, which are pleasant to the taste and a little gelatinous, will refresh the parched mouth; the gum, say the Arabs, is very good and cooling to eat.   Some Fehját who rode in the kúfl, would stay in the next menzil of Bíllî to seek for er'n roots in the Tehláma side of the mountain.   The er'n, which is a gnarled stub of massy wood, resembles the stool of ling-wort.   I have not found the plant, nor seen any heather kind, growing in Arabia.   The chips, which they soak in water to tan their leather, are of a cedar colour.   Two or three days, a raw skin is laid in a pan with the er'n water; but the hide is tanned to so little depth, that such crude leather, if it be a water-skin, will after some time putrefy; when it is chapped, it must be steeped anew: corrupt are thus most of their girbies, so that they infect the water in them.   For a knot of er'n root, which is in the husbandry of every nomad and oasis housewife, a real is paid at Teyma.

In all this day's passage of the Harra the sand-rock nowhere comes to light, but is covered with the immense pan of basaltic lavas.   We tread first after mid-day the high vulcanic platform of the mountain, after much ado in climbing of the fasting camels.   A black vulcanic gravel plain is there before us to the horizon, in which there rise single black cones, and twin crests; [they were crater hills; and in those the vulcanic craters have been broken down upon a side, by the outrunning lavas and the blast of the eruption].   In all these I thought already I saw the distant forms of vulcanic hills.   Mild was the summer day's heat in all the Harra height, here 5000 feet above the sea level: the rarity of the air, was our shelter from the extremity of the sun, which now shone' upon us only in friendly wise.   We felt a light wafting breath in the higher denes; a tepid air streamed at large over this vast headland of the mountain.   Somewhere in the lava soil we see yellowish loamy earth under the loose stones, tufa or it might be burned chalk-rock, which upon this Harra lies in few scales above the deep sandstone; and I have found it singed to ochre, by the old lava's over-streaming.   Such Harra land is more often a vast bed and banks of rusty and basaltic bluish blocks (*dims, róthm,* which after their crystalline nature are rhomboid;) stubborn heavy matter, as iron, and sounding like bell-metal: lying out eternally under the sand-driving desert wind, they are seen polished and shining in

the sun. Because of this cumber of stomes and sharp cutting
lavas, the Harra country is hard to pass, out of the paths, for
any other than Harra-bred camels. The heavy poised stones
sliding and toppling to the tread, the herdsmen's feet are oftentimes sorely bruised ; for which, and because the stones are
as glowing coals in the summer sun, the Beduin hinds in the
Harra commonly sit all day upon the croups of their browsing
camels.

This Titanic desolation, seeming in our eyes as if it could
not bear life, is good Beduin ground and heritàge of the bold
Moahîb *Abu Shamah*. Wholesome is that high attempered air,
they have cattle enough, and those mountaineers are robust
Beduin bodies of rude understanding, more than the nomads
which I have seen, in the plains about them. In this difficult
vulcanic country, their small cattle can be seldom robbed ; and
milk of the flocks is in less scarcity among them, which is
the health and wealth of the poor nomads. When their
stout old sheykh came visiting the Fejîr, later in this summer
at el-Héjr, Zeyd, with the nomad hilarity, took up the word
with him thus, in the mejlis, *Ya Tollog, râiyat el-Harra* which
may signify " Ha Tollog, thou that art lord of the Harra ! " Finding, as we marched, where a flock was lately passed, we hoped
soon to meet with those friendly Aarab, and lodge that night in
their menzil. .

We rode in the further mountain way by ruins of dry-built
walling ; a kind of simple breast-works and small enclosures,
such as the cotes which shepherds build now to fold their
lambs, (from the nightly wolf,) upon the mountains of Syria :
besides these, there are some narrow cells that might be taken
for graves laid above ground. Other narrow cells there are
with a groove and cullis door :—some such I have seen baited
by hunters in the Sinai desert ; they are traps, they told me,
to take the leopard (nimmr), and other land-loping beasts
of the flesh-eaters.—There is another kind, which are round
builded heaps and are perhaps barrows, the nomads say of them,
"they are beacons, and mark the site of springs which were of
yore, but the old knowledge is lost." If I asked any Beduin
passengers of these things, he answered listless, hardly willing
to open the mouth, in that heat,—" Things of the former world,
and before the Moslemîn." Some answered, " Tell us Khalîl!
those old kafirs, thy forefathers, they made them not ? " And
other voices said, " They are of the Helalát."

Not finding the Moahîb, we begun already to descend by
the western basaltic coombs of the mountain ; and came
to pits of water, where the Arabs alighted to draw for their

thirsting and fasting camels : for save that little they may browse, after the evening halt, when they are loosed out an hour to pasture, the kúfl camels fast upon the whole journey ; but because of sweating they cannot pass for thirst. At other times the querulous huge creature, that seems overburdened with his own vast bulk, will groan, if but a fly light or a date-stone fall from his rider upon him ; but compelled to any great pain, the camel marches to the end with a silent fortitude. The wayfaring Aarab having no troughs with them, with the driving-stick and their hands now scrape hollows in the hard-burned ground ; and upon these spreading leathers, they pour in their buckets full, drawn of the corrupt (long stagnant) and tepid well-water. Every man drives up his beasts, with *weeaho ! weeaho ! weeaho !* encouraging them to drink ; and as they justle with the heavy long necks together, he calls them to stand by with *wòh-ho ! wòh-ho ! wòh-ho !*

We pass sometimes a *dàr el-Aarab*, or old worn camping-ground : the site is commonly a bottom, sheltered from the weather and their enemies' eyes, where the nomads lodge two or three days in the year, as the seasons come about again. These dàrs are where the wild stones have been gathered aside, and there is a clear room to build the worsted booths, and for their cattle to lie down in : they remain doubtless from the old generations. Further, as the sun was low, we came in the flank of the Harra, to some nomad tents ; these Aarab were *H'roof* a kindred of Bíllî. There came out men, whilst we rode by, with a forced voice of bounty to bid us in, crying, " Alight folk ! we have mèreesy in the byût, we have léban and samn." I rode with an acquaintance to a booth which stood upon the stony bank at a hollow seyl-side, and alighted with a present of tittun. I found the good housewife at home, her forelock hanged braided as a horn, with a threaded bead upon it,—the manner in some north-west districts. She sat and rocked the blown milk-skin upon her knees, and bade me have patience a moment, till her butter came, and she might pour me out of the churn-milk to drink. Her great Bíllî sheep-dog followed negligently with the frank air of an host (more often they are loud-mouthed and ruffling with strangers), and came to lie down by us. Afterward I knew this hospitable poor woman, who was a widow alone, and her not less honest son; when later, they came summering to our Aarab, and built their booth among us in the valley Thirba.

From the brink of the Harra, the high rugged border of the Teháma lower land lie dimly before us. In our first de-scending, the sand rocks came again to sight ; and I marked

where a billow of surging lavas stood, stiffened like some hollow
wave, upon the valley wall of sandstone. In the next sand
cliff I saw rudely scored Himyaric legends. We arrived in
the dusk at a nomad encampment, in the underlying plain;
they were Bíllî of the fendy *Sehamma*, sheykhs *Mahanna* and
his uncle *Fodil*: it was Mahanna who would on the morrow
conduct the Fejîr kúfl to el-Wejh. Our Aarab dispersed, some
to seek comfort at the beyts of their acquaintance; some to
lodge by themselves in the sand, as poor souls ashamed to take
hosts. I alighted with another at Mahanna's tent, and lay
down suffering; they marking this, with a kind inquietude,
brought me léban to drink, and I slept as the dead. The
Belûwy sheykh called me in the beginning of the night to sit
up and eat; I saw the brittled carcase of a goat steaming before
us in a vast trencher, Mahanna had killed and seethed the sacrifice of hospitality. Kindly he bade the stranger draw nearer and
'stretch forth the hand' to meat, saying in this that 'he made
much of Motlog's recommending me; he was very happy to see
me.' Mahanna was a man at the middle age, of a certain noble
simplicity and humanity, which the harsh and hasty world's
schoolery might interpret an amiable ineptitude of mind: he
was of half melancholy humour at home, and a hardy leader in
the field. Our amity increased till the autumn months when
I forsook their dîras. The Sehamma are allied neighbours
of the Moahîb; other fendies of Bíllî, besides the H'roof, are
el-Gùeyîn, *Zubbàla*, *Aradát*, *Wâbissa*, *Sarâbta*, *Graya*, *Hareyry*,
Grâuty, *Sweymly*, *Fueyhy*, *Jemán*. In their genealogies *Bíllî*
is named jid or patriarch of the tribe, and his sons after him
M'khâlid and *Kh'zám*. All their wandering ground is from
hence to the sea four journeys over. The Sehamma kindred
are forty households: here stood pitched twenty booths of them.

As the morrow began to be light, Mahanna encouraged me
to mount, our kúfl being about to remove; but I answered he
needs must leave me, I could no further. In the last weeks of
heat and drought I had swallowed little but water; it was a
burden to me to breathe that simûm air of the Tehâma: with
what anguish must I cross the rest of that rugged lowland
country, frying in the sun, with the slow-footed camels, to fall
perhaps from the saddle, or give the last breath before the kúfl
should enter el-Wejh. I thought I would seek Abu Sinûn
upon the Harra, the Moahîb menzil was not far from hence;
and might I breathe again upon the mountain, and find there
a little milk, I should recover health. "How! (asked the good
man in a perplexity) should he leave me so many days only
with the hareem?" a friendly Fejîry voice answered for me,

" Khalîl knows billah all the custom (*dîn*) of the Aarab, he is as
one of us." As Mahanna was taking his thelûl to ride after the
departing kúfl, I put in his palm a few piastres, saying this ·
was for a little tittun, which he should bring back, as any
Beduin will for a friend, from the market town. " But tell me
(said the good simple man) how much make these silverlings, or
shall I call one who can count money ? " The nomads reckon
only by reals, smaller coins are almost unknown among them ;
besides, these nomads are far from the road and defile not their
hands with the haj surra. Mahanna now mounted with his lance,
the Fukara caravaners passed forth unarmed ; and yet beyond
the Sehamma all the Bíllî land was hostile to those Annezy ;
but in his conduct they were well assured, and would be even
entertained by the way. Mahanna's fee is upon every camel
a real.

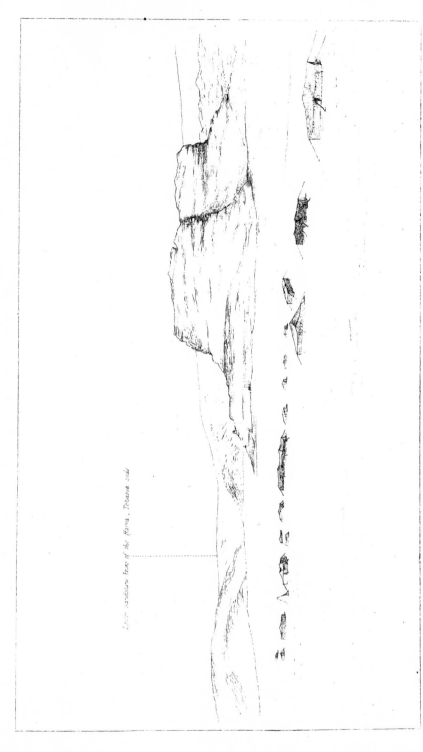

Large semicircular front of the Harra, Persian side.

Plate IV to face p. 385

Encampment of BiLLÎ AARAB

CHAPTER XIV.

WANDERING UPON THE HARRA WITH THE MOAHÎB.

View of volcanoes. "Nazarene houses." The ancients of these countries. Fabulous tales. The BENY HELÁL. *The Seyl el-Arem. The old heroic generation. Their sepulchres. Mahanna's mother. The Shizm. The Yahûd Kheybar. The Billi clans. Diseases. Muzayyins Our kûfl come again from Wejh. The sheykh's mare perishes of thirst. Men of another menzil discourse with the Nasrány. Mahanna's housewife. Seeking the Moahîb upon the Harra. The wonderful vulcanic country. Antique graves there not of the Mohammedan Beduins. We ride at adventure looking for the Aarab. Mishwat. A contention in hospitality. The Moahîb and Sbáa tribesmen of Annezy. Alliances of the tribes. A Beduin host's breakfast. Thanks after meat. The Moahîb sheykh Tollog. Aby Sinûn the Moor's household. His thriving in the Nomad life. The Moahîb camp in the Harra. The crater hills. A Howeytát sheykh comes in to sue for blood-money. Their wonder-talk of the Nasára. A vulcanic hill. The face of the Harra;—intolerably cold in winter. Scarcity of water. Abu Sinûn come again from a journey. His voyage from the West Country. Tollog bids the Nasrány depart. Housewives talk with the stranger. Fáiz the herdsman.*

THE Sehamma were pitched [*v.* pl. IV.] near the upper Tehâma mountain, *J. Sléih*, and nigh the chief watering-place of their district, *Ummshash.*—There were in sight from our tents three two-headed mountains upon the Harra, which (attentively considering them through the glass) I could not doubt to be cinder-hills of volcanoes. The Beduins told me they were burned stones and black sand. In the sandy site of the menzil I saw old ground-courses of building, and upon the next higher soil certain built and vaulted stone-heaps, *rijjûm*, which were ten or twelve feet over : the most are broken through, and a narrow cell is seen within them ; I afterward saw very many of them upon all the Aueyrid, standing almost upon every rising ground. The nomads say of them they are " houses of the Nasarenes," or the old kafirs which were the people of this land before their fathers, the Moslemîn. The like, or not much unlike these, I have seen in Sinai ; there they

are called *Namûs*, pl. *Nawamîs*, which the Tówara
Beduins fabulously inter-
pret "gnats' houses," saying in that horrid maze
of forlorn droughty valleys
had been " channels run-
ning down in old world's
times, and fenny pools which bred
clouds of midges, so that the ancient
people (whom they also call Nasâra)
built these stone cottages, wherein
recovering themselves at nightfall
and kindling fires. the reek defended
them from the insect plague." *Namûs* is spoken also in Syria and the
Arabic countries, corruptly, for *Nagûs*,
which is said for any such family
place of sepulture of the not Moslemîn, as those in the Christian grave-
yards; it may be an ecclesiastical word
formed to the Greek,—the nursing
tongue of the Christian religion,
(νέκυς, a corse). I have found a
Namûs in Sinai, in the way of those
coming from Suez, half a journey
before the Greek monastry, wherein
the Beduins use even now to lay
their dead. When I came there, in the
year 1874, seeing a doorway stopped
with stones and faggots, I would
have removed some sticks to look in,
but the old Beduin cameleer made
signs with the hand (for yet I had not
learned much Arabic) that men lay
therein, stark upon their backs with
closed eyes, and with the other he
stopped his nostrils. I have counted
in some wild Sinai valley (W. Zileyly)
about thirty round and oval nawamîs
standing nigh together : the most are
ruinous, and always dry-built, as these
in Arabia. The bee-hive shaped rijjûm of the Aueyrid are rude,
but not unworkmanlike put up.—Are they not barrows, graves
of principal persons of the old village and nomad inhabitants ?

All the Nasâra they suppose to be one kindred, and to have held these desert countries in the beginning, until 'their fathers had driven them out.' "Wellah, they said, were not those your ruined villages, Khalîl, which we see in many places, and even in this mountain ? And art thou not one sent before them, to spy out the land ?—it is likely the heathen still pretend to inherit it." Others said, " It is the B. Helál that would have the country again ; " and some added darkly " this tiding is indeed come to us, but thinkest thou they will break in upon us ? Where be the old springs, which we find not ? Canst thou not tell us, out of thy books, where to find the springs and hidden treasures ? As the Lord liveth ! we will reward thee only to show us the water."—" Listen (one said), and I will tell you a thing ;—is not such a ground of ruins known to us all ? Being, I say, upon a time in Syria, there comes a Nasrâny to me, when he understood I was from this country,—he had, too, a book in his hand !—and ' Tell me thou Beduwy, said he, is there not such a ruined site—he named it !—in your dîra ? ' ' Ay billah ! I answered him, there be walls of some dead *géria*.'—'A great treasure should lie thereabout ; well ! answer me, [it is a formula I have heard in other like tales,] your Aarab drink they in copper, or in silver vessels ? '—' Some of our vessels, billah, are copper tinned, but the more part wooden bowls.'—' Then that treasure is yet there,' so, said the Nasrâny, ' Wilt thou carry me thither, and finding the riches, we may divide all truly together ? ' That I promised him upon my religion, and when the day was come in which our people mounted to ride homeward, I went to take up the Nasrâny. ' I would go with you, he said, and so we might enrich ourselves, but the khála is fearful, and how could I return, over that great wilderness to mine own house ? ' "—Such talk was often in my ears in Arabia ! Because I had been long at el-Héjr, the Aarab hereabout looked upon me as a Nasrâny, who in his books could " see the invisible," and a treaure-seeker.

Some enquired, ' Had I visited Tûnis in my voyages, and were the Beny Helál yet a great people in those dîras ? ' The B. Helál, as they make account of them, were the multitude of many Nejd tribes, assembled upon a time when the land had suffered seven rainless years. Their cattle dying the Aarab, removing out of all places, came together, an innumerable host, to seek a land which the Lord had blessed with showers and the rabîa. The Belka village country was at first wasted by them : then they went down to Egypt, where some tribes stayed, but the most of them passed forth towards the sun-setting, and seized new pasture lands in the

25—2

Barbary countries : the tradition says that they seated themselves principally in the marches of Tûnis. In every tribe,
in every oasis where I came in Arabia, the simple people
have questioned me, a wayfarer from the furthest Occident,
' Had I met with the Beny Helál ? ' If I said, ' They should
be neighbours of ours,' they took it well ; and if I had said " I
am a B. Helály," they would so have regarded me. Certain
Moors, passenger-adventurers in Arabia, especially any tall men,
will vaunt themselves " sons of the Beny Helál." The lays
of the B. Helál are chanted in every wild hamlet of worsted
booths, in the immeasurable wilderness,—an unwritten scripture
(which moves the younger sort) of the ostentation of liberality,
and of prowess in the field, but barbarous, as leaping out of
just measure, and beyond the limits of human endeavour. There
is many a man, in ten nomads, who cannot patter his formal
prayer, but in an hundred there is hardly some child, upon
whose tongue is no bold rime of the B. Helál.

This tradition so lively in all the breadth of nomadic Nejd may
be of some main descent of the Kabâil in their later antiquity.
—But what is the *Seyl el-Arem?* It is a molehill-mountain
record of the fabulous Mohammedan authors. The Beduw
have no tradition of the " dam-breach " of Mâreb and—upon so
small an accident—the old dispersion of the tribes from one
market town of Arabia Beata. Nejd in apperance and likelihood, has been a nomad land from the beginning. This
were as quaint a story in their hearing, as that of the tower
of Babel. When I was at Hâyil, a like tale was brought in
from er-Riâth ; we had tidings, in the great kahwa, of another
rat which had eaten, of late, and let water through a side
of the Wady Hanîfa.

That old heroic generation are reputed authors of all
deep desert wells, and water-pits lined with dry stone building,
and of any other considerable works, and colossal stone-laying,
seen up and down, in the northern waste countries and, southward, at least as far as that Teháma which lies about Mecca.
Such works, in the lazing eyes of the Aarab, are of the giants,
and the giants are the Beny Helál.

There are graves, set out in many places, in the Arabian
wilderness, more than twenty feet in length ; and such are said to
be of the B. Helál. In like sort, we may see the graves of
certain biblical patriarchs and prophets in Palestine, now in
custody of the Moslemîn, that are drawn out to a demesurate
length, after their higher age and dignities, some sixty, some
an hundred feet long. Eve's grave is set out (for is she
not called mother of mankind ?) to almost as many paces at

Jidda ; to the oratory upon our great mother's navel, being more
than the height of a tall cedar ;—her babes, at the birth,
(saving her reverence) should be greater than elephants. If thus
were the first woman, what should Adam be ? we would not
more than one fathom of the human flesh, lest we should not
be able to bear it.

I answered to those Beduins, " The Nasâra will not invade
you, this was never a land of ours : and, besides their own, they
have other great lands beyond the seas, not long discovered,
and full of the benediction of Ullah ; lands of waters and green
as the garden of Damascus. In them is a temperate air, *barâd*,
without great heat or cold, and there is room for you all my
friends, they would receive you freely and welcome you thither.
Who has sent me to spy out your sand and stones ? by my faith I
would not visit this country at any man's bidding. I am a *sûwahh*,
and surely, if I had esteemed worldly things, I had not forsaken the town to come to this hunger and thirst, and heat of
the desert."—" Ay, wellah ! (murmured Mahanna's mother, who
stood by us, spinning), theirs is a better land, and what should
they seek for here, where—O my God!—is nothing, save *eth-
thùmma wa ej-jûa*, bare thirst and hunger."   Beautiful in her
age was this mother of a Beduin sheykh, and he grey-haired ;
and doubtless she had been very fair, as many of the Bíllî
women. They are, as their neighbours of Annezy, open-faced :
many of them are brown-haired : (brown-haired women, I hear,
to be seen also among the B. Atîeh) but baked in the sun in
a hungry and thirsty country, they are always lean and want
freshness of colour.

In the Sehamma dîra, which is the high mountainous
Teháma, next under the Aueyrid, are many ruined sites of
hamlets and villages. Here is told also, for a natural wonder,
of some cave or bath of Stygian water, *Hammam es-Shízm*, at
the head of a mountain, where the nomads go to wash themselves and their camels for the healing virtues ; but they say if
any man drink of it he would perish. This water is greenish
and sour (I thought it might be of copper rust) ;—they say
fabulously, "the Shízm will not flow in the month of the Haj,
the water is then retired to Mecca."

Two or three households there were of W. Aly in this Bíllî
menzil; that had remained behind, for the sheykhs' carriage of
rice from Wejh, shrews full of evil meaning and fanatical knavish
humour, so that the Bíllî whispered at their backs, *Yahúd
Kheybar !* The like they will say (the ill-will of neighbours) of
the Fukara, being tribes which inherited the Jewish Kheybar ;
and generally the southern Annezy,—saving only Kahtân—

are the most Jew-natured of the Beduin Arabs.   A good
Allayda lad was with the rest, *Thaifullah,* who in that spirit of
the wild Arabs, which covets commendation, where is little
merit, questioned me with simplicity, ' How looked I upon the
Aarab ? '   I answered, likening them to the tolh, a pleasant
tree in the wilderness with her branches of few evergreen leaves
and sharp spines and with some sweet blossoms in the time, the
block is next to unprofitable timber.   " Wellah, Khalîl (he
cried), *ent sabt,* thou hast shot into the mark." Such words
please their idle ears.

These Bíllî are the pleasantest of all the nomad Arabians.
Free and light hearts, the best of them were men of mild and
ingenuous utterance, but sooner kind than very hospitable. They
were well-faring, their camels were in good number, and at sunset
I saw a little flock couched before every beyt : that is a comfortable sign of livelihood in the desert. They are, as lately said, not
leaners upon a surra, which brings no blessing, but undaunted
Beduins, that hope only in themselves.   Nevertheless, the Bíllî
clans nigh the seabord take a toll for the Egyptian haj-road, and
the Bíllî great sheykh has, they told me, his common residence (as
a pensioner of the government) at Cairo. Like them are their
Jeheyna neighbours, tribesmen of magnanimous manners. That
is a great tribe of old nobility ; they are praised among the Arbân
as observers of the ancient hospitality. Upon the Bíllî northern
marches are Howeytát,—their robust foeman and cattle robbers :
for fear of them they live in discomfort of heart, and all the open
desert is more unquiet without the domination of Ibn Rashîd.
Every day Mahanna's son mounted, with his lance in hand, upon
a swift thelûl, and rode to view the ground before the pasturing
camels : so he remained, watching in advance, till evening.—Did
the young sheykh make them a sign, the herdsmen, gathering
their beasts, would drive all homeward at a run. I asked him,
" If you met with any cattle thief ? " said he, with an atrocious
look : " I would pierce him with this spear, ha ! "

I saw in my medical practice that these Tehâma Beduins
suffer not only many kinds of rheums and ophthalmia, but are
infected with the *morbus gallicus.*   The evil has passed into
their blood from the seabord in late years ; and if you will
believe them, few have escaped altogether untainted. Because
of this their allies, of the inland Aarab, are now afraid to
wed with persons of the Tehâma tribes, saying " The flesh
of them is indeed not wholesome."   Aarab kindreds will say
the like for other maladies. I have asked a nomad smith :
' Did not his kindred match with Teyma sânies ? ' he said, " Well !
we have taken of their daughters, and might take them again,

but we left it for a leprosy we found in their blood." The
cruel pestilence was come to the Moahîb, who now abstained
from these inter-marriages. I knew among them only one
afflicted person, a poor coughing old woman of thirty years, in
our menzil, with muffled voice, and loathsome to look upon, and
yet they said she had been the fairest of the hareem! A
Sehamma wife who came to the hakîm was whole then in
appearance, but her young child suffered. An Allaydy wedded
six years before with one of these fair tribeswomen, but the
corroding mischief latent in her veins had since corrupted
all his vital powers ; he showed me upon his hands horrible
open ulcers. They call the disease *hub el-Frenjy,* Frankish
button, and *el-bellush,* and *thá el-melúk,* king's evil, and with
an horrible irony, *el-mubárak,* the benison. All their hope was
in the use of red lead in some violent form or other, which
they fetched from Wejh. A leprous disposition of the blood
is common among the misdieted Arabians. So Arabs commending a maiden in marriage, will often add this word : *wa lahm-ha
zain,* ' her flesh also is well and sound.'

I saw more muzayyins in the camp of the Sehamma ; it was
early in the morning when the children would be " purified."
As I came by the first tent the child a moment before had
been made a Moslem ; but so rude was the surgery that he
of the knife must be called back again. The child lamented
for himself ; *weyley !* woe is me. Thereby lay an ewe, for the
guest meal, gurgling in her blood with the throat cut ; and now
the child's father severed the sheep's head from the body.
I came to a second muzayyin tent ; here a sâny was the surgeon.
I saw him whetting his blade, and one held a sheep ready to be
slaughtered. The father encouraging his little son, set up the
child and held him to ride round on the sacrificial sheep's back ;
then he seated him again in his place, so drawing his cutlass and
with a back stroke houghing him, he cut down the mutton ;
he also cut the throats of a goat and a kid. They now
seated the child upon a vast metal charger reversed, which
at other times is for the large nomad hospitality, " the table
of God in the wilderness," some horse-dung being powdered
under him. This smith stood still striking a rude razor blade
to a fair edge, upon his sinewed arm. He drew then the fore-
skin through a pierced stone shard, and there tied with a thread.
" Look thou cut not over much," said the mother. Holding her
child, with the other she blinded his eyes, and encouraged
him with the mother's voice and promises of sweet milk and fat
things. The sâny, with a light stroke, severed the skin at
the knot ; then he powdered the wound with charcoal, and gave

up the child, which had not felt a pain, to his mother ; and she comforting him in her bosom, bade him be glad that he was now entered into the religion of Islam. Their boiled rice and mutton was largely distributed before mid-day, and portions were borne through the camp, to the friends who were not present. I saw the maidens and young married women caroling in the next hours before the muzayyins.

Upon the morrow there rode by our tents Abu Sinûn, coming again from Wejh with loaded camels ; he went up to his people in the Harra ; but promised he would return or send for me after three days. The eighth morning we saw Mahanna, riding in upon his thelûl, before the returning kûfl ; the Beduins reported the heat to be now intolerable at el-Wejh, the night without breath of air, and even the townspeople could not slumber. Their convoy arrived in an afternoon, and they had ended their affairs in town before nightfall, and departed with the expeditious impatience of nomads. There they de-livered what camels they led with them to sell, to the public brokers, who, crying them up and down the sûk, had sold all in one hour to the highest bidders,—the India rice salesmen and camel shippers of the place. The dealers pay not in money to the Beduins, unless that which is over in a broken price, but in sacks of their merchandise : they ship the sale beasts upon the Arab hoys to Suez. An excellent young hurr or he-thelûl of Motlog's, fetched him but fifteen reals in rice for his summer provision ; certainly he had not parted with the same at home for twenty-five reals in white money. A great bearing-camel of Zeyd's, now a little old, valued at twenty reals in the desert, brought him no more than eleven reals worth of rice, and Zeyd must pay about the half for the carriage. Zeyd was out of humour at this decay of his thrift, and swore a mighty oath in the mejlis, and ' Another time, he said, except he went down with his own head ! (that is himself) ;' he counselled also the sheukh to send no more by other hands. Those of the kûfl were poor tribesmen hired as carriers, mostly for the sheykhs ; there went no sheykh upon this servile errand with them. The cameleers received for their cattle hire, upon every sack carried, one and a half reals : three India rice sacks are a camel-burden ; upon some of very robust growth they may lay four sacks. To come and go between el-Erudda and "the Salt Sea," is twelve summer journeys, in a raging heat ; the half lies over steep moun-tains, or by very cragged ground ; and the cattle make forced marches almost without tasting herbage. The owner who goes with his beast is not paid for himself, in the Arabic countries ; and besides there is a real for the safe conduct :

every camel returning from such voyage has lost his spring
fatness, and his selling value is lower by five reals. The men
return along with them in evil plight; and, will you reckon
it with them, they allow themselves to be losers; only, without
diminishing their stock, the poor carriers may thus obtain for
their need a little ready money.

In this menzil died Mahanna's old mare; she had lately
foaled. The mare is that which the nomad sheykh holds most
precious among his cattle. When the foal was fallen from this
sack of bones, they tied up her dry dugs (as it is done with the
milch camels); and the healthy foal was bound in the sheykh's
tent, to be reared of their sour milk and mereesy: the decrepid
dam they abandoned to die, and cut her off from water. As
I lay awake I saw her return by night and smell miserably to
the water-skins in the tent, she gnawed the hay out of the
camels' pack-saddles for hunger. I asked the Arabs, "Wherefore not end her lingering pain with a gun-shot?" I thought
them cruel, but they thought my words such, and outlandish!
—Only the dog (which alone of all his beasts eats of man's bread),
has no citizenship in the nomad life. Man abhors in this parasite brute of half human mind, the mockery of his own evil
nature: upon this crouching creature of his morsels he may
visit for every cause, his ill-humour, as it were upon an enemy;
yet, in the border-land towns, religious citizens, having a vow,
do sometimes cast a dole of bread to the carrion hounds in
their sûks.—Those of our household looked back every idle
hour into the desert, to see when the mare would lie down
to die; the third mid-day she was fallen and could not rise.
At the break of day the rákhams were come, with the brown
ágab, to devour the putrifying carcase; these sharn-birds also
haunt the nomad menzils in the wide wilderness, not very far
inland: they depart before winter. Whilst they are with the
Aarab they lie wheeling upon the wing all day, stooping and
hovering at little height above the menzil. The rákham is
stiff-feathered, her white wings are tipped black, the bill is
yellowish: being "hook-bill birds" after the Aarab's Mohammedan lore, the flesh is forbidden meat, yet they will give
it to their children to 'expel worms,' and Beduins think their
hollow bones make them the best short pipe-stems. The foul
hopping birds, when they were dull of their gory feast, sat
heavily by upon the shelves of rocks, and hardly men's threatening
voices might raise them. In few hours the fetor of a battle-
field was in our nostrils, which the night remitted. Ill odours
are very hateful to the Arabs, and when the new day was
light, Mahanna, only murmuring that the mare was dead, bade

his housewife strike the tent, and the people hastened **to** remove.

We journeyed three leagues northward, and alighted, having ever above us, at the right hand, the immense Harra mountain. This desert is sand, full of sandstone crags ; there I heard again the cheerful voice of the rock partridge, and saw her brood running and cowering, under the stone ledges. Whilst we rode I descried some basalt rocks, which spouted from the fiery veins beneath, had of old burst through this brittle floor of sandstone. In the same passage, upon a rising ground, *Zenaiba,* I saw other small builded heaps of stones, and beside them upon the soil were set out plain grave chambers.

At evening there came-in a company of Bílli from another menzil ; and much they wondered to meet with a Nasrâny in their kinsmen's booths. With jealous hostile glances their eyes were still fastened upon me. One chanted some staves (it might be an ancient lay), of the *Rûm* (Romans, Byzantines), their forefathers' border enemies. " A race full of ingenuity, adversaries not to trust." And they took me to be of that hostile heathen nation, which conspired continually to beat down the saving religion of Islam. After supper, when we had broken meat together and they heard good reported of me, they were become of my counsel. Some of them desired that I should come to the know-ledge of Ullah, also being a Moslem I might ever inhabit with them—' then every man bringing some goat or sheep, they would gather a little flock to sustain me, I should receive of them im-mediately a camel, and a maiden to wife.' They thought it like a despite that, a lone man in their midst, I should be so bold as to profess a strange religion : and they Aarab of the khála, only subject to their own rash wills. They said also, ' But have we not heard it told of them that the Nasâra are upright men, of such good faith in their idolatry, that pity is they be not enlightened ? if this man converted he would make a good Moslem ; the Christian blood also was better than their own, so that any of us entering the religion became wellah a sherîf.'

Mahanna was a good man, and his sheykhly wife a good woman, but they were not well met. For a light displeasure he had lately uttered—to the half—words of divorce : her mind was in doubt and heaviness, and she was great with child ; yet would she take, she said, a water-skin upon her shoulder, and wend upon her bare feet alone over the hot sands, to her own kindred, who were sheukh in another menzil. She was " good to the guest ; " cheerfully she ground for me my corn, and she brought of that little milk which she could have from her neighbours ;

for the foal drank all here in her beyt. One day, when she had
baked a cake of my corn under the coals, she took a little léban,
and smiling like a sorrowful house-mother, she bid me rise to
dine ; and after that she said, "'lie down to sleep, and it will do
thee more good, and comfort thyself, that thou die not in this
land of hunger." She suffered corroding intestinal pains, a common Arabian disease. I gave her laudanum powder, and she
slumbered in the noon heat ; awaking, she told me she had
dreamed much, and was the better, but would not afterward
use it, for her unborn babe's sake. I studied to accord them,
saying to Mahanna, in a few more weeks she might bear him
a son, the consolation of an Aarab household.

More days passed, and when we had no tidings of Abu Sinûn,
I agreed with an old man for the kid which he had given me to
cure his grandchild's eyes, to guide me upon the Harra to the
Moahîb. We ascended north-eastward upon an ancient lava-
stream, such an one as those vast floods which I had seen issue
from Vesuvius a few years before. The molten stone had seyled
down the Arabian valley of sandstone, when the Aueyrid was
nearly as we see at present. When we were come upon the main
lava-field above, it seemed like nothing so much as an immeasurable cow-shard : a startled troop of gazelles scudded before
us ; here they are robust, and *nearly of the colour of basalt;*
—gazelles are white in the sand plains. After the lava crusts
we rode upon black sand, and upwards under a crater hill ; and
beyond I saw a wonderful new and horrid world of vulcanic
rusty hills and craters,—black powder, sharp lava slag, and
cinders, was this soil under our camels' feet. The volcanelli
appeared standing so thick that bye and bye looking about us I
counted above thirty at once. After that, I saw again upon the
basalt platform a cluster of barrows, and thereby an ancient
grave-kist of flags set out lengthwise. We passed in another
place some ancient burying ground ; the old man *Abeydillah,*
with his chin pointing to the graves, enquired, ' What did I see,
and what were my thoughts of them ? '—" Is this some mákbara
of your Aarab ? "—" Nay, they be no graves of the Beduw which
thou seest there with many great stones upon them. The use
is not so in our time ; they are of the former world, *el-auellîn ;*
now dost thou not know them ! wellah, Khalîl ! be they not of
your old heathen folk ? "—A lichen grows not in this land of
sunny drought, and the baked soil is merely naked, without
blade : in the passage of time, of human observation, there is no
sensible elemental waste,—it might hardly be discerned, at
first sight, if the graves were of ten years past or a thousand.—
' They were of the world before them ; the people of those times

were kafirs, kafirs be the Yahûd and Nasâra; Khalîl is a
Nasrâny; therefore these lying here in graves are the old dead
ancestors of Khalîl.' In this sort they reason, and it is strong
enough ground in the people's religion to build a man's fanaticism
upon it.

Many broken hollows in the waste uneven vulcanic field are
grown up with a few desert acacia trees and barren broom
bushes. These sunk thickets were full of locusts, which we saw
sitting thick as rain-drops upon all the thorny branches, from
whence they flew up in a storm of rustling wings, a sight that
quickened the weary heart of the old nomad. " Ha! cried he,
Khalîl, hast thou now no spell to drive them away? take thy
paper man, for I say this is a time to write, and not those
ninneries which thou didst enquire daily of the Aarab; canst
thou not make, thus, that they fly out of our dîra?" I said,
" But what thinkest thou, is read in God's Word? that these
are ' the Lord's great army.' " He answered with a pious sigh,
as the Beduw will receive every saw sounding to religious
edification, " Heigh! they be indeed as the army of Ullah." In
a place I saw the sand-rock appearing through the Harra platform, thereby a climbing billow of columnar basalt that resembled bilge timbers of some long ship's side;—chilled by the
heel and petrifying upwards, while the height was carried slowly
outward, the planetary metal is suspended like the spring of a
Moorish arch.

In this, we began to think where should be the Aarab:
Abeydillah said, ' If we did not see them yonder, we might not
find them in this daylight,' we must look for them upon
another water. This is all that can be predicted in the case, for
the Beduins are shifting from day to day, and alighting in new
menzils. It was el-j(g)aila, the giddy forenoon heat, we had
taken no water, and carried nothing with us to eat: the sunny air
flickered over all the radiant beach of hot lava stones. Abeydillah could not see well, he said, he had trusted to my eyes;
when I answered that I was not far-sighted, he began to be a
little amazed, he had not foreseen this case. " Khalîl, here
come riding, many times, robbers of the Howeytát, and how,
if we cannot see them nor our friends neither? alas! that
you did not tell me at the menzil you could not see, then we
were not come hither. I am purblind, and what shall we do
now? "—" I have this glass to see at a distance; tell me thou
to which part, and I shall see as the best." We rode a little
further, and said my companion, " I see, there, a little glim-
mering of a white thing, Khalîl! look forth."—" Well! I see
a white camel, feeding."—" These are the Aarab, let us cross

to them." So we came to Moahîb herdsmen, with the great
cattle ; they showed us a rising ground, from whence we might
see their people's menzil.

There came one running down to us, like a giant from the
next crater hill ; his *ganna* (that is the Beduins' short loaded
club-stick, in his hand) : "Abeydillah ! " he shouted, as he
came nigh, with heated countenance and robust voice, of his
great chest, and half out of breath, " why hast thou brought
us the kafir ?—ha ! peace be with thee, and well met." While I
was wondering how anyone could know me in these parts, he
went on with boisterous speech, to behave himself so wildly, laying the other stalwart hand to my nâga's bridle, and, poising and
shaking the murderous oaken mace in his fist, that I thought
each next instant the burly body might turn, and with a
bitter stroke have clapped out my brains. I asked Abeydillah
in a whisper, what must I think of it ? and he, " Wellah, I
cannot tell, Khalîl."—" By God, I took you for two thieves
(cries that Mahûby) as I looked from yonder hill, and saw you
come riding over the Harra ; so I was lying in wait, to have
risen upon you at unawares."—" Upon you be peace ! and
(Abeydillah said now, laughing) Wellah, O *Mishwat*, didst thou
take us for habalîs ! where be your Aarab ? "—" The people
removed to-day, come on, I say, O Abeydillah, the menzil lies
in the bottom, there, beyond that rising ground."

He strode before us ;—and as he went by some outlying
booths, a man came forth, and saying something to Abeydillah, who rode in front, he took hold on his bridle : then
Mishwat turned back, and laying to his hand, he drew against
him. Reading only their urgent looks, and not hearing what
they meant, I supposed that one had challenged my rafîk for
an old debt, and would attach his thelûl, which I saw he led
away with Abeydillah ; and at the tent side he pulled down
the brute upon his knees.—This was a contention in hospitality
of the poor Beduins ! Mishwat said he found us, and had accompanied us, therefore we were his guests ; but the other answered
him, ' We should not pass his beyt ! ' Said Abeydillah, "*Noakh*
Khalîl, alight then ! it is here we shall breakfast." The pleasant
old man, one of their next neighbours and allies, was a friend of
them both. Mishwat entered with us : he was a cousin of the Moahîb
sheykh, and next after him in the councils of the tribe. The
government was in him, as the elder of the house, in the sheykh's
absence, and before the sheykh's sons ; yet the Beduin sheykh
dying is succeeded by his own son. Mishwat was a hearty
man, but fanatic, suspicious, fond, of an ox-like humour ; his
strength lay in his stubborn brawns and large breast, and little

in his brains, which indeed were not very well settled. Our
host who put upon us this gentle force, was a poor man, of very
hospitable mind ; and in these Beduins of the mountain there
remains something, say their nomad neighbours, of the old
hospitality.   His family tents were three, which in all the
general menzils, he pitched a little apart to the westward, at
the camp's end, where any coming from that quarter must needs
pass them.   The man soon after departed, with a few more, to
eat of the date harvest, at Kheybar ; they would encamp with
the W. Aly, and glean for themselves and buy dates in those
feverish valleys.   A wife of the Moahîb sheykh went down with
them.—This small fendy of southern Annezy have no inheritance
at Kheybar.   As we sat, his old mother entered : women's
greetings are short, "The Lord strengthen you ! peace." The
hospitable house-mother came with her butter-milk skin, and
shook it and poured out for us, to the last drop ; then she
lifted the mighty bowl-full of refreshing nourishment to our
hands, with the kinds words, *Isshrub wa erwîk,* "Drink, and
quench thy thirst ;" this was now sent round, since the guest-
meal could not so soon be made ready.

This small outlying Moahîb kindred, remaining in the Hejâz
borders, between Annezy and Bíllî, is reckoned to them both ;
they are by adoption Bíllî, and by lineage a fendy of that great
sub-tribe of Annezy in the north, *es-Sbáa,* nomads of the district
es-Shimbel (called of shimbel, a corn measure of twelve midds,
modius), north-eastwards of Damascus.   Anciently the Sbáa
were Aarab of the W. er-Rummah country, north of the Harrat
Kheybar, and under el-Kasîm ; where wander now the midland
Heteym.   There is an ancient Moahîb colony of husbandmen,
"keepers of kine," in *el-Hasa,* (that is very far from hence, in
East Nejd).   The Moahîb, now few, which have been more than
thirteen generations in the Aueyrid, entered perhaps strong in
number, since they dispossessed the B. Sokhr. All the Aueyrid
they even yet reckon to be theirs by right, for they once possessed it ; though, diminished to a small kindred, they hold only
the southern third part.   There are besides, families of the
Moahîb living with their Sbáa kinsmen in Syria, and other
booths of them with the B. Sokhr in Belka. The Moahîb dîra
eastward, under the Harra, marches with the haj road, and
from a little above el-Akhdar to Medáin.   Westwards they
descend to the Jau, to Ummshash, to *Ensheyfa,* in the Sehamma
country, to pasture and water.   The Sehamma friends go up
in like manner to the Moahîb summering in the Harra, or
lodge by them, in the western valleys.   Thus, if one of their

dîras should fail, the other may serve them both. This is a neighbourly custom of the desert, whereby the tribes assure themselves in ill years, and in dangers ; and they are easily received (as we saw lately the Fejîr) one by another, to their kheyr Ullah, the Lord's common providence. Large is the tolerance, the religious forbearance, of Arabian hospitality, but friendship must keep an even balance, which, also in the desèrt religion, is as glass, that being drawn to a length, may then snap short, and the divorced parts are hardly to be knit again : and after long indulgent amity, comes variance, as their several interests are touched, which are before other, of pasture and water. When brawls happen all day between tribesmen, about their pits, and days of watering, great must be the policy of the sheukh of tribes lying together, to separate the herdsmen's and waterers' differences. Last year there happened a grave quarrel for pasture in the Sehamma dîra, between those friendly Aarab hosts and the *Serahîn*, a kindred of the Moahîb, of whom the rest held with the Sehamma against their trespassing kinsmen. Upon both sides, men ran to arms, the Moahîb are sturdy swelling hearts to fight and, in the bickering, a Sehamma tribesman was slain by a Serahîny.

When strangers are seen to arrive, it is presently known in the menzil, and men of Abeydillah's acquaintance came in one by one to greet him and enquire tidings. Our host, as they would rise again, gently bade them sit still, which is to say, " remain thou and eat with us." A long space passed till there was had in the mighty wooden charger, which among honest nomad households, is not the least necessary of their goods and utensils : this sign of hospitality is seen like a shield trussed up with their gear upon the baggage-camel in the ráhlas. The vast trencher, hoarded with cooked rice, was now set down before us, and in the midst was a pan of their precious samn melted ; into this they dip each morsel, (an half handful, pressed by the eater's fingers into a ball,) and carry it to the mouth so handsomely that he is an unfeatly fellow who spills any little drop. The host mildly cheers his guests, bidding them approach and sit round, he says " Though it be a poor mess yet take ye in good worth such as Ullah sendeth." A host commonly sits not down to the dish, his heart is fed to see his guests eat, he is there to serve us ; but here all sat together as brethren. The Arabs say always before meat or drink, *Bismillah*, in the name of God. The rice is served from the caldron ; and though, in summer, they first let it stand a good while, (in the oasis clay houses the mess is set by some time in the casement,) it is yet so hot that, when we have eaten

what is uppermost we scald our fingers : then the Aarab sitting
round withhold their hands for a moment, whilst some one of
them fans the reeking victual with the lap of his mantle. Mishwat
was my neighbour, a hospitable shrew in his heart, though his
brows looked dangerous ; now he bent upon me at the bread
and salt a pair of friendly meaning eyes : he pushed me with
the elbow, and nodded, saying, "Eat strongly, and it will do
thee good ; this is the manner as thou seest me do ; when the
dish is before a man he should eat heartily, eat thou and
enlarge thy breast, here among the Beduw." He thrust forth
the stalwart forearm and made rice balls, and laid them by me.
He had nearly been our host to-day, and was therefore a solicitous
friend in the guest-meal. Mishwat, though out of my memory,
remembered me for good ; he had passed in the winter by our
kella at Medáin, where, asking me to fill his pipe-head, I had
filled his hand, and he hoped well there came good store of the
brain-steeping drug in my deep camel-bags,—the thing which
he loved best, beside the hope of his son, and the consolation
of his jowwar, under the nomad heaven. Mohammed Abu Sinûn
was his sister's husband.

When any have done eating, they hold still their hands at
the dish till the rest be satisfied, and then all say together, blessing the host and rising, "*Khálaf Ullah aleyk ya mazîb.*" Who
answers for himself heartily, *háni* or *sáhah, auáfy :* or we may
say *káthir Ullah fothilakom,* "the Lord multiply thy virtuous
bounty." Later it came to my knowledge that out host had
spent upon this guest-meal nearly all the victual which remained by him in this low season. They had hereafter but
milk, and that not enough, and mereesy. The Aarab can live for
long months so slenderly nourished, that it seems to us they
endure without food. Startling is this occasional magnanimity of the Beduw in the religious sacrifice of hospitality ;
men who in their other dealings are commonly of so merely
vile, fraudulent, self-loving mind and envious misanthropy.
The most honour of a man's life is the people's praise of his
bounty. The Beduin is moved to the bountiful receiving
of guests where his nature is very sensible ; vainglorious, he
would be catching at an estimation in the world : also the
nomad's natural religion is working within him, whose days
are wanderings between the empty earth and sky, with perils
evermore about them. Faithfully he receives God's guests,
who is the Host of all, and the Giver of all good ; and,
this doing, he looks for a blessing and the divine protection. A strained giving of thanks I have not heard ; they
tell me it may be homely said sometimes, *Káthir Ullah*

lebánakom, The Lord multiply your milk ; *'bilakom*, give you increase of great cattle ; *ghrannámakom*, of flocks ; *eyyàlakom*, of many children ; and even *kilábakom*, multiply the watch-hounds of your menzils (so may ye lead your lives with the less loss and danger).

Abu Sinûn only now came in to salute me ; I went with him to deposit my bags in his beyt, and then we walked together to visit the Moahîb sheykh, Tollog, to whom Abeydillah committed me at my request Teslîm, in trust, from Mahanna. The burly mountaineer sheykh looked yet green in his old age, for he was by many years the oldest man of them all, and did not seem such ; he might have matched in their time with his housewives' grandmothers. He returning at the moment from his afternoon prayers, received me kindly, and, when we had drunk coffee in his tent, there was served for us here another guest-meal of rice. I found a Fejîry of Zeyd's menzil in the company, come to treat with the sheykh to suffer him and his kinsmen, (exiles for his sake who was wounded by the Fehjy) to wander with the Moahîb. We remained silently sitting out the day's heat till the sun's going down, then we returned to the Moor's menzil.

His was a very long winter booth, so great I had not seen any in Arabia, of four apartments ; in which lodged, besides his household, two families of brethren : the men were his shepherd and two hinds, one or other of whom accompanied him upon his trading journeys betwixr Tebûk and the coast. A stranger, of the hard western alloy, he seemed a man of large understanding and civil prudence among the negligent, bird-witted Arabians. There is many a way before them to gain by honest endeavour, where they find none, or they will not go under the burden. Mohammed the carrier was grown in short time to welfare :—might not a few such spirits, dispersed among the wandering tribes, become the school-masters of Arabia ? The nomads lie every day of their lives upon their hungry maws, waiting for the mercy of Ullah : this is the incurious misery of human minds faint with the hunger of generations and grown barren in the desert. Abu Sinûn was in few years come up out of nothing, and now he matched the best of them : but that soon thriving of his honest industry was a leanness to the Aarab ; his was as the life of an alien in their menzils, and they esteemed him of too grudging humour. Beardless he had come down to these countries to be a nefer of the garrison at el-Akhdar ; a dozen years later, with an asthma, he seemed to-day a man past the middle age. I asked Mohammed, how had he found confidence to take up the nomad life, and where learned he this trade of flocks and camels ?—In the Beduins' hearing, he made me no answer.

On the morrow, Mohammed must set out for el-Akhdar with that rice he had lately brought up from Wejh ; and thence to Tebûk. The Moghreby who, for shortness of breath, could not take rest in the open Beduin booth, lay down among his flock abroad to sleep. Loading in the dawn, he departed with the hind, bidding his housewife have a care of me until his coming again. This Moahîb camp, of thirty beyts, was pitched in a coomb of the lava ground : only a few broom bushes, not the pasture of any cattle, grew among the huge vulcanic stones. The housewives' tent-pins, which could not be struck down in the rock soil, were here made fast above ground with weight of basalt blocks ; upon these the beyt cords strained securely. In the lava clefts and gravel of the sharp Harra about, appeared only few springing blades of herbage, and rare harsh bushes of the desert : locusts had devoured the thin spring of grasses, so that wild hay for the sheykh's filly was fetched from a day's distance in the underlying sand plain ; there was no other horse in this small Hara tribe.

We removed and encamped next amidst innumerable vol-canelli, *hilliân,* the greater of those about us might be 500 feet in height, above the mountain plain ; there seemed to be some such crater-hill in about every square mile. From hence, three hours to the southward, over the open lava field, is seen the great volcano cone *Anâz,* with a long train of vulcanic bergs and craters. [*v.* pl. v.] Anâz the giant *hilla* amongst the hilliân is named by the Aarab *sheykh el-Aueyrid :* next after Anâz upon the Harra is *J. Usshúb,* (which stands over el-Héjr,) called therefore *ibn amm-hu,* " his cousin," in the laughing mouth of the nomads. Nigh to our high mountain menzil they told me there was a ruined site !

Whilst we lodged here there came in (with a Mahûby rafîk) three men of the Howeytát, their next foemen in the Teháma. This was a sheykh, *Abu Bátn,* a companion, and his hind. Abu Batn sought the *midda,* or payment made between enemies for the blood of the slain :—a man of theirs had been shot in a foray upon the Moahîb. An enemy's life is assessed among them at five camels. The midda is not withheld between hostile tribes which, as these, are but reavers of each others' camels : only where there is blood-feud, as between the Fejîr and B. Atîeh, there is no atonement ; that fire which is in their hearts for old homicides may endure for generations, and who of either part falls into his foeman's hands is in danger to be slain without

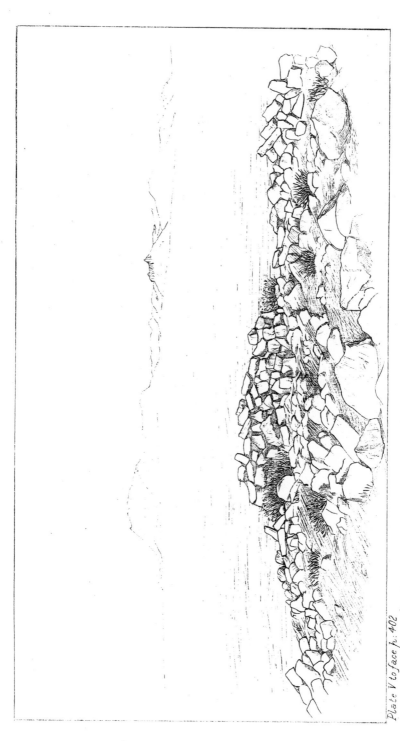

Plate V to face p. 402

JEBEL 'ANÂZ, seen over the lava plain of the Harra (altitude nearly 6000 feet) from the Northward and distant 11 miles : in the foreground part of an antique circle of heaped stones.

remedy. The Aarab, in their suffering manner of life (their cup of life is drawn very low, and easily stirred at the dregs), which eagers the blood and weakens the heart, are of a jealous frenetic heat towards their enemies ;—of this also is the Semitic fanaticism. They are, in any warfare, as the wasps of mankind, too much tempted in their nature to sting the adversary, even though they leave some of their own bowels in them : so it is well in their ghrazzus that they have a second thought, in remembrance of the midda, which must be paid out of their own, if they should kill even a foeman. I asked, " What if you deny them satisfaction ? " *Answer:* " We durst not, or none of all our lives would be sure from day to day ; the first of us met by any of them, they would kill him outright."

These strangers seeing Abu Sinûn's tent so widespread, were gone to alight there, they had not perhaps confidence to enquire for the sheykh in the menzil of their enemies. *Hamdy*, Mohammed's wife, boiled them the guest-meal of rice ; but after that Tollog called them to his own booth ; they should be the sheykh's guests. They and he were all worthy men, of a sheykhly moderation, and spoke, as they could, kindly together ; those required but reason, and these meant not to defraud or delay them. Abu Bátn, a man in years, and a poor-seeming sheykh (unless perhaps *sordidatus*,— and that I have seen in the Beduish Kerak, in Moab), was suer for the blood :—he treated with the tribesmen that had slain his own son. Commonly the ghrazzus meet with only a few herdmen, who cannot resist them ; but some of the Moahîb, finding Howeytát in their country, had set furiously upon them in defence of their cattle, and shot through one of their bodies. " Ah-ha ! and eigh me ! " sighed the unhappy father of a valiant son, that this day lay rotting in his shallow burial before the time ; " we ride only a cattle-lifting, but ye slay men : " so he ended with a great drawn sob ; Tollog sighed after him, as he was a father, and they sat on in silence.

When I questioned with these strangers of their dîra, they answered me without signs of the wild Beduins' jealousy of a hostile religion. The Aarab can sit long in sober solemnity, and they cheer themselves the next while with some elvish mockery : now said *Shwoysh*, brother of the Moor's wife, between jollity and bitterness, in those strange and hostile tribesmen's hearing, and they also smiling, " We are gôm, Khalîl, with the Howeytát, —and there may be a few good men of them such as these, but all the rest are wicked !—Aarab of theirs have set up their summer camp upon a water of ours in the Teháma,—God send them confusion ! I say, hast thou not amongst thy medicines

any baneful thing, that we may put it in the wells, and
poison them, and we will reward thee."—" My religion bids
us to deal with all men as brethren; your silver, above ground
and under it, cannot move me." Gravely the Howeytát smiled,
and " Well spoken! " they said. I answered, at some time I
hoped to visit them. ' If I came down to their dîra (said Abu
Bátn), I should be welcome.'—Our menzil was left standing
till the Howeyties departed, " lest in the ráhla they should see
more of the Harra." A nomad passing in strange marches, will
look curiously upon the landmarks, to remember them another
day : even the rankest hostile riders have little knowledge of
this vulcanic country.

I wished to ascend the great crater-hill Anâz, and look
far over this lava country : but if any agreed to accompany
me, the sheykh secretly forbad him ; Tollog reserved the advantage to himself and his own sons. He supposed I might be
good to the discovering of springs or treasure : a Beduwy,
he could not otherwise think than that I came to enrich
myself, and he would be enriched with me. The Fejîr sheukh,
men of more urbane minds, had better understood the Haj
officers ; but these were men stiff in their opinions, and heavy
mountaineers. Tollog, travailing in his heart of all that he
had ever heard strange of the Nasâra, enquired of me at the
coffee hearth, " Khalîl, Wellah, is there not a vessel for the
air—tell me this, and let the company hear it—in which
the Nasrânies may fly? "—" Very true, Tollog ; a great bubble
in a silk bag, greater than this booth, and that may float
in the air." *Tollog :* " But tell us more ! is there not a ship
which is made to sail under the face of the water, with all
her Arabs, and that may rise again? "—" From whence (I
asked) had he this? "—' Of a son of his uncle (that is a Sbáite)
of Syria, who had taken a western woman, very rich, of those
lands beyond seas, or he wist not where.'
We removed again, and when we encamped, I looked round
from a rising ground, and numbered forty crater hills within
our horizon ; I went out to visit the nighest of them. To go a
mile's way is weariness, over the sharp lava field and beds of
wild vulcanic blocks and stones. I passed in haste, before
any friendly persons could recall me ; so I came to a cone
and crater of the smallest here seen, 300 feet in height, of
erupted matter, pumice and light rusty cinders, with many
sharp ledges of lavas. The hill-side was guttered down by
the few yearly showers in long ages. I climbed and entered
the crater. Within were sharp walls of slaggy lava, the further

Plate VI. to face p. 405

Height of the Harrat el-'Aueyrid: the top of Jebel 'Anâz, seen over the vulcanic desert, part broken down—that was before the bore of out-flowing lavas—and encrusted by the fiery blast of the eruption. Upon the flanks of that hilla, I found a block of red granite, cast up from the head of some Plutonic vein, in the deep of the mountain. Red granite, called by these nomads *hajr el-kra*, in some parts of the Harra lies not far under, they say it is seen near Anâz ; and below the Aueyrid mountain. In the Jau, are some antique ruins, built of great blocks of the same mineral : I understand from them that it is the rock of the next lower-lying *Shéfa* country, and of those mighty crested land-marks, appearing in the north-western horizon, mountains of the Teháma, *Wuttid* and *Jowla.* (*v.* the panorama, pl. vII., p. 416.) Of the hajr el-kra, the Beduw work out their best quern-stones : they have no tools, but when they choose a block, they hammer incessantly upon it, with another hard stone, till they have beaten it down to that shape they would ; and they drill the hole of the pin, beating upon a nail. I found a natural pit under the crater hill of yellow tufa, breathed of old from the vulcanic gulf, and in the great slag-stones about, many common greenish vulcanic crystals (chrysolite).

We look out from every height, upon the Harra, over an iron desolation ; what uncouth blackness and lifeless cumber of vulcanic matter !—an hard-set face of nature without a smile for ever, a wilderness of burning and rusty horror of unformed matter. What lonely life would not feel constraint of heart to trespass here ! the barren heaven, the nightmare soil ! where should he look for comfort ?—There is a startled conscience within a man of his *mesquîn* being, and profane, in presence of the divine stature of the elemental world !—this lion-like sleep of cosmogonic forces, in which is swallowed up the gnat of the soul within him,—that short motion and parasitical usurpation which is the weak accident of life in matter. Anâz appeared, riding as it were upon the rocky tempest, at twelve miles distance ;—I despaired of coming thither, over so many vulcanic deeps and reefs of lavas, and long scalding reaches of basalt rolling stones. (*v.* pl. vI.)

As we removed again over the Harra, I thought I could not have dreamed of such a direful country ; it is like that (a thousand fold) which wearies the eye that looks down from Vesuvius to the south-eastward, where a European will hardly adventure with heavy heart to bewilder his feet ;—but that had brought forth, in Arabia, léban and samn to the poor nomads. Where the Aarab alight in some cragged place, some wild bottom, it is our homestead of two or three desert nights and daylights, and there the hideous scars of basalt, the few thorn-tree scrogs and barren broom bushes, wear to our familiar acquaintance, and they become even of our human affections, so that we are unwilling to leave them ;—and doubtless the home-born Mahûby is thus affectioned to his foster Harra. They reasoning as simple men, commonly suppose a great part of the world to be thus, lava country : not their children alone, but men and women have enquired of me, " Is your dîra, Khalîl, Harra or sand plains ? "

—Beside the Aarab and their cattle, there is nearly no life upon the Harra. In this pure airy height hardly the flies follow us, which abound even in the waste nomad dîras. There is here but a small black solitary bird of slender form, less than a thrush, with certain white feathers, the *sweydîa*, which is, as our little red-breast, a cheerful neighbour to mankind. Many a time the passenger hears at unawares her short descant ringing upon the waste moors, in perplext desert ways, in the awe and the Titanic ruins of desolate mountains, with a silver sweetness, as it were the voice to his soul of some benign spirit. Of great ground beasts, only wolves prowl in the wind of our mountain menzils : they are more in number upon the Harra, and bolder than in the plain dîras. The nights, so serene in Arabia, were yet fresh at this altitude in the first weeks of June ; even the summer days are here airy. I found one morning, at the sun-rising, 79° Fahr., 90° at the jaila, and about mid-day 95° in the tent's shadow. This high land is intolerably cold in winter ; Beduin passengers can hardly stand against the biting blast of it : even the wild beasts have then forsaken the Harra. The Moahîb at that time retire to the Teháma, and shelter themselves in the bottom of the Wady Jizzl ; where they find plenty of dry tamarisk timber, *tûrfah*, which will glow all night in their closed worsted tents : and the Beduins having but a loose cotton tunic upon their lean bodies, and a wide mantle, and the most of them lying down without a coverlet, yet they can say " we suffer little then or nothing from the cold." In the day-time they comfort themselves with sips of coffee or milk made hot ; the winter mid-day sun is always warm there.

That we had to drink in the lava country is pool-water, black, thick and fetid. Commonly after two or three camel waterings the pool is drawn to the dregs, and that water will sooner foul than whiten linen ; yet of this the nomads are fain to fill their garbies and be thankful :—there is none other. But worse ! some will go down to wash themselves, if they see no sheykh by to forbid them, and will there steep and wring out their rusty tunics :—and always, where the nomad finds water enough,

there he makes religion to wash the body ; in the menzils a man
will carry out from the tent a bowl of water, and go to purify
himself in some secret place of the desert. The nomads might
cleanse the pools (which now they must needs abandon at half-
water,) from the feculent lees of generations ; they have wit
enough, but not public virtue for a common labour ; and the
sheykh's authority cannot compel his free tribesmen. There
are found now and then stirring spirits among them who, betwixt free will and their private advantage, will cleanse some
wells which were stopped.

Now came Abu Sinûn again from el-Khúthr and Tebûk
and with him some men of that village and camel drivers of
B. Atîeh. One day he rested with us, and on the morrow they
would descend towards el-Wejh. " Khalîl, what a strange
chance (said he) that thou findest me here, and that I meet
with thee in this waste. Moghreby I, and thou Engleysy !
—Ah ! where be the cool Morocco mountains, the waters running in the valleys, and all that blessing of Ullah ?—those
sown fields of corn, the orchards full of pleasant fruits, lemons,
oranges, citrons, the vine, and the pomegranate, which we press
into our summer drinks, the fat gourds running upon the ground,
and refreshing melons ?—which good things am I not a fond
man to forsake, for this wretchedness of the Beduw and burning rocks without a shadow from the sun ? "—" But thou hast
found God's blessing here, Mohammed ; what may a man desire
above an easy fortune ? "—" Ah well ! a man who can shift for
himself should find it in what country he is ; " and he said,
with a peaceable sigh, that ' his life would not be long '; it
seemed to him unhappiness to perish at last in these deserts,
leaving his son after him to be a Beduwy. He asked, betwixt sad
and smiling, ' Would I not, when I returned to the West, carry
the child (an ungracious boy) along with me ? ' Mohammed's
camels were to-day more than twenty, and all those good ones;
his goats and his sheep, after the yeaning, would be not fewer
than an hundred ; already he saw no man richer than himself
among these " weak " nomads.

He told me of his embarking from the West with other men
of Morocco : they sailed upon pilgrimage and, as Moghrâreba
adventurers, to seek fortune. In the high seas huge tempests
overtook them, their vessel was carried many days in the
fury of the wind, and they not seeing the sun or stars were
driven eastward, till they fell upon the coast of Anatoly, and
saved themselves in the haven of Smyrna. Giddy and weak
from shipboard, and lately escaped the fear of death, they
heard themselves kindly spoken with there in a stragne land in

their own tongue, and were hospitably entertained too by the
health officer, and he was a ' *Taliâny* ' (those of the quarantine
in the Levant are mostly Italian). Mohammed asked me, with
a smile of good remembrance, if Italians and Engleysies were
not one nation? and he was not much pleased when, in reverence of the truth, I answered him barely " Nay."

Not without peril were Mohammed's journeys betwixt
Tebûk and Wejh. Thrice commonly he went and came in the
hot summer's season, and some years four times, each double
journey being about five hundred desert miles. If any hostile
ghrazzu met with him and robbed his camels, his loss would be
more than he might recover in many a painful voyage. He had
been stripped last year and his thelûl taken from under him, only
crossing the Héjr plain, betwixt W. Thirba and the kella. In
their coming down from the north they had seen a small foray of
six riders, but were not espied by them. Abu Sinûn turned then
and descended with this news to Mahanna ;—the Sehamma
had immediately removed. Mohammed hearing there the last
tidings of our ráhlas, was able to ascend directly from thence
to our menzil, thirty miles distant from the place in which he
had left us. The nomad marches may hardly be traced in the
vulcanic field ; for seldom a little sand appears in all that lava
crust and waste of stones which might receive the footprints.
These Aarab tell me, that in their breaking up an encampment, the household of any absent tribesman use to grave a
line upon the forsaken dâr, showing the bearing of the new
menzil ; or else their sign is a spray of broom or a broken
bough of acacia. Those who are bred in the khála have
an excellent skill of the way, and yet strangers exercised in
the nomad life may become Beduins. Beduins may confidently seek out unknown menzils in immense deserts, where
they have a knowledge of the waters, and which therefore are
not to them inhospitable. When the place of the Aarab
whom they would find is unknown, they must roll in their
minds a sort of running problem,—' At this season we must
look for them in such a quarter ; ride we to that or that
water, and we shall find the traces of them, if they be at all in
those parts,—if no, let see now in which other quarter of their
dîra the Aarab are likely to be.' If by the way they find some
breadth of the desert a bare soil without blade, they understand
that no winter rain had fallen there ;—then certainly the Aarab
are not come thither, and they turn to seek them in another
part : thus even in a great nomad district, they may very
soon come to their friends. Beduins returning from a longer
absence, and from far countries, Syria, Mecca, Mesopotamia,

enquire of friendly Aarab by the way ; and they put in for tidings to the market villages as Teyma and el-Ally.

'I might accompány him to-morrow,' said Mohammed ; but I finally answered "Nay," being yet too feeble to forsake the mountain air, and in that raging sun to pass the heated plains of the Teháma. I lodged in my tent, I removed upon my own nâga, I received nothing of the wandering Arabs but water. If I drank any milk I took care to repay it to their advantage ; upon Abu Sinûn I had bestowed for his rice-bowls of my three guest-days as many reals. Every few weeks there went down marketers of Bíllî to el-Wejh ; I might wait a time, but as each breath of air refreshed my spirits, I mused anew of breaking into Arabia. The stranger's presence with the Aarab was not welcome to the jealous old sheykh ; Tollog even laid a blame upon the Moghreby for my sake, and, said Mohammed, "I cannot do against the sheykh's bidding, although I would have you dwell here with me ; you are one, they say, come before the Franks that would take the country. Tollog is hot of heart and will not be contraried, and remember, Khalîl, that these are Beduw, having no notice of the world." I asked Tollog of it in the mejlis, "Go with Mohammed, said he, to-morrow, he will bring thee to el-Wejh ; Khalîl, you cannot longer accompany the Aarab."—"And wherefore, O Tollog ? "—" El-gâbily, to-morrow, I mount in a ghrazzu (feigned reasons, which he spoke with his old Beduin courtesy) ; besides, the Aarab are about to remove far off, into a very thirsty country, so that thou couldst not suffer it."—" Tollog, you Beduins are very thirsty souls, and I drinking less may endure with the Aarab, whether thirst or hunger ; only send me not unfriendly away in this deadly heat to die in the Teháma. No, Tollog, I will remain with you and the Aarab."—" Wellah, Khalîl, that may not be ; it were also better for thee to return to thine own people, and not die : depart to-morrow with Abu Sinûn, but drink now thy coffee, and speak we no more of this."

In my host's household all that summer's day (as Tollog would), they poured me out no water to drink ; that suffering this thirst I might be the more willing to depart. The guest will endure in silence ; but at half afternoon, despising their brittle ceremonial which is contrary to reason and humanity, I went to ask a draught, which is never denied, at one of the neighbour booths. I thought to agree with a Beduin herdsman, whom I had seen well disposed, to guide me to Anâz, and then, descending from the Harra, I might visit *Béda* and *Middián*, which they said is a ruined village in the Teháma, and pass from thence to el-Wejh. His housewife told me he was gone a water-

ing, and would return soon. She invited me to sit in their
tent, and poured me out putrid water and léban ;—should she
not also, she asked, with a feminine hypocrisy, run and slay a
kid for me ? She called her gossips, and led them to see the
Nasrâny in her beyt. The men from home, the nomad women
will come motherly and sisterly, to sit down timidly and loose
the tongue and feed their feminine curiosity in communing with
a stranger. After the first words, these poor hareem were
for my part, condemning the ill-will and ignorance of their
Aarab, that misspoke of my religion, ' which was not wicked,
as men said ; —but how did we pray ?—Khalîl, wilt thou say
for us something out of your prayers ? do you pray in your
own language ? and that is not *Araby.*'. I recited to them
with the canonical solemnity the Lord's Prayer. " How now !
they cried out, we are unjust, look you he prays devoutly, these
are good men," and they added the proverb, " There be none less
Moslems than the Moslemîn." So said those housewives,—
daughters of Nature, and not immodestly, " We would enquire of thee, if it be true which we hear, that the Nasâra
are not circumcised, and how then may the man live with his
wife ? " They asked had I not a medicine for one of their young
husbands, by whom the young woman his jâra had not conceived in the years two or three of their marriage. The gossips
praised her wifely ' patience, that she had not forsaken him, but
this year out, and the fault remaining, she was minded to leave
him.'

Fâiz, her husband, who now came in, was not willing to
accompany me, for the sheykh had sharply forbidden him. Fâiz
was one who gave me notice of the country without much
suspicion. One of these afternoons he had traced me out,
with his camel-stick, in the sand, the figure of the Harra,
setting up stones for the mountains, and the net of seyl-beds
and valleys below, with the Hareyry and the W. el-Humth.
When we looked up the sun was setting, and the people
rising, went apart to their prayers. Fâiz exclaimed then, not
seeing me about to fall upon my knees, " Where is thy Lord
God ? It is the hour to ask thy petition of Ullah ! " Fâiz
at this summer's end perished in the Héjr plain before
Wady eth-Thirba, enveloped in the Bishr ghrazzu, which
reaved, in that unhappy day, nearly all these tribesmen's
great cattle. Of too stubborn mettle, Fâiz strove among an
hundred armed enemies ; he could not so soon yield all that
he had in the world, and his trust too of Tollog's camels :—a
cruel shot of some wild hand put an end to that poor man's
impertinent resistance.

APPENDIX TO CHAP. XIV.

NAMÛS : in the *Kamús*, or Ocean Lexicon of the endless Arabic tongue, we find *nak(g)ús* a bell, [*v.* above pp. 307, 308]—and the nawamîs are bell-shaped : we find also *namús* a lair,—especially a hunter's shroud ; and where are nawamîs there are very commonly certain stone cells with cullis doors which the nomad people tell us are traps to take the leopard and the hyena. The Sinaitic nawamîs are semblable to the *rijjúm* of the Harrat Aueyrid and of Kheybar, which, it will be shown further on, are by all likelihood barrows. —Sir Henry C. Rawlinson thinks that the [Sinai] word *namús* may very well be taken to signify tombs ; he says "As the *m* and the *v* were indistinguishable, the true form should be navûs, which was a word known wherever Arabic was known. *Navús* was originally Persian, but was adopted in Arabic and applied to any old cemetery. It had always been supposed to be a corruption of, or a cognate word with the Greek ναός, and there were hundreds of navúses about Mesopotamia, which are mentioned in the old authors."

CHAPTER XV.

OUR LIFE UPON THE HARRA.

Tollog commands and the Nasrâny resists. A redoubtable bowl of lében. They fear also the tea-making of the Nasrâny. Tollog visited in the dark. The Shéfa country. Topology. The Aueyrid Harra. Planetary antiquity of the Harra. A great vulcanic eruption; Vesuvius. Is lava the Arabic laba? It is an art to enquire of the Beduw. The sheykhs have no great land-knowledge. The ancient tribe of Jeheyna. The height of the Harra. Tollog visits the stranger in his tent. Tollog sick. Phantom camel. The sheep of the Nomads. The wolf by night. The Nomads' watch-dogs. The shepherd's life. Rubbâ the herdsman. Rachel is rokhal of the Aarab. Murrain in the land. Wool-wives. Goats of the Nomads run wild. Gazelle fawns bred up by the Nomads. The milk season. The Moahîb descend to the plain deserts. Jaysh. A troop seen. Descent into W. Gârib. The grave-heap of Abu Zeyd's mother. The children's pastimes. Mehsan the Bountiful journeying from the North is robbed by a ghrazzu. Abu Selim the Moorish eye-pricker.

BEFORE the sun was fairly risen I heard Tollog's loud rough voice,—he had walked over himself to the Moor's beyt—bidding Mohammed, " Convey that Frenjy away to-day with thee! " he laid also his injunction upon the hind who should accompany the Moor not to leave me behind them. His last shouted word was, ' Wellah, when I was gone, I would return to take the country.' —I reminded Mohammed of his old promises, they had drawn me hither. He was bound, he answered, by the sheykh, yet he allowed that if I remained, there could no man compel me. The Aarab also were *rahîl*, about removing; Mohammed was ridden forth : as his men would now have constrained me I judged it prudent to resist them ;—or when other fanatical Aarab heard that this tribe had driven me out, would they not attempt the like, where I entered their menzils and dîras? and my heart was already set upon going to Kheybar. I was mounted, the Beduins removed, and those that were to follow Mohammed beat forward my old nâga. —They swore by my life I should that way with them! The poor brute, bellowing and tottering under their tempest of

blows, and constrained by my bridle, fell down many times
under me. ' *Etrush,* drive forward ! I might not stay, cried
the tormentors ; wellah, if I remained, the Aarab would strip
me and murder me.'—" Friends, there is none will do me
any hurt, were it only for fear of the Dowla." But they
cried out in their villanous disdain,—" Nakedness of the mother
of the Dowla ! " As I said, " In the next coming down, would
not M. Saîd (the Haj Pasha) require it of them ? " they cried
again, " Nakedness of his wife for Mohammed Saîd ! Khalîl,
come now, by the Lord thou shalt come away ! "—" *Beneyyi,* I
said, calling him by his name, are we not of old acquaintance ;
desîst, lad ! "—" Khalîl, but Tollog is a masterful man, *jabbàr,*
.he rules us at his pleasure, and I am in dread that for this he
will take my thelûl."—" If he seize thy thelûl for me, be sure,
as I am a faithful man, I will restore it." One of them laid
hand upon the headstall, and grinning the teeth he came
with his club-stick against me : these were servants, without a
sheykh amongst them. " Nay, Beneyyi cried, no violence ! " the
Aarab not forgetting at such a time that the stranger is a guest
of Ullah ! Seeing then that neither threats nor entreaties could
move me, and that their market company was gone a long
mile before them, they abandoned the Nasrâny, and ran forward
to overtake them.

The nomads, removing in that vast cragged ground, were
gone out of my sight ; my dizzy nâga strove to break away
after those that yet appeared journeying down to el-Wejh. I
made her kneel, till they were gone under the horizon : with
the bridle I could not hold in her mad force. Though I cried
to her never so much, she would not suffer me to mount
peaceably ; I leapt upon her back, some of my things fell,
but I hazarded not the staying to recover them ; she sprang
up under me, and broke away at a gallop, and I turned her
head after the removing nomads.—A horrible distress it were,
to be bewildered in these hideous lavas, like the floor of a furnace in the sun, and without water ! I rode with this burden at
heart, lest I should see the people no more ; my eyesight was
never good. It was not long when, by the will of Heaven, I
espied their wandering train, which had been hidden awhile
among cragged bottoms of the vulcanic field.

I rode apart from them, uncertain if now there would
any of the Aarab revile me. I had no saddle ; my baggage, tied with a girding cord, was loose and sliding.
Some honest man who went by upon his thelûl alighted
to aid me. It was not long before I came up with a client
of Mohammed, one whom I had befriended with medi-

cines, and having this morning great thirst, I called to him by name, "*Aŷd!* canst thou pour me out to drink?" With some delay and ill-humour, he brought me léban in a bowl. I marked his strange behaviour, and someone saying of those about me, *temût,* "thou wilt die," I thought it was not good. Aŷd, who should himself have sipped first, barely handed me the bowl: another said, "there is no harm in it."— "I have done, I answered without drinking, and requite you Ullah." Aŷd went again to his wife's camel, and made as though he poured all back into the neck of the semîly; but he stole aside then and, luring the hounds which followed, poured some to them in a hollow of the lava rock; seeing I observed him, he returned with the air of a man who cannot tell what next to do. "Is not Ullah, I said to him, above us? what, O man! is in the léban?"—"See, there is nothing amiss, my own brother (the bedrid herdsman, my patient) shall drink it," and he went to him with the bowl: when the sick man had swallowed it all, I took Aŷd by the hand, and granted that his milk was excellent. The man had a sidelong glance. Covert murder by envenoming is a thought of the hearts of the Arabians, therefore they always taste before you; and yet I believe it is a crime nearly not committed in the desert. We journeyed in a great heat till noon, when the Arabs encamped: as I alighted apart, those of the Moghreby's household called to me, saying, 'Why did I not pitch my tent among them?' These nomads encamp, by kindreds and fellowships, in five or six by-menzils: yet they incline to pitch in length, which is the Bílli-wise; and the Sehamma encampment was nearly as a street of tents. (*v.* pl. IV., p. 385.)

At evening, having purified a little water with charcoal, I sat making tea, and the tribesmen of the common sort, who lay about the hearth, looked on with half suspicious malignity. When I lifted the lid, and a vapour exhaled as of sweet-smelling roses, the Beduins gave back hastily, and cries one: "It is pernicious, take it up thou! and carry it away."— "Nothing more wholesome, I said to them, than this blessed savour, which is of the trees of Paradise." Another cried, "Akhs, that he would have it away! for now my head turns." I would go then to make peace with Tollog: one told me "His beyt is near," another whispered to him, "Say it is far off;" so he said,"Nay, it is far off."—"And how, fellow, is it both near and far off?" *Aŷd:* "We know, Khalîl, that thou knowest all things, [that by thy book thou canst divine and see the invisible,] but go not, there are habalîs upon the Harra."—"Then one of you lend me a weapon, I will borrow thy sword awhile."—

" Nay, but upon payment."—" At least I may take this staff
of a friend." It was the sick herdsman's, who lived by my
daily alms of medicine, but the ungracious wretch denying,
I flung down the stake upon the stones. The ill-conditioned
company murmured, and said his evil-eyed brother Aŷd, " We
are the Beduw, we be no townspeople ! "

Tollog's booths, because this dâr was so narrow, were built
upon another clear ground at nearly a mile's distance. I trod
on, in the vulcanic field, over thick beds of loose blocks and
stones in the dark till I saw his watch-fire. " Lord ! (said
Tollog, as I entered from the gloom, and sat down amongst
them), thou comest thus abroad at night ? nay Khalîl, without even a weapon in thy hand ! " The goodly old man
now received me with kindness. I said, " I could not sleep
except I had seen thee, nor might come till now, being sick
and weary in the day's heat. Tollog, you will not forbid me to
breathe the common air ; for this I came upon your mountain."
Tollog : " But we are the Beduw, *mesakîn* (mesquins), leading
our lives in great extremities. We are afraid lest anything befall thee amiss, and a blame should be laid upon the Moahîb ;
some rash fellow might kill thee, a Nasrâny, and bring thy
blood upon us !—Hast thou no dread of the wolf, nor fearest the
land-lopers ! Wellah, Khalîl, wilt thou not tell it us, what is in
thy mind to do here ? Hast thou a skill to find hidden things,
and to see the invisible ? "—" I have none indeed : you have
caught some false suspicion of my books, which are but a sewing
together of men's sayings. You have kasasîd which recite to
you their excellent conceits ; so have we, and their words, that
should not die with them, written in paper books ; but the
Aarab are untaught."—" Ay, wellah, untaught ! " answered
Tollog.—" Also if any be sick, I am here to serve him, I will
never refuse any ; and they may pour me out a little léban,
as I am a thaif-Ullah amongst you. What brought me here,
sayest thou ? and wherefore have I enquired of ruins ? I tell you
I seek some ancient inscriptions, as you heard at el-Héjr ; and
that is for no gain, but for the pleasure of some learned men,
Moslemîn and Nasâra, that study the old language like your own
in which they are written." *Tollog :* " But what of those written
stones which you removed from el-Ally ?—when you had visited
them, we heard they were not found in the morning."—" Do not
believe this folly, I would have bought a written stone from one ;
and consider that at Stambûl is a great kasr to this purpose,
where are gathered all such strange and rare things, from the
quarters of the world. The Pasha favoured me,—for he knows the
ahl sûwahh—also I am of the Engleys, allies of the Sûltàn, and

therefore your friends. What did Abu Sinûn hear, last journey,
at Wejh ? "—" Yet methought they were not wholly with el-
Islam : did they not show us some evil turn of late years·? Wed
you then with the daughters of Islam ? ".—" We are far off, we
come sailing in our ships to Stambûl ; by yonder coast you
might, most days, see our shipping."—" Shall I not eat at least a
pair of liras of thee, eigh Khalîl," said finally the old man.—" You
Aarab are too ungenerous, when they see the stranger, passing
poor and afflictedly in their country, they would even strip
him."—" But we will show thee the ruined places, and, Khalîl,
whereso thou wouldst go, it shall be free to thee."—" I will see
none, I have few reals ; I ask but to breathe this mountain air
awhile, O Tollog !—or wilt thou drive me out of the dîra ? "—
" Go now only with this young man, who will attend thee home,
and thy camel will be to-morrow upon the haj way ; rise, thy
nâga they say is strayed."—" What of to-morrow ? wilt thou
then drive me away ? "—" Return now, and you will be with
your hosts."—" By that beard, Tollog ! it were not a thing to be
spoken of among the honourable Beduins."—" Thou art with
us ; only go no more out by night alone, and unarmed ; "
—and he sent one with a lance to bring me again to our
menzil.

In another march, a little descending upon the side of the
Harra, we found the hummu heat by so much greater. We
looked from this menzil, far down through the giddy heat, into
the Jau ; and thereover to a frowning coast terraced with black
basalt, and beset with crater hills, the Khúthery Harra. (See
the panorama pl. vii.) Seaward, lay stretched out before
us, the mountainous falling Teháma country, such as we see
dimly from the brow of Edom ; or when we look down from the
Hejâz above Mecca upon a horrid obscurity of lower mountains
sinking to the Teháma of Jidda. The Shéfa country is all that
we see here below us, as a hedge of mountains ; one day's way
over, say the Beduins ; and after that is better travelling. The
Red Sea they call simply " The Sea, the Salt Sea."—Zeyd upon a
time answered me, when I asked him the sea's name, *Bahr eth-
Thellam*, ' Sea of the glooming (West).'—In like manner our
Saxon king, Alfred, in his book of Geography : " Ireland is dim,
where the sun goeth on settle." Two mighty mountain landmarks ride aloft, upon all that cragged lowland (see the same
plate) : these nomads call them Jowla and Wuttid (tent-peg).
Betwixt them, is no more than a pathway ; they rise in a long
ranging granite coast, lying north and south, half a day over,
whose name I could not certainly learn, whether it be *el-
Hadàd, Enzân, Negâba*. It is a day or more between the

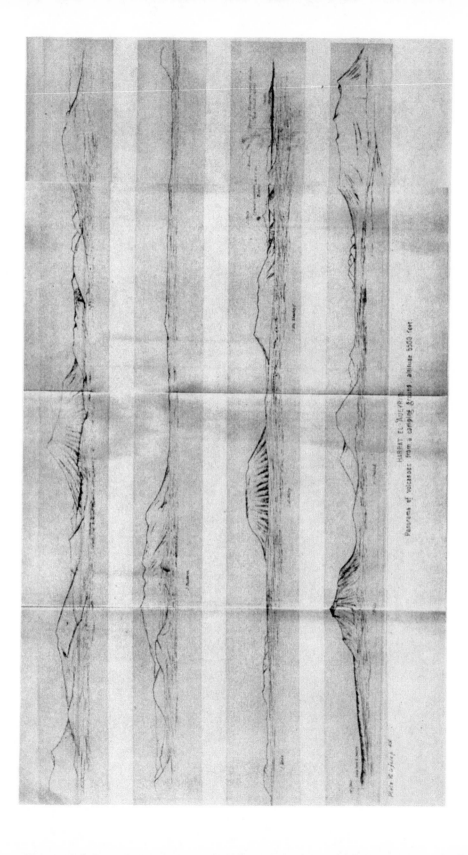

HARRAT EL 'AUERIB.

Panorama of volcanoes from a camping ground, altitude 5300 feet.

Hadàd and the Aueryid. All this within the Hadàd is named
properly es-Shéfa, and all that without et-Teháma ; but even
the Aueyrid, in their solemn style, is comprehended in the
Shéfa. Otherwise the Moahîb say, (for Beduw seldom agree in
their setting of bounds, to the open desert,) " All is et-Teháma,
outwards to the sea, from the brink of the Harra."

In the Teháma-Shéfa lies el-Ferâ. It is a plain bottom,
with some growth of cane reeds : and there come down the
seyls from Jowla and Wuttid upon the one hand, and those from
the valleys and many breaches of the Aueyrid, upon the other.
These are the heads on this side of the Harra, of the great Hejâz
water-ways of W. el-Humth. This upper valley bottom, next
below the Ferâ, is called W. Nejl, which receives the seyl waters
from the Jau, and afterward W. Nejid. W. Nejid descends from
a two-headed sandstone mountain, *Shòrafat en-Nejid.* This is
not Nejd, the name in their speech of the great upland country,
which is the best part of that the ancient geographers have
called " Nomad Arabia." There is a diversity in the Beduins'
utterance of the two words ; they wondered and laughed that a
foreign tongue could not walk so finely after them. W. Nejid
lies in the caravaners' way, between Ally and el-Wejh : it is
two days from the inland town, and in it they journey one
day. Ferâ too, is not sounded alike with Ferrá, the name
of an Harb oasis in the mountains betwixt the Harameyn.
Another wady descends from the west side of the Shòrafat, to
the seaward, named also *W. Nejid ;* this passes Béda and goes
out above Wejh. Béda is a ruined site with dôm, or branched
wild nut-palms : there is a standing hamlet of tents of Bíllî,
the husbandmen of a few palms. The place is one natural day's
journey, said Mohammed the Moghreby, from the sea town.
After W. Nejid, there seyl into the valley which descends from
the Ferâ (now W. Jizzl), the deep wadies of that Harra side,
Aurush, Dokhàn, Thá, Gaila, in which are *gerýa,* or hamlets
of tents of Moahîb husbandmen. The valley receives upon the
other hand, the seyl waters coming down from the wadies of
the Hareyry : of which certain, as *W. Jaida,* are palm wadies
and husbanded by Bíllî Beduins.

The Aueyrid vulcanic platform mountain, is three members,
lying north and south, an hundred miles nearly. It is in most
places reckoned a summer journey to go over : yet betwixt the
opposite heads of W. Thirba and W. Aurush is only half a day's
passage. Land names are often repeated in Arabia ; a part of
J. *Ajja* (the mountains of Shammar,) is named el-Aueyrid, and
well known is el-Aruth in east Nejd. In all is the signification
" wide-stretching." The upper member of the Aueyrid, that

is next under Tebûk, is named (of the inhabiting nomads),
Harrat es-Sŷdenyîn, a fendy reckoned to B. Atîeh, their
hareem wear the braided forelock, hanging as a horn, upon
the forehead, with a threaded bead : it is said " they were of
old a kindred of Bíllî, from the Teháma mountain *Seyd,* not
far from Wejh."—The beginnings of any nomad kindred, tribe,
or nation, they commonly fetch from some mountain, though
it may now lie far distant from them ;—so even Kahtân, reckoned
the noblest blood of the South Arabians, from a mountain in
el-Asîr.   A tribe invading another nomad dîra seize upon a
mountain ; and the name of their old Jebel stronghold, though
they may be since removed into other seats, is long remembered
in their tradition.—The platform of the Sŷdenyîn Harra mountain " is plain and wadies, with a few hilliân."

The third Harra, in the midst, is named, as said, of the
Beduins *el-Khuthéra,* also a fendy of B. Atîeh. The *W. Rumûtha*
descending from the north-west part, between the hills Sheybàn
and Witr, passes out north-eastwards, and seyls inland towards
Tebûk ; where cutting the haj road it is counted the border of
the Moahîb, the furthest of the southern Annezy.   From the
east of the mountain descends, we may remember, a main valley,
el-Akhdar, which crosses the pilgrim way by the kella ; the
length to its going-out in the sandy desert, near the height of
Tebûk, is reckoned four journeys. Westward under the northern
Harrats wander the *S'bût,* also a fendy of B. Atîeh ; with them
is found an old usage, mentioned by Wallin, who once crossed
these parts from Mueylih to Hâyil, namely, to send out their
cattle and call them in at evening to the ringing of a bell.
This might seem outlandish in Arabia, but the like have other
kindreds of the Maazy and Howeytát.   The Jau divides the
Khúthery from the third and last Harra of the Moahîb. *Jau*
(plur. *jîan*) is said of a low water-ground, with wells in the
desert ; so we may say jîan in general for the low well-grounds
of a tribe, as *jîan Bishr.*   The great Jau is a hollow plain,
betwixt the sandstone undercliffs of the Harra, shelving from
the eastward ; the mouth upon that side is partly shut by
certain sandstone bergs. There-through is a path of the ghrazzus ; thus they avoid the difficult passage of the Harra for any
not homeborn thelûls, and to themselves little known. The way
lies therein between el-Wejh and the village of Tebûk ; seven
journeys for loaded camels. This Jau is counted as naturally
setting limits between Ahl Gibly and Ahl es-Shemàl, or the
northern and south-country Aarab.   The third and southern
Harra, with which we have here to do, is a prodigious sherd of
old vulcanic matter, with a multitude of crater-hills, upon a

platform mountain of sandstone. The mean height of the lava
floods, in the northern parts which I have visited, I find to be
above 5000 feet ; the head of Anâz, the greatest of the hilliân,
may be 7600 feet.

The head of the W. el-Humth, upon the west side of the
Harra, is the seyl coming from *W. Gârib ;* which descends thence
by the *Thorrèyd,* and the plain of el-Héjr, to el-Ally ; and passes
from Ally to Bîr el-Ghrannem, receiving the seyl waters of W.
es-Sódr : and this dry waterway is presently joined by that
western branch of the W. Jizzl which descends from the Shéfa.
Next under the long train of the Aueyrid is the lesser Harra
lately mentioned, el-Hareyry, likewise a platform of lavas upon
a sandstone mountain ; therein are few hilliân. The Hareyry
is higher than the Harra, and of a rounded figure ; it is of
Bíllî tribesmen.

In the train of Harras we see a spectacle of the old vulcanic
violence that tormented this border of the Arabian peninsula.
I have followed these Harras almost to Mecca ; that is through
nearly seven degrees of latitude. The midst of the Aueyrid
may be a hundred and twenty miles from the desolate Red
Sea side ; where I have seen raised coral reefs, documents of
other land and water levels in older times of the world.

When we look upon the Aueyrid, it were no light task to
divine the story of that stupendous physiognomy of nature ! A
sandstone platform mountain is overlaid, two thousand square
miles, to the brink, by a general effusion of lavas : then beyond
the vulcanic crust, all around, we see a wasted border of undercliffs and needles of the sandstone rock, down to the low-lying
plains.—It seems thus that the lava floods have preserved the
infirm underlying sand-rocks, whilst the old sandstone country
was worn down and wasted by most slow decays, in such sort
that this Aueyrid mass now stands six hundred fathoms aloft,
like a mighty mountain, which was in old time even with
the floor of the now low-lying sandstone plains !

Viewing the great thickness of lava floods, we can imagine
the very old beginning of the Harra,—those streams upon
streams of basalt, which appear in the walls of some wady-
breaches of the desolate Aueyrid. Seeing the hilliân are no
greater, we may suppose that many of them (as the Avernine
Monte Nuovo) are the slags and the powder cast up in one strong
eruption. The earlier over-streaming lavas are older than the
configuration which is now of the land :—we are in an amazement, in a rainless country, to see the lava-basalt pan of the
Harra, cleft and opened to a depth of a hundred fathoms to
some valley-grounds, as Thirba. Every mass is worn in grooves

in the infirmer parts, by aught that moves upon it ; but what is this great outwearing of 'stones of iron,' indomitable and almost indestructible matter ! We see in the cliff-inscriptions at Medáin, that the thickness of your nail is not wasted from a face of soft sandstone, under this climate, in nearly two thousand years !

Every pasty mass is crazed in the setting ; and such kind of chinks we may suppose to be opened in the sandstone frame of this mountain shouldered upon an invading head of the planetary lavas ; and that, swelling with tremendous violence, the lavas should be˙ infused into many natural clefts, and, by some of them rising to the soil, there break forth with that infinite spitting and spouting of the super-heated fiery vapour of water, entangled and embodied in the lake of molten stone, which, with issue of lavas, is the stupendous elemental rage of a vulcanic eruption. In the year 1872 I was a witness of the great eruption of Vesuvius. Standing from the morning alone upon the top of the mountain, that day in which the great outbreak began, I waded ankle-deep in flour of sulphur upon a burning hollow soil of lava : in the midst was a mammel-like chimney, not long formed, fuming with a light corrosive breath ; which to those in the plain had appeared by. night as a fiery beacon with trickling lavas. Beyond was a new seat of the weak daily erup- tion, a pool of molten lava and wherefrom issued all' that strong dinning noise and uncouth travail of the mountain ; from thence was from time to time tossed aloft, and slung into the air, a swarm of half-molten wreathing missiles. I approached the dreadful ferment, and watched that fiery pool heaving in the sides and welling over, and swimming in the midst as a fount of metal,— and marked how there was cooled at the air a film, like that floating web upon hot milk, a soft drossy scum, which endured but for a moment,—in the next, with terrific blast as of a steam-gun, by the furious breaking in wind of the pent vapours rising from the infernal *magma* beneath, this pan was shot up sheetwise in the air, where, whirling as it rose with rushing sound, the slaggy sheet parted diversely. and I saw it slung out into many great and lesser shreds. The pumy writhen slags fell whissing again in the air, yet soft, from their often half- mile high parabolas, the most were great as bricks, a few were huge crusts as flag-stones. The pool-side spewed down a reek- ing gutter of lavas.

At afternoon, the weight of molten metal risen in the belly of the volcano hill (which is vulcanic powder wall and old lava veins, and like the plasterer's puddle in his pan of sand,) had eaten away, and leaking at mid-height through the corroded hillsides, there gushed out a cataract of lava. Upon some unhappy persons who approached there fell a spattered fiery shower of vulcanic powder, which in that fearful moment burned through their clothing, and, scorched to death, they lived hardly an hour after. A young, man was circumvented and swallowed up in torments by the pursuing foot of lava, whose current was very soon as large as Thames at London Bridge.—The lower lavas rising after from the deep belly of the volcano, and in which is locked a greater expansive violence, way is now blasted to the head of the mountain, and vast outrageous destruction upward is begun.

Before the morrow, the tunnel and cup of the mountain is become a cauldron of lavas, great as a city, whose simmering (a fearful earth-shuddering hubbub) troubles the soil for half a day's journey all round. The upper liquid mineral matter, blasted into the air, and dispersed minutely with the shooting steam, is suddenly cooled to falling powder ; the sky of rainy vapour and smoke which hangs so wide over, and enfolds the hideous vulcanic tempest, is overcharged with electricity ; the thunders that break forth cannot be heard in that most tremendous dinning. The air is filled many days, for miles round, with heavy rumour, and this fearful bellowing of the mountain. The meteoric powder rains with the wind over a great breadth of country ; small cinders fall down about the circuit of the mountain, the glowing up-cast of great slags fall after their weight higher upon the flanks and nearer the mouth of the eruption ; and among them are some quarters of strange rocks, which were rent from the underlying frame of the earth (5000 feet lower),—upon Vesuvius, they are limestone. The eruption seen in the night, from the saddle of the mountain, is a mile-great sheaf-like blast of purple-glowing and red flames belching fearfully and up-rolling black smoke from the vulcanic gulf, now half a mile wide. The terrible light of the planetary conflagration is dimmed by the thick veil of vulcanic powder falling ; the darkness, the black dust, is such that we cannot see our hands, nor the earth under our feet ; we lean upon rocking walls, the mountain incessantly throbs under us : at a mile's distance, in that huge loudness of the elemental strife, one cannot almost hear his own or his neighbour's voice.—Days pass and the hidden subterraneous passions slowly expire, the eruption is at an end.

The vulcanic womb delivered of its superfluous burden, the column of lava is fallen, in the last oscillations, to the hollow roots of the hill ; where the fiery force remains under much crusting over and cooling. Massy hardening in any great conduit, to not many fathoms, may be hardly, as we have experience, in two or three generations. If many ages pass of repose, the old vulcanic tunnel, near the floor of the earth, may be then somewhat deeply sealed. As for any pocket of the molten mineral, low seated, as a lake beneath, we cannot suppose it to be set by cooling, in very long space as measured by years of the planet ; nor intermeation to cease with the molten magma of the deep of the earth. When the vulcanic outbreak revives, we may suppose such womb of molten metal swelling forth to a new delivery ;—it might be incensed by some percolation of sea-water. Slowly must the basaltic stop-rock relent again upon the rising vulcanic heat ; or sudden way may be opened by rending upward of the irrepressible elemental force.—Is this word 'lava,' *laba* in the Arabic, come into our new European languages from the Moorish Italian of Sicily ? where the usurping Arabs found so much which they name *laba*. Laba of the Arabians (where I treat of the great Harras best known to me, the Aueyrid, and the Harrat Kheybar) is not all that which we understand by lava, but is said of the basaltic-massy, the drawn and sharp-set and nearly vitreous kinds : the slags, the drossy, the clinker crusts, cinder and pumice-stone are not called laba.—Thus far of the vulcanic country.

The coming together of the branches of W. Jizzl, below the Hareyry, and of W. el-Humth from the southward, and of the W. el-Îss of antique name, are set forth in the map after that which I received of the Aarab. In W. el-Îss are sixty (that may be six, or else many) springs, and one hundred and eighty (eighteen or many) wells, ruins of dead villages and dôm palms. The dôm grows about many abandoned sites of habitation in dewless Arabia, where the ground-water is near ; as we might see the homely briar and the nettle spring in more northern countries. In the *W. Kora,* whose head is in the Hareyry, are other dead villages, ruins in clay which are said to be not inconsiderable. Amidst a ruined clay village site in these parts is commonly a kella or stronghold of rude stone building. This name of W. Kora, which signifies, the Aarab told me, Valley *Rugged,* is common in the country. There is a W. Kora southward, whose head is in the Harrat Kheybar, (therein are ruined sites, oozing ground, and dôm palms,) and which gives into the great Wady el-Hümth by Sujwa. The Teháma wadies *Amudán* and *Therry* descend from a sandstone mountain district next the Hareyry through deep sand country, to the W. el-Humth ; they are of the Barakát (a fendy of Bílli), and of Jeheyna Aarab.

—It is an art to examine the Beduins, of these countries ; pains which I took the more willingly, that my passing life might add somewhat of lasting worth to the European geography. Of the Peninsula of the Arabs, large nearly as India, we have been in ignorance more than of any considerable country in the world which remains to be visited. There are difficulties in these enquiries ; the rudeness of the common sort of minds, and the few sheykhly men who are of a better understanding, dwelling all the days of their destitute lives in the tent shadows, are those that have least topical knowledge. The short levity of the most will glance from your question, they think thy asking vain, and they think thee fond.—You shall have also their wily crooked answers, yielded with little willingness by these free-born wretches, jealous of their wandering grounds and waters. Their sober men who would say their meaning truly, are unreclaimed minds, that were never chastened by any feeling after knowledge ; they can hardly keep one measure of length and breadth. Such will tell thee sooth—as they would not falsify landmarks—within their own dîras ; but commonly the land which lies beyond is not much in their knowledge.   I have sometimes wondered to see among persons of worth how divided might be their opinions of the next dîras ; and many an honest man failing of his matter and still willing to please thee will tell thee in the end a fable.   Before my going into Arabia I lived some months with the nomads of Sinai and beyond Jordan, and found these slipping places in the magnanimous voices of the desert : other years I passed in households of the mixed Semitic people of Syria, and at my setting out from Damascus had learned nearly the bent of their bows. Being with the Aarab I listened gladly to the telling of honest men, which were of my fellowship and acquaintance. Many times, in discoursing with all kinds of persons, I drew from them unaffected answers, and of some chance word might perceive further landmarks. I noted the responses of strangers, and required them again of my friends ; I examined again the same persons, and conferring the answers of several, found where firm ground lay, and commonly rejecting that which I could not see confirmed, I have shunned, to my possibility, to build in unprofitable manner.

    Motlog, sheykh of the Fejîr, a wary man in the policy of his tribe, was unready in land knowledge : one day as I was asking a tribesman in his tent, who had forayed in those parts, of the great W. el-Iss, he asked further for himself : " Let me see, how lies the W. Iss from el-Héjr ? " We may take this for an example of the homely ignorance of the sheykhs and nomad people, in anything which not nearly concerns them. The great old valley, not far off, was in hostile land of the Jeheyna, from whom they live divided by mountains. I suppose there is hardly any tribesman who could tell us as much as that which I have compiled in the chart published in this book, even of the desert land between Tebûk and Kheybar. The ancient tribe of Jeheyna, praised as *ikhtiarîn*, for their magnanimous hospitality, are besides Prayers, say the Aarab neighbours, and Fasters too, in their religion. The Jeheyna inhabit a very cragged dîra, and as the Arabs seem to say in good part granitic. I have also seen petrified shells " Miriam's nails," *zófr Miriam umm Sinnakît*, which were from limestone rock of that country. Even Ibn Rashîd thinks it too hard an enterprise to invade them.—The nomads, whose lean lives are of the showers, are curious observers of all the lying of the land ; there is no ragged wretch amongst them, that cannot answer thee everywhere in their marches, whither the drops run down of the Lord's blessing of rain.

The 15th of June we were come nigh the highest of the Harra platform, five miles north of Anâz, where the barometer showed 6800 feet above the sea level, but even here was a mid-day " clear heat," which beat scalding upon the worsted booths. Hamdy's long beyt was overblown with a flaw of wind at midnight. That short summer night we passed very unquietly ; for besides, the camels strayed, and we thought we heard strange voices in the Harra : then *Rubba*, the sick herdsman, as it drew towards morning, with some little freshing of the air, awakened in a new anguish, and groaned so loud and long that his brethren thought him dying. I heard him making his moan as another psalmister, *ya Rubby ! ana ajist min hâl-y, wa ent tekúbbny*, " I am weary of my being, O Lord, and thou dost cast me off ! " Then he lamented sore, as if he were bewailing his own funerals. I called to him to hold his peace, if he might, and let us now take some rest, for the barking dogs had kept us watching. Upon this, his brother began to sing outrageously. When on the morrow I blamed him, he said that Rubba losing heat, they had believed him at the point of death. —" And why sang ye so lustily ? "—" Well, I see, said he, thou dost not know our custom, to sing the death away."

At sunrise the Aarab removed ; as we passed near Anâz, I saw the crest as a comb of cragged lavas. Now I had viewed the mountain upon three sides about, and everywhere it is a perfect cone. That stack of vulcanic powder seemed to me as much or more than the hill of Vesuvius above the observatory. From the highest of the Harra platform, there is a wonderful

spectacle over a lower vulcanic country, whither we now descended by the crater-hill sides and sharp shelves of lavas. The
under-Harra is a lower vulcanic terrace : there again the ruddy
sand-rocks come to sight, from under the spent lava streams,
and are thinly scattered with loose lava crusts. In this horrid
region we encamped, 1500 feet beneath our last menzil : the
Aarab sought a pool, *Abu Thain ;* and there, finding water, they
would rest a few days. Then, all the pool-waters wasted, they
must finally forsake the Harra height and go down to drink in
the Tehâma ; or to the plain of Medáin Sâlih. Here among
lava crags and *musherifs,* or high overlooking grounds, enclosing
about us, I found flint stones, and upon the next *bottîn,* or
rising hill, a shelf of chalk with cockle-shells, burned to an
ochre colour, by the old overflowing of shallow lava, now dis-
solved and scattered in few great sliding blocks.

Here Tollog would have me show him my quaint things of the
Nasâra : one of these afternoons, though heavy with age, he walked
over alone, to visit me. Gazing through my double telescope,
" Lord ! he exclaimed, *Sàlema's* héjra, there in the end of the
menzil, seems to me to stand even with this next beyt ! "—Then
looking through them reversed, when he saw all things vanished
to an infinite distance, he went on musing to himself under his
breath, " *Shûf,* look, Tollog ! "—Whilst he handled my medicine-
book, turning over leaves to see the pictures, with the rude fingers
of one who knows no letters, I said, " Shall I write thy name ?—
see here ! TOLLOG."—" Khalîl, said he, shrinking with a sudden
apprehension, I do pray thee write not my name ! " Seeing him so
out of countenance, I rent the paper in little pieces and buried
them under the harra stones, which made him easy again.

The old sheykh fell sick soon after ; and then there came no
loving wife to call the hakîm,—such are hardly found where a
man may have many, and they are so transitory,—but his aged
sister, weeping. Tollog lay under an awning, which his hareem
had spread for him between tall broom bushes of the seyl-strand,
es-shâeb : yesterday he had drunk a bowl of mereesy, heated,
and was much oppressed. I gave him drops of croton oil, and
a draught in the evening ; the day after he was himself again,
and sitting in the mejlis he boasted of Khalîl's effectual remedy.
Upon this there came to me all their people, " to be purged like
Tollog ; " and they think they may be helped by nothing so
much, in their most diseases ; also the medicine was wonderfully
pleasant to them, because they received it (sweetness and fatness together) upon a morsel of sugar, and for this benefit the
housewives brought me handfuls of rice and mereesy. As for

Tollog, he was a fatherly man, and at all times very good to me; when any guest-supper was in his sheykhly tent, he sent to the stranger the portion of the thaif-Ullah; and the most house-holders did the like, when they had any sacrifice.

These few hill-men, not forsaking the old hospitality, are, we have seen, commended by their tribes: yet there was a strange tale told at this time in their tents. ' A certain Belùwy or Bíllî tribesman, was going over the Harra; and, at the sun setting, where he halted to pass the night, a strange camel appeared to him, standing over him, and the camel uttered a manner of human speech, " These murrains and the great drought they come oftener upon you, and the locusts, not as befoːetime, but now year by year, and ye wot not wherefore :— wherefore go the Beduw back from the custom of the fathers? ye suffer the wayfaring man to pass by your byût, and the hungry man goes from you empty! " ' The Arabs spoke of the phantom by twos and threes in their tents and in the mejlis, and this was now a tale current in all the country. Some asked me,—a book-man,—' how I looked upon it? ' all the people knew him who had seen the phasm, to be " a good understanding man."

Secure in a nearly impervious dîra the Moahîb are sheep keepers as well as camel-Beduins, and though the greatest of their mixed flocks was less than an hundred head. The sheep of the nomads are not all of one kind in Arabia; there is the great upland sheep of Nejd, and a small kind (such as our Welsh mutton), in the border country above Mecca. In the great sheep is a gaunt bony frame, the face is aquiline, the fleece is rough and hairy; the flesh is lean and woody,—but that meat is yet warm with the life, which they cast into their nomad pot. The Harra is good coverȶ for wolves, which all these moonless nights troubled our menzils. The long-coat and great-tailed Bíllî dogs after sunset, when the day grew dark, rose and swaggered forth of themselves, beyond the fire-light. The canine guards ruffle it up and down, between the robber wolf and the couching flock without defence, from time to time baying fearfully with an hollow throat: but if the dog champions be gone by, and ᵗthe wolf approaches, then the flocks which wind him shrink and suddenly rush together; —the herdsman's heart leaps, he steps upon his feet, and thinks to make all good with a great shout. The Beduins at the hearth stare into the thick night; the shepherd, taking up his club-stick, goes forth now and flings stones, chiding to his hounds, which course again to him with furious affray, and all the encampment is presently on a bark. The peaceable camels lie by chawing the cud through the long night, still careless of these alarms, or, if some one of them be risen affrighted, the brute is seen in the flickering fire-light hobbling upon three legs, for the fourth is knee-bound, until, yielding to the voice and handling of the least child, he fall upon the knees and will couch down again. But if "grey-legs" sprang in, it is too likely he ravished some weanling, (and though their little velvet heads be all tied, in loops, on a ground line), and we hear in the dark the lamb or the kid's feeble death-cries out of the wolf's jaws. Thus the larger flocks,—which lie also more exposed—lost some little ones every moonless night in our dim menzils upon the Harra. The Aarab bear all such crosses with religious patience. Hamdy, our housewife, lost two goats in six dark nights, and she said only, "The wolf, *eth-thib*, snatched them, the cursed one ! "

Their hounds bark on till midnight, when the nomads go to rest, and till the morrow's light, when the dogs' throats are so husk, they may not almost bark any more. These Beduin hounds are seen blear-eyed in the day-time, wooden-weary with long watch, and nearly voiceless. The nomad people seldom call to their hounds, naming them ; yet all the dogs know their names, which are often jesting by-names, as the Beduins use of human mortals. Such are *Ummthail,* "mother, or she of the great tail :" *Abusinnán,* "father of teeth." Certain dogs' names appear again in some names of tribes and kindreds of the Aarab, as *Aduàn,* a fendy of Maazy in the Hisma above Akaba el-Missry, and *Shalán,* a fendy (named after their sheykh's house) of northern Annezy, and *Ibn Sim'ry* is a fendy of Heteym (called after the sheykh's house) near Kheybar. Some other of their dogs' names are : *Sowwán* (whose mother was *Sowwa*), *Nuzzán* (whose mother was Nuzza), *Mushy, Rushdán, Dogmán, Ammera, Oweyish, Turr'fa, El-háfera, Nim-rân, Hajjilân, Adilla, Huddebán, Ajilân* (nimble), *Tóga, Zuggi-mán, Dubbilán, Seherán, Hòwama, Sim'rán, Buggán, Aida, Waga, Wadda, Fejjuán, Auda, Khuzayn.*

When the sun is half an hour high, the shepherd casts his mantle upon his shoulder, calls to the flock, and steps forth ; and they getting upon their knees and feet, troop out after him to the pasture :—the hounds follow not with the ghrannem. The goats and sheep feed forward with their loitering herds-man till the gaila ; then he calls in his scattered flock, and if it be not the watering day, he leads them to shadows of rocks or some desert thorn ; and there he milks a goat to his break-fast. The sheep hang their heads together, in the breathless heat, the goats couch by themselves, the herdsman stretches his idle length upon the soil to take his noonday slumber, until the sunny hours be gone round to the half-afternoon ; then rising, he leads forth again to the pasture, till the going down of the sun, when he calls them, and the sheep and goats follow their herd to the booths of the Aarab. There the ewes and the goats, that have swelling dugs, throng under the hands of their known housemother, that she milk them soon ; many press into the shelter of the nomad tent and lie down there. As for the herdsman, though he have nothing to put under his teeth, yet the udders are always ready, and he is satisfied with this daily sustenance : therefore though he go all day barefoot under the scalding sun and breathe the air as flames, his lot may be esteemed the more tolerable in the desert life. The human body fed with milk in the sunny drought, is slender, full of pith, of perfect endurance ; yet between beggarly pride and the Beduin indolence, there is none will take up the herdsman's life, but it be of bare necessity. They had liever lie and drowse out the daylight heat upon their empty maws in the tent shadows, and suffer hunger until the cattle are come home at evening. But the herdsman may sing in the desert, his adventure is light ; and if the troop be robbed, few among them were his own. His care is of the beasts of other men, who pall in the cheerless byût all the empty day long, and when it is night may hardly find rest : but he is blithe with the daily turns of his honest business, and hearty of the air of the field.

The nomad sheep drink every second day, but the Beduin graziers in their wide dîras, may not come at all times so soon to water : the herdsmen send forward to fetch in water upon asses. *The ass,* which sweats little, *is hardly less than the camel a beast of the wilderness.* The wild ass yet lives in the north-east, that is towards the rivers of the Syrian desert. To every head of cattle the nomads give a certain name ; and in every great mixed flock, if their herdsman, whose voice they know, " call to any beast by name, he will look up." We sat one evening by Hamdy's fire, and Rubba, the sick shepherd, told me over the names of the sheep and goats, that stood by, or lay chawing their cuds about us. The droves when mingled at the drinking places may be in this wise separated ; " the herdsmen leading up from the water, call out their own by their names." Rubba was a good simple man, though he never requited his hakîm with a thank. Eighteen months before, foraying against the Sherarát, he had received *sotwh,* a sword-wound in the hip : the old mischief badly healed, now rankled inwardly ; he lay all day groaning, and I procured him the night rest with opiates ; and being a broken man, he might have died without some timely relief of his sufferings. His wife had forsaken him long ago, he was a *mesquîn* in Mohammed's great tent : all his fellowship was with the small cattle. He knew every case in the life of each one of them, from the yeaning : he said, they were to him as the issue of his own body ; and was any one of them slain it grieved him ; he ate then of the meat " for his necessity, but it was unwillingly."

The ewes of these uplands yean in the year once, and bear almost never twins ; the goats may bring forth again out of the common time, which, for all the Aarab's cattle, is the season of the spring pasture. The male lamb, *kharûf*, is in the Nejd Beduins' mouths as often called *tully*, pl. *tulliân ;* the female *rókhal* (Rachel of the Bible), plural *rokhâl ;* which may be said also of the young females of goats and camels. We have seen a murrain had destroyed the Fejîr flocks : sheep, they tell me, may never thrive in their marches, and a cause is the sharp sand which they eat in with the minute herbage. I have seen such which they call " sand-struck " sheep, stand all day heartless, as poultry with the pips ; nature soon gives out, and they are dead. At that time, the Moahîb were in the Jau, where likewise many of their small cattle died, with pain and swelling. The nomads think there was a malignity in the year's herbage, not only their own dubbush perished, but they saw the locusts lay dead in heaps under the bushes, and the carcases of two or three ostriches lying in their desert, and many hares. Camels were affected, but purged with a dose of butter they recovered, and of all the *tursh*, they lost two only. The small stock they treated with milk, but in ten sick hardly one recovered. The belly, at the death, was always much swollen.—I have known thus all the hares perish in one year in a Scandinavian valley (Numedal).

Beduin housewives sell their wool in the border countries·; but it is little worth, that which is shipped to Europe from Syria hardly serving for carpet weaving and gross blanket stuffs. The nomad gossips admired the fineness of some woollen which I wore about me : " It is silk (they answered each other, feeling it between their fingers), this is not woollen." Little it is which have any poor southern Arabs, and they sell none, for there come no border-land tradesmen into these dîras to buy wool ; the hareem lay up all they have, for spinning, and their yarn for tent weaving, but this they will sell to each other, sometimes. In shearing the sheep's fleece and clipping their goats' wool and hair, they observe no certain time : but as the housewife sees any beast, whose coat is long grown, she bids the herdsman hold it fast, whilst with a rude blade and the natural expeditious disorder of the Arabs, she crops that which comes to her hand ; so losing above the third part they let the bleater go. The soft wool is left hanging matted about the necks and flanks of their camels until it fall of itself ; and only then will she take that little which may be plucked betwixt the thumb and forefingers. All this hair and wool, of sheep, goats, and camels, they shake together for their rough spinning, the house-wife only separating her colours, the brown camels' and the white sheep's wools ; for the nomad webster-wives work in white bands upon the rusty blackish ground of their common tent weaving, and put-to the ornament of fringes.

Goats are here the most of their mixed herd-flock, as are the sheep in Nejd : goat milk is these nomads' sustenance, the beasts have little or no rammish odour. It happens sometimes that goats, frayed by wolves or abandoned in the flight by ghrazzus, have been found afterward, grown wild in the desert, and the Aarab must approach to take them as they would stalk game. I have asked why they did not tame young bedûn ? and, since the wild mountain buck is more robust and better meat, they might cross them with their goats and improve the stock. They answered, " It would be lost labour, the bedûn cannot be tamed, their wildness always remains in them." I have often seen gazelle fawns with the Beduin flocks ; commonly the strange fawn is tied by a leg to the shank of a milch goat ; others I have seen fostered in the tent, of camel milk : the Beduwy, when the cattle came home, bore it in his arms to suck a teat of the foster nâga. The Aarab have several calls to the kinds of their beasts, to drive, to bring, to stay them. We may say there is one cattle-speech among them, yet nothing sounds more diversely in the nomad tribes.

. The pleasant milk season was now nearly spent, even in the cool height of the Harra. In these happier months butter-milk from the semîly is poured out to any who come in, in friendly beyts :—butter-milk is " the Lord's bounty." Among the Aarab there is no better report of a man's life than to be called in his country *karîm*, a liberal soul ; so nothing more hateful than the lean niggard's name, *bakhîl*. Their milk-vessels are bowls of wooden ware ; some, well turned, are from the haj market, others, square-shaped, are rudely wrought and hollowed by the desert smiths. A few sheukh have basins of tinned copper : many are the names of such utensils, *jiddýha, mahallib, helwîa* or *hellowîa, zilfa, henâba*. Arabia is very thinly stored with live stock ; we may wonder that the nomad cattle do not increase in the wilderness !—but yet more that this people and their beasts may ever thrive there many years together. It is an unfostering soil of sun-stricken drought, which corrodes all life : the fatal plagues of Mecca return in every generation ; the Beduw are all their lives riding in ghrazzus, and it is affirmed that many fall thus ; in some rainless years there is no rabîa ; their cattle are all years wasted by hostile forays : it is " a land which eateth up the inhabitants thereof."

The 24th June the Aarab removed from this lower Harra platform : the last pools were drunk to the dregs, and now they must descend to the plains for water. We journeyed down through a wilderness of vulcanic bergs, upon lava field, and in shallow wadies of the lower burned country. Midway in the ráhla there appeared to us a band of men standing upon a lofty vulcanic sierra. I asked "What be they?" *Answer:* " *Jaysh !* those are foemen, and what shall we do now ? "—It is their elvish humour to give a false alarm : I saw the Aarab pass on quietly, and being secretly so well armed, I heard them with indifference,—should not one thing happen to us all ? " See you, said they, how he fetches this confidence out of his books ! " " How say you ! is not jaysh an army ? "—" No, Khalîl, that is your town speech. The Beduw say jaysh [troop] of the thelûls and their warfaring riders." Those we saw were some of our own tribesmen, they had been two days out, hunting the bedûn.

Before noon we were come down to the brink of the valley head, Gârib ; here is the edge of the Harra. W. Gârib is a formidable breach in the sandstone mountain skirts, and opens as a deep before us, into which I wondered how we might descend upon camels. At the brink, where all the people alighted, I saw two great cairns, funeral heaps perhaps (which the ancients raised in the noblest sites), or else cast up here for guide-stones. Men and cattle we got down heedfully by the steep and cragged places ; the inured Harra camels can maintain themselves stiffly even among rolling stones. This going down the Beduins say was not formerly so difficult, but " a star falling four years before had shattered the ancient passage." In the brow the sandstone body of the mountain appears. Above is the precipitous edge of the Harra, with a long cornice of the coal-black pan of lava, of which some is fallen down in wild ruins of shales and basaltic rocks. We may read here in a natural monument that this valley breach is newer than the shallow outermost vulcanic overflowing. There is a tabular crag in the midst, of sandstone, upon whose head, though widely sundered now from either side, there has flowed out an equal pan of lava. In the deep below is seen a basalt rock risen in the lower sandstone.

The valley head into which we descended, is full of great lava blocks and pumice, this drift not less abruptly ending, than the tongue of a glacier, upon the lower plain sands. To the border of the black upon the yellow-grey, is reckoned the W. Aly right of pasture, from the outer lowland. Soon after noon the Beduins alighted and the hareem set up their byût upon these hot sands, being yet at the height of 4700 feet. The lower sandstone valley is about a mile over, betwixt high cliffs, and the stagnant heat seemed so much greater as we were now come down from the Harra ; and immediately the milk of the flocks and camels began to give out ; in the days following it was diminished to the half. The Aarab, finding water of some natural cistern in a glen head, would take their rest here a few days. Over the valley appeared an hamlet of nomad tents : these were the Serahîn,—the Moahîb fendy lately reconciled to their own tribesmen.

Under the opposite cliff of the wady, I came to a place in which are many timathîl, or scored rock-inscriptions, and outlined images of cattle, very lively portrayed by those old hands ; there is also a great barrow of cast stones, " the graveheap of Abu Zeyd's mother." Children of the menzils came down upon me, armed as it were against some savage beast which appeared in their dîra, with slings, *merdàha*, in their hands. The flock of little knaves whirled out their stones from a good distance ; when I showed them I might make the stones sing back over their ears, they put their hope in their heels. Tollog, hearing in the mejlis of the graceless children, was displeased ; " Woe worth them !—and is the world come to this, he murmured, that eyyàl of the Beduw have no respect of the *ghrarîb*, stranger, and the thaif-Ullah ! it makes not whèther he be Moslem or Nasrâny. Khalîl is an honest young man, and wellah, they are hounds that offend him, cursed ones, and Yahûdies ; and thou, Khalîl, do not heed them : but I say, if any durst do so again, wellah, I shall cut off their heads, and cast them into the well-pit."—Salutary words of the old sheykh that, forbidding the children, he forbad also the fathers: the knaves doubtless being set on by their fanatical elders.

The children's pastimes are few in the Beduin encampment; the little son is very often put to herding, he keeps the lambs and kids not far from the beyts: the eyyàl here made little three-cornered shales and naming these shards their "gaûds and camels," they set them over against each other in the sand, calling to their playfellows *taal shûf,* "come and see!"—and some have a toy, *ferneyny,* of a shard pierced with two eyes, and twice stringed with a sewing thread, that the mothers spin finely for them of their best camel down; this stone or else it is a shive of wood, is slung in the midst, and with a cast in the air they twist up the two threads into a double twine, and then drawing out and slacking, their gig spins with a loud whirring. I have seen the nomad boys set a trap by wells, to take the rock-partridge; it was a stone flag, lightly stayed upon a stick, and for bait the little birders had made a hollow and poured water under.—'Masque' is a word taken up in our tongues, of the Arabic *maskhara:* I have seen even the Beduin children run a mumming; and we may wonder that this masking humour in the Semitic blood has never grown in their settled countries to stage playing or public spectacles. I was soon a friend of the children, and some of them one evening visited me at my tent, having their young faces blackened with charcoal, and the mothers had made them solemn beards of their sheep's wool. They were *Sudàn,* they cried, or "black men," come from a far country, and he of the best beard was their sheykh among them. After the long nomad greetings, which are, for the most, to say over a dozen times with bashful solemnity the same *cheyf-ent, cheyf-ent,* "How dost thou? and how heartily again?" they had little more to tell me, and fled away to play at wild horses.—The humanity of the Semitic salutations, turned in the towns to hypocrisy, is noted in the New Testament.

Here Mehsan had passed little before our coming; the bountiful W. Aly sheykh returning from Damascus brough his eye-salver along with him. Above Tebûk, as they came riding by the haj way, they were crossed by a ghrazzu of Sherarát, and fell into the hands of enemies. The robbers found the medicine boxes in the hakîm's saddle-bags, they saw he was a stranger. "But who art thou, they said to the other, Wullah?" The sheykh answered, "O ye of the Sherarát, I am Mehsan Allayda."—"And thou be'st Mehsan Allayda—eigh, fellows! this is that bountiful man—in thy bags, O Mehsan, should be *sugar.*" (Coffee is made in Mehsan's tent, in ramathan, with sugar.) Said Mehsan (handing out the loaves himself), " Here, take ! and let the dogs of the Sherarát eat them ! " " Do ye hear, mates ! said the agîd, we have taken the thelûls and their stuff ; we will not strip them, for this is Mehsan the Bountiful, wellah, we will do him no dishonour." The hakîm asked for himself ' Would they give him again his medicines ? '—" Nay, these shall go with us, for we think the hareem should know them : but give the stranger his books again, and let them go now with Ullah.—And we are sorry thou must walk, Mehsan ; it is not very far, as thou knowest, to the village."—Mehsan received that day a small usury of his great principal of human kindness !—the honest fame went of him even among enemies. They came to Tebûk, that night, on their feet, and hiring there thelûls they rode by the *derb el-bukkra,* inward of the haj road, where they looked to be safer, and to come the sooner to some friendly Aarab.—Such is the fugitive life of those that inhabit Arabia, most miserable of mankind !

The hakîm was a Moor of Morocco, *Abu Selím :* I heard he told the Aarab he had known me in Damascus, ' I was his countryman, and an honest man, and he was himself an Engleysy : ' this were to say, that at a need he would betake himself, from pursuit of the Turkish catchpoles, to the friendly English consulate : his person was unknown to me, and I have since ascertained that he was not known there. Perhaps he had heard, from the returning Haj officers, of my adventure in Arabia ; and they might bid him enquire friendly for me. Aby Selím was very expert with his needle, inheriting the fine skill of his father, an eye-salver in the West Country. Abu Selím's name, first vaunted in the Moorish colony, was now in all mouths of the Mohammedan Damascenes ; yet might he not practise openly, being without diplomas, in the government cities. His praise had been soon blown to the outlying Syria ; he went thither often, where no impertinent magistrate enquired of his school license, also many eye-sick Arabs resorted to this hakîm in Damascus. I had counselled Mehsan to consult the learned missionary-physicians, at Beyrût ; but even Damascus Moslems preferred the Moghreby with his granddam's lore, before those learned in the Frankish schools of medicine. I have heard Abu Selím extolled by Moors for his liberal singularity : when he entered a coffee-house he would beckon to the teller at the door to take no money from any man who went out,—they should all be his guests, for the water-pipe and the cup, whilst he sat with them.

Abu Selím had heard of his patient, when Mehsan the

blind visited him. " And what (said he) wilt thou give me for the cure of thine eyes ? " *Mehsan :* " Say this thyself. What is it if I spend gold whether the white or red, so I might have my sight again ? "—" An hundred lira " (pounds, Turkish money).—" Well, be it an hundred lira."—" Look ! Mehsan, I will cure thee without money, and afterwards go down with thee to your dîra in the Hejâz, to practise among the tribes, for a time." Mehsan had partly recovered his sight, he could now see dimly.

Abu Selím, after this hap by the way, went down, to buy new medicines, to Medina :—he was this summer after with Mehsan at Kheybar, but I have since heard of him nearly that of the Evangelist : " He could not make there many cures, because of their unbelief." He found it as good to sit idle, and better than to labour for the faithless, graceless generation of Beduw. Yet, a busy Moghreby head, he had made talk at Kheybar, where he promised them a water vein, so strong that if opened it would turn a water-mill, but they must give him an hundred lira. Moreover, he had discovered, he told them, ' the site of an ancient *kinîsy* (synagogue) of the Yahûd ; and so they would dig for him he promised to take up the old scrolls, in which might be found written where those old (Mosaic) Kheyâbara had buried their worldly treasure.' The people bruited his talk ; but when will Arabs unite to attempt any new thing ? there is none would put out his penny in the hope to catch ten pounds : so they let the wise man go, but the Kheyâbara yet spoke of Master Abu Selím's strange talk when I came thither.

CHAPTER XVI.

THE AARAB FORSAKE THE HARRA AND DESCEND TO THEIR
SUMMER STATION IN WADY THIRBA.

A son born to old Tollog. The Senna plant. The women's camel-crates. Their ráhlas in the summer heat. Surgery in the desert. The Thorréyid passage. The rose-laurel of Syria. The desert valley Thirba. Multitude of great and well-built barrows. Dead villages. The springing wells in Thirba. Their summer station. The people's hunger. Life bare of all things. The hot day of famine. They suppose the Nasrâny to be an exile. The Arabs are tale-bearers. They are pleased with the discourse of the stranger. Questions and answers in religion. The barrows. The menhel. Birds at the water. Burying-place and prayer-steads. The Melûk. Burial of the dead. Tollog's sacrifice. Blood-sprinkling. Korbàn. The tribes would not descend this year to Kheybar. The Nasrâny proffers to increase their waters. The Moahîb in doubt whether they should submit to Ibn Rashîd. They bring their weapons to the Nasrâny. The nâgas coming home to water. The watering. The elephant, the swine, the lion, are but names to them. Darÿesh.

BREAKING up from W. Gârib, we pitched five hours to the S.W. in the Agorra ; great was the midsummer heat even in that high ground ! Here a womanly fair young girl, so nigh as he could have mind the fifteenth of his many marriages, bore to Tollog her first-born son and recomforted the old heart in his heavy age. The last day of June we descended southward by the haj road ; where I saw again the wheel-rut of the Jurdy cannon. Among the bergs, upon our left-hand, stands a bee-hive shaped sandstone mountain, *J. Merzûm*, which seemed to me capped with basalt, although at some miles from the Harra side. In this desolate passage I saw many blossoming plants of senna, with the head of yellow flowers, nearly like a ground pea. My old nâga cropped the noxious herb, that is not often browsed by camels, and when the nomads see them they drive their beasts further ; but those riding next by me looked on with the Beduish malice, and held their peace ; afterwards they said, " Wherefore, Khalîl, let thy nâga eat of that which is venomous ! "

Somewhat more brave is the desert march of the Moahîb than the ráhla of the Fejîr ; for these sheykhly housewives ride gaily mounted in saddle-frames *múksir*, with some caparison of coloured carpets. The creaking múksirs are basket-frames of withy rods, firmly knit and compacted with steeped camel neck-sinews, (which dry, are of an ivory whiteness and hardness,) and with thongs of raw leather. The most are square crates, in which a wife may sit cross-legged, and her young children with her ; and overhead is a bowed cross-rod or two, upon which she may cast her mantle, for a tilt, to house them in from the flaming sun. Another litter they have in these parts, and it is perhaps of the Arabian antiquity, for such I have seen in a ráhla of nomads in the little Algerian *Sáhara*. That is a long fantastic wicker frame, like nothing so much as a wind-mill sail, laid overthwart the camel's chine: into this straight cage the maiden creeps, and the swagging creaky arms of her litter, bouncing against tree and cliff, and thrusting upon nigh riders in the ráhla, make it a very uneasy carriage. I have asked how, being in their minds, they could use such faulty furnitures. "For ornament, Khalîl ! and the young women would ride gallantly." The hareem hang crimson shreds about their litter-frames, and upon the saddle-tree they put a housing with long fluttering tails of leather. So their women's riding makes a brave show, in the fantasy of the Aarab, in their wandering processions. The men pass forth riding, with only their arms, upon the stalking thelûls. In the heat, they mostly march in silence, to speak were to open the mouth to the droughty flaming air which brings thirst : they ride breathing through their kerchiefs, *thorrîb*, of which a lap is drawn up under the girdle of the head (*meyhsub*, or *maasub*, *agâl*), so that of such a masked visage little more is seen than the two robber-like black eyes.

These journeys, in the summer heat, they themselves think very distressing : the wilderness is dazzling, stricken by the barren sunshine, the brain is swooning ; so all the Aarab are withdrawn at this season to their great summer water-stations, and remain in standing camps. The herding-men and children fare with us unshod over glowing sand and burning stones·; the boys not seldom are bare-headed and naked. Some days they pass thus twenty or thirty miles way, still fasting and carrying only a little water-skin with them. Thus they are broken early to the necessity of the khála, and they learn to observe earnestly their landmarks : but the fierce sun scorching their naked bodies, and exposed to sudden flaws of wind, there are many rheums bred in their young limbs, which grow with them

and will vex them in their after age. At noon we turned out
of the way, a little above Menzil el-Haj, and entered a long
breach in the sandstone skirts of the Aueyrid; this is *eth-Thor-
réyid,* and the seyl-passage from W. Gârib to the valley plain of
el-Héjr. The cross-cleft country sandstone here is wasted into
a natural maze of blind and crooked straits, dividing through
the mountain. The Beduins alighted soon within, unloading
their stuff by menzils under the cliff-shadows, and loosed out
their bearing camels; for here *yugaialún,* they would pass these
meridian hours in rest till the mid-afternoon.

His brethren set down the sick herdsman in their arms,
moaning, in great anguish of his uneasy riding,—and solaced is
the rude man, in pain, to hear his own moaning. His brother
Benneyi was ready in this extremity, I saw he handled a pack-
needle, and was endeavouring with this to attain the rankling
abscess at the hip-joint. He pricked it effectually, and there
ran out in the sand a wonderful waste of corrupt matter. The
lookers-on pinched their nostrils, and stood off; his brethren
drew up quickly a lap of their kerchiefs. The Aarab stop their
nostrils where is the least thought of any infection, which they
can imagine to be as a kind of ill-odours in the air. In Semitic
cities we find some nice opinions of this kind, as that aphorism
of the Damascenes, "Who is lately vaccinated, should smell
no flesh-meat;" good odours they esteem comfortable to the
health, and so our old physicians held them (that which we perceive in smelling to sweet roses). The Aarab make therefore
nose-medicines, little bunches of certain herbs and odours, to
hang a day or two in their nostrils, and in the nostrils of their
camels. One evening at Medáin, a scorpion showed itself at
our hearth-stone; all gave back, one struck the vermin with a
stick, and raked it on the embers! "Out! cries Haj Nejm, now
thou hast singed the scorpion!" and they all rose from the
place; but a little of the insect's juice sprinkling upon Hasan's
forehead, he brushed it away with the back of his hand, and
laughing, his only care was lest he should smell the roasting
stench. Arabs are delighted with perfumes; the nomad housewives make treasure of any they have, with their medicines:
they often asked me, "Hast thou no perfumes to sell?" When
the Arabians commend a place they say, "There is a good
air and sweet water!" but to tell you the ill nature of an
ugly site, as el-Ally or Kheybar, they will say, "It lies drowned
in a corrupt air, and thou drinkest there an unwholesome
water."

Some of the herdsmen that passed with the flocks stayed
to enquire the way forward, so obscure is this mountain laby-

rinth, even to the Aarab. By this (they told me) the Syrian
haj road had once passed!—but that here was any common
passage of the old trade-road caravans appeared not, that I could
discern, by any timathîl upon those sandstone precipices. In
thievish country, with cavernous cliffs all along, full of strong-
holds at the ground and natural lodges, as galleries, upon
either hand, it were no good thoroughfare for caravaners. In
these miles-long straits, are many trees of the acacia thorn,
and a myrtle-leaved kind of great wild bareen fig-tree, *el-
uthub;* and in the bottoms some greenness of weeds, a sign
that the seyl water lies not far under.—But I saw nowhere the
rose-laurel, whose blossoming thickets are the joy of our eyes
in all fresh sites of the lime-rock wilderness towards Syria.
Beautiful at Petra, how beautiful in the torrents of Jordan!—
and those wild gardens of exceeding beauty where of old stood
the town of Caesarea Philippi!—but oh the delicious groves of
water blossoms which blow by that blissful strand of the lake of
Galilee! Who that was a Christian, should not remember them
in his grave, if it were possible!

Soon after our issuing to the Héjr plain, the sun set, and
we rode on in the brown twilight, coasting the undercliffs of
the Harra. It was now night, and we dismounted hastily, glad
to lie down, though still fasting and supperless, and to pillow the
head upon some wild block in the vulcanic drift. The travelled
cattle's udders had not a drop in them; nor would any man stir
from the ground, where he had alighted, to gather a few sticks
for an evening fire, all were afraid in that dark place to tread
upon *deybàn,* serpents. The nomads have a dread of these
poisonous vermin. A serpent having been seen in a beyt,
(which gliding among the baggage-sacks was not taken,) I have
known the family forsake their shelter, and remain abroad for
some days, until they thought the danger past.

Thus we rested out the short summer night till the day
beginning to rise, the Aarab loaded again and we set forward,
to pitch the standing camp this day in W. Thirba. We rode
on over a world of vulcanic cumber, fallen out from the eaves of
the Aueyrid, until it drew again to the jaila, when we came to
that valley mouth which opens, nearly in face of the Mezham,
in the enclosing cliffs of the plain of Medáin Sâlih. This large
valley bottom is a desolate bed of grit and of vulcanic stones,
strands and shelves, banks and terraces, horrid heaps without
number in a great torrent ground. All such work of laying and furrowing again is of *a vibrating water-stream:* but
from whence that abundant operation of water under a rainless climate? The weak autumn freshets, coming down after

showers in the high mountain, or in winter of any melting
snow, must be very soon sunk up under such a vast litter of
sand and stones.

When we had ridden in the valley two hours, we came by
many builded heaps, *rijûm*, in the midst of this wilderness
of banks and stones. Certain of them I saw built up in
part from a torrent channel ; —had the seyl beds ceased to be
ways of water in those old builders' days? Are those the
graves of their sheykhly families?—but of what antiquity?
The upland Semitic life is ever rude, thus they may be
from the time of the temple-tombs of the Héjr merchants—
which to guess only after the appearance, might be from the
morning of the human world! Monuments of human hands,
even ruined graves are a comfortable sight in this Titanic
landscape.

The valley walls are, at the mouth, sand-rock overflowed
by the Harra lavas ; then the sandstone sinks under the rising
wady floor. An hour above, the walls are bluish swarthy
streams upon streams of basalt, in all their height, nearly an
hundred fathoms. Higher, where opens a side valley, upon
the south side, we rode by some ancient ruins. The Arabs
showed me there a broken conduit and old plots of buildings :
I saw dry-laid masonry of the wild lava blocks and long walls,
to the midst of the valley, in this wilderness of stones, terraces,
platforms, enclosures of the ancient houses :—but lost is the
name of that dead settlement, and they call it *el-Géria*, ' The
Village.' Next over the wady stand many rijûm together,
they are workmanly dry-built, and further many more barrows
appear in a cluster upon the shelving valley side. With the
Beduins is no tradition of those who lived of old time in their
world : " Builders, they say, of the dead villages were the Yahûd
or Nasâra."

Some water-springs do yet remain above, and W. Thirba
is not abandoned by Moahîb husbandmen ; they are from the
valley (over against this) W. el-Aurush, but they had forsaken
Thirba this year for dread of Bishr ghrazzus egged on by the
Shammar Emir. We rode by their few cleared plots, amidst
that huge waste of harra stones, in the ground next the wells ;
there our Aarab drew bridle, and each household alighted
upon these platforms where they would. Year after year, upon
their little terraces of vulcanic grit, without any dressing, they
raise barley and wheat, pumpkins, melons, and a little tobacco ;
and all these kinds are better than can be grown in the yellow
sand-soil at el-Ally. The watering channels are led down from
the springs, whose heads are under a delicious green grove of fruit-

bearing wild fig-trees, *hamâta.* As their slender harvest is up, the Beduin colonists return from these outlying seed grounds to their own tent-village, géria.—W. Aurush is also a stony valley, but with many husbanded palms, watered by a spring above, upon the wady side.

There were solitary nomad tents in the forlorn valley before us, of Towwâla, W. Aly. Leaving their beyts a-building and the hareem, to that fresh grove resorted all our Beduins, to see the springing clear wells, which are pits opened back in black earth of the rising valley-side and walled with dry stone building : the water rises in the ground-rock of basalt.—Oh joyful refreshment to see the paradise covert of a thick green grove, and water fleeting ! Here we should be in rest awhile, with springing water to refresh our dried-up veins. Since a day or two, in our journeys, I had not almost tasted food, to-day I dined of these pleasant wild fruits, figs no greater than hazel nuts, and the taste not unlike wood strawberries ; but the rind is rough, and they scorch the tongue and throat. Therefore the Beduins would not pluck them, or it might be they think it not becoming their manly dignities ; for they willingly ate with me of those which I had gathered. The mid-day heat here in the tent shadow, at an height of 4500 feet, was now in the mean a degree or two above 100 F. ; but the great heat was yet to begin, and would be " in the reigning of the dog-star," said the Aarab.

Here was their summer home, the nomads were in rest, having that which they need most for themselves and their cattle's lives, which is water enough. Their provisions were fallen low since the year's beginning, when they had a little money of the haj surra, yet for this they did not trouble their hearts ; although, they had not much more to put under their teeth than that little mereesy which remained in their sacks. Of such mingled with water they keep a bowl standing by them, and sup of it often in the long daylight, which is so " long (says the Scripture) without bread."

It were but a short journey, yet none thought of going down to buy food at el-Ally, they would first thither when the sferry, or autumn time, should be nearly in. The hareem of poor households suffer most, for the men can take a turn upon the Harra to keep the camels, and drink their fills, when, they say, they ' multiply the léban.' I called to a poor neighbour woman going by my tent, who with a kerchief had covered her mouth and nostrils, ' did she ail anything ? ' " Aha, she answered, I am as I think thou art, *khormán,* a-hungred, the Lord send us some relief ! " So they are often heard saying, " To-day we have not *loosed the spittle* (their word for breaking the fast), and now the

sun sets ! " The flocks and great cattle are in the mountains ;
every other morrow the dubbush were led down to drink, and
their housewives went out to the springs to milk them : but
they found daily less in the dugs, and soon almost nothing ; for
the small cattle were teeming anew, *téghrurriz el-ghrannem.*
The camel troops were driven down every third day to the
watering. The Aarab mingled then the nâgas' milk with
mereesy, and drank, and felt a little refreshment. Since I
could not send to the town, I had nothing left but the slender
handfuls of rice which some more honourable housewives
brought to the mudowwy for medicines. I boiled one good
handful in water, and mixed a little mereesy, and it sustained
my life for that day ; it was like a holiday when I might drink
a little milk at the cattle watering. Some days I boiled tea,
in which is a cordial perfume that does wonderfully comfort
the spirits in great languishing. Sorry were the Aarab to mark
my wasted plight ; the stranger is a public guest, and when
women neighbours saw me go upon the scalding stones to
gather stalks for a cooking fire, one or other have commonly
proffered themselves, saying to me with kindness, *Khalîl, athan
lak oweyish,* " Shall I prepare for thee a little victual ? " and the
next gossip commended her, saying, " Leave it in her hands,
Khalîl, *wa iswat-ha tâyib,* for she can make it very well."

Such was their summer indigence! yet there were households, besides the sheykhs', which fared better than they seemed.
The best they found was now a slender mess of bare rice and
water, which their hareem cooked secretly, either closing their
booths, or else by night, for fear of smell-feasts ; since at such
times they must bid him who comes to them. The destitute
people, as any one is seen approaching whilst they are eating a
morsel, say quickly under their breaths, *ghrátta !* " Cover it from
sight." Yet if one surprise them, they begin with great instance
to bid him sit down and partake with them. A worthy man will
refuse then, or if he be a friend of theirs, he seats himself, and
tasting only a mouthful rises again, protesting, *wellah ghradeyt,*
" I have done eating, and it is enough." Almost as the birds must
the poor Beduins live at such times of the year, when the milk
is up, until the new dates. As the sun's vast flaming eye rose
each day upon us with new bringing of suffocating hours, the
remembrance revives in our fainting breasts of our want, with
the hollow thought " What shall be for this day's life ? "—and the
summer I passed thus fasting and Beduin-wise, lying upon the
elbow. Yet in this low state, there was hardly a week when some
householder had not a sacrifice, whether the year's mind of his
ancestors, for the birth of a son, for his recovery from sickness,

or for the health of his camels. Then a man's friends assembled
to the distribution of boiled flesh : they look also for the thaif-
Ullah, and I went, lest any should forget me ; but were they
my neighbourly acquaintance, or patients, or the sheykh, they
would send me a portion.

Bare of all things of which there is no need, the days
of our mortality are so easy and become a long quiescence !
Such is the nomad life, a long holiday, wedded to a divine
simplicity, but with this often long tolerance of hunger in the
khála. The sun returns all too early after the short summer
night's refreshment, and wakens the Aarab, who will lie no
longer as they see the day is dawning, when good Moslems
should say the first prayers. The men come together, at the
coffee-booth, to taste the morrow's cup. Children drive their
little weanling troops to the next bushes and the valley sides.
The hareem take up their spinning : of other housewifery they
go now nearly empty-handed ; there is no ráhla, there is no
butter-making nor daily milking. There is not a handmill
heard any more in the menzil ; they have no more ado to
fetch water.

The sun born above the horizon, the oven-like strong
heat is suddenly upon us ; in an hour the tent-poles are
hot to the touch. The Beduins lie all day in the booths
breathless and (in so extreme drought) without sweating :
only in those few lingering hours when the sun's eye stands
directly over our foreheads, is the day to us, who lie down,
very oppressing. The sun at length westing to the valley brow
of the Harra, and the comfortable shadows advancing to cover
our tents, the day's languishing heat is forgotten. The housewives come abroad to breathe the air, and they sit before the
beyts spinning. The men, *ez-zílm*, risen, draw to the sheykh's
mejlis and the coffee-tent ; there is the " club " of the tribe, and
commonly I went to take my place among them till the evening. The wady sides blush, the black Harra seems to blossom
in her dire vulcanic hills. The sun looks last askance upon
the bald spire of *Sheraan*, appearing from hence through the
mouth of W. Thirba ; that is a high sandstone mountain backward of the Rikb el-Héjr, and principal landmark at the midst
of the Fejîr dîra. When the light forsakes the earth, the day's
heat is radiated into the thin mountain atmosphere : a new
breathing coolness is come from the Harra, and the serene
Arabian night is above us, without dew or chilling. After
we had taken somewhat I remained to chat in our menzil ; or
amed went to seek human fellowship at some tent of acquaintance. The Beduw lie couched about their evening hearths,

and are out of countenance if they see a stranger less than light-hearted among them ; *eysh b' hu*, they say, ' What aileth him ! ' They took notice if at any time I fell into a study : " Khalîl is sad and silent ! it may be he has seen some mishap to-day (in my books, of second sight), there is one dead, perhaps, of his kindred and fellowship." The Beduins asked me daily if I did not feel a home-sickness ? They whispered ofttimes that I were a banished man. " Khalîl, how long wilt thou be missing from thy place and fellowship ? "—" It may be ten years." They said then " The time of exile among Khalîl's Aarab is ten years, which ended, Khalîl will go home to his house. Hast thou no blood-guiltiness upon thee ; is it not this that brings thee hither ? Tell us, art thou an outlawed man ? and else, we cannot imagine what thou art ! "

—Blood-guiltiness they think to be a misfortune in one's life, rather than a stain in human fellowship. The manslayer who flees to tribe or town, is taken in to the public hospitality ; and a lodging will be assigned him if he came so bare that he may hire none : the charitable call him to meat, and the company have no dainty to dip with the homicide hand in the dish. In their sight he is an unhappy fugitive, not an ex-communicated person : his fault is human and not divine (which only hath no remission), he blasphemeth not Ullah.—If they saw me stay the head in my hand the Beduins said, " Wherefore thus, Khalîl ? it is not well ! " When I gazed at the clear beauty of the moon, they said, " Look not so fixedly on him, it is not wholesome." There is no danger, I think, to sleep abroad, with open face in the bright moonlight ; for so do the poor nomads all the summer months of their lives : in Syria they have an opinion, that the moon, more than any sunlight, will blacken their faces. If any time I fell asleep, for languishing, after the assr, they roused me kindly, saying : " Slumber not at this hour, Khalîl, it is not for thy health."

Though it be a passion to a liberal conscience, one cannot be too circumspect in speech with the Arabs. Their half-hearings of my simple sayings were often so misreported, that I was amazed to hear my words as they set them forth again : and many a thing they fathered upon me, which I neither did not uttered ; but the sheukh were content, always, with my frank word of denial. A mother brought me her sick child ; and since I had taken him kindly by the hand, they said I was skilled in palmistry. It was reported that I fetched treasure from the rijûm, so (said one) " Since thou hast now silver, wilt thou not buy of me a thelûl that I have ? " Some young men entering where I sat to read in my tent, because

I let the book fall, they said, " Look you, he has found in it the misfortune of one dear to him ! "

When I spoke with the Beduins words out of the common human conscience, which are for every time under all the aspects of heaven, they heard with a pleased wonder and responded with a comely gravity, *aleynak sâdik*, " Thy saying is very good sooth." The idle Aarab have delight also in any playful word of the understanding ; they esteem him whose words move their better minds, and they favour him who is the daily waker of any mirth among them. Men yield half their soul with the smile, nothing is more comfortable to the spirits, nothing so human as laughter ; they can hardly another while contend with him, of whom they have any moment enjoyed the happy forgetfulness of themselves.

In our firelight evening talk, the Aarab asked of me a hundred questions ; which ever, like the returning wheel, reverted to that which possessed their Semitic souls, the sentiment of religion. The women curiously enquired of that great *sheykha*, the sovereign lady of my nation, ' whom Khalîl affirmed to be of power more than any man in the world ! ' A child answered, " Wellah, how great is she ? tell us is she greater than thy tent yonder ? " They asked if I were not a sheykh, and had a mare in my own land ? They heard my answers with a pleased suspense ; one or other would interpose if they saw me weary and say, " O you that question him, where is your courtesy, why will ye molest the stranger ? " But chiefly they admired, when they heard of me the good manners of the Christians. " We have asked Khalîl (they said) the *suâlif* of the Nasâra ; and wellah they whom we esteemed kafirs, are God-fearing wellah more than we which are named the people of Ullah : neither is Khalîl hostile, whatso any man say, but of one mind with the Aarab." Sometimes they exclaimed, *el-hâchy Khalîl helw*, ',my talk was sweet ' in their hearing. They desired most, as all the Arabs, to hear of the *jizzat en-Nasâra*, or kind of Christian wedlock, and admired whilst I related to them at length, the inalienable chaste bond of the Messianic marriage !

And I have wondered at the darkness of these poor hill-Beduw, in matter of Semitic religion ! They said to me, " We are mesakîn and ignorant ! in any religious doubt we go to ask the Alowna, that know letters and are readers of the Scripture." Amongst these—they were praying Beduins, more than their neighbours westward and northward—some had not heard of a life to come after our natural decease ! Only they said that those who displeased Ullah " should fall down to Jehennem."

One asked at our evening fire: "Is there aught after a man's death, Khalîl, and tell us, (the thought of an indigent people who, in the sacrifice of hospitality, must many times defraud their own bowels,) if any have given *sádaka*, alms for God, shall he find it again?" Sádaka is the willing God's-tribute and godly kindness of an upright man, spared out of his own necessity, to the relief of another; I answered with that Scripture, "He who giveth alms lendeth to the Lord; and as you sow so shall you reap hereafter."—"We have heard that all shall be a fire, and then what, Khalîl?"—"The Nasâra and Moslemîn believe that the dead shall rise in their bodies, to appear before Ullah to judgment, in a wady that is before the walls of The Holy (City), *el-Kúds*."—"Ah! where is that Holy (City), and where lies *el-Khalîl* (City of 'The Friend,' Abraham's dwelling, or Hebron)? We have heard that the souls shall be gathered into a pit under the "hanging-stone there': what is this, Khalîl? and when that stone shall fall, is it not the end of the world? Sawest thou that stone, as men say, hanging in the air; and seemed the stone to be nigh unto falling?"—The cavern and its cover, 'the falling-stone,' is a pit, (named in the Mohammedan mythology of Abraham and the Patriarchs,) or inconsiderable ceiled chamber, all hewn in the limestone rock, in the temple precinct of Mount Moriah, and over it is built the mosque of Omar: it is such as a small water-cellar, and like it are many cisterns of the ancient husbandry seen in the country about Jerusalem. —"And the Judgment passed, what shall become of us?"— "The faces of the just shall be clear as the sun-light, and angels lead them into the gardens of God; where, says the Book, they shall not remember the sorrow of the world any more; but the wicked shall fall down to the fire, where their torment is never ended."—"Shall we see and know our fathers and acquaintance? also speak to us of your religion. When was Îsa?"—"The religion of Îsa ben Miriam, from the spirit of Ullah, that is higher than the heaven! forbids all evil meaning and dealing, and bids men live in devout fear and love of the Lord which made them, with godly love towards our neighbour; harmless and quietly leading our lives, not hating any as an enemy, and easy of forgiveness." The Beduins repeated the words after me with a religious admiration: but it seemed strange to them, that a man must love his adversary in this malicious world, and indeed not just. "And is tobacco, Khalîl, Iblîs his water; and shall smoke 'drinkers' fall down to hell burning?"—"Childish folly! —what is Iblîs or Sheytàn?" They could not tell, and wondered that these two names were of one meaning:—my lore also seemed to them marvellously quaint!

I went one afternoon to visit those beehive-like rijûm, nigh
our camping-ground ; well built barrows seated upon the waste
soil with an enduring weight and solidity. I numbered of them
more than one hundred and fifty. Some are partly fallen, all
the rest have been broken through. These round heap-buildings,

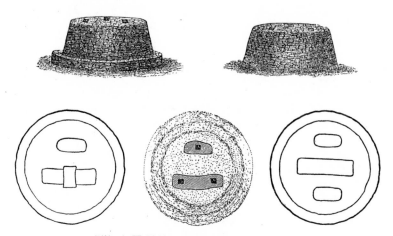

Rijûm in W. Thirba ; section and plans of the same.

or drawn slightly to the oval, are twenty-five feet wide, and
ten feet in height. Within are narrow deep cells, one or two,
or even three in a rijm, and provided with trap mouths. By
these man-holes I let myself down into some of the barrows,
where I always found a sepulchral air ; but I saw no bones lying
in any of them. The cells are built diminishing upwards, and
closed over with slabs : upon this is filled in a rubble of loose
stones ; the tunnel mouths appear as wells in the heads of the
rijûm. There is built a ledge, or advancing foot, about the ground
courses of some of the barrows (*v.* fig.). They are all of dry
building, very well laid of the basalt blocks of the valley. In
W. Aurush are other such barrows, some also in *W. Shellál* I
saw later, but they are less workmanly built up. Greater than
any rijûm in the valley are certain which appear from hence,
upon the wady brink, where a giddy sheep-path led upwards
to the Harra ; but I was too feeble to ascend upon my feet.
The sheykhs told me those are but circuits of walling. I asked
the Arabs, " Are not the rijûm sepulchres of the ancients ? "
Answer : " We have thought so, but some of us searching the last
year, found no bones in them."

Some days I sought shelter in the cool fig-tree thicket, in the hottest hours—not without suspicion of those feverish shadows. There the flocks come to the lukewarm watering, the Beduin housewives return to fill their girbies, and men refresh themselves with bathing. Two are the well-heads, the upper, without the grove, is better; the temperature of the water is 83° Fahrenheit. The well-spring within the grove (a little sulphurous smelling) flows into a small clay pool (birket) of the absent Beduin husbandmen, it is the head of their irrigation. Those wild fig trees (hamât) bear a very small leaf, like the garden mulberry; the sap is so acrid, that touched to the skin it will raise a blister, which burns for a day or two. A few wild fig trees may be found in these deserts, they spring (of the wild birds' sowing) about water. A wild grove as this I have not seen in Arabia: thereby is a mákbara or tribesmen's burying place and, in their belief, a *menhel*, or descending place of the angels or fairies.

In these thick shadows, I have seen long whip-snakes, and spiders great as the palm and fingers of a man's hand: little dragon-flies of several colours glanced in that teeming broken light. Over the clay pool, I saw all day a fluttering cloud of the small grey birds of the desert, which fly in to water from the dry wilderness; and there are dun-swallows, and blue roving rock-doves, birds which haunt about water-holes in Arabia. Next below the pool in the open valley is a desert thorn, grown to great timber, to whose thin grey shadows resort the men of the encampment: there they stretch themselves to slumber upon the ground rather than in the close tents, and waste the desolate meridian hours. The basalt valley-steep behind the grove and water is a covert of red-legged stone partridges of the wilderness: we heard them calling with ripe and merry note, the livelong summer's day. Here only I have seen a butterfly in the khála, fluttering forth like a falling blossom in the desert air. The Aarab called it *sherràra,—aisûn* say the townsmen of Medina.

In the stony wild of the valley by the grove, is the burying place of the sheykhs of the Moahîb. I saw there some ruined ground walls of old dry building; and among the great heaps of stones lie a few forms of graves and *musullies*, praying-steads, such as we saw that of Ibn Rashîd at el-Héjr, where as much ground as a man may bow himself in is enclosed from the common by a horseshoe of laid stones, whose bent is toward Mecca. In these I have seen tribesmen come, to pray at the graves of their ancestors. The Beduins are loth to pass that way by night, saying ghosts do walk there, which are of the kafirs, dwellers of old time in the valley.

The *menhel el-melûk* is thereby, 'a lighting place of the Power of the air.' But, when they saw I derided their superstition, "Khalîl, said the coffee drinkers, it 'is true indeed; and though we have not seen them, our fathers have seen them! There are tribesmen now living who will swear upon their faith that they have heard the tread of their feet in the dance, the sound of them, and the song, by night, and have understood their words; and that was sometime when, come hither a-hunting, they lodged alone in these grounds in Thirba;—and they were very sure that no Aarab lay encamped in all the valley." These Beduins say further, "Did one pluck any bough, he should be caught away in the air, and be seen no more; or forgetting his mind, be driven continually, without eating or drinking, through the khála." They told me of the mischief of one not much before, a wealthy Tuâly—he had been well known to most of them,—who (in despite of their superstition) set fire to one of those possessed trees growing in the Jau; "but not much after a grievous sickness took him, his bowels gushed out from beneath, and he ended miserably: his children likewise perished, and his many cattle;" the man had been the owner of forty camels. Here was a sign of the silent heaven in their own times, which put in solemn record of books (had those Beduw the superfluous art of letters), might pass, under all their seals, to later generations! The Beduins always granted me that none living had seen the angel visions,— the relation was come down to them from their ancients. "If such manifestations be not of the melûk, they asked, what were they?" The melaika are seen in the air like horsemen, tilting to and fro; 'in your approaching, billah, they vanish away.'

Some *menâhil* there are in these parts of Arabia, in every nomad dîra. They are commonly trees, and even shrubs of the khála. Thither the tribesmen coming in their ráhlas, the sick person will sacrifice a sheep, for his health, or a goat, with blood-sprinkling. He cooks the flesh in the place, and divides it to his friends, and leaves some hanging upon the branches: then he lies down to slumber full of his superstitious faith that the melaika will descend upon him in vision, and speak precepts for his health. "The sick will awaken whole and sound; but if anyone in health be so hardy as to slumber there, he will rise upon the morrow a broken man." There are two menâhil in the Jau, one of them is a bush *sárhah*, and the other is a sort of evergreen oak *butm* or *thirwa;* the possessed trees are behanged with old beads, votive shreds of calico, lappets of coloured stuffs, and

other vile baggage. Another is that great desert thorn before
the kella at el-Héjr. — Is their superstition of the menhel-
trees a remnant of the tree-worship, which we know was in
ancient Arabia ?

The like we may see continued, in field and town, in the
Arabic border-countries. Trees, places of accepted prayer,
are found thus garnished in the open lands from Syria to
Morocco : every returning worshipper suspends a rag for his
prayer which was heard in that place. Many you may see are
bushes which lend no shadow in the heat to the sun-beaten
and thirsty wayfarer, who kneels down there. In the *W.
Barada,* near Damascus, where certain heathenish festival
customs do yet remain amongst the Moslemîn, I have visited
two groves of evergreen oaks, which are *wishing-places* for the
peasantry. If the thing fall to them for which they vowed,
they will go to the one on a certain day in the year to break
a crock there ; or they lay up a new stean in a little cave which
is under a rock at the other. There I have looked in, and
saw it full to the entry of their yet whole offering-pots : in
that other grove you will see the heap of their broken potsherds. [The groves are in the valley coast westward above
the village *Zibdány.*]—These are common beliefs of the superstitious half-rational human conscience in the whole world.
More are the examples than need be numbered, of this kind of
apparition of angels, in Moses' books, and in the sacred histories
of the first full times of Irsael. We have a startling example
[though it be an ancient interpolation] in the new Scriptures :
at his seasons the Power of the air descended to trouble a
cistern at Jerusalem, and who went down first into the water,
he was healed of his infirmity.

I questioned these Beduins of their funeral customs. The
deceased is buried the same day or, if he die at evening, upon
the morrow. The corse is washed, and decently lapped in a
new calico cloth : they scrape out painfully, with a stick and
their hands, in the hard-burned soil, a shallow grave. The feet
of the dead are laid towards Mecca, and over the pitiful form of
earth they heap a few stones, to assure the human clay ; yet I
have seen their graves in the desert mined by foul hyenas, and
the winding-sheets lay half above ground. A Mahûby told me
that " a man's head is shaved, and the hair is scattered to the
wind ; " if he spoke truly, it is not known in other parts of
Arabia. He said also " a woman's hair is not cut, they bury
her comb with her ; a stake of the tent is set up at the
housewife's grave-head." They sprinkle a woman's bier with
perfumes when she is carried out. When one is dead, his

kinsmen sacrifice at his grave a ewe, but without sprinkling of blood ; they boil and distribute the meat to the funeral company. In the next religious festival, the friends of the deceased assemble to his next kinsman, who has sacrificed according to his ability—the nomads are in this of a large-hearted piety—it should be a cow-camel ; but because their households were so indigent, and it were impossible to cut off this womb of the stock, they buy for three or four sheep or goats some *fâtir*, a decrepid nâga that has lost the front teeth, and is past bearing : this beast they release from all burdens and let fatten for certain months.—For the deceased woman, they keep no sacrifice.

As I sat down some hot after-midday by the *hamât* there came *Miblis*, Tollog's other fair young wife, with five or six water-skins : I asked her wherefore so many to-day ? she answered, " To-night Tollog keeps *a liberality*, he slaughters a camel-calf ; Khalîl, see thou fail not to be there."—Sitting later in the afternoon mejlis I heard that the sheykh kept the year's mind to-day and would sacrifice for his father and his grandsire. When the sun was near setting Tollog went out, called to bring him a knife, and tucked up his sleeves,—for every householder should slay his own sacrifice : there stood a nâga and her calf before the tent. Some voices cried, " Ho ! why thus, Tollog ? and the suckling calf is a female. Take a sheep, thou, or else a goat, and sacrifice it in her stead." *Hamed*, the sheykh's son, answered them,—upon whom this charge must one day come to sacrifice for his father yet living before us, " But she refuses the teat, and we have determined to kill her." The worth of such a calf were three or four reals, and every month she rises one in value. These were Pickthanks' words of course, which could not move the old sheykh's bountiful humour. The by-standers, as he bade them, laid on rough hands and flung down the howwâra bleating and struggling. The dam, seeing their hard usage, made up to her young one and, wreathing down her long neck, uttered an affectionate murmur in her vast throat, and was full of trouble. Tollog carved the victim's long neck with a deep gash, next the breast ; the miserable mother, tracing to and fro, smelled to the spouting blood ; her kneeling calf, with the head upheld, bearing an appearance of life. The brittled carcase was soon in the pots, and the pots bubbling over the weak nomad fire of a few sticks and camel-dung. Tollog's guest-meal, with a mighty mess of rice cooked in the broth, was ready a little before midnight. I had departed to sleep, but the good old man did not forget the stranger ; his messenger wakened me, putting in a savoury bowl under the skirt of my tent ; " This is from Tollog, he said, rise and take.thy supper." Such suckling meat is sweet as veal and tender. Seldom the nomads eat other flesh than the meat of their sacrifices ; 'but it be some beast that will not thrive, or is likely to die on their hands ;—it is little they taste of any game.

⌐—And to speak shortly of their sacrifices in the desert : when a man child is born, the father will slay an ewe, but the female birth is welcomed in by no sacrifice. Something has been already said of their blood-sprinkling upon break-land, and upon the foundation of new building ; this they use also at the opening or enlarging of new walls and waters. Again when their ghrazzu riders return with a booty, *feyd* or chessab, the women dance out with singing to meet them : and the (live) chessab, which they say ' is sweet,' is the same evening smeared with the blood of a victim. *Metaad,* a neighbour of mine, sent me a present of the meat of a fat goat which he had sacrificed for the health of a sick camel ; and " now, said the Aarab, it would certainly begin to amend." Rubba, the poor herdsman, made a supper to his friends, dividing to them the flesh of a she-goat, the thank-offering which he had vowed in his pain and sickness. Swoysh sacrificing the year's mind, for his grandsire, distributed the portions at his tent, but we sat not down to a dish. They are persuaded that backwardness to sacrifice should be to their hurt. All religious sacrifices they call *kurbân.* I have seen townsmen of Medina burn a little bakhûr, before the sacrifice, for a pompous odour ' acceptable to God,' and disposing our minds to religion.—Where all men are their own butchers, perhaps they are (as the Arabs) more rash-handed to shed human blood. When they sacrifice to the jan they sacrifice to demons. If one sacrifice for health, the death of the ewe or the goat they think to be accepted for his camel's or for his own life, life for life. [So the slaughter of a ram redeemed Abraham's son's life.] The sacrifices eaten in fellowship in the desert a little allay these nomads' almost incessant famine ;—and they are as a calling of the Lord the Allgiver, in his guests, a mystical communion of their bread and salt with Him !

I waited to go on to Kheybar. The barren days passed over me, and Kheybar seemed never the nearer, and less daily my ability to travel. The date fruits in those hot valleys were already ripening. Certain Moahîb would have gone thither, with the Fejîr ; but we had since word that the

Fukara went not this year to Kheybar, and they durst not, few together, cross a country so infested (at this season) by hostile ghrazzus. Messengers of the Fejîr sheykhs had returned from Kheybar, bringing word that ' great part of the fruit of their trees was devoured by the locusts, also the Medina soldiery were there to take dues of them' ; and we now heard that therefore the sheykhs and tribesmen had determined to abandon their harvest. The Dowla tax is a real mejîdy upon six camels, or for forty head of small cattle,—milder and lighter, they say, than the exaction made by the gatherers of Ibn Rashîd, which also is not much ; yet it cuts the Beduins to their hearts that have no experience of public burdens.

How might the Fukara sheykhs live without their Kheybar dates ?—" By selling away some of their great cattle, for victual, in the villages ; " but the poor tribesmen's families, what should they do ?—" They can hire out their best camels, to draw wells in the oases, for so many measures of dates by the month." The great infirm brute may not long apply his strength ; his hump failing, he must be dismissed to the wilderness ; a well-team may, they say, endure to labour not more than an hundred days. There are well-owners who drive the same camels continually, but they are at last very lean and weak. Indigent persons in a low time, must cast themselves upon their more welfaring tribesmen, asking to-day to drink a little léban, in God's name, and to-morrow for somewhat to eat. I have seen the grudging housewives yield the dole with deadly scarcity ; but that little, for the fear of Heaven and the tongues of men, is not ever denied them. Since the Fukara would not go up to Syria, they had devised to pitch this summer no standing camps, but to march with their camels ; thus every household might drink milk at evening. There was none' in our menzil who would adventure to conduct me to Kheybar. I yet desired to see Kheybar, and, as my strength diminished, I thought there to put the bourn of my voyage in Arabia ; wherefore should I macerate my life continually in the greatest jeopardy ? or suffer this distress of soul, to kick against the fanaticism of the whole Ishmaelite country ?

The Moahîb entreated me to discover for them the old waters. Their desire of such lasting benefit is above their more than Hebrew cupidity of tháhab. For the mine of water, yielding butter and milk continually, they would forsake all transitory advantage. Sitting in the mejlis, some of the sheykhs questioned me, ' Would I not open for them certain dead waters in Thirba ? ' I asked, ' Had they not attempted this themselves ? '—" Ah ! Khalîl, the Aarab are affinîn, corrupt, good-for-

nothing.' *Tollog :* " So Khalîl find us the water, let him take
up what treasure he will and it shall be his own ! " There was
lately a springing well under the further side of the valley,
but it had been stopped by a shoot of stones, and the Beduins
could not join themselves to reopen their well-pit. " I will go
about the work, so you find me every morning two or three
men for my labourers." Tollog answered, " But who will go
out with thee ? he would first ask to be paid his wages, and
we have no power to compel any 'man."—" If you are so
heartless, who can help you ? "—" You may well say it,—the
Beduw ! Khalîl, the Beduw ! But at least, Khalîl, show us the
head of the water, whose broken conduit you. saw the day we
rode into the valley by the géria." I said, if they mounted
me, we might go and seek it ; but even in this they could not
determine anything.

I had seen the signs of ground-water in the Thorreyyid,
and coveted to leave them some lasting advantage and good
remembrance of a Nasrâny's sojourn and guestship in their
dîra. Shallow pits to ground-water, which the Aarab may
reach with their hands, are called *themîla,* pl. *themeyîl.* I
said, 'Let them send me with a few upon this expedition,
and I asked but the milk of a nâga.' In that languishing heat
of the year, there will none be at any pains ; many doubted
in their illiberal souls, whether—for the sake of a little milk
—the stranger would not mislead them, seeing that I had
not enquired of their rewards ;—for it is impossible they should
suppose that a man can wish no other thing than merely well
toward his neighbours. I said therefore, " No more of this ;
and I know, Tollog, that if a spring were opened there would be
contentions among you, (el-Aarab *yuhowwishûn,*) for the rights
of water. There are factious spirits even in so small kindreds,
it is a little will rip up the scars of their old sores ; and the
sheykh may not always contain the hot-heartedness of his
Aarab : I knew they had bickerings over these waters at the
grove. Tollog answered : " Ullah ! and that is sooth ; (he added
wondering), but whence has Khalîl all this knowledge of the
Aarab ! "

Some would persuade me, 'since I was now come so far that
I might hardly hope to return to my own country, to remain in
W. Thirba, and plant this valley ; they would learn of me and
I should be as their tribesman.'—' And when the people re-
moved—? ' *Answer :* ' They would build me a kella, they would
leave some men with me ; I should open the hidden waters, and
the valley would grow green of our industry.' I enquired,
' Wherefore fetched they not some villagers from el-Ally, and the

fruits might be divided between them?' It was answered, "The Alowna are too faint hearts to sojourn here."—I have asked also the Alowna, Why, there lying much wady nigh about them where the water is not far under, and garden ground so dear in their close settlement, they did not send a colony into some of the ruined valleys? *Answer:* "But those would live ever in dread, what for the insecurity of the wild country, and for the small faith of the Beduw."

A grave matter was handled in the mejlis, 'whether the tribe should not submit themselves to Ibn Rashîd;'— that was the contention of the Serahîn sheykhs. Formerly these Moahîb, Abu Shamah, had yielded the zikâ, or tithing, to the *Jebel;*—to Abdullah first prince, and in the beginning of Telâl's time. It is but a light real upon every five camels, worth 180 or 200 reals, and the same for thirty head of small cattle, worth 100 reals. Trusting in their Harra mountain, they had ever since withheld this small tribute; and when upon a time the warlike Abeyd, returning from an expedition in the Tehàma, lighted on the Moahîb menzil in the flank of the Aueyrid, those sturdy mountaineers ran upon the hill sides and spared not to shoot down upon his hostile squadron. Abeyd, seeing he could not drive them out of the wild rocks, held off, carrying no more away with him than the spoil of one Mahûby beyt; but "there fell down among them those that had been wounded by the shot of the Moahîb, in all the way to Teyma."

One day when they had long and earnestly deliberated in the mejlis of their policy towards Ibn Rashîd, they described little before the sunsetting the new moon, *el-hilâl.* Tollog rose, and all the men with him, and coming abroad they gazed at the friendly star appearing; then looking up to heaven they prayed fervently, 'That in the time of this moon it might be well with them, and that the Lord would deliver them from their enemies.' Afterward Tollog said to me, "And what thinkest thou? they of the Jebel (the government of Ibn Rashîd), because we deny them the zikâ, call us *mushrakîn*, idolaters; Khalîl, didst thou see in thy travels any Aarab that pray more than we? The Beduins that you met with in the north parts, *ahl es-Shemàl,* they pray?—what sayest thou?—nay, I think little at all, they be nigher your kin, the Nasâra." I began to answer that I held them to be therefore the better, but the stout old sheykh did not thus understand me: "You judge rightly, said he; you have seen that we are better than the northern folk; they pray no more than the kafirs, but we are Moslemîn.

Is it well for us not to pay zikâ to Ibn Rashîd ? "—" Since the
zikâ is light, were it not better to secure yourselves thus, in
front, than, being assailed upon that side, to lose perhaps at
once many camels ? "—" Wellah true ! and we have nothing to
fear from the backward, where, besides the Howeytát, they are
all our friends."

After their opinion that *all arts are of the Nasâra,* these
tribesmen resorted to me in the long hours with swords and
cutlasses, asking would I try the temper for them ; this they
affect to discern for themselves smelling to the steel, or they
breathe upon their blades, and watch the vapour fading
away. Some put in my hands their long guns ; and when
any inscriptions were upon their arms they desired that I
should read them.—To speak in few words of the kinds of
weapons among them : the long Arabian guns are always
matchlocks. The best according to the superscriptions are old
pieces of Europe ; and (saving some made lately in Spain,
Barbary and Egypt), they are of the centuries past. It is
perhaps half a dozen or half a score of generations since those
were in the hands of our ancestors ; by whom cast off, they
have been sold far away in the markets of the East. They call
the best *el-Lazzâry,*—and I read upon them the trade-mark,
in Latin letters, *Lazzarino Cominazzi!* Next after these are
el-Májar, old pieces named—of which the nomads can give no
account—of Hungary, and perhaps brought by the Turks
to the border cities. In the third degree is *el-Engleysy* ; that
is also but a name among them, of which they know no more.
There is no imprint upon the Engleysy guns. In every kind
they esteem a quality of metal, the Arabian smiths are in
this very sufficient judges. Of the temper comes, they think,
the gun's delivery of the ball ; whether it be, as our fathers
said of their bows, quick or dull shooting. " Good metal, they
answer, should show always clean and neat, and shining in
the mouth as a coffee-cup." The baser metal will foul easily ;
but all must foul soon, with their gross charges of coarse-
grain weak powder. I have seen their long pieces cast level, a
light ill-made bullet to the distance of nearly two hundred
yards.

The older the arms, so they may yet serve, the more are
they esteemed among the Arabs. The world was stronger,
they think, in the old days, but some of their firelocks are
worn so nigh that, with any overcharge they must needs burst ;
and the owner, giving God thanks, if he escaped scatheless, will
carry his gun to the next sâny to have it clouted up again,

and trust in Ullah it will be never the worse. So highly do
they value their best pieces, that a gun reckoned excellent is
hardly to be had among them for reals.' These Southern Aarab
are so low in the welfare of the world that you may hardly find
three guns or four swords in five men's hands. He who has
none is provided with some old pike, not better than a stick
of even length and weight, or, although a footman, he bears
the formidable horseman's lance, *shelfa*. The poorer nomad,
who would be a gunman, may buy him a piece, one of the
bastard kinds, for his three or five reals ; they are counterfeited
Lazzaries, Barbary or Egyptian, with false stamps badly set
upon them. The nomad is not an hunter, he has seldom
need to fire his gun, even in the ghrazzus when commonly
they do but lift cattle from a few herdsmen, and ride away
hastily to outgo the pursuit. The guns in the hands of the welfaring and sheykhly sort are commonly of a middle estimation ;
for such Beduins will pay sixteen or seventeen reals. Other
fire-arms amongst southern nomads are a few crazy horse-pistols ;
I have seen they are European from our grandsires' times ; the
best of them they call *el-Engleysy*.

Of their side-arms the Persian scimitar and then the Indian,
are of fine temper and so much arched as were lately our cavalry
officers' sabres ; that is held the better shape in the East. They
say the truth, "the effectual sword cut is the stroke with a
sawing draught." The hatchet stroke they think uncunning ;
it will not well bite and open. The plain-handed stroke is, they
say, weak : but the back stroke is that wherein a man may
assemble all his force, and with the finest blades in a valid hand,
the neck of a mother's son may be severed at a stroke. I saw
also swords among these few Moahîb which were of Occidental
countries ; two of them ship-cutlasses that long ago " had been
taken out of a vessel stranded on the coast." The motto was
in Latin, *Pro Deo et patria.* Upon another I read a German
legend ; it was a scimitar, of iron, and made perhaps for
the Oriental markets. Mishwat among the rest brought me
his sword. As I turned it in my hand he fixed his eyes
strangely, but when I felt with a finger down the edge of his
blade, "Khalîl ! not so (he cries), it is not well ! why handle
el-fumm es-seyf, the mouth of my sword ? " He feared I
might weaken the steel with which another day he must
meet his foemen in the field. As for other tools a knife,
khûsa, might hardly be found in three tents of these poor
nomads ; a little clasp-knife, such as they saw me use, they
call *rîsh :* the crooked girdle-knife, *khánjar*, is seldom seen
among them, which the Beduins name rather *kiddamîyyah*

and *shibrîyyah :* for all such are wares of the far border lands, and this is a deep wilderness of dearth and misery.

Their camels come again to the watering in the third afternoon. We see in their far-off appearing (that comfortable sight in the dead land) the long ostrich-like necks, and the tall moving dun bulks at the head of the Harra valley, then we hear them lowing as they come : the nâgas bear home full-swelling udders for the poor households, and we shall drink this afternoon a sweet refreshment. Man's body reposing, is preserved with little food in that serene and purest dry air ; the hungry gnawing is slowed by often coffee and tobacco drinking, and his flesh is wasted only little and little in this vacation from all labour. It is the slumber by day steeping the spirits, and the clear upland Arabian night's coolness which recomforts our weariness. The herdsmen come in before the beasts to camp, to see how their households fare, and their great cattle pass down of themselves to the watering, *maweyrid :* there all the men are presently gathered of the small Moahîb kindred : the sheukh, save Tollog and his elder son, go down also to the watering labour.

The troughs, *hawd*, are set ready, one for every owner-ship of camels : the hawds are shallow basins, a yard wide, of seamed camel leather, hanging in a foot-frame of withy rods. The rivelled bucket-bags, having in the midst a cross-tree of wood to hold them open, have been steeped and suppled. Every waterer who stands in a well draws with a chant and heaves his bucket to his fellow's hands, and he answering with the return of their perpetual refrain, runs to empty this water-burden in the hawd. The water-men, to be more expedite, tuck up their tunics ; the long wing-like sleeves (once seen in ancient Europe, now the guise of Arabia), which droop to the ground, they have tied upon the nape of their necks. You shall see then the Beduins are lithe bodies, the arms dry and tough, with small brawns : the manly breast, even in young men, is commonly shagged. Very often the weleds wear bracelets, *mathûd*, upon the upper arm : of such there is mention in the old scripture, in the story of the death of Saul. Their bracelet is but a copper band ; he will bestow it upon the " uncle's daughter " whom he shall have purchased to himself, in the day of their marriage. The Aarab waterers hearten and quicken them-selves to their efforts—it is long and they are weak—with this cheerfulness of the song. The more burdenous, say they, of their tasks is the *weyrid :* but every rude labour is heavy upon men in long hunger and languishing. Beduins are valorous, in this sort, about any endeavour that their necessity may cast upon them. Then they can rouse themselves erect and magnanimous ; whence that saying in the oases, " The Beduw are all heart : " but the famine upon them, it is a short fit, a man's brains unsettle over the fainting stomach, he submits himself to Ullah, and must sit down again.

That loud chant of Beduins at labour is but some stave of three or four words in cadence, with another answering in rime, being words which first happen to their minds, and often with little sense ; and when they have sung a couplet somewhile, they will take up a new.—And this is a shepherd's rime which he made of me in the booths : *yâ Khalîl ! zéy el-fîl,* " O Khalîl ! sib to the elephant."—That beast of another continent is only known to them in name ; the like may be said of the lion and the swine, which are names only (and such in sense as we use them) to these middle Arabians. The lion is not found in Arabia proper, unless, as I have heard southern men relate, it be in a province of el-Yemen. The swine is wild in all the high Syrian border : the Aarab often asked me, what beast is that of the prayerless Nasâra, which is forbidden in the Apostle's religion to be eaten ; some have answered among them, that had been in the north, and would seem wise, " We have seen his traces, and wellah he has gazelle's feet, with the snout, ye would say, of a hound."—The waterers have asked me in the heat of their labour, why stood I by gazing, and did not come down to help them ?—" Fellows, you see these wasted arms ? I am weakened with hunger, I cannot draw and drudge ; but let my old nâga drink a little which remains in the troughs, and God will requite you." When they heard my words they answered, " Wellah, he says truth ; God help thee, Khalîl ; and have no care for this, but sit down, that it is we will water her."

The great camels coming from the summer pasture, where they have gone and sweated in the eye of the sun till the third daylight (and therefore the best camels are those, in their sight, that sweat least), will drink long out at the watering, every beast, say the waterers, to the quantity of three or four girbies,—this is less, by a third, than a nomad horse would drink in the same summer's days' space ; and then swollen and groaning with the swallowed burden, they are driven to the menzil, where the beneficent animals couch again in their troops before the Beduin households. All night the drenched beasts dribble water, and camels at all times, even in the journey and drought, stale more often and little than other animals. It is found in the morning, that they have digested

the water : their great veins are seen no longer starting from the
hairy hide, and their vast bodies are returned nearly to the
natural figure. The sun risen, they are driven again to the
watering, that they may drink a little more ; and then turning
away of themselves *yusuddirûn*, they " breast " upward, passing
on by the way of the mountains to their slender pasture,
where in the long hot months are but languishing evergreen
plants, commonly of bitter sap or saline, and very little harsh
forage. I have asked the Aarab, " Is there no bowel, in these
beasts' intestines, for the storing of water ? " they answered me,
" No, Khalîl, or how (and every camel is finally slaughtered)
have we never found it ? " From the first days of autumn
the camels then *âzab*, or pasturing apart from the menzil,
return not to the watering till the *fifth* daylight :—from whence
then is that abundance of saliva ? that they may swallow their
droughty fodder.

The Nomad households watch their beasts departing ; and
have patience till the third day, when they shall drink léban
again. As the water is too little for their troops at once, all the
menzils have not the same watering days. Thus in some bye-
evenings I might obtain a little milk. One afternoon, where
Hamdy showed me, (she was a good hostess careful of my health,)
I crossed over the wady to the Serahîn. " It is to Darŷesh, she
said, thou shouldst go, the man has four milch camels." This
was the Serahîny sheykh, a very fond and scolding splenetic
person. As I entered in the dusk, he cried with a braving
sour look, " What wouldst thou here ? " I pointed silently to
the many couched camels before his tent. He smiled with a
fool's solemnity, " And why, he said, come hither from thy
Aarab ?—dost thou not know that there is danger between us,
to the cutting off of heads ; and what hast thou to do with
our léban ? "—" The stranger has no cattle, wilt thou not give
me a draught for my medicine ? "—" Well, well, Khalîl (said
the company), sit down till the milking time, and it shall be
brought to thee." This dog-face, whom I had often seen in
Tollog's kahwa tent, always professed against me a fanatical
bitter enmity ; he shot through me with his glancing eyes
at the mejlis, but had not before spoken with the kafir ! " Ha !
he said, as now his mouth was open, if I might find thee
one day in the wilderness, and my gun were in my hand,
then would I shoot thee dead ! "—" Take thy gun to-morrow,
except thou be'st a coward, and fire thy shot, and I will fire
another ; by the Lord I think not to spare thee."—" Now
look you, how the Nasâra be *ahl kellimy*, a people of the
very word ; they say not a thing as we and mean it not :—

Khalîl, we are the Beduw and, if I said aught, it was not so in earnest, and I wish thee no hurt." The hind now brought in the pleasant frothing milk-bowls and " Drink, Khalîl, and refresh thyself," said the wooden Darŷesh, setting before me a good one. I went homeward and he showed me the path ; but misgoing in the feeble starlight, I fell headlong from the gravel-cliff where their booths stood, upon the torrent stones below.

CHAPTER XVII.

THE MOAHÎB SUMMER CAMP IN WADY THIRBA.
VISIT TO EL-ALLY.

Meteoric rumour in the mountain. Women cover the throat. The colocynth. Charms for love. Fair women. Miblis. Hamed's kasîda. The Nasrâny called to name one of their daughters. Beduins weary of the songs of the desert. Names of Beduin women. A childing woman. Strife betwixt young tribesmen. Tollog's apology for his many marriages. A Beduin slayer of himself. The nomads' splenetic humour, and their religious mind. Hamdy. The plagues of Mecca. The summer famine. The old hermits. False war news. Is St. Sergius, since his death, become a Moslem? Wejh. Certain Nasarenes dwelling there. Mahanna arrives to require blood-money. One from Kheybar arrived at el-Ally. The Nasrâny departs for el-Ally. Horeysh. The Akhma. Summer night at el-Ally. Mûsa's coffee-house. The jummaa or Semitic faction. The hospitable kâdy. Whether the righteous man may ' drink smoke'? Return with Horeysh. He yields the Nasrâny his thelúl. Ghosts in Thirba. Come again to the Beduw. The Nasrâny accused by Horeysh, is acquitted by the sheykhs.

ONE of these nights, a little before dawn, a sudden awful rushing sound startled the Beduw from their dreams; for a thunder-din resounded marvellously through the waste mountain above us: it seemed as if this world went to wrack. I was awake, and heard it at the full; the sound was double, a loud lasting uproar in the head of the Harra; then some shorter, it might be a vast echo that rumbled in the valley. A moment I dreaded to see the old vulcanic flames, that slumber so long under this soil, and the lava-floods break forth upon us: then I thought some vast rock had fallen in the distant Harra; or was it the noise of a shoot of stones in the abrupt ahead of the wady? It was a lofty sound such as is heard in the calving of ice in the glacial mountains. The Beduins, with ears full of the strange rumour, were ere day come together at the kahwa. Some neighbours, as they went by, stayed to ask the Nasrâny, " What is it? "—" You do not know your own dîra! "—" But fetch thy books and see; wilt thou not tell us, Khalîl? "—" Was it a rock falling? "—" It was more; there are

wennys in this dîra." The most in the mejlis were of opinion
that a " star " had fallen ; the sheykh's son at the moment was
untying his filly and saw the shooting star, whereupon that
thunder-noise followed.   An old wife who was sitting up,
when she heard the rumour, felt the ground tremble under
her.—In every man's memory was a luminous meteor, which
five years before had passed " nigh over head, with a loud
rumour, at midday, tending north and shedding in the sky a
long smoky train : it was seen at one time, in all the country
(nearly a thousand miles) lying betwixt Mecca and Damascus ;
so that in every dîra the people supposed it had fallen within
their borders." They remembered another in the last ten years,
which shot over the earth in the night-time, casting a noonday-
gleam upon the dark wilderness.   " The sound of it was *ker-
ker-ker-ker;* "—but thus say the Aarab in their talk of all
travelling noises.

When there sat down to talk with me at my tent door any
of these open-faced tribeswomen, of younger age—they came
to enquire for medicines—she drew up her kerchief to cover
the throat and the lower jaw. I asked them wherefore thus ?
" They did so (they said) because it became them, before a
sheykhly person." [In Greece, lately under Turkey, it is a
custom of the elder women, when they go abroad, to wimple
the throat with a kerchief, and the lower face,—the like is
seen in European countries, in many older images of Mary.]
When absent, I left my tent always open and unwatched, though
the Beduins warned me, " Be not so imprudent." I have almost
never lost anything in the menzils of the Aarab.

Two drops of my croton oil remedy, now in such favour
among them, is an ordinary dose : when I gave four drops
to the Aarab they felt no more than a little uneasiness ; I
gave six drops, nor might this always move the nomad
ironsides, and certain of them felt no more, than if my oil
had been poured upon the Harra. As I was wondering, they
reckoned upon their fingers, and found it was Friday, ' a day,
in which no remedy were good to be taken, and therefore the
medicine might not work.' Finally, to some of this human brood
of the desert, I give eight drops, without their feeling other
than with an effectual purging to be a little indisposed.   I
complained to them, " Ye ruin me with the expense of medicines ; the doses I give you would be death to other persons."
" Ay, said they, give, Khalîl, give ! it is a strong people the
Beduw ! "—In the better-dieted Arabian towns, I have found
an ordinary high dose suffice. These Aarab purge themselves

with seeds of the colocynth; but it is only when they have great
need, and few times in their lives ; the pulp is very bitterness.
Suppositories made of it, are said to be effectual for sick languishing of robust persons. They know the senna plant, but
make little use of it.

These rude Semites have little hope in any skill of human
prudence ; they wait upon heaven, and desire hijâbs of magical
men ; and when a man possesses a good hijâb, it is a comfortable suspension of his understanding, a mad confidence that
God will do for him as in his dreams. They came to me with
Fattish b'il kitâb ya Khalîl! fécher (or *fassir*) ! 'Search thou,
make divination in the book,' because they oftentimes found me
reading. " And canst thou not discern there the mind and intents
of men ? "—" Who have lied to you thus ? "—" The Alowna allege
such things."—" And was not that to catch your money ? "—
" Wellah Khalîl knows everything ! but mayst thou not see in
thy book where are the enemies, and whether one absent be in
life or is deceased ? See you not your own household, Khalîl, so
far off, and how they fare ? " Thus there came many in vain to
consult me. " Alas ! (said a poor forsaken housewife) look in thy
book, and tell me shall I recover my goodman's love.—Oh ! hast
thou no charm for love ? give me at least some writing that I
may be pleasing in his sight again." And said a young man,
" Well, Khalîl, take thy reed and a paper-leaf, and move this upon
that but a moment ! and wilt thou not receive money, yet for my
sake give me the writing, that where I love I may be beloved,—
heigh ! at the least that she weep for me ! " And husbands came
to beg a hijâb which should reclaim to them the estranged, the
fugitive, the unkind, and yet beloved jâra. "How may paper
and ink-blot save you ? "—" Yet being written, Khalîl, with the
name of Ullah, we have seen them also very availing."

And thus there came to me Miblis, the old sheykh's fair young
wife, and fairest of the daughters of the nomads. Among these
Moahîb and Sehamma, Bîllî fendies, are some brown-haired
women and even yellowish, they are *mezûnas* or " beauties ' ;
nevertheless, baked in the sunny drought, and thirsting and
hungering continually in a barren country, they want flesh and
freshness of colour. A younger sister of Tollog was of a blond
womanly beauty, and Shwoysh's housewife of a certain fine-
drawn lovely feature,—her amorous looking might trouble a
young man's soul. I remember one day to have met near el-Ally
with a lone Beduwîa wife and a young maiden, her daughter,
that without knowledge of herself, were to our eyes a vision of
amiable beauty in that frightful desert. We found them sitting
half afraid like partridges in the bushes to await the goodman,

who had walked into the town. " We are, they said, Bílli of the Moahîb ;" but they were not of Tollog's Aarab. An ornament, here, of the younger women is a necklace of dull vitreous beads, which are brought from Mecca.

" Could I bring again the love of her husband ? " asked Miblis, with a wayward light in the pleasant assured eyes of a wife : —and whether she spoke or moved there was a grace in all. So when any men, and more oftentimes the hareem, asked me of our hareem, I showed them with my finger Miblis of the sweet voice and nut-brown hair, and said, " She that sits yonder is like them ! " Her face of the beautiful perverse eyes, that seemed to lurk in ambush, was drawn beneath the oval, and might be likened to some pleasant fruit, among the irissprinkled amber sheaves of her full side-locks. An envelope of gracious clay, but of crude alloy, a mask wherethrough there shined no beautiful light of the spirit.

Tollog was often displeased with the young wife, whom his eye had chosen for the beauty of her body out of a poor house ; and the bitter-sweet young woman loved her fresh old lord, who had raised her to this honour among the hareem. She had borne him from her virginity two boys, the fairest in the tribe ; yet sometimes, for little cause, she savagely beat them, and seemed then to be nearly without natural affection. A skin-deep beauty is a joyless treasure, and hearty Tollog, himself of a sturdy humour, could not always abide the young woman's headstrong conditions. He had another very goodly young wife that had borne him a son, in the Agorra : to her booth went the old sheykh to lodge, and bade Miblis alight out of his menzil. She came to build her beyt with us ; and with beautiful rueful smiles besought an hijâb of the stranger, ' because she dreaded her husband might say the word of divorce.' I counselled her the hijâb of wifely meekness, to bear herself without froward behaviour. She promised, and Tollog soon after spoke to her kindly, in a ráhla, and bid her pitch beside him again.

Tollog had lived through three men's ages ; and in this last he governed his tribe. He had always taken wives at his list, and feeling his heart yet green, he seemed a father of the tribe, and indeed he was the worthiest amongst them all :—the Arabian sheukh are commonly such. There was no tribesman old enough to remember Tollog's youth ; the elder ones had seen Tollog, in their young years a man of middle age. He was the father of three grown sons living, and a daughter, besides the fair children, all males, born to him of the two goodly young spouses in his heavy age. The two elder sons, by one wife, were young men and fathers. Mishwat the sheykh's next cousin had taken their divorced mother ; she was to-day the elder of his two wives. Her sons of Tollog inherited the mother's shrewd conditions ; Hamed, the first, was a worthy young man, modest as becomes the great sheykh's son in his father's day, of good counsel in the mejlis, and a valiant leader of the ghrazzus. There was in the dregs of his nature a smouldering bestiality, not common with the Aarab. I have seen him savagely beat his stubborn beast with a stake ; this was in his family and these Beduin mountaineers' thick blood.

Hamed I found contrary at first, and jealous of the Nasrâny ; he was impatient with a young man's fanatical opinion, to see me in the *menzil el-Aarab.* The kahwa, which is the guest and the mejlis tent, was now Hamed's booth, the old sheykh and father coveting his own repose, or whether it were for his young wives' sake that he would have it so. I answered Hamed upon a day, since he did me wrong, *ya gomâny!* ' O mine enemy ! and why an enemy ? ' Hamed bit his lip, the sheykh's son is always coy in the lifetime and presence of his father. After weeks his suspicious misliking died, and he became my settled friend. Hamed wreaked himself in the meantime with a mocking rime of Khalîl mounted upon *el-Khuèyra,* that is my poor camel. A long daylight and the summer night, Hamed's head travailed ; at the next afternoon coffee-hearth he rehearsed his hard-born kasîda : old Tollog took up the best lines in hearty good humour, and repeated some of his son's conceits with kindly laughter, and said nothing ungenerous. We had amongst us a kassâd, the rimester was of the B. Atîeh ; Hamed was his prentice in the gentle skill.

Abdullah, Hamed's brother, his shrewish mother's own son, pitched his booth in her menzil, beside the tent of his " uncle " Mishwat. There the young man had grown up much like them both. At my first coming, with the Semitic caressing, which we see, in stronger countries, among the deceitful arts of women, he affected to be the friend of the Nasrâny ; and Hamdy alighting from every râhla beside her brother, he was continually our neighbour. Seeing a little ruddy boy with him, I asked, " Whose child is this, it is thine, Abdullah ? "—" His mother says so," answered the nomad shrew. The young wife was again at her time, and bore a daughter, and now Abdullah said " *sâhiby,* his entire friend, Khalîl must give him a name for her ;" some one of those beautiful names of women, which, he thought, must be in the speech of my far country, it should be a sweet word of foreign sound,—' he was weary of the Aarab names, they were *muáffin,* musty-like in his hearing.' " Well, *Miriam*."—" No not Miriam, it is a sláve's name in these parts." I said over some more and ended, seeing I could not please their dainty ears. ' Sarah was not ill,' it is a name heard among them ; but Khalîl's English names they found too slight and dumb sounding for their full-mouthed utterance : I heard later they would name her *Banna*. The Arabs having a presumptuous opinion of themselves, yet of a high indolent fantasy distempered with melancholy, they are ever dispraisers of their own things. They believe their speech to be above all tongues, and themselves to be the first of the nations, for their warlike valiance. But in their idle lives, the Beduins have a surfeit of the bibble-babble in the byût, where they find not other business than the clapping of tongues in all their waking hours ; their heads ache of weaving cobwebs in their very emptiness. They are cloyed with a new-made song, with the sententious ditties of the desert poets, that search a man's wit, and that raise his blood, that counsel his life. Hard to please, they find but one barren artifice in them all ; I have heard Beduins mocking that irksome, because never changed, and solemn yawning stave, in the Muse of their desert Nature, which must bring in all riding, *ya ent râkabin*, ' Ah ! thou who sittest mounted ' (upon a thelûl).—The mind is a kind of corroding mobility, and in a little circuit is bye and bye weary ; like the tethered beast which has eaten and stamped down, and would range further.

Some names of the Beduin hareem are : *Sàlema* and *Selma* (of peace), *Hámdy* (of praise), *Khothra* (that was born in a green place), *Umteyra* (born in rain), *Therrýa* (born in an oasis field of millet, thúra), *Bokhýta* (of fortune, hap), *el-Fosîha* (the well-spoken), *Auwèytha*, *er-Romla*, *Dalèyel* (of *dalîl*, shewer of the way), *Bussîyeh*, *Furja* (pleasance), *Gorma* (bountiful, which they turn in jesting, *nibs*, or in anger, to *Worma* gorbellied), *Sabera* (of patience), *Atheba* (of sweetness), *Umm es-Sûf* (mother of wool, that is wool-wife), *Hówsha* (scold), *Jáffila*, *el-Háddefa*, *el-Féha*, *el-Fushíla*, *Girtha*, *Gitthera*, *Šebbâ*, *Ateja*, *el-Lejîma*, *Naha*, *Deghrèyma*, *Rakýyeh*, *Khadýjy*, *Wajjid*.

I saw Abdullah's wife returning from the desert an hour after child-bearing ; she was faintly pacing home, supported among her female neighbours, that had played the midwives : and as she passed by their tents the next housewives ran forth to meet her, silently taking the places of the former, and set under her elbows their hands, and so they will all bear her forward one after other, and the last bring her to her own beyt again. This is women's kindness to women. A day or two after,

I found her standing by the booth; already she went about
her household business. The young woman smiled in her pale
weakness when I asked how the child did,—her own brother
would not have enquired of the babe, which was a female.
I asked of a young wife in our menzil, if their hareem brought
forth easily? She seemed a little abashed that a man had
asked such thing of her, then she said with a smile and a little
rueful cry, "I have borne but one; *ih! ih!* it was a smart
indeed."

The Beduins told me of an older sôn of Tollog, *rajjàl,*
"a *man* (they said, with an emphasis, so they speak of
manly worth), more than either of these, and by another
mother :" he died years before, being then almost at the middle
age. Tollog had besides a younger son, a sturdy young man
seldom seen in the menzil, for he herded his father's and his
brother Hamed's camels upon the Harra. One of these morrows, there was a strife in the watering between Tollog's young
herding son and another of his own age. They were old haters
of each other, and being there without weapons they caught up
stones, and each of them in their ferocious contention spilt his
adversary's blood. I passed by his beyt and found Darŷesh, who
had a daughter of Tollog's, declaiming of the matter—tribesmen
are pensive for any blood shed among them—and "Wellah!
said this barren hoarse voice, with counterfeit irresolute gesture,
who cannot take a man's head off at need, he were no sheykh
indeed."

Beduins of the common sort are garrulous tale-bearers, and
in this altogether ungenerous: I did not much question of persons, because the word would be quickly blown to them again.
That the Nasrâny had enquired of Tollog's marriages was immediately reported in the mejlis. The next day, at my coming
into the coffee club Tollog met me with a robust good humour,
and the full eyes of a man having somewhat made ready to
say, "Ay, Khalîl, wives I have wedded many; yet I would
not have thee to think that I take of the hareem *hy Yellah!*
the first met and welcome in God's name, but it is upon good
advisement; (and, here his voice falling to a sort of comic
lamentation) but now it is not so with me, alas, as it was once,
also you see that this beard is hoary :" then shamelessly he said,
before his grown sons, with the ribald simplicity of Beduins,
of whose hap even in this kind nothing can be hid; "I am not
very well in the opinion of my jowwar, and this makes all our
checking; have you not a medicine that may help a man?
were it but to live in peace in mine own household !" Whilst
the old wight spoke he smiled heartily, his sons looked merrily

upon it, the company laughed out. Tollog ruled the Aarab, but he could not tame the pride and melancholy of his own jâras. All day in the public tent he smoked of his galliûn, and 'it was when the dear consolation of dokhàn failed him (he told me with a broad gravity betwix mirth and ruth), that the anger came upon him, and he beat his innocent hareem.'

Mishwat was sturdy, but he could not be master with his wives : Abdullah's mother could so daunt him with her tongue ! the other, a younger woman, had lately fled from him. Mishwat sighed manly when he spoke of her ; she was gone from her place in the household, but not out of his aching heart : "She is beautiful, he said to me, she has horns, that reach down to her middle." Seldom or never have the nomad women very long hair, and it is not thick. Side-locks are worn by men at their natural length : so it is said in praise of a young man's fortunate beauty, "he has great and long horns." Mohammed Ibn Rashîd, the Shammar prince, hardly at the middle age, is of less than princely looks, but the Beduins say, commending him, "It is a fair young man, he has goodly horns." Elder men at length renounce this ornament of their regretted youth, but there are some which do never wear them. Mishwat when I twitted him that it was little honourable not to pay the price of his medicines, answered, "Well, I am thy debtor, but have patience until I am myself again and *èherris*, may prevail over the hareem."

This was Tollog's family : the sheykh had formerly a brother ; I learned with wonder that he had shot himself ! I could not hear in what bitterness of his own soul ; when I enquired secretly it was answered, 'That was long ago, they could not tell.' As seen in Mishwat their cousin, and in the sometimes short humour of Tollog himself and the impatience of his sons, there were natural faults of addled and inflamed brains in that sheykhly family. The soul in these Semites cleaveth to the dust, but their religious confidence is in a heaven nigh them, and the community of human kindness is largely round about them. Seldom is the great offence of man's desolate spirit committed amongst them. How should his soul despise and despair of God's Providence, unto whom there enters not a doubt of the Religion ? God's hand lies light upon them in every time of trouble, and born to the unprofitable wilderness, they are by nature long-suffering. The, towards man, sordid and faithless Semitic spirit leans upon Ullah in devout quiescence. They see the Lord's hand working in all about them, the name of God is in their names, they call upon God in every mouthful of words.

—Telâl, the magnanimous prince of Shammar, shot himself
in some frenetic melancholy !—for the Emir's miserable death
is clear hitherto of other suspicion.   I have asked of erudite
town Arabians : " What will be awarded to such unhappy soul
at the last ? "   They answered, " He is for the burning ! "—In
the ferment of our civil societies, from which the guardian
angels seem to depart, we see many every moment sliding
at the brink.   What anguishes are rankling in the lees of
the soul, the heart-nipping unkindness of a man's friends, his
defeated endeavours ! betwixt the birth and death of the mind,
what swallowing seas, and storms of mortal miseries ! And when
the wildfire is in the heart and he is made mad, the incontinent
hands would wreak the harm upon his own head, to blot out
the abhorred illusion of the world and the desolate remembrance
of himself.   Succoured in the forsaken hour, when his courage
swerved, with the perfume of human kindness, he might have been
to-day alive.   Many have looked for consolation, in the imbecility
of their souls, who found perhaps hardness of face and contradiction ;   they perished untimely in default of our humanity.

Infinite are the distempers of the human spirit, man is a
prodigy of misery.   Under other climates there are many beside
themselves for religion, requiring in this dulness of the churl of
the flesh, the perfect will of the spirit :—but this is not in the
elvish simplicity of the Arabs,—they are Naturals in religion.
They have so little conscience of the stink of sin in themselves,
they see not the leprosy of their own souls.   There is an eager
blood, a maleficent weakness of some human fibre, that were his
Adam in heaven it should not avail him ; and as flies lighting
upon wounds, so are to such persons the common vicissitudes of
this life.   Even in the wilderness the inveterate pricks of the
world are strewed up and down under their bare feet : within
are the inarticulate jarrings of the human spirit, and there is no
savour in men's lives.   The Aarab are pleasant heads, lightly
given, but also full of musing melancholy ; and as there is a
hairbrained camel in every troop, and in every flock some dizzy
sheep, so commonly in their nomad menzils are some scorned
and bewildered persons.

The Aarab are in apprehension every hour of the wolf and
the enemy, and in thought of their religion.   As I wandered in
the valley a shrill voice called to me from her tent *Ley tahow-
wam*, " what dost thou here to wander ? art thou not afraid of the
cruel wild beast ? knowest thou not that *the stranger is due to
the hyena* (*hàg eth-thúba*) ? "—Kasîm caravaners to Mesopotamia
say the like of the lion.   Where I entered, this kind of persons
wearied me with their querulous religion.   " *Khalîl, fen Rubbuk ?*

where is they Lord God ? or canst thou say this as we ? *yâ Rubby*, ah Lord my God ! and pronounce *Ullâhu akhbar*, God is all might." Then some would cry " Do ye not hear that he can speak these things as well as the Moslemîn ? why say they then that he is an heathen man ? One word more, Khalîl, recite after me, *Ullah er-Rahmàn er-Rahîm*, ' The mild-hearted God, yearning with mercy and pity' ; hark, fellows ! he says it ; how say they then that the Yahûd and the Nasâra cannot utter the Lord's name ? "

They prefer the opinion of a stranger in thing beside the religion, as if there should be an happier birth of the under-standing, and men's fortunes were better under stars not their own. Often in their splenetic fantasy they speak bitterly of their own nation ; my hostess Hamdy, cousin-german of the sheykh, a robust ' sheykha of the hareem,' and full of womanly worth, when many importuned her for a little tittun which her husband had brought from the coast, and seeing them still busy about me ; " How long, she cried, will ye weary the stranger ? send them away, Khalîl, akhs ! the Beduw are altogether *hátab lil-nar*, ' fuel for hell-fire.' " This nomad widow, after her first husband, and before the Moghreby married her, had said her word ' she would not wed with a Beduwy.' She had now of Abu Sinûn two young sons ; but born of this mixed blood, they seemed of an ill changeling kind amongst the Aarab. Yet now there was come nigh to her that stress of heart of the Arabian wife in her middle age ; the goodman would bring a new bride home to his household.

A diligent wife, and liberal, as she durst be under her Moorish husband, and a good work-woman, was Hamdy ; her hands made his thelûl head-stalls, and his white woven saddle-bags, with the long tassels gaily dyed. I saw no other fault in her than a little of that thick-blooded unforbearing, which was in her family, with her own elder son of the former husband. Fair-faced was the boy, twelve years old, well-grown, and of an excellent spirit ; he herded the kids and lambs of his " uncle's " household : and naked, since his birth, went the half-orphan child among the Aarab, under the sun by day, and under the cold night stars. The spousal money that the Moor had given to Mishwat, her half-brother, was a she-camel ; that was here about the twentieth part of the most welfaring man's stock. Mishwat bestowed the nâga upon his sister Hamdy again. Later, in the day of the calamity of these tribesmen, when they were bereaved at once of all their camels, and saved were those of Abu Sinûn only and Thâhir's household, encamped by themselves upon the Harra, the Moor showed himself a generous

giver : he delivered·two good nâgas to the now destitute Mishwat
and gave three to Tollog, of his troop of twenty camels. Not
only the Beduwîa sheykha Hamdy spoke despitefully of the
Aarab, such a checking is often heard among them ; a young man
coming to ask medicine, another cried out, " Give him nothing,
he is a rotten one." " *Yakta umrak*, the other answered him,
with a deadly look; The Lord cut thee off ! and Khalîl, believe
him not :" the former added, " He is as that which I blow from
my nostrils, and fuel, wellah, for hell burning ! "

All households·in this small nomad clan are kindred ; for
seldom does any tribesman take an housewife from without.
The Moahîb.are burly bodies, and manly in warfare. Not
twenty years past, they had mounted eighty riders in the
ghrazzus—now they were but half that number of warfaring
men—and were then more rich in flocks and camels. Tollog's
brother *Muámer* was in that time sheykh, Muámer's sons died :
the small-pox and *Abu tawfish* (they would say the cholera)—
the plagues of Mecca—destroyed the Aarab. When the dead
is buried, their loss is not held in any bitter remembrance : can
Moslemîn dispute with God's Providence ? Notwithstanding
the affinity in all their wedlock there was none deformed or
lunatic of these robust hill-Beduins. When they heard our
opinion of the natural inconvenience of marriage within the
first degree, some thought it likely. " But at least it is not
always so, they answered ; for this we see among cattle, and
nevertheless their offspring is good."

I suffered their summer-famine with the nomads. They who
are brought low by hunger in so serene cherishing atmosphere,
without the seeds of ferments, are not soon carried into wasting
diseases. The Beduin body is as a light-timbered ship, which
may lie stranded till the spring-tide, when with one great
eating; he may replenish his fainting nature, and his blood is
renewed after many days of evil fare. The Beduw can always
tell wonderful tales of some man they knew; who upon a time
being very sharp-set; had eaten a mutton. It is, they believe, of that little camel-milk they have to drink, that their
bodies are made nimble and light; and hardened to a long
patience of fatigue and hunger. When there is none, they help
themselves with a little mereesy; but it is so lean, that they
confess they laze deadly upon it. It is seldom in their lives
that they must make a shift to endure with a squalid diet of
locusts ; which; they say, may hardly hold life in them until
better times. The often abstinences of the less welfaring
amongst them enfeeble and corrode the viscera ; and there is no

people which are more molested with this kind of diseases : also
dwelling in a rainless land they taste not the sap of the timely
fruits of the earth. Languor of hunger, the desert disease, was
in all the tents. *Máana lón,* " We have nothing left," said the
people one to another. The days passed by days in this weakness of famine, in forgetfulness of the distant world, and the
wasting life of the body. The summer night's delightful freshness in the mountain is our daily repast ; and lying to rest
amidst wild basalt-stones under the clear stars, in a land of
enemies, I have found more refreshment than upon beds and
pillows in our close chambers.—Hither lies no way from the
city of the world, a thousand years pass as one daylight ; we
are in the world and not in the world, where Nature brought
forth man, an enigma to himself, and an evil spirit sowed in
him the seeds of dissolution. And, looking then upon that
infinite spectacle, this life of the wasted flesh seemed to me
ebbing, and the spirit to waver her eyas wings unto that divine
obscurity.—I thought I might number twenty and more flitting
meteors in every hour.

And I mused in these nights and days of the old hermits
of Christian faith that were in the upper desert countries—
and there will rise up some of the primitive temper in every
age to renew and judge the earth ; how there fled many
wilfully from the troublesome waves of the world, devising
in themselves to retrieve the first Adam in their own souls,
and coveting a sinless habitation with the elements, whither,
saving themselves out of common calamities, they might
accomplish the time remaining of their patience, and depart
to better life. A natural philosophy meditates the goodly
rule and cure ; religious asceticism is sharp surgery to cut
away the very substance of man's faulty affections ; sorting
wonderfully with that fantastic pride and maidish melancholy
which is also of the human soul, that has weariness of herself in
the world, and some stains even in the shortest course. The
soul that would rid herself out of all perplexed ways, desireth
in her anger even the undoing of this hostile body, only ground
of her disease. Mohammed bade spare that pale generation of
walkers-apart, men of prayer blackened in the desert, a kind of
spiritual Nimrods, going about in fairyland of religion to build
of themselves a stair to heaven. And cause was that certain
of them, "having the spirit of prophecy," had saluted in the
young caravaner the secret signs of his future apostleship. But
Mohammed in the koran, with the easy felicity of the Arabian
understanding, notes the heartless masking of these undoers,
for God, of themselves and the human brotherhood : " Ullah

sent the Evangil by His apostle Îsa-bin-Miriam, unto the Christian nation ; but the way of the Eremites is out of their own finding."

Now came Abu Sinûn again ; he had been so long that his wife and friends were in much thought for him, nor yet returned he home to rest, but on the morrow must go down, with fresh camels, to draw more rice from el-Wejh. The Moor carried upon his summer journeys besides bare rice, only a little mereesy ; he marched by night in the flaming Tehấma lowlands. Mohammed brought us news from Wejh. " The Moslemîm had made sheep-slaughter, killing and taking alive 230,000 of the Nasrânies ; only 30,000 were fallen ' martyrs ' upon the side of Islam :—hearest thou this, Khalîl ! The Lord be glorified !— the Engleys be also of the Sooltàn's part ! The Lord grant victory to the Sooltàn ! The armies of the religion have over- run the enemies' country, they are marching upon the great city of the Muscôv, and when that is taken, they will carry away, in chains, the great King of the Yellow, and he shall make restitution of all territory conquered aforetime from the Mos- lemîn. Not by land only, by sea also, have they brought them to mischance ;—seven great battle-ships are foundered of the Muscôv ! " Mohammed was newsman to his nomads, (to whose herdsmen's ears there was much in his foreign argument of little or no understanding), with the easy smiling utterance of a substantial man in knowledge, yielding to teach the ignorant. —How might I interpret the Moor's war news ! When I left Syria the Turks were warring with Servia and the Montenegrins. Strange had been the portents then denounced to us in Damascus. ' St. George, who, since his death—they tell you—is become a Moslem, had appeared in Montenegro chasing with his spear the Christian hounds ; the mountains had removed at his presence to two hours' distance.'—Not George only, but they believe and affirm that our Lord Îsa also, and his mother Mary are become Moslems ; and that the creation had not been created but for *our Lord Mohammed* (confused anciently with the Platonic WORD of the Christian Scriptures), *the first before every creature.* One *Sergius* was an old Christian saint at Damascus, " but he is now of Islam ; " you may see his shrine in the sûk by a street fountain, the bars of his windows are all behanged with votive rags. Upon a morrow, in the beginning of the rebellion, Sergius his lamps were found full of gore, also his fountain ran blood, prodigies which great learned turbans interpreted to presage ' great destruction of Christian blood ! ' The nomads say of the inhabitants of their rice-port Wejh,

" they are inhospitable to the stranger, a people of mis-sounding (Egyptian and mixed) speech." The summer sea-side heat is, to these nomads, of a dry upland air, intolerable. Some tribesmen telling the tale there of ' a Nasrâny wandering with the Aarab, who wrote up their belâd,—and could the sea townsfolk tell them aught of my country people, or where my land lay ? ' it was answered, ' if the Nasrâny came hither they would receive him.' At Wejh, the Beduins told me, are certain Nasâra, " two or three men together, with great red beards, honest persons although kafirs, they lodge by themselves in a kella, and set on their heads broad hats ;—but tell us, is it sooth that no kafir may endure to look upon the *séma?* look up, Khalîl, if thou be'st able." I bade them remember that every year they see Damascus and Persian hajjies, tie a leathern lap upon their foreheads, to shield their eyes from the sunshine.—But this is an opinion which I have found in all my Arabian travels ; I came almost nowhither where some children and women have not said to me, ' Lift up thy eyes thou to the séma ! ' A devout Kahtâny, whom I knew later in Kasîm, said of the townsmen of *Nejrán,* where he had been often : " They are not as the right Moslemîn,—they call not to prayers in (all) the same words that we—but like the Persians, and wear their turbans advanced to cover their eyes, lest (he added) they should see up to the Lord of them."—The three worthy men in a tower might, I thought, be (Greek or Frankish) light-house people.

Now came Mahanna, who had ridden to us over the Harra to require the *midda* for his tribesman fallen in the last year's bickering. The Sehamma sheykh lodged in the kahwa booth, from whence he was morning and evening bidden out with the mejlis company to a guest-meal, which some hospitable Mahûby friend had prepared for him, and they sat down to a mess of rice cooked in water, seasoned with Teyma salt and pepper, and coloured with saffron. These were sheykhly households, the hosts, in these low times, made the magnanimous excuses of nomads ; and some there were, I think, who spent then at once nearly all their living. Mild were the man's manners, nice was also his task to touch a fresh healed wound amongst reconciled brethren ; and of great natural policy are the sheykhly nomads. They hold fast to that they can have, and with a witty grace forsake the thing which they should never obtain. Mahanna smiled friendly to find me here, he was glad when Tollog praised me heartily ; and the good man stretched out his long galliûn asking me for a little tittun.

Mahanna on the morrow sent one back with tidings to

his tribe, the number of nâgas could not yet be determined
between them : there lay danger in this difference which touched
the most vehement passions of nomads. Mahanna demanded
forty she-camels, the ransom for blood betwixt tribesmen. The
Serahîn said that the price should be five camels, as between
tribe and tribe in their enmities ;—for the man was slain as
an enemy, and they had paid at that time five she-camels :
now they saw Mahanna return to require of them other thirty
and five ! Mahanna and Tollog could have agreed to some
reasonable composition, but they had to do with Darŷesh the
splenetic Serahîny sheykh.

Mahanna having no tittun would *khôtr,* go down to buy at
el-Ally, Hamed and Shwoysh rode with him. Such an expedition of few men, wayfaring peacefully in the desert, they call
a *turkîeh.* Before mounting, they came to ask me how they
might avoid the oasis fever,—which is called " the Hejâz fever "
in Nejd, and is such in their weak bodies, that one may hardly
come to his perfect health again. El-Ally fever is long-lasting,
more than deadly. The Beduw are very sensible of ferments
and damps, and the unnatural night-chillness, cast by the
irrigated plots ; and not seldom they bear home invisible
wounds of disease and death from their market villages.

When they returned Mahanna told me he had spoken in
the village with one come over from Kheybar, who would ride
home on the morrow, *bâchir,* and was willing to convey me back
with him. Though Kheybar and el-Ally lie but a long thelûl
journey asunder, the villagers pass their lives without ever
visiting each other, and el-Medina is market-town to them both.
A steer had been stolen from Kheybar by Beduins ; and when
word came to them that the beast was at el-Ally, the villager
rode over with a Beduwy rafîk to require his own again. ' I
might be in time, said Mahanna, if I set out on the morrow.'
It was not easy to find a rafîk to " the medina ; " and he with
whom I was accorded overnight failed me in the morning.

When the day was light, seventeeen camels, to quit their
midda, were driven up to the kahwa tent ; yesterday instead
of some of the camels Mahanna had accepted as many palm
stems in Wady Aurush,—any good stem is valued at a camel.
But now I heard Mahanna reject all their proffers, and cry out
that ' the Aarab would return to their feud, and there naught
remained between them but the black death ;—wellah, he would
not now be contented with fewer than forty nâgas.' Mahanna
mounted his thelûl, and turning the back rode forth without
leave-taking towards the valley head, to go home over the Harra.

Such sternness in show was but a policy of the man to draw forth
other camels ; besides it were not for his honour, without a
seeming difficulty, to compose so grave a matter. The Moahîb,
who had certainly looked for this event, watched Mahanna
depart and dispersed to their watering.

I found Tollog sitting at the spring, with those who awaited
their turn at the watering. " Who is there, said Tollog, will
ride to the town with Khalîl ? " A sheykh, *Seydàn,* who of a
certain magnanimity of nature, always favoured the stranger,
answered, " If there be none other my own brother shall ride with
thee, for his wages." This was *Horeysh,* and we finding him
at home the man went to fetch his thelûl, but soon returned to
my tent grinning the teeth and saying, I should give him
somewhat more, which I granted. A Beduin would have the
fee in his hand at the setting out, and will then do his
endeavour. My money must be changed at el-Ally, but now
said Horeysh with a barbarous malevolence, which his brother
blamed, he would not trust me, ' I was a Nasrâny.' I gave him
the silver to exchange it there himself, and we departed.

As we journeyed we fell in with another small travelling
fellowship, a Serahîny conveying his sister and her young son
to the oasis. The nomad woman's husband, an Ally villager,
had sent for their boy to be bred up in the settled life. With
them went a man driving two or three head of small cattle, I
knew him by his duskish fallen visage to be of the town. He
was a butcher, come with a little tobacco to sell to the Beduw,
and now he returned with live meat. They shouted salaam to
some of our shepherds at the wady mouth ; and mounting by
the low valley coast, we came over to another wady, whose
mouth is in the sandstone mountain borders and the upper
parts in the basaltic Harra,—waterless, unvisited by the nomad
graziers, and lying in a sort of elemental silence. The wooden
gait of the camel awakened in me some uneasy hollow feeling
of famine, and I hardly remembered that in my life before
these Arabian months, I had daily breakfasted. We came on
in that huge forest of sandstone undercliffs, el-Akhma, which
is the outer border of the Aueyrid. At noon they alighted,
as is the wont of summer wayfarers, under the shadow of a
tall cliff, to wear out the hottest mid-day hours. I found there
a scored Himyaric inscription [*Doc. Epig.* xxvi. 50] ; but dreaded
by these unreasonable delays to come too late to el-Ally.

When we mounted again, the summer's day was wasted to
the third part. I reached down to take up the butcher's water-
skin which he bore upon his back, that he might drive the
less wearily, and not be separated from us riders in this insecure

neighbourhood ; but the butcher said, ' Nay ! he would not be divided from the girby that was his mother.' The Beduins answered him, half wondering, " Ay verily, man, it is thy mother ! " —so much the Arabians think of going an hour or two without water ! Finally, we had sight of the palms of the village, in the twilight ; when we alighted at the gate it was night, and we had ado to drive in our cattle, which smelling the close streets feared to enter the gloom under the overbuilt chambers. My old nâga dashed her head to the walls so cruelly that I thought she must have done herself a mischief. A villager or two returning late home answered our salutation and came on friendly with us Beduins. The narrow ways of the tepid Hejâz town seemed to be full of a sickly sweetness of rose water. We halted in an open place where Horeysh sought an acquaint-ance *Farhàn ;* and, leaving our couching camels knee-bound, the young men who had brought us forward laid my great bags. upon their honest shoulders, and went before us to the door. We sat upon the earthen banks, which are made beside all entries, and there they fetched us out a bowl of dates, and another of their unwholesome water ;—we had not tasted food in this daylight now past. That was a store-room, where they laid my things, and locked the door upon them for the night. Then we were shown by these friends to the clean terrace of an empty house, where we might sleep.

We arrived, as I had foreseen, *múbty,* too tardy ; the Khey-bar villager had departed this forenoon,—which they call, when past the mid-day, *el-beyrih,* " yesterday."—Those few hours lost by the treacherous slowing of Horeysh, were the occasion to me of another year's languishing and jeopardy in Arabia, since my set purpose was to visit Kheybar. Here, the dead night-heat is not sensibly diminished from the noon-day ; we lay half-breathless, till the new sun rose, and could not sleep for a moment. There are no beds in this country ; wayfarers lie down to rest, with the forearm for a pillow, upon the bare floor matting :—you may oftentimes see poor marketing Beduins napping at noon in the town or village, as the lad Jacob, with a stone laid under their heads ! Even the Ally villagers may hardly sleep in this long hot season of the year. The most pass their summer nights in the orchards, where they have bowers of palm-stalks and palm matting. There they guard the ripening fruits, and a little breath rises upon them of the dampish air, and a coolness towards morning. The light come, we took again our camels in the street. The suffering cattle may lie thus empty, at the villages, three or four days, commonly to return overloaded with the householder's provision of dates,—more than they might bear in their health ; you may meet with these poor brutes hardly tottering homeward from the inhospitable settlements.

We drove our cattle to the coffee-house of the kâdy Mûsa, a Hejâz man truly of the primitive Moslem mind ; and he then coming in from his night's rest in the *busatîn*, received me with the smiles of his hospitable benevolence. The morrow's kahwa fire was kindled, the coffee-server, *káhwajy*, roasted in the flames and pounded with an idle rhythm. The familiars arriving from the orchards to the early cup, men of Mûsa's sûk, shuffled off their sandals in the entry, and when they saw me and my Beduin rafîk sitting at the hearth, they greeted me mildly, " Is it thou, Khalîl,—from whence ? " and stepped over to take hands with me. Here is not the bird-like ruffling urbanity of the sheykhs of the desert and the Nejd villages, of whom the words might be said in mirth which Isaiah cast once in the teeth of the daughters of Judah, ' They are haughty, and walk with stretched forth necks and wanton eyes, jetting and mincing as they go.' But at el-Ally is seen the sober and lenient lowland carriage of men homely-wise.

—This is the hall and coffee-club of Mûsa's partiality, his *jummaa*. The jummaa is that natural association of house-holds, born in affinity, that are reckoned to the same jid, or first-father, and are confederate under an elder, the head of their house, inheriting the old father's authority. In these bonds and divisions by kindreds, is the only corporate life and security in an anarchical infested country. In-coming strangers are reckoned to the alliance of their friends. Freed men are clients of the lord's household ; and their children, with the children of incorporated strangers, are accounted parentage with the children of ancestry : they are ' uncle's sons ' together of the same jummaa.

Political mixed factions do seldom rise in Arabia ; for no man's prepotency, even in the towns, can enable him, if he be born without the sheykhly blood, to take upon him public authority. In every oasis-town are many kinships, and very oftentimes of more than one lineage ; and he only can rightly rule—as take for example the emir of Aneyza—who is natural head of the old sheykhly house, and namely of those Beduin fathers, that were founders of their palm colony in the desert. In some town a side faction may chance to come up and prevail, as the house of Ibn Rashîd, in Hâyil, then favoured by the Waháby, and now grown to be the greatest name in High Arabia.—A mingled jummaa was the gathering of the people in Mohammed's religion, which—to-day a partiality of nations—

we see even yet shows forth the canine lineaments of the Arabian faction.

The jummaas in the oases are fraternities which inhabit several quarters. When townsmen fall out, that are not of the same fellowship, their elders seek to accord them friendly ; but in considerable and self-ruling oases, as Aneyza, the townsmen carry their quarrels to the emir sitting in the mejlis, as do the nomads to their great sheykh. Until the civil benefit of the Waháby government, the villagers were continually divided against each other, jummaa against jummaa, sûk against sûk, in the most settlements of Upland Arabia.—I heard in my jeopardy at Kheybar that, ' if the stranger's life be endangered in one sûk and he flee to another, they would defend him.'

Mûsa brought a piece of a water-melon to refresh us, and soon he led us to breakfast ; such at el-Ally is buttered girdle-bread, with a bowl of their sulphur-smelling water. Disappointed of Kheybar, I was in some perplexity. It is perilous for a man not of the religion to return to the short tolerance of the Moslemîn, therefore I everywhere to my possibility prepared also a retreat to their fair remembrance. Should I abide in the town ? where all day the sweat fell in great drops from our foreheads, with a stagnant air, and the nights unrefreshed. In the oases is food in abundance ; but I chose to put back into the airy wilderness. Good old Tollog had said at my departure, foreseeing we might miss the Kheybary, " So thou art a man to stay with the Beduw, turn again, Khalîl, and remain with us until the new pilgrimage." And now said the kâdy Mûsa, " Khalîl, wouldst thou dwell in the town, remain here with me, and welcome."—I had chosen Mûsa for my host, and he indulged towards the Nasrâny guest his natural benevolence : mildly he questioned with me of many things, and gave always a pleasant turn to my answers, in the public ear. When some friendly hand reached me his galliûn, another began to raise the old question, ' Whether the upright might drink smoke ? ' Some honest bibbers, *sherràb*, made answer, ' they thought a man did not much amiss in it ; ' other neighbours, who were more superstitious, murmured it could not be altogether blameless ; and one looking very crabbedly upon it, the next sitter spoke to him, with an elbow-dint, " Dost thou not sow tobacco thou, and raise it in they field, that is joining to mine ? "—At his word he of the formal countenance made a shift to excuse himself, ' Well, he did but sell some to the Beduw ; were not the Beduw (he asked us) kafirs already, and fuel for hell-fire ? ' Mûsa, beginning now to think that ours was some too fine-drawn and brittle observance in religion, asked me, "And how say the Nasâra?—is smoke-drinking a fault among you? is it harrâm!" I answered with a sudden word, "Ullah created the harrâm!" which falling from the mouth of the Nasrâny, was very welcome to the mild religious humour of this Hejâz sheykhly villager: he was besides a brother of the galliûn, and he went on a while repeating under his breath the pious sophism, that "Ullah created not forbidden thing."

When I asked Horeysh for my silver, he answered with grinning horse-teeth, 'he had laid it out for barley in the town.' I responded, since he had spent my money, he should carry back my heavy bags upon his thelûl, and I would ride upon her. The kâdy said my word was just, and so said the bystanding villagers, who are disposed of themselves, as the people in Job, to cry out upon the deceitful Beduw,—and they all misliked this brutish fellow Horeysh. Even the young Serahîny, who had ridden down with us, coming by, gave his voice against his own tribesman. So finding the world was contrary, Horeysh (as Beduins will always) submitted to them with a good grace.

As we were departing in the cool of the day, I conceded that he should mount his own thelûl awhile, that bore my baggage, and we rode forth from the hot stagnant air and plague of flies in the oasis. The lofty mountain shadows already fell upon our path: we came in face of the sepulchral cliffs of el-Khreyby, and rose on under the Harra, leaving the Héjr way ascending to the right hand. Before us lay low glistening clay grounds, grown up with tall knot-grass; there we must pass a thicket of tamarisks, often a covert for land-loping Howeytát: Beduins therefore spur on their beasts to come by them at a trot. My old nâga could only run as a camel; I rode at foot pace, hardly for faintness maintaining myself upon her, and Horeysh trotted out of my sight. When we were far come in the Akhmar, I saw my rafîk again, and called to him, 'Since he would save himself alone upon the thelûl, would he lend me his cutlass?'—My pistol was bound in the camel-bags which were upon his dromedary. Horeysh answered, 'He would escape in any danger, without regard of me; why should he lend me the sword? and could I not ride faster, he would abandon me.' The fellow would not linger a moment. This brought us nearly up to the Howwâra;—the black platform head is a pan of basalt, which has flowed out evenly from the Aueyrid, but lies now sundered from the mountain by the distance of many hundred yards!

D. T.   31

The sun setting, I bid my rafîk await me, and, dismounting, I lay down faintly in the sand. He granted then that I should mount upon his thelûl, but my heavy bags must go upon my own nâga.—"My loaded nâga cannot bear a rider, but mount behind me."—"It is not far now, and I will drive on foot." He helped me to the saddle, but, as ever I was up and moving, he ran to take his beast's bridle again. With the heel I chased her quickly from him, and being now at my ease, and fortune in my hand, and the night coming on, I would maintain my advantage with this Horeysh, who was an uncouth carl, very strong, and armed with a cutlass : I might, at need, find my way to the Aarab in Thirba, or over the plain to the kella of Medáin. When I looked round, I saw this heavy Beduin had got silently upon the back of my distressed nâga. I bade him descend and mount with me radîf ; but goading the jaded brute, he passed by me, in his wild riding. I called to him to come down ; and when he heard the swift footing of his own ponderous dromedary which bore me upon him, Horeysh let himself slide to the ground from the narrow croup, and standing upon his feet he cast back a deadly look, dreading (he afterward affirmed to the Aarab—yet not knowing me to be an armed man,) that a shot from the Nasrâny would have pierced his sides.—He went now on foot, and sometimes he ran out·on a sudden to catch his thelûl's bridle, but I swerved yet more swiftly from him. *Aly houn-ak, aly houn-ak, ya Khalîl !* ' Stay ! have a care with her,' cries the great sot who would do thus, although I offered him peaceable riding. The Beduwy thought, as a Beduwy, that the Nasrâny bereaved him of his thelûl and would ride away with her. "If I were a robber, man, I know not the paths in a strange country, or how should I forsake my nâga with the things on her ? "—" Wellah it is sooth, Khalîl."—" Are we not companions ? "—" I did but wish to drink a little water."—" Come drink thou, and mount behind me." I drew up, and taking my counsel, when he had drunk his draught he mounted, and we jolted on together, driving the baggage camel.

At the mouth of our wady, Horeysh instead of riding under the near cliffs, led me over among pathless beds and banks of rolling stones, and worn seyl channels. The cause I could not guess, till Horeysh asked in a small voice, ' Were the ghosts in this wady ghosts of the Nasâra or ghosts of the Yahûd ? ' The wretch was now in ghastly fear of the Nasrâny, whom a little before he had offended, lest the bogles here of some of my ancestors should have set upon him.—" Aha ! he answered with chattering teeth, the melaika ! " About midnight we drew nigh to the

desolate menzil, where the first black booths were Hamdy's:
the watch-dogs were awake, and sprang up with open throats
against us. I said (their names) *Rushdàn!* *Âdilla!* and they
came cowering and fawning upon me.

When I had alighted Horeysh shouted in despite, as he rode
forth, " Ho people ! I bring ye again the—I wot not whether—
Yahûdy or Nasrâny." The day-slumbering nomads are light
night-sleepers ; the old quean Sàlema, came presently out with
other women neighbours, and they helped me to unload ;—this
is a good turn of the hareem to a man come home from wayfaring, and they will ask of thee a little tobacco. " Gossips ! "
cried she,—her vein was inextinguishable of the nomad ribald
hilarity, " Ah-hî-hî-hî ! This is billah your eye-salver come again ! "
A man or two soon stept over from the next booths and sat
down by me to enquire tidings of the oasis, and to receive of one
returning a little tobacco. They came shivering out from slumber,
their striped mantles closely wrapped about them ; and here is a
difference between the daylight and night temperatures of more
than thirty degrees : one mixed me a bowl of mereesy, and the
hareem would have set up my tent, but I thought it easier to
lie down immediately under the shining stars,—the hot dawn
would be all too soon rising upon us.

At daybreak the Beduins are stirring ; when little after I
opened my eyes, Mishwat was standing over me, and then came
Wâyil, a just and friendly Serahîny sheykh :—they went to sit
together in Hamdy's tent ; when I joined them they began to
question with me, asking what was it had chanced betwixt me
and Horeysh.—I now perceived that not without danger I had
lain abroad dreaming. Horeysh had accused me to his sheykhly
brother, ' the Nasrâny would have taken his sword from him,
and have broken away upon his thelûl, and (which was not so).
had cursed their father.' Seydàn swore, in the first heat of his
short-minded resentment, to make sharp work for his brother's
wrong, and he rose ' to hew the head off, he cried, of that Nasrâny;'
the sheykhs hardly appeased him, saying it were but just that
Khalîl's answer should be heard. Mishwat was a friend to me
in his sober mind, he hated in his doting humour " the God's
adversary" ; it had done his heart good, and yet the man had
been sorry, to see his sister's guest overtaken by any mortal
accident : Wâyil, a true man, one who ever favoured my
part in the mejlis, were it only with his kindly-looking
silence, was come over to enquire of this thing from me and to
put off any iniquitous violence. He assented to my words ;
even Mishwat showed by his eyes to consent in his unstable

mind to my defence. Seydàn now arrived; he seeing me already befriended came solemnly and sat down beside us. I greeted him with peace, but he turned away his face. Wâyil bade him think reasonably upon it, he should find that Khalîl was not in fault; but Seydàn answered hardly, " The man is a Nasrâny, I say cut his head off, and there is none that will require his blood at our hand." In the midst of his big words, his heart began to relent. There came over to us the men of the next byût, to see this strife, for Seydàn was a perilous man in his anger. I perceived then their minds without disguise, as they cried for and against me; amongst other of Abdullah, the unworthy son of Tollog, who with a fanatical malignity, gave his voice that ' my mind had been to have done Horeysh a mischief.'—Is it not a saying of the wise to "keep no company with a fool"; but what shall he do who may not choose? it is better, sometime, to go guided by a fool than not to go at all. The fellowship of Horeysh cost me my then missing Kheybar. There I should have been a guest of Motlog, sheykh of the W. Aly, to whom I had been long since commended, and from whose menzil I might have set out peaceably to Hâyil. —To Kheybar I afterward attained only at the price of long pains and perils, and suffered there an intolerable captivity. The Aarab, who love to be suddenly out of hand in any matter and return to sit out their indolent humour, when they saw there would be no contention, rose to go their ways again.

With my pistol hidden under my shirt I led down my nâga to the watering: but come again I deposited the weapon in my tent, and walked over to the coffee club, where the sheukh sat. Tollog I found, and Hamed and Mishwat and Wâyil and Darŷesh, only Seydàn was absent. I sat down, and then they bid me " tell my adventures to the sheykh,' and with rising good humour they began to smile. So said Tollog, " And how seest thou Horeysh? "—" I should not wonder if his head were not *matîn bi'l-hail,* a very sound piece," which word set them all heartily laughing. *Tollog:* "Wellah Horeysh is *fâsid* " (one depraved in his life and understanding). " And Khalîl, give me thy hand," cried Hamed; " and Khalîl, give me thy hand," cried Wâyil; and " thy hand here, Khalîl," and " thy hand," said Mishwat and Darŷesh:—they were all the sheykhs of the Moahîb besides Seydàn. They could not forbear this Beduin jollity and, between mirth and good will, as every man took my right hand, he wished me health and gave me thanks, *àfia,* upon it. And said Wâyil, " He speaks sooth, by God, Khalîl lies not."—" Ay, Billah! (answered Tollog), and now we are reconciled again we with thee, Khalîl, are one, and thou art wellah as one of mine own sons :—and, he added kindly, it is not only thou that art a stranger in this dîra, but all we are incomers, and Khalîl is *ikhtiyàr* (that my heart was not divided from them in mirth and affection), and he is of el-Aarab *et-tayyibîn,* the Engleys are good Arabs." *Wâyil :* " But tell us something of your second sight, Khalîl, read me what is written here in my palm " (he stretched out his hand). *Tollog :* " Ay look, Khalîl, that some say *Solomon* is written there."— " I see nothing, but you will not believe me." And they : " Wellah, Khalîl deceives not the Arabs."—*Tollog :* " Khalîl, what seest thou of our filly tied yonder ? I had her a weanling of Annezy, for three camels."

CHAPTER XVIII.

THE FUKARA SUMMERING AT EL-HÉJR.

Tollog removes with the most households. Thâhir. The Simûm. Alarm in the night. The ghrazzu. Locusts again. The son of Horeysh assails the Nasrâny. Thâhir casting bullets. His words of the Melûk. Bride-money. Blood-money, how discharged. Phlebotomy. Set out to go to Tollog in W. Shellâl. Salâmy. The Khuèyra nâga finds her way. The Aarab in the valley. Reconciled with Horeysh. Malicious tale of Abdullah. How dare the Nasâra make war against el-Islam ? A maker of lays. Fable of an enchanted treasure. Thâhir's daughter wife of Tollog. The grinning looks of Nomad herdsmen. Mishwat's sacrifice. Strife of tribesmen at the weyrid. A lonely passage to Medáin Sâlih. Portrait of a Fejîry sheykh. Come again to the Fukara. Visit Haj Nejm in the kella. A fanatical W. Aly sheykh. Motlog and Tollog's words to the Nasrâny. Ibrahîm the Haj post. The Héjr monuments. A foray of Mahanna. Lineage of the Sherarât unknown to themselves. Moahîb sheykhs ride to make their submission to Ibn Rashîd. Warmth of the air at night. Marriage with an uncle's divorced wife. El-Ally revisited in the first days of the new dates. Howeychim. Ramathán month. The summer heat at el-Héjr. Motlog's eldest son Therrÿeh. A Syrian hajjy living with our Aarab. The Kella palms. Evening with Haj Nejm. A new journey to el-Ally. Alarm in returning by night. Darÿesh and Doolan find the footprints of Horeysh.

THE unlucky adventure of Horeysh confirmed me with the sheukh, for he was an unwelcome spirit among them ; but it stirred up enmity of the fanatical common sort who thought they had now a cause to be avenged upon the Nasrâny. Tollog soon after, with most of the households, removed three hours distant to the W. Shellâl ; but the people of Hamdy's menzil, and of her cousin *Thâhir's* menzil, remained still in Thirba. The day after, for dread of night thieves, we joined our menzil to Thâhir's, which was in face of the upper spring. Our house-wives would build their tents nigh by the water, where all the ground is a dunghill, but one, when I counselled them to alight further back, taking in her palm a piece of camel-dung, answered me, " What ill is there ! I smell to this, and we would put it in our mouths ; it is the smell of our livelihood, and sweet to the Beduw." I went therefore to pitch my tent beside Thâhir.

This was a worthy man, of a liberal natural conscience, now advancing in years, strenuous of soul and body as any I have found among nomads ; I had treated his wife for ophthalmia.

The listless lazing of the booth at home was not for Thâhir, he must be doing, and he was ready to take upon himself every hardy and even public enterprise. He wore the long Arabian tunic, as the herdsman, cut above the knee, not to encumber his valiant limbs. Alone upon his thelûl, or else with a chosen rafîk, he often rode to view the empty wilderness in advance of the nomad tribesmen ; sometimes he lurked in ambush to cut off the wild beast, or even the strange human life that passed within the stroke of his gunshot : his sons told me he never spared any,—and so necessity whets their teeth that the Beduw have little or no conscience in what violence they do abroad. Thâhir, who became now my " uncle " and homely friend, had as likely been my murderer had he met with me before in the wilderness ! This desert man was an hunter as none other of his tribesmen, and only few among Beduins. That was his goodly daughter, fairest among the younger tribeswomen, who had borne to Tollog a son in the Agorra ;—the old sire had said in espousing her he hoped in Ullah to beget a man of mettle to the likeness of her father. In Thâhir's company I spent now the most of my hours : he was of the riper sort of fresh understandings, full of pithy talk, of an even hilarity ; and passing his years, a nomad and solitary hunter, in the Titanic wilderness, he had gotten of his own meditation in that contemplative kind of life more than a great inheritance of natural knowledge. He was keen of eyesight, and of no less hard vigour of bodily endurance, and one of the few among Beduw who had grown by the ghrazzu : he had won so many camels, that of a man " weak " in the beginning, he was now among the first for the number of his great cattle ; and Thâhir with his forcible integrity and not less prudence of mind, was like a leader to the poorer part of his tribesmen. " Khalîl (said the strong robber with a manly smile) wherefore go about for milk ? when it is I who have the many nâgas." Yet in the day of the camels' coming home again, he used somewhat of the hunter's sleight in the performance. Thâhir when he had allayed the precious humour with water, although in my debt for his wife's medicines, brought me only a niggard draught of this thin milk ; but that was with a manly grace which became him well.

Thâhir roused by famine would take his long gun, and a handful of mereesy to stay the yearning of hunger, and he

wandered immediately out of] sight; I have known him thus
a summer daylight and that night absent, and return very
weary on the morrow from some great distance where he had
lurked to meet with a wild goat or thobby ;—and besides he
would spy out the signs of all that had passed of late in the
wilderness. The dust was not laid of the late adventure with
Horeysh, and it was well to dwell in this man's friendship,
who maintained my cause and feared not to blame the other.—
A strong simûm one of these nights blew down upon us,—it is
the hot breath of the Teháma blowing over the Harra : that
thin tepid air cannot fill the gasping chest nor quicken the
blood, and there follows some uneasiness and head-ache. These
hot winds, which the Aarab call thus, "infeĉted," are common
in the long summer half of the year ; but no Beduin of the many
I questioned had ever heard speak of any man suffocated in
them.—I found the simûm the most days blowing in the high
desert between el-Kasîm and the tropical Mecca country, where
I passed in the hottest of the summer season, and when all
the atmosphere was on fire in the sun : I have felt for an hour
or two very faint upon it. Camels, it is said, may die, for
want of breath, in the hot wind : the feeble brutes are then
in their worst plight ; and so huge bulks living only of weak
fodder, may the sooner perish. Shortly after my passing
W. Fâtima, I heard reported in Jidda, that many of the villagers'
camels had since died in the simûm of the unwholesome provender.

In the night-time I startled from sleep, at a rumour in
Thâhir's tent,—men were coming and going in the starlight :
what this should be I knew not, but let it pass, since my lot
was cast in with Thâhir's ; and, turning to repose, would not
break our life's only refreshment.   I heard before the morning
a strange sweet cadence of a woman's voice (like that blithe whistle
of the wood-grouse in Northern Europe) which is even now
in my remembrance. As the stars were paling, I looked up
and saw one standing over me, an ill-looking Beduin ; he bore
in his arms a great basalt block, and feinted, when he saw
my open eyes, to let his load fall upon my breast. " Cursed
one, he craked, ho ! thou Nasrâny that sleepest here ! if now
I let this stone slide it should do away the life of an enemy
of Ullah." I knew the malignant wretch, one of a broken-witted
brutish behaviour, and unwelcome at every coffee-hearth. He
had a good will to wreak upon me the despite lately done to
the religion in Horeysh. As he marked me take no heed of
him and his burden was heavy, the fellow by and by cast it

from him, and went his way with a less mad opinion of Nasrânies ; he never troubled me more.

Word had been brought over the Harra in the night-
time from Tollog in W. Shellál ;—Darŷesh with *Haleyma*, a
certain Fejîry dwelling with us, riding out in quest of the
Fejîr had seen a ghrazzu, more than an hundred men, upon
thelûls with some led horses, passing in the Héjr plain ! they
could not tell what tribesmen those were,—they might be
the dreaded Bishr. I asked Thâhir, " Are they not gone by,
what now do you dread ? "—" Lest they should put in to
Thirba to water." " *Nuhéj*, said his housewife, ' we will flit ' at
afternoon, as ever the bearing camels—they had sent for them
in the night—be come down."—" What if ye be taken tardy ? "
—*Thâhir :* " We will climb to the valley sides and shoot down
upon them ; the Moahîb spare for nothing, it is well known,
in the presence of their enemies." Afterward they thought
the great ghrazzu must be passed from us, and when the camels
were come, they sent them up again to the Harra.

This day, the last in July, we felt cool and refreshed, yet
I found in the shadow 97°. Already the Beduins began to say
the midsummer fever of the air abated, but Thâhir, more
learned in the nomad school, said that certain hot stars were
yet to rise in the horizon ; the greatest heat of all that hot
year was nearly a month afterward. The people were troubled
on the morrow with the remembrance of the ghrazzu, and
sorry that they had not removed ; their cattle being now in the
Harra, they would have lost, at the worst, all their household stuff. The black booths, standing in uneven vulcanic
ground, could not be discerned from the valley mouth five
miles distant. I asked Thâhir if that armed troop might not be
of the Fukara ? We afterward knew them to be the Fejîr indeed,
that in a long time had not forayed ; they rode out then, and
some men of Bishr with them, against the Beny Atîeh. We
had word later that thirty camels had been taken by them. I
asked " And no more ? " They sheykhs answered, " But it is
very well." In the autumn I heard Motlog, their leader,
boast that this ghrazzu had been a ghrazzu indeed, " ay, wellah !
a ghrazzu."—They fell upon a hamlet of their enemies' tents
at evening ; and those in the byût forsook them and fled at
the sight of their foemen. The Bishr drew off by themselves,
and rode through the Jau, to rob cattle in the Teháma ; late
in the day, finding Bíllî children keeping sheep-flocks, they
compelled the little herdsmen to tell over the owners' names,
and took to slaughter whose beasts they would, killing " fifty
head to their suppers,"—but being here far (above an hundred

miles) from home, they drove away none of the slow-footed small cattle.

We saw " pillars " of locusts again, the desolation of the land that is desolate, reeling high above the soil in the evening wind, from the westward and driven towards el-Ally and Kheybar : the deep clouds of flickering insects passed without dimming the waning sunlight.

At the next watering, a lad (one of those come down from the mountain with the cattle) ran upon me with his spear ; but the bystanders withheld him. He was the son of Horeysh, and would have avenged his father's despite upon the Nasrâny ; —they think it no felony to assail an unarmed man. The lad sat afterwards in Thâhir's tent, they were his cousins and he was better than his father ; whilst I spoke with him he laid down his ruffled humour. Another day when I was bathing, a young man started up in a bush and stood threatening me with a great stone and his Beduin mace, in one and the other hand. When I reviled him as an impudent coward, he sneaked back again ; and finding him at the evening watering I drew him out before the people,—the fellow would then have struck at me with his cutlass, but was derided by the bystanders. He was a son of the old ribald quean Sàlema ; they were of the absent herdsmen, and I had not known their faces before.

Thâhir sat casting bullets. Their lead is bought in the haj market, or fetched from Medina. The ingot was hollowed between two stone plates, he had shaped them himself ; such hammering work in stone is (as said) of the nomad Arabs, and rude was the form, as is all the handywork of this most unhandsome Semitic race. For every ball he put in a pebble, and upon that he cast a thick film of lead. I said : " Your bullets are too light and not well centred or round, how should they fly true ? "—" But lead is dear in this country." With these starting balls he thought he could shoot within an arm's length at the distance of two hundred paces ; but he allowed that his penny was not well spared, if he missed a gazelle or a wild goat worth two or three reals. Thâhir, with a frank liberty of mind, which becomes the strong man of good understanding, doubted not to answer my questioning of his country (so far as I have found) faithfully. In these and the like discourses, I wore out the long hours of the languishing summer days, yet even Thâhir's talk reverted every hour to the religion, the factious passion of their Semitic souls. Clear was the sight of this man's spirit ; and when I spared not to say to him, " Is not the people's menhel-worshipping a dishonouring of God, a remnant of the heathen superstition in your nomad dîras ? " Thâhir, musing a moment of that opinion of angels, in which he had been bred up, answered hardily, " Nay, wellah, it is not good, it is superstitious." Thâhir, at the hour when others rose to pray, was not of so forward mood ; and some religious wretches chiding with the worthy man, he gave them as quick a word, " Go pray ! (and yawning) *wellah ana ajizt*, but I am weary, I, of this pray-praying,"—Adam in all his days waiting upon a kind Providence above him, and empty still !

Some of the Beduins found an idle pleasure to enquire my mind of such and such persons :—as in all small familiar fellowships, the malicious sparkles of human hearts are rife amongst them. I have sometimes, in safer hearing, tried answers with them ; as *Selím*, Thâhir's elder son, asking me, " What is Mishwat ? "—" Is he not a little broken headed ? "— and like words, which meeting their hearts in the midst, were received with merry laughter and wonder.

Selím now returned to us from W. el-Aurush, whither he was gone a-wooing. His mother told me they had not to pay bride-money, the daughter-in-law being one of their own kins-folk : his father would endow their son's marriage with two of the cow-camels and a few head of the lesser cattle. The most Beduins are of too slender livelihood to give payments for wives, the price is seldom to be delivered. There is a kind of honest fiction used among them, and a man who is bound to pay camels shall be able oftentimes to acquit himself for as many reals. When one would discharge himself of a heavy blood money—it is forty camel kine for the killing of a tribes-man—and, poor soul, his stock all told is not perhaps four or five camels, he is happy who has many honest friends, for they will all then intercede for him. His gun, that cost three or four reals, they will procure to be taken at thirty, in the stead of one camel, his cooking pot to be reckoned at fifteen, his cutlass, hardly worth three dollars, let it go for ten. Every friend will be instant with the heir of the blood to release to him somewhat for his friendship and good acquaintance sake, as " O *Murtaad!* thou son of Abdullah, yet one nâga, I say remit him this one, for the love of me." But the kinsman " owner of the blood " will make it wonderfully strange and has merchants' ears for them, since this is both to his honour and advantage.—The crime is now past, and the many indifferent persons will give their voices for the faulty tribesman, that peace may be restored with reason : if anything yet remain, his friends may undertake for him that he will acquit himself by determinate payments.

Thâhir felt some megrims, and would have his son Selím let him a little blood in the neck. The young man, who had inherited the witty hands of his hunter father, came with the end of a cow-horn which was pierced in the tine ; by this Selím, who had made with his knife a few scotches, sucked up the skin, and with a stop of leather, ready on his tongue, he closed the hole. Thâhir, cupped in the head, neck, and back, felt lightened, he covered the blood with a little heap of dust, and one who came in asking " What is this heap ? " he answered, " Blood which I have buried." (So it is read in Ezekiel, that blood should be covered with dust.) There are such phlebotomists, cauterizers, tooth-drawers, and barbers to find in all the greater menzils. Not seldom their cauterizings leave slow sores ; some ill-blooded patients have shown me such breaking forth again after many years. You may see young women that have not spared branding their faces for an headache !

Abu Sinûn came safely again ;—and now he had accomplished three summer journeys between Tebûk and Wejh. Seven days he was a silent man ; and after that, finding the air of the tent too close for him, he was ready to ride in a ghrazzu, of which Hamed should be the leader, in a few days. " But why wear out thy life thus ? *is Mohammed a Beduwy* to go cattle lifting ? " At this word he looked up, and " *Tóma*, Khalîl, said he with a weary breath, *tóma !* it is the desire of having, and more having, thus the world is made ; I live with the Beduw, and I do as the Beduw, also I may win a camel."—I determined to go with the first wayfaring company, to the Aarab in W. Shellâl, before I perished here with hunger, for that which I brought from el-Ally I had given to Hamdy. In the lower wady I should be nearer the oasis. Mohammed, who would ride in a day or two to the town, might leave me abreast of that valley.

On a morrow, as the great drenched cattle yusuddirûn, were " breasting " up from the watering, we took our riding camels. Thâhir bade me friendly farewell, with " peace " ; we rode forth and I lost soon the fresh sight of the green grove in the desolate valley. With Abu Sinûn went *Salâmy*, a brother of Thâhir, but very unlike him, and one *Hâdy* a Tuâly, wedded with a sister of Seydàn. It was the first day in the month *Shaabân.* In the way a lad awaited us, who asked one of our company to take him up, he went also to the wady ; the ill-faced fellow was a son of Hamdy's former Beduin husband. It is a good turn not denied to tribesmen, he appealed to

Salâmy, who answered " Nay ! " but called him anon, " Come and ride." From near the wady mouth we ascended by a sheep-path that lay over the skirts of the Aueyrid, where the tread was perilous for camels. All theirs came empty : as we went on foot I looked every instant that my decrepit and burdened nâga would slide and fall from the precipices.—There might be some malice in this of Salâmy, a finely depraved counterfeit fellow, who against all their wills had led us upon the dangerous passage.

We passed down after an hour into deep valley grounds ; where I found a tall shrub like the myrtle, which I had not seen before. Then crossing more ridges and the next great valley, we came nearly up to the wady. I was riding a little advanced with Salâmy.—" Lend me your pan, said he, to drink a little water, and in that reach me a little dokhàn."—" They are deep in my saddle-bags, I am deadly weary ; but I will make my nâga kneel, so come thou and take them thyself." The man, hitherto full of smiling dissimulation, received my simple answer, when few steps remained till our parting company for ever, with malignant speech.

There we came to a mountain cleft which opened, above the mouth, into the W. Shellál : and the lad alighting, Salâmy prescribed to him not to show the Nasrâny the way to the Aarab, but pass on hastily before the weak pace of my nâga. The dizzy camel strove to follow with the rest, but making her couch down I bound her knees whilst they were in sight. The passage by which the lad had entered gave into a plain-like vulcanic valley, in whose hard black soil I could preceive no traces of the nomads' cattle ; and the boy, covered by the uneven ground, was already gone out of my sight. I made forward where the wady seemed to rise, and a sharp soil strewed with prickly burrs was under my bare feet. When I got upon my dizzy nâga again I saw the boy before me and the large wady divided in front. I gave the Khuèyra her head, and when she had gazed all round she was still and paced securely, so that it seemed to me the poor beast must know her path. The brute had been taken years back in a foray upon the Harb. One of her former owners, a Bishry whom I met with afterward at Hâyil, told us that such was her beast's knowledge of all the country, that in certain expeditions ' she had served them for dalîl or shewer of the way : ' and whether we wandered in the Harra or how wide it were towards Nejd, she seemed to have this land-knowledge everywhere. Putting her to the trot I passed the unlucky lad, *Kreybîsh* by name, who crouched for dread and had covered his face. Riding towards the main arm of the dividing valley, where many tolh trees appeared, the Khuèyra mended her pace ; then I saw rijûm, and ruinous dry walling of an old dead settlement. I passed some rocks and beheld the first Beduin booth. The sitters within pointed for me where I might find the rest, and where Mishwat lodged, Hamdy's half-brother ; it was in his menzil I should set up my tent.

Trees and stones had dispersed the old order of the nomad hamlet. I found Mishwat's menzil by a piece of his wife's tent-cloth weaving, it was stretched as in Thirba upon the desert soil before the booth, which was shut close for the immoderate ground-heat. "*Márhaba*," welcome, said a lively voice within ; it was his housewife who, looking under the tent skirts, bade me alight and enter out of the sun. She came abroad immediately, bringing me a bowl of water, 'for, said she, I must be nigh dead of thirst:' the burning heat of the earth whilst I was unloading my few things baked my bare feet. If the Aarab, in their fanaticism, had not received me well, the very hounds of their menzil welcomed my coming again : here was a lost dog of Hamdy's which had followed the Aarab from Thirba, and Rushdàn ran with casts of joy, making much of me in such terms as he could. The mind of Nature in the poor brute discerned much better than his half-rational masters, that there is no difference between a Nasrâny and the Moslemîn.

Now came Mishwat and Abdullah, who had seen me arriving, from the coffee-tent. Mishwat, feeling the weight of my medicine box, "Here, said he, are Khalîl's bundles of reals ! " I opened the box before them, in which were some heavy drugs as sugar of lead, and I said if he found money he might keep it himself. Mishwat drew back, he would not stain the honour of an host.—"But why linger here, Khalîl ? " He led me into the tent's shadow, where his wife mixed for their alighted guest a bowl of mereesy ; then she went to cook for me a little mess of rice in water. I had nearly not eaten in many days ; and it was famine-time with the Aarab.

When I had visited the mejlis, where the sheykhs received me friendly again, I walked over to Seydàn. " Call Horeysh, I said, and let this quarrel fall, for I am not in fault, my friend." Horeysh, whose booth was nigh, came to his brother's voice and, seeing me there, he sat down apart. " Come, Horeysh, answer me by God, *Bullah ana khalaft aleyk :* Have I wronged thee in the road, as we came from el-Ally ? " Thus conjured to answer another, in the hearing of God, the Beduwy durst not forswear himself. Horesyh's tongue tottered a little, " Well, he answered, I cannot say thou didst." *Seydàn :* " *Bess !* it is enough."—" Reach me then thy hand, and though thou didst deceive me." *Seydàn :* "Ay, Horeysh, give Khalîl the hand, and now well ! Khalîl and Horeysh are again frineds ; thou art true, Khalîl, to the rafîk, but so are we."—" Beduins are commonly the best of way-fellows."—" Yet not all, and there are few besides us, with whom a stranger might trust himself ; of all the tribes about us, there is none whose name has not been blotted with such manner of crimes ; but it was never told of the Moahîb, that a man had betrayed his rafîk."—" Yet to-day I suffered something like this of Mahuby companions." (The sheukh had not heard that I arrived alone.)—" Ah I tell thee that Salâmy is always false." Of another he said,—the young Serahîny, of my former company to el-Ally, called, for his long side-locks, 'Father-of-horns'—" Well it was thou didst not journey home in my brother's stead with Abu Krûn, for he is *néjis,* of a foul impious spirit, and God wot he had not spared to kill thee." The same Salâmy, lately visiting W. Shellál, had been bearer from me of a bundle of tittun for Tollog, but the sheykh had never received it. "How strange, quoth the old man, and the dog was here ! he has 'drunk ' it himself, but when was there any good in Salâmy ? "

Abdullah related to me maliciously that he had been these days on a visit in *W. Jáida,* a valley of the Hareyry, where he found a great ghrazzu of Bíllî, three hundred and eighty horse-men—the Aarab, in such tales, commonly multiply by ten—come in from an inroad they had made upon the Saadîn, Harb tribesmen upon the haj way next above Medina. *Abdullah :* "And as I was telling them of the wandering Nasrâny, who wrote up the béled, they said, 'If he come to us, by God we will do for him !' "—I answered, I had not met with more hospitable and friendly Beduw than Bíllî.

The cattle were upon the Harra and here being no pasture bushes, I went to keep my nâga a mile or two higher in the valley. Having hoppled the fore-legs with a cord, I loosed her out in the Beduin manner, and, shadowing in the hollow bank of the seyl, I soon fell asleep. When I awoke it was past mid-afternoon, and I had ado to find my nâga again, which was of one colour with the wild wady ground ; so mounting upon her bare croup I rode homeward. But the sheukh laughed, where they sat in the mejlis tent, to see the stranger come riding by them in the herdsman's manner : "Look ! I heard them say, wellah Khalîl is become altogether a Beduwy."

The Beduins lay here pitched about a pond-like water-hole, which, drawn to the dregs in a morrow's watering, is risen again by the half-afternoon ; that water is, they said, "of the winter,"

that is the (autumn) rain sinking in seyl ground, for there is no
spring under. When the nomads are absent, this is a drinking
place for birds and wild creatures from the mountain wilderness, and thereby I saw was made a hunter's shroud of rudely
laid stones, and covered with felled acacia timber. One morning, when the sheykhs were gone to the weyrid, only Hamed
remained with me in the kahwa, and a Serahîny, and their
ignorant thoughts falling upon the Sultan's warfare, Tollog's son
asked of me, ' What were now those great wars in the world, and
how is the power of el-Islam weakened ? so that the Nasâra durst
in these days make war upon the Sultan of the Moslemîn ! ' I
showed them, rolling the coffee-cup box, that ' this world's course
is as the going round of a wheel. The now uppermost was
lately behind, and that lately highest is beginning to descend.'
Such kind of sententious talk to the ears and eyes is always
heard with childish assent by the Arabs.

There came in a stranger, that poet of the Beny Atîeh, so
poor a man that in this world he had nothing besides his
bare shirt ; he lately lay sick of a fever, and was this summer
guesting with the Moahîb. The poul soul cast upon them is not
contemned by the Beduw : his place is still at the coffee-hearth,
sitting amongst the sheukh. The best of them are clad not
much better than he, and he will be serviceable to them in what
little offices he may. *Aly* was a maker of ribald lays ; such
are much tasted by the Aarab,—and where is not a merry
vein well accepted in the world ? All are glad to forget
themselves and the long hours. Aly made well ; I have heard
his staves quoted by old Tollog himself smiling hugely, all the
company were pleasant upon it ; and the sheykhly housewives
answered them, freshly laughing, with merry words from their
apartment.

The poor gleeman, chopfallen, and hollow with hunger, sat
down wearily, of late he had found no more to eat than a
cricket ; all this week, he told us, there had passed through his
gullet no more than the smoke of a little tittun, and water.
The sheykhs now returning, " Alas ! " said he, and is it thus the
Moahîb deal with their guests ?—I die, and ye shall bury me
here in Shellâl ; for wellah I may never have strength to go
from hence, except I set out to-morrow,—and I had departed
before, but was in dread to be met with by some of the Fukara."
The Aarab hearing his sorrowful complaint, sat silent : then Tôl-
log said kindly, " O Aly, we are sorry for thee, but seest thou into
what straitness we be fallen ourselves : "—an ungenerous word
was not cast in his teeth, for that were against the reverence of
God's hospitality.—The Beduins willingly plead for each other,

and one will make a vaunt for another, it is but the cost of
breath, saying, (that biblical sentence) " He is better than I,"
so Hamed had praised his poet to me, that I might bestow upon
him fever medicines. " This, he said, is Aly, poor, but a man
of such a principal sheykh's fellowship, in much account with
the haj pasha."—" O Aly, I know the Pasha has as good see
your tribesmen all hanged." Aly smiling set a good face upon
it, the Beduins would be taken for sons of the valiant, though
it were with some expense of their honesty. " Also I heard in
the Haj that some of you are savages : say, what kindred is
that of B. Atîeh, which go all naked, and they know not bread,
and there is none other world, they say, than that they see
about them ;—cold the elves must lie of a winter's night ! "
Aly answered with a pleasant lying wit, " Ay, billah, they are
reckoned to us, but yet we hardly know them : at the fall of
the day they dig themselves down in the sand to the necks, and
sleep warm enough."

The poor merrymaker reported to me the fable of *Gerŷeh,*
which is a journey to the north from Tebûk : there is but the
ruined ground of a walled village, lying in such heaps as the
Kheryby. Great treasures are fabled to be there buried, and
that every Friday the money pieces roll out of the ground, and
run of themselves over the desert plain till sunset. Beduins have
asked me with a grave curiosity, " Could this be sooth ? " Beduins
are clear-sighted in their short natural horizon, and they easily
incline in worldly things to incredulity. Another B. Atîeh man
added, " In the neighbourhood is a sandstone cliff (he had not
visited it), and therein a gateway, and beyond that a gallery
hewn in the rock, in whose walls are side-chambers, wellah, as
the shops in a bazaar, and a great treasure lies behind a door im-
penetrable, which (where all is enchantment) is kept by a black
man with his drawn sword.—Come thou ! said the Beduwy, and
take up the treasures, and they shall be freely thine, so thou
wilt show us the hidden waters ! "

Tollog rose and beckoned me out with him : the old sire
led me to his own booth, where he brought me into the
closed apartment of his comely young housewife, Thâhir's
daughter, justly reckoned a beautiful woman amongst them.
She lay fostering her babe, and leaning, elbow-wise, on a Turkey
carpet of cheerful colours. The young wife looked up with mild
eyes : in that with a graceful gesture she reached forth a bowl
full of dates, and with womanly pensive voice gently persuaded
me to eat. Tollog went out to the camel troughs, and brought
the guest water to drink ; so the old sheykh left me with
Thâhir's daughter to dine, and returned himself to the mejlis.

This covert hospitality of a bountiful sheykh was a sign to me how low were the chief households. Seldom was there lack in Tollog's tents ; a sheykh of Aarab, he received also a khûwa, two camel-loads of dates, from Tebûk, and as much from Teyma. —At Teyma some of these tribesmen had possessed a few stems of palms, but whilst they were enemies of Ibn Rashîd, they could not come thither ; notwithstanding, their rights in the plants remained inalienable. My hostess said gently, ' She heard that I had pitched by her parents ; and their treatment of me, was it well ?—but, Khalîl ! eat, eigh me ! why dost thou not eat ? or maybe thou canst not ? '

Horeysh had taken upon himself the káhwajy's office, " And how dost thou, Horeysh ? "—" Right well ; and how is *Ayûn bilâ sinûn*, eyes without teeth ? " he asked this maliciously of my nâga jade : but his pleasantry did not call a smile upon any of their faces.—Why did not his housewife tell him that his two jaws were such hedges of tushes, as might have become a camel ? The nomads have very often great horse-teeth and white as if they were scoured by the sour milk : many young cattle-herders in the Beduin tribes show them with an incessant dog-like grinning. Herding all days from their first childhood, companions of rocks and bushes and the cattle in the wilderness, they grow up almost void of human understanding. Under the day-long beating of the sun their brow is frounced out, the lips are drawn up, and by stiffening of the muscles become set in that posture ; the light heart and natural wit of the Beduins is fallen in them for lack of human fellowship into a kind of imbecility.—I remember a young Syrian Nasarene who told me he had found in the scripture a terrible saying against the Beduw ; and fetching his (missionary) bible, he turned me up a leaf and read that ' the locusts which proceeded from the pit bottomless had hairs as the hair-locks of women, and their teeth were as the teeth of lions ! ' The poor marketing Beduins I have heard compared in the Kasîm town-speech to a flight of locusts, *míthil el-jerâd.*

In W. Shellál was a mountain wind, flowing down as the plains below were heated, which dulled the scalding beams of the summer day's sun, and increased till the half-afternoon, blustering then so strongly from the Harra head of the valley, that I have had my little tent overblown.

We had word that the Fukara were about to encamp at el-Héjr, as every year they lodge one autumn month about those waters. I thought then to return to them, they would soon journey to Teyma, from whence I might pass to

Hâyil. When Mishwat found me as I sat under some ruinous walling, in the lee of the tepid blast, reading, " Khalîl ! he cried, now deny it not, thou wast here to take up some treasure." At evening, he offered a young sheep for the health of his camels,—*mesquin !* unwitting of the Will above, and the event determined against him ! a month later they were in the power of the enemy. The ewe he had cast silent and struggling to ground (the head of every sacrifice is turned towards Mecca) ; the Mishwat, kneeling upon it, in the name of God, drew his sword across her throat. Some of the spouting blood he caught in the bowl, and with this he passed devoutly through the troop ; and putting in his fingers he bedaubed with a blood-streak the neck and flank of every one of his couching great cattle. The mutton went to the pot. When any beast is slaughtered and brittled, the great bowels are borne out and cast away at little distance by the hareem ; the small fatty gut and chitterlings, hastily roasted in the hearth, are divided as sweet morsels by the nomads lads and children. The slaughter-blood, which has flowed upon the ground, is smelled to but refused by the nomads' hounds. Pieces of the liver, amongst the Fejîr, I saw cast into the fire-pit, and eaten broiled by the minors of the household, before the guest-supper. The head is likewise cast in and roasted, the brain is eaten only by women, the men have a superstition that it should dull their eyesight.

The morrow was of the weyrid, and then there arose a scolding contention among them. The Aarab could not agree about the price of a thelûl in heads of small cattle, whereof a Serahîny owner would quit his contribution to the midda which must be paid to Mahanna. The Arabs are iniquitous in any bargain, and the frenetic clamouring of Darŷesh soon set all the waterers by the ears ; I saw from my tent the Serahîny sheykh casting his wooden arms and that the capon and his adversary had lifted their drawn swords. Old Tollog went out from the coffee-tent to appease them ; but he re-entered by and by, shrinking the shoulders, when his voice was not heard in their strife. The Moahîb are heady and sturdy, and angry Darŷesh was a nettle to have stung them all into a garboil. After the first breath spent in shouting, peaceable men's words began to prevail, and the Arabs drew off, every man to his own, with their cattle. Wâyil, as he came, shouted to his housewife that she should strike the beyt, he would remove at the instant ; a little after he suffered himself to be persuaded to his quiet and the common good.

This morning the sheukh would ride to the Fukara encamped at el-Héjr, to treat of the common welfare, and do away a coldness which was grown between them since the Haj ; they desired to be accorded with Motlog, and joining his Aarab to make one camp with them.   Tollog mounted with Hamed, Wâyil and Darŷesh : Mishwat, contrary to his overnight words, would not ride, and my nâga was now ' breasted up ' with his cattle towards the Harra.   A young shepherdess, *Gottha*, daughter of the widow *Thanwa*, proffered herself to run and fetch her :—many times the poor Beduins lend themselves to this kind of service, for the sheykh and the stranger.   An hour passed ere the camel could be led in again ; though the sheykhs had long since departed upon their thelûls, I thought I might adventure to ride alone as I came.   Mishwat said over quickly the last counsels, what landmarks I should ' put upon this or leave upon that hand : ' I gave his housewife, as she desired, some ' fever medicine,' and they bade me speed well.

The desolate valley yawned out widely, the footprints were insensible, on the hard vulcanic bottom, of those that had ridden before me.   I looked therefore ever to the lower soil, —so I must find a natural outlet of the torrent water ; in this sort I came through, without failing, to the Howwâra.   Thereabout lie small balls upon the sand of some mineral matter fallen from the wasting sand-cliff, the most are in clusters which resemble the dropping of ruminant animals ; those which may roll in their guns, are taken up for bullets by the poorer tribesmen.

Badly mounted, a man might now overtake me on foot :—I hoped not to be met with by habalîs ; it was in this short passage to the kella that Abu Sinûn had been " taken."   Besides a wild contention for life, it would be published that the Nasrâny carried a manner of dangerous pistol ; and were that seized from me, I should be left naked in all my travels, amidst armed enemies.   The way was full of such hollow rocks as might serve ill-meaning wretches for lurking places ;—and who, finding me here, and his deed unespied, would spare the Nasrâny !   The spires and pinnacles of mount Ethlib were soon after in sight ; then troops of the Aarab's camels, that were driven slowly over the plain.   Having passed those few miles, I came to booths of some Solubba under the kella, and learned that the sheykh's tents were pitched at the wells under the Borj rocks.

Riding further, I overtook some sheykhly tribesman : seen from the backward, I already guessed him by the smooth sidesweeping, square from the shoulders, of his stiff striped mantle, and the delicate and low bare-footed gait, to be a coffee-fellow of Zeyd's:—the head is elated from a strutting breast, arms kimbowed from the hips, the man holds a mincing womanish pace. This is sheykhly carriage in the wilderness, and of the principal personages. They are noblemen born, lapped in the stern delicacy of the desert life, and sit, as men-gossips, sipping coffee-cups in the mejlis, all the day-time of their lives. The housewives do all for them in the tents, these tent-dwelling men find nothing abroad to do, and they seldom ride in a ghrazzu. Under his gay kerchief you shall see perhaps a politic man's visage, with a smooth feminine grace, great sharp-set ambitious eyes, watching with an indolent wildness under those severe and comely brows. In all the Fejîr sheukh, that, as said, are germains, is a family likeness of the voice and bearing.

I alighted before that booth where I found couched the thelûls of the Moahîb sheykhs, who had arrived before me. There sat a great assembly within, and that was Motlog's tent. The Fukara saw me again with a cold fanatical countenance. This humour of theirs was for their companion Zeyd's sake (the hablûs) ; and besides, as told, no kafir may return among the Moslemîn and be welcome : only a young man coming in after me took me, with hearty greeting, by the hand, and he was a Mahûby, in exile, one of Tollog's Aarab. The Moahîb sheykhs cast upon me silently their friendly looks, and nodded with smiles of cheerful remembrance. Said Tollog, "Ha, Khalîl! had we known thou wast coming, I would have awaited thee;" then turning to those malevolent Aarab, he said, "Khalîl has been living this while with us, and wellah his talk is very reasonable and pleasant ; although he be a Nasrâny, he is a weled very well minded toward the Moslemîn."—The Moahîb did not love the Fukara, whom in despite they call *el-Fúggera* and Yahûd Kheybar. Tollog now spoke of their affairs, "Wellah, O thou Motlog, and you the Fukara, I know it has been said ' the Moahîb and the Fukara be not well together.' "—The Tehâma was in these days full of Aarab, and the summer pasture was scant, therefore Tollog desired now to wander awhile with the Fukara, which Motlog, for certain respects (due to Ibn Rashîd), heard unwillingly. Also Tollog came to take counsel with the Fukara, for his tribe's submission : Wâyil and the Serahîn would otherwise make their several peace. They felt they might no longer live safe from Bishr, whom Ibn Rashîd egged on incessantly to infest them. At noon a great breakfast heap of cooked rice was borne in, which had been long a-cooling in the woman's apartment. The breathless heat in the Héjr plain was now immoderate.

The sheukh rose from the dish to go drink coffee in the

kella, and visit Haj Nejm. The old man was astonished and smiled to see me again : I found there, Zeyd, Méhsan, and other friends. The guests were soon seated in a long row, upon Nejm's holiday carpets, under the west wall of the gallery : but the Beduins could not forbear debating some of their petty differences, and I saw Wâyil twice called out to swear in a disputed matter upon his sword ; a formal oath of which they have a wholesome superstition. The Beduin soldier lad Mohammed cried bravely, in presence of the Moahîb, ' Wellah ! except he bound one of them, the first (after this) upon whom he might lay his hands ! ' Tollog the sheykh answered him with a fatherly gravity : " My son, we have nothing at all that is thine." The Beduins rose again when the sun was setting, to return to the menzil. Motlog killed a sheep for his guest-meal ; but a third of the night was spent, when the seethed flesh (with the best pieces laid above of the great tallow-tail and the liver), was served upon a mighty mess (the whole might be a barrow-full) of Wejh rice. The guests drew nigh, and reaching forth the right hands, in the name of Ullah, they begin to eat—rending their first morsels of the tail (*thail*), which, in the live sheep, is a swagging foot-wide lap, that may nearly cover the hind quarters, and many pounds weight ;—they think it very sweet and wholesome. The Aarab, as often as I told them that our small fleeced-cattle had but wiggle tails, have answered me, " Then the sheep of the Nasâra must be of evil kind." When they have done, the guests rise, blessing their host (who by nothing is so well paid as to hear his hospitable performance commended) ; in this wilderness-life, where is no superfluity of water, they wipe their greasy hands upon the next tent-stuffs, or rub them upon their scabbards, the tent-poles or any saddle-tree by them. Nomads sip not whilst they eat, the bowls of water or milk are set apart for their drinking after meat. Only much later, a caldron was fetched in, full of the mixed mutton broth and camel milk ; and the guests poured out for themselves in bowls.

I wondered with a secret horror at the fiend-like malice of these fanatical Beduins, with whom no keeping touch nor truth of honourable life, no performance of good offices, might win the least favour from the dreary, inhuman, and for our sins, inveterate dotage of their bloodguilty religion. But I had eaten of their cheer, and might sleep among wolves. The fortune of the morrow was dark as death, all ways were shut before me. There came in a W. Aly sheykh, and principal of that tribe's exiles, he was an hereditary arbiter or lawyer

among them, in the custom of the desert : the arbiter sitting
by and fixing upon me his implacable eyes, asked the sheykhs
of the Moahîb in an under-voice ' Why brought they the Nasrány ? ' They said, ' Khalîl was come of himself.' Then turning
to Hamed he whispered a word which I well overheard, " Why
have ye not left him—thus ? " and he made the sign of the
dead lying gaping upright.   Hamed answered the shrew in
a sort of sighing, *Istugfir Ullah*, " Lord, I cry thee mercy ! "
Târiba (the man's name,) was of a saturnine turning humour ; and upon a time afterward, with the same voice, he
defended me at Teyma, against the splenetic fanaticism of
some considerable villager, threatening me that ' except I
would convert to the religion of Ullah and His Apostle, as
I carelessly passed by day and by night in the lanes and
paths of the oasis, a God-fearer's gunshot might sometime end
my life.' Târiba answered him with displeasure, " Wellah, the
Beduw be better than ye ! " Târiba's cavilling was now also for
my greeting (as they use), *salaam aleyk*, ' peace be with you.' It
is " the salutation of Islam and not for the mouths of the heathen,
with whom is no peace nor fellowship, neither in this world nor
the next : " also he would let the people know that I was a
khawâja. This is the title of Jews and Christians in the mixed
Semitic cities of the Arabian conquest.

   Motlog said in the morning, " *Henna rahîl*, we are about removing : and thou, Khalîl, canst not remain with the Aarab,
neither do I permit thee, nor is there any of them who will
receive thee."—" I tell thee they will all receive me ; do you
account me an enemy ? "—" Well, I do not take thee for an
enemy, but the life of the Beduw is uneasy, and in this summer
heat thou wast best remain in the g(k)ella." The Moahîb sheykhs
answered friendly for me : " Khalîl is no novice, he is like one
of the Beduw, and we have heard it of Abu Sinûn that his
Aarab are of the Sooltàn's alliance."—" Here is Zeyd, Khalîl's
' uncle,' said Motlog, let him go with Zeyd." But Zeyd answered, " Khalîl is now out of my hands, and I will no more
answer for him ; besides when he was with me, and we were so
much friends, Khalîl called me *hablûs !* " The Aarab now dispersed from the morning cup, and Tollog rising, called me
apart. " Khalîl, said the good old sheykh, if you do not like
this people, we now are going, and you can return in our company ; or else later, when you find it well for yourself, come
again to us and welcome, and be with us till the returning
Haj."

   —The Moahîb sheykhs loosed the thelûls' knee-strings and
let their beasts rise, which lay before Motlog's tent, fasting,

since yesterday. They climb to their saddles, as the tall cattle are standing; only Tollog, in his unwieldy age, got him upon his kneeling thelûl: so they rode forth. There was but a last shouted word of their affairs, without turning the head, and no leave-taking. This is school to depart on the morrow betimes: —the overnight's full-fed guest is dismissed upon his morning way empty. I remained uneasy at Motlog's tent, for his W. Aly housewife was shrewish, so that her own step-children called her "gipsy woman," *Solubbîa;* my last handful of provisions spent, I walked over to the booths about the next wells, where that W. Aly sheykh lodged, *Ibrahîm es-Sennad,* who was the haj post: the man, a little fanatical humour apart, was of friendly worth and of my acquaintance.

I found him reposing in his summer tent, for the gaila heat was soon upon us. Surprised to see me enter, he bade the housewife take away the falcon on the perch, and to set me his thelûl saddle for a leaning pillow. The man who had received me at first with a half-averted look, now said friendly, "Thou art welcome;—and hearest thou, wife, make ready, that Khalîl may breakfast, and let it be immediately." In our talk I enquired of the guestship of the Beduw. "A guest, he answered warmly, whoso he be, and the stranger, is the guest of Ullah, and *azîz,* as one dearly beloved." Of Motlog's house-wife he said, 'She came of no good kin, a sheykh's daughter among them of small estimation:' he added a little after, "Hearken, Khalîl, if you have spent all, although my credit be low at el-Ally, where in these days I have laid up my sword in pawn for a little barley, I will be thy surety to Haj Nejm for a few reals until the coming Haj." Yet in our talk he indulged his self-pleasing fanaticism, 'one Moslem in the exchange of prisoners, in the jehâd, he affirmed to be rated against ten Nasâra.' He would ride before Ramathán with Khálaf and Mohammed the Sherâry, for their affairs to Damascus, and return with the Haj, and bade me be of their company.

Lodged now, the third time, before those ghastly grinning ranges of the Héjr monuments—like rat-holes, in the distant aspect, under mountain banks of squalid sandstone rock—I found nothing in them which I had not viewed already.

Mohammed ed-Deybis was willing to accompany me to Kheybar, for large wages; there he might take up a load of dates for his poor household, and return with the Aarab: but on the morrow he excused himself, saying, "Khalîl, it is for this (he clapped his hand to the neck-bone)! and I am a father of children." I found another, *Jâzy,* but afterward he drew back, saying, "It would be too rash riding." I found a likely

young man of the Khamâla, who had a good thelûl; for ten reals
he would mount me upon another, and for the price I might
leave him my nâga. But he likewise failed at the time ; and in
all this was Zeyd's hand that hindered, he alleging himself still
careful of my safety as he would answer for me to the Dowla.

We had word that Mahanna foraying nigh Kheybar with eight
companions, had lifted fifty Heteym camels, of which there fell
seven to his share :—yet we heard afterwards that these had
been restored to their owners, as taken upon Aarab not their
declared enemies. So the Beduw will many times be fair-policy
men and magnanimous, for any sufficient·cause. But it is a
marvel how in the languor and heat of the year, these weary
Beduins, taking no more than handfuls of mereesy with them,
can foray many days together, certain of deadly fatigue, uncertain to bring anything home, or even to come again alive to their
worsted menzils. Another guest of Motlog's was a young Sherâry,
who arrived to treat about some reaved camels. When I enquired, who was the jid or father of his tribe ? he answered,
" The Aarab have no remembrance of antiquity, but you may
find it in your books ; look if it be not there." There was
a guest also of the half tribe of W. Aly in the north, who in
the last Haj came down riding upon his thelûl to visit the
southern kinsmen. These months he had guested it with them
as a fugitive, and now lodged from tent to tent with the
Fukara, till the next ascending pilgrimage.

Thr fourth day the Moahîb sheykhs returned to us, leading
a dromedary ; the younger men, Hamed and Wâyil, would
ride with this peace-offering to Ibn Rashîd. Motlog made
again a guest-supper ; and, when the morrow was light, the
two friends, for such they were, took their beasts to set forward.
All the Aarab of the Emir's jurisdiction being yet hostile before hired, they hired a Fejîry rafîk, who though of Tollog's
ancient acquaintance, made it strange with him to bargain for
this voyage : and yet the fellow was sure of a change of clothing, besides, at Hâyil. From hence they counted seven days
riding (of nomads) to "THE JEBEL." So old Tollog returned
with a lad back-rider, alone, to the W. Shellâl.—Cool seemed
the nights after the great heat of these daylights in the close
Héjr plain ; yet I have found at the lowest (in the dawning),
73° Fahrenheit, more often 76°. Girbies hanged to the air from
the sunset, as they incessantly sweat out humour, in an hour or
two yielded water which seemed to our drinking of an icy
chillness,—tried by the thermometer I found 52°. The water in
the wells under the Borj is cooler and much better than water
drawn from ' the nâga's well ' in the kella.—Tepid and flat is

every water that I have tasted in Arabia, and unlike the
good ground-waters of our climate, as the simûm wind is unlike any wholesome air!—After these wells have been drawn
out at a camel-watering, the water is risen again in a few
hours. The savour to their palates is not one in all ; the water
of the well two hundred paces north-west from the kella is the
better tasting. If the waterers lose any of their gear in the
pits, I have seen them let down a child for it—to-day it was a
son of the sheykh Motlog—tying him under the arms : the Arabs,
as said, have excellent heads to adventure themselves thus, and
the boy went down cheerfully into that dripping depth and
darkness.

Some marketers descended to el-Ally, and I rode with them.
The most were Fehját, a beggarly crew, carrying loads of wild
hay upon their camels, which they would barter for dates. In
the company, went some tribeswomen on foot : one of them, a
poor creature, had been a wife of Rahyêl, Motlog's brother ; and
when she was divorced, his elder nephew Therrŷeh had taken
her, it seemed in a sort of adulation. To Motlog's son the
poor jâra had borne a daughter, and then, because unlike his
springing years, he had put her away. Now, a lone woman,
she carried a tinned bowl of two or three shillings, to buy a
pair of sheep-skins for new girbies in her widowed booth. Another time I asked Therrŷeh himself of his not convenient
marriage, " Is it well? " He answered, " Ay, it is well ; " but his
father Motlog, in whose tent we were speaking, responded with
an emphasis, " Nay wellah ! it is not well." As we rode in the
Akhma among crags and cliffs, there was a sudden cry of a
ghrazzu at our backs ; but soon those thelûl riders were known
to be tribesmen, and marketers to the town.

At el-Ally I went to buy some provision of Sâlih the Mos-
lemany ; but now I found him no truer dealer than another, and
his wife came running after me in the street to make resitution.
The Alowna are sordid in their dealings. If you buy a thing
and they receive a greater piece of money, it is likely they will
refuse to render the difference, or to receive their own again,
saying only, " You may have the rest in goods ; " and they lie in
their answers, that they have not a 'thing, which afterward
upon better hopes they bring forth. A thirsting stranger may
pass by many of their doors asking to drink a little water,
and they answer, " Here is no water," though he see the full
girby swinging in their entry. We found the villagers' prices
risen thirty per cent. since they had notice that the Fukara
were encamped at el-Héjr.

Beautiful is the green pageant of the oasis, after the burning barren dust of the desert. I saw the thousand crowns of palms now richly loaded with purple-ripe, and yellow and red clusters of this land's food-fruit; the first gathered were yet good cheap, twenty sahs for a real. In their thick orchards only the cry of some gay fruit-eater bird startles from time to time the teeming stillness of a tropical vegetation, where I found but a midday heat of 93°. The sun rises late, and is early set behind their deep valley coasts; but all the nights are of heavy heat without refreshment. In the most garden grounds I saw a leafy riot of great-grown pumpkins and sweet-smelling kinds of water-melons.

I re-entered the town at mid-afternoon, when the villagers assemble, to sip the cup in the kahwas of their sheykhs. At the first found I stepped over the threshold; room was made for the stranger, and I sat down amongst them.—A voice soon said to me in the taunting vein of these villagers, which in their shallow half negro, half feverish mirth, "Here sits an uncle's son of thine, and thou dost not know him!" I saw it was a lithe young man, with a countenance between shrewish earnest and light scoffing humour, his skin was white and ruddy in comparison with these sweeps' visages of the Alowna. The fellow sat in a new Turkey red cap, with great swinging tassel of blue silken,—many of these haj-way villagers affecting the Damascus usage. His father, a Nasrâny, was come trading, or a fugitive, hither from Egyptian parts, and at el-Ally they had made him a Mosleman. This was *Howeychim* his son, who now saluted me, "How dost thou? and I, as thou, am Engleysy (he would say, of the free Nasâra). My father was of those countries: when he was here, they were too many for us, they caught him, and they beat him, till he confessed *Mohammed rasûl Ullah.* Khalîl, the dogs had the upper hand, and here am I, the Lord be praised, a Moslem:—and say thou ' There is none other God than the Lord, and His apostle Mohammed,' and inhabit amongst us, and palms shall be given thee." The coffee drinkers answered for their parts, " We do promise this; and hearken, Khalîl,—what were two little words? pronounce them with us, and it shall do thee no hurt. Khalîl, believe in the saving religion, and howbeit thou care not for the things of this life, yet that it may go well with thee at the last.—Neighbours, Khalîl is an honest man, but blind, it may please Ullah to give him light; and if no, it is His will, and here is a town of the Moslemîn, he is free to come and go without question among us."

Howeychim invited me to his garden, saying he would give

me some water-melons, but being there he made me pay for
them beyond the market price; and when we returned with
these in our hands, he answered the infirm gossiping humour
of all who met with us, " Wellah they are *bakshîsh* which I
have bestowed upon the Nasrâny!" The impudent Harebrains
went half-leaping before me! and when he saw me come feebly
dragging after, " What is this! he cries, thou art a young man,
and I have fifty years upon my back:" and this seemed likely;
the fellow considered, though he might have passed for twenty
years younger. " But thou art a pretty boy, and can skip it
more than a wild goat."—" Ah, sayest thou this because I am
beardless? it was the rats came and bit off my beard by night."
Howeychim had besides, a busy working head to attempt a
thing. Not many years past, he had imagined to plant the
empty soil, of profitable loam, which lies half a mile above
the oasis, under el-Khreyby; and there he built a redout,
wider than a house or two, which yet remains, and is called
after his name. Such a " kella " is a close of four high walls,
for surety, wherein the husbandmen may quickly shelter themselves, from the incursions of hostile Beduins. But Howeychim
found few of his stomach at el-Ally, such pithless townsmen
would not follow the projector, and his stirring hopes were fallen
to the ground. More than all, in his heart brooded an impotent
ambition, to climb one day over all their heads to be captain
of the town. The year before he had been to see Kheybar,
and finding one there [afterward my entire friend], Mohammed
el-Nejûmy of Medina,—of whom, in his robust mirth, I had
this tale—a hardy strong man, he had opened his purpose to
him, and namely, that they twain should return to el-Ally, and
make themselves masters there by the sword. Said he, ' his
townsmen the Alowna were such very natural cowards, that the
same would be toys to them, wellah, but the swapping off a
few heads, and over the rest they might lord it at their own
list.'—When I found that my nomad company would not move
before morrow, I returned to Musa's kahwa, where I had
alighted, and that good man strewed down garden stalks to my
camel: the night I passed, dreading the dampish air of the
palms, upon his terrace roof.

More of our Beduins came in the morning, and among them
Zeyd. They told us that the Aarab removed yesterday (after
our departure), and were now at the wells el-Atheyb, nearer to
the town. I had left my bags standing before Motlog's beyt; but
my friends bade me be easy, for the hosts " must in honour have
carried them with them." I returned to the Aarab with Zeyd,
who had taken up dates and rice upon credit till the next Haj.

—The nomad people lodging here dispersedly, on a long ascending sand, between high cliffs of the Akhmar and the Harra mountain, we rode by their menzils for more than three miles. The next evening came Mahanna, to treat of his conveying another kúfl to Wejh. He had alighted at Motlog's tent, but Rahŷel made the guest-supper, killing at sunset a good sheep ; late in the evening, he called us all and we rose from Motlog's, to go over to his booth. Mahanna, as we sat about the dish, observing me with a friendly eye,—" Is it always thus, he said to Zeyd, who sat and supped by me, that Khalîl eats not ? how hard must it be for a man, as he was bred, to lead the life of the Beduw ! "

Ramathán, the fasting month, was nearly in, which kindles in Moslem spirits, even of the wild Aarab, a new solemnity of religion ; the Beduins, aping the town guise, which they had seen at Medina, now stood out from the byût at the hours, and making ranks, they rehearsed the formal prayer, bowing the empty foreheads and falling upon the petticoated knees together. If the sheykh Motlog were there he prayed not as an Imam before the rest, but standing like a truant amongst them. All the Moslemîn are equal in the performance of their religion. A lewd, mad and lousy derwish may savagely reprehend his prince in such matter, and the great man must take all in godly patience. Motlog, whose manly breast savoured not of mumming, was oftentimes molested by some abject calling upon him that 'now was the hour ; *goom yâ, súl !* ho ! to the prayers, up thou Motlog, rise and pray ! '—the zealots being such that he might have said of them with Job, " I would not have set them among the dogs of my flock ! " Yet rising with a patient submission, Motlog, the great sheykh, went then to asquit himself of the duty in religion. The greatest sheykh durst not do otherwise ; it is for his peace and safety among his Mohammedan brethren,—intolerable among them were the reproach of irreligion. Such few of the nomad hareem as are taught, kneel down in this religious month before their beyts, to say the formal prayers ; and seldom at other times is any woman seen praying.

The heaven showed all that night, in the full of the moon, a beautiful day-like blue depth and nearly starless. The moon, near the morning, was totally eclipsed, and the Arabs told me, they had seen the sky red as blood, which they took for " a token of great heat." At sunrise I found 83° F., the day followed without breath of air, at half-afternoon I found 40·5° Cent., the heaven was overcast, and the Aarab, full of languor, lay down in the great mountain shadows. The day after the heat rose

to 41·5° C. (110° F.); in that afternoon the Beduins removed, and
we returned to el-Héjr. In the way, seeing that my loosely-
girded baggage was sliding and falling, a poor woman riding
nigh me alighted of her own good will, and she came barefoot
in a place of thorns, to help the stranger:—there is this natural
goodness in the Aarab.

Alighting again at Medáin, the nomad households pitched
in their old steads, and made the evening fires upon the ashes of
their former hearths. At the next sunrise, the coolest hour of
the natural day, I found 86° F. and the afternoon heat was
again 41·5° C. The noisome flies of el-Héjr, everywhere a
swarming plague, as much in the shadowing of lofty cliffs as in
the tent's feeble shade, made it not possible in the whole daylight to find rest. I went to shelter by the Diwán, a cliff
passage in which the sun never shines ; but even there was the
cloud of sordid insects. Where I sat, there came tripping
a little fly-catcher bird, slender and slate-coloured and somewhat as our common wagtail, which coursing nimbly upon
the tormenting flies, snatched her prey without ever missing :
I spread upon her my kerchief, and took and caressed the little
friendly bird without hurt, and let her go from my hand : but for
all this she only removed a little and did not fly from me.

Motlog's wide booth was a common afternoon napping place
of loitering tribesmen : there the impertinent tongues of Ramathán zealots often barked upon the Nasrâny, till I called upon
a day to Therrŷeh, " Oh the plague of flies, the heat, and the
barren words of these dubbush ; they know even what is good
for man better than the Lord that made them."—" Thou
sayest the truth, they are dubbush."—" But what worship they ?
the aphrodisia and the galliûn !—these be your hallows, O
Aarab."—" Ah-ha-ha ! Khalîl, wellah, they could not deny it, upon
these all their vain thoughts be set ; the Beduw worship the one
and the other." He was the sheykh's elder son, but Sâlih
his next brother, a robust young man of a sturdy turbulent
humour, was best beloved in their father's eyes, and born of a
more sheykhly mother ; in the father's right he already inherited
a principal sheykh's surra. Motlog favoured Sâlih, who began
to be considerable in the tribe, and Therrŷeh seeing himself
supplanted at home, had learned to be a courtier. Every day
he was busy to visit his father, (little warm to him,) and this
seemed to be in way of adulation : Therrŷeh had made himself
a great beyt as Motlog's, and his menzil was apart with Aarab ;
he had many camels, and the young man was a valiant leader
of the ghrazzus. I have heard him say among his friends with
a kind of melancholy " —but I am no sheykh ! " They answered

cheerfully, " Thou art *sheykh es-sheûkh*, a sheykh of sheykhs."
Sâlih yet inhabited in his father's menzil, where his tent,
new woven of the best, was but a modest hejra.—Therrŷeh
taking carelessly in his hand the book in which I was reading,
he pleased himself with my pencil to draw upon a leaf—in their
manner—figures of men and animals. (See next page.)

Of the many slumberers out of the sun in the sheykh's tent
was one whom I perceived to be no Arabian ; ' some lost derwish
(I thought) of the haj caravan : ' and yet his visage was swarthier
than the most of their Beduin faces. He told me he was a
gardener of Beyrût, and had remained here with the Aarab
from the third Haj before : with the money he then had he
purchased a couple of camels, the Khamâla bestowed upon
him a housewife, and she had borne him two children in the
meanwhile. His mind, he said, was soon to return home, and
he would carry up his Beduin family with him. He was weary
in the desert ; he thought this summer heat was no greater
than in his Phoenician country. He was an ill-eyed fellow,—
there go many criminals with the Haj, and escape justice : and
surely a dull-spirited peasant would not forsake the plenty of his
good things, without cause, for the deadly life of the Beduw !

Zeyd would now have received me more willingly than I
had any mind to return to him :—said Méhsan, who was a good
man, " Ay wellah we have neglected thee, Khalîl, but why stay
longer at Motlog's, where thy baggage is left in the open, and
the dogs rip up all with their sharp claws, when thou art
absent, to devour your few provisions ; but we are as thine own
household, and the stuff will be in surety in our beyt." I
gladly removed to their tent ; and at evening we went together
to drink coffee at the kella, where this sheykhly man of mild
and friendly manners, and a patient player of the Arabic
draughts, was always welcome to the techy Moghrebies. Though
we had supped Haj Nejm would have us taste his rice mess ;
and they ever welcomed me whether I came to sit in their
stone porch, where is some draught of air, at noonday, or I
visited them at the coffee-hearth in the cool of the evening.
Those few palms which Haj Nejm had defended from the spring
locust, now stood with full burdens ripe to the harvest ; I saw
the yellow fruit-stalks bowing under the beautiful leafy crowns,
all round, in goodly great clusters : the weight of these, tree-
mammels, under that female beauty of long leafy locks, was
in every stem, they reckoned, a camel's burden (3 cwt.). The
Héjr dates are ready at one time with the dates of Teyma,
which is not till twenty days after the ingathering at el-Ally,
which lies four hundred feet lower.

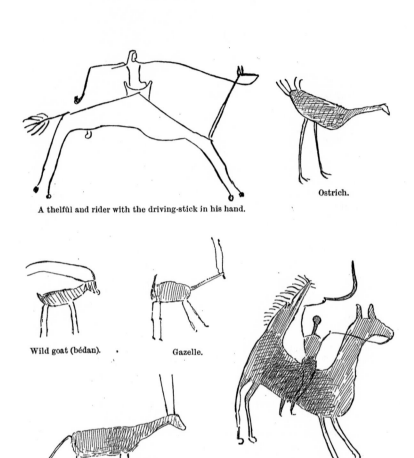

A thelfûl and rider with the driving-stick in his hand.

Ostrich.

Wild goat (bédan).

Gazelle.

W'othŷhi.

Mare and rider with his sword.

A sheykh and his wife.

A woman (showing the long "horns" and the *haggu*).

—This last evening Haj Nejm fell into his old argument of the western countries. He said generously to the gaping audience, " Ye ought not to esteem of Khalîl and those like him as kafirs, for they believe as we in the most things necessary. *Saiduna Îsa* (our Lord Jesu), son of our Lady Miriam, the Lord of them, is indeed an holy prophet of Ullah. So have they Mûsa, Daûd, and the ancient prophets ; and they say like the Moslemîn, that Ullah is one God, and beside Him there is none other. Mark ye, this only remains between us, that they say not, as we, of our Lord Mohammed,—whom magnify Ullah, and give him peace—that he is the Apostle of Ullah. And wot ye, Khalîl's people, the Engleys, are the friends of Islam, and neighbours to us a little way over the narrow sea, from Fez and Marâkish and so nigh that either coast country appears to the inhabitants of the other beyond the water : the speech of the Engleys is *waar*, rugged-like "—[yet called *helw*, sweet, in the Syrian countries, and even *loghrat et-teyr,* ' a tongue as the chittering of birds.'] Then he returned to murmur, with homely affection, of his West Country, ' full of fresh springs under an wholesome climate, whose fortunate and peaceful inhabitants' lives are drawn out to an extreme old age ! ' He counted upon the fingers of his two hands, ' how many days a man might wander to what part he would and not see an end of palms ! and lastly, the rough and barren desert spreading out two months' journey southward to the Sudàn (land of black men) ; whither went great yearly caravans of Morocco merchants, calling at Timbuctû, and the adventurers to the deep country beyond, for the rich traffic in slaves, and gold and ivory, and ostrich feathers.' He said over the many good seabord towns : and extolled the great capital cities. ' In Fez, the mosques were three hundred, so that in the hours of prayer you may hear a crying upon all sides of muétthins from the many steeples ; the hammàms too in like number : a river flows through the town, of which they draw pure water. It was a fair sight to look upon the lines of high-built streets, and the houses made so that a family may lodge apart [with the Mohammedan household jealousy,] in every stage ; the sûks also well garnished with all things needful to the daily life, and where every craft is lodged by itself, so that in one short passage ye may be provided with all you lack without lost labour of seeking hither and thither.'—" *Esma !* hearken ! " answered the Arabs, assenting with a grave attention to every new taking of the old man's breath ; and when he had done they said, " Haj Nejm, thou hast many marvellous things to relate, and of thine own knowledge : Eigh, wellah ! he who has travelled has seen much, and

D. T. 33

which of us, except he heard it, had ever thought on all this ?
Large is the world, it is no doubt, and wonders be therein, more
than we wot of :—ay ! Haj Nejm, what are we the Beduw,
but dubbush, a silly drove of small cattle !"—In our coming
home, Méhsan said to me, " I like Haj Nejm, and pleasantly
he talks, if one might always follow him, but, billah, what
for his Moghreby terms, I understand not much better than
the half of his speech." I found no need of an interpreter :
the strange names of foreign countries and alien things had
perplexed the lively simple wit of the desert-bred Beduwy.

The heat seemed already less ; these were like the first days
of autumn, yet I found in the afternoon, as before, 40·5° or 41° C.
Old Nejm had finally thrust the half Beduwy lad, Mohammed,
from the kella ; he came to harbour for the night with us in
Méhsan's tent, who, for the boy's falcon, granted to carry him on
the morrow to el-Ally, from whence he might go over to his
nomad mother's kindred. In the dawning Méhsan mounted,
with the lad radîf, and I mounted to visit the town with them.
The Beduin boy let his wife fare on foot, until some marketing
tribesman coming by us on his thelûl took her up, unwillingly, to
ride behind him. We went by a lone Beduin grave, set round
with wild flags of sandstone,—a great W. Aly sheykh, said they,
rested there. Near the end of the Akhma, they showed me a
hollow cliff, *Makhzan el-Jindy*, " the soldier's ware-room : "—
whereby the former haj-road had passed to el-Ally. " A soldier's
wife travailing in the march, died, and her husband hastily buried
her there ; and because no woman was in the caravan to give it
suck, he forsook her babe under the rock's shadow. The father
as he came by again in the ascending pilgrimage (seventy days
after) found his child yet alive, which had been suckled by gazelle
dams of the wilderness."—We drew bridle in the town, at noon,
before Mûsa's kahwa : the kâdy lay now sick of fever. I visited
the good man in his house, and left some quinine with him.

Finding Howeychim I went home with him to buy provisions, and he brought me to his ware-room, where I saw
great heaps laid up, after their kinds, of the new in-gathering
of dates. He bade me sit down before the best and break my
fast ; and brought a little samn in the foot of his lamp-
dish. Whilst we were talking there was some noise in the
street and shuffling of feet at his outer door, Howeychim
caught up his tin, to hide it from any hungry Beduwy that
might break in upon him. A goat had run into his entry,
and the poor desert man who came driving this meat instead of
money to town made two steps after his own in the villager's
doorway. But Howeychim outrageously reviled him and cried,

" Out, Beduwy hound, from my house, thou and thy goat together !—curse thee, and God curse thy father that begat
thee ! " The poor man excused himself, ' he did but seek his
cattle ; ' not daring to dispute in the oasis, where any contentious
nomad would be followed with hue and cry and even scornfully
mishandled. Howeychim said of the Fukara, *ma fî árzal
minhum,* " There are none viler among the nomads."

After nightfall I went out to seek our Beduin company
among the palms ; they would depart about midnight, at the
moon rising. I found Méhsan and a few with him, napping
upon, mats spread in his merchant's plantation, and coffee
drinking.—We journeyed upward in the night, and after long
riding, being come in the open before el-Hejr, and the old moon
showing little light, we saw fire struck with the flint before
us, as if some had waylaid us, and in this kindled the matches
of their long guns ;—the Arabian life is full of such apprehensions. Then our Beduins fled fast upon their thelûls ; the
hareem on foot ran hither and thither ; two men who came
with us driving back a few head of sheep, beat their cattle
furiously to the rocks' dim shadows. I looked round in the
doubtful light for Méhsan, my rafîk, and saw him scouring
over the plain : I hastened after him, and since our tribe held
the country we were all gone down unarmed. My old nâga
running and bellowing, with a very hard snatching gait, twice
sank down under me, and as I had her up again, she held
on so vehemently that I feared she might cast the young, said
to be of a few months in her. A skin of dates, which I carried
for a poor woman, broke from my saddle. I asked " What is
this ado, Méhsan ? "—" The habalîs ! " said he ; yet by and by,
by the counter shoutings, we understood that all was a false
alarm. But Méhsan's strong thelûl roused, and feeling the
freshness of the night, broke away mainly, and ran on under
him to Medáin Sâlih. Arriving there a moment before the
dawn, I found Méhsan sitting pensive in his beyt where he
had alighted half an hour before me. Surprised in this folly—
he had forsaken his rafîk—he blessed, in an irony, the fathers'
kin of such scatterlings as were come along with us, calling
them all " Beduw," and " mad bodies." The cause of this trouble
in the night was a young negro, Motlog's freed man, who passing
late, had but struck fire to his galliûn, when he heard us coming,
thinking to return now in some friendly company.

Mishwàt, Shwoysh, and Seydàn of the Moahîb friends visited
our menzil : Shwoysh, who had so fair a wife at home, would
persuade a fugitive housewife that he had among the Fukara
to return with him. Also Darŷesh, removing with his house-

hold from Tollog, was come in to pitch under the kella. He had
of late ridden out with Doolan and another far in the north to
the Ruwàlla dîra 250 miles distant ; and they now returned
from beyond Jauf weary men and empty handed.   In riding
near Thirba, they had found my nâga's and the thelûl's footsteps, and the print of Horeysh's bare feet.   Darŷesh told them
the tale, and they alighted to consider them : and now Doolan
laughed to me, " ha-ha-ha ! Khalîl, yes, hî-hî-hî ! we found it all
wellah in the sand, and there we sat down for mirth. *Afuah*
(*el-afu*) wellah, *aysht* Khalîl, gramercy, God give thee health
upon it : " and the poor man putting the hands upon my shoulders,
his knees sank for laughing.   It did their hearts good that the
Nasrâny had unseated the bully Horesyh (and in their eyes,
taken his dromedary).   " Wellah, thou art mine own uncle's son,
Khalîl,—and how seeset thou Darŷesh ? "—He could not forbear
to go and tell Darŷesh, that I had answered " A coxcomb, a
proud fellow ; " and the Serahîny sheykh when he met me again,
seemed to stand higher in the neck, and found it not amiss
that the stranger had taken knowledge of his magnanimity.
Doolan now went lame, his camel had kicked him, and heavy
is a stroke of the great-limbed brute's padfoot ; he was very
low in the world, and the herdsman's place was given to
another.   " *Ma n' ash,*" said the poor Fehjy, " we have nothing
left," and crackled his thumb-nail behind the vacant teeth.
The Moahîb were again in Thirba.   The well-spring flowed
more weakly, and that was, some of them ungraciously said,
since the Nasrâny's bathing and his " writing " the water ; yet
had I not laboured there a morning to clear the channels ?
and the current was stronger than before, so that the Beduins
said " The stranger merited, billah, that every waterer should
milk a goat for him."

In the serenity of this climate I read in the barometer, the
daily tides of the atmosphere.   The height of Medáin Sâlih
[mean of 105 observations] may be 2900 feet, nearly.

CHAPTER XIX.

TEYMA.

Final departure from Medáin Sâlih, with the Aarab. An alarm at sun-rising. Disaster of the Moahîb. Journey towards Teyma. Watching for the new moon. The month of Lent begins. Teyma in sight. Husbandmen. A distracted poor woman. An outlying grange. Ramathán. The new.ripening dates. Townsmen's talk at our coffee fire. A troubled morrow. A wayfaring man may break his fast. Hásan. Ajeyl. Visiting the sick. The custom of spitting upon sore eyes. Khálaf sheykh of Teyma. Lenten breakfast after sunset. Lenten supper at midnight. A Beduin's ' travellers' tales.' A nomad of the north discourses favourably of the Nasâra. An exile from el-Ally. A fanatic rebuked. Antique columns. A smith's household. Teyma is three oases. A mare of the blood upon three legs. Fowling at Teyma. Migration of birds. The Nasrâny observes not their fast. Méhsan pitched in a hauta or orchard of Teyma. A pastime of draughts. Women fasting. Méhsan's impatience with his household. The autumn at hand. " El-Islam shall be saved by the Beduw." Their opinion of the Christian fasting.

FINALLY, after other days of great heat, which were the last of that summer, the 28th of August, the Aarab removed from el-Héjr. Once more their " faces were toward " the Teyma country, and I mounted among them with such comfort of heart as is in the going home from a scurvy school-house ;—delivered, at length, from the eye-sore and nose-sore of those mawkish mummy-house cliffs, the sordid kella and perilous Moghrâreba of Medáin Sâlih. Now, leaving the Turkish haj-road country, I had Nejd before me, the free High Arabia !

We passed the enclosed plain to the south-eastward. I saw many falcons carried out by the thelûl riders in this ráhla ; they had purchased the birds of the gate Arabs ; and there are Beduin masters who in the march carry their greyhounds upon camel-back, lest the burning sand should scald their tender feet. Four days we journeyed by short marches to the eastward, and the nomads alighting every forenoon dismissed their cattle to pasture. The summer heat was ended for us in those airy uplands. At the morrow's sunrise whilst we sat a mo

ment, before the ráhla, over a hasty fire, I read the thermometer, 73° F. ; yet it seemed a cold wind that was blowing
upon us.

I would leave now the wandering village, and set out with
Méhsan, and a company of poorer tribesmen who went to pass
Ramathán at Teyma, where the new dates were ripening. The
tribe would come thither a month later in the last days of Lent,
to keep their (Bairam) festival at the village and in the date
gathering to buy themselves victuals.

When the sun rose of the first of September, and we were
departing from the menzils, we heard cries, in the side of the
camp, *El-Gôm!* Tribesmen ran from the byút girded in their
jingling gunners' belts, with long matchlocks, or armed with
pikes and lances.   The sheykhs went to take their horses,
foot-farers hastened forward, and shouted. Only a few aged
men remained behind with the hareem ; by and by they
'thought they heard shots yonder.' Now Zeyd went by us,
a little tardy, at a hand gallop. Stern were the withered looks
of his black visage and pricking sheykhly upon the mare
to his endeavour, with the long wavering lance upon his virile
shoulder, and the Ishmaelite side-locks flying backward in the
wind, the son of Sbeychan seemed a martial figure. Even boys
of mettle leapt upon thelûls which were theirs, and rode to
see the battle : this forwardness in them is well viewed by
the elders.   Méhsan cast down his load and followed them,
unarmed, upon his mad thelûl. It was not much before we
saw the head of our tribespeople's squadron returning :—the
riding of an hundred mounted upon dromedaries is (as said)
a gallant spectacle ; they come on nodding in the lofty saddles
to the deep gait of their cattle, with a glitter of iron, and the
song of war, in a sort of long flocking order.

Then we heard a sorry tiding of the calamity of our friends !
The herdsmen first abroad had found strange camels in the
desert ; they knew them by the brand ⊃ to be cattle of
the Moahîb and shouted, and the cry taken up behind them
was heard back in the menzils.—Therrŷeh leading out the
armed band, the keepers of those cattle came to greet them—
with ' *Gowwak ya Therrŷeh*, we are of the Auwájy and have
" taken " the Moahîb yesterday ; wellah, all their camels in the
Héjr plain, beside Thirba.'—The Fukara being their friends
upon both sides, could not now go between them ; but if the
Moahîb had been removing and encamping with the Fukara
in their dîra, the Bishr might not have molested them. Silent
and pensive our Teyma company gathered again, we were forty
riders ; and many a man went musing of his own perpetual

insecurity in the face of these extreme slips of fortune. Our familiar friends had been bereaved in one hour of all their living ; and their disaster seemed the greater, since we have seen their sheykhs had ridden—it was to have outgone this danger, but they came too late—to make their humble submission to the Emir. The Aarab sigh a word in sadness which is without contradiction, and cease complaining, " It has happened by the appointment of Ullah ! "

After two hours' riding we come to drink and fill our girbies at a solitary well-pit of the ancients, cased with dry stonework ; there grew a barren wild fig-tree. In that day's march we went by three more small well-pits, which are many (wherever the ground-water lies not deep) in all the waste emptiness of the Arabian wilderness : these may suffice to the watering of their lesser cattle.

Sultry was our journey, and we alighted at half-afternoon, where we found shadows of some great rocks with tolh trees, and pasture for the camels. The men rested and drank coffee : the housewives also kindled fires and baked scanty cakes, under the ashes, of their last barley meal. After an hour or two, when men and beasts were a little refreshed from the burdenous heat, we mounted and rode on again in the desert plain, till the sun was nigh setting ; then they drew bridle in ground where an encampment of ours had been in the spring time. " Companions, I exclaimed, this is Umsubba ! " but it dismayed the Aarab, with a sort of fear of enemies, to hear a stranger name the place, and though it is marked by that tall singular needle of sandstone (*v.* fig. p. 303).

At the watch-fires they questioned among them, had they well done to break their fasts to-day, which some of these Beduin heads accounted to be the first in the holy month : but Méhsan, who was of an easy liberal humour, held that no man were to blame for eating ' until he saw the new moon (it is commonly at the third evening), and then let him fast out his month of days.' Some answered : " In the town they reckon now by el-Hindy (Indian art, arithmetic), and they say it is unfailing, but what wot any man of us the Beduw ! " Now in the gloaming we perceived the new moon nigh her setting, and of the third day's age : the Beduins greeted this sign in heaven with devout aspirations, which brought in their month of devotion. The dwellers in the desert fast all months in their lives, and they observe this day-fasting of a month for the religion. But Ramathán is to the Beduins an immoderate weariness full of groans and complaining ; so hard it is for then to abstain from drinking and even from tobacco till the summer sun sets : in those weeks is even a separation of wedded folk. The month of Lent which should be kept clean and holy, is rather, say the nomads and villagers, a season of wickedness, when the worst sores break forth and run afresh of human nature. Not more than a good half of these fanatical nomads observe the day-fasting and prayers ;— the rest are " ignorants,"—this is to say they have not learned to pray, yet they cherish little less fanaticism in their factious hearts, which is a kind of national envy or Semitic patriotism. —For herding-men, fried all day in the desert heat, it is very hard and nearly impossible not to drink till the furnace sun be set. Men in a journey have a dispensation ; the koran bids them fast to the number of days omitted and hallow the month, at their home-coming.

We set forward very early on the morrow, long and sultry lay the way before us, which to-day the Beduins must pass thirsting ; and when the morning heat rose upon us, we were well advanced towards Teyma,—the landmark J. Ghrenèym now appearing—and came to that bald soil which lies before the town, a floor of purple sand-rock with iron-stone and shingles, where the grassy blade springs not and you may seldom see any desert bush. We perceived in the early afternoon the heads of the oasis palms, and approached the old circuit of town walling. The first outlying orchards are nigh before us,—an Eden to our parched eyes from the desert ; then we see those full palm-bosoms, under the beautiful tressed crowns, the golden and purple-coloured food-fruits. Locust flights had passed this year over all the villages, and hardly more than half their trees had been saved at Teyma. The company dispersed, every fellowship going to pitch upon their friends' grounds. I followed with Méhsan's fellowship, we made our camels stumble over some broken clay walls into an empty field : the men as we alighted cried impatiently to their housewives to build their booths ; for the thirsty Beduins would be out of this intolerable sun-burning.

Some labourers, with hoes in their hands, came out of the next gates ; I asked them to fetch a twig of the new dates (their Semitic goodness to strangers), and to bring me a cup of water. " Auh ! what man is this with you, O ye of the Fukara (said the villagers, wondering), who eats and drinks in Ramathán, and the sun is yet high !—for shame ! dost thou not know Ullah ? " and the torpid souls gaped and fleered upon me. One said, " Is not this Khalîl the kafir, he that was here before ? ay, he is he."—" Upon you be the shame, who forbid my eating, that am a wayfaring man, *musáfir*."—" Ha ! (said the voice of a poor woman, who came by and overheard them) this stranger says truth, it is ye the men of Teyma, who fear not Ullah," and she passed on hastily. By and by as I was going in with them, she, who seemed a poor Bedlam creature, met me again running, and took hold without saying word on my mantle, and opening her veil, with a harrowed look she stretched me out her meagre hands, full of dates and pomegranates, nodding to me in sign that I should receive them; she lived where we went in to water.—The poor woman came to me again at evening like one half distracted, and shrinking from sight. "Stranger, she said, eigh me! why didst thou not eat all my fruit? I ran for them as ever I heard thee speak. Know that I am a poor woman afflicted in my mind.—Ah Lord! He who has given has taken them away; I have lost my children, one after other, four sons, and for the last I besought my Lord that He would leave me this child, but he died also —aha me!—and he was come almost to manly age. And there are times when this sorrow so taketh me, that I fare like a madwoman; but tell me, O stranger, hast thou no counsel in this case? and as for me I do that which thou seest,—ministering to the wants of others—in hope that my Lord, at the last, will have mercy upon me."

—The Teyma men had thwacked their well-team, with alacrity, and made them draw for the guests. Our host's place was a poor grange, lying a little before the main orchard walls of Teyma. In the midst was his house-building, *kasr*,—dark clay-built rooms about a long-square space, which was shadowed from the sun by a loose thatch upon poles of the palm leaf-branches. His was a good walled palm-orchard and corn ground, watered day and night from a well of two reels and dullûs : yet such a possession may hardly suffice to the simple living of an Arabic household from year to year. Of the uncertain fruits of his trees and seed-plots, that which was above their eating, he sold for silver to the Beduw ; he must pay for timely help of hands, the hire of well-camels, for his tools, for his leathern well-gear ; and the most such small owners will tell you, what for their many outgoings and what for their old indebtedness, they may hardly hold up their heads in the world.

The Arabs very impatiently suffering the thirst of the first Ramathán days, lie on their breasts sighing out the slow hours, and watching the empty daylight till the "eye of the sun" shall be gone down from them. When five or six days are past, they begin to be inured to this daylight abstinence, having so large leave in the night-time. If their Lent fall in the corn harvest, or at the ingathering of dates, the harvesters must endure for the religion an extremity of thirst : but in Ramathán the villagers give over all that they may of earnest labour, save the well-driving that may never be intermitted. Their most kinds of dates were ripe in the midst of the fast ; but they let them still hang in the trees.—The owner of the plantation, to whom I said again my request, delayed, as it were with unwillingness. " It is a pain (one whispered to me) for men, weak with thirst and hunger, to see another eat the sweet and drink water ; "—the master lingered also to make a little raillery (as the Arabs will, for they love it) at that contempt in the stranger of their high religious custom. Then he went out and gathered me date-twigs of the best stems, upon which hanged, with the ripe, half-ripe purple berries, which thus at the mellowing, and full of sappy sweetness, they call *belah ;* the Arabs account them very wholesome and refreshing. Even the common kinds of dates are better meat now than at any time after,—the hard berry, melted to ripeness in the trees, is softly swelling under the sun with the genial honey moisture.

We returned to our cottage friends at evening, when the Arabs refreshed, and kindling their cheerful galliûns, seemed to themselves to drink in solace again. Fire was made in the cold hearth-pit, and coffee-pots were set, a drink not often seen in that poor place. Later came in some persons from the town, and their talk with us new-comers was of the ruined haddàj, ' The Teyâmena, they told us, were persuaded that the pit fell-in after my having " written it," and when they saw me again in their town, wellah, the angry people would kill me.' Because they had thus drunk with me in fellowship, they counselled me not to adventure myself in Teyma ;— let my Beduin friends look to it, as they would have my life saved. Méhsan answered (who was a timid man), " As ever the morrow is light, Khalîl must mount upon his nâga, and ride back to Zeyd."—" Consider ! I said to them, if I were guilty of the haddàj falling, I had not returned hither of my free will. May our bodies endure for ever ? ancient house-buildings fall, also that old well must decay at some time."—" But after it was fallen, we heard that you refused to rebuild it ! "—So we left them for the night.

The first moments of the morning sun, were of those which I oftentimes passed very heavily in Arabia, when I understood of my bread-and-salt friends, that my lonely life was atrociously threatened, and they earnestly persuaded me to sudden flight. Some of our hareem came to me when I awoke,—Méhsan was gone out in the cool, before dawn, to sell a

new saffron gown-cloth in the town ; and the men were abroad
with him—Zeyd's sister, my hostess, and the women besought
me to depart in haste, ' lest I should be slain before their eyes.'
—The nomad wives had been over-night to visit their gossips
in the settlement, and in their talk they said the Nasrâny
had arrived in the company. " The Nasrâny ! cried the Teyma
housewives,—is not that, as they say, a son of the Evil One ? is
he come among you ! Now if ye have any care of Khalîl's life,
let him not enter the town,—where yet would God ! he may
come, and be slain to-morrow : some of our men are sworn
upon the death of him."—" And why think ye evil of this man ?
now a long time he is living among the Beduw, and other
than his name of Nasrâny, they find no cause in him."
—" Yet know certainly that he is a wicked person, and of the
adversaries of Ullah ; they say.moreover, he is a sorcerer. Heard
you not tell that the haddàj was fallen ? and men do say it
was his eye.—Ye have not found him maleficent ? but what he
may be no man can tell, nor wherefore he may be come into the
land of the Aarab. Who ever heard before that a Nasrâny
came hither ? and our people say he ought not to live ; it were
also a merit to kill him."

" Khalîl, said Méhsan's wife, the Teyâmena are determined
to kill thee for the haddàj, and if they come, we are few and
cannot resist them. They are not the Beduw, that have a good
mind towards you, and a regard for the Dowla, but the headstrong and high-handed people of Teyma, so that whilst we
lodge here, we live ourselves wellah in dread of them : the
Teyâmena are treacherous, *melaunnin*, of cursed counsels ! "—
Said Méhsan, who now arrived, " Akhs ! while Khalîl sits here,
some of them will be coming ; Ullah confound the Teyâmena !
Mount, Khalîl, and prevent them ! "—The women added, " And
that quickly, we would not have thee slain." The children
cried, " Ride fast from them, uncle Khalîl." Sâlih the old
grey-headed gun-bearer of Zeyd's father, and Zeyd's own man,
was very instant with me that I should mount immediately
and escape to the Beduw, " Our Aarab (he said) are yet where
we left them, and my son and another are about to ride
back with the camels ; mount thou and save thyself with the
young men ; and remain with Zeyd, and amongst thy friends,
until time when the Haj arrive."—" And if all this cannot
move thee, said the old man and Méhsan, Khalîl, thou hast
lost thy understanding !—and companions, this man whom we
esteemed prudent (in his wise books), is like to one that hath
a jin : up now ! that thy blood be not spilt before our faces.
When they come, we can but entreat and not withhold them,

—wellah it is a cursed people of this town.—We know not
what he may have seen (in his books) ; yet stay not, Khalîl,
rise quickly, and do thou escape from them with the lads ! Ah,
for these delays ! he does not hear the words of us all, and
sitting on here he may have but few moments to live :—and yet
Khalîl does nothing ! " *Another voice,* " It may be that Ullah
has determined his perdition ; well ! let him alone." I blamed
them that trusted to the fond words of silly hareem.—" And
what if the Teyâmena come, I might not dissuade them with
reason ? "—" They that will be here presently are hot-heads, and
hear no words."—There is an itch between pain and pleasure,
which is such a mastering cruelty in children, to see one
shaped like themselves overtaken in some mortal agony, and
his calamitous case not to touch them ; and now, as I looked
about me, I saw a strange kindling in some of this ring of
watching wild eyes, there a writhing lip, and there some inhuman
flushing even in those faded women's cheeks. " Eigh ! what and
if the Lord have determined his death !—we see, he cannot hear,
or hearing that he cannot understand ! We say but this once
more ; mount, Khalîl ! whilst there is any space. Wellah we
would not that thy blood be spilt beside our byût, by the rash-
handed people of Teyma, and we cannot deliver thee."—" Friends,
when I was here before, I found them well disposed."—" Then
thou wast in company with a great sheykh, Zeyd, and now
there is none here to shelter thee !—but since we have endeavoured and cannot persuade thee, may not the event be such
as we would not !—it is now too late, and Ullah will provide."

In this there approached two younger men of the town,
and they spoke pleasantly with us. One of them, Hásan Ibn
Salâmy, the Beduins told me, was of the principal town sheukh ;
that other was a Shammar Beduwy of the north, lately become
a flesher at Teyma,—he brought this new trade into the Beduin-
like town. The Shammary boasted to be a travelled young man,
he had visited Sham as well as Irâk, and now he looked for the
praise of a liberal mind. Being one of the most removable heads,
he had gone out at the first rumour of the stranger's arriving,
and led that sheykh, his neighbour in the sûk, along with him.
The weled would see for himself, and bring word whether that
Nasrâny were not of some people or tribe he had visited, or
it might be he had passed by their béled in his caravan journeys : besides, he had a thought, there might be a *shatâra*, or
mastery in the hand of the Nasrâny, for building up their haddàj,
and he would win a thank for himself from the village sheukh.
The Teyâmena had built their well-wall, since the spring, now
three times, and the work was fallen. The best village archi-

tect of the spacious and lofty clay-brick Teyma houses was their master-builder in the second and third essays, for not a small reward,—fifty reals. As ever the walling was up, the land-owners had mounted their wheel-gear ; and the teams were immediately set labouring upon the distempered earth, so that the work could not stand many days ; the weak soil parted for-ward, and all had fallen again. The Teyâmena knew not what more to do, and when Ramathán was in, they let it lie : also the workmen (seeing their time) demanded higher wages,—and they labour in Lent only half-days.

The last ruin of the walls had been a fortnight before. ' If I had a shatâra to build, said the Beduwy, the sheykhs would enrich me, giving me what I myself would in reason.' Hásan confirmed the word, being himself *râiyat*, or one of the principal owners, with his sûk, of the haddàj, and namely of that part which was fallen. I said, ' I would go in to see it, if they thought the town was safe.'—" Fear nothing, and I am *thâmin* (said Hásan) engaged for thee to these friends here ; and if thou art not fasting come down to my house, where I will have thy breakfast made ready ; and we will afterward go to visit the haddàj ; but as for the wall falling, it was from Ullah, and not of man's deed." I was fainting from hunger, and had my weapon bound under my tunic, so hearing they would lead me to breakfast, I rose to follow them. " And these thou mayest trust," said the Beduins ; nevertheless, Méhsan's wife took me by the sleeve as I departed, to whisper, " Khalîl, we know him—a great sheykh, yet he may be leading thee to destruction : have a care of them, *iftah ayûn-ak*, open thine eyes, for they are all treacherous Teyâmena."

As we were entering at the town's end I called to him, " Hásan ! art thou able to defend me if there should meet with us any evil persons ? " And he, with the slippery smiling security of an Arab, who by adventure is engaged for an-other, and in the Semitic phrase of their speech : " There is nothing to fear, and I have all this people in my belly." We came in by alleys of the town to the threshold of Hásan's large dàr. We sat down on a gay Turkey carpet, in the court before his kahwa, and under a wide shelter-ing vine, whose old outspread arms upon trellises, were like a wood before the sun of sappy greenness : there came in a neighbour or two. Water from the metal, *'brîk*, was poured upon my hands, and the host set a tray before me of helw dates—this kind is full of a honey-like melting sweetness—gathered warm out of the sun, and pomegranates. —They wondered to see me eat without regarding the public

fast, but as smiling hosts were appeased with this word :
Imma ana musâfir, " but I am a wayfaring man." They smiled
when I told of the nomads' distrust of them, for my sake,
and said, " It is like the Beduw! but here, Khalîl, thou hast
nothing to fear, although there be some dizzy-headed among
us like themselves ; but they fear the sheukh, and, when they
see I am with thee, *khálas !* there an end of danger."

We walked forth to the great well-pit, where I heard such
voices, of idle young men and Beduins—" Look, here he comes,
look, look, it is the kafir ! will the sheykhs kill him ? is not this he
who has overthrown the haddàj ? Or will they have him build
it again, and give him a reward, and they say it shall be better
than before." Hásan bade me not mind their knavish talk ; and
when we had passed round he left me there, and said that
none would offer me an injury. This butterfly gallant, the
only ornament of whose bird's soul was a gay kerchief of a
real, would not be seen in the kafir's company,—it was not
honest : and where is question of religion, there is no sparkle
of singular courage in these pretended magnanimous, to set
one's face against the faces of many. So I came to some grave
elder men who sat communing together under a wheel-frame :
as I saluted them with peace, they greeted me mildly again ;
I asked would there be any danger in my walking in the
town ? " Doubt nothing, come and go, they said, at thine own
pleasure in all the ways of Teyma, and give no heed to the
ungracious talk of a few blameworthy young men."—The
Shammary was gone with word to " the *Emir ;* " thus he called
the chief sheykh in the town (under Ibn Rashîd), *Khálaf el-
Ammr.*—He (for the Arabs) is Emir, in whom is the word of
command, *amr :* thus, *emir el-kâfila* ruler of an Arabian town-
caravan ; and in arms they say, likewise, ' emir of ten ' and ' emir
of an hundred.' The Beduwy told how he had found me willing,
and he made them this argument, ' Their ancient well is of
the old kafirs' work, and Khalîl is a kafir, therefore could
Khalîl best of all rebuild the haddàj.'

I asked my way to *Aj(k)eyl's* dàr, he had been one of those
Teyma merchant-guests in the kella (before the Haj) at
Medáin. With a sort of friendliness he had then bidden
me, if I came afterward to Teyma, to lodge in his house.
Homely was his speech, and with that bluntness which persuaded me of the man's true meaning. Nevertheless the
Beduins bade me mistrust Ajeyl, " a dark-hearted covetous
fellow that would murder me in his house, for that tháhab "
or metal of money, which Arabians can imagine to be in every
stranger's hold. Zeyd had said to me, " Ajeyl killed his own

brother, in disputing over a piece of silver ! " Therrŷeh added,
" Have a care of him, that certainly Ajeyl is a churl."—Zeyd
said then a good word, " Thou art too simple, Khalîl, if thou hast
not discerned it already, that coveting of money is before all
things in the Aarab : having this in mind, thou wilt not be
deceived ; trust me, it is but upon some hope of winning, if
any man bind himself to further a Nasrâny. It is hard
for thee to pass the distance from hence, to the Ghrenèym
mountain ; but this must thou do,—I tell thee, Khalîl, thou
mayest travel in the Aarab's country only by tóma ; "—that is
in casting back morsels to their sordid avarice.

I went now to see if after his promises I might not lodge
in some room of Ajeyl's house. ' Every place, he answered, is
taken up, but he would speak with his father.'—A young man
of the town led me away to visit his sick mother. In another
large dàr I found the woman lying on the ground far gone in
a vesical disease, which only death could remedy. Thâhir the
householder promised me much for the healing of this old wife,
and would have the hakîm lodge in his house ; but the man
was of such a grim inflamed visage, with a pair of violent eyes,
and let me divine so much of his fanatical meaning (as if
he would have made me a Mosleman perforce), that, with
a civil excuse, I was glad to be abroad again and out of their
neighbourhood.—Another led me to see a dropsical woman
near the haddàj ; the patient was lying (so swollen that those
who entered with me mocked) under a palm, where her friends
had made her an awning. She promised, she would not fail to
pay the hakîm, when he had cured her. In visiting the sick I
desired in my heart to allay their heathenish humour with the
Christian charity ; but I considered that whatso I might do, it
must ever be unavailing, and that it would endanger me to
empty a part of my small stock of medicines ;—my only passport when all else should fail in this hostile country.

A young mother, yet a slender girl, brought her wretched
babe, and bade me spit upon the child's sore eyes ; this ancient
Semitic opinion and custom I have afterwards found wherever
I came in Arabia.—Meteyr nomads in el-Kasîm, have brought
me some of them bread and some salt, that I should spit in it
for their sick friends.—Her gossips followed to make this request
with her, and when I blamed their superstition they answered
simply, that ' such was the custom here from time out of mind.'
—Also the Arabians will spit upon a lock which cannot easily
be opened.

Ajeyl excused himself saying ' a Beduin woman of their
acquaintance had alighted here yesterday, who occupied their

only room, and that to dismiss the guest became not his
beard : yet he would help me, so that I should not be deceived, when I would buy anything in the town.' Nevertheless,
as I bought wheat another day of himself, the sahs which Ajeyl
numbered to me were of short measure.

I thought if I might lodge at Khálaf's, it would be well.
He had spoken of my rebuilding the haddàj ; I might resolve
that simple problem, when I should be a little refreshed,—so to
wall up the great water-pit that it should stand fast, more than
before, and leave them this memorial of a Christian man's
passage ; also the fair report would open the country before me.
Khálaf with the men of his household and certain guests were
sitting crosslegs on the clay bench at his own court door in
the street, whereover was made a rude awning of palm branches,
and silently awaiting the sun's going down, that he might enter
to his evening breakfast. I saw him a'slender tall man of mild
demeanour, somewhat past the middle age ; and have found in
him a tolerant goodness and such liberality of mind as becomes
a sheykh : he was a prudent householder, more than large in
his hospitality. Khálaf's world being this little palm village
in the immense deserts, and Hâyil the village capital, and his
townspeople fewer than the souls in a great ship's company,
yet there appeared in him the perspicuous understanding, and,
without sign of natural rudeness, an easy assured nobility of
manners (of their male society), which may be seen in the best
of nearly all the Arab blood. The Arabs are never barbarous,
they are of purer race than to be brutish ; and if they step from
their Arabian simplicity, into the hive of our civil life (as it is
seen in Bombay), their footing is not less sure than another's,
and they begin by and by to prosper there.

I sat down in his company, and few words were spoken
besides greetings ; they were weak with fasting. When I rose
to be gone he beckoned me friendly to sit still : as the sun was
sinking, Khálaf and they all rising with him, he led me in,
' to drink coffee, the evening, he said, was come.' Within was
his pleasant house-court, the walls I saw decently whitened
with *jîss*, gypsum ; we sat down upon long carpets before the
hearth-pit, whited as well, in the Nejd-wise, and where already
his slave-lad stooped to blow the cheerful flames, and prepared
coffee ;—this, when the sun was gone down, should be their
first refreshment. You will see a bevy of great and smaller
tinned coffee-pots in the Nejd village fire-pits which they use
for old coffee-water store, pouring from one to another. They
sat now, with empty stomachs, watching earnestly the fading
sunlight in the tops of the palm trees, till we heard the welcome

cry of the muétthin praising God, and calling the devout
Moslemîn to their prayers. It is then a pious man may first
put in his mouth a morsel and strengthen himself; the coffee
was immediately served, and as one had drunk the cup, he
went aside, and spreading down his mantle evenly before him
towards the Sanctuary of Mecca, he began to recite the formal
devotion. After prayers there is fetched-in the first night-
meal *futûr* or breakfast; this was, at Khálaf's, bare date-stalks
fresh gathered from the tree. They took their food, though
they had been languishing all day with thirst, without drinking
till the end; and after the dates slices were set before us of a
great ripe but nearly tasteless melon, an autumn kind which
is common at Teyma.

Two young men of Tebûk sat here as guests, clad in their
holiday apparel; they were come to buy Teyma dates in the
harvest. They told me 'there is no well named after Moses
in their hamlet.'—Those poor villagers reckon themselves to
the Beny Sókhr, once masters of so wide a country. Wherefore their poor clan should be called Kaab'ny they could not
tell, "unless it were, of the Kaaba at Mecca." The distance
they reckon all one from them to Wejh, Teyma and Maan,—
five journeys with loaded camels. They draw their rice from
Wejh; but corn and (Syrian) clothing stuffs are better at Maan.
Between Teyma and their village, they told me, is an even
sandy khála with no seyl strands.—That Shammary also sat
down with us, and entertained the company with tales of his
travels; he boasted to be come to a people that worshipped
Sheytàn and The Evil, and he had heard such words spoken
among them: "Let me alone, that I with this lance might rake
down Ullah out of his throne in heaven!" As a Beduin truant
he laughed strangely himself at this blasphemy; and "akhs!
akhs!" answered him the village audience, grinning their teeth
with elvish horror. Later in the evening came in some Fukara,
Weyrid, Jèllowwy ,Feràya, that arrived after us, and they being
men of my friendly acquaintance, we sat coffee-drinking till
late hours. It was not well to go out then in the moonless
night, to seek my Beduin fellowship that had removed I knew
not whither, and I lay down with my arm for a pillow by the
hearth-side to sleep. It seemed to me little past midnight
when the company rose to eat the second night-meal, it was of
dates only,—this is a wretched nourishment; and then the Arabs
lay down anew under the cool stars, till the grey daylight of
the returning fast, when they rose to their prayers. I spoke
to Khálaf, on the morrow, and he said, 'He would give me a
chamber in his house-building, in a day or two:'—but at that

D. T.   34

time, he answered, ' It was a store-room, full of corn, which his housewife said could not be voided at present.'—His superstitious hareem might think it not lucky to harbour the Nasrâny in their dàr.

The open space about the haddàj serves for a public place. Thither come the citizens of the desert town, freshly clad, with their swords in their hands, when the sun descends in the afternoons, to sit upon the clay banks a long hour ; and it is the loitering place of any idle nomad strangers in the oasis. There I oftentimes found a man whom I supposed by his looks to be a sâny : " And have I not, he said, seen thee in Syria ? it was such a year at Keriateyn " (that is the last inhabited place before Palmyra). One day when many came about us, he began to speak of the Nasarene religion ; his tribesmen, he told them, had daily dealings with the Nasâra upon the borders of Syria : " Ye may trust them before all men, and when we are among them, if they see any of us not rise to prayers, they say : *Goom, sully ala dînak ya Musslim : goom yâ ! sull !* ' Up, Moslem, and call upon the Lord after thy religion ; to the prayer, man, go pray ! ' and else wot well they will not . trust us." This nomad touched then, with a word of understanding, the insociable nature of those twin bodies of religious faith. Said he, " It is a little thing that divides us ; they believe in Ullah and the prophets, only they account not Mohammed to be a prophet of Ullah : for all the old prophets, say they, have been of the blood of Beny Israel, but Mohammed is from without, and not one of the stock of the prophets." And saying again they were good folk, he repeated that common Mohammedan word, ' Sup with the Jew (when thou comest in a country where the unbelievers be) but sleep under the roof of the Nasrâny.' This man was come down two years before in a company of his poor Annezy tribesmen, es-Sbáa, whose wandering ground stretches in the northern Syrian dîras toward Aleppo. His tribe were of the old Annezy inheritance at Kheybar, and—the Beduin landowner's rights, although long forsaken, are inalienable—they had come to wander in the south with Bishr, that they might eat of their own palms at Kheybar : they were now about returning to Syria, and he invited me to go up along with them.

Another stranger whom I found living in the town was from el-Ally, Selím, a banished man for homicide, yet every year he received his own fruits from thence. Some day, as we were speaking in Ajeyl's yard, *Greyth*, father of Ajeyl, a fanatic of sour embittered blood, began to insist with me, that the Nasâra were " uncle's sons (tribesmen) of the Yahûd."—" Why this

malevolence, O Abu Ajeyl, only for my name of another religion !
consider man, am I not born in it by the will of heaven ? but if
thou canst show me that your religion can make a man better
than mine, then I will become a Mosleman. We are not Jews,
but ye, believe me, who are ignorant of these things, are of one
stock, of one parentage, and one tongue—with whom ? I say with
the Yahûd." Greyth winced ; I turned to the half negro Selím,
a lettered man, and he testified for me out of their scriptures,
dividing the descents from the fathers of the new world, Sem,
Ham, Yâfet.

There was a young smith *Seydàn* who sought me out ; and
many an Arabian sâny imagined he might learn a mastery
of the Nasrâny, since from us they suppose the arts to spring
and all knowledge. When a lad he had come with his family,
footing it over the deserts two hundred miles from Hâyil
his birth-place, to settle at Teyma. He was one of those
who last winter passed by the kella of Medáin to el-Ally. I
entered their workshop to bespeak a steel to strike fire with the
flint,—a piece of gear of great price in the poor desert life,
where so cheerful is the gipsy fire of sweet-smelling bushes :—
there is a winter proverb of the poor in Europe, " Fire is half
bread ! " Their steel is a band of four inches, which is made
two inches, the ends being drawn backward upon itself. When
he had beat out the piece, the long sunlight was low in
the west. " We may not all day labour, said the young smith,
in Ramathán ; " and rising, with a damp clout he wiped his
honest smutched face, and as he shut up the shop he invited
me home to drink coffee in his dàr. He led me round by the
way, to see some inscription that was in a neighbour's house.
There I found a few great antique embossed letters upon the
threshold of dark bluish limestone, in the kind which I had
found before at Teyma. [*Doc. Epigr.* pl. xxvii.] The smith's
house was the last in going out of the town beyond Khálaf's,
small, but well-built of clay bricks. The former year he and
his brother had made it with their own hands upon a waste
plot next the wilderness, and in Hâyil wise ; they thought but
meanly of the Teyma architecture.

Another time he brought me a little out of the town (yet
within the walls) eastward, to see some great antique pillars.
We came to a field of two acres, wherein stands their great
clay-built mesjid. I saw certain huge chapiters, lying there,
and drums of smooth columns, their thickness might be twenty-
seven inches, of some bluish limestone, and such as there
is none (I believe) in a great circuit about. The sculpture is

34—2

next to naught ; we found not any inscription. These mighty
stones have not, surely, been transported upon the backs of
camels. I thought this might be the temple site of ancient
Teyma ; and wonderful are such great monuments to look upon
in that abandonment of human arts and death of nature which
is now in Arabia ! A stranger in these countries should not be
seen to linger about ruins, and we returned soon.

Seydàn was telling me great things by the way of Hâyil : he
supposed his Arabian town (nearly three thousand souls), for
the well-purveyed sûks, the many dàrs of welfaring persons,
the easy civil life and the multitude of persons, who go by
shoals in the public place, and the great mesjid able to receive
them all, should be as much as es-Sham [Damascus, 130,000] !
We sought further by the town and through the grave-yard,
looking (in vain) upon all headstones for more antique inscriptions. There was one till lately seen upon a lintel in Ajeyl's
camel yard, but it had fallen and was broken, and the pieces they
told us could no more be found ; also a long inscription was on
a stone of the haddàj walls, which were fallen down. [Since
writing these words in 1879 the haddàj inscription has been
seen by Huber and the learned epigraphist Euting some years
after me. Euting supposes the inscription, which is dedicatory,
and in the same Aramaic letters as the other inscriptions
which I found at Teyma, may be of four or five centuries
before Jesus Christ.]

Sometimes in these Ramathán half days we walked a mile
over the desert to an uncle of his, who with the gain of his
smith's labour had bought a good *hauta* (orchard) in · the
Ghrerb, or outlying little west oasis. When we came thither
the sâny, who would have me cure his· son's eyes, fetched
lemons and pomegranates, and leaving me seated under his
fruit-tree shadows, they went in to labour at the anvil, which
the goodman had here in his house in the midst of his
homestead. One day the young smith, who thought vastly
of these petty hospitalities, said to me, " Khalîl ! if I were come
to your country wouldst thou kill a sheep for me, and give
me somewhat in money, and a maiden to wife ? " I said,
' I would not kill any beast, we buy our meat in the market-
place ; I would give him money if he were in want ; and he
might have a wife if he would observe our law ; he should find
that welcome in my dàr which became his worth and my honour.'
We sat at Khálaf's ; and the young smith answered ; " See what
men of truth and moderation in their words are the Nasâra !
Khalîl might have promised now—as had one of us—many
gay things, but he would not." To reward Seydàn I could but

show him the iron-stone veins of the desert about ; he wondered
to hear that in such shales was the smith's metal ;—but how
now to melt it ! Their iron, which must be brought in over
the desert five or six hundred miles, upon camels, from the
coast, is dear-worth in Arabia.

Teyma oasis is three (*v.* the fig. p. 287) : the main, lying in
the midst, is called of the Haddàj ; outlying from the two ends
are *es-Sherg* and *el-Ghrcrb*, the " east and west hamlets," and
these are watered only from wells of the ancients which have
been found from time to time. In all of them, as the " man of
medicine," I had friends and acquaintance, especially in the
Sherg ; and whereso I entered, they spread the guest-carpet
under some shadowing greenness of palms or fig-trees : then
the householder brought the stranger a cooling cucumber or
date-stalks, and they bade me repose whilst they went about
their garden labour.—Cheerful is the bare Arabic livelihood in
the common air, which has sufficiency in few things snatched
incuriously as upon a journey ! so it is a life little full of superfluous cares. Their ignorance is not brutish, their poverty is
not baseness. But rude are their homes ; and with all the
amorous gentleness of their senses, they have not learned to
cherish a flower for the sweetness and beauty, or to desire
the airy captivity of any singing bird.

Shâfy, one among them, led me out one morrow ere the sun
was risen (that we might return before the heat), to visit some
antique inscription in the desert. When we had walked a mile
he asked me if I were a good runner.—" Though (he said) I
am past my youth, I may yet outrun a thelûl and take her ;
see thou if I am nimble," and he ran from me. While he
was out there came one with the ganna or Arab
club-stick in his hand ; and from Teyma a horseman sallied
to meet me. I began to wish that I had not gone to this length
unarmed. Those were men from the Sherg, though they seemed
Beduins, who came to see whether we found any treasures.
The rider with a long lance came galloping a strange crippling
pace ; and now I saw that this mare went upon three legs ! her
fourth was sinew-tied. The rest laughed, but said the cavalier
Atullah, ' his mare was of the best blood, billah, and he was thus
early abroad to breathe her ; she bred him every year a good
filly or a foal.' The inscription was but a rude scoring in
Arabic. Atullah, a prosperous rich man and bountiful householder, would have us return with him. His orchard grounds
were some of the best in Teyma : and besides this fortune he
had lighted lately upon the mouth of an ancient well nigh his

place, in the desert. The welfaring man brought me a large
basket of best fruits, and bade me return often.

Where I walked round the oasis I found some little rude
buildings of two or three courses of stones, thatched with sticks
and earth. They are gunners' shrouds, that may contain a man
lying along upon his breast. At a loop in the end his gun is
put forth, and a little clay pan is made there without, to be
filled, by the hareem, before the sun, with two or three girbies
of water. The wild birds, wheeling in the height of the air and
seeing glistering of water, stoop thither to drink from great distances ; their gun is loaded with very small stones. Commonly
five birds are killed from such a kennel, ere the half-afternoon,
when the villagers, that are not labourers, go home to coffee
and think the busy-idle day is done : I have seen nearly all their
dead birds were buzzards and falcons and the rákham, in a word
only birds of prey,—and yet it is seldom one may perceive
them riding aloft in the desert. I asked of some " Do you eat
these puttocks ? "—" We eat them, ay billah, for what else
should we shoot them ? if they be not very good meat, it is the
best we may take ; and what we would not eat ourselves we may
cast to the hareem, for the hareem anything is good enough."
—The Teyâmena are blamed for eating vile birds ; most
nomads would loathe to eat them. So the answer was easy
when Arabians have cast it in my beard that the Nasâra eat
swine's flesh. " If God have commanded you anything, keep it ;
I see you eat crows and kites, and the lesser carrion eagle.
Some of you eat owls, some eat serpents, the great lizard you
all eat, and locusts, and the spring-rat ; many eat the hedgehog,
in certain (Hejâz) villages they eat rats, you cannot deny it !
you eat the wolf too, and the fox and the foul hyena, in a
word, there is nothing so vile that some of you will not eat."
These young villagers' pastime is much in gunning. They
pace with their long guns in the sunny hours, in all the
orchard ways, and there is no sparrow sitting upon a leaf that
possesseth her soul in peace. You hear their shots around
you, and the soft singing of their balls over your head. Here
also in the time they strike down certain migratory birds. I
have seen small white and crested water-fowl, and a crane,
saady, shot at this season in their plantations ; the weary
birds had lighted at the pools of irrigation water. The Arabs
think these passing fowl come to them from the watered
Mesopotamia (four hundred miles distant). In the spring they
will return upwards. Being at Tôr, the Sinai coast village,
in March 1875, I saw a flight, coming in from the seaward, of

great white birds innumerable,—whether storks or rákhams
I cannot tell ; they passed overhead tending northward.

When certain of the town were offended with the Nasrâny
because I kept not their fast, others answered for me, " But why
should we be hard on him, when billah the half of the Beduw fast
not, whom we grant to be of el-Islam ; Khalîl is born in another
way of religion, and they keep other times of fasting. Are not
en-Nasâra the people of the Enjîl, which is likewise Word of
Ullah, although now annulled by the koran *el-furkân.*"—In the
Medina country I heard their book, besides *furkân* (' the reading which separates the people of God from the worldly ignor
ance '), named more commonly " The Seal," *el-khátm,* a word
which they extended also, for simplicity, to any book ; for they
hardly know other than books of the religion. As I walked
about the town some from their house doors bade me come in ;
and, whilst I sat to speak with them, dates were put before me ;
—yet first to satisfy their consciences they asked, " Art thou a
musâfir (traveller) ? "

Méhsan, Sâlih, and our nomad households' booths were now
pitched in an orchard field of Féjr's, my host in the spring, when
with Zeyd I had visited Teyma. The camels being in the wilderness, they had removed upon asses borrowed of their acquaintance ; and commonly if one speak for an ass in the Arabian
villages (though no hire will be asked) it is not denied him.
[Comp. Matt. xxi. 2, 3 ; Mark xi. 2—6 ; Lu. xix. 30—34.] In
this hauta at the walls of the oasis I pitched my little tent
with them. Here were corn plots, and a few palm trees full of
fruit ; yet the nomads and their children will not put forth
their hand to the dates which are not fallen from the trees.
Méhsan, when his last real was spent, knew not how longer to
live ;—these are the yearly extremities of all poorer Beduins !
They must go knock at men's doors in the market village, to
see ' who will show them any good ' and lend them at thirty in
the hundred above the market price, till their next tide, which
is here of the haj surra. Méhsan purchased upon credence the
fruit of a good date tree in our field to satisfy his children's
hunger this month ; and when they were hungry they climbed
to the palm top to eat.

Méhsan was a sickly man, and very irksome was the fast,
which divided our Beduins all day from their galliûns and even
from the water-skin ; they slumbered under the palms from the
rising sun, only shifting themselves as the shadows wore round
till the mid-afternoon. The summer heat was not all past, I
found most mid-days 97° Fahrenheit under the palm-leaf awn-

ings of the coffee-courts of Teyma houses. At noon the fasting
Beduins wakened to rehearse their formal prayers, when they
feel a little relief in the ceremonial washing of the hands, fore-
arms and feet with water—which they need not spare in the oasis
—and to cool their tongue ; for taking water into the mouth
they spout it forth with much ado again.   Coming to themselves at vespers, they assembled after their prayers under
the high western wall, which already cast the evening shadow,
there to play at the game of *beatta*, which may be called a
kind of draughts ; the field is two rows of seven holes each,
beyts, which in the settled countries are made in a piece of
timber, *múngola ;* but with these nomads and in the Hejâz
villages they are little pits in the earth.   I have not seen this
playing in Nejd, where all their light pastimes were laid down
in the Waháby reformation, as dividing men's souls from the
meditation of The Living God.   In every hole are seven stones ;
the minkala was the long summer game of Haj Nejm in the
kella at Medáin, and these Beduins had been his patient playfellows.   "Ay wellah (said the old man Sâlih), Haj Nejm is
min ashîraty, as mine own tribesman."   Instead of the clear
pebbles of the Héjr plain (which are carried even to Damascus),
they took up bullets of camel-dung, *jella,*—naming their pieces
gaûd (camel foals), and the like.   I never saw right Arabians
play to win or lose anything ;—nay certes they would account
one an impious sot who committed that (God-given) good
which is in his hand to an uncertain adventure.   We saw
carders at el-Ally and shall see them at Kheybar, but these are
villages of the Hejâz infected from the Holy Cities.—Galla
slaves have told me that the minkala game is used in their
country, and it is doubtless seen very wide in the world.

Who had the most pain in this fast ? Surely Méhsan's
sheykhly wife with a suckling babe at her breast ; for with a
virile constancy Zeyd's sister kept her Lent, neither drinking nor
eating until the long going-down of the sun. For this I heard
her commended by women of the town,—' her merit was much
to admire in a simple Beduish creature ! ' Even religious women
with child fast and fulfil the crude dream of their religion,
to this they compel also their young children. She was a good
woman, and kind mother, a strenuous housewife, full of affectionate service and sufferance to the poor man her husband ;
her's was a vein like Zeyd's, betwixt earnest and merry, of the
desert humanity.   The poor man's sheykhly wife was full of
children ; which, though the fruitful womb be God's foison
amongst them, had made his slender portion bare, for their
cattle were but five camels and half a score of dubbush, be-

sides the worsted booth and utensils :—hardly £60 worth in all.
Therefore Méhsan's livelihood must be chiefly of the haj surra.
Because he was an infirm man to bear the churlish looks of
fortune, he snibbed them early and late, both wife and children,
but she took all in wifely patience. There is among them no
complaining of outrageous words (not being biting injuries as
ent kelb, ' thou an hound ! ') ; such in . a family and betwixt
kindred and tribesmen have lost the sound of malevolence in
their ears. Now this child,—now he would cry down that, with
" Subbak ! the Lord rip up thy belly, curse that face ! " or his
wife, not in an instant answering to his call, he upbraided as a
Solubbîa, gipsy woman, or *bàghrila,* she-mule (this beast they
see at the kellas) ; and then he would cry frenetically, *Inhaddem
beytich,* the Lord undo thee, or *Ullah yafúkk'ny minch,* the Lord
loose me from thee ! and less . conveniently, " Wellah some
bondman shall know thee ! " But commonly a nomad father
will entreat his son, if he would have him do aught, as it
were one better than himself, and out of his correction. When
he had chided thus and checked all the household as undutiful
to him, Méhsan would revert to the smiling-eyed and musing
nomad benevolence with us his friends.

A light wind rising breathed through our trees,—first
bathing, after the many summer months' long heat, our languishing bodies ! We were thus refreshed now the most afternoons, and the sun rose no more so high ; the year went over
to the autumn. At the sun's going down, if anyone had invited us, we walked together into the town ; or when we had
supped we went thither " seeking coffee " and where with friendly
talk we might pass an evening. The tent-lazing Beduins are
of softer humour than the villagers inured to till the stubborn
metal of the soil, with a daily diligence :—the nomads surpass
them in sufferance of hunger and in the long journey. As we
sit one will reach his galliûn to another, and he says, *Issherub
wa keyyif rás-ak,* Drink ! and make thy head dream with
pleasance. All that is genial solace to the soul and to the
sense is *keyyif,*—the quietness after trouble, repose from labour,
a beautiful mare or thelûl, the amiable beauty of a fair woman.

Some nights if any nomad weleds visited us, our hauta
resounded, as the wilderness, with their harsh swelling song,
to the long-drawn bass notes of the rabeyby. I asked, " What
think ye then of the Emir's letter ? " [his injunction to the
Teyâmena to put away the viol.] *Answer ;* " Ibn Rashîd may
command the villagers, but we are the Beduw ! "—As this was
a great war-time, their thoughts fell somewhiles upon that
jehâd which was now between Nasâra and Islam. A Beduwy

arriving from Jauf brought in false tidings,—' The Sooltàn of
the Moslemîn had sallied from Stambûl, to take the field, and
the lately deposed Murâd marched forth with him, bearing the
banner of the Prophet ! '—" But wot well (sighed Méhsan) whenever it may be at the worst for el-Islam, that the conquering
enemies *shall be repulsed at the houses of hair !* [the religion of
the Apostle shall be saved by the Beduw.] Wellah *wakid !* it
is well ascertained, this is written in the book ! "—also the
poor man was recomforted since this end of miseries was foretold
to the honour of the Aarab.   I said, " Yet for all your boasting
ye never give a crown, nor send an armed man for the service
of the Sooltàn ! "—" What need, they answered, could the [mag-
nific] Sooltàn have of us *mesakín* (mesquins) ? "

Sometimes the Beduw questioned me of our fasting ; I told
them the Nasâra use to fast one day in the week, and they
keep a Lenten month ; some observe two or even more.—" And
what is their fasting ?—till the going down of the sun ? "—
" Not thus, but they abstain frcm flesh meat, and some of them
from all that issues from the flesh, as milk and eggs, eating only
the fruit of the ground, as bread, salads, oil of olive, and the
like ;—in the time of abstinence they may eat when they will."
" Ah-ha-ha ! but call you this to fast ? nay wellah, Khalîl ! you
laugh and jest ! "—" But they think it a fasting diet, ' as the
death,' in those plentiful countries,—to eat such weak wretchedness and poor man's victuals."—" God is Almighty !   Well, that
were a good fasting !—and they cried between wonder and
laughter—Oh that the Lord would give us thus every day
to fast ! "

CHAPTER XX.

THE DATE HARVEST.

Damsels to wed. Fair women. The people of Teyma untaught. Their levity noted by the Beduins. The well camels. Labourers at the ruined haddàj. Beduins swimming in the haddàj. Project to rebuild the haddàj. Ibn Rashîd's Resident. Ibn Rashîd a Hâkim el-Aarab. *The Medina government cast their eyes upon Teyma. Unreasonable patients. Oasis ophthalmia. The evil eye. Exorcism. Zelots in Ramathán. The ruined site of Mosaic Teyma. Reported necropolis of antique Teyma with inscriptions. The seven ancient boroughs of this province. A new well-ground. African slave-blood in the Peninsula. The Arabian bondage is mild. Ramathán ended, Bairam festival. A whistler. The music of Damascus. The Fukara arrive. Beduins of Bishr flocking into the town. The date-gathering. An Harb dancing woman. Misshel's words. Better news of the Moahîb. The visit of Hamed and Wâyil to Ibn Rashîd. Nomad butchers. Méhsan's petition. The "wild ox" or wothýhi. The ancient archery. The Aarab friends are slow to further the Nasrány's voyage. The Bishr at Teyma. An Heteymy sheykh. Dispute with Zeyd's herdsman. Last evening at Teyma. Zeyd.*

In the field, where we dwelt, I received my patients. Here I found the strangest adventure. A young unwedded woman in Teyma, hearing that the stranger was a Dowlâny, or government man, came to treat of marriage: she gave tittun to Méhsan's wife and promised her more only to bring this match about ; my hostess commended her to me as ' a fair young woman and well-grown ; her eyes, billah, egg-great, and she smelled of nothing but ambergris.' The kind damsel was the daughter of a Damascene (perhaps a kella keeper) formerly in this country, and she disdained therefore that any should be her mate of these heartless villagers or nomad people. We have seen all the inhabitants of the Arabian countries contemned in the speech of the border-country dwellers as " Beduw," —and they say well, for be not all the Nejd Arabians (besides the smiths) of the pure nomad lineage ? The Shâmy's daughter resorted to Méhsan's tent, where, sitting in the woman's apartment and a little aloof she might view the white-skinned man from her father's countries ;—I saw then her pale face and not very fair eyes, and could conjecture by her careful voice and countenance—Arabs have never any happy opinion of present things,—that she was loath to live in this place, and would fain escape with an husband, one likely to be of good faith and kind ; which things she heard to be in the Nasâra. When it was told her I made but light of her earnest matter, the poor maiden came no more ; and left me to wonder what could have moved her lonely young heart : ' Her mind had been, she said, to become the wife of a Dowlâny.'

Some of the Teyâmena bade me remain and dwell among them, ' since I was come so far hither from my country '—it seemed to them almost beyond return,—and say *La îlah ill' Ullah wa Mohammed rasûl Ullah.* They would bestow upon me a possession, such as might suffice for me and mine when I was a wedded man. But seeing an indifferent mind in me, " Ha ! he has reason, they said, is not their flesh better than ours ? the Nasâra have no diseases,—their hareem are fairer in his eyes than the daughters of Islam : besides, a man of the Nasâra may not wed except he have slain a Moslem ; he is to bathe himself in the blood, and then he shall be reputed purified." But others answered, " We do not believe this ; Khalîl denies it : " one added, " Have we not heard from some who were in the north, that no kind of wedlock is known amongst them ? " I answered, " This, O thou possessed by a jin ! is told of the Druses ; your lips all day drop lewdness, but a vile and unbecoming word is not heard amongst them."—" The Druses, quoth he ? Ullah ! is not that the name of the most pestilent adversaries of el-Islam ?—Well, Khalîl, we allow all you say, and further, we would see thee well and happy ; take then a wife of those they offer you, and you will be the more easy, having someone of your own about you : and whenever you would you may put her away."—" But not in the religion of the Messîh." —" Yet there is a good proverb, It is wisdom to fall in with the manner, where a man may be."

When they said to me, " We have a liberty to take wives and to put them away, which is better than yours : " the answer was ready, " God gave to Adam one wife ; " and they silently wondered in themselves that the Scriptures seemed to make against them.—There was another young woman of some Dowlâny father in the town ; and as I sat one day in the smith's forge she came in to speak with us : and after the first word she enquired very demurely if I would wed with her. *Seydàn :* " It is a fair proffer, and thou seest if the woman be well-looking ! she is a widow, Khalîl, and has besides two young sons : "—Seydàn would say, ' also the boys shall be a clear gain to thee,' and like as when in buying a mare the foal is given in with her.'—" Shall I marry thee alone, mistress, or thee and thy children ? Come I will give thee a friend of mine, this proper young man ; or wouldest thou have the other yonder, his brother, a likely fellow too if his face were not smutched." But the young widow woman a little in disdain : " Thinkest thou that I would take any sâny (artificer) for my husband ! "

The fairest of women in the town were Féjr our host's wife —fair but little esteemed, " because her hand was not liberal "— and another the daughter of one Ibrahîm an Egyptian, banishing himself at Teyma, for danger of his country's laws or of some private talion. One day I was sitting on the benches when the stately virgin came pacing to us, with a careless grace of nature ; I marked then her frank and pleasant upland looks, without other beauty : the bench-sitters were silent as she went by them, with their lovely eye-glances only following this amiable vision. One of them said, as he fetched his breath again, " You saw her, Khalîl ! it is she of whom the young men make songs to chant them under her casement in the night-time ; where didst thou see the like till now ? Tell. us what were she worth, that one, happy in possessing much, might offer to her father for the bride money ? " *Ibrahîm el-Misry* had lived some years at Teyma, he dealt in dates to the Beduins ; he was from the Delta, and doubtless had seen the Europeans ; if he were seated before his coffee-door, and I went by, he rose to greet me. Some day when he found me poring in a book of geography at Khálaf's, I turned the leaf, and read forward of that river country ; and he heard with joy, after many years, the names of his own towns and villages, often staying me to amend my utterance from the skeleton Arabic writing. Said some who came in, " Is Khalîl *kottîb !* (*lit.* a scribe) a man who knows letters." Khálaf answered, " He can read as well as any of us ; " the sheykh himself read slowly spelling before him :—and what should their letters profit them ? The sheykh of the religion reads publicly to all the people in the mosque on Fridays, out of the koran ; and he is their lawyer and scrivener of simple contracts,—and besides these, almost no record remains in the oases : they cannot speak certainly of anything that was done before their grandfathers' days.

Abd el-Azîz er-Român, sheykh of one of the three sûks, was unlettered ; there was no school in Teyma, and the sons must take up this learning from their fathers. Some young men of the same sheykhly family told me they had learned as far as the letters of the alphabet,—they made me hear them say their *álef, ba, ta, tha, jîm*—but come thus far in schooling,

they *yakub-hu,* cast it down again : they might not cumber
their quick spirits, or bind themselves to this sore constraint of
learning. Every morrow the sun-shiny heat calls them abroad
to the easy and pleasant and like to an holiday labour of their
simple lives. Learning is but a painful curiosity to the Arabs,
which may little avail them,—an ornament bred of the yawning
superfluity of welfaring men's lives. These Shammar villagers
are commonly of the shallowest Arabian mind, without fore-wit,
without after-wit ; and in the present doing of a plain matter,
they are suddenly at their wits' end. Therefore it is said of
them " the Teyâmena are juhâl, untaught, not understanding
the time." The Annezy say this saw, " *Es-Shammar, ayûnu-
hum humr,*—of the red eyes ; they will show a man hospitality, yet the stranger is not safe amongst them ; " but this is
no more than the riming proverbs which may be heard in all
the tribes of their neighbours.

These townsmen's heartless levity and shrewish looseness of
the tongue is noted by the comely Beduw. Teyma is not
further spoken of in Arabia for their haddàj, than for that
uncivil word, which they must twitter at every turn, " The devil
is in it, *iblîs! iblîs!* "—as thus : " This child does not hear
me, *iblîs!* dost thou disobey me ? *iblîs!* What is this broken,
lost, spoiled, thing done amiss ? It is the devil, *iblîs! iblîs!* "
So, at anything troublesome, they will cry out " alack ! and
iblîs! " It is a lightness of young men's lips, and of the women
and children ; their riper men of age learn to abstain from the
unprofitable utterance. When I have asked wherefore they
used it, they answered, " And wast thou two years at Teyma,
thou couldst not choose but say it thyself ! " I found the
lighter nomad women, whilst they stayed at Teyma, became
infected with this infirmity, they babbled among many words,
the unbecoming *iblîs ;* but the men said scornfully, " This
iblîs, now in the mouths of our hareem, will hardly be heard
beyond the first ráhla ; their *iblîs* cannot be carried upon the
backs of camels, *henna el-Beduw!* "—The strong contagion
of a false currency* in speech we must needs acknowledge
with " harms at the heart " in some land where we are not
strangers !—where after Titanic births of the mind there remains
to us an illiberal remissness of language which is not known in
any barbarous nation.—Foul-mouthed are the Teyâmena, because
evil-minded ; and the nomads say, " If we had anything to set
before the guest, wellah the Beduins were better than they : "
and, comparing the inhabitants of el-Ally and Teyma, " Among
the Alowna, they say, are none good, and all the Teyâmena are
of a corrupt heart."—Their building is high and spacious at

Teyma, their desert is open, whereas everything is narrow and straitness at el-Ally.

The building up again (*towwy*) of the haddàj was for the time abandoned: forty-four wheels remained standing, which were of the other two sheykhs' quarters. Khálaf and those of his sûk whose side was fallen, wrought upon the other sûks' suânies in by-hours, when the owners had taken off their well-teams. The well nâgas, for they are all females—the bull camel, though of more strength, they think should not work so smoothly and is not so soon taught—are put to the draught-ropes in the third hour after midnight, and the shrieking of all the running well-wheels in the oasis awakens the (Beduin) marketing strangers with discomfort out of their second sleep. The Teyma housewives bring in baskets of provender, from the orchards, for their well camels, about sun-rising; it is that corn straw, sprinkled down with water, which is bruised small in treading out the grain, and, with which they have mingled leaves of gourds and melons and what green stuff they find. Though such forage would be thought too weak in Kasîm, the camels lose little flesh, and the hunch, which is their health, is well maintained; and sometimes a feed is given them in this season of the unripe date berries. Good camels are hired by the month from the nomads, for an hundred measures of dates each beast, that is five reals.—Their sweet-smelling fodder is laid to the weak labouring brutes in an earthen manger, made at the bottom of every well-walk. Thus the nâgas when they come down in their drawing, can take up a mouthful as they wend to go upward. They are loosed before nine, the sun is then rising high, and stay to sup water in the *suryân* (running channels),—a little, and not more, since labouring in the oasis they drink daily: they are driven then to their yards and unharnessed; there they lie down to rest, and chew the cud, and the weary teamsters may go home to sleep awhile. The draught-ropes of the camel harness are of the palm fibre, rudely twisted by the well-drivers, in all the oases; —and who is there in Arabia that cannot expeditely make a thread or a cable, rolling and wrapping between his palms the two strands? To help against the fretting of the harsh ropes upon their galled nâgas, the drivers envelop them with some list of their old cotton clothing. At two in the afternoon the camels are driven forth again to labour, and they draw till the sun-setting, when it is the time of prayers, and the people go home to sup. They reckon it a hard lot to be a well-driver, and break the night's rest,—when step-mother Nature rocks us again in her nourishing womb and the builder

brain solaces with many a pageant the most miserable of
mankind,—and hours which in comparison of the daylight,
are often very cold. They are the poorest young men of the
village, without inheritance, and often of the servile condition,
that handle the well-ropes, and who have hired themselves to
this painful trade.

Later I saw them set up two wheel frames at the ruined
border of the haddàj, and men laboured half days with camels to
dig and draw up baskets of the fallen stones and earth. Seeing
the labourers wrought but weakly in these fasting days, I said
to a friend, " This is slack work." He answered, " Their work is
fâsid, corrupt, and naught worth."—" Why hire you not poor
Beduins, since many offer themselves ? "—" This is no labour
of Beduins, they are too light-headed, and have little enduring
to such work."

Khálaf, Hásan and Salâmy, the sheykhs of the sûk, sent for
their thelûls (which are always at pasture with the nomads in
the desert) : they would ride with Beduin radîfs to Hâyil, and
speak to the Emir for some remission of taxes until they might
repair the damage. Villager passengers in the summer heat
yugáillûn, alight in every journey for ' nooning,' where they may
find shadow. The sheykhs fasted not by the way—they were
musâfirs, though in full Ramathán : villagers pass in seven days
thelûl riding to J. Shammar,—it is five Beduin journeys.

The well side fallen, one might go down in it, so did many
(the most were Beduins), to bathe and refresh themselves in
these days. That is the only water to drink, but the Arabs
are less nice in this than might be looked for : I felt the
water tepid even in that summer heat. There remains very
little in the haddàj walls of the ancient masonry, which has
fallen from time to time, and been renewed with new pans
of walling, rudely put up. The old stone-laying is excellent,
but not cemented. In the west walling they showed me a
double course of great antique masonry ; and where one stone
is wanting, they imagine to be the appearance of a door,
" where the hareem descended to draw water in the times of
Jewish Teyma." As I was at the bottom, some knavish children
cast down stones upon the Nasrâny. Oftentimes I saw Beduins
swimming there, and wondered at this watercraft in men of the
dry deserts ; they answered me, " We learned to swim, O stranger,
at Kheybar, where there are certain tarns in the Harra borders,
as you go down to the W. el-Humth," that is by the *Tubj* : they
were tribesmen of Bishr.

I had imagined, if those sheukh would trust me in it, how
the haddàj might be rebuilt : but since they were ridden to

Hâyil, the work must lie until their coming again. In their former building the villagers had loosely heaped soil from the backward ; but I would put in good dry earth and well rammed ; or were this too much enlarging the cost I thought that the rotten ground mixed with gravel grit might be made lighter, and binding under the ram likely to stand. The most stones of their old walling were rude ; I would draw some camel-loads of better squared blocks from the old town ruins. And to make the new walls stand, I thought to raise them upon easy curves, confirmed against the thrust by tie-walls built back, as it were roots in the new ground, and partings ending as knees toward the water. I confided that the whole thus built would be steadfast, even where the courses must be laid without mortar. That the well-building might remain (which I promised them) an hundred years after me, I devised to shore all the walling with a frame of long palm-beams set athwart between their rights and workings.—But I found them lukewarm, as Arabs, and suspicious upon it, some would ascertain from me how I composed the stones, that the work should not slide ; they enquired ' if I were a mason, or had I any former experience of stone-building ? ' and because I stood upon no rewards, and would be content with a thelûl saddled, they judged it to be of my insufficiency, and that should little avail them.

Upon a clay bench by the haddàj sat oftentimes, in the afternoons, Ibn Rashîd's officer or *mutasállim*, and in passing I saluted him, friendly, but he never responded. One day sitting down near him,—he was alone, for no man desired Saîd's company,—" What ails thee ? I said, thou art deaf, man, or dost thou take me for an enemy ? " Saîd, who sat with his slow-spirited swelling solemnity, unbent a little, since he could not escape me, that dangerous brow, and made his excuses : ' Well, he had been in Egypt, and had seen some like me there, and—no, he could not regard me as an enemy ; the Engleys also *yuháshimûn* (favour) the Sûltàn el-Islam.' The great man asked me now quite familiarly, " Tell me, were the ancients of this town Yahûd or Nasâra ? "—" For anything I can tell they were like this people !—I showed him the many kerchiefed and mantled Arabs that went loitering about the well—Yahûdies, billah." Saîd shrewdly smiled, he might think the stranger said not amiss of the Teyâmena.—The sum of all I could learn (enquiring of the Arabs) of Ibn Rashîd's custom of government is this : ' He makes them sure that may be won by gifts, he draws the sword against his adversaries, he treads them down that fear him ; ' and the nomads say, " He were no right *Hâkim* (ruler), and he hewed no heads off."

Though hard things be said of the Ruler by some of the nomads, full of slipping and defection, one may hear little or no lamenting in the villages. The villagers think themselves well enough, because justly handled.

When Kheybar was occupied, the Turkish government of Medina had a mind to take Teyma.—The year before this a squadron of Ageyl, with infantry and a field-piece, had been sent from thence upon a secret expedition to the north ; it was whispered they went to occupy Teyma : but when the soldiery had made two marches a new order recalled them, and they wheeled again for Kheybar. It was believed that the great ones in Medina had been bought off, in time, with a bribe from Hâyil. The Turks love silver, and to be well mounted ; and the Shammar " *Súltàn el-Aarab* " is wont to help himself with them in both kinds ; he fishes with these Turkish baits in the apostle's city. The Teyâmena live more to their minds under the frank Nejd government ; they would none of your motley Turkish rule of Medina, to be made dogs under the churlish tyranny of the Dowla.—It was affirmed to me by credible persons, that a stranger who visited Teyma few years before, had been afterward waylaid in the desert and slain, by order of Khálaf, because they guessed him to be a spy of the Dowla ! The poor man was murdered, lest he should bring the ugly Dowla upon them ; I heard among the Fukara ' he was *abd*, a negro.'

I could not thrive in curing the sick at Teyma ; they who made great instance to-day for medicines will hardly accept them to-morrow with a wretched indifference ; the best of them can keep no precept, and are impatient to swallow up their remedies. *Dareyem*, one of the sheykhs, was dropsical ; his friends were very earnest with me for him. Coming home heated from a Friday noon prayer, before Ramathán, he had drunk a cold draught from the girby ; and from that time he began to swell. I mixed him cream of tartar, which he drank and was the better, but soon began to neglect it, ' because in seven nights I had not cured him,' and he refused to take more. I said to the friends, " I suppose then he may hardly live a year or two ! "—but now they heard this with a wonderful indifference, which made my heart cold. " The death and the life, they answered, are in the hands of Ullah ! " There came others to me, for their eyes ; but they feared to lay out sixpence or two pottles of dates for the doctor's stuff, and some of them, because they had not received it for a gift, went home cursing me. Nomads in the village resorted to the hakîm more frankly, and with better faith, for the old cough, aching in the bones, their many intestinal diseases,—the mischiefs of the desert ; and Annezy tribesmen, for the throbbing ague-cake of Kheybar.

In the month of Lent a kind of rheumatic ophthalmia is rife ; the cause of it (which may hardly be imagined in countries of a better diet) is the drinking of cold water to bedward, as it is chilled in the girbies ; and perhaps they slept abroad or uncovered, and the night's chill fell upon them towards morning, when they are in danger to waken with the rime about their swollen eyelids. The course of the disease is ten days with a painful feeling in the nearly closed eyes of dust and soreness, and not without danger of infiltration under the cornea of an opaque matter ; and so common is this malady in the Nejd settlements, that amongst three persons, there is commonly some one purblind. Ophthalmia is a besetting disease of all the Arab blood, and in this soil even of strangers : we see the Gallas suffer thus and their children, but very few of the negroes ; I found the evil was hardly known at Kheybar, though they all lead their lives in the same country manner. Méhsan and another in our field, encamping upon the oasis soil, *gâra*, had already been in the dark with prickly eyes ; but it passed lightly, for the malady is of the oases, and not of the dry deserts. I drank every evening a large draught out of the suspended girbies, looking devoutly upon the infinity of stars !— of which divine night spectacle no troublous passing of the days of this world could deprive me : I drank again at its most chillness, a little before the dawning. One morrow in the midst of Ramathán, I felt the eyes swell ; and then, not following the precept of the Arabs but grounding upon my medical book, I continually sponged them. " In this disease put no water to the eyes," say the Arabs ; washing purged the acrid humour a moment and opened the eyes, yet did, I believe, exasperate the malady.— But the Arabians carry too far their superstition against water, forbidding to use it in every kind of inflammation.

Ten twilight days passed over me, and I thought ' If the eyes should fail me !—and in this hostile land, so far from any good.' Some of the village, as I went painfully creeping by the ways, and hardly seeing the ground, asked me, " Where be now thy medicines ! " and they said again the old saw, " Apothecary, heal thyself." After a fortnight, leaving the water, the inflammation began to abate ; I recovered my eyes, and, Heaven be praised ! without worse accident. The eyesight remained for a time very weak, and I could not see so well as before, in the time of my being in Arabia ; and always I felt a twitching at the

35—2

eyes, and returning grudges of that suffered ophthalmia, if I but sipped cold water by night,—save the few times when I had supped of flesh meat. I have seen by experience, that one should not spare to drink water (competently) in the droughty heat of the day, to drink only when the sun is set; and in the people's proverbs, in the water-drinking Arabic countries, it is counted ' one of the three most wasting excesses of the body to drink water to bedward.' Some friendly Teyâmena, sorry to see my suffering plight, said to me : " This is because thou hast been eye-struck—what ! you do not understand *eye-struck?* Certainly they have looked in your eyes, Khalîl ! We have lookers (God cut them off !) among us, that with their only (malignant) eye-glances may strike down a fowl flying ; and you shall see the bird tumble in the air with loud shrieking *kâk-kâ-kâ-kâ-kâ.* Wellah their looking can blast a palm tree so that you shall see it wither away.—These are things well ascertained by many faithful witnesses."

Where I passed by the sûk, many—they were Beduins— silently held me out their hands from the benches, they supposed I should be skilled in palmistry : many looked to find in the Nasrâny the power of exorcism, and entreated me in behalf of their sick friends (for this they esteem the great skill in medicine, to bind and cast out the jan). They could hardly tell what to think when, despising their resentment, I openly derided the imposture of the exorcists ; I must well-nigh seem to them to cast a stone at the religion : yet afterward at Hâyil, I found exorcists only living under tolerance,—such kind of ungodly superstition, and pretended dealings of brain-sick men with the nether world, is not, perchance, to the reformed stomach of the Waháby religion.

The strangest fantasy which I found at Teyma, (which resembles the nomads' tales of the menâhil,) is that they have of a neighbouring phantom oasis, *Aueynát Masállat el-Amáñ.* " It is three hours riding form Teyma upon the north-west, and is often beheld by the Beduw. Slaves and horses issue from the enchanted appearance of palms ; but all fadeth soon if a man approach them."

In a village, in Lent, I could not altogether escape (that contagious pestilence of minds) the Mohammedan zelotism. The Teyâmena, slippery merchants, and swimming in all looseness of carnal living, are unreproved Moslemîn in the formal observance of the faith, with fasting and prayers. Here, as in Nejd, the people are as freshly devout, as if they were new believers in a young religion, or as if Mohammed himself were but lately deceased from among them : in a word, they are all busy with religion to buy God's blessings ;—religion is the only earnest business and is the only pastime of their empty lives. The Waháby plowed and purged this soil from much over-growth of old bastard weeds, and their renewing will not soon be forgotten in the public conscience. To taunt and mock, to check and enviously cross one another, these are the ungenerous *argutiae* of the Arabic temper : zelotism in these countries harbours in the more depravedly embodied of human souls. Re-ligion when she possesses the better minds is amiable, humane and liberal ; but corrupting in envious disgraced natures must needs give up some baneful breath of self-loving and fanaticism, which passes among them for laudable fruit of the spirit that is of their religious patriotism.—Patriotism and Religion! In the one and the other there seem to us to be sweetly comprehended all virtues ; and yet in the excess they are springs from which flow out extreme mischiefs !—The zelots would cry upon me, *Goom !* *utlub rubbuk,* " Rise up thou, and call upon the Lord thy God." They were slender and ill-favoured growths of young lads, and unhappy shrews that were come up from these ! Like words were spit upon me from the petulant tongues of certain little estimable women : and I mused in spirit, that those should be Heaven's brokers, who would be shunned in the rest by every man of integrity ! Yet they durst not insult the Nasrány in the village, because I was with the Beduw, and in the countenance of their own sheykhs.

I knew a young-middle-aged man, Ibrahîm, of the spirited Romàn family, unlike his kindred, a sober man in his talk, and lettered, who seemed to have been worn, in weathers of the world, to a not common moderation of mind. He had lived in exile, perhaps for no small forfeit, at *Yánba en-Núkhl,* and now at length (the ransom paid) he was returned home. I found him very poor, and he never bade me over his cottage threshold, where there was no coffee-hearth ; but he always responded liberally when I enquired anything in his hearing. He invited me one day to accompany him in the cool of the afternoon, when he would show me the sûr and ruins of old (Mosaic) Teyma. The ancient town-walling, little ruined, we see riding high as a dyke banked up with sand-drifts upon the desert, a mile above the oasis, southward. The wall-head where we came is great blocks of sandstone rudely laid. They showed me a hillock even with the wall-height, and thereupon a heap of building-stones ; this they call ' *Kasr Bédr Ibn Jôhr,* Prince of old Teyma of the Yahûd.'—Of any " Emir *Samuel,* Jewish ruler of Kheybar and

Teyma " (of old renown), there is no memory in either village
tradition : the unlettered inhabitants of Teyma are new comers,
and the Arabians keep no records. They told me " within the
compass of this wall, there lies buried *Wajjàj*, under the sand, that
is another such great well-pit as the hàddàj." Two freedmen
accompanied us of the same sheykhly family ; they came bravely
apparelled with the barbaric vanity of the negro blood, and
carrying their swords. With loud laughter they skipped among
the ruins, and ran down as children out of school to ask me
" Would I not be content to live at Teyma and dig up the
Wajjàj ? (the site is unknown) and all that waste soil in the
sûr circuit should become fruitful gardens."

I found, by observation of the aneroid, that the old town
lay fifty feet above the village,—wells then in that site must
be sunk doubly deep ; but that were not more than is found in
many Nejd villages. Some old broken irrigation channels appeared above the soil. These old water-conduits are continually
before their eyes, but there are none who will follow them up, to
find their heads.—If any forward spirit were born amongst them
should he not fall into the same slumbering slackness ? A man's
two hands may not accomplish a great enterprise ; if there will
none accompany him, his heart should cease by and by
to encourage him ! The small conduits are of rude-set untrimmed flags ; such are commonly seen in old ruined sites of
Arabia. They think that springs might be found under their
soil ; in digging clay, some have lighted upon old water-ducts.
I heard them talk of hiring cunning persons from el-Ally to
search for springs : words which may be upon their tongues for
many more years !

Later, when the Fukara were come in and held the country
upon that side about, I adventured into the desert to view all
these ruins. Following them far round, I crossed the old walled
town-enclosure ; all within was plain sand and the gravel of the
desert, without any plots of ancient street, or foundation stones
of houses. The masonry of the great sûr is of rudely-wrought
sandstone-blocks laid to a face, in earthy clay for mortar : the
midst between the stone faces is filled in with the same, which,
not crumbling under this climate, becomes yet harder with
time. Thus the old work is as a clay wall faced with masonry ;
the whole may have a fathom thickness, and (where the sûr
can be viewed above the overflowing desert sand) more than
three in height. I saw in a place a low tower, (was it a
sepulchre ?) filled with clay ; in another a postern, whose jambs
were of simple great stones. Little red shivers of silex or cornelian lie strewed upon the old town-site ; which are foreign to

this country. [The like is seen in ancient sites upon the Persian Gulf coast.]—But looking all along by the walls, for other antique inscriptions of Teyma, I found none : my eyes were yet dim, of the suffered ophthalmia, and I passed with the steps of a fugitive, alone and unshod, and sinking in the deep drifted and burning sand.—There are other village ruins, springs and broken channels, at *Erbah,* sandstone bergs appearing in the horizon to the south-eastward at a few miles' distance from Teyma. Also upon the rising ground beyond the oasis salines eastward, is seen some ancient round building, it might have been a stronghold, or as they imagine, *heykal,* ' a temple ' of the heathen and over-looking all Teyma : it is great, they pretend, as Kasr Zellûm ; I could not visit it.

Besides Ibrahîm told me,—where I cannot yet fully trust him, since his words were not confirmed to me by the nomads,—" there is a ground, *el-Khubbu (Khúbbah) b'il Wady Mahàjja,* under the Ghrenèym mountain, in which are many tall stones pitched on end, showing a sculpture above of human eyes and the nose and tressed horns, and below some *naksh* or uncouth scored inscription." His words brought to my mind that stone (*v.* fig., p. 296) which I had found in Kasr Zellûm ! Was it more likely that Ibrahîm should tell the truth, or go about to lie to the stranger in such matter ? He might speak of the necroplis of Teyma, in times of the Bible ! and much I desired to visit the site. When I asked Méhsan he answered that ' he had kept goats when a child upon all that side of Ghrenèym,—what was this khubbu ! wellah, to his knowledge there was nothing such, and he did not believe it.' Sorry I was in these busy times, and when strange nomads were flocking from all sides into the town, that I could not be assured in the matter. I could not hear that anyone had ever found so much as a piece of ancient money at Teyma, whether silver or gold, or even of copper. Old trove-money is accounted lucky and good for charms, in the Arab countries ; the finders carry it to the smith to be made into rings, or ornaments of their hareem and children. Shâfy showed me an amphora, which he had found (empty) in digging his ground ; one such as the oil-jars of Southern Europe ;—now there is not an earthen vessel used in these parts of Arabia ! Strewed potsherds of the ancients, and broken glass, I found between the oasis' walls and the saline bottoms of Teyma. They say antique Teyma was the old borough in the sûr, with the three open suburbs, the West, the East, and the Haddàj, which are now : but that is worth remembrance which they tell after the tradition, " Seven were the ancient townships of this country ; Teyma, el-Hejr, Mubbîa(t), *Umgassur,* Kheybar, el-Khreyby, Mogeyra.''

I went one day to see where a lately found ancient well had been re-opened. The son of the well-finder was driving a camel at the well, to raise water upon their new holding, which was already walled-in from the desert and had been ploughed and balked out in seed plots ; this water was cooler, but not so well tasting as that which springs in the haddâj. The young man climbed over his clay wall (there are foot-holes in all their high orchard walling, so they may be scaled even by women), and returned to me with a present of pomegranates : in the Arabic countries, whoso enters a man's field or orchard is a guest of that ground, and the honest owner will fill his hand, if there be any seasonable fruits. So, still driving the nâga with his voice, the lad sat down to parley with me. The well of seven fathoms had been cleared by the labour of three journey-men, at six-pence or eight-pence, in twenty-five days, that is for ten or twelve reals ; and this new ground of two to three acres, yet unplanted, he said to be worth two to three hundred reals, that may be near £18 an acre. There was yet to spend for setting out roots of young palms ; and the not light yearly charges for camel hire and team driving. The young sets will bear fruit as bushes, in five or six years, and be grown to goodly young stems, in fifteen, yielding dates at the full,—this were a yearly harvest worth hardly an hundred reals : so that the profit of the fortunate field, at the last, is not much more than should rise of the principal laid up of so many expenses. When any hauta is sold at Teyma, a part payment is made with such scarcity of silver as they have, the rest to be delivered in dates and in household gear, as brazen vessels ;— which beside the seldom seen sitting-carpet, are nearly the only moveables in these Arabian dwellings. The dates may be sold out of hand for reals, to the marketing Beduins.

The closing-in of this new hauta had advanced the compass of the oasis towards the desert : there is no public sûr about Teyma, but the township stands enclosed by the orchard walls of private persons. There are four or five ways, at the public paths' ends, into the settlement,—the outlying are shut by gates ; yet foot-passengers may pass in at all hours, creeping upon the breast through a man-hole in the side wall (which is very irksome),—the like is seen in some Syrian villages lying in the desert, as Keriateyn before Palmyra.—I found one early morn-ing a great company of Sherarát, waiting to enter, without the northern gate ; and some of the town were there, to seek first

bargains among these poor people, who had brought in with
them, to sell, samhh and samn : they came, lean and ragged
from their suffering life in the desert, to buy victual in the
village at the date harvest, and were of a quiet dejected demeanour. The gate a little later was opened to them, and they
went to lodge in an empty hauta, upon that side of the oasis.

To speak of the African blood in these countries; there are
bondsmen and bondswomen and free negro families in every
tribe and town; many are home-born and free-born, *muwalladín*.
A few persons may be seen, at Teyma, of the half-negro blood;
they are descended from freedmen, who grown to substantial
living have taken poor white women of the sunna or smiths'
caste, which is reckoned illiberal.—A pleasant looking young
Heteym woman in the kella at M. Sâlih was the wife of a
negro askar, Nejm's freedman who had been sent to keep the
cistern at Moaddam. She was happy-faced, and (maugre a little
natural sensibility of their slaves' colour) kindly affectioned to
her children, that were negroes with better lineaments than
those of the full blood. I have seen none of the lithe Gallas
at Teyma, nor among nomads. This is because the first cost
were more, and their strength is less for any rude labour.
There are many Galla slaves in the Sacred Cities; and not few
in the little tyrannies of Upper Arabia, as Hâyil and Boreyda,
servitors and armed men of the Emirs : they are tall and well-
grown as Arabs, hardy and gentle at once, obedient as slaves
and of a spirit which carries them at his word upon every
warfare. A stout negro lad might yet be purchased of the
returning Haj, in these parts, for sixty reals (the value of two
camels or a common thelûl). There is besides a negro kind
of them, with clear ruddy-brown looks :—but the blacks are not
fewer nations and kindreds than white-skinned men. I have
questioned with many negroes, slaves from their youth in Arabia,
—they were all from the Upper Nile countries, and had been
robbed by the Arab forays.

A poor (now freed) woman who served at *Thuèyny's*, er-
Romàn, in his orchard house next by us, where I passed the
most mid-days, told me her heart yet yearned for her own land,
her kinsfolk and her father's house. She sighed and said,
'Ah! that the Lord would give her to see it again!' A land
which in comparison with this naked misery of the soil of
their bondage is very full of the beneficence of nature, and
from whence she had been ravished when almost grown. It
was one day as she kept her father's goats upon the hill
sides by the river with another girl. She saw her play-

fellow surprised, at little distance, by the Arab riders ; then she climbed into the thick of a tree, but was espied by them and they robbed her also.—To-day she was a free woman again, but in a hungry and strange land, very far from her own country, that lay she could not now tell whither, and she named to me Dungola. The border Arabs are ever waspish raiders into more peaceable and plentiful settled countries. Her people, she said, were happy : there is no use of money amongst them ; if any is hungry in their villages, he may go into the gardens and eat his fill freely. Their clothing is good cotton stuff of their own weaving : they have no need that any foreign thing should be brought in among them."—I asked, ' How went her people clothed ? ' When she answered, " They wear but a loin-cloth," a young negro girl that stood by and listened to the ' aunt's ' talk, and had been robbed from thence before her remembrance, derided her African people with laughing shrieks of " *Iblis ! iblis !—hi-hi-hi !* they be not then better than wild men ! " The condition of a slave is always tolerable and is often happy in Arabia : bred up as poor brothers of the sons of the household, they are a manner of God's wards of the pious Mohammedan householder, who is *ammy,* the ' eme ' of their servitude, and *abúy,* ' my father.' Slave-holding among them is harsher in the mixed Holy Cities (where is the churlish military obedience and Turkish violence, and where some poorer citizens make merchandise of their slaves' labour). It is not many years, " if their house-lord fears Ullah " before he will give them their liberty ; and then he sends them not away empty ; but in Upland Arabia (where only substantial persons are slave holders) the good man will marry out his freed servants, male and female, endowing them with somewhat of his own substance, whether camels or palm-stems.

The free negroes are commonly seen lusty and thriving ; they are rich men's children by adoption, where the poor disherited Arabs must hire themselves to every man's task as day labourers. But also of the natural stalwart condition of negro bodies, they fare well enough of a feeble diet and shoot up strongly in lean soil, where you see only pithless and languishing growths of the country Arabs. Nature, as was said above, has set a sorry mark upon all the date-eater village folk of Nejd,—that blighted, unprosperous, hollow caste of the human visage, which once looked upon is ever had in remembrance. The diet of the Teyâmena is dates in the day-time, and most evenings dates, but bread is then served in the better houses, or porridge boiled with fat gobbets of pumpkin. In those Africans there is no resentment that they have been made slaves—they are often captives of their own wars—even though cruel men-stealers rent them from their parentage. The patrons who paid their price have adopted them into their households, the males are circumcised and—that which enfranchises their souls, even in the long passion of home-sickness—God has visited them in their mishap ; they can say, "*it was His grace,*" since they be thereby entered into the saving religion. This therefore they think is the better country, where they are the Lord's free men, a land of more civil life, the soil of the two Sanctuaries, the land of Mohammed :—for such do they give God thanks that their bodies were sometime sold into slavery !

At length the last sun set in Lent, and Ramathán was ended. As the new day dawned, I walked with Méhsan to breakfast in the town. " Hie, Khalîl, it is a feast day, and we shall be merry ; God be praised, said he, that now the Lent is past ! "—" Thou art like one delivered from prison."—" Wellah, as thou sayest, out of imprisonment ! and I may now strike light to my galliûn. I go to break the fast with the acquaintance ;—knowest thou the custom to eat something at every friendly dàr ? The people will eat their fill to-day ! Here be two ways, go round breakfasting with those you know, and where you enter say, *Aÿd-ak mubárak,* ' blessed be your feast ' :—or come on ! I and thou will go breakfasting about together."

Fresh appeared the villagers with holiday faces in this morning sun, they had laid up merits in Lent ; and to-day they put on their new apparel for the year. Many now perfume their kerchiefs, their beards, their mantles, over the chafing-dish of incense, some go sweetened with rose-water. The holiday-makers issued from all doors, and enter over all thresholds, visiting and greeting from house to house. Where men come in, there the festival dish is set down to them of sopped flat-bread sweetened ; a swarm of human flies fall to their knees about it, at the instant ; and lifting their right hands full, in hot haste to the mouth—once, twice, thrice—the bare metal appeared. So they rise and throng on breakfasting to the next and the next houses, till they have walked through the neighbourhood : and after that, with well-lined ribs, they will go sit in some friendly dàr to drink coffee. Where they come in they say " Blessed be thy festival," and it is answered them again, *Aaddi aley-na,* pass unto us ; and we are keeping this feast, *wa henna aÿidín.* All the rest of the day they gad up and down in their first-worn garments, and ruffle it in Bagdad kerchiefs of golden silk with purple cotton, very glorious in a colourless country. A young man clad before only in a poor tunic stained

with his honest labour, I saw to-day an highflyer in their clay
streets like a stage king, with his mantle of scarlet fine.

The Resident for Ibn Rashîd passed through the sûk in the
forenoon, in the pomp of his lord's new apparel, to visit Khálaf.
Khálaf, of a perspicuous and liberal mind, was but then returned from Hâyil ; and for those fourteen Ramathán days by
the way, in which they had eaten, he now fasted not at all,
in spite of the zelots, who of their natural vility were busy-
bodies, questioners of other men's religion in the town. I have
seen him patiently bear with their scurvy importunity, since
he could not shun them ; Khálaf was of the sheykhly mildness,
but a man inwardly of his own counsel. The Teyma sheukh
had not fared amiss in Hâyil, where the Emir bestowed upon
each of them a camel and 60 real-mejîdies, (which they call
as often ghrazziát), for their charges about the well-building,
besides the accustomed change of clothing, that is the sum
value of £50 sterling. Khálaf had sore eyes, and I made him a
bottle of medicine ; it might be because he had but slenderly
deserved of the Nasrâny, that he accepted it without thanks, and
looking fixedly in my face. The poor nomad wives and children
had no new garments to put on, but blithely they danced out
the hour in our hauta. When the Beduin friends insisted with
me to let them see our holiday dance, I would not make a
breach in their mirth, but, foreseeing their natural judgment,
I was half-ashamed to show them the manner.—With that stern
congruity which is in their wild nature, they found it light :
' Oh ! what was that outlandish skipping and casting of the
shanks, and this footing it to and fro ! '—it seemed to them
a morris dance ! but when they heard more, of our caroling,
that his arm about her middle, every man danced it forth
bosom to bosom with every fair woman, they thought of us but
scorn and villany.

Many Aarab were come to town, and as I went abroad
I heard one whistling—a surprising sound in the Arabic
countries ! where it would be taken for one's whistering to
the jan. I found him to be a Fejîry of my acquaintance, and
asked where learned he that ribaldry ? " In the time of our
being in es-Sham."—There he might have heard it of some
coxcomb Nasrâny, light-heads to take up a toy, of any Jack-
would-be-a-gentleman passenger Frank in their country.—In
that there came to us a Solubby, riding upon an ass, and
singing ; he snivelled deep, and brayed so wonderfully loud !
and I called to this companion, " Thinkest thou they sing
better in Syria ? "—The cheerful young Solubby arriving anon
answered for himself, " No, wullah ! I too have been in the

North;" and with great heart, he laughed to scorn the eunuch-like trickling warbles,—intolerable also in our ears for their barbaric remissness—of the musicants [the best are Jews] of Damascus. I never heard a woman sing (other than the girls' festival chanting of single staves) in these countries.—Where be the Aphrodisiastic modulations of the fair singing women in these Arabian deserts of ' the Time of Ignorance ' ? The hareem sing not in their new Arabian austerity of a masculine religion.

In this festival afternoon came the Fukara, the tribe had alighted at two hours from the town ; they watered the cattle at their friends' running channels, in Teyma. Zeyd rode to us upon his mare, and through a breach of the wall towards the wilderness the camels were driven in to drink. Our people in the hauta had lacked fuel ; now the hind brought his cloak full of jella, which as said, is excellent firing. The tribesmen had well supped, they told us, in Ramathán, having taken many foxes.—But I saw not my nâga among the camels of Zeyd's Aarab, standing to drink at the suryân ! " She has strayed ! " answered the young herdsman.

Three days they keep the Bairam feast, but in the second I saw the villagers put off the new garments, and go about their harvest labour. The dates, past the full ripening, were falling in the trees ; the nomads were now flocking into the town, to be buyers in the date-gathering, and all Beduw are impatient to be sped of marketing business, and be gone to their wandering menzils, where they have left their wives and children in the booths without defence, and the cattle in the open field. Companies of Bishr arrived every hour from the eastward : the Fukara wondered at the multitude of faces which, Zeyd told me, they had not before known. These Bishr, cut off from their landed inheritance at Kheybar, came in this year to victual themselves at Teyma, where dates are as good or better, and cheaper than in the villages and hamlets of the Jebel : many of them had not been here in their lives. Among these headlong troops entering the town, some have hailed me, " O man ! this way leads whither ? where is the haddàj ? "— Teyma seemed no more the former oasis with this daily hubbub up and down, and the hitherto clean ways were full of pestilent ordures. The villagers being in their orchards, all house-doors were shut ; men and hareem were at the ingathering in their hautas (*yajidún en-núkhl*), where their climbers in the trees cut and let down with a cord the frails of food-fruit. The barefoot family trains pass homeward every hour shuffling and stooping in the ways under great basket-loads to their cottage ware-rooms. They wrought all day, and the next and the third daylight after, till the sun's going down ; and now breakfasting again at noon since Ramathán, they felt their strength revive.—The Beduw are seen flitting from hauta to hauta, and entering where they list to eat of the sweet hospitality. The Teyâmena hastened the more that the season was lateward ; in their second harvest day the sky was troubled. They carried in the last fruit when it was already wetted ; in such case the dates will ferment. Showers fell, every man was in the orchards, even the many-wheeled haddàj was forsaken and silent : they told me, for these few days after harvest, and rain falling upon the heads of their palms, the trees would take no hurt.

I saw a Beduwîa wife, decked in poor wild bravery, as it were a gipsy queen ; she went caroling in the hautas with a gay banner : a stranger, the people wondered and mocked, the hareem approached timidly to touch her outlandish apparel, and where she came she was bidden to sit down and eat. Hearing she was of Harb, the first I had seen of that Beduin nation, neighbours of the Harameyn, I regarded her silently. And she, with a great breath, not less astonished to see that white man there,—" A Nasrâny say ye ! " ' Ha ! she had heard this name, and how came any Nasrâny hither ? were we not children of the Evil One ? yet I did greet her with fair words, and with blessing ! ' I said, " The Arabs bid God curse all that is not theirs, but we beseech God to have mercy upon all mankind ; I heartily pray Ullah bless thy household, and thy children, and thy cattle." She answered, " Ah now ! how many be the false hearsays in the world,—ay billah, ay billah ! Look ye, he must be one of a good peaceable kind of folk." Trays of the food-fruit in the stalk were brought down from the best trees, and she was called apart to eat with the hareem. I was bidden where I stood with some sheykhs, and we sat down together with our rich host Thuèyny er-Român, whose was this great harvest-ground : Misshel el-Aúájy was one of them— he that is great sheykh of Bishr.

Afterward, as there was peace (of this eating together) between us, I said to Misshel, I was for going to Hâyil and Kheybar, and would return with him eastward in the deserts, from whence I might find some market-goers to J. Shammar, and ride along with them. The burly man (he was such for a Beduwy) answered the stranger with a sturdy sharpness, in that hollow ringing voice, which is of the drought of the desert. " But we go now to seek *él-gúsh f'il khála*, wild bushes in the empty waste, for our camels, and far distant ; we go not to

J. Shammar.—Kheybar quoth he! Kheybar where?—but know, Khalîl, there is no man will guide thee thither: the Dowlat is there! and wellah I tell thee there is naught but the cutting of wezands between us. Nay! put this from thy mind, of going to Nejd; also thou canst not come with us."—" Tell me, Misshel, whether you hold me for a friend or an enemy?" He responded with eyes of rapine, after a little pause, " Well, I take thee for neither! nor friend nor enemy;—(the shrew murmured)—but I would to God I might once have the spoiling of thee." Misshel, this " Ruler of the seven tribes," was sheykh in particular of his own Auájy, the heaviest bodies and most formidable in warfare of all the country. It was his tribesmen that had " taken " this year the general ghrazzu of the Wélad Aly, more than a hundred lances, and lately in one day all the cattle of the Moahîb. Last year they had crossed arms with the Dowla at Kheybar, where many of them were fallen; Mohammed Ibn Rashîd egged them on. Misshel is praised in the people's tongue as ' a mighty spearsman';—it seemed the man could be a bearer down of right and goodness with a more robust iniquity.—Proudly Abd el-Azîz er-Romàn had showed me Misshel's lance, laid along upon the tenter-pegs in the clay wall of his kahwa, where this sheykh often lodged; it might be nearly fourteen foot in length. The great sheykh of Aarab was a friend of his youth, so also was Motlog el-Fejîry. Bishr tribesmen have boasted to me thus of Misshel's shelfa, " The head is large as an hand-breadth, and waggleth billah as a tongue, athirst to lap up his enemies' blood."

Also Abd el-Azîz had been out in Ramathán, riding round to the nomads to take up well-camels: descending toward el-Héjr, he went first to visit the small tribe of Moahîb in Thirba, lately accounted their enemies—he had not known them before—but now friends being reconciled with Ibn Rashîd. They feasted him largely, a goat here, a sheep there, had been killed for his supper, so that he admired (which he showed me spreading out his hands and opening the eyes) their ancient hospitality; and yet only little before they had lost all their camels. He saw them yet in the sorrow of that immense disadventure; but they were lifting up their heads again. The nomad neighbours of Bílli had been good to them in gifts. Tollog's great cattle were even more than before; Mahanna had sent him seven camels. He found the old man low and broken, though the bereaved tribesmen were in a manner re-established, every man after the number, the ability, and free-giving kindness of his friends:—and that is like a day of judgment in the desert

world, wherein each soul receiveth according to his proper deserts, the liberal man more and he that was at all times a
jocundity to his friends. Before this moon was out the Moahîb
were camel masters to half their former strength : their flocks,
that were upon the Harra, had not been taken. But Abd el-
Azîz made me mourn, falsely reporting the deaths of many of
my former friends, till I learned from Shwoysh, now in exile for
a dispute with Tollog, who came to Teyma with the Fukara,
that only Fâiz was fallen.—The Teyma sheykh had ridden
further, to el-Ally, where he had never been before, since this is
an Hejâz village in the friendship of the Dowlat of Medina.
A nomad was his back-rider, and so well were they mounted,
that he accomplished this voyage in Ramathán of not less
than three hundred miles in a few days,—but not fasting.
When now I asked this man to commend me to Misshel, he
suborned certain Beduins to tell me a forged tale : ' It was
impossible that I should pass with any of the Bishr to Hâyil,
they were fallen (it was false) under the Prince's displeasure,
he having commanded them to restore the Moahîb cattle to
their owners and they would not.'—But all with whom I spoke
set themselves against my going to Nejd ; they would have
me ' *return thither from whence I was come into their country.*'

In Hâyil, Hamed and Wâyil had attended the coming home
of the Emir,—he was ridden out upon a foray. Ibn Rashîd,
when he arrived, accepted their submission and the thelûl, and
dismissed the men home. As they rode peaceably homeward
bearers of good tidings, over the deserts (from Hâyil are about
an hundred leagues to Thirba), and were come to the mid-way
in dîrat of Bishr, they saw pasturing camels, which were none
other in their eyes than their own cattle !—Then they saw on
them the brand-mark of the Moahîb indeed. They alighted
for the night at a great tent, and that was Misshel's. After
supper they heard from their host's lips (it was he who had
made them bare) of their home calamities ; and Misshel gave
Hamed, for the old man his father, one of his own nâgas.—
Reckoning days, they found the day of their disaster to fall
within the time, when having brought their submission, they
were in Hâyil, awaiting the Emir. In the morning therefore
they mounted, to ride back thither :—but would the (lately
hostile) Emir ordain the restitution of their cattle ?
—Mohammed Ibn Rashîd received them sternly. The
ruler had accepted three thelûls since they were here, which
the Auájy sent him immediately, out of their booty. The
Emir was well pleased with this final punishment of his old

foes, though he had now received them as tributaries. Bitter is the heart, and the sword is sharp, of him who rules over the wandering tribes of the khála! but in truth he might not else contain them.

A Sherâry neighbour of our hauta slaughtered an old camel in Bairam, and sold portions of the meat against dates : he laid up this provision for his family in the short winter. I went to buy of him, and he was a gentle butcher, calling me at every turn ' the son of his brother.' Another day a Fehjy neighbour slaughtered an old nâga,—that nomad family husbanded a small palm ground without the walls, and were become as settlers. The slaughter-beast was worth five reals, but selling the joints, he laid up a larger provision. I went to him, but he would not sell meat for money, saying, ' Who would buy let him bring dates.' That which was not sold in the first day, they boiled in the broth and blood :—thus, though it be unlawful, they eat the blood—the koran letter is unknown to them. I saw the sale till the third day, the meat then beginning to stink ; but these townsmen and the Aarab will eat the flesh of game thus tainted, which, as the wild goat and the antelope, are shot at a day's distance in the wilderness : yet they took it well when I refused to taste of such worms' meat with them. Having bought of the flesh, Méhsan's daughter, the little maiden that served me, boiled it, and I called my Beduin friends to supper ; but such old camel is not very good to eat.

The autumn rain fell upon us, as we sat abroad after supper : the lately sunny world seemed swallowed up in gloom. The rainy evening closed in dimly, and wild flaws of wind beat upon our nakedness of worsted housing. As the cold drops fell through the worn tent-cloth, Méhsan questioned me of my country,—I was soon now to depart from them. When he heard that we had an abundance of the blessings of Ullah, bread and clothing, and peace, and how if any wanted the law succoured him,—and the night's dark storm was breaking with discomfort upon us,—he began to be full of melancholy, and to lament the everlasting infelicity of the Aarab, whose lack of clothing is a cause to them of many diseases, who have not daily food nor water enough, and wandering in the empty wilderness, are never at any stay ; and these miseries to last as long as their lives. And when his heart was full, he cried up to Heaven —such informal praying of a man's spirit they call *duâa*— *Úrhum yâ Rubb! khálkat, elathi Ent khalakta: úrhum el-mesakín, wa el-juaanín, wa el-aryanín! úrhum yâ'llah,—yâ'llah!* " Have mercy, ah Lord God, upon Thy creature, which Thou createdst :—pity the sighing of the poor, the hungry, the naked, have mercy ! have mercy upon them, O Ullah ! " Yet after their complaint in the present, wherein they see themselves orphans of a niggard Providence, so lively is the human humour of faith and hope in them, that they will say anon, which Méhsan now added devoutly—*Ullah karîm,* " The Lord, He is bountiful."

The Teyâmena seldom taste flesh-meat, but game is some-times brought to town by Solubbies, living here beyond the walls in booths and home-born, poor smiths in iron and tinkers. They ride out upon their asses to the open khála a-hunting, and return on foot, driving home their beasts laden with venison ; and all the meat is commonly bought from them, ere they be past the sûk. The best of them was *Mátar,* a pleasant fellow, and I often talked with him of his hunting. When I enquired of the wild ox, wothŷhi, he showed me a thick-bodied white ass of theirs, and said, " The wothŷhi is like her !—She is white haired (as all great game of the sand-plains), without hunch, and has crop ears, with the tail of a cow, and the ending bunch of hairs." The wothŷhi is fleetest of game, the meat is esteemed above all venison ; the hide of the bull, which is very thick, is said to make the best sole leather for sandals. I saw in 1875 the hides brought to Maan from the Sherarát desert. The rod-like horns were common at Teyma ; the most are brought in by the Sherarát and bestowed upon their town friends, who have them, in their ware-rooms, to break up any hard clotted store of old dates : I saw that the Teyma Solubba families used them for tent-pegs.—I spoke to Mátar of the ancient archery, he answered, " Many times I and my companions have found iron arrow-heads of a finger's length in the mountains, as we were hunting the bedûn, wellah like the heads of little spears,—we found not the shafts, because the wood has perished." He had seen images of men scored upon the rocks, "holding bows in their hands, and having on their heads a long cap ! "—That were now an outlandish guise in Arabia.

There fell daily showers, and a cold wind breathed over the desert, the sky was continually overcast. The visiting nomads were about to depart, and I desired to go eastward with them,—forsaking the well-building, rather than longer abide their loitering leisure. The year was changing, and must I always banish my life in Arabia ! My friends were very slow to help me forward, saying, ' What had I to do in Hâyil that I must go thither ? and after Teyma I should no longer be safe with Aarab that knew not the Dowla.' As for Ibn Rashîd, they said, " He is *néjis* (polluted, profane), a cutter-off of his

nigh kinsfolk with the sword: " and said Abd el-Aziz, who col-
lected the Emir's dues, " Word is come of thee to Ibn Rashîd !
—that ' a Nasrâny, whom no man knoweth, is wandering with
the Aarab, and *writing*,' and he was much displeased. The
Beduw eastward will fear to receive thee lest the Emir should
require it of them."

I hoped to depart with Bishr, their marketing families lay
in an outlying hauta of Thuèyny's ; there I went to visit them.
Each household lodged apart upon the ground amongst their
pack-saddles and baggage, and in the rain by day and night
they were without shelter : only the sheykh Misshel lay under
a tent-cloth awning. Misshel was coffee-drinking in the town,
but I found Askar (he who had been wounded), a young man in
whom was a certain goodness and generosity of nature, more
than in his blunt-witted father : Askar received my greeting
with a comely *yâ hulla !* he was pleased when the stranger
enquired of his hurt, and that thus I should know him.
The rain fell as we sat about the camp-fire, where they were
making coffee : theirs was the best I had tasted in Arabia,
—not of casting in a few beans Teyma-wise, but as Nejders the
best part of an handful. By and by I asked, which of them
would accompany me to Hâyil ? one said, ' He cared not if it
were he ; when they returned from Teyma, he must needs go
thither : what would Khalîl give, and he would set me down in
the midst of the town ? '—" I will give thee three reals." The
rest and Askar dissuaded him, but the man accepted it, and
gave his right hand in mine, that he would not draw back from
this accord, and Askar was our witness. The help to needy
Beduins of a very little money, to buy them a shirt-cloth and
a mantle, made my journeys possible (as Zeyd foretold), among
lawless and fanatical tribes of Arabia :—but I have hardly
found Beduins not better than the Fukara. These Bishr nomads, not pensioners of the haj road, but tribesmen living by
their right hands in their own marches, are more robust-
natured, and resemble the northern Beduins. They are clad
from el-Irâk, and they bind the kerchief upon their foreheads
with a worsted head-band in great rolls as it were a turban.

On the morrow one of those nomads took me by the mantle
in the street to ask me, ' Would I go to his dîra to cure
a tribesman who had suffered many years a disease of the
stomach, so that what food he took he rejected again ? ' I saw
the speaker was a sheykh, and of Zeyd who was standing by he
enquired ' had they found the Nasrâny a good hakîm, in the
time of my living amongst them ? ' I was pleased with the
man's plain behaviour and open looks. Though he seemed a

great personage, he was an Heteymy, *Hannas Ibn Nômus*, sheykh of the *Noâmsy ;*—that is a kindred of Heteym now living in alliance with Misshel, and inhabiting the nomad district of the Auájy, where they had found a refuge from their enemies. Zeyd said to me, " There is nothing to fear if thou go with him : Hannas is a very honest man : billah I would not so leave thee in the hands of another."

The Fejîr watered once more at Teyma ; I saw the great cattle of our households driven in, and after the watering their burden camels were couched by the booths : for Méhsan and the rest would remove in the morning and return to the desert. Among the beasts I found my old nâga, and saw that she was badly galled on the chine ; the wound might hardly be healed in fifteen or twenty days, but I must journey to-morrow. I brought nomad friends to look at her, who found that she had been ridden and mishandled, the marks of the saddle-tree cords yet appearing in the hairy hide. It could not be other than the fault of Zeyd's herdsman Îsa, a young man, whom I had befriended. So taking him by the beard before them all, I cursed ' the father of this Yahûdy.' The young man, strong and resolute, laid hands upon my shoulders and reviled me for a Nasrâny ; but I said, " Sirrah, thou shouldst have kept her better," and held him fast by the beard. The tribesmen gathered about us kept silence, even his own family, all being my friends, and they had so good an opinion of my moving only in a just matter. Îsa seeing that his fault was blamed, must suffer this rebuke, so I plucked down the weled's comely head to his breast, and let him go. An effort of strength had been unbecoming, and folly it were to suffer any perturbation for thing that is without remedy ; I had passed over his fault, but I thought that to take it hardly was a necessary policy. Also the Arabs would have a man like the pomegranate, a bitter-sweet, mild and affectionate with his friends in security, but tempered with a just anger if the time call him to be a defender in his own or in his neighbour's cause. Îsa's father came by and by to my tent, and in a demiss voice the old hind acknowledged his son's error ; " Yet, Khalîl, why didst thou lay upon me that reproach, when we have been thy friends, to name me before the people Yahûdy ? " But as old Sâlih saw me smile he smiled again, and took the right hand which I held forth to him.

I found Zeyd, at evening, sitting upon one of the clay benches near the haddàj ; he was waiting in the midst of the town, in hope that some acquaintance of the villagers coming by, before the sun's going down, might call him to supper. Returning after an hour I found Zeyd yet in the place, his almost black visage set betwixt the nomad patience of hunger and his lordly disdain of the Teyâmena. Zeyd might have seemed a prosperous man, if he had been liberal, to lay up friendship in heaven and in this world ; but the shallow hand must bring forth leanness and faint willing of a man's neighbours again. I stayed to speak a word with Zeyd, and saw him draw at last his galliûn, the remedy of hunger : then he called a lad, who issued from the next dàr, to fetch a live coal, and the young villager obeyed him.

In the first hour of this night there fell upon us a tempest of wind and rain. The tall palms rocked, and bowing in all their length to the roaring gusts it seemed they would be rent by the roots. I found shelter with Méhsan in the house of Féjr our host ; but the flat roof of stalks and rammed earth was soon drenched, and the unwonted wet streamed down inwardly by the walls. Méhsan spoke of my setting forth tomorrow with the Bishr, and, calling Féjr to witness, the timid friendly man sought to dissuade me, ' also Zeyd, he said, had forsaken me, who should have commended me to them ; it was likely I should see him no more.'—" Should I wonder at that ? —Zeyd has no heart," they answered both together : " Ay, billah, Zeyd has no heart," and repeated *ma láhu kalb*, He has no heart ! Féjr was suffering an acute pain of ' the stone,' *el-hása*, a malady common in these parts, though the country is sandstone ; yet sometimes it may be rather an inflammation, for they think it comes of their going unshod upon the burning soil. When the weather lulled, we went towards our wet tents to sleep out the last night at Teyma.

CHAPTER XXI.

THE JEBEL.

Depart from Teyma with Bishr. Journey eastward in the rain. Misshel the great sheykh makes and serves coffee. Women of Bishr. Ibn Mertaad. Hospitality of a sheykh in the wilderness. Come to Misshel's tents. Misshel's threats. Depart with a company for Hâyil. A journey with thelúl riders. The Nasrâny esteemed a Beduwy and a cattle thief. Arrive at tents by night. A Beduin who had served in the Ageyl. A Shammar sheykh in the desert. He wishes well to the Engleysy. Nejd Arabia is nearly rainless. Questions and answers of the Beduw. Extreme fatigue of riding. An appearance of water. Askar's counsel. Arrive at the first Shammar village. Môgug. Judgment given by the sheykh for the Nasrâny. Their kahwa. A liberal-minded young scholar. An Irâk Beduwy accuses the Nasrâny. The Nejd speech. Depart for Hâyil. Rîa-es-Self. A perilous meeting in the rîa. Bishr and Shammar not good neighbours. View of the mountain landmark of Hâyil. Gofar. Veiled Nejd women. Public hospitality at Gofar. Outlying Gofar in ruins. Desert plain before Hâyil. Passengers by the way. Horsemen. Approaching Hâyil. Beduin guile. Abd el-Aziz. Enter Hâyil. The public place. The Kasr. Mufarrij. The public kahwa. The guest-hall or mothîf. The Prince's secretary. The Nasrâny brought before the Prince Ibn Rashîd. The audience. A Mohammedan book-tale of the Messiah. An unlucky reading. A seal. Walk in the Kasr plantation with Mohammed the Emir. Their deep wells of irrigation. The wothŷhi.

THE women of the hauta loaded the tents and their gear, and I saw our Aarab departing before the morning light. Zeyd rode in upon his mare, from the village where he had slept; 'If I would now go with him, he would bring me, he said, to the Bishr and bind them for my better security;' but Zeyd could not dwell, he must follow his Aarab, and I could not be ready in a moment; I saw the Fukara companions no more. A stranger, who passed by, lent me a hand in haste, as I loaded upon my old nâga : and I drove her, still resisting and striving to follow the rest, half a mile about the walls to those Bishr, who by fortune were not so early movers. There, I betook myself ro *Hayzàn*, the man who had agreed to conduct me : and of another I bought the frame of a riding-saddle, that

I might lay the load upon my wounded camel. They were charging their cattle, and we set forward immediately.

Leaving Teyma on the right hand, we passed forth, between the Érbah peaks and Ghreneym, to the desert; soon after the bleak border was in sight of the Nefûd, also trending eastward. We journeyed on in rain and thick weather; at four of the afternoon they alighted, in the wet wilderness, at an height of 600 feet above Teyma, and the hungry camels were dismissed to pasture. The Beduin passengers kindled fires, laying on a certain resinous bush, although it be a plant eaten by the cattle, and though full of the drops of the rain, it immediately blazed up. They fenced themselves as they could from the moist wind and the driving showers, building bushes about them; and these they anchored with heavy stones.

We removed at sunrise : the sudden roaring and ruckling hubbub of the Beduins' many camels grudging to be loaded, made me remember the last year's haj journeys ! before ten in the morning, we had Helwàn in front, and clearer weather. The Bishr journeyed a little southward of east, Birrd (Bírd) was visible: at two, afternoon, we alighted, and dismissed the camels to pasture ; the height was here as yesterday, nearly 4000 feet. The rain had ceased and Hayzàn went out hawking. There were two or three men in this company who carried their falcons with them, riding on the saddle peaks, in their hoods and jesses, or sitting upon the master's fist. Sometimes the birds were cast off, as we journeyed, at the few starting small hares of the desert ; the hawks' wings were all draggled in the wet : the birds flew without courage wheeling at little height, after a turn or two they soused, and the falconer running in, poor Wat is taken. Thus Hayzàn took a hare every day, he brought me a portion from his pot at evening, and that was much to the comfort of our extenuated bodies. I missed Hannas and his cousin *Rayyàn*, in the way; they had left our journeying Aarab to go to their people encamped more to the southward, above the *Harrat Kheybar*. To-day I was left alone with the Auájy,—somewhat violent dealing and always inhospitable Beduins, but in good hope of the sooner arriving at Hâyil. We sat down to drink coffee with the sheykh, Misshel, who would make it himself. This "ruler of the seven tribes" roasted, pounded, boiled, and served the cheerful mixture with his own hand. Misshel poured me out but one cup, and to his tribesmen two or three. Because his shrew's deed was in disgrace of my being a Nasrâny I exclaimed, " Here is billah a great sheykh and little kahwa ! Is it the custom of the Auájy, O Misshel, that a guest should sit among you who are all drinking, with his cup

empty ? " Thus challenged, Misshel poured me out unwillingly,
muttering between the teeth some word of his fanatical humour,
yâ fárkah !

The third day early, we came in sight of J. Irnàn ; and I
said to my neighbour, " Ha, Irnàn ! " A chiding woman, who
was riding within ear-shot, cried out, " Oh, what hast thou
to do with Irnàn ? " At half-afternoon we alighted in high
ground, upon the rising of Ybba Moghrair, where I found by
the instrument, 4000 feet. Some camels were now seen at
a distance, of Aarab *Ibn Mertaad*, allies of theirs. When
we were lodged, there came a woman to my tent ; who asked
for needles and thread (such trifles are acceptable gifts in the
khála) ; but as she would harshly bargain with the weary
stranger I bade her begone. She answered, with an ill look,
" Ha ! Nasrâny, but ere long we shall take all these things
from thee." I saw, with an aversion [of race], that all these
Bishr housewives wore the *berkoa* or heathenish face-clout,
above which only the two hollow ill-affected eyes appeared.
This desolation of the woman's face was a sign to me that I
journeyed now in another country, that is jealous (and Waháby)
Nejd ;—for even the waste soil of Arabia is full of variety.

The fourth morning from Teyma, we were crossing the high
rugged ground of sandstone rocks behind Ybba Moghrair.
Strange is the discomfort of rain and raw air in Arabia,
when our eyes, wont to be full of the sun, look upon wan
mists drooping to the skirts of these bone-dry mountains !
wind, with rain, blew strongly through the open wilderness in
the night-time. We lodged, at evening, beside some booths of
Mertaad Arabs, and I went over by and by to their cheerful
watch-fires. Where I entered the fire-light before a principal
beyt, the householder received me kindly and soon brought
me in a vast bowl of fresh camel-milk. They asked me no
questions,—to keep silence is the host's gentleness, and they had
seen my white tent standing before sunset. When I was rising
to depart, the man, with a mild gesture, bade me sit still.
I saw a sheep led in to be sacrificed ;—because Misshel had
alighted by them, he would make a guest-supper. *Ajid* Ibn
Mertaad, this good sheykh, told me his Aarab went up in
droughty years to the Shimbel, and as far as Palmyra, and
Keriateyn ! I lay down and slumbered in the hospitable security
of his worsted tent till his feast was ready, and then they sent
and called Misshel and the Auájy sheykhs. Their boiled
mutton (so far from the Red Sea coast) was served upon a
mess of that other rice-kind, temmn, which is brought from

el-Irâk, and is (though they esteem it less) of better savour and
sustenance. Misshel, and every man of these Bishr tribesmen,
when they rose after supper and had blessed their host, bore
away—I had not seen it before—a piece of the meat and a bone,
and that was for his housewife journeying with him.

Upon the morrow, the fifth from Teyma, we ascended over
the very rugged highlands eastward by a way named the *Derb
Zilláj*, where the height was 4500 feet, and I saw little flowerets,
daughters of the rain, already sprung in the desert. At noon
we reached Messhel's menzil of only few tents standing together
upon this wide sandstone mountain platform where we now
arrived, *el-Kharram*, the altitude is 5400 feet : the thermometer
in the open showed 80° F. From hence the long mountain train
appeared above the clouds, of Irnàn, in the north, nearly a day
distant.

At afternoon there came in two strange tribesmen, that
arrived from a dîra in the southward near Medina : they said,
there was no rain fallen in the Jeheyna dîra, nor in all the country of the W. el-Humth ! A bowl of dates was set before them ;
and the Beduin guests, with the desert comity, bade me [a guest]
draw near to eat with them :—Misshel, although I was sitting in
his tent, had not bidden the Nasrâny ! I took and ate two of
the fruits, that there might be " the bread and salt " between us.
I had with me a large Moorish girdle of red woollen ; Misshel
now said, I should give it him, or else, billah, he would ' take
me ' and my things for a booty. The girdle of the settled
countries, *kúmr*, is coveted by the nomad horsemen, that
binding thus the infirmer parts of the body they think a man
may put forth his strength the better. ' The girdle, I said, was
necessary to me ; yet let Misshel give me a strong young camel,
and I would give him my old nâga and the girdle.'—This man's
camels were many more than two hundred ! ' Well then, Misshel
answered, he would take me.'—" See the date-stones in my
hand, thou canst not, Misshel, there is now ' bread and salt '
between us."—" But that will not avail thee ; what and if to-
morrow I drive thee from us, thou and thy old nâga, canst
thou find a way in the wilderness and return to el-Héjr ? "—
" I know it is four journeys south of west, God visit it upon thee,
and I doubt not it may please Ullah, I shall yet come forth."—
" But all the country is full of habalîs."—" Rich Misshel, wouldst
thou strip a poor man ! but all these threats are idle, I am thy
guest."—They believe the Nasâra to be expert riders, so it was
said to me, ' To-morrow would I meet Misshel on horse-back,
and I should be armed with a pistol ? ' I answered, ' If it must
be so, I would do my endeavour.'—" Nay, in the morning

Khalîl shall mount his old nâga (said Misshel again) and ride
to Medáin Sâlih ; " so with a sturdy smile he gave up the
quest, seeing he could not move me. His younger son, who
sat dropsical in the father's tent, here said a good word, ' Well,
let Khalîl sleep upon it,—and to-morrow they would give me
a nâga for the Khuèyra and the girdle.'—In their greediness
to spoil the castaway life, whom they will not help forward, the
Arabs are viler than any nation !

Hayzàn in the morning bade me prepare to depart, Askar
and some companions were setting out for Hâyil, and we might
ride with them ; he enquired ' Was my old nâga able to run
with thelûls ? '—" She is an old camel, and no dromedary."—
" Then we must ride apart from them." Hayzàn, when he had
received his money, said he could not accompany me himself,
' but this other man,' whom he feigned to be his brother, besides
he named him falsely.—Hard it were to avoid such frauds of
the Beduins ! Misshel said, " Well, I warrant him, go in peace."
I made the condition that my bags should be laid upon his
thelûl, and I might mount her myself ; so we set forward.

This rafîk looked like a wild man : Askar and his fellowship
were already in the way before us ; we passed by some shallow
water-holes that had been newly cleared ; I wondered to see
them in this high ground. We came then to the brow, on
the north, of the Kharram mountain, here very deep and
precipitous to the plain below ; in such a difficult place the
camels, holding the fore-legs stiff and plumping from ledge
to ledge, make a shift to climb downward. So, descending,
as we could, painfully to the underlying sand desert, and
riding towards a low sandstone coast, *Abbassîeh*, west of
Misma, we by and by overtook Askar's company. Coming
nigh the east end of the mountain, they thought they
espied habalîs lurking in the rocks, " Heteym of the Nefûd,
and foemen," where landlopers had been seen the day before.
" Khalîl (said Askar), can your nâga keep pace with us ? we are
Beduw, and *nenhash (nahájj)* ! we will hie from any danger upon
our thelûls ; hasten now the best thou canst, or we must needs
leave thee behind us, so thou wilt fall alone into the hands
of the robbers." They all put their light and fresh thelûls
to the trot : my old loaded nâga, and jaded after the long
journey from Teyma, fell immediately behind them, and such
was her wooden gait I could not almost suffer it. I saw all
would be a vain effort in any peril ; the stars were contrary
for this voyage, none of my companions had any human good
in them, but Askar only. My wild rafîk, whom I had bound
at our setting out by the most solemn oath, ' upon the herb stem,'

that he would not forsake me, now cried out, 'Wellah-billah, he would abandon me if I mended not my pace (which was impossible); he must follow his companions, and was their rafîk,' so they ran on a mile or two.

The last days' rain had cooled the air; this forenoon was overcast, but the sun sometimes shone out warmly. When with much ado I came up to my flying fellowship, I said to Askar, "Were the enemies upon you, would you forsake me who am your way-fellow?" "I would, he said, take thee up back-rider on my thelûl, and we will run one fortune together; Khalîl, I will not forsake thee." They were in hope to lodge with Aarab that night, before we came to the Misma mountain, now before us. The plain was sand, and reefs of sandstone rocks, in whose hollows were little pools of the sweet rain-water. At half-afternoon they descried camels very far in front; we alighted, and some climbed upon the next crags to look out, who soon reported that those Aarab were rahîl, and they seemed about to encamp. We rode then towards the Misma mountain, till we came to those Beduins; they were but a family of Shammar, faring in the immense solitudes. And doubtless, seeing us, they had felt a cold dread in their loins, for we found them shrunk down in a low ground, with their few camels couched by them, and the housewife had not built the beyt. They watched us ride by them, with inquiet looks, for there is no amity between Annezy and Shammar.—That which contains their enmities is only the injunction of the Emir. I would have asked these Beduins to let me drink water, for all day we had ridden vehemently without drawing bridle, and the light was now nearly spent; but my companions pricked forward. I bade my rafîk lend me at last his more easy thelûl, that such had been our covenant; but the wild fellow denied me, and would not slack his pace. I was often, whilst they trotted, fallen so far back as to be in danger of losing them out of sight, and always in dread that my worn-out nâga might sink under me, and also cast her young.

At Askar's word, when they saw I might not longer endure the fellow assented to exchange riding with me, and I mounted his dromedary; we entered then at a low gap in the Misma near the eastern end of this long-ranging sandstone reef. My companions looked from the brow, for any black booths of Aarab, in the plain desert beyond to the horizon. One thought he saw tents very far distant, but the rest doubted, and now the sun was setting. We came down by the deep driven sand upon the sides of the mountain, at a windy rush, which seemed like a bird's flight, of the thelûls under us, though in the even any horse may overtake them. The seat upon a good thelûl " swimming," as say their ancient poets, over sand-ground, is so easy that an inured rider may sometimes hardly feel his saddle.

We descended to a large rain-pool in the sand-rock, where they alighted, and washed, and kneeling in the desert began to say their sunset prayers ; but Askar, though the night was coming on, and having nothing to dry him, washed all his body, and his companions questioning with him, " That thus behoved a man, he said, who has slept with his wife ; " and then let him return with confidence to ask his petition of Ullah :—the like Moses commanded. Moslems, whether in sickness or health, if the body be sullied by any natural impurity, durst not say their formal prayers. Many patients have come to me lamenting that, for an infirmity, ' they might not pray ' ; and then they seem to themselves as the shut out from grace, and profane. Thus they make God a looker upon the skin, rather than the Weigher and Searcher-out of the secret truth of man's heart. We rode now in the glooming ; this easy-riding lasted for me not far, for the darkness coming on, *Nasr* my rafîk could not be appeased, and I must needs return to my old nâga's back, ' For, he said, I might break away with her (his thelûl) in the night-time.' In Nasr's eyes, as formerly for Horeysh, I was a Beduin, and a camel-thief ; and with this mad fantasy in him he had not suffered me earlier in the day to mount his rikàb, that was indeed the swiftest in the company ; for Askar and the rest who were sheykhs had left at home their better beasts, which they reserve unwearied for warfare.

We had ridden two hours since the sunset, and in this long day's race the best part of fifty miles ; and now they consulted together, were it not best to dismount and pass the night as we were ? We had not broken our fast to-day, and carried neither food nor water, so confident they were that every night we should sup with Aarab. They agreed to ride somewhat further ; and it was not long before we saw a glimpsing of Beduin watch-fires. We drew near them in an hour more, and I heard the evening sounds of a nomad menzil ; the monotonous mirth of the children, straying round from the watch-fires and singing at the houses of hair. We arrived so silently, the dogs had not barked. There were two or three booths. When the Aarab perceived us, all voices were hushed : their cheerful fires, where a moment before we saw the people sitting, were suddenly quenched with sand. We were six or seven riders, and they thought we might be an hostile ghrazzu. Alighting in silence, we sat down a little aloof : none of us so

much as whispered to his companion by name ; for the open
desert is full of old debts for blood. At a strange meeting, and
yet more at such hours, the nomads are in suspense of mind and
mistrust of each other. When, impatient of their mumming,
I would have said Salaam ! they prayed me be silent. After
the whisperers within had sufficiently taken knowledge of our
peaceable demeanour, one approaching circumspectly, gave us
the word of peace, *Salaam aleyk*, and it was readily answered
by us all again, *Aleykom es-salaam*. After this sacrament of
the lips between Beduw, there is no more doubt among them
of any evil turn. The man led Askar and his fellowship to his
beyt, and I went over to another with Nasr my rafîk and a
nomad whom we had met riding with his son in the desert
beyond Misma. The covered coals were raked up, and we
saw the fires again.

What these Aarab were we could not tell, neither knew
they what men we were ; we have seen the desert people ask no
questions of the guest, until he have eaten meat ; yet after some
little discoursing between them, as of the rain this year, and
the pasture, they may each commonly come to guess the other's
tribe. When I asked my rough companion " What tribesmen
be these ? " he answered in a whisper, ' he knew not yet ; ' soon
after we understood by the voices that they had recognized
Askar in the other tent. He was the son of their own high-
sheykh ; and these Aarab were Wélad Sleyman, a division of
Bishr, though the men's faces were nearly unknown to each
other. Our host having walked over to the chief tent to hear
the news, we were left with his housewife, and I saw her
beginning to bray corn with a bat, in a wooden mortar, a manner
not used by the southern Beduw of my former acquaintance ;
but bruised corn is here as often served for the guest-meal as
temmn. The year was now turned to winter in the waste wilderness, they had fenced round their booths from the late bitter
rain and wind with dry bushes.

There came in one from the third remaining tent, and
supped with us. I wondered, seeing this tribesman, and he
wondered to look upon me : he a Beduwy, wearing the Turkey
red cap, *tarbûsh*, and an old striped gown *kumbâz*, the use
of the civil border countries ! When I asked what man he was,
he answered that being "weak" he was gone a soldiering to
Sham and had served the Dowla for reals : and now he was
come home to the nomad life, with that which he esteemed a
pretty bundle of silver. In this the beginning of his prosperity
he had bought himself camels, and goats and sheep, he would
buy also my old nâga for the price I set upon her, seven reals,

to slaughter in the feast for his deceased father.—Where Beduins
are soldiery, this seemed to me a new world! Yet afterwards,
I have learned that there are tribesmen of Bishr and Harb,
Ageyl riders in the great cities. The Beduin who saw in
the stranger his own town life at Damascus, was pleased to
chat long with me, were it only to say over the names of the
chief sûks of the plenteous great city. He should bring his
reals in the morning; and, would I stay here, he would
provide for my further journey to Hâyil, whither he must go
himself shortly.—But when my rafîk called me to mount before
the dawn, I could not stay to expect him. Afterwards finding
me at Hâyil, he blamed me that I had not awaited him, and
enquired for my nâga, which I had already sold at a loss. He
told me that at our arriving that night, they had taken their
matchlocks to shoot at us; but seeing the great bags on my
camels, and hearing my voice, they knew me to be none of the
nomads, and that we were not riding in a ghrazzu.

We hasted again over the face of the wilderness to find a
great menzil of Aarab, where my fellowship promised themselves
to drink coffee. Sheykhs accustomed to the coffee-tent think
it no day of their lives, if they have not sipped kahwa; and
riding thus, they smoked tittun in their pipe-heads incessantly.
We arrived in the dawning and dismounted, as before, in two
fellowships, Askar and his companions going over to the sheykhly
coffee-tent : this is their desert courtesy, not to lay a burden
upon any household. The people were Shammar, and they
received us with their wonted hospitality. Excellent dates
(of other savour and colour than those of el-Ally and Teyma)
were here set before us, and a vast bowl—that most comfortable
refreshment in the wilderness—of their camels' léban. Then
we were called to the sheykh's tent, where the sheykh himself, with magnanimous smiles, already prepared coffee. When
he heard I was an hakîm, he bade bring in his little ailing
grand-daughter. I told the mother that we were but in passage, and my remedy could only little avail her child. The
sheykh, turning to my companions, said therefore, 'That I must
be some very honest person.'—" It is thus, Askar answered him,
and ye may be sure of him in all." The sheykh reached me
the bowl, and after I had supped a draught, he asked me, ' What
countryman I was?' I answered "An Engleysy," so he whispered in my ear, " Engreys !—then a Nasrâny ? " I said aloud,
" Ay billah; " the good sheykh gave me a smile again, in which
his soul said, " I will not betray thee."—The coffee ready, he
poured out for me before them all. When my companions had

swallowed the scalding second cup, they rose in their unlucky running haste to depart : the sheykh bade me stay a moment, to drink a little more of his pleasant milk and strengthen myself.

We rode on in the waste wilderness eastward, here passing out of the Misma district, and having upon the right-hand certain mountains, landmarks of that great watering-place *Baitha Nethîl.* From the Kharram we might have ridden to Hâyil eastward of the mountain *Ajja ;* but that part they thought would be now empty of the wandering Beduins. This high and open plain,—3800 feet, is all strewed with shales as it were of iron-stone ; but towards noon I saw we were come in a granite country, and we passed under a small basalt mountain, coal-black and shining. The crags rising from this soil were grey granite ; *Ibrân,* a blackish mountain, appeared upon our horizon, some hours distant, ranging to the northward. A little later we came in Nefûd sand and, finding there wild hay, the Beduins alighted, to gather provender. This was to bait their cattle in the time when they should be lying at Hâyil, where the country next about is *máhal,* a barrenness of soil hardly less than that which lies about Teyma. To make hay were unbecoming a great sheykh : and whilst the rest were busy, Askar digged with his hands in the sand to the elbow, to sound the depth of the late fallen rain, this being all they might look for till another autumn, and whereof the new year's herb must spring. Showers had lately fallen, sixteen days together ; yet we saw almost no sign in the wilderness soil of small freshets. When Askar had put down his bare arm nearly to the shoulder, he took up the old sandy drought ; the moisture of the rain had not sunk to a full yard ! The seasonable rains are partial in Arabia, which in these latitudes is justly accounted a nearly rainless country. Whilst it rained in the Kharram no showers were fallen in the Jeheyna dîra ; and so little fell at Kheybar, a hundred miles distant, that in the new year's months there sprang nearly no rabîa in those lava mountains.

We had not ridden far in this Nefûd, when at half-afternoon we saw a herd of camels moving before us at pasture in their slow dispersed manner ; we found beyond where the nomad booths were pitched in an hollow place. Beduins, when encamping few together, choose deep ground, where they are sheltered from the weather, and by day the black beyts are not so soon discerned, nor their watch-fires in the night-time. These also were Shammar, which tribe held all the country now before us to the Jebel villages ;—they were scattered by families as in a peaceable country of the Emir's dominion, with many

wells about them. Flies swarming here upon the sand, were a
sign that we approached the palm settlements. Whenever we
came to tents in this country the Aarab immediately asked of
us, very earnestly, " What of the rain ? tell us is there much
fallen in the Auájy dîra ? " My companions ever answered
with the same word, *La tanshud,* " Ask not of it." If any
questioned them, ' Who was this stranger they brought with
them ? ' the Auájy responded, with what meaning I could not
tell, " *El-kheyr Ullah.*" The sheykh in this menzil would have
bought my nâga, engaging as well to convey me to Hâyil after
a few days in which I should be his guest.

I thought at least we should have rested here this night
over ; but my companions when they rose from supper took
again their thelûls to ride and run, and Nasr with them ; they
would not tarry a moment for me at the bargain of the nâga.—
Better I thought to depart then with these whom I know, and
be sure to arrive at Hâyil, than remain behind them in booths
of unknown Beduins ; besides, we heard that a large Shammar
encampment lay not much before us, and a coffee-sheykh : Askar
promised to commit me to those Aarab, if he might persuade my rafîk to remain with me. I was broken with this
rough riding : the heart every moment leaping to my throat,
which torment they call *katu 'l-kalb,* or heart-cutting. They
scoured before me all the hours of the day, in their light
riding, so that with less than keeping a good will, death at
length would have been a welcome deliverance out of present
miseries. The Aarab lay pitched under the next mountain ;
but riding further in the darkness two hours, and not seeing
their watch-fires, the Auájy would then have ridden on all that
long night, to come the earlier, they said, to Hâyil. They must
soon have forsaken me, I could not go much further, and my
decrepit nâga fainted under me : by and by Askar, overcome
by drowsiness, murmured to his companions, " Let us alight
then and sleep." A watch-fire now appeared upon our right
hand, which had been hidden by some unevenness of the ground,
but they neglected it, for the present sweetness of sleeping : we
alighted, and binding the camels' knees, lay down to rest by
our cattle in the sandy desert.

We had not ridden on the morrow an hour when, at sun-
rising, we descried many black booths of a Beduin encampment, where the Auájy had promised me rest : but as ever
the scalding coffee was past their throats, and they had swallowed a few of the Shammary's dates, they rose to take their
dromedaries again. Such promises of nomads are but sounds in

the air; neither would my wild and brutish rafîk hear my words, nor could Askar persuade him: "Wellah, I have no authority," said he; and Nasr cried, "Choose thee, Khalîl, whether thou wilt sit here or else ride with us; but I go in my company." What remained, but to hold the race with them? now to me an agony, and my nâga was ready to fall under me. As we rode, "It is plain, said Askar, that Khalîl may not hold out; wilt thou turn back, Khalîl, to the booths? and doubt not that they will receive thee."—"How receive me? you even now lied to them at the kahwa, saying ye were not Auájy, and you have not commended me to them: what when they understand that I am a Nasrâny? also this Nasr, my rafîk, forsakes me!"—"We shall come to-day, they said, to a settlement, and will leave thee there." We had neglected to drink at the tents, and riding very thirsty, when the sun rose high, we had little hope to find more rain-pools in a sandy wilderness. Afterward espying some little gleam under the sun far off, they hastened thither,—but it was a glistering clay bottom, and in the midst a puddle, which we all forsook. The altitude of this plain is 3700 feet, and it seemed to fall before us to J. Ajja which now appeared as a mighty bank of not very high granite mountain, and stretching north and south. The soil is granite-sand and grit, and rolling stones and rotten granite rock. We passed, two hours before noon, the ruins of a hamlet of one well which had been forsaken five years before. Askar said, "The cattle perished after some rainless years for want of pasture, and the few people died of the small-pox,"—not seldom calamities of the small out-settlements, in Arabia. When I asked the name of the place, he answered shortly, *Melûn Tâlibuhu*, which might mean " Cursed is everyone that enquireth thereof."

We found a pool of clear rain in the rock, which, warmed in the sun, seemed to us sweeter than milk. There we satisfied our thirst, and led our beasts to drink, which had run an hundred and thirty miles without pasture or water, since the Kharram. His companions before we mounted went to cut a little more dry grass, and Askar said to me, "Khalîl, the people where we are going are jealous. Let them not see thee writing, for be sure they will take it amiss; but wouldst thou write, write covertly, and put away these leaves of books. Thou wast hitherto with the Beduw, and the Beduw have known thee what thou art; but, hearest thou? they are not like good-hearted, in yonder villages!" We rode again an hour or two and saw the green heads of palms, under the mountain, of a small village, where, they said, five or six families dwelt, *Jefeyfa.*

Upon the north I saw *J. Tály,* a solitary granitic mountain
on the wilderness horizon. My company, always far in advance,
were now ridden out of my sight. I let them pass, I could
no longer follow them, not doubting that with these landmarks before me I should shortly come to the inhabited. There
I lighted upon a deep-beaten path,—such are worn in the
hard desert soil, near settlements which lie upon common
ways, by the generations of nomad passengers. I went on
foot, leading my fainting camel at a slow pace, till I espied
the first heads of palms, and green lines of the plantations of
Môgug. At length I descried Nasr returning out of the distance to meet me. At the entering of the place my jaded camel
fell down bellowing, this a little delayed us ; but Nasr raised
and driving her with cruel blows, we entered Môgug about an
hour and a half after noon.

I wondered to see the village full of ruins and that
many of their palms were dead and sere, till I learned that
Môg(k)ug(k) had been wasted by the plague a few years before.
Their house building is no more the neat clay-brick work
which we see at Teyma, but earthen walls in layers, with
some cores of hard sun-dried brick laid athwart in them ;
the soil is here granitic. The crumbling aspect of the place
made me think of certain oases which I had seen years
before in the Algerian Sáhara. Their ground-water is lukewarm, as in all the Arabian country, and of a corrupt savour ;
the site is feverish, their dates are scaly, dry, and not well-
tasting. We went towards the sheykh's kahwa, where the
companions had preceded us, and met with the good sheykh
who was coming forth to meet me. He led me friendly by the
hand, and bade his man straw down green garden stalks for
our camels. When we were seated in the coffee-room there
entered many of the villagers, who without showing any altered
countenance—it might be for some well-said word of Aškar
beforehand—seemed to regard me favourably. Seeing all so
well disposed, I laid before the sheykh my quarrel with Nasr,
and was supported by Askar, he allowing that my nâga could
not go forward.

Even now they would mount immediately, and ride all
night to be at Hâyil ere day. ' He would go in their company,
said Nasr, and if I could not ride with them, he must
forsake me here.' The sheykh of Môgug ruled that since the
camel could not proceed, Nasr, who had taken wages, must
remain with me, or leaving so much of his money as might pay
another man (to convey me to Hâyil) he might depart freely.
The elf, having, by the sheykh's judgment, to disburse a real,

chose rather to remain with me. Askar and his fellowship rose
again hastily from the dates and water, to ride to Hâyil. This
long way from the Kharram they had ridden, in a continued running, carrying with them neither food nor water-skins, nor coffee :
they trusted to their good eyesight to find every day the Aarab.
All were young men in the heat of their blood, that rode in a
sort of boast of their fresh endurance and ability. I asked
Askar, wherefore this haste, and why they did not in any place
take a little repose. *Answer :* " That we may be the sooner at
home again ; and to stay at the menzils by the way were unbecoming (*ayb*)." When they were gone, the villagers sitting
in the kahwa—they were Shammar—blamed my companions
as *Annezy !* These narrow jealousies of neighbours often fur
thered me, as I journeyed without favour in this vast land of
Arabia.

Here first I saw Bagdad wares, from the sûk at Hâyil : the
men of Môgug no longer kindled the galliûns with flint and
steel, but with the world-wide Vienna *Zündhölzer*,—we were
in the world again ! Dim was their rudely-built coffee-hall,
and less cleanly than hospitable ; the earthen floor where we
sat was littered with old date-stones of the common service
to daily guests. The villagers were of a kindly humour ;
and pleased themselves in conversing with the stranger, so far
as their short notice might stretch, of foreign countries and
religions : they lamented that the heathen yet resisted the
truth, and more especially the Nasâra, in whom was a well
of the arts, and learning. They reached me from time to
time their peaceable galliûns. I thought the taste of their
bitter green tobacco, in this extremity of fatigue, of incomparable sweetness, and there was a comfortable repose in those
civil voices after the wild malignity of the Bishr tongues. A
young man asked me, ' Could I read ?—had I any books ? '
He was of Môgug, and their schoolmaster. I put in his hand
a geography written in the Arabic tongue by a learned
American missionary of Beyrût.—The young man perused and
hung his head over it in the dull chamber, with such a thirsty
affection to letters, as might in a happier land have ripened
in the large fields of learning : at last closing the book, when
the sun was going down, he laid it on his head in token
how highly he esteemed it,—an Oriental gesture which I have
not seen again in Arabia, where is so little (or nothing) of
" *Orientalism.*" He asked me, ' Might he buy the book ?—
(and because I said nay) might he take it home then to read
in the night ? ' which I granted.

A tall dark man entered the kahwa, I saw he was a stranger from the north, of a proud carriage and very well clad. Coldly he saluted the company, and sat down : he arrived from *Gofar* where he had mounted this morning. The dates were set before him, and looking round when he remembered one or two sitting here, with whom he had met in former years, he greeted them and, rising solemnly, kissed and asked of their welfare. He was a Shammary of Irâk ; his Beduin dîra lay 250 miles from hence. Long and enviously he looked upon me, as I sat with my kerchief cast back in the heat, then he enquired, " Who is he ?—eigh ! a Nasrâny, say ye ! and I knew it : this is one, O people ! who has some dangerous project, and ye cannot tell what ; this man is one of the Frankish nation ! " I answered, " It is known to all who sit here, that I am an Engleysy, and should I be ashamed of that ? what man art thou, and wherefore in these parts ? " —" I am at Hâyil for the Emir's business !—wellah, he said, turning to the company, he can be none other than a spy, one come to search out the country ! tell me what is reported of this man ; if he question the Aarab, and does he write their answers ? "—A villager said, ' Years before one had been here, a stranger, who named himself a Moslem, but he could guess, he was such as Khalîl, and he had written whatsoever he enquired of them.'

The villagers sat on with little care of *Nasr's* talk (that was also his name), misliking, perhaps, the northern man's lofty looks, and besides they were well persuaded of me. The sheykh answered him, " If there be any fault in Khalîl, he is going to Hâyil, and let the Emir look to it." Nasr, seeing the company was not for him, laid down his hostile looks and began to discourse friendly with me. At evening we were called out to a house in the village ; a large supper was set before us, of boiled mutton and temmn, and we ate together.

Nasr told me the northern horses abound in his dîra ; he had five mares, though he was not a sheykh, and his camels were many ; for their wilderness is not like these extreme southern countries, but full of the bounty of Ullah. As he saw my clothing worn and rent—so long had I led my life in the khála—he bade me go better clad before the Emir at Hâyil, and be very circumspect to give no cause, even of a word that might be taken amiss, amongst a people light and heady, soon angry, and [in which lies all the hardship of travelling in Arabia] unused to the sight of a stranger. Here first in Nejd I heard the *nûn* in the ending of nouns pro-

nounced indefinitely, it is like an Attic sweetness in the
Arabian tongue, and savours at the first hearing of self-
pleasing, but is with them a natural erudition. The sultry
evening closed in with a storm of lightning and rain; these
were the last days of October. In this small village might be
hardly 150 souls.

Upon the morrow we stayed to drink the early kahwa;
and then riding over a last mile of the plain, with blue and
red granite rocks, to the steep sides of Ajja, I saw a passage
before us in a cleft which opens through the midst of the
mountain, eighteen long miles to the plain beyond; this strait
is named, *Rîa es-Self*. The way at first is steep and rugged:
about nine o'clock we went by a cold spring, which tumbled
from the cliff above!—I have not seen another falling water
in the waterless Arabia. There we filled our girby, and the
Arabs, stripping off their clothing, ran to wash themselves;
—the nomads, at every opportunity of water, will plash like
sparrows. Not much further are rude ground-walls of an
ancient dam, and in a bay of the mountain unhusbanded palms
of the Beduins; there was some tillage in time past. At the
highest of the rîa, I found 5100 feet.

A poor Beduwy had joined our company in the plain,
he came, driving an ass, along with us, and was glad when I
reached him an handful of Teyma dates to his breakfast. Later,
at a turn of the rock, there met us three rough-looking tribesmen of Shammar, coming on in hot haste, with arms in their
hands. These men stayed us; and whilst we stood, as the Arabs
will, to hear and tell tidings, they eyed me like fiends. They
understanding, perhaps, from some of Askar's malicious fellowship, of the Nasrâny's passing to-day by the rîa, had a mind
to assail me. Now seeing themselves evenly matched, they
said to him of the ass, and who was their tribesman, " Turn thou
and let us kill him ! "— " God forbid it (the poor man answered
them), he is my fellow ! " They grinning savagely then with all
their teeth, passed from us. " Now Khalîl ! (said Nasr,) hast thou
seen ?—and this is that I told thee, the peril of lonely riding
through their country ! these are the cursed Shammar, and, had
we been by ourselves they would have set upon thee,—Ullah
curse the Shammar ! "—" Have we not in the last days tasted of
their hospitality ? "—" Well, I tell thee they are fair-faced and
good to the guest in the beyts, but if they meet a solitary man,
kh'lûy, in the khála, and none is by to see it, they will kill him !
and those were murderers we saw now, lurkers behind rocks, to
cut off any whom they may find without defence.

There is but the Emir's peace and no love between Bishr and Shammar. Not many years before, a bitter quarrel for the rights of the principal water station of their deserts, Baitha Nethîl, had divided these nigh dwellers. Baitha Nethîl is in the Bishr borders, and they could not suffer it patiently, that Shammar came down to water there, and in that were supported by the Emir Telâl. For this they forsook even their own dîra, and migrating northward, wandered in the wilderness of their Annezy kindred in Syria, and there remained two or three years : but, because they were new comers in those strange marches, many foraying enemies lifted their cattle ;—and the Bishr returned to their own country and the Emir.

—In the midst of the rîa the granite mountain recedes upon the north side and there are low domes of plutonic basalt, which resemble cones of volcanoes. We heard there a galloping tumult behind us, and a great shuffling of camels' feet over the gritty rocks ; it was a loose troop of *ajlâb*, or " fetched," dromedaries, the drove of a camel broker. The drovers went to sell them " in Jebel Shammar." These tribesmen were Bishr, and in their company our apprehensions were ended. A driving lad cried to me, " Hast thou not some kaak (biscuit cake of Damascus) to give me ? in all this day's going and running I have tasted nothing." It was late in the afternoon when we came forth, and as I looked down over the plain of Gofar, the oasis greenness of palms lay a little before us. The sun was setting, and Nasr showed me the two-horned basalt mountain, *Sumrà* Hâyil, which stands a little behind the village capital, upon the northward. Gofar, written Káfar, and in the mouth of the nomads Jiffar, lies, like Môgug, enclosed by orchard walling from the desert. In the plain before the town, I read the altitude 4300 feet. We entered by a broad empty way, between long walls, where we saw no one, nor the houses of the place. It was sunset, when the Arabian villagers go in to their suppers. There met us only a woman,—loathly to look upon ! for the feminine face was blotted out by the sordid veil-clout ; in our eyes, an heathenish Asiatic villany ! and the gentle blooded Arabian race, in the matter of the hareem, are become churls. —Beginning at Káfar, all their women's faces, which God created for the cheerfulness of the human world, are turned to this jealous horror ; and there is nothing seen of their wimpled wives, in sorry garments, but the hands ! We dismounted by a mosque at the *munâkh*, or couching place of strangers' camels, where all passengers alight and are received to supper : the public charge for hospitality is here (upon a com-

mon way) very great, for, by the Arabian custom, wayfarers
depart at afternoon, and those who ride from Hâyil to the
southward pass only that first short stage, to sleep at Gofar.

Arriving with the drovers, we were bidden in together to
sup of their scaly lean dates and water ; dates, even the best,
are accounted no evening fare to set before strangers. He
who served us made his excuses, saying that the householder
was in Hâyil. The citizens of Gofar, *Beny Temím*, are not
praised for hospitality, which were sooner to find in Hâyil,
inhabited by Shammar. Nasr my rafîk, who had showed himself more treatable since the others' departure, afterwards
began to blame the passers-by in the street, because none had
bidden me to coffee and to sleep in their houses, saying,
' Would they leave an honourable person to lodge in the open
ways ! ' Nasr strawed down equally, of his store of dry provender, to his thelûl and to my poor nâga ; then he made dough
of some barley-meal I had bought at Môgug and kneaded
it with dates, and thrusting this paste into her mouth by
handfuls, he fed my weary beast. There we lay down by our
cattle, to pass this starry night, in the dust of their village
street.

We mounted at break of day : Nasr would be at Hâyil in
time to go to breakfast in the guest-hall, with Askar and his
fellowship. I wondered, to see that all that side of Gofar town,
towards Hâyil, was ruinous, and the once fruitful orchard-
grounds were now like the soil of the empty desert,—and tall
stems, yet standing in their ranks, of sere and dead palms. We
rode by cavernous labyrinths of clay-building under broken
house-walling, whose timbers had been taken away, and over
sunken paths of the draught-camels, where their wells now lay
abandoned. When I asked, " What is this ? " Nasr answered,
Béled mât, " a died-out place." The villagers had perished, as
those of Môgug, in a plague which came upon them seven years
before. Now their wells were fallen in, which must be sunk
in this settlement to more than twenty-five fathoms. The
owners of the ground, after the pestilence, lacked strength to
labour, and had retired to the inner oasis.

Beyond Gofar orchard walls is that extreme barrenness of
desert plain (máhal) which lies before Hâyil ; the soil, a sharp
granite-grit, is spread out between the desolate mountains
Ajja and *Selma*, barren as a sea-strand and lifeless as the dust
of our streets ; and yet therein are hamlets and villages, upon
veins of ground-water. It is a mountain ground where almost
nothing may spring of itself, but irrigated it will yield barley

and wheat, and the other Nejd grains. Though their palms grow high they bear only small and hot, and therefore less wholesome kinds of date-berries. We found hardly a blade or a bush besides the senna plant, flowering with yellow pea-like blossoms. The few goats of the town must be driven far back under the coast of Ajja to find pasture. After two hours Nasr said, " Hâyil is little further, we are here at the mid-way ; women and children go between Hâyil and Gofar before their (noon) breakfast." Thus the road may be eleven miles nearly. Hâyil was yet hidden by the brow of the desert,—everywhere the horizon seemed to me very near in Nomad Arabia. Between these towns is a trodden path ; and now we met those coming out from Hâyil. They were hareem. and children on foot, and some men riding upon asses : " Ha ! (said a fellow, and then another, and another, to Nasr) why dost thou bring him ? " —So I knew that the Nasrâny's coming had been published in Hâyil ! and Nasr hearing their words began to be aghast. ' What, he said, if his head should be taken off ! '—" And Khalîl, where is the tobacco-bag ? and reach me that galliûn, for billah, my head turns." We had ridden a mile further, when I espied two horsemen galloping towards us in a great dust. I began to muse, were these hot riders some cruel messengers of the Emir, chevying out from Hâyil upon my account ?—The name of Nasrâny was yet an execration in this country, and even among nomads a man will say to another, " Dost thou take me for a Nasrâny ! that I should do such [iniquitous] thing."— Already the cavaliers were upon us, and as only may riders of the mild Arabian mares, they reined up suddenly abreast of us, their garments flying before them in the still air ; and one of them shouted in a harsh voice to Nasr (who answered nothing, for he was afraid), " All that baggage is whose, ha ? "—so they rode on from us as before ; I sat drooping upon my camel with fatigue, and had not much regarded what men they were.

We saw afterward some high building with battled towers. These well-built and stately Nejd turrets of clay brick are shaped like our light-houses ; and, said Nasr, who since Telâl's time had not been to Hâyil, " That is the Emir's summer residence." As we approached Hâyil I saw that the walls extended backward, making of the town a vast enclosure of palms. Upon our right hand I saw a long grove of palms in the desert, closed by high walls ; upon the left lies another outlying in the wilderness and larger, which Abeyd planted for the inheritance of his children. Now appeared as it were suspended above the town, the whitened donjon of the *Kasr*,—such clay buildings they whiten with jiss. We rode by that summer residence which stands at the way-side; in the tower, they say, is mounted a small piece of artillery. Under the summer-house wall is a new conduit, by which there flows out irrigation water to a public tank, and townswomen come hither to fetch water. This, which they call *mâ es-Sáma*, is reckoned the best water in the town; from all their other wells the water comes up with some savour of salty and bitter minerals, "which (though never so slight) is an occasion of fever." We alighted, and at my bidding a woman took down the great (metal) water-pan upon her head to give us to drink. Nasr spoke to me not to mount anew; he said we had certain low gateways to pass. That was but guile of the wild Beduwy, who with his long matted locks seemed less man than satyr or werwolf. They are in dread to be cried down for a word, and even mishandled in the towns; his wit was therefore not to bring in the Nasrâny riding at the (proud) height of his camel.

I went on walking by the short outer street, and came to the rude two-leaved gateway (which is closed by night) of the inner sûk of Hâyil. There I saw the face of an old acquaintance who awaited me,—Abd el-Azîz, he who was conductor of Ibn Rashîd's gift mare, now twelve months past, to the kella at el-Héjr. I greeted him, and he greeted me, asking kindly of my health, and bade me enter. He went before me, by another way, to bring the tiding to the Emir, and I passed on, walking through the public sûk, full of tradesmen and Beduw at this hour, and I saw many in the small dark Arab shops, busy about their buying and selling. Where we came by the throng of men and camels, the people hardly noted the stranger; some only turned to look after us. A little further there stepped out a well-clad merchant, with a saffron-dye beard, who in the Arabian guise took me by the hand, and led me some steps forward, only to enquire cautelously of the stranger 'From whence I came?' A few saffron beards are seen at Hâyil: in his last years Abeyd ibn Rashîd had turned his grey hairs to a saffron beard. It is the Persian manner, and I may put that to my good fortune, being a traveller of the English colour, in Arabia. The welfaring men stain their eyes with kahl; and of these bird-like Arabians it is the male sex which is bright-feathered and adorned. Near the sûk's end is their corn market, and where are sold camel-loads of fire-wood, and wild hay from the wilderness. Lower I saw veiled women-sellers under a porch with baskets where they sit daily from the sunrise to sell dates and pumpkins; and some of them sell poor ornaments from the north, for the hareem.

We came into the long-square public place, *el-Méshab,* which is before the castle, *el-Kasr.* Under the next porch, which is a refuge of poor Beduin passengers, Nasr couched my camel, hastily, and setting down the bags, he withdrew from me ; the poor nomad was afraid. Abd el-Azîz, coming again from the Kasr, asked me why was I sitting in that place ? he sat down by me to enquire again of my health. He seemed to wish the stranger well, but in that to have a fear of blame,—had he not also encouraged my coming hither ? He left me and entered the Kasr gate, to speak anew with the Emir. Abd el-Azîz, in the rest a worthy man, was timid and ungenerous, the end of life to them all is the least displeasure of Ibn Rashîd, and he was a servant of the Emir. A certain public seat is appointed him, under the Prince's private kahwa upon the Méshab, where he sat in attendance with his company at every mejlis. The people in the square had not yet observed the Nasrâny, and I sat on three-quarters of an hour, in the midst of Hâyil ;—in the meanwhile they debated perhaps of my life within yonder earthen walls of the castle. I thought the Arabian curiosity and avarice would procure me a respite : at least I hoped that someone would call me in from this pain of famine to breakfast.

In the further end of the Méshab were troops of couched thelûls ; they were of Beduin fellowships which arrived daily, to treat of their affairs with the Emir. Certain of the Beduw now gathered about me, who wondered to see the stranger sitting under this porch. I saw also some personage that issued from the castle gate under a clay tower, in goodly fresh apparel, walking upon his stick of office, and he approached me. This was *Mufarrij, rájul el-Mothîf,* or marshal of the Prince's guest-hall, a foreigner, as are so many at Hâyil of those that serve the Emir. His town was Aneyza in Kasîm (which he had forsaken upon a horrible misadventure, afterwards to be related). The comely steward came to bid the stranger in to breakfast ; but first he led me and my nâga through the Méshab, and allotted me a lodging, the last in the row of guest-chambers, *mákhzans,* which are in the long side of this public place in front of the Kasr : then he brought me in by the castle-gate, to the great coffee-hall, which is of the guests, and the castle service of the Emir. At this hour—long after all had breakfasted and gone forth—it was empty, but they sent for the coffee-server. I admired the noble proportions of this clay hall, as before of the huge Kasr ; the lofty walls, painted in device with ochre and jiss, and the rank of tall pillars, which in the midst upheld the simple flat roof, of ethel timbers and palm-stalk mat-work, goodly stained and varnished with

the smoke of the daily hospitality.   Under the walls are benches
of clay overspread with Bagdad carpets.   By the entry stands

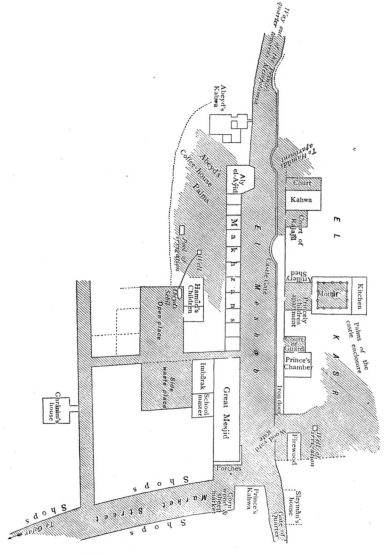

a mighty copper-tinned basin or " sea " of water, with a
chained cup (daily replenished by the hareem of the public

kitchen from the mâ es-Sáma); from thence the coffee-server draws, and he may drink who thirsts. In the upper end of this princely kahwa are two fire-pits, like shallow graves, where desert bushes are burned in colder weather; they lack good fuel, and fire is blown commonly under the giant coffee-pots in a clay hearth like a smith's furnace. I was soon called out by Mufarrij to the guest-hall, *mothîf;* this guest-house is made within the castle buildings, a square court cloistered, and upon the cloisters is a gallery. Guests pass in by the Prince's artillery, which are five or six small pieces of cannon; the iron is old, the wood is ruinous.

The Beduins eat below, but principal sheykhs and their fellowships in the galleries; Mufarrij led me upstairs, to a place where a carpet was belittered with old date-stones. Here I sat down and dates were brought me,—the worst dates of their desert world—in a metal standish, thick with greasy dust; thy left me to eat, but I chose still to fast. Such is the Arabian Ruler's morning cheer to his guests—they are Beduw—and unlike the desert cleanness of the most Arabian villages, where there is water enough. Till they should call me away I walked in the galleries, where small white house-doves of Irâk were flittering, and so tame that I took them in my hands. I found these clay-floor galleries eighty feet long; they are borne upon five round pillars with rude shark's-tooth chapiters. Mufarrij appearing again we returned to the kahwa where coffee was now ready. A young man soon entered shining in silken clothing, and he began to question me. This Arabian cockney was the Prince's secretary, his few words sounded disdainfully : " I say, eigh ! what art thou ?—whence comest thou, and where-fore hast thou come ? " I answered after the nomad sort, " Weled, I can but answer one question at once ; let me hear what is thy first request : " he showed himself a little out of countenance at a poor man's liberal speech, and some friendly voice whispered to me, " Treat him with more regard, for this is *Nasr.*" So said this Nasr, " Up ! the Emir calls thee : " and we went out towards the Prince's quarters.

There is made a long gallery under the body of the clay castle-building, next the outer wall upon the Méshab ; by this we passed, and at the midst is an iron-plated door, kept by a young Galla slave within ; and there we knocked. The door opens into a small inner court, where a few of the Emir's men-at-arms sit in attendance upon him ; at the south side is his chamber. We went through and entered from the doorway of his open chamber into a dim light, for their windows are but casements to the air, and no glass panes are seen in all Nejd. The

ruler Mohammed—a younger son of Abdullah ibn Rashîd, the
first prince of Shammar, and the fourth Emir since his father—
was lying half along upon his elbow, with leaning-cushions
under him, by his fire-pit side, where a fire of the desert bushes
was burning before him. I saluted him " *Salaam aleyk*, Peace
be with thee ; " he lifted the right hand to his head, the
manner he had seen in the border countries, but made me no
answer ;—their hostile opinion that none out of the saving
religion may give the word of God's peace ! He wore the long
braided hair-locks for whose beauty he is commended in
the desert as ' a fresh young man.' His skin is more than commonly tawny, and even yellowish ; lean of flesh and hollow
as the Nejders, he is of middle height : his is a shallow
Nejd visage, and Mohammed's bird-like looks are like the
looks of one survived out of much disease of the world,—and
what likelihood was there formerly that he should ever be the
Emir ?

"Sit down ! " he said. Mohammed, who under the former
Princes was conductor of the " Persian " Haj, had visited the
cities of Mesopotamia, and seen the manners of the Dowla.—
The chief of the guard led me to the stranger's seat. In the
midst of a long carpet spread under the clay wall, between
my place and the Emir, sat some personage leaning upon
cushions ; he was, I heard, a kinsman of Ibn Rashîd, a venerable
man of age and mild countenance. The Emir questioned me,
" From whence comest thou, and what is the purpose of thy
voyage ? "—" I am arrived from Teyma, and el-Héjr, and I
came down from Syria to visit Medáin Sâlih."—" *Rájul sadûk*,
wellah ! a man to trust (exclaimed that old sheykh). This is
not like him who came hither, thou canst remember Mohammed in what year, but one that tells us all things plainly."
Emir : " And now from Teyma, well ! and what sawest thou
at Teyma—anything ? "—" Teyma is a pleasant place of palms
in a good air."—" Your name ? "—" Khalîl."—"Ha ! and you have
been with the Beduw, eigh Khalîl, what dost thou think of
the Beduw ? *Of the Beduw there are none good :*—thou wast
with which Beduins ? "—" The Fukara, the Moahîb, the Sehamma beyond the Harra."—" And what dost thou think of the
Fejîr and of their sheykhs ? Motlog, he is not good ? "—" The
Fukara are not unlike their name, their neighbours call them
Yahûd Kheybar." The Emir, half wondering and smiling,
took up my words (as will the Arabians) and repeated them to
those present : " He says they are the Yahûd Kheybar ! and
well, Khalîl, how did the Aarab deal with thee ? they milked
for thee, they showed thee hospitality ? "—" Their milk is too

little for themselves." The Emir mused and looked down, for
he had heard that I wandered with the Beduins to drink
camel milk. " Ha ! and the Moahîb, he asked, are they good ?
and Tollog, is he good ? "—The Emir waited that I should say
nay, for Tollog was an old enemy or ' rebel ' of theirs.—" The man
was very good to me, I think he is a worthy Beduin person."
To this he said, " *Hmm hmm !*—and the Sehamma, who is their
sheykh ? "—" Mahanna and Fóthil."—" And how many byût are
they ? "

He said now, " Have you anything with you (to sell) ? and
what is thy calling ? "—" I have medicines with me, I am
an hakîm."—" What medicines ? *kanakîna* (quinine) ? "—" This
I have of the best."—" And what besides ? "—" I have this and
that, but the names are many ; also I have some very good
chai, which I will present to thee, Emir ! "—" We have chai
here, from Bagdad ; no, no, we have enough." [Afterward it
was said to me, in another place,—" He would not accept thy
chai, though it were never so good : Ibn Rashîd will eat or
drink of nothing which is not prepared for him by a certain
slave of his ; he lives continually in dread to be poisoned."]
Emir : " Well ! thou curest what diseases ? canst thou cure the
mejnûn ? " (the troubled, by the jan, in their understanding) :—
the Emir has some afflicted cousins in the family of Abeyd,
and in his heart might be his brother Telâl's sorrowful remembrance. I answered, " *El-mejnûn hu mejnûn,* who is a fool
by nature, he is a fool indeed." The Emir repeated this wisdom
after me, and solemnly assenting with his head, he said to those
present, " *Hu sâdik,* he saith truth ! " Some courtiers answered
him " *Fi tarîk,* but there is a way in this also." The Aarab suppose there is a *tarîk,* if a man might find it, a God-given way,
to come to what ènd he will.—" And tell me, which beasts thou
sawest in the wilderness ? "—" Hares and gazelles, I am not a
hunter."—" Is the hare unlawful meat !—you eat it ? (he would
know thus if I were truly a Christian). And the swine you
eat ? " I said, " There is a strange beast in the Sherarát wilderness, which they call wild ox or wothŷhi, and I have some horns
of it from Teyma."—" Wouldst thou see the wothŷhi ? we have
one of them here, and will show it thee." Finally he said, " Dost
thou ' drink ' smoke ? " The use of tobacco, not yet seen in the
Nejd streets but tolerated within doors, is they think unbecoming in persons of more than the common people's dignity
and religion. Mohammed himself and Hamûd his cousin
were formerly honest brothers of the galliûn ; but come up
to estimation, they had forsaken their solace of the aromatic
Hameydy. The Emir said further, " So you are Mesîhy ? "

—that was a generous word! he would not call me by the reproachful name of Nasrâny; also the Emir, they say, "has a Christian woman among his wives."—Christians of the Arabic tongue in the great border lands name themselves *Mesíhiyûn*.

He bade Nasr read in a great historical book which lay upon a shelf, bound in red (*Akhbâru-'d-Dúal wa athâru-'l-Uwwal*), what was written therein of the prophet *Isa ibn Miriam;*—and the secretary read it aloud. The Mohammedan author tells us of the person, the colour, the human lineaments of Jesus, "son of the virgin;" and the manner of his prophetic life, how he walked with his disciples in the land of Israel, and that his wont was to rest in that place where the sun went down upon him. The Emir listened sternly to this tale, and impatiently.—"And well, well! but what could move thee (he said) to take such a journey?" I responded suddenly, "*El-elûm!* the liberal sciences;" but the sense of this plural is, in Nejd and in the Beduin talk, *tidings*. The Ruler answered hastily, "And is it for this thou art come hither!" It was difficult to show him what I intended by the sciences, for they have no experience of ways so sequestered from the common mouth-labours of mankind. He said then, "And this language, didst thou learn it among the Beduw, readest thou *Araby?*"— He bade Nasr bring the book, and put it in Khalîl's hands. Mohammed rose himself from his place, [he is said to be very well read in the Arabic letters, and a gentle poet though, in the dispatch of present affairs of state, he is too busy-headed to be longer a prentice in unprofitable learning]— and with the impatient half-childish curiosity of the Arabians, the Emir Ibn Rashîd himself came over and sat down beside me.—"Where shall I read?"—"Begin anywhere at a chapter,— there! and he pointed with his finger. So I read the place, '*The king* (such as one) *slew all his brethren and kindred.*' It was *Sheytân* that I had lighted upon such a bloody text; the Emir was visibly moved! and, with the quick feeling of the Arabs, he knew that I regarded him as a murderous man. "Not there! he said hastily, but read here!—out of this chapter above" (beating the place with his finger); so I read again some passage. *Emir*: "Ha, well! I see thou canst read a little," so rising he went again to his place. Afterward he said, "And whither wouldst thou go now?"—"To Bagdad."—"Very well, we will send thee to Bagdad," and with this word the Emir rose and those about him to go forth into his palm grounds, where he would show me the 'wild kine.'

Nasr then came with a letter-envelope in his hand, and

asked me to read the superscription. " Well, I said, this is not
Arabic ! "—" Ay, and therefore we wish thee to read it."—" From
whom had ye this letter ? "—" From a Nasrâny, who came from
the Haurân hither, and *this we took from him.*" Upon the seal I
found in Greek letters *Patriarchate of Damascus,* and the legend
about it was in Latin, *Go ye into all the world and preach
this gospel to every creature.* They were stooping to put on
their sandals, and awaited a moment to hear my response ;
and when I recited aloud the sense *Ukhruju fî kulli el-
álam* ...... the venerable sheykh said piously to the Emir :
" Mohammed, hearest thou this ?—and they be the words of
the Messîah ! "

All they that were in his chamber now followed abroad with
the Emir ; these being his courtier friends and attendance.
Besides the old sheykh, the captain of the guard, and Nasr,
there was not any man of a good countenance amongst them.
They of the palace and the Prince's men wear the city gown,
but go ungirded. Mohammed the Emir appeared to me, when
we came into the light, like a somewhat undergrown and hard-
favoured Beduwy of the poorer sort ; but he walked loftily and
with somewhat unquiet glancing looks. At the irrigation well,
nigh his castle walls, he paused, and showing me with his
hånd the shrill running wheel-work, he asked suddenly, " Had I
seen such gear ? "—" How many fathoms have ye here ? "—
" Fifteen." He said truly his princely word, though I thought
it was not so,—for what could it profit them to draw upon the
land from so great depths ? I walked on with Mohammed
and the old sheykh, till we came to his plantation, enclosed
in the castle wall ; it seemed to me not well maintained. The
Emir stayed at a castor-oil plant (there was not another in
Hâyil) to ask " What is that ? " He questioned me, between
impatient authority and the untaught curiosity of Arabians,
of his plants and trees,—palms and lemons, and the thick-
rinded citron ; then he showed me a seedling of the excellent pot-herb *bâmiya* and thyme, and single roots of other
herbs and salads. All such green things they eat not ! so unlike is the diet of Nejd Arabia to the common use in the Arabic
border countries.

Gazelles were running in the further walled grounds ; the
Emir stood and pointed with his finger, " There (he said) is
the wothŷhi ! " [*v.* p. 327—8.] This was a male of a year and
a half, no bigger than a great white goat ; he lay sick under
a fig-tree. Emir :—" But look yonder, where is a better, and
that is the cow."—" Stand back for fear of her horns ! the
courtiers said about me, do not approach her." One went

out with a bunch of date twigs to the perilous beast, and stroked her; her horns were like sharp rods, set upright, the length I suppose of twenty-seven inches. I saw her, about five yards off, less than a small ass; the hide was ash-coloured going over to a clear yellow, there was a slight rising near the root of her neck, and no hump, her smooth long tail ended in a bunch. She might indeed be said " to resemble a little cow "; but very finely moulded was this creature of the waterless wilderness, to that fiery alacrity of their wild limbs. " *Uktub-ha!* write, that is portray, her!" exclaimed the Emir. As we returned, he chatted with me pleasantly; at last he said " Where are thy sandals? "— " Little wonder if you see me unshod and my clothing rent, it is a year since I am with the Beduw in the khála."—" And though he go without soles (answered the kind old sheykh), it is not amiss, for thus went even the prophets of Ullah."—This venerable man was, I heard, the Emir's mother's brother: he showed me that mild and benevolent countenance, which the Arabs bear for those to whom they wish a good adventure.

The Emir in his spirituous humour, and haughty familiar manners, was much like a great sheykh of the Aarab. In him is the mark of a former contrary fortune, with some sign perhaps of a natural baseness of mind; Mohammed was now " fully forty years old," but he looked less. We came again into the Kasr yard, where the wood is stored, and there are two-leaved drooping gates upon the Méshab; here is the further end of that gallery under the castle, by which we had entered. The passage is closed by an iron-plated door; the plates (in their indigence of the arts) are the shield-like iron pans (*tannúr*) upon which the town housewives bake their girdle-bread.—But see the just retribution of tyrants! they fear most that make all men afraid. Where is—the sweetest of human things— their repose? for that which they have gotten from many by their power, they know by the many to be required of them again! There the Emir dismissed the Nasrány, with a friendly gesture, and bade one accompany me to my beyt or lodging.

CHAPTER XXII.

HÂYIL.

WHEN this day's sun was setting, Mufarrij called me to the Mothîf gallery, where a supper-dish was set before me of mutton and temmn. When I came again into the coffee-hall, as the cup went round there began to be questioning among the Beduin guests and those of the castle service, of my religion. I returned early to my beyt, and then I was called away by his servants to see one, whom they named "The Great Sheykh."—'Who was, I asked, that great sheykh?' they answered "*El Emir!*" So they brought me to a dàr, which was nearly next by, and this is named Kahwat Abeyd. They knocked and a Galla slave opened the door. We passed in by a short entry, which smelled cheerfully of rose-water, to that which seemed to my eyes full of the desert a goodly hall-chamber. The Oriental rooms are enclosures of the air, without moveables, and their only ornaments are the carpets for sitting-places, here laid upon the three sides of the upper end, with pillowed places for " the Emir " and his next kinsman. All was clay, the floor is beaten clay, the clay walls I saw were coloured in ochre ; the sitters were principal persons of the town, a Beduin sheykh or two, and men of the princely service ; and bright seemed the civil clothing of these fortunate Arabs.—They had said *'The Emir'!* and in the chief place I saw a great noble figure half lying along upon his elbow.!—but had I not seen the Prince Ibn Rashîd himself this morning ? If the common sort of Arabs may see a stranger bewildered among them, it is much to their knavish pleasure.

This personage was *Hamûd,* heir, although not the eldest son, of his father Abeyd ; for *Fáhd,* the elder, was *khíbel,* of a troubled understanding, but otherwise of a good and upright behaviour ; the poor gentleman was always much my friend.—The princely Hamûd has bound his soul by oath to his cousin the Emir, to live and to die with him ; their fathers were brethren and, as none remain of age of the Prince's house, Hamûd ibn Rashîd is next after Mohammed in authority, is his deputy at home, fights by his side in the field, and he bears the style of Emir. Hamûd is the Ruler's companion in all daily service and counsel.—The son of Abeyd made me a pleasant countenance, and bade me be seated at his right hand, and when he saw I was very weary, he bade me stretch the legs out easily, and sit without any ceremony.

Hamûd spoke friendly to the Nasrâny stranger ; I saw he was of goodly great stature, with painted eyes, hair shed [as we use to see in the images of Christ] and hanging down from the midst in tresses, and with little beard. His is a pleasant man-like countenance, he dissembles cheerfully a slight crick in the neck, and turns it to a grace, he seems to lean forward. In our talk he enquired of those marvellous things of the Nasâra, the telegraph, 'and glass, was made of what ? also they had heard to be in our Christian countries a palace of crystal ; and Baris (Paris) a city builded all of crystal ; also what thing was rock oil,' of which there stood a lamp burning on a stool before them : it is now used in the principal houses of Hâyil, and they have a saying that the oil is made from human urine. He wondered when I told them it is drawn from wells in the New World ; he had heard of that *Dínya el-jedîda,* and enquired to which quarter it lay, and beyond what seas. He asked me of my medicines, and then he said, " Lean towards me, I would enquire a thing of thee." Hamûd whispered, under the wing of his perfumed kerchief, " Hast thou no medicine, that may enable a man ? " I answered immediately, " No, by thy life."—

38—2

" No, by my life ! " he repeated, turning again, and smiled
over to the audience, and laughed cheerfully, " ha ! ha ! "—for
some crabbed soul might misdeem that he had whispered of
poison. Also that common oath of the desert, " By thy life,"
is blamed among these half-Wahábies. Hamûd said, with the
same smiling demeanour, " Seest thou here those two horsemen
which met with thee upon the road ? "—" I cannot tell, for I was
most weary."—" Ay, he said with the Arabian humanity, thou
wast very weary ; ask him ! " Hamûd showed me with his finger
a personage, one of the saffron-beards of Hâyil, who sat leaning upon cushions, in the place next by him, as next in dignity
to himself. This was a dull-witted man, *Sleymàn*, and his
cousin. I asked him, " Was it thou ? " but he, only smiling,
answered nothing. *Hamûd :* " Look well ! were they like us ?
be we not the two horsemen ?—It was a match, Khalîl, to try
which were the better breathed of our two mares ; how seest
thou ? the horses of the Engleys are better, or our Nejd horses ? "
—Hamûd now rising to go to rest (his house is in another
part), we all rose with him. In that house—it stands by the
public birket which is fed from the irrigation of this kahwa
palm-yard—are his children, a wife and her mother, and
his younger brothers ; but, as a prince of the blood, he has a
lodging for himself (where he sleeps) within the castle building.
The Hâyil Princes are clad as the nomads, but fresh and cleanly
and in the best stuffs ; their long wide tunic is, here in the town,
washed white as a surplice, and upon their shoulders is the
Aarab mantle of finer Bagdad woollen, or of the black cloth of
Europe. They wear the haggu upon their bodies, as in all
nomad Arabia.

I was but ill-housed in my narrow, dark, and unswept cell :—
they told me, a Yahûdy also, at his first coming, had lodged
there before me ! This was a Bagdad Jew, now a prosperous
Moslem dwelling at Hâyil and married, and continually in-
creasing with the benediction of the son-in-law of Laban ; the
man had a good house in the town, and a shop in the sûk,
where he sold clothing and dates and coffee to the nomads : his
Hâyil wife had borne him two children. The gaping people
cried upon me, " Confess thou likewise, Khalîl, ' There is one
God, and His apostle is Mohammed,' and thine shall be an
equal fortune, which the Emir himself will provide." From the
morrow's light there was a gathering of sick and idle townsmen to the Nasrâny's door, where they sat out long hours
bibble-babbling, and left me no moment of repose. They asked
for medicines, promising, ' If they found them good remedies
they would pay me, but not now.' When I answered they

might pay me the first cost for the drugs, this discouraged them ; and nothing can be devised to content their knavish meaning. I said at length, " None of you come here to chaffer with me, for I will not hear you," and putting my door to upon them, I went out. As I sat at my threshold in the cool of the afternoon, Hamûd went by with his friends ; he stayed to greet me, and bade me come to supper, and showed me his sword, which he carries loosely in his hand with the baldric, like the nomads, saying, " What thinkest thou of it ? "—they suppose that every son of the Nasâra should be schooled in metal-craft. As I drew his large and heavy blade out of the scabbard—the steel was not Damascened—Hamûd added, " It is Engleys " (of the best Christian countries' work): he had this sabre from Ibn Saûd, and "paid for it one thousand reals." " It seems to be excellent," I said to him, and he repeated the words smiling in their manner, " It is excellent." The sword is valued by the Arabians as the surest weapon ; they all covet to have swords of the finest temper.

At sunset came a slave from Abeyd's coffee-hall to lead me to supper. Hamûd sups there when he is not called to eat with the Emir ; his elder son *Mâjid*, and the boy's tutor, eat with him ; and after them, the same dish is set before the men of his household. His simple diet is of great nourish-ment, boiled mutton upon a mess of temmn, with butter, seasoned with onions, and a kind of curry. When the slave has poured water upon our hands, from a metal ewer, over a laver, we sit down square-legged about the great brazen tinned dish upon the carpet floor. " *Mudd yédak*, Reach forth thine hand " is the Arabs' bidding, and with " *Bismillah*, In the name of God," they begin to eat with their fingers. They sit at meat not above eight or ten minutes, when they are fully satisfied ; the slave now proffers the bowl, and they drink a little water ; so rising they say " *El hamd illah*, The Lord be praised," and go apart to rinse the mouth, and wash their hands :—the slave lad brought us grated soap. So they return to their places refreshed, and the cheerful cup is served round : but the coffee-server—for the fear of princes—tasted before Hamûd. There is no banqueting among them. Arabians would not be able to believe, that the food-creatures of the three inhabited elements (in some happier lands) may hardly sustain an human entrail ; and men's sitting to drink away their understanding must seem to them a very horrible heathenish living. Here are no inordinate expenses of the palace, no homicide largesses to smooth favourites of the spoil of the lean people. Soon after the sunrising, the Shammar princes breakfasted of girdle-bread and butter with a draught of milk; at noon a dish of dates is set before them; at sunset they sup as we have now seen: Prince and people, they are all alike soberly dieted. The devil is not in their dish; all the riot and wantonness of their human nature lies in the Mohammedan luxury of hareem.— I remember to have heard, from some who knew him, of the diet of the late Sultan of Islam, Abd el-Azîz, otherwise reproached for his insatiable luxury. Only one dish—which his mother had tasted and sealed—was set before him, and that was the Turks' every-day *pilaw* (which they say came in with Tamerlane) of boiled rice and mutton; he abstained (for a cause which may be divined) from coffee and tobacco. I heard Hamûd say he had killed the sheep in my honour; but commonly his supper mutton is bought in the sûk.

An hour or two after, when the voice of the muétthin is heard in the night calling to the last prayer, Hamûd never fails to rise with the company. A slave precedes him with a flaming palm leaf-branch; and they go out to pray in the mosque, which is upon the further part of the Méshab, [*v.* the fig. p 587,] ranging with the guest-chambers, but separated by a small thoroughfare from them.—Princes of men, they are bond-servants to a doting religion!

When Hamûd returns, a little *sajjeydy* or kneeling-carpet reserved only to this use is unrolled by the slave in waiting before him; and the princely man falling upon his knees towards Mecca says on to great length more his formal devotion. One evening I asked him, ' But had he not already said his prayers in the mesjid ? '—" Those, Hamûd answered, which we say in the mesjid are a man's legal prayers, and these are of the tradition, sunna." The sitters in the coffee-hall did not stint their chatting, whilst Hamûd prayed,—there prayed no man with him. The rest were not princes, why should they take upon them this superfluous religion! and the higher is a Moslem's estate, by so much the more he must show himself devoted and as it were deserving of God's benefits. Hamûd never fails at the mosque in the hours; and in all the rest with the cheerful air of a strong man he carries his own great fortune, and puts by the tediousness of the world. He might be a little less of age than the Emir; in his manly large stature he nearly resembles, they say, the warlike poet his father: Hamûd and the Emir Mohammed are not novices in the gentle skill inherited from their fathers in this princely family; —their new making is extolled by the common voice above the old.

The Prince Mohammed goes but once, at el-aṣṣr, to prayers

in the great mesjid ; he prays in an oratory within the castle,
or standing formally in his own chamber. And else so many
times to issue from the palace to their public devotion, were
a tediousness to himself and to his servitors, and to the townspeople, for all fear when they see him, since he bears the
tyrant's sword. And Mohammed fears !—the sword which
has entered this princely house ' shall never depart from them
—so the Aarab muse—until they be destroyed.' He cut down
all the high heads of his kindred about him, leaving only
Hamûd ; the younger sort are growing to age ; and Mohammed
must see many dreams of dread, and for all his strong security,
is ever looking for the retribution of mankind. Should he
trust himself to pass the Méshab oftentimes daily at certain hours ?—but many have miscarried thus. Both Hamûd
and the Emir Mohammed affect popular manners : Hamûd
with an easy frankness, and that smiling countenance which
seems not too far distant from the speech of the common people ;
Mohammed with some softening, where he may securely, of his
princely asperity, and sowing his pleasant word between ; he
is a man very subtle witted, and of an acrid understanding.
Mohammed as he comes abroad casts his unquiet eyes like a
falcon ; he walks, with somewhat the strut of a stage-player,
in advance of his chamber followers, and men-at-arms. When
Hamûd is with him, the Princes walk before the rout. The
townspeople (however this be deemed impossible) say ' they
love him and fear him : '—they praise the prince under whose
sufficient hand they fare the better, and live securely, and
see all prosper about them ; but they dread the sharpness, so
much fleshed already, of the Ruler's sword.

The evening after, Mohammed sent for me to his apartment : the clay walls are stained with ochre. When I said to
the Emir, I was an Englishman, this he had not understood
before ! he was now pleasant and easy. There sat with him a
great swarthy man, Sâlih, (I heard he was of the nomads,)
who watched me with fanatical and cruel eyes, saying at length
in a fierce sinister voice, " Lookest thou to see thy land again ? "
—" All things, I answered, are in the power of Ullah."—" Nay,
nay, Sâlih ! exclaimed the Emir, and Khalîl has said very
well, that all things are in the hand of Ullah." Mohammed
then asked me nearly Hamûd's questions. " The telegraph
is what ? and we have seen it (at Bagdad in time of his old
conductorship of the ' Persian ' pilgrims) : but canst thou not
make known to us the working, which is wonderful ? "—" It is a
trepidation—therewith we may make certain signs—engendered

in the corrosion of metals, by strong medicines like vinegar."
Emir : " Then it is an operation of medicine, canst thou not
declare it ? "—" If we may suppose a man laid head and heels
between Hâyil and Stambûl, of such stature that he touched
them both ; if one burned his feet at Hâyil, should he not feel it
at the instant in his head, which is at Stambûl ? "—" And glass
is what ? " He asked also of petroleum ; and of the New Continent, where it lay, and whether within ' the Ocean.' He listened
coldly to my tale of the finding of the New Land over the great
seas, and enquired, " Were no people dwelling in the country
when it was discovered ? " At length he asked me, ' How did
I see Hâyil ? and the market street, was it well ? but ah (he
answered himself) it is a *sûk Aarab !* ' little in comparison
with the chief cities of the world. He asked ' Had I heard of
J. Shammar in my own country ? ' The ruler was pleased to
understand that the Nasâra were not gaping after his desert
provinces ; but it displeased the vain-glory of the man that
of all this troublous tide of human things under his governance, nearly no rumour was come to our ears in a distant
land. Hamûd asked of me another while the like question,
and added, " What ! have ye never heard of Ibn Saûd the
Waháby ! " When I had sat two hours, and it might be
ten o'clock, the Emir said to the captain of the guard, who
is groom of his chamber, " It is time to shut the doors ; " and
I departed.

In the early days of my being in Hâyil, if I walked
through their sûk, children and the ignorant and poor Beduw
flocked to me, and I passed as the cuckoo with his cloud of
wondering small birds, until some citizen of more authority
delivered me, saying to them, ' Wellah, thus to molest the
stranger would be displeasing to the Emir ! ' Daily some
worthy persons called me to coffee and to breakfast ; the
most of them sought counsel of the hakîm for their diseases,
few were moved by mere hospitality, for their conscience
bids them show no goodness to an adversary of the saving
religion ; but a Moslem coming to Hâyil, or even a Frankish
stranger easily bending and assenting to them, might find
the Shammar townspeople hospitable, and they are accounted
such.

And first I was called to one *Ghrânim,* the Prince's
jeweller, and his brother *Ghruneym.* They were rich men,
of the smiths' caste, formerly of Jauf, where are some of
the best sânies, for their work in metal, wood, and stone,
in nomad Arabia. Abeyd at the taking of the place found
these men the best of their craft, and he brought them

perforce to Hâyil. They are continually busied to labour
for the princes, in the making and embellishing of sword-
hilts with silver and gold wire, and the inlaying of gun-
stocks with glittering scales of the same. All the best
sword-blades and matchlocks, taken (from the Beduw) in
Ibn Rashîd's forays, are sent to them to be remounted, and
are then laid up in the castle armoury. Of these, some
very good Persian and Indian blades are put in the hands
of the Emir's men-at-arms. In his youth, Ghrânim had
wandered in his metal trade about the Haurân, and now he
asked me of the sheykhs of the Druses, such and such whom
he had known, were they yet alive. The man was fanatical,
his understanding was in his hands, and his meditations
were not always of the wise in the world : so daily meeting me, Ghrânim said before other words, "Khalîl, I am
thine enemy!" and in the end he would proffer his friendly
counsels.—He had made this new clay house and adorned it
with all his smith's art. Upon the earthen walls, stained with
ochre, were devices of birds and flowers, and koran versets in
white daubing of jiss,—which is found everywhere in the desert
sand : the most houses at Hâyil are very well built, though
the matter be rude. He had built a double wall with a casement in each, to let the light pass, and not the weather. I saw
no sooty smith's forge within, but Ghrânim was sitting freshly
clad at his labour, in his best chamber ; his floor was spread with
fine matting, and the sitting places were Bagdad carpets. His
brother Ghruneym called away the hakîm to his own house
to breakfast : he was hindered in his craft by sickness and the
Emir ofttimes threatened to forsake him. His son showed
me an army rifle [from India] whereupon I found the Tower
mark ; the sights—they not understanding their use!—had
been taken away.

The Jew-Moslem—he had received the name *Abdullah*, "the
Lord's servitor," and the neophyte surname *el-Moslemanny*—
came to bid me to coffee. His companion asked me, 'Did
my nation love the Yahûd?' "We enquire not, I answered,
of men's religions, so they be good subjects." We came to
the Jew's gate, and entered his house : the walls within were
pleasantly stained with ochre, and over-written with white
flowerets and religious versets, in daubing of gypsum. I read :
"THERE IS NO POWER BUT OF GOD ;" and in the apostate's
entry, instead of Moses' words, was scored up in great letters
the Mohammedan testimony, "There is none other God than
(very) God, and Mohammed is the apostle of (very) God."
Abdullah was a well-grown man of Bagdad with the pleasant

elated countenance of the Moslemîn, save for that mark (with peace be it spoken) which God has set upon the Hebrew lineaments. Whilst his companion was absent a moment, he asked me under his breath " Had I with me any—" (I could not hear what).—" What sayest thou ? " " *Brandi,* you do not know this (English Persian Gulf word)—brandi ? " His fellow entering, it might be his wife's brother, Abdullah said now in a loud voice, ' Would I become a Moslem, his house should be mine along with him.' He had whispered besides a word in my ear—" I have a thing to say to thee, but not at this time." It was seven years since this Bagdad Jew arrived at Hâyil. After the days of hospitality he went to Abeyd saying, he would make profession of the religion of Islam ' upon his hand ' ; —and Abeyd accepted the Jew's words upon his formal hand full of old bloodshed and violence. The princely family had endowed the Moslemanny at his conversion with " a thousand reals," and the Emir licensed him to live at Hâyil, where buying and selling,—and Abdullah knew the old art,—he was now a thriving tradesman. I had heard of him at Teyma, and that ' he read in such books as those they saw me have '; yet I found him a man without instruction,—doubtless he read Hebrew, yet now he denied it.

A merchant in the town, *Jâr Ullah,* brought me a great foreign folio. It was a tome printed at Amsterdam in the last century, in Hebrew letters ! so I said to him, " Carry it to Abdullah, this is the Jews' language."—" Abdullah tells me he knows it not."—This book was brought hither years before from the salvage of a Bagdad caravan, that had perished of thirst in the way to Syria. Their dalîl, " because Ullah had troubled his mind," led them astray in the wilderness ; the caravaners could not find the wells, and only few that had more strength saved themselves, riding .at adventure and happily lighting upon Beduins. The nomads fetched away what they would of the fallen-down camel-loads, ' for a month and more.' There were certain books found amongst them, a few only of such unprofitable wares had been brought in to Hâyil.

It was boasted to me that the Jew-born Abdullah was most happy here ; ' many letters had been sent to him by his parents, with the largest proffers if he would return, but he always refused to receive them.' He had forsaken the Law and the Promises ;—but a man who is moved by the affections of human nature, may not so lightly pass from all that in which he has been cherished and bred up in the world !

Jâr Ullah invited me to his spacious house, which stands

in the upper street near the Gofar gate : he was a principal
corn-merchant. One *Nasr*, a fanatical Harb Beduwy of the
rajajîl, meeting with us in the way, and *Aneybar* coming
by then, we were all bidden in together : our worthy host,
otherwise a little fanatical, made us an excellent breakfast.
Aneybar was a *Hábashy*, a home-born Galla in Abdullah ibn
Rashîd's household, and therefore to be accounted slave-
brother of Telâl, Metaab and Mohammed : also his name is of
the lord's house, Ibn Rashîd. This libertine was a principal
personage in Hâyil, in affairs of state-trust under the Emirs
since Telâl's time. The man was of a lively clear understanding,
and courtly manners, yet in his breast was the timid soul-
not-his-own of a slave : bred in this land, he had that suddenness
of speech and the suspicious-mindedness of the Arabians.—
When I came again to Hâyil Aneybar had the disposing of
my life ;—it was a fair chance, to-day, that I broke bread
with him !

Hamûd bade me again to supper, and as I was washing,
" How white (said one) is his skin ! " Hamûd answered in a
whisper, " It is the leprosy."—" Praised be God, I exclaimed,
there are no lepers in my land."—" Eigh ! said Hamûd (a
little out of countenance, because I overheard his words), is
it so ? eigh ! eigh ! (for he found nothing better to say, and
he added after me) the Lord be praised." Another said,
" Wellah in Bagdad I have seen a maiden thus white, with
yellow hair, that you might say she were Khalîl's daughter."—
" But tell me (said the son of Abeyd), do the better sort in your
country never buy the Circass women ?—or how is it among
you to be the son of a bought-woman, and even of a bond-
woman, I say is it not-convenient in your eyes ? "—When it
seemed the barbaric man would have me to be, for that un-
common whiteness, the son of a Circass bond-woman, I responded with some warmth, " To buy human flesh is not so
much as named in my country : as for all who deal in slaves we
are appointed by God to their undoing. We hunt the cursed
slave-sail upon all seas, as you hunt the hyena." Hamûd was
a little troubled, because I showed him some flaws in their
manners, some heathenish shadows in his religion where there
was no spot in ours, and had vaunted our naval hostility,
(whereby they all have damage in their purses, to the ends
of the Mohammedan world).—" And Khalîl, the Nasâra eat
swine's flesh ? "—" Ay billah, and that is not much unlike
the meat of the wabar which ye eat, or of the porcupine.
Do not the Beduw eat wolves and the hyena, the fox, the

thób, and the spring-rat ?—owls, kites, the carrion eagle ? but I would taste of none such." Hamûd answered, with his easy humanity, " My meaning was not to say, Khalîl, that for any filth or sickliness of the meat we abstain from swine's flesh, but because the Néby has bidden us ; " and turning to Sleymàn, he said, " I remember *Abdullah,* he that came to Hâyil in Telâl's time, and cured *Bunder,* told my father that the swine's flesh is very good meat."—" And what (asked that heavy head, now finding the tongue to utter his scurvy soul) is the wedlock of the Nasâra ? as the horse covers the mare it is said [in all Nejd] the Nasâra be engendered,—wellah like the hounds ! "

And though they eat no profane flesh, yet some at Hâyil drink the blood of the grape, *mâ 'el-enab,* the juice fermented of the fruit of the few vines of their orchards, here ripened in the midsummer season. Mâjid told me, that it is prepared in his father's household ; the boy asked me if I had none such, and that was by likelihood his father's request. The Moslemîn, in their religious luxury, extremely covet the forbidden drink, imagining it should enable them with their wives.

When coffee was served at Hamûd's, I always sat wondering that to me only the cup was not poured ; this evening, as the servitor passed by with the pot and the cups, I made him a sign, and he immediately poured for me. Another day Mâjid, who sat next me, exclaimed, " Drinkest thou no kahwa, Khalîl ? " As I answered, " Be sure I drink it," the cup was poured out to me,—Hamûd looked up towards us, as if he would have said something. I could suppose it had been a friendly charge of his, to make me the more easy. In the Mohammedan countries a man's secret death is often in the fenjeyn kahwa. The Emir where he enters a house is not served with coffee, nor is coffee served to any in the Prince's apartment, but the Prince called for a cup when he desired it; such horrible apprehensions are in their daily lives !

Among the evening sitters visiting Hamûd in the Kahwat Abeyd was a personage whom they named as a nobleman, and yet he was but a rich foreign merchant, *Seyyid Mahmûd,* the chief of the *Meshâhada* or tradesmen of Méshed, some thirty-five families, who are established in Hâil; the bazaar merchandise (wares of Mesopotamia) is mostly in their hands ; Méshed (place of the martyrdom of) Aly is at the ruins of *Kûfa,* they are Moslems of the Persian sect in religion.

These ungracious schismatics are tolerated and misliked in Ibn Rashîd's town, howbeit they are formal worshippers with the people in the common mesjid. They are much hated by the fanatical Beduins, so I have heard them say, " Nothing, billah, is more néjis than the accursed Meshâhada." Men of the civil north, they have itching ears for political tidings, and when they saw the Engleysy pass, some of them have called me into their shops to enquire news of the war,—as if dwelling this great while in the deserts I had any new thing to relate !—for of the Turkish Sûltàn's " victories " they believed nothing ! The (Beduin-like) princes in Hâyil have learned some things of them of the States of the world, and Hamûd said to me very soberly : " What is your opinion, may the Dowlat of the Sûltàn continue much longer ? "—" *Ullah Âlem* (God knoweth)."—" Ay ! ay ! but tell us, what is that your countrymen think ? "—" The Sûltàn is become very weak."—Hamûd was not sorry (they love not the Turk), and ₫he asked me if I had been in el-Hind ;—the Prince every year sends his sale horses thither, and the Indian government they hear to be of the Engleys. Hamûd had a lettered man in his household, Mâjid's tutor, one formed by nature to liberal studies. The tutor asked me tidings of the several Nasâra nations whose names he had heard, and more especially of Fransa and Brûssia, and *el-Nemsa*, that is the Austrian empire. " All this, I said, you might read excellently set out in a book I have of geography, written in Arabic by one of us long resident in es-Sham, it is in my chamber." —" Go Khalîl, and bring it to me," said Hamûd, and he sent one of his service to light before me, with a flaming palm-branch.

" How ! (said Hamûd, when we came again,) your people learn Arabic ! " I opened my volume at the chapter, *Peninsula of the Aarab.* Hamûd himself turned the leaves, and found the sweet verses, " Oh ! hail to thee, beloved Nejd, the whole world to me is not as the air of Nejd, the Lord prosper Nejd ; " and with a smile of happiness and half a sigh, the patriot, a kassâd himself, gave up the book to his man of letters, and added, wondering, " How is this ?—are the Nasâra then *ahl athâb*, polite nations ! and is there any such beautiful speaking used amongst them ? heigh !—Khalîl, are there many who speak thus ? " For all this the work was unwelcome among them, being written by one without the saving religion ! I showed the lettered man the place where Hâyil is mentioned, which he read aloud, and as he closed the book I said I would lend it him, which was (coldly) accepted. I put also in their hands the Psalter in Arabic of " Daûd Father of Sleymàn," names which they hear with a certain reverence, but whose *kitâb* they had never seen. Even this might not please them! as coming from the Nasâra, those ' corrupters of the scriptures'; and doubtless the title savoured to them of ' idolatry,'—*el-Mizamîr* (as it were songs to the pipe); and they would not read.

" Khalîl, said Hamûd, this is the Seyyid Mahmûd, and he is pleased to hear about medicines; visit him in his house, and he will set before thee a water-pipe,"—it is a keyif of foreigners and not used in Nejd. Hamûd told me another time he had never known any one of the tradesmen in Hâyil whose principal was above a thousand reals; only the Seyyid Mahmûd and other two or three wholesale merchants in the town, he said might have a little more. Of the foreign traders, besides those of Méshed, was one of Bagdad, and of Medina one other;—from Egypt and Syria no man. Hamûd bade me view the Emir's cannon when I passed by to the Mothîf:—I found them, then, to be five or six small ruinous field-pieces, and upon two were old German inscriptions. Such artillery could be of little service in the best hands; yet their shot might break the clay walling of Nejd towns. The Shammar princes had them formerly from the Gulf, yet few persons remembered when they had been used in the Prince's warfare, save that one cannon was drawn out in the late expedition with Boreyda against Aneyza; but the Emir's servants could not handle it. Two shots and no more were fired against the town; the first flew sky-high, and the second shot drove with an hideous dint before their feet into the desert soil.

—To speak now of the public day at Hâyil: it is near two hours after sunrise, when the Emir comes forth publicly to the Méshab to hold his morning mejlis, which is like the mejlis of the nomads. The great sheykh sits openly with the sheukh before the people; the Prince's mejlis is likewise the public tribunal, he sitting as president and judge amongst them. A bench of clay is made all along under the Kasr wall of the Méshab, in face of the mesjid, to the tower-gate; in the midst, raised as much as a degree and in the same clay-work (whereupon in their austere simplicity no carpet is spread), is the high settle of the Emir, with a single step beneath, upon which sits his clerk or secretary Nasr, at the Prince's feet. Hamûd's seat (such another clay settle and step, but a little lower) is that made nigh the castle door. A like ranging bank and high settle are seen under the opposite mesjid walls, where the sheukh sit in the afternoon shadow, holding the second mejlis, at el-assr. Upon the side, in face of the Emir, sits always the kâdy, or man of the religious law; of which

sort there is more than one at Hâyil, who in any difficult process
may record to the Emir the words, and expound the sense, of
the koran scripture. At either side of the Prince sit sheykhly
men, and court companions ;. the Prince's slaves stand before
them ; at the sides of the sheukh, upon the long clay bank, sit
the chiefs of the public service and their companies ; and mingled
with them all, beginning from the next highest place after
the Prince, there sit any visiting Beduins after their dignities.
—You see men sitting as the bent of a bow before all this mejlis,
in the dust of the Méshab, the *rajajîl*, leaning upon their
swords and scabbards, commonly to the number of one hundred
and fifty ; they are the men-at-arms, executors of the terrible
Emir, and riders in his ghrazzus ; they sit here (before the tyrant)
in the place of the people in the nomads' mejlis. The mejlis
at Hâyil is thus a daily muster of this mixed body of swords-
men, many of whom in other hours of the day are civilly
occupied in the town. Into that armed circuit suitors enter
with the accused and suppliants, and in a word all who have
any question (not of state), or appear to answer in public audience
before the Emir ; and he hears their causes, to every one shortly
defining justice : and what judgments issue from the Prince's
mouth are instantly executed. In the month of my being at
Hâyil might be daily numbered sitting at the mejlis with the
Emir about four hundred persons.

The Emir is thus brought nigh to the people, and he is
acquainted with the most of their affairs. Mohammed's judgment and popular wisdom is the better, that he has sometime himself tasted of adversity. He is a judge with an
indulgent equity, like a sheykh in the Beduin commonwealths,
and just with a crude severity : I have never heard anyone
speak against the Emir's true administration of justice. When
I asked if there were no handling of bribes at Hâyil, by those
who are nigh the Prince's ear, it was answered, " Nay." The
Byzantine corruption cannot enter into the eternal and noble
simplicity of this people's (airy) life, in the poor nomad country ;
but (we have seen) the art is not unknown to the subtle-
headed Shammar princes, who thereby help themselves with
the neighbour Turkish governments. Some also of Ibn Rashîd's
Aarab, tribesmen of the Medina dîras, have seen the evil
custom : a tale was told me of one of them who brought a
bribe to advance his cause at Hâyil, and when his matter
was about to be examined he privily put ten reals into the
kâdy's hand. But the kâdy rising, with his stick laid load
upon the guilty Beduin's shoulders until he was weary, and
then he led him over to the Prince, sitting in his stall, who gave

him many more blows himself, and commanded his slaves to
beat him. The mejlis is seldom sitting above twenty minutes,
and commonly there is little to hear, so that the Prince
being unwell for some days (his ordinary suffering of head-
ache and bile), I have seen it intermitted ;—and after that
the causes of seven days were dispatched in a morning's
sitting ! The mejlis rising and dispersing, as the Prince is
up, they say *Thâr el-Emir !*—and then, what for the fluttering
of hundreds of gay cotton kerchiefs in the Méshab, we seem
to see a fall of butterflies. The town Arabians go clean and
honourably clad ; but the Beduins are ragged and even naked
in their wandering villages.

The Emir walks commonly from the mejlis, with his companions of the chamber, to a house of his at the upper end
of the Méshab, where they drink coffee, and sit awhile : and
from thence he goes with a small attendance of his rajajîl
to visit the stud ; there are thirty of the Prince's mares in the
town, tethered in a ground next the clay castle, and nearly
in face of the Kahwat Abeyd. After this the Emir dismisses
his men, saying to them, "Ye may go, *eyyâl*," and re-enters
the Kasr ; or sometimes with Hamūd and his chamber friends
he walks abroad to breathe the air, it may be to his summer
residence by the mâ es-Sáma, or to Abeyd's plantation : or
he makes but a passage through the sûk to visit someone
in the town, as Ghrânim the smith, to see how his orders
are executed ;—and so he returned to the castle, when if
he have any business with Beduins, or men from his villages,
and messengers awaiting him, they will be admitted to his presence. It is a busy pensive life to be the ruler at Hâyil,
and his witty head was always full of the perplexity of this
world's affairs. Theirs is a very subtle Asiatic policy. In
it is not the clement fallacy of the (Christian) Occident, to
build so much as a rush upon the natural goodness (fondly
imagined to be) in any man's breast ; for it is certain they
do account most basely of all men, and esteem without re-
morse every human spirit to be a dunghill solitude by itself.
Their (feline) prudence is for the time rather than seeing very
far off, and always savours of the impotent suddenness of
the Arab impatience. He rules as the hawk among buzzards,
with eyes and claws in a land of ravin, yet in general not
cruelly, for that would weaken him. An Arab stays not in
long questioning, tedious knots are in peril to be resolved by
the sword. Sometimes the Prince Ibn Rashîd rides to take
the air on horseback, upon a white mare, and undergrown, as are
the Nejd horses in their own country, nor very fairly shaped.

I was sitting one after-sunset upon the clay benching at the castle-gate when the Prince himself arrived, riding alone : I stood up to salute the Emir and his horse startled, seeing in the dusk my large white kerchief. Mohammed rode with stirrups, he urged his mare once, but she not obeying, the witty Arab ceded to his unreasonable beast ; and lightly dismounting the Emir led in and delivered her to the first-coming hand of his castle service.

Beduin companies arrived every day for their affairs with the Prince, and to every such company or *rubba* is allotted a makhzan, and they are public guests (commonly till the third day) in the town. Besides the tribesmen his tributariés, I have seen at Hâyil many foreign Beduins as *Thuffir* and *Meteyr*, that were friendly Aarab without his confederacy and dominion, yet from whom Ibn Rashîd is wont to receive some yearly presents. Moreover there arrived tribesmen of the free Northern Annezy, and of Northern Shammar, and certain migrated Kahtân now wandering in el-Kasîm.

An hour before the morning's mejlis the common business of the day is begun in the oasis. The inhabitants are husbandmen, tradesmen (mostly strangers) in the sûk, the *rajajîl es-sheukh*, and the not many household slaves. When the sun is risen, the husbandmen go out to labour. In an hour the sûk is opened : the *dellâls*, running brokers of all that is put to sale, new or old, whether clothing or arms, cry up and down the street, and spread their wares to all whom they meet, and entering the shops as they go with this illiberal noise, they sell to the highest bidders ; and thus upon an early day I sold my nâga the Khuèyra. I measured their sûk, which is between the Méshab and the inner gate towards Gofar, two hundred paces ; upon both sides are the shops, small ware-rooms built backward, into which the light enters by the doorway,—they are in number about one hundred and thirty, all held and hired of the Emir. The butchers' market was in a court next without the upper gate of the sûk : there excellent mutton was hastily sold for an hour after sunrise, at less than two-pence a pound, and a small leg cost sixpence, in a time when nine shillings was paid for a live sheep at Hâyil, and for a goat hardly six shillings. So I have seen Beduins turn back with their small cattle, rather than sell them here at so low prices :—they would drive them down then, nearly three hundred miles more, to market at Medina ! where the present value of sheep they heard to be as much again as in the Jebel. The butchers' trade, though all the nomads are slaughterers, is not of persons of liberal condition in the townships of Nejd.

Mufarrij towards evening walks again in the Méshab : he comes forth at the castle gate, or sends a servant of the kitchen, as often as the courses of guests rise, to call in other Beduin rubbas to the public supper, which is but a lean dish of boiled temmn seconds and barley, anointed with a very little samn. Mufarrij bids them in his comely-wise, with due discretion and observance of their sheykhly or common condition, of their being here more or less welcome to the Emir, and the alliance or enmities of tribesmen. Also I, the Nasrâny, was daily called to supper in the gallery ; and this for two reasons I accepted,— I was infirm, so that the labour had been grievous to me if I must cook anything for myself, and I had not fuel, and where there was no chimney, I should have been suffocated in my makhzan by the smoke, also whilst I ate bread and salt in the Mothîf I was, I thought, in less danger of any sudden tyranny of the Emir ; but the Mothîf breakfast I forsook, since I might have the best dates in the market for a little money. If I had been able to dispend freely, I had sojourned more agreeably at Hâyil ; it was now a year since my coming to Arabia, and there remained but little in my purse to be husbanded for the greatest necessities.

In the Jebel villages the guest is bidden with : *summ !* or the like is said when the meat is put before him. This may be rather *'smm* for *ism*, in *b' ismi 'llah* or bismillah, " in God's name." But when first I heard this summ ! as a boy of the Mothîf set down the dish of temmn before me, I thought he had said (in malice) *simm*, which is ' poison,' and the child was not less amazed, when with the suddenness of the Arabs I prayed Ullah to curse his parentage :—in this uncertainty whether he had said poison I supped of their mess, for if they would so deal with me I thought I might not escape them. From supping, the Beduins resort in their rubbas to the public kahwa : after the guests' supper the rajajîl are served in like manner by messes, in the court of the Mothîf ; there they eat also at noon their lean collation of the date-tribute, in like manner as the public guests. The sorry dates and corn of the public kitchen have been received on account of the government-tax of the Emir, from his several hamlets and villages ; the best of all is reserved for the households of the sheykhly families. As the public supper is ended, you may see many poor women, and some children, waiting to enter, with their bowls, at the gate of the Kasr. These are they to whom the Emir has granted an evening ration, of that which is left, for themselves, and for other wretched persons. There were daily served in the Mothîf to the guests, and the rajajîl, 180 messes of barley-bread and temmn of second quality, each might be three and a quarter pints ; there was a certain allowance of samn. This samn for the public hospitality is taken from the Emir's Beduins, so much from every beyt, to be paid at an old rate, that is only sometimes seen in the spring, two shillings for three pints, which cost now in Hâyil a real. A camel or smaller beast is killed, and a little flesh meat is served to the first-called guests, once in eight or ten days. When the Prince is absent, there come no Beduins to Hâyil, and then (I have seen) there are no guests. So I have computed may be disbursed for the yearly expenses of the Prince's guest-house, about £1500 sterling.

—Now in the public kahwa the evening coffee is made and served round. As often as I sat with them the mixed rubbas of Beduins observed towards me the tolerant behaviour which is used in their tents ;—and here were we not all guests together of the Emir ? The princely coffee-hall is open, soon after the dawn prayers, to these bibbers of the morning cup ; the door is shut again, when all are gone forth about the time of the first mejlis. It is opened afresh, and coffee is served again after vespers. To every guest the cup is filled twice and a third is offered, when, if he would not drink, a Beduwy of the Nejd tribes will say shortly, with the desert courtesy, *Káramak Ullah,* ' the Lord requite thee.' The door of the kahwa is shut for the night as the coffee-drivelling Beduw are gone forth to the last prayers in the mesjid. After that time, the rude two-leaved gates of this (the Prince's) quarter and the market street are shut,—not to be opened again ' for prayer nor for hire ' till the morrow's light ; and Beduins arriving late must lodge without :—but the rest of Hâyil lies open, which is all that built towards Gofar, and the mountain Ajja.

The Emir Mohammed rode out one half-afternoon with the companions of his chamber and attendance to visit *ed-dubbush,* his live wealth in the desert. The Nejd prince is a very rich cattle-master, so that if you will believe them he possesses " forty thousand " camels. His stud is of good Nejd blood, and as *Aly el-Aýid* told me, (an honest man, and my neighbour, who was beforetime in the stud service,—he had conducted horses for the former Emirs to the Pashas of Egypt,) some three hundred mares, and an hundred horses, with many foals and fillies. After others' telling Ibn Rashîd has four hundred free and bond soldiery, two hundred mares of the blood, one hundred horses : they are herded apart in the deserts ; and he has " an

39—2

hundred bond-servants " (living with their families in booths
of hair-cloth, as the nomads), to keep them. Another told me
the Emir's stud is divided in troops of fifty or sixty, all mares
or all horses together ; the foals and fillies after the weaning
are herded likewise by themselves. The troops are dispersed in
the wilderness, now here, now there, near or far off,—according
to the yearly springing of the wild herbage. The Emir's horses
are grazed in nomad wise ; the fore-feet hop-shackled, they are
dismissed to range from the morning. Barley or other grain
they taste not : they are led home to the booths, and tethered
at evening, and drink the night's milk of the she-camels,
their foster mothers.—So that it may seem the West Nejd
Prince possesses horses and camels to the value of about a
quarter of a million of pounds sterling ; and that has been
gotten in two generations of the spoil of the poor Beduw.
He has besides great private riches laid up in metal, but his
public taxes are carried into the government treasury, *beyt
el-mâl*, and bestowed in sacks and in pits. He possesses much in
land, and not only in Hâyil, but he has great plantations also
at Jauf, and in some other conquered oases.—I saw Mohammed
mount at the castle gate upon a tall dromedary, bravely
caparisoned. In the few days of this his peaceable sojourn
in the khála, the Prince is lodged with his company in
booths like the Beduins. He left Hamûd in Hâyil, to
hold the now small daily mejlis ;—the son of Abeyd sits not
then in the Prince's settle, but in his own lower seat by the
tower.

Hamûd sent for me in his afternoon leisure : " Mohammed
is gone, he said, and we remain to become friends." He
showed me now his cheap Gulf watches, of which he wore two
upon his breast, and so does his son Mâjid who has a curious
mind in such newels,—it was said he could clean watches !
and that Hamûd possessed not so few as an hundred, and the
Emir many more than he. Hamûd asked me if these were not
" Engleys," he would say ' of the best Nasâra work.' He was
greedy to understand of me if I brought not many gay things
in my deep saddle-bags of the fine workmanship of the Nasâra :
he would give for them, he promised me with a barbarous
emphasis, FELûS ! ' silver scales ' or money, which the miserable
Arab people believe that all men do cherish as the blood
of their own lives. I found Hamûd lying along as the nomads,
idle and yawning, in the plantation of Abeyd's kahwa, which, as
said, extends behind the makhzans to his family house in the
town (that is not indeed one of the best). In this palm-
ground he has many gazelles, which feed of vetches daily littered

down to them, but they were shy of man's approach : there I
saw also a bédan-buck. This robust wild goat of the mountain would follow a man and even pursue him, and come
without fear into the kahwa. The beast is of greater bulk
and strength than any he-goat, with thick short hair ; his colour
purple ruddle or nearly as that blushing before the sunset of
dark mountains.

This is a palm-ground of Abeyd, planted in the best manner.
The stems, in the harsh and lean soil of Hâyil, are set in rows,
very wide asunder. I spoke with Aly, that half-good fanatical
neighbour of mine, one who at my first coming had felt
in my girdle for gold, he was of Môgug, but now overseer at
Hâyil of the Prince's husbandry. This palm foster answered,
that 'in such earth (granite grit) where the palms have
more room they bear the better ; the manner which I showed
him of setting trees could not avail them.' Hamûd's large
well in this ground was of fifteen fathoms, sunk in that hard
gritty earth ; the upright sides, baked in the sun, stand fast
without inner building or framework. The pit had been
dug by the labour of fifteen journeymen, each receiving three
or four piastres, in twenty days, this is a cost of some £10.
Three of the best she-camels drew upon the wheels, every one
was worth thirty-five reals. The price of camels in Arabia had
been nearly doubled of late years after the great draughts for
Egypt, the Abyssinian wars, and for Syria. It surprised me
to hear a Beduwy talk in this manner,—" And billah a cause
in the lessened value of money ! " If rainless years follow
rainless years there comes in the end a murrain. It was not
many years since such a season, when a camel was sold for a
crown by the nomads, and languishing thelûls, before worth
sixty in their health, for two or three reals, (that was to the
villagers in Kasîm,) sooner than the beasts remaining upon
their hands should perish in the khála.

Mâjid, the elder of Hamûd's children, was a boy of fifteen
years, small for his age, of a feminine beauty, the son (the Emirs
also match with the nomads) of a Beduin woman. There accompanied him always a dissolute young man, one Aly, who had
four wives and was attached to Hamûd's service. This lovely pair
continually invaded me in my beyt, with the infantile curiosity
of Arabs, intent to lay their knavish fingers upon any foreign
thing of the Nasâra,—and such they hoped to find in my much
baggage ; and lighting upon aught Mâjid and his villanous
fellow Aly had it away perforce.—When I considered that they
might thus come upon my pistol and instruments, I wrested

the things from their iniquitous fingers, and reminded them of the honest example of the nomads, whom they despise. Mâjid answered me with a childish wantonness : " But thou, Khalîl, art in our power, and the Emir can cut off thy head at his pleasure ! " One day as I heard them at the door, I cast the coverlet over my loose things, and sat upon it, but nothing could be hidden from their impudence, with *bethr-ak! bethr-ak!* " by thy leave ; "—it happened that they found me sitting upon the koran. " Ha ! said they now with fanatical bitterness, he is sitting upon the koran ! "—this tale was presently carried in Mâjid's mouth to the castle ; and the elf Mâjid returned to tell me that the Emir had been much displeased.

Mâjid showed himself to be of an affectionate temper, with the easy fortunate disposition of his father, and often childishly exulting, but in his nature too self-loving and tyrannical. He would strike at the poorer children with his stick as he passed by them in the street and cry, " Ullah curse thy father ! " they not daring to resent the injury or resist him,—the best of the *eyyâl es-sheukh;* for thus are called the children of the princely house. For his age he was corrupt of heart and covetous ; but they are all brought up by slaves ! If he ever come to be the Prince, I muse it will be an evil day for Hâyil, except, with good mind enough to amend, he grow up to a more humane understanding. Mâjid, full of facility and the felicity of the Arabs, with a persuading smile, affected to treat me always according to his father's benevolence, naming me ' his dear friend '; and yet he felt that I had a cold insight into his ambitious meaning. So much of the peddling Semite was in him, that he played huckster and bargained for my nâga at the lowest price, imagining to have the double for her (when she would be a milch cow with the calf) in the coming spring : this I readily yielded, but ' nay, said then the young princeling, except I would give him her harness too,' (which was worth a third more).— I have many times mused what could be their estimation of honour ! They think they do that well enough in the world which succeeds to them ; human deeds imitating our dream of the divine ways are beautiful words of their poets, and otherwise unknown to these Orientals.

As I walked through their clean and well-built clay town I thought it were pleasant to live there,—save for the awe of the Ruler and their lives disquieted to ride in the yearly forays of the Emir : yet what discomfort to our eyes is that squalor of the desert soil which lies about them ! Hâyil for the unlikelihood of the site is town rather than oasis, or it is, as it were, an oasis made *ghrôsb,* perforce. The circuit, for their plantations are not very wide, may be nearly an hour; the town lies as far distant from the Ájja cliffs (there named *el-M'níf*). Their town, fenced from the wholesome northern air by the bergs *Sumrâ Hâyil*, is very breathless in the long summer months. The Sumrâ, of plutonic basalt, poured forth (it may be seen in face of the Méshed gate) upon the half-buried grey-red granite of Ajja, is two members which stand a little beyond the town, in a half moon, and the seyl bed of Hâyil, which comes they say from Gofar, passes out between them. That upon the west is lower; the eastern part rises to a height of five hundred feet, upon the crest are cairns; and there was formerly the look-out station, when Hâyil was weaker.

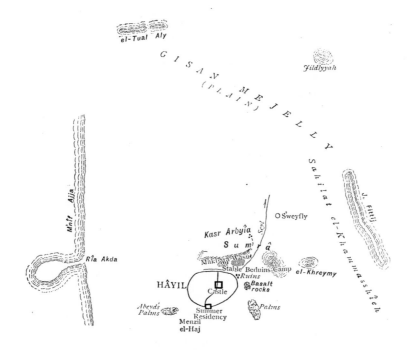

The higher Samrâ, *Umm Arkab*, is steep, and I hired one morning an ass, *jáhash*, for eightpence to ride thither. The thick strewed stones upon this berg, are of the same rusty black basalt which they call *hurrî* or *hurra*, heavy and hard as iron, and ringing like bell-metal. Samrâ in the nomadic speech of Nejd is any rusty black berg of hard stone in the desert; and

in the great plutonic country from hence to Mecca the samrâs
are always basalt.   The same, when any bushes grow upon it,
is called *házm*, and házm is such a vulcanic hill upon the
Harras.   I saw from the cairns that Hâyil is placed at the
midst in a long plain, which is named *Sâhilat el-Khammashîeh*,
and lies between the M'nîf of Ajja (which may rise in the
highest above the plain to 1500 feet), and that low broken
hilly train, by which the Sâhilat is bounded along, two leagues
eastward, toward Selma, *J. Fittij ;* and under us north-eastward
from Hâyil is seen *el-Khreyma*, a great possession of young
palms,—the Emir's ; and there are springs, they say, which
water them !

Some young men labouring in the fields had seen the
Nasrâny ascending, and they mounted after us.   In the desert
below, they said, is hidden much treasure, if a man had wit
to find it, and they filled my ears with their "*Jebel Tommîeh !*"
renowned, "for the riches which lie there buried," in all Nejd ;
—Tommîeh in the Wady er-Rummah, south of the *Abanát* twin
mountains.   After this, one among them who was lettered, sat
down and wrote for me the landmarks, that we saw in that empty
wilderness about us.   Upon a height to the northward they
showed me *Kabr es-Sâny,* ' the smith's grave,' laid out to a
length of three fathoms : " Of such stature was the man ; he lived
in time of the Beny Helál : pursued by the enemies' horsemen,
he ran before them with his little son upon his shoulder, and
fell there."   All this plain upon the north is *G(k)isan M'jelly,*
to the mountain peaks, *Tuâl Aly,* at the borders of the Nefûd,
and to the solitary small mountain *Jildíyyah,* which being less
than a journey from Hâyil, is often named for an assembling
place of the Emir's ghrazzus.   There is a village northward of
Hâyil two miles beyond the Sumrâ, *S'weyfly ;* and before
S'weyfly is seen a ruined village and rude palm planting and corn
grounds, *Kasr Arbŷiyyah.*   Arbŷiyyah and S'weyfly are old
Hâyil ; that is to say the ancient town was built, in much
better soil and site, upon the north side of the Sumrâ.   Then
he showed me with his hand under the M'nîf of Ajja the place
of the *Ria Ag(k)da,* which is a gap or strait of the mountain
giving upon a deep plain-bosom in the midst of Ajja, and
large so that it might, after their speaking, contain *rúba ed-
dínya,* " a fourth part of their (thinly) inhabited world."   There
are palms in a compass of mighty rocks ; it is a mountain-
bay which looks eastward, very hot in summer.   The narrow
inlet is shut by gates, and Abeyd had fortified the passage
with a piece of cannon.   The Riâ Agda is accounted a sure
refuge for the people of Hâyil, with all their goods, as Abeyd

had destined, in the case of any military expedition of the
Dowla, against " the JEBEL," of which they have sometimes
been in dread. Northward beyond el-M'nîf the Ajja coast is
named *el-Aueyrith.*

I came down in the young men's company, and they invited
me to their noonday breakfast of dates which was brought out
to them in the fields. Near by I found a street of tottering
walls and ruinous clay houses, and the ground-wall of an ancient
massy building in clay-brick, which is no more used at Hâyil.
The foundation of this settlement by Shammar is from an
high antiquity; some of them say " the place was named at
first, *Hâyer,* for the plentiful (veins of ground-) water," yet
Hâyil is found written in the ancient poem of Antar. [Ptolemy
has here Ἀῤῥη κώμη.—*v.* Sprenger in *Die alte Geogr. Arabiens.*]
The town is removed from beyond the Sumrâ, the cause was,
they say, the failing little and little of their ground-water.
Hâyil, in the last generation, before the beginning of the
government of Ibn Rashîd, was an oasis half as great as Gofar,
which is a better site by nature; yet Hâyil, Abdullah Ibn
Rashîd's town, when he became *Muhafúth,* or constable under
the Waháby for West Nejd, was always the capital. To-day
the neighbour towns are almost equal, and in Hâyil I have
estimated to be 3000 souls; the people of Gofar, who are Beny
Temîm, and nearly all husbandmen, do yet, they say, a little
exceed them. In returning home towards the northern gate, I
visited a ruined suburb *Wâsit* " middle " (building), which by
the seyl and her fields only is divided from Hâyil town. There
were few years ago in the street, now ruins, " forty kahwas," that
is forty welfaring households receiving their friends daily to
coffee.

Wâsit to-day is ruins without inhabitant; her people (as
those in the ruined quarter of Gofar and in ruined Mŏgug) died
seven years before in the plague, *wába.* I saw their earthen
house-walls unroofed and now ready to fall, for the timbers had
been taken away: the fields and the wells lay abandoned.
The owners and heirs of the soil had so long left the waterer's
labour that the palm-trees were dead and sere: few palms
yet showed in their rusty crowns any languishing greenness.
Before I left Hâyil I saw those lifeless stems cut down, and
the earth laid out anew in seed-plots. There died in Wâsit
three hundred persons; in Hâyil, ' one or two perished in
every household (that were seven hundred or eight hundred);
but now, the Lord be praised, the children were sprung up
and nearly filled their rooms.' Of the well-dieted princely
and sheykhly families there died no man! Beduins that

visited Hâyil in time of the pestilence perished sooner than
townsfolk ; yet the contagion was lighter in the desert and
never prevailed in their menzils as a mortal sickness.   The
disease seized upon the head and bowels ; some died the
same day, some lingered awhile longer.   Signs in the plague-
struck were a black spot which appeared upon the nose, and
a discolouring of the nails ; the sufferings were nearly those of
cholera.   After the pest a malignant fever afflicted the country
two years, when the feeble survivors loading the dead upon
asses (for they had no more strength to carry out piously
themselves) were weary to bury.   A townsman who brought
down, at that time, some quinine from the north, had dispensed
' ten or twelve grains to the sick at five reals ; and taken
after a purging dose of magnesia, he told me, it commonly
relieved them.'   This great death fell in the short time of
Bunder's playing the Prince in Hâyil, and little before the
beginning of Mohammed's government, which is a reign they
think of prosperity, " such as was not seen before, and in which
there has happened no public calamity."   Now first the lordship of Shammar is fully ripe : after such soon-ripeness we
may look for rottenness, as men succeed of less endowments
to administer that which was ' acquired of late by warlike
violence, or when this tide of the world shall be returning from
them.

  After Wâsit, in a waste, which lies between the town walls
and the low crags of the Sumrâ, is the wide grave-yard of
Hâyil.   Poor and rich whose world is ended, lie there alike
indigently together in the desert earth which once fostered
them, and unless it be for the sites here or there, we see
small or no difference of burial.   Telâl and Abeyd were laid
among them.   The first grave is a little heap whose rude head-
stone is a wild block from the basalt hill, and the last is like
it, and such is every grave ; you shall hardly see a scratched
epitaph, where so much is written as the name which was a
name.   In the border Semitic countries is a long superstition
of the grave ; here is but the simple nomad guise, without
other last loving care or adornment.   At a side in the mákbara
is the grave-heap of Abeyd, a man of so much might and
glory in his days : now these are but a long remembrance ;
he lies a yard under the squalid gravel in his shirt, and upon
his stone is rudely scored, with a nail, this only word, *Abeyd
bin-Rashíd*.   When I questioned Mâjid, ' And did his grandsire, the old man Abeyd, lie now so simply in the earth ? ' my
words sounded coldly and strange in his ears ; since in this
land of dearth, where no piece of money is laid out upon

thing not to their lives' need, they are nearly of the Wife of Bath's opinion, " it were but waste to bury him preciously," —whom otherwise they follow in her luxury. When one is dead, they say, *khálas!* " he is ended," and they wisely dismiss this last sorrowful case of all men's days without extreme mourning.

Between the mákbara and the town gate is seen a small menzil of resident nomads. They are pensioners of the palace ; and notwithstanding their appearance of misery some of them are of kin to the princely house. Their Beduin booths are fenced from the backward with earthen walling, and certain of them have a chamber (kasr) roofed with a tent-cloth, or low tower of the same clay building. They are Shammar, whose few cattle are with their tribesfolk in the wilderness ; in the spring months they also remove thither, and refresh themselves in the short season of milk. As I went by, a woman called me from a ragged booth, the widest among them ; ' had I a medicine for her sore eyes ? ' She told me in her talk that her sister had been a wife of Metaab, and she was " aunt " of Mohammed now Emir. Her sons fled in the troubled times and lived yet in the northern dîras. When she named the Emir she spoke in a whisper, looking always towards the Kasr, as if she dreaded the wings of the air might carry her word into the Prince's hearing. Her grown daughter stood by us, braying temmn in a great wooden mortar, and I wondered to see her unveiled ; perhaps she was not married, and Moslems have no jealous opinion of a Nasrâny. The comely maiden's cheeks glowed at her labour ; such little flesh colour I had not seen before in a nomad woman, so lean and bloodless they all are, but she was a stalwart one bred in the plenteous northern dîras. I counted their tents, thirty ; nearer the Gofar gate were other fifteen booths of half-resident Shammar, pitched without clay building.

APPENDIX TO VOL. I.

[*The following very valuable note by the learned author of* Syrie Centrale *was not received in time to be printed in its place after Chap. VI. in this Volume.*]

The Nabatean sculptured Architecture at Medáin Sâlih. Note by M. le Marquis de Vogüé (*Membre de l'Institut*).

Funchal 24 janvier 1886.

Vous me demandez, Monsieur, de vous donner mon avis sur le style des monuments que vous avez découverts, au prix de si grands efforts et de si grand dangers. Votre question, m'embarrasse un peu : je suis à Madère, séparé, depuis plus d'un an, de mes livres et de mes notes : je ne puis donc écrire que de souvenir : les réflexions que me suggèrent vos dessins n'auront pas le développement que j'aurais aimé à leur donner : je vous les adresse néanmoins, avec j'espoir qu'elles pourront vous être de quelque utilité.

Le principal intérêt du groupe de tombeaux de Médaïn-Salih réside dans ce fait qu'il est daté : il offre donc une base indiscutable pour les rapprochements archéologiques. Tous ces monuments ont été exécutés dans le premier siècle de notre ère, et, pour la plupart, dans la première moitié de ce même siècle. Ils sont d'une remarquable uniformité. On voit qu'ils ont tous été exécutés à la même époque par des artistes de la même école, en possession d'un petit nombre de modèles. On s'étonnerait, à première vue, qu'une région aussi anciennement habitée ne renfermât pas de monuments de sa longue existence, si le fait n'était pas général. La Syrie et la Palestine, malgré la grande antiquité de la civilisation dans ces contrées, ne renferment presque plus de monuments antérieurs à l'époque grecque : à part quelques rares exceptions, les innombrables tombeaux, taillés dans le roc, qui sillonnent toutes les montagnes de ces régions, sont postérieurs à Alexandre, et généralement même postérieurs à Jésus Christ. Telle est du moins mon opinion, et les monuments que vous avez découverts lui apportent une confirmation nouvelle.

La forme générale de ces tombeaux est celle d'une tour à demi évidée dans la surface du rocher : à la base de la tour une porte donne accès dans la chambre sépulcrale : la surface de la tour est coupée par des bandeaux, ou corniches, qui en rompent l'uniformité ; le sommet est couronné par une sorte de crénelage à merlons taillés en escalier. Quelques unes des façades de ces tours sont décorées de pilastres : c'est le petit nombre ; vos dessins en mentionnent surtout quatre qui méritent de nous arrêter quelque temps : ce sont les monuments provenant l'un du Borj, l'autre de Kasr-el-Bint, reproduits à la page 104 et à la page 105 de votre volume, puis les monuments désignés sous les noms de Beït-Akhraémat (p. 114) et Mahal-el-Mejlis (p. 116).

Le premier est orné de deux pilastres portant une architrave et une corniche ; les pilastres devaient avoir des chapiteaux corinthiens : mais ils sont restés inachevés : le tailleur de pierre s'est borné à les dégrossir : il a ménagé, à leur base, des anneaux pour les deux rangées de feuilles d'acanthe ;—à leurs angles supérieurs, deux saillies pour les volutes et les feuilles qui les supportent ;—au centre de l'abaque, une saillie pour le fleuron. Les moulures de l'architrave sont empruntées à l'art grec ; la corniche est au contraire imitée de la corniche égyptienne ; quant aux créneaux ou pinnacles, imités des tombeaux de Pétra, ils semblent un souvenir de l'art Assyrien. La porte est décorée dans le même style hybride : les pilastres qui la flanquent sont corinthiens inachevés ; l'architrave est imitée du dorique de basse époque ; le fronton est imité de l'ionique ; des acrotères informes ornent les angles du fronton, que surmonte la figure grossière d'un aigle. Le dessin que vous avez donné (Pl. XLI de la publication de l'Académie), à une plus grande échelle, d'une porte semblable, permet d'en apprécier plus complètement le caractère. Les triglyphes et les rosaces sont du style que l'on appellerait *toscan*, si la date et le lieu n'excluaient toute intervention des architectes romains. Il faut se reporter à Jérusalem, aux tombeaux de la vallée de Josaphat, pour en trouver d'analogues.

Le second tombeau, celui de Kasr-el-Bint, est presque semblable au précédent : l'architrave est plus complète et surmontée d'une frise : mais les détails sont absolument les mêmes : les chapiteaux ne sont qu'ébauchés.

. Les monuments dits Mahal-el-Mejlis et Beït-Akhraémat ne diffèrent des deux premiers que par de plus grandes dimensions et une plus grande richesse. L'un a quatre pilastres et une succession de bandeaux ; l'autre a deux ordres de pilastres et une porte très ornée : mais le style est identiquement le même ; ils sont également inachevés.

La disposition intérieure de ces tombeaux est celle des monuments analogues de Syrie et de Palestine : une chambre sépulcrale, taillée dans le roc, et munie de *loculi* pour recevoir les corps : les *loculi* sont creusés ou dans le sol de la chambre, ou dans les parois latérales, parallèlement à ces parois : on en trouve qui sont superposés trois à trois, de chaque côté d'une grande niche rectangulaire : toutes ces formes se retrouvent en Syrie et Palestine : mais les tombeaux de ces régions renferment en outre deux formes que nous ne voyons pas ici, du moins dans les monuments que vous avez dessinés : c'est la forme dite *arcosolium* si répandue dans la Syrie du Nord, et les *fours* perpendiculaires à la paroi du rocher, si nombreux autour de Jérusalem. Néanmoins tous ces monuments sont de la même famille. Les *loculi* portent, dans les inscriptions de Médaïn-Salih, le nom de *Goukh*, très voisin du mot *Kouk* par lesquels les Juifs les désignent.

Le seul monument non funéraire de ce groupe est celui qui est désigné sous le nom de Liwân. C'est une grotte artificielle, ouverte au dehors par un portique aujourd'hui écroulé, et qui servait de lieu de prière ; les nombreuses stèles votives sculptées sur le rocher ne laissent aucun doute à ce sujet. L'une d'elles est accompagnée d'une inscription où se lit le mot *mesgeda* qui est caractéristique, et qui est devenu le mot arabe *mesjed*, " mosquée." . La grotte a été exécutée avec soin : une corniche en fait le tour à l'intérieur ; des pilastres ornent les angles ; le tout est formé d'éléments grecs.

Les détails reproduits sur les planches XXXVIII, XL, XLI de la publication de l'Académie sont aussi empruntés à l'art grec ; mais on les dirait imités de monuments de basse époque : les colonnettes accouplées, les arcs placés soit en décharge, soit en porte-à-faux sur des architraves ou des pilastres sont des formes que nous étions habitués à considérer comme l'œuvre des architectes romains : les monuments de Pétra avaient bien déjà ébranlé cette opinion ; mais comme ils ne sont pas datés, la discussion était permise ; tandis qu'à Médaïn Salih la présence des dates défie toute contradiction.

En résumé, les monuments que vous avez découverts confirment ce que l'étude des monuments de Pétra et de Siah, dans le Haouran, ainsi que la numismatique, avaient déjà fait connaître, c'est qu'au point de vue de l'art le royaume Nabatéen était profondément pénétré par la Grèce : à peine les arts antérieurs de l'Asie sont-ils représentés par quelques rares réminiscences. Les artistes étaient nabatéens ; ceux de Siah et de Pétra avaient un véritable talent ; ceux de Médaïn Salih étaient des tailleurs de pierre qui attaquaient le rocher avec vigueur et ampleur, mais ne savaient pas sculpter les détails : pour achever leurs œuvres ils attendirent sans doute de Pétra des sculpteurs qui ne vinrent jamais.

Les modèles grecs imités per ces artistes orientaux renfermaient des formes dites de décadence : il faut donc faire remonter avant l'ère chrétienne l'origine de ces formes. Enfin, en imitant les monuments grecs, les artistes orientaux en mélangeaient les ordres, associant les triglyphes doriques aux chapiteaux corinthiens, aux frises ioniques, et même à la corniche égyptienne. Ces associations hybrides déjà remarquées dans les tombeaux qui entourent Jérusalem, cessent donc d'être une exception : elles constituent un fait général qui caractérise une région et une époque (la fin de l'ancienne ère et le commencement de la nouvelle) ; la discussion que les monuments de Jérusalem avaient soulevée se trouve ainsi définitivement close, et ce n'est pas un des moindres services rendus par votre courageuse exploration que d'avoir débarrassé la science des théories fantaisistes qui ont un moment égaré certains esprits.

Veuillez agréer, Monsieur, l'expression de ma sincère estime et de mes sentiments très distingués.

M. DE VOGÜÉ.

LONDON : PRINTED BY WILLIAM CLOWES AND SONS, LIMITED, STAMFORD STREET, S.E. 1.

COSIMO is a specialty publisher of books and publications that inspire, inform, and engage readers. Our mission is to offer unique books to niche audiences around the world.

COSIMO BOOKS publishes books and publications for innovative authors, nonprofit organizations, and businesses. **COSIMO BOOKS** specializes in bringing books back into print, publishing new books quickly and effectively, and making these publications available to readers around the world.

COSIMO CLASSICS offers a collection of distinctive titles by the great authors and thinkers throughout the ages. At **COSIMO CLASSICS** timeless works find new life as affordable books, covering a variety of subjects including: Business, Economics, History, Personal Development, Philosophy, Religion & Spirituality, and much more!

COSIMO REPORTS publishes public reports that affect your world, from global trends to the economy, and from health to geopolitics.

CPSIA information can be obtained at www.ICGtesting.com
Printed in the USA
BVOW04s2143101214

378677BV00001B/254/P